NCERT EXEMPLAR

Problems - Solutions

Mathematics 10th

BEST Solution
Guaranteed •••

NCERT EXEMPLAR
Problems - Solutions
Mathematics 10th

Author
Mohd. Adil Tauheed

arihant
SUCCESS AND NOTHING LESS

Fully Updated as per Latest **Rationalized NCERT**

arihant
SUCCESS AND NOTHING LESS

ARIHANT PRAKASHAN (Series), MEERUT

Administrative & Production Offices

Regd. Office

'Ramchhaya' 4577/15, Agarwal Road, Darya Ganj, New Delhi -110002
Tele: 011- 47630600, 43518550

Head Office

Kalindi, TP Nagar, Meerut (UP) - 250002
Tel: 0121-7156203, 7156204

Sales & Support Offices

Agra, Ahmedabad, Bengaluru, Bareilly, Chennai, Delhi, Guwahati, Hyderabad, Jaipur, Jhansi, Kolkata, Lucknow, Nagpur & Pune.

PRICE ₹275.00

PO No : TXT-XX-XXXXXXX-X-XX

Published by Arihant Publications (India) Ltd.

For further information about the books published by Arihant, log on to www.arihantbooks.com or e-mail at info@arihantbooks.com

Follow us on

PREFACE

NCERT Exemplar Problems, published by the NCERT, are designed to provide students with a diverse range of quality questions in formats such as Multiple Choice Questions, Short Answer Question with Reasoning, Short Answer Questions, and Long Answer Questions, catering to varying levels of difficulty.

These problems are essential for success in school and board exams, as well as competitive exams like engineering and medical entrances. Regular practice with these problems prepares students to tackle challenging questions effectively.

This book, **NCERT Exemplar Problems-Solutions Mathmatics 10th**, offers precise and detailed solutions to all the questions in the NCERT Exemplar Mathematics textbook. Each solution is complemented by explanatory notes and authentic explanations, enabling students to deepen their conceptual understanding and enhance their analytical skills.

Key features

- **Thinking Process** Provides simple steps to approach and solve the question, clearing up any confusion.
- **Concept Insight** Explains the main ideas and concepts needed to answer the questions correctly.
- **Mistake Alert!** Points out common mistakes students might make and helps them avoid these errors.

I hope this book proves to be a valuable resource, aiding students in their academic journey and leading them to great success.

Author

CONTENTS

Note (*) This Chapter has been deleted from Latest NCERT.

Chapter

01

Real Numbers

Multiple Choice Questions (MCQs)

Choose the correct answer from the given four options in the following questions:

***Q.1** For some integer m, every even integer is of the form

(a) m (b) $m+1$ (c) $2m$ (d) $2m+1$

Ans. *(c)* We know that, even integers are … – 4, –2, 0, 2, 4, …
So, it can be written in the form of $2m$.

where, $m = \text{Integer}$

or $m = \cdots, -1, 0, 1, 2, 3, \ldots$

$\therefore$ $2m = \cdots, -2, 0, 2, 4, 6, \ldots$

Alternate Method

Let 'a' be a positive integer. On dividing 'a' by 2, let m be the quotient and r be the remainder. Then, by Euclid's division algorithm, we have

$$a = 2m + r, \text{ where } 0 \le r < 2 \text{ i.e., } r = 0 \text{ and } r = 1.$$

$$\Rightarrow \quad a = 2m \text{ or } a = 2m + 1$$

when, $a = 2m$ for some integer m, then clearly a is even.

***Q.2** For some integer q, every odd integer is of the form

(a) q (b) $q+1$ (c) $2q$ (d) $2q+1$

Ans. *(d)* We know that, odd integers are 1, 3, 5, ⋯
So, it can be written in the form of $2q + 1$.

where, $q = \text{integer}$

or $q = \cdots, -1, 0, 1, 2, 3, \ldots$

$\therefore$ $2q + 1 = \cdots, -3, -1, 1, 3, 5, \ldots$

Alternate Method

Let 'a' be given positive integer. On dividing 'a' by 2, let q be the quotient and r be the remainder. Then, by Euclid's division algorithm, we have

$$a = 2q + r, \text{ where } 0 \le r < 2$$

$$\Rightarrow \quad a = 2q + r, \text{ where } r = 0 \text{ or } r = 1$$

$$\Rightarrow \quad a = 2q \text{ or } 2q + 1$$

when $a = 2q + 1$ for some integer q, then clearly a is odd.

Note (*) *Topics related to these question have been removed from latest NCERT.*

***Q.3** $n^2 - 1$ is divisible by 8, if n is

(a) an integer (b) a natural number
(c) an odd integer (d) an even integer

Ans. *(c)* Let $a = n^2 - 1$

Here n can be even or odd.

Case I $n =$ even *i.e.*, $n = 2k$, where k is an integer.

$$\Rightarrow \quad a = (2k)^2 - 1 \Rightarrow a = 4k^2 - 1$$

At $k = -1$, $a = 4(-1)^2 - 1 = 4 - 1 = 3$, which is not divisible by 8.

At $k = 0$, $a = 4(0)^2 - 1 = 0 - 1 = -1$, which is not divisible by 8.

Case II $n =$ odd *i.e.*, $n = 2k + 1$, where k is an integer.

$$\Rightarrow \quad a = (2k+1)^2 - 1$$

$$\Rightarrow \quad a = 4k^2 + 4k + 1 - 1 \quad [\because (a+b)^2 = a^2 + 2ab + b^2]$$

$$\Rightarrow \quad a = 4k^2 + 4k \Rightarrow a = 4k(k+1)$$

At $k = -1$, $a = 4(-1)(-1+1) = -4(0) = 0$, which is divisible by 8.

At $k = 0$, $a = 4(0)(0+1) = 0$, which is divisible by 8.

At $k = 1$, $a = 4(1)(1+1) = 4(2) = 8$, which is divisible by 8.

So, we can conclude from above two cases, if n is odd, then $n^2 - 1$ is divisible by 8.

***Q.4** If the HCF of 65 and 117 is expressible in the form $65m - 117$, then the value of m is

(a) 4 (b) 2 (c) 1 (d) 3

Thinking Process Apply Euclid's division algorithm until the remainder is 0. Finally we get divisor, which is the required HCF of 65 and 117. Now, put $65m - 117 =$ HCF (65, 117) and get the value of m.

Ans. *(b)* By Euclid's division algorithm,

$$b = aq + r, \; 0 \le r < a \quad [\because \text{dividend} = \text{divisor} \times \text{quotient} + \text{remainder}]$$

$$117 = 65 \times 1 + 52$$

$$65 = 52 \times 1 + 13$$

$$52 = 13 \times 4 + 0$$

$\therefore$ HCF (65, 117) = 13 ...(i)

Also, we have, HCF (65, 117) = $65m - 117$ ...(ii)

From Eqs. (i) and (ii), we get

$$65m - 117 = 13 \Rightarrow 65m = 130 \Rightarrow m = 2$$

Q.5 The largest number which divides 70 and 125, leaving remainders 5 and 8 respectively, is

(a) 13 (b) 65 (c) 875 (d) 1750

Thinking Process First, we subtract the remainders 5 and 8 from corresponding numbers 70 and 125, respectively and then get HCF of resulting numbers, which is the required largest number.

Note (*) *Topics related to these question have been removed from latest NCERT.*

Ans. *(a)* As, 5 and 8 are the remainders of 70 and 125 respectively. So, after subtracting these remainders from the numbers, we have the numbers $65 = (70 - 5)$, $117 = (125 - 8)$, which is divisible by the required number.

$\therefore$ Required number = HCF of 65, 117 [for the largest number]

Now, $117 = 3 \times 3 \times 13$ [$\because$ dividend = divisor × quotient + remainder]

$\Rightarrow$ $65 = 5 \times 13$

$\therefore$ HCF (65, 117) = 13

So, 13 is the largest number which divides 70 and 125, leaving remainders 5 and 8 respectively.

Q.6 If two positive integers a and b are written as $a = x^3y^2$ and $b = xy^3$; x, y are prime numbers, then HCF (a, b) is

(a) xy (b) xy^2 (c) x^3y^3 (d) x^2y^2

Ans. *(b)* We have, $a = x^3 y^2 = x \times x \times x \times y \times y$

and $b = xy^3 = x \times y \times y \times y$

$\therefore$ HCF of a and b = HCF $(x^3y^2, xy^3) = x \times y \times y = xy^2$

[since, HCF is the product of the smallest power of each common prime facter involved in the numbers]

Q.7 If two positive integers p and q can be expressed as $p = ab^2$ and $q = a^3b$; a, b being prime numbers, then LCM (p, q) is

(a) ab (b) a^2b^2 (c) a^3b^2 (d) a^3b^3

Ans. *(c)* We have, $p = ab^2 = a \times b \times b$

and $q = a^3b = a \times a \times a \times b$

$\therefore$ LCM of p and q = LCM $(ab^2, a^3b) = a \times b \times b \times a \times a = a^3b^2$

[since, LCM is the product of the greatest power of each prime factor involved in the numbers]

Mistake Alert ! *Students might get confused while calculating the LCM and HCF i.e., they might take the least and highest power to calculate the LCM and HCF, respectively.*

Q.8 The product of a non-zero rational and an irrational number is

(a) always irrational (b) always rational

(c) rational or irrational (d) one

Ans. *(a)* Product of a non-zero rational and an irrational number is always irrational

i.e., $\frac{3}{4} \times \sqrt{2} = \frac{3\sqrt{2}}{4}$ (irrational).

Q.9 The least number that is divisible by all the numbers from 1 to 10 (both inclusive) is

(a) 10 (b) 100 (c) 504 (d) 2520

Ans. *(d)* Factors of number from 1 to 10 are

$$1 = 1$$
$$2 = 1 \times 2$$
$$3 = 1 \times 3$$

$$4 = 1 \times 2 \times 2$$
$$5 = 1 \times 5$$
$$6 = 1 \times 2 \times 3$$
$$7 = 1 \times 7$$
$$8 = 1 \times 2 \times 2 \times 2$$
$$9 = 1 \times 3 \times 3$$
$$10 = 1 \times 2 \times 5$$

$\therefore$ LCM of numbers from 1 to 10 = LCM (1, 2, 3, 4, 5, 6, 7, 8, 9, 10)

$$= 1 \times 2 \times 2 \times 2 \times 3 \times 3 \times 5 \times 7 = 2520$$

***Q.10** The decimal expansion of the rational number $\frac{14587}{1250}$ will terminate after

(a) one decimal place
(b) two decimal places
(c) three decimal places
(d) four decimal places

- **Concept Insight** In terminating rational number, the denominator always have the form $2^m \times 5^n$.

Ans. ***(d)*** Rational number $= \frac{14587}{1250} = \frac{14587}{2^1 \times 5^4}$

$$= \frac{14587}{10 \times 5^3} \times \frac{(2)^3}{(2)^3} = \frac{14587 \times 8}{10 \times 1000}$$

$$= \frac{116696}{10000} = 11.6696$$

2	1250
5	625
5	125
5	25
5	5
	1

So, the given rational number will terminate after four decimal places.

Short Answer Questions with Reasoning

*** Q.1** Write whether every positive integer can be of the form $4q + 2$, where q is an integer. Justify your answer.

Ans. *No,* by Euclid's division lemma, $b = aq + r, 0 \le r < a$

[$\because$ dividend = divisor $\times$ quotient + remainder]

Here, b is any positive integer and $a = 4 \Rightarrow b = 4q + r$ for $0 \le r < 4$ *i.e.,* $r = 0, 1, 2, 3$

So, this must be in the form $4q$, $4q + 1$, $4q + 2$ or $4q + 3$.

***Q.2** 'The product of two consecutive positive integers is divisible by 2'. Is this statement true or false? Give reasons.

Thinking Process The product of two consecutive positive numbers *i.e.,* $n(n + 1)$ will always be even, as one out of n or $(n + 1)$ must be even.

Ans. *True,* two consecutive positive integers can be n and $(n + 1)$. So, one integer out of these two must be divisible by 2. So, product of two consecutive positive integers is divisible by 2.

Note (*) *Topics related to these question have been removed from latest NCERT.*

***Q.3** 'The product of three consecutive positive integers is divisible by 6'. Is this statement true or false? Justify your answer.

Ans. *True,* three consecutive positive integers can be n, $(n+1)$ and $(n+2)$.

So, atleast one number of these three must be divisible by 2 and one must be divisible by 3. So, product of three consecutive positive integers is divisible by 6.

***Q.4** Write whether the square of any positive integer can be of the form $3m+2$, where m is a natural number. Justify your answer.

Ans. *No,* by Euclid's division lemma, $b = aq + r, 0 \le r < a$. Here, b is any positive integer and $a = 3 \Rightarrow b = 3q + r$ for $0 \le r < 3$

So, any positive integer is of the form $3k$, $3k+1$ or $3k+2$.

Now, $(3k)^2 = 9k^2 = 3m$ [where, $m = 3k^2$]

and $(3k+1)^2 = 9k^2 + 6k + 1$

$= 3(3k^2 + 2k) + 1 = 3m + 1$ [where, $m = 3k^2 + 2k$]

Also, $(3k+2)^2 = 9k^2 + 12k + 4$ [$\because (a+b)^2 = a^2 + 2ab + b^2$]

$= 9k^2 + 12k + 3 + 1$

$= 3(3k^2 + 4k + 1) + 1$

$= 3m + 1$ [where, $m = 3k^2 + 4k + 1$]

which is in the form of $3m$ and $3m+1$. So, square of any positive number cannot be of the form $3m+2$.

***Q.5** A positive integer is of the form $3q+1$, q being a natural number. Can you write its square in any form other than $3m+1$, *i.e.,* $3m$ or $3m+2$ for some integer m? Justify your answer.

Ans. *No,* by Euclid's division lemma, $b = aq + r, 0 \le r < a$

Here, b is any positive integer and $a = 3 \Rightarrow b = 3q + r$ for $0 \le r < 3$

So, this must be in the form $3q$, $3q+1$ or $3q+2$.

Now, $(3q)^2 = 9q^2 = 3m$ [where, $m = 3q^2$]

and $(3q+1)^2 = 9q^2 + 6q + 1$

$= 3(3q^2 + 2q) + 1 = 3m + 1$ [where, $m = 3q^2 + 2q$]

Also, $(3q+2)^2 = 9q^2 + 12q + 4$

$= 9q^2 + 12q + 3 + 1$

$= 3(3q^2 + 4q + 1) + 1$

$= 3m + 1$ [where, $m = 3q^2 + 4q + 1$]

So, square of a positive integer is of the form $3q+1$ is always in the form $3m+1$ for some integer m.

Q.6 The numbers 525 and 3000 are both divisible only by 3, 5, 15, 25 and 75. What is HCF (525, 3000)? Justify your answer.

Ans. The numbers 3, 5, 15, 25 and 75 divides the numbers 525 and 3000. That mean these terms are common in both 525 and 3000. So, the highest common factor among these is 75.

Note (*) *Topics related to these question have been removed from latest NCERT.*

Q.7 Explain why $3 \times 5 \times 7 + 7$ is a composite number.

● **Concept Insight** A number which has more than two factors is known as a composite number.

Ans. We have, $3 \times 5 \times 7 + 7 = 105 + 7 = 112$

Now, $112 = 2 \times 2 \times 2 \times 2 \times 7 = 2^4 \times 7$

So, it is the product of prime factors 2 and 7 *i.e.*, it has more than two factors. Hence, it is a composite number.

Q.8 Can two numbers have 18 as their HCF and 380 as their LCM? Give reasons.

Ans. No, we know that HCF is always a factor of LCM but here 18 is not a factor of 380.

*** Q.9** Without actually performing the long division, find if $\frac{987}{10500}$ will have terminating or non-terminating (repeating) decimal expansion. Give reasons for your answer.

Ans. $\because \frac{987}{10500} = \frac{47}{500} = \frac{47}{5^3 \times 2^2} = \frac{47}{5^3 \times 2^2} \times \frac{2}{2} = \frac{94}{5^3 \times 2^3} = \frac{94}{(10)^3} = \frac{94}{1000} = 0.094$

Yes, after simplification denominator has factor $5^3 \times 2^2$ and which is of the type $2^m \cdot 5^n$. So, this is terminating decimal expansion.

Mistake Alert ! *Students often forget to wirte the fraction in simplest form, before finding the prime factors of the denominator.*

***Q.10** A rational number in its decimal expansion is 327.7081. What can you say about the prime factors of q, when this number is expressed in the form $\frac{p}{q}$? Give reasons.

Ans. 327.7081 is terminating decimal number. So, it represents a rational number and also its denominator must have the form $2^m \times 5^n$.

So, $327.7081 = \frac{3277081}{10000} = \frac{p}{q}$ (say)

$\therefore \quad q = 10000 = 2 \times 2 \times 2 \times 2 \times 5 \times 5 \times 5 \times 5 = 2^4 \times 5^4 = (2 \times 5)^4$

So, the prime factors of q are 2 and 5.

Short Answer Questions

*** Q.1** Show that the square of any positive integer is either of the form $4q$ or $4q+1$ for some integer q.

Thinking Process Use Euclid's division algorithm, put the value of divisor as 4 and then put the value of remainder from 0 to 3 and get the different form. Now, squaring every different form and get the required form.

Ans. Let a be an arbitrary positive integer. Then, by Euclid's division algorithm, corresponding to the positive integers a and 4, there exist non-negative integers m and r, such that

Note (✱) *Topics related to these question have been removed from latest NCERT.*

$$a = 4m + r, \text{ where } 0 \le r < 4$$

$\Rightarrow \quad a^2 = 16m^2 + r^2 + 8mr$ ...(i)

where, $0 \le r < 4$ $[\because (a + b)^2 = a^2 + 2ab + b^2]$

Case I If $r = 0$, then put $r = 0$ in Eq. (i), we get

$a^2 = 16m^2 = 4(4m^2) = 4q$ [where, $q = 4m^2$ is an integer]

Case II If $r = 1$, then put $r = 1$ in Eq. (i), we get

$$a^2 = 16m^2 + 1^2 + 8m \times 1$$

$= 4(4m^2 + 2m) + 1 = 4q + 1$ [where, $q = (4m^2 + 2m)$ is an integer]

Case III If $r = 2$, then put $r = 2$ in Eq. (i), we get

$$a^2 = 16m^2 + 2^2 + 8m \times 2 = 16m^2 + 4 + 16m$$

$= 4(4m^2 + 1 + 4m) = 4q$ [where, $q = (4m^2 + 4m + 1)$ is an integer]

Case IV If $r = 3$, then put $r = 3$ in Eq. (i), we get

$$a^2 = 16m^2 + 3^2 + 8m \times 3 = 16m^2 + 9 + 24m = 16m^2 + 24m + 8 + 1$$

$= 4(4m^2 + 6m + 2) + 1 = 4q + 1$ [where, $q = (4m^2 + 6m + 2)$ is an integer]

So, the square of any positive integer is either of the form $4q$ or $4q + 1$ for some integer q.

***Q.2** Show that cube of any positive integer is of the form $4m$, $4m + 1$ or $4m + 3$, for some integer m.

Thinking Process Use Euclid's division algorithm. Put the value of remainder from 0 to 3 to get the different forms of any positive integer. Now, cubing to every different form of positive integer and get the required forms.

Ans. Let a be an arbitrary positive integer. Then, by Euclid's division algorithm, corresponding to the positive integers a and 4, there exist non-negative integers q and r, such that

$$a = 4q + r, \text{ where } 0 \le r < 4$$

$\Rightarrow \quad a^3 = (4q + r)^3 = 64q^3 + r^3 + 12qr^2 + 48q^2r$

$[\because (a + b)^3 = a^3 + b^3 + 3ab^2 + 3a^2b]$

$\Rightarrow \quad a^3 = (64q^2 + 48q^2r + 12qr^2) + r^3$ ...(i)

where, $0 \le r < 4$

Case I If $r = 0$, then put $r = 0$ in Eq. (i), we get

$$a^3 = 64q^3 = 4(16q^3)$$

$\Rightarrow \quad a^3 = 4m$ [where, $m = 16q^3$ is an integer]

Case II If $r = 1$, then put $r = 1$ in Eq. (i), we get

$$a^3 = 64q^3 + 48q^2 + 12q + 1$$

$$= 4(16q^3 + 12q^2 + 3q) + 1$$

$= 4m + 1$ [where, $m = (16q^2 + 12q^2 + 3q)$ is an integer]

Note (*) *Topics related to these question have been removed from latest NCERT.*

Case III If $r = 2$, then put $r = 2$ in Eq. (i), we get

$$= 64q^3 + 48q^2 \times 2 + 12q \times 2^2 + 2^3$$
$$= 64q^3 + 96q^2 + 48q + 8 = 4(16q^3 + 24q^2 + 12q + 2)$$
[where, $m = (16q^3 + 24q^2 + 12q + 2)$ is an integer]

Case IV If $r = 3$, then put $r = 3$ in Eq (i), we get

$$= 64q^3 + 48q^2 \times 3 + 12q \times (3)^2 + (3)^3$$
$$= 64q^3 + 144q^2 + 108q + 27$$
$$= 64q^3 + 144q^2 + 108q + 24 + 3 = 4(16q^3 + 36q^2 + 27q + 6) + 3$$
$$= 4m + 3 \quad [\text{ where, } m = 16q^3 + 36q^2 + 27q + 6 \text{ is an integer}]$$

Hence, the cube of any positive integer is of the form $4m$, $4m + 1$ or $4m + 3$ for some integer m.

***Q.3** Show that the square of any positive integer cannot be of the form $5q + 2$ or $5q + 3$ for any integer q.

Ans. Let a be an arbitrary positive integer.

Then, by Euclid's divisions algorithm, corresponding to the positive integers a and 5, there exist non-negative integers m and r such that

$$a = 5m + r, \text{ where } 0 \le r < 5$$
$$\Rightarrow \quad a^2 = (5m + r)^2 = 25m^2 + r^2 + 10mr \quad [\because (a + b)^2 = a^2 + 2ab + b^2]$$
$$\Rightarrow \quad a^2 = 5(5m^2 + 2mr) + r^2 \quad \ldots(i)$$

where, $0 \le r < 5$

Case I If $r = 0$, then putting $r = 0$ in Eq. (i), we get

$$a^2 = 5(5m^2) = 5q$$

where, $q = 5m^2$ is an integer.

Case II If $r = 1$, then putting $r = 1$ is Eq. (i), we get

$$a^2 = 5(5m^2 + 2m) + 1 \Rightarrow q = 5q + 1$$

where, $q = (5m^2 + 2m)$ is an integer.

Case III If $r = 2$, then putting $r = 2$ in Eq. (i), we get

$$a^2 = 5(5m^2 + 4m) + 4 = 5q + 4$$

where, $q = (5m^2 + 4m)$ is an integer.

Case IV If $r = 3$, then putting $r = 3$ in Eq. (i), we get

$$a^2 = 5(5m^2 + 6m) + 9 = 5(5m^2 + 6m) + 5 + 4$$
$$= 5(5m^2 + 6m + 1) + 4 = 5q + 4$$

where, $q = (5m^2 + 6m + 1)$ is an integer.

Case V If $r = 4$, then putting $r = 4$ in Eq. (i), we get

$$a^2 = 5(5m^2 + 8m) + 16 = 5(5m^2 + 8m) + 15 + 1$$
$$\Rightarrow \quad a^2 = 5(5m^2 + 8m + 3) + 1 = 5q + 1$$

where, $q = (5m^2 + 8m + 3)$ is an integer.

Hence, the square of any positive integer cannot be of the form $5q + 2$ or $5q + 3$ for any integer q.

Note (*) *Topics related to these question have been removed from latest NCERT.*

***Q.4** Show that the square of any positive integer cannot be of the form $6m+2$ or $6m+5$ for any integer m.

Ans. Let a be an arbitrary positive integer, then by Euclid's division algorithm, corresponding to the positive integers a and 6, there exist non-negative integers q and r such that

$$a = 6q + r, \text{ where } 0 \le r < 6$$

$\Rightarrow \quad a^2 = (6q + r)^2 = 36q^2 + r^2 + 12qr \quad [\because (a + b)^2 = a^2 + 2ab + b^2]$

$\Rightarrow \quad a^2 = 6(6q^2 + 2qr) + r^2 \quad$ ...(i)

where, $\quad 0 \le r < 6$

***Case* I** If $r = 0$, then putting $r = 0$ in Eq. (i), we get

$$a^2 = 6(6q^2) = 6m$$

where, $m = 6q^2$ is an integer.

***Case* II** If $r = 1$, then putting $r = 1$ in Eq. (i), we get

$$a^2 = 6(6q^2 + 2q) + 1 = 6m + 1$$

where, $m = (6q^2 + 2q)$ is an integer.

***Case* III** If $r = 2$, then putting $r = 2$ in Eq (i), we get

$$a^2 = 6(6q^2 + 4q) + 4 = 6m + 4$$

where, $m = (6q^2 + 4q)$ is an integer.

***Case* IV** If $r = 3$, then putting $r = 3$ in Eq. (i), we get

$$a^2 = 6(6q^2 + 6q) + 9 = 6(6q^2 + 6q) + 6 + 3$$

$\Rightarrow \quad a^2 = 6(6q^2 + 6q + 1) + 3 = 6m + 3$

where, $m = (6q + 6q + 1)$ is an integer.

***Case* V** If $r = 4$, then putting $r = 4$ in Eq. (i), we get

$$a^2 = 6(6q^2 + 8q) + 16 = 6(6q^2 + 8q) + 12 + 4$$

$\Rightarrow \quad a^2 = 6(6q^2 + 8q + 2) + 4 = 6m + 4$

where, $m = (6q^2 + 8q + 2)$ is an integer.

***Case* VI** If $r = 5$, then putting $r = 5$ in Eq. (i), we get

$$a^2 = 6(6q^2 + 10q) + 25 = 6(6q^2 + 10q) + 24 + 1$$

$\Rightarrow \quad a^2 = 6(6q^2 + 10q + 4) + 1 = 6m + 1$

where, $m = (6q^2 + 10q + 1)$ is an integer.

Hence, the square of any positive integer cannot be of the form $6m + 2$ or $6m + 5$ for any integer m.

***Q.5** Show that the square of any odd integer is of the form $4q+1$, for some integer q.

Ans. By Euclid's division algorithm, we have $a = bp + r$, where $0 \le r < 4$ ...(i)

On putting $b = 4$ in Eq. (i), we get

$$a = 4p + r, \text{ where } 0 \le r < 4 \quad i.e., r = 0, 1, 2, 3 \quad \text{...(ii)}$$

If $r = 0 \Rightarrow a = 4p$, $4p$ is divisible by $2 \Rightarrow 4p$ is even.

If $r = 1 \Rightarrow a = 4p + 1$, $(4p + 1)$ is not divisible by 2.

Note (*) *Topics related to these question have been removed from latest NCERT.*

If $r=2 \Rightarrow a=4p+2=2(2p+1)$, $2(2p+1)$ is divisible by $2 \Rightarrow 2(2p+1)$ is even.

If $r=3 \Rightarrow a=4p+3$, $(4p+3)$ is not divisible by 2.

So, for any positive integer p, $(4p+1)$ and $(4p+3)$ are odd integers.

Now, $a^2=(4p+1)^2=16p^2+1+8p=4(4p^2+2p)+1=4q+1$

$[\because (a+b)^2=a^2+2ab+b^2]$

It is a square which is of the form $4q+1$, where $q=(4p^2+2p)$ is an integer.

and $a^2=(4p+3)^2=16p^2+9+24p=4(4p^2+6p+2)+1=4q+1$

$[\because (a+b)^2=a^2+2ab+b^2]$

It is a square which is of the form $4q+1$, where $q=(4p^2+6p+2)$ is an integer.

Hence, for some integer q, the square of any odd integer is of the form $4q+1$.

***Q.6** If n is an odd integer, then show that n^2-1 is divisible by 8.

Ans. Let $a=n^2-1$ ...(i)

Given that, n is an odd integer.

$\therefore$ $n=1, 3, 5, ...$

From Eq. (i), at $n=1$, $a=(1)^2-1=1-1=0$, which is divisible by 8.

From Eq. (i), at $n=3$, $a=(3)^2-1=9-1=8$, which is divisible by 8.

From Eq. (i), at $n=5$, $a=(5)^2-1=25-1=24=3\times 8$, which is divisible by 8.

From Eq. (i), at $n=7$, $a=(7)^2-1=49-1=48=6\times 8$, which is divisible by 8.

Hence, (n^2-1) is divisible by 8, where n is an odd integer.

Alternate Method

We know that an odd integer n is of the form $(4q+1)$ or $(4q+3)$ for some integer q.

***Case* I** When $n=4q+1$

In this case, we have

$$(n^2-1)=(4q+1)^2-1=16q^2+1+8q-1 \quad [\because (a+b)^2=a^2+2ab+b^2]$$
$$=16q^2+8q=8q(2q+1)$$

which is clearly divisible by 8.

***Case* II** When $n=4q+3$

In this case, we have

$$(n^2-1)=(4q+3)^2-1 \quad [\because (a+b)^2=a^2+2ab+b^2]$$
$$=16q^2+24q+8=8(2q^2+3q+1)$$

which is clearly divisible by 8.

Hence, (n^2-1) is divisible by 8.

***Q.7** Prove that if x and y are both odd positive integers, then x^2+y^2 is even but not divisible by 4.

Thinking Process Here, we have to take any two consecutive odd positive integers. After that squaring and adding both the numbers and check it is even but not divisible by 4.

Ans. Let $x=2m+1$ and $y=2m+3$ are odd positive integers, for every positive integer m.

Then, $x^2+y^2=(2m+1)^2+(2m+3)^2$

$$=4m^2+1+4m+4m^2+9+12m \quad [\because (a+b)^2=a^2+2ab+b^2]$$
$$=8m^2+16m+10=2(4m^2+8m+5) \text{ or } 4(2m^2+4m+2)+2$$

Hence, x^2+y^2 is even for every positive integer m but not divisible by 4.

Note (*) *Topics related to these question have been removed from latest NCERT.*

***Q.8** **Use Euclid's division algorithm to find the HCF of 441, 567 and 693.**

Thinking Process First we apply Euclid's division algorithm between two larger numbers and get the HCF between these two numbers. After that we take the third number and resulting HCF of two numbers and apply again Euclid's division algorithm and get the required HCF.

Ans. Let $a = 693$, $b = 567$ and $c = 441$

By Euclid's division algorithm,

$$a = bq + r \qquad \text{...(i)}$$

[$\because$ dividend = divisor × quotient + remainder]

First we take, $a = 693$ and $b = 567$ and find their HCF.

$$693 = 567 \times 1 + 126$$
$$567 = 126 \times 4 + 63$$
$$126 = 63 \times 2 + 0$$

$\therefore$ HCF (693, 567) = 63

Now, we take $c = 441$ and (let) $d = 63$, then find their HCF.

Again, using Euclid's division algorithm,

$$c = dq + r \Rightarrow 441 = 63 \times 7 + 0$$

$\therefore$ HCF (693, 567, 441) = 63

***Q.9** **Using Euclid's division algorithm, find the largest number that divides 1251, 9377 and 15628 leaving remainders 1, 2 and 3, respectively.**

Ans. Since, 1, 2 and 3 are the remainders of 1251, 9377 and 15628, respectively. Thus, after subtracting these remainders from the numbers.

We have the numbers, $1251 - 1 = 1250$, $9377 - 2 = 9375$ and $15628 - 3 = 15625$ which is divisible by the required number.

Now, required number = HCF of 1250, 9375 and 15625 [for the largest number]

By Euclid's division algorithm,

$$a = bq + r \qquad \text{...(i)}$$

[$\because$ dividend = divisor × quotient + remainder]

For largest number, let $a = 15625$ and $b = 9375$

$$15625 = 9375 \times 1 + 6250 \qquad \text{[from Eq. (i)]}$$
$$\Rightarrow \quad 9375 = 6250 \times 1 + 3125$$
$$\Rightarrow \quad 6250 = 3125 \times 2 + 0$$

$\therefore$ HCF (15625, 9375) = 3125

Now, we take $c = 1250$ and $d = 3125$, then again using Euclid's division algorithm,

$$d = cq + r$$
$$\Rightarrow \quad 3125 = 1250 \times 2 + 625$$
$$\Rightarrow \quad 1250 = 625 \times 2 + 0$$

$\therefore$ HCF (1250, 9375, 15625) = 625

Hence, 625 is the largest number which divides 1251,9377 and 15628 leaving remainders 1, 2 and 3, respectively.

Note (*) *Topics related to these question have been removed from latest NCERT.*

Q.10 Prove that $\sqrt{3}+\sqrt{5}$ is irrational.

Ans. Let us suppose that $\sqrt{3}+\sqrt{5}$ is rational.

Let $\sqrt{3}+\sqrt{5}=a$, where a is rational.

Therefore, $\sqrt{3}=a-\sqrt{5}$

On squaring both sides, we get

$$(\sqrt{3})^2=(a-\sqrt{5})^2$$

$$\Rightarrow \quad 3=a^2+5-2a\sqrt{5} \qquad [\because (a-b)^2=a^2+b^2-2ab]$$

$$\Rightarrow \quad 2a\sqrt{5}=a^2+2$$

Therefore, $\sqrt{5}=\dfrac{a^2+2}{2a}$ which is contradiction.

As the right hand side is rational number while $\sqrt{5}$ is irrational. Since, 3 and 5 are prime numbers. Hence, $\sqrt{3}+\sqrt{5}$ is irrational.

Q.11 Show that 12^n cannot end with the digit 0 or 5 for any natural number n.

Ans. If any number ends with the digit 0 or 5, it is always divisible by 5.

If 12^n ends with the digit zero it must be divisible by 5.

This is possible only if prime factorisation of 12^n contains the prime number 5.

Now, $12=2\times2\times3=2^2\times3$

$$\Rightarrow \quad 12^n=(2^2\times3)^n=2^{2n}\times3^n$$

Since, there is no term containing 5.

Therefore, there is no value of natural number n for which 12^n ends with digit 0 or 5.

Q.12 On a morning walk, three persons step off together and their steps measure 40 cm, 42 cm and 45 cm, respectively. What is the minimum distance each should walk, so that each can cover the same distance in complete steps?

Thinking Process Students need to find the minimum distance to cover the same distance in complete steps *i.e.*, a number which if divisible by all the given numbers. Therefore, find LCM of the numbers.

Ans. We have to find the LCM of 40 cm, 42 cm and 45 cm to get the required minimum distance.

For this, $40=2\times2\times2\times5$

$$42=2\times3\times7$$

and $45=3\times3\times5$

$$\therefore \quad \text{LCM}(40, 42, 45)=2\times3\times5\times2\times2\times3\times7$$

$$=30\times12\times7=210\times12=2520$$

$\therefore$ Minimum distance each should walk is 2520 cm. So that, each can cover the same distance in complete steps.

***Q.13** Write the denominator of rational number $\frac{257}{5000}$ in the form $2^m \times 5^n$, where m, n are non-negative integers. Hence, write its decimal expansion, without actual division.

Ans. Denominator of the rational number $\frac{257}{5000}$ is 5000.

Now, prime factorisation of $5000 = 2 \times 2 \times 2 \times 5 \times 5 \times 5 \times 5 = (2)^3 \times (5)^4$, which is of the type $2^m \times 5^n$,

where $m = 3$ and $n = 4$ are non-negative integers.

$\therefore$ Rational number $= \frac{257}{5000} = \frac{257}{2^3 \times 5^4} \times \frac{2}{2}$

[multiplying numerator and denominater by 2]

$$= \frac{514}{2^4 \times 5^4} = \frac{514}{(10)^4}$$

$$= \frac{514}{10000} = 0.0514$$

Hence, 0.0514 is the required decimal expansion of the rational number $\frac{257}{5000}$ and it is also a terminating decimal number.

Q.14 Prove that $\sqrt{p} + \sqrt{q}$ is irrational, where p and q are primes.

Ans. Let us suppose that $\sqrt{p} + \sqrt{q}$ is rational.

Again, let $\sqrt{p} + \sqrt{q} = a$, where a is rational.

Therefore, $\sqrt{q} = a - \sqrt{p}$

On squaring both sides, we get

$$q = a^2 + p - 2a\sqrt{p} \qquad [\because (a-b)^2 = a^2 + b^2 - 2ab]$$

Therefore, $\sqrt{p} = \frac{a^2 + p - q}{2a}$, which is a contradiction as the right hand side is rational number while $\sqrt{p}$ is irrational, since p and q are prime numbers.

Hence, $\sqrt{p} + \sqrt{q}$ is irrational.

Long Answer Questions

***Q.1** Show that the cube of a positive integer of the form $6q + r$, q is an integer and $r = 0, 1, 2, 3, 4, 5$ is also of the form $6m + r$.

Ans. Let a be an arbitrary positive integer. Then, by Euclid's division algorithm, corresponding to the positive integers 'a' and 6, there exist non-negative integers q and r such that

$$a = 6q + r, \text{ where, } 0 \le r < 6$$

$$\Rightarrow \quad a^3 = (6q + r)^3 = 216q^3 + r^3 + 3 \times 6q \times r(6q + r)$$

$$[\because (a+b)^3 = a^3 + b^3 + 3ab(a+b)]$$

$$\Rightarrow \quad a^3 = (216q^3 + 108q^2r + 18qr^2) + r^3 \qquad \ldots(i)$$

where, $0 \le r < 6$

Note (*) *Topics related to these question have been removed from latest NCERT.*

***Case* I** If $r = 0$, then putting $r = 0$ in Eq. (i), we get

$$a^3 = 216q^3 = 6(36q^3) = 6m$$

where, $m = 36q^3$ is an integer.

***Case* II** If $r = 1$, then putting $r = 1$ in Eq. (i), we get

$$a^3 = (216q^3 + 108q^2 + 18q) + 1 = 6(36q^3 + 18q^2 + 3q) + 1$$

$\Rightarrow$ $a^3 = 6m + 1$, where $m = (36q^3 + 18q^2 + 3q)$ is an integer.

***Case* III** If $r = 2$, then putting $r = 2$ in Eq. (i), we get

$$a^3 = (216q^3 + 216q^2 + 72q) + 8$$

$\Rightarrow$ $a^3 = (216q^3 + 216q^2 + 72q + 6) + 2$

$\Rightarrow$ $a^3 = 6(36q^3 + 36q^2 + 12q + 1) + 2 = 6m + 2$

where, $m = (36q^3 + 36q^2 + 12q + 1)$ is an integer.

***Case* IV** If $r = 3$, then putting $r = 3$ in Eq. (i), we get

$$a^3 = (216q^3 + 324q^2 + 162q) + 27 = (216q^3 + 324q^2 + 162q + 24) + 3$$

$$= 6(36q^3 + 54q^2 + 27q + 4) + 3 = 6m + 3$$

where, $m = (36q^3 + 54q^2 + 27q + 4)$ is an integer.

***Case* V** If $r = 4$, then putting $r = 4$ in Eq. (i), we get

$$a^3 = (216q^3 + 432q^2 + 288q) + 64$$

$$= 6(36q^3 + 72q^2 + 48q) + 60 + 4$$

$\Rightarrow$ $a^3 = 6(36q^3 + 72q^2 + 48q + 10) + 4 = 6m + 4$

where, $m = (36q^3 + 72q^2 + 48q + 10)$ is an integer.

***Case* VI** If $r = 5$, then putting $r = 5$ in Eq. (i), we get

$$a^3 = (216q^3 + 540q^2 + 450q) + 125$$

$\Rightarrow$ $a^3 = (216q^3 + 540q^2 + 450q) + 120 + 5$

$\Rightarrow$ $a^3 = 6(36q^3 + 90q^2 + 75q + 20) + 5$

$\Rightarrow$ $a^3 = 6m + 5$

where, $m = (36q^3 + 90q^2 + 75q + 20)$ is an integer.

Hence, the cube of a positive integer of the form $6q + r, q$ is an integer and $r = 0, 1, 2, 3, 4, 5$ is also of the forms $6m, 6m + 1, 6m + 2, 6m + 3, 6m + 4$ and $6m + 5$ *i.e.*, $6m + r$.

***Q.2** Prove that one and only one out of n, $(n + 2)$ and $(n + 4)$ is divisible by 3, where n is any positive integer.

Thinking Process Since, n is positive integer, then put $n = 1, 2, 3, \ldots$ in the given numbers and makes the order triplets, then we see that any one digit in a triplet is divisible by 3.

Ans. On dividing 'n' by 3, let q be the quotient and r be the remainder.

Then, $n = 3q + r$, where, $0 \le r < 3$

$\Rightarrow$ $n = 3q + r$, where, $r = 0, 1, 2$

$\Rightarrow$ $n = 3q$ or $n = 3q + 1$ or $n = 3q + 2$

***Case* I** If $n = 3q$, then only n is divisible by 3.

but $n + 2$ and $n + 4$ are not divisible by 3.

Note (✱) *Topics related to these question have been removed from latest NCERT.*

Case II If $n = 3q + 1$, then $(n + 2) = 3q + 3 = 3(q + 1)$, which is only divisible by 3, but n and $n + 4$ are not divisible by 3.

So, in this case, $(n + 2)$ is divisible by 3.

Case III If $n = 3q + 2$, then $(n + 4) = 3q + 6 = 3(q + 2)$, which is only divisible by 3, but n and $(n + 2)$ are not divisible by 3.

So, in this case, $(n + 4)$ is divisible by 3.

Hence, one and only one out of n, $(n + 2)$ *and* $(n + 4)$ is divisible by 3.

Alternate Method

Let $a = n$, $b = n + 2$ and $c = n + 4$

$\therefore$ Order triplet is $(a, b, c) = (n, n + 2, n + 4)$

Where, n is any positive integer *i.e.*, $n = 1, 2, 3,...$

At $n = 1$; $(a, b, c) = (1, 1 + 2, 1 + 4) = (1, 3, 5)$

At $n = 2$; $(a, b, c) = (2, 2 + 2, 2 + 4) = (2, 4, 6)$

At $n = 3$; $(a, b, c) = (3, 3 + 2, 3 + 4) = (3, 5, 7)$

At $n = 4$; $(a, b, c) = (4, 4 + 2, 4 + 4) = (4, 6, 8)$

At $n = 5$; $(a, b, c) = (5, 5 + 2, 5 + 4) = (5, 7, 9)$

At $n = 6$; $(a, b, c) = (6, 6 + 2, 6 + 4) = (6, 8, 10)$

At $n = 7$; $(a, b, c) = (7, 7 + 2, 7 + 4) = (7, 9, 11)$

At $n = 8$; $(a, b, c) = (8, 8 + 2, 8 + 4) = (8, 10, 12)$

We observe that each triplet consist of one and only one number which is multiple of 3 *i.e.*, divisible by 3.

Hence, one and only one out of n, $(n + 2)$ and $(n + 4)$ is divisible by 3, where, n is any positive integer.

***Q.3** Prove that one of any three consecutive positive integers must be divisible by 3.

Ans. Let three consecutive positive integers are $x, x + 1$ and $x + 2$.

On dividing x by 3, let q be the quotient and r be the remainder by Euclid's division algorithm,

$$x = 3q + r, \text{ where } 0 \le r < 3$$

$$\Rightarrow \quad x = 3q \text{ or } x = 3q + 1 \text{ or } x = 3q + 2$$

Case I If $x = 3q$, then only x is divisible by 3, but $(x + 1)$ and $(x + 2)$ are not divisible by 3.

Case II If $x = 3q + 1$, then $x + 2 = 3q + 1 + 2 = 3q + 3 = 3(q + 1)$ which is divisibly by 3, but x and $(x + 1)$ are not divisible by 3.

So, in this case, only $(x + 2)$ is divisibly by 3.

Case III If $x = 3q + 2$, then $x + 1 = 3q + 2 + 1 = 3q + 3$

$= 3(q + 1)$ which is divisible by 3, but x and $(x + 2)$ are not divisible by 3.

So, in this case only $x + 1$ is divisible by 3.

Hence, one of any three consecutive positive integers must be divisible by 3.

Note (✱) *Topics related to these question have been removed from latest NCERT.*

Alternate Method

Any three consecutive positive integers must be of the form $n, (n+1)$ and $(n+2)$, where n is any natural number. *i.e.*, $n = 1, 2, 3, \ldots$

Let, $a = n, b = n+1$ and $c = n+2$

$\therefore$ Order triplet is $(a, b, c) = (n, n+1, n+2)$, where n is a positive integer *i.e.*, $n = 1, 2, 3, \ldots$ ...(i)

At $n = 1$; $(a, b, c) = (1, 1+1, 1+2) = (1, 2, 3)$

At $n = 2$; $(a, b, c) = (1, 2+1, 2+2) = (2, 3, 4)$

At $n = 3$; $(a, b, c) = (3, 3+1, 3+2) = (3, 4, 5)$

At $n = 4$; $(a, b, c) = (4, 4+1, 4+2) = (4, 5, 6)$

At $n = 5$; $(a, b, c) = (5, 5+1, 5+2) = (5, 6, 7)$

At $n = 6$; $(a, b, c) = (6, 6+1, 6+2) = (6, 7, 8)$

At $n = 7$; $(a, b, c) = (7, 7+1, 7+2) = (7, 8, 9)$

At $n = 8$; $(a, b, c) = (8, 8+1, 8+2) = (8, 9, 10)$

We observe that each triplet consist of one and only one number which is multiple of 3 *i.e.*, divisible by 3.

Hence, one of any three consecutive positive integers must be divisible by 3.

***Q.4** For any positive integer n, prove that $n^3 - n$ is divisible by 6.

Ans. Let $a = n^3 - n$

$\Rightarrow$ $a = n(n^2 - 1)$

$\Rightarrow$ $a = n(n-1)(n+1)$ $[\because a^2 - b^2 = (a-b)(a+b)]$

or $a = (n-1)n(n+1)$

We know that if a number is divisible by 6 if and only if it is divisible by 2 and 3.

Now, we prove that a is divisible by 3.

On dividing n by 3. Let q be the quotient and r be the remainder.

Then, $n = 3q + r$, where $0 \le r, < 3$

i.e., $n = 3q$ or $3q+1$ or $3q+2$

***Case* I** If $n = 3q$, then $a = (3q-1)(3q)(3q+1)$

Clearly, a is divisible by 3.

***Case* II** If $n = 3q+1$, then $a = (3q)(3q+1)(3q+2)$

Clearly, a is divisible by 3.

***Case* III** If $n = 3q+2$, then $a = (3q+1)(3q+2)(3q+3)$

$\Rightarrow$ $a = (3q+1)(3q+2) \times 3 \times (q+1)$

Clearly, a is divisibly by 3.

Therefore, we can say that $a = n^3 - n$ is divisible by 3.

Now, we prove that a is divisible by 2.

On dividing n by 2. Let q be the quotient and r be the remainder.

Then, $n = 2q + r$, where $0 \le r < 2$

i.e., $n = 2q$ or $2q+1$

Note (*) *Topics related to these question have been removed from latest NCERT.*

Case I If $n = 2q$, then $a = (2q-1)(2q)(2q+1)$

Clearly, a is divisible by 2.

Case II If $n = 2q+1$, then

$$a = (2q)(2q+1)(2q+2)$$

Clearly, a is divisibly by 2.

$\therefore$ We can say that $a = n^3 - n$ is divisible by 2.

Therefore, $n^3 - n$ is divisible by 6.

***Q.5** Show that one and only one out of $n, n+4$, $n+8, n+12$ and $n+16$ is divisible by 5, where n is any positive integer.

[**Hint** Any positive integer be written in the form $5q, 5q, +1, 5q+2, 5q+3, 5q+4$]

Ans. On dividing on n by 5, let q be the quotient and r be the remainder.

Then, $n = 5q + r$, where $0 \le r < 5$.

$\Rightarrow \quad n = 5q + r$, where $r = 0, 1, 2, 3, 4$.

$\Rightarrow \quad n = 5q$ or $5q + 1$ or $5q + 2$ or $5q + 3$ or $5q + 4$.

Case I If $n = 5q$, then only n is divisible by 5.

Case II If $n = 5q + 1$, then $n + 4 = 5q + 1 + 4 = 5q + 5 = 5(q+1)$, which is divisible by 5.

So, in this case, only $(n + 4)$ is divisible by 5.

Case III If $n = 5q + 2$, then $n + 8 = 5q + 2 + 8 = 5q + 10$

$$= 5(q+2) \text{ which is divisible by 5.}$$

So, in this case only $(n + 8)$ is divisibly by 5.

Case IV If $n = 5q + 3$, then $n + 12 = 5q + 3 + 12 = 5q + 15 = 5(q+3)$, which is divisible by 5.

So, in this case only $(n + 12)$ is divisible by 5.

Case V If $n = 5q + 4$, then $n + 16 = 5q + 4 + 16 = 5q + 20 = 5(q+4)$, which is divisible by 5.

So, in this case, only $(n + 16)$ is divisible by 5.

Hence, one and only one out of $n, n+4, n+8, n+12$ and $n+16$ is divisible by 5, where n is any positive integer.

Alternate Method

Given numbers are $n, (n+4), (n+8), (n+12)$ and $(n+16)$, where n is any positive integer.

Then, let $n = 5q, 5q+1, 5q+2, 5q+3, 5q+4$ for $q \in N$

[by Euclid's division algorithm]

Then, in each case if we put the different values of n in the given numbers.

We definitely get one and only one of given numbers is divisible by 5.

Hence, one and only one out of $n, n+4, n+8, n+12$ and $n+16$ is divisible by 5.

Note (✱) *Topics related to these question have been removed from latest NCERT.*

Chapter

02

Polynomials

Multiple Choice Questions (MCQs)

Choose the correct answer from the given four options in the following questions:

Q.1 If one of the zeroes of the quadratic polynomial $(k-1)x^2 + kx + 1$ is -3, then the value of k is

(a) $\frac{4}{3}$ (b) $\frac{-4}{3}$ (c) $\frac{2}{3}$ (d) $\frac{-2}{3}$

- **Concept Insight** If α is the one of the zeroes of the quadratic polynomial $f(x) = ax^2 + bx + c$, then $f(\alpha)$ must be equal to 0.

Ans. *(a)* Given that, one of the zeroes of the quadratic polynomial say $p(x) = (k-1)x^2 + kx + 1$ is -3, then $p(-3) = 0$

$$\Rightarrow \quad (k-1)(-3)^2 + k(-3) + 1 = 0$$

$$\Rightarrow \quad 9(k-1) - 3k + 1 = 0$$

$$\Rightarrow \quad 9k - 9 - 3k + 1 = 0$$

$$\Rightarrow \quad 6k - 8 = 0$$

$$\Rightarrow \quad k = 4/3$$

Q.2 A quadratic polynomial, whose zeroes are -3 and 4, is

(a) $x^2 - x + 12$ (b) $x^2 + x + 12$ (c) $\frac{x^2}{2} - \frac{x}{2} - 6$ (d) $2x^2 + 2x - 24$

Ans. *(c)* Let $ax^2 + bx + c$ be a required polynomial whose zeroes are -3 and 4.

Then, sum of zeroes $= -3 + 4 = 1$ $\left[\because \text{sum of zeroes} = \frac{-b}{a}\right]$

$$\Rightarrow \quad \frac{-b}{a} = \frac{1}{1} \Rightarrow \frac{-b}{a} = \frac{-(-1)}{1} \quad \ldots(i)$$

and product of zeroes $= -3 \times 4 = -12$ $\left[\because \text{product of zeroes} = \frac{c}{a}\right]$

$$\Rightarrow \quad \frac{c}{a} = \frac{-12}{1} \quad \ldots(ii)$$

From Eqs. (i) and (ii), we get

$$a = 1, b = -1 \text{ and } c = -12$$

$\therefore$ Required polynomial $= 1 \cdot x^2 - 1 \cdot x - 12$

$$= x^2 - x - 12 = \frac{x^2}{2} - \frac{x}{2} - 6$$

We know that, if we multiply or divide any polynomial by any constant, then the zeroes of polynomial do not change.

Alternate Method

Let the zeroes of a quadratic polynomial are $\alpha = -3$ and $\beta = 4$.

Then, sum of zeroes $= \alpha + \beta = -3 + 4 = 1$

and product of zeroes $= \alpha\beta = (-3)(4) = -12$

$\therefore$ Required polynomial $= x^2 -$ (sum of zeroes)$x +$ (product of zeroes)

$$= x^2 - (1)x + (-12) = x^2 - x - 12$$

$$= \frac{x^2}{2} - \frac{x}{2} - 6$$

Q.3 If the zeroes of the quadratic polynomial $x^2 + (a+1)x + b$ are 2 and –3, then

(a) $a = -7, b = -1$
(b) $a = 5, b = -1$
(c) $a = 2, b = -6$
(d) $a = 0, b = -6$

Ans. *(d)* Let $p(x) = x^2 + (a+1)x + b$

Given that, 2 and –3 are the zeroes of the quadratic polynomial $p(x)$.

$\therefore$ $p(2) = 0$ and $p(-3) = 0$

$\Rightarrow$ $2^2 + (a+1)(2) + b = 0$

$\Rightarrow$ $4 + 2a + 2 + b = 0$

$\Rightarrow$ $2a + b = -6$ ...(i)

and $(-3)^2 + (a+1)(-3) + b = 0$

$\Rightarrow$ $9 - 3a - 3 + b = 0 \Rightarrow 3a - b = 6$ ...(ii)

On adding Eqs. (i) and (ii), we get

$$5a = 0 \Rightarrow a = 0$$

Put the value of a in Eq. (i), we get

$$2 \times 0 + b = -6 \Rightarrow b = -6$$

So, the required values are $a = 0$ and $b = -6$.

Q.4 The number of polynomials having zeroes as –2 and 5 is

(a) 1 (b) 2 (c) 3 (d) more than 3

Ans. *(d)* Let $p(x) = ax^2 + bx + c$ be the required polynomial whose zeroes are –2 and 5.

$\therefore$ Sum of zeroes $= \frac{-b}{a}$

$\Rightarrow$ $\frac{-b}{a} = -2 + 5 = \frac{3}{1} = \frac{-(-3)}{1}$ ...(i)

and product of zeroes $= \frac{c}{a}$

$\Rightarrow$ $\frac{c}{a} = -2 \times 5 = \frac{-10}{1}$ (ii)

From Eqs. (i) and (ii), we get

$$a = 1, b = -3 \text{ and } c = -10$$

$\therefore$ $$p(x) = ax^2 + bx + c = 1 \cdot x^2 - 3x - 10$$
$$= x^2 - 3x - 10$$

But we know that, if we multiply or divide any polynomial by any arbitrary constant, then the zeroes of polynomial never change.

$\therefore$ $$p(x) = kx^2 - 3kx - 10k \quad \text{[where, } k \text{ is a real number]}$$

$\Rightarrow$ $$p(x) = \frac{x^2}{k} - \frac{3}{k}x - \frac{10}{k}, \quad \text{[where, } k \text{ is a non-zero real number]}$$

Hence, the required number of polynomials are infinite *i.e.*, more than 3.

Mistake Alert ! *Students might forget the minus sign while finding the sum of zeroes of a quadratic polynomial.*

***Q.5** Given that one of the zeroes of the cubic polynomial $ax^3 + bx^2 + cx + d$ is zero, the product of the other two zeroes is

(a) $\frac{-c}{a}$ (b) $\frac{c}{a}$ (c) 0 (d) $\frac{-b}{a}$

Thinking Process Firstly, we find the sum of product of two zeroes at a time and put the value of one of the zeroes *i.e.*, zero, we get the required product of the other two zeroes.

Ans. *(b)* Let $p(x) = ax^3 + bx^2 + cx + d$

Given that, one of the zeroes of the cubic polynomial $p(x)$ is zero.

Let α, β and γ are the zeroes of cubic polynomial $p(x)$, where $\alpha = 0$.

We know that,

Sum of product of two zeroes at a time $= \frac{c}{a}$

$\Rightarrow$ $$\alpha\beta + \beta\gamma + \gamma\alpha = \frac{c}{a}$$

$\Rightarrow$ $$0 \times \beta + \beta\gamma + \gamma \times 0 = \frac{c}{a} \quad [\because \alpha = 0, \text{ given}]$$

$\Rightarrow$ $$0 + \beta\gamma + 0 = \frac{c}{a} \Rightarrow \beta\gamma = \frac{c}{a}$$

Hence, product of other two zeroes $= \frac{c}{a}$.

***Q.6** If one of the zeroes of the cubic polynomial $x^3 + ax^2 + bx + c$ is -1, then the product of the other two zeroes is

(a) $b - a + 1$ (b) $b - a - 1$ (c) $a - b + 1$ (d) $a - b - 1$

Thinking Process Firstly, we find the value of constant term 'c', by using $p(-1) = 0$. After that we find the product of all zeroes and put the value of one of the zeroes. Finally, we get the required result.

Ans. *(a)* Let $p(x) = x^3 + ax^2 + bx + c$

Let α, β and γ be the zeroes of the given cubic polynomial $p(x)$.

$\therefore$ $$\alpha = -1 \quad \text{[given]}$$

Note (✱) *Topics related to these question have been removed from latest NCERT.*

and $p(-1)=0 \Rightarrow (-1)^3+a(-1)^2+b(-1)+c=0$

$\Rightarrow$ $-1+a-b+c=0 \Rightarrow c=1-a+b$ ...(i)

We know that,

$$\text{Product of all zeroes} = -\frac{\text{Constant term}}{\text{Coefficient of } x^3} = -\frac{c}{1}$$

$\Rightarrow$ $\alpha\beta\gamma = -c$

$\Rightarrow$ $(-1)\,\beta\gamma = -c$ [$\because \alpha = -1$]

$\Rightarrow$ $\beta\gamma = c \Rightarrow \beta\gamma = 1-a+b$ [from Eq. (i)]

Hence, product of the other two roots is $1-a+b$.

Alternate Method

Since, -1 is one of the zeroes of the cubic polynomial $f(x)=x^3+ax^2+bx+c$ *i.e.*, $(x+1)$ is a factor of $f(x)$.

Now, using division algorithm,

$$\begin{array}{r|l} & x^2+(a-1)x+(b-a+1) \\ \hline x+1 & x^3+ax^2+bx+c \\ & x^3+x^2 \\ & \underline{-\quad -} \\ & (a-1)x^2+bx+c \\ & (a-1)x^2+(a-1)x \\ & \underline{-\qquad -} \\ & (b-a+1)x+c \\ & (b-a+1)x+(b-a+1) \\ & \underline{-\qquad -} \\ & (c-b+a-1) \end{array}$$

$\therefore$ $x^3+ax^2+bx+c=(x+1)\times\{x^2+(a-1)x+(b-a+1)\}+(c-b+a-1)$

$\Rightarrow$ $x^3+ax^2+bx+(b-a+1)=(x+1)\{x^2+(a-1)x+(b-a+1)\}$

Let α and β be the other two zeroes of the given polynomial, then

$$\text{Product of zeroes} = (-1)\,\alpha\cdot\beta = \frac{-\text{Constant term}}{\text{Coefficient of } x^3}$$

$\Rightarrow$ $-\alpha\cdot\beta = \dfrac{-(b-a+1)}{1} \Rightarrow \alpha\beta = -a+b+1$

Hence, the required product of other two zeroes is $(-a+b+1)$.

Q.7 The zeroes of the quadratic polynomial $x^2+99x+127$ are

(a) both positive (b) both negative

(c) one positive and one negative (d) both equal

Ans. *(b)* Let given quadratic polynomial be $p(x)=x^2+99x+127$.

Let α and β are the zeroes of quadratic polynomial $p(x)$.

$\therefore$ $\alpha\beta = 127$ and $\alpha+\beta=-99$

As $\alpha\beta$ is positive, then either both α and β are positive or both α and β are negative.

But $\alpha+\beta$ is negative.

$\Rightarrow$ Both α and β, are negative.

Hence, both zeroes of the given quadratic polynomial $p(x)$ are negative.

Alternate Method

We know that,

In quadratic polynomial, if either $a > 0, b > 0, c > 0$, or $a < 0, b < 0, c < 0$, then both zeroes are negative.

In given polynomial, we see that

$$a = 1 > 0, b = 99 > 0 \text{ and } c = 127 > 0$$

which satisfy the above condition.

So, both zeroes of the given quadratic polynomial are negative.

Mistake Alert! *Students need not to simplify the given quadratic polynomial.*

Q.8 The zeroes of the quadratic polynomial $x^2 + kx + k$ where $k \neq 0$,

(a) cannot both be positive
(b) cannot both be negative
(c) are always unequal
(d) are always equal

● **Concept Insight** Sum of two or more positive numbers is always greater than zero.

Ans. *(a)* Let α and β are the roots of the quadratic polynomial $p(x) = x^2 + kx + k$, where $k \neq 0$

Then, $\alpha + \beta = -k$ and $\alpha\beta = k$ ...(i)

As, $k \neq 0, \alpha$ and $\beta \neq 0$

From Eq. (i), $\alpha + \beta = -\alpha\beta$

$\Rightarrow$ $\alpha + \beta + \alpha\beta = 0$ ...(ii)

Eq. (ii), cannot have both value of α and β as positive because sum of 2 or more positive value cannot be zero.

Q.9 If the zeroes of the quadratic polynomial $ax^2 + bx + c$, where $c \neq 0$ are equal, then

(a) c and a have opposite signs
(b) c and b have opposite signs
(c) c and a have same signs
(d) c and b have the same signs

● **Concept Insight** Square of any numbers is always greater than or equal to zero.

Ans. *(c)* The zeroes of the given quadratic polynomial $ax^2 + bx + c$, $c \neq 0$ are equal. If coefficient of x^2 and constant term have the same sign *i.e.*, c and a have the same sign. While b *i.e.*, coefficient of x can be positive/negative but not zero.

e.g., (i) $x^2 + 4x + 4 = 0$ (ii) $x^2 - 4x + 4 = 0$

$\Rightarrow$ $(x + 2)^2 = 0$ $\Rightarrow$ $(x - 2)^2 = 0$

$\Rightarrow$ $x = -2, -2$ $\Rightarrow$ $x = 2, 2$

Q.10 If one of the zeroes of a quadratic polynomial of the form $x^2 + ax + b$ is the negative of the other, then it

(a) has no linear term and the constant term is negative
(b) has no linear term and the constant term is positive
(c) can have a linear term but the constant term is negative
(d) can have a linear term but the constant term is positive

Ans. *(a)* Let $f(x) = x^2 + ax + b$

and by given condition the zeroes are α and $-\alpha$.

$\therefore$ Sum of the zeroes $= \alpha - \alpha = a$

$\Rightarrow \qquad a = 0$

$\therefore \qquad f(x) = x^2 + b$, which cannot be linear.

and product of zeroes $= \alpha \cdot (-\alpha) = b$

$\Rightarrow \qquad -\alpha^2 = b$

which is possible when, $b < 0$.

Hence, it has no linear term and the constant term is negative.

Q.11 Which of the following is not the graph of a quadratic polynomial?

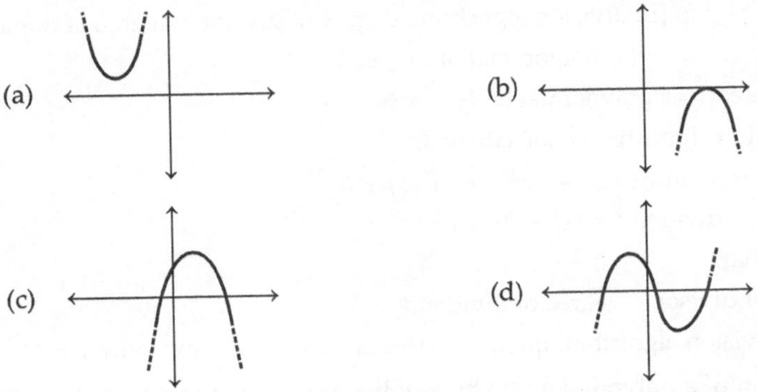

Ans. *(d)* For any quadratic polynomial $ax^2 + bx + c$, $a \neq 0$, the graph of the corresponding equation $y = ax^2 + bx + c$ has one of the two shapes either open upwards like $\cup$ or open downwards like $\cap$ depending on whether $a > 0$ or $a < 0$. These curves are called parabolas. So, option (d) cannot be possible.

Also, the curve of a quadratic polynomial crosses the X-axis on at most two points but in option (d) the curve crosses the X-axis on the three points, so it does not represent the quadratic polynomial.

Short Answer Questions with Reasoning

Q.1 Answer the following and justify.

*(i) Can $x^2 - 1$ be the quotient on division of $x^6 + 2x^3 + x - 1$ by a polynomial in x of degree 5?

*(ii) What will the quotient and remainder be on division of $ax^2 + bx + c$ by $px^3 + qx^2 + rx + s$, $p \neq 0$?

*(iii) If on division of a polynomial $p(x)$ by a polynomial $g(x)$, the quotient is zero, what is the relation between the degree of $p(x)$ and $g(x)$?

*(iv) If on division of a non-zero polynomial $p(x)$ by a polynomial $g(x)$, the remainder is zero, what is the relation between the degrees of $p(x)$ and $g(x)$?

(v) Can the quadratic polynomial $x^2 + kx + k$ have equal zeroes for some odd integer $k > 1$?

Ans. (i) *No*, because whenever we divide a polynomial $x^6 + 2x^3 + x - 1$ by a polynomial in x of degree 5, then we get quotient always as in linear form *i.e.*, polynomial in x of degree 1.

Note (*) *Topics related to these question have been removed from latest NCERT.*

Let divisor = a polynomial in x of degree 5 $= ax^5 + bx^4 + cx^3 + dx^2 + ex + f$

quotient $= x^2 - 1$

and dividend $= x^6 + 2x^3 + x - 1$

By division algorithm for polynomials,

dividend = divisor × quotient + remainder

$= (ax^5 + bx^4 + cx^3 + dx^2 + ex + f) \times (x^2 - 1)$ + remainder

= (a polynomial of degree 7) + Remainder

[in division algorithm, degree of divisor > degree of remainder]

= (a polynomial of degree 7)

But dividend = a polynomial of degree 6

So, division algorithm is not satisfied.

(ii) Given that, Divisor $px^3 + qx^2 + rx + s, p \neq 0$

and dividend $= ax^2 + bx + c$

We see that,

Degree of divisor > Degree of dividend

So, by division algorithm, quotient = 0 and remainder $= ax^2 + bx + c$

(iii) If division of a polynomial $p(x)$ by a polynomial $g(x)$, the quotient is zero, then relation between the degrees of $p(x)$ and $g(x)$ is degree of $p(x)$ < degree of $g(x)$.

(iv) If division of a non-zero polynomial $p(x)$ by a polynomial $g(x)$, the remainder is zero, then $g(x)$ is a factor of $p(x)$ and has degree less than or equal to the degree of $p(x)$. *i.e.*, degree of $g(x) \leq$ degree of $p(x)$.

(v) *No*, let $p(x) = x^2 + kx + k$

If $p(x)$ has equal zeroes, then its discriminant should be zero.

$\therefore$ $$D = B^2 - 4AC = 0 \quad ...(i)$$

On comparing $p(x)$ with $Ax^2 + Bx + C$, we get

$$A = 1,\ B = k \text{ and } C = k$$

$\therefore$ $$(k)^2 - 4(1)(k) = 0 \quad \text{[from Eq. (i)]}$$

$\Rightarrow$ $$k(k-4) = 0 \Rightarrow k = 0, 4$$

So, the quadratic polynomial $p(x)$ have equal zeroes only at $k = 0, 4$.

Q.2 Are the following statements 'True' or 'False'? Justify your answer.

(i) If the zeroes of a quadratic polynomial $ax^2 + bx + c$ are both positive, then a, b and c all have the same sign.

(ii) If the graph of a polynomial intersects the X-axis at only one point, it cannot be a quadratic polynomial.

(iii) If the graph of a polynomial intersects the X-axis at exactly two points, it need not be a quadratic polynomial.

*(iv) If two of the zeroes of a cubic polynomial are zero, then it does not have linear and constant terms.

*(v) If all the zeroes of a cubic polynomial are negative, then all the coefficients and the constant term of the polynomial have the same sign.

Note (✱) *Topics related to these question have been removed from latest NCERT.*

*(vi) If all three zeroes of a cubic polynomial $x^3 + ax^2 - bx + c$ are positive, then at least one of a, b and c is non-negative.

(vii) The only value of k for which the quadratic polynomial $kx^2 + x + k$ has equal zeroes is $\frac{1}{2}$.

Ans. (i) *False,* if the zeroes of a quadratic polynomial $ax^2 + bx + c$ are both positive, then

$$\alpha + \beta = -\frac{b}{a} \quad \text{and} \quad \alpha \cdot \beta = \frac{c}{a}$$

where α and β are the zeroes of quadratic polynomial.

$\therefore$ $c < 0, a < 0$ and $b > 0$

or $c > 0, a > 0$ and $b < 0$

(ii) *True,* if the graph of a polynomial intersects the X-axis at only one point, then it cannot be a quadratic polynomial because a quadratic polynomial may touch the X-axis at exactly one point or intersects X-axis at exactly two points or do not touch the X-axis.

(iii) *True,* if the graph of a polynomial intersects the X-axis at exactly two points, then it may or may not be a quadratic polynomial. As, a polynomial of degree more than 2 is possible which intersects the X-axis at exactly two points when it has two real roots and other imaginary roots.

(iv) *True,* let α, β and γ be the zeroes of the cubic polynomial and given that two of the zeroes have value 0.

Let $\beta = \gamma = 0$

and $f(x) = (x - \alpha)(x - \beta)(x - \gamma)$

$= (x - \alpha)(x - 0)(x - 0) = x^3 - \alpha x^2$

which does not have linear and constant terms.

(v) *True,* if $f(x) = ax^3 + bx^2 + cx + d$. Then, for all negative roots, a, b, c and d must have same sign.

(vi) *False,* let α, β and γ be the three zeroes of cubic polynomial $x^3 + ax^2 - bx + c$.

Then, product of zeroes $= -\frac{\text{Constant term}}{\text{Coefficient of } x^3}$

$\Rightarrow$ $\alpha\beta\gamma = -\frac{c}{1}$

$\Rightarrow$ $\alpha\beta\gamma = -c$ ...(i)

Given that, all three zeroes are positive. So, the product of all three zeroes is also positive *i.e.,* $\alpha\beta\gamma > 0$

$\Rightarrow$ $-c > 0$ [from Eq. (i)]

$\Rightarrow$ $c < 0$

Now, sum of the zeroes $= \alpha + \beta + \gamma = -\frac{\text{Coefficient of } x^2}{\text{Coefficient of } x^3}$

$\Rightarrow$ $\alpha + \beta + \gamma = -\frac{a}{1} = -a$

But α, β and γ are all positive.

Thus, its sum is also positive.

Note (*) *Topics related to these question have been removed from latest NCERT.*

So, $\alpha + \beta + \gamma > 0$

$\Rightarrow \quad -a > 0$

$\Rightarrow \quad a < 0$

and sum of the product of two zeroes at a time $= \dfrac{\text{Coefficient of } x}{\text{Coefficient of } x^3} = \dfrac{-b}{1}$

$\Rightarrow \quad \alpha\beta + \beta\gamma + \gamma\alpha = -b$

$\because \quad \alpha\beta + \beta\gamma + \alpha\gamma > 0 \quad \Rightarrow \quad -b > 0$

$\Rightarrow \quad b < 0$

So, the cubic polynomial $x^3 + ax^2 - bx + c$ has all three zeroes which are positive only when all constants a, b and c are negative.

(vii) *False*, let $f(x) = kx^2 + x + k$

For equal roots. Its discriminant should be zero *i.e.*, $D = b^2 - 4ac = 0$

$\Rightarrow \quad 1 - 4k \cdot k = 0 \Rightarrow 4k = 1 \Rightarrow k^2 = \dfrac{1}{4}$

$\Rightarrow \quad k = \pm\dfrac{1}{2}$

So, for two values of k, given quadratic polynomial has equal zeroes.

Short Answer Questions

Find the zeroes of the following polynomials by factorisation method and verify the relations between the zeroes and the coefficients of the polynomials.

Q.1 $4x^2 - 3x - 1$

Thinking Process Firstly, we use the factorisation method *i.e.*, splitting the middle term of quadratic polynomial and find its zeroes. After that use the formula of sum of zeroes and product of zeroes for verification.

Ans. Let $f(x) = 4x^2 - 3x - 1$

$= 4x^2 - 4x + x - 1$ [by splitting the middle term]

$= 4x(x-1) + 1(x-1) = (x-1)(4x+1)$

So, the value of $4x^2 - 3x - 1$ is zero when, $x - 1 = 0$ or $4x + 1 = 0$ *i.e.*, when $x = 1$ or $x = -\dfrac{1}{4}$.

So, the zeroes of $4x^2 - 3x - 1$ are 1 and $-\dfrac{1}{4}$.

$\therefore$ Sum of zeroes $= 1 - \dfrac{1}{4} = \dfrac{3}{4} = \dfrac{-(-3)}{4} = -\dfrac{\text{Coefficient of } x}{\text{Coefficient of } x^2}$

and product of zeroes $= (1)\left(-\dfrac{1}{4}\right) = -\dfrac{1}{4} = \dfrac{\text{Constant term}}{\text{Coefficient of } x^2}$

Hence, verified the relations between the zeroes and the coefficients of the polynomial.

Q.2 $3x^2 + 4x - 4$

Ans. Let $f(x) = 3x^2 + 4x - 4$

$= 3x^2 + 6x - 2x - 4$ [by splitting the middle term]

$= 3x(x+2) - 2(x+2) = (x+2)(3x-2)$

So, the value of $3x^2 + 4x - 4$ is zero when $x + 2 = 0$ or $3x - 2 = 0$ *i.e.,* when $x = -2$ or $x = \frac{2}{3}$. So, the zeroes of $3x^2 + 4x - 4$ are -2 and $\frac{2}{3}$.

$\therefore$ $$\text{Sum of zeroes} = -2 + \frac{2}{3} = -\frac{4}{3} = -\frac{\text{Coefficient of } x}{\text{Coefficient of } x^2}$$

and $$\text{product of zeroes} = (-2)\left(\frac{2}{3}\right) = \frac{-4}{3} = \frac{\text{Constant term}}{\text{Coefficient of } x^2}$$

Hence, verified the relations between the zeroes and the coefficients of the polynomial.

Q.3 $5t^2 + 12t + 7$

Ans. Let
$$\begin{aligned} f(t) &= 5t^2 + 12t + 7 \\ &= 5t^2 + 7t + 5t + 7 \quad \text{[by splitting the middle term]} \\ &= t(5t + 7) + 1(5t + 7) \\ &= (5t + 7)(t + 1) \end{aligned}$$

So, the value of $5t^2 + 12t + 7$ is zero when $5t + 7 = 0$ or $t + 1 = 0$

i.e., when $t = \frac{-7}{5}$ or $t = -1$.

So, the zeroes of $5t^2 + 12t + 7$ are $-7/5$ and -1.

$$\therefore \text{Sum of zeroes} = -\frac{7}{5} - 1 = \frac{-12}{5} = -\frac{\text{Coefficient of } t}{\text{Coefficient of } t^2}$$

$$\text{and product of zeroes} = \left(-\frac{7}{5}\right)(-1) = \frac{7}{5} = \frac{\text{Constant term}}{\text{Coefficient of } t^2}$$

Hence, verified the relations between the zeroes and the coefficients of the polynomial.

Q.4 $t^3 - 2t^2 - 15t$

Ans. Let
$$\begin{aligned} f(t) &= t^3 - 2t^2 - 15t \\ &= t(t^2 - 2t - 15) \\ &= t(t^2 - 5t + 3t - 15) \quad \text{[by splitting the middle term]} \\ &= t[t(t - 5) + 3(t - 5)] \\ &= t(t - 5)(t + 3) \end{aligned}$$

So, the value of $t^3 - 2t^2 - 15t$ is zero when $t = 0$ or $t - 5 = 0$ or $t + 3 = 0$

i.e., when $t = 0$ or $t = 5$ or $t = -3$.

So, the zeroes of $t^3 - 2t^2 - 15t$ are -3, 0 and 5.

$$\therefore \text{Sum of zeroes} = -3 + 0 + 5 = 2 = \frac{-(-2)}{1} = -\frac{\text{Coefficient of } t^2}{\text{Coefficient of } t^3}$$

Sum of product of two zeroes at a time
$$\begin{aligned} &= (-3)(0) + (0)(5) + (5)(-3) \\ &= 0 + 0 - 15 = -15 = \frac{\text{Coefficient of } t}{\text{Coefficient of } t^3} \end{aligned}$$

$$\text{and product of zeroes} = (-3)(0)(5) = 0 = \frac{\text{Constant term}}{\text{Coefficient of } t^3}$$

Hence, verified the relations between the zeroes and the coefficients of the polynomial.

Q.5 $2x^2 + \frac{7}{2}x + \frac{3}{4}$

Ans. Let $$f(x) = 2x^2 + \frac{7}{2}x + \frac{3}{4} = 8x^2 + 14x + 3$$
$$= 8x^2 + 12x + 2x + 3 \quad \text{[by splitting the middle term]}$$
$$= 4x(2x + 3) + 1(2x + 3)$$
$$= (2x + 3)(4x + 1)$$

So, the value of $8x^2 + 14x + 3$ is zero when $2x + 3 = 0$ or $4x + 1 = 0$,

i.e., when $x = -\frac{3}{2}$ or $x = -\frac{1}{4}$.

So, the zeroes of $8x^2 + 14x + 3$ are $-\frac{3}{2}$ and $-\frac{1}{4}$.

$\therefore$ $$\text{Sum of zeroes} = -\frac{3}{2} - \frac{1}{4} = -\frac{7}{4} = \frac{-7}{2\times 2}$$
$$= -\frac{(\text{Coefficient of } x)}{(\text{Coefficient of } x^2)}$$

and $$\text{product of zeroes} = \left(-\frac{3}{2}\right)\left(-\frac{1}{4}\right) = \frac{3}{8} = \frac{3}{2\times 4}$$
$$= \frac{\text{Constant term}}{\text{Coefficient of } x^2}$$

Hence, verified the relations between the zeroes and the coefficients of the polynomial.

Q.6 $4x^2 + 5\sqrt{2}x - 3$

Ans. Let $$f(x) = 4x^2 + 5\sqrt{2}x - 3$$
$$= 4x^2 + 6\sqrt{2}x - \sqrt{2}x - 3 \quad \text{[by splitting the middle term]}$$
$$= 2\sqrt{2}x(\sqrt{2}x + 3) - 1(\sqrt{2}x + 3)$$
$$= (\sqrt{2}x + 3)(2\sqrt{2}x - 1)$$

So, the value of $4x^2 + 5\sqrt{2}x - 3$ is zero when $\sqrt{2}x + 3 = 0$ or $2\sqrt{2}x - 1 = 0$,

i.e., when $x = -\frac{3}{\sqrt{2}}$ or $x = \frac{1}{2\sqrt{2}}$.

So, the zeroes of $4x^2 + 5\sqrt{2}\,x - 3$ are $-\frac{3}{\sqrt{2}}$ and $\frac{1}{2\sqrt{2}}$.

$\therefore$ $$\text{Sum of zeroes} = -\frac{3}{\sqrt{2}} + \frac{1}{2\sqrt{2}}$$
$$= -\frac{5}{2\sqrt{2}} = \frac{-5\sqrt{2}}{4}$$
$$= -\frac{(\text{Coefficient of } x)}{(\text{Coefficient of } x^2)}$$

and $$\text{product of zeroes} = -\frac{3}{\sqrt{2}} \cdot \frac{1}{2\sqrt{2}} = -\frac{3}{4} = \frac{\text{Constant term}}{\text{Coefficient of } x^2}$$

Hence, verified the relations between the zeroes and the coefficients of the polynomial.

Q.7 $2s^2 - (1 + 2\sqrt{2})s + \sqrt{2}$

Ans. Let
$$f(s) = 2s^2 - (1 + 2\sqrt{2})\,s + \sqrt{2}$$
$$= 2s^2 - s - 2\sqrt{2}s + \sqrt{2}$$
$$= s\,(2s - 1) - \sqrt{2}\,(2s - 1)$$
$$= (2s - 1)\,(s - \sqrt{2})$$

So, the value of $2s^2 - (1 + 2\sqrt{2})\,s + \sqrt{2}$ is zero when $2s - 1 = 0$ or $s - \sqrt{2} = 0$,

i.e., when $s = \frac{1}{2}$ or $s = \sqrt{2}$.

So, the zeroes of $2s^2 - (1 + 2\sqrt{2})\,s + \sqrt{2}$ are $\frac{1}{2}$ and $\sqrt{2}$.

$\therefore$ Sum of zeroes $= \frac{1}{2} + \sqrt{2} = \frac{1 + 2\sqrt{2}}{2} = \frac{-[-(1 + 2\sqrt{2})]}{2} = -\frac{\text{(Coefficient of } s)}{\text{(Coefficient of } s^2)}$

and product of zeroes $= \frac{1}{2} \cdot \sqrt{2} = \frac{1}{\sqrt{2}} = \frac{\text{Constant term}}{\text{Coefficient of } s^2}$

Hence, verified the relations between the zeroes and the coefficients of the polynomial.

Q.8 $v^2 + 4\sqrt{3}v - 15$

Ans. Let
$$f(v) = v^2 + 4\sqrt{3}\,v - 15$$
$$= v^2 + (5\sqrt{3} - \sqrt{3})v - 15 \quad \text{[by splitting the middle term]}$$
$$= v^2 + 5\sqrt{3}\,v - \sqrt{3}\,v - 15$$
$$= v(v + 5\sqrt{3}) - \sqrt{3}(v + 5\sqrt{3})$$
$$= (v + 5\sqrt{3})(v - \sqrt{3})$$

So, the value of $v^2 + 4\sqrt{3}\,v - 15$ is zero when $v + 5\sqrt{3} = 0$ or $v - \sqrt{3} = 0$,

i.e., when $v = -5\sqrt{3}$ or $v = \sqrt{3}$.

So, the zeroes of $v^2 + 4\sqrt{3}v - 15$ are $-5\sqrt{3}$ and $\sqrt{3}$.

$\therefore$ Sum of zeroes $= -5\sqrt{3} + \sqrt{3} = -4\sqrt{3} = -\left(\frac{\text{Coefficient of } v}{\text{Coefficient of } v^2}\right)$

and product of zeroes $= (-5\sqrt{3})\,(\sqrt{3})$
$$= -5 \times 3 = -15 = \left(\frac{\text{Constant term}}{\text{Coefficient of } v^2}\right)$$

Hence, verified the relations between the zeroes and the coefficients of the polynomial.

Q.9 $y^2 + \frac{3}{2}\sqrt{5}y - 5$

Ans. Let $f(y) = y^2 + \frac{3}{2}\sqrt{5}y - 5$
$$= 2y^2 + 3\sqrt{5}\,y - 10$$
$$= 2y^2 + 4\sqrt{5}\,y - \sqrt{5}\,y - 10 \quad \text{[by splitting the middle term]}$$
$$= 2y\,(y + 2\sqrt{5}) - \sqrt{5}\,(y + 2\sqrt{5})$$
$$= (y + 2\sqrt{5})\,(2y - \sqrt{5})$$

So, the value of $y^2 + \frac{3}{2}\sqrt{5}y - 5$ is zero when $(y + 2\sqrt{5}) = 0$ or $(2y - \sqrt{5}) = 0$

i.e., when $y = -2\sqrt{5}$ or $y = \frac{\sqrt{5}}{2}$.

So, the zeroes of $y^2 + \frac{3}{2}\sqrt{5}y - 5$ are $-2\sqrt{5}$ and $\frac{\sqrt{5}}{2}$.

$\therefore$ Sum of zeroes $= -2\sqrt{5} + \frac{\sqrt{5}}{2} = \frac{-3\sqrt{5}}{2} = -\frac{(\text{Coefficient of } y)}{(\text{Coefficient of } y^2)}$

And product of zeroes $= -2\sqrt{5} \times \frac{\sqrt{5}}{2} = -5 = \frac{\text{Constant term}}{\text{Coefficient of } y^2}$

Hence, verified the relations between the zeroes and the coefficients of the polynomial.

Q.10 $7y^2 - \frac{11}{3}y - \frac{2}{3}$

Ans. Let

$$\begin{aligned} f(y) &= 7y^2 - \frac{11}{3}y - \frac{2}{3} \\ &= 21y^2 - 11y - 2 \\ &= 21y^2 - 14y + 3y - 2 \quad \text{[by splitting the middle term]} \\ &= 7y(3y - 2) + 1(3y - 2) \\ &= (3y - 2)(7y + 1) \end{aligned}$$

So, the value of $7y^2 - \frac{11}{3}y - \frac{2}{3}$ is zero when $3y - 2 = 0$ or $7y + 1 = 0$,

i.e., when $y = \frac{2}{3}$ or $y = -\frac{1}{7}$.

So, the zeroes of $7y^2 - \frac{11}{3}y - \frac{2}{3}$ are $\frac{2}{3}$ and $-\frac{1}{7}$.

$\therefore$ Sum of zeroes $= \frac{2}{3} - \frac{1}{7} = \frac{14 - 3}{21} = \frac{11}{21} = -\left(\frac{-11}{3 \times 7}\right)$

$$= -\left(\frac{\text{Coefficient of } y}{\text{Coefficient of } y^2}\right)$$

and product of zeroes $= \left(\frac{2}{3}\right)\left(-\frac{1}{7}\right) = \frac{-2}{21} = \frac{-2}{3 \times 7}$

$$= \left(\frac{\text{Constant term}}{\text{Coefficient of } y^2}\right)$$

Hence, verified the relations between the zeroes and the coefficients of the polynomial.

Long Answer Questions

Q.1 For each of the following, find a quadratic polynomial whose sum and product respectively of the zeroes are as given. Also, find the zeroes of these polynomials by factorisation.

(i) $\frac{-8}{3}, \frac{4}{3}$ (ii) $\frac{21}{8}, \frac{5}{16}$ (iii) $-2\sqrt{3}, -9$ (iv) $\frac{-3}{2\sqrt{5}}, -\frac{1}{2}$

Thinking Process

(i) Firstly we use the concept or method of formation of a quadratic polynomial, *i.e.*, $f(x) = x^2 -$ (sum of the zeroes) $x +$ (product of zeroes).

(ii) After making a quadratic polynomial we factorise it by splitting the middle term and get the required zeroes.

Ans. (i) Given that, sum of zeroes $(S) = -\frac{8}{3}$

and product of zeroes $(P) = \frac{4}{3}$

$\therefore$ Required quadratic polynomial, $f(x) = x^2 - Sx + P$

$$= x^2 + \frac{8}{3}x + \frac{4}{3} = 3x^2 + 8x + 4$$

Using factorisation method, $f(x) = 3x^2 + 6x + 2x + 4$

$$= 3x(x+2) + 2(x+2) = (x+2)(3x+2)$$

The value of $3x^2 + 8x + 4 = 0$

when $x + 2 = 0$ or $3x + 2 = 0$

$\Rightarrow$ $x = -2$ or $x = -\frac{2}{3}$

Hence, the zeroes of $f(x)$ are -2 and $-\frac{2}{3}$.

(ii) Given that, $S = \frac{21}{8}$ and $P = \frac{5}{16}$

$\therefore$ Required quadratic polynomial, $f(x) = x^2 - Sx + P$

$$= x^2 - \frac{21}{8}x + \frac{5}{16}$$

$$= 16x^2 - 42x + 5$$

Using factorisation method, $f(x) = 16x^2 - 40x - 2x + 5$

$$= 8x(2x-5) - 1(2x-5)$$

$$= (2x-5)(8x-1)$$

The value of $16x^2 - 4x + 5 = 0$

when $(2x-5) = 0$ or $8x - 1 = 0$

$\Rightarrow$ $x = \frac{5}{2}$ or $x = \frac{1}{8}$

Hence, the zeroes of $f(x)$ are $\frac{5}{2}$ and $\frac{1}{8}$.

(iii) Given that, $S = -2\sqrt{3}$ and $P = -9$

$\therefore$ Required quadratic polynomial,

$$f(x) = x^2 - Sx + P = x^2 + 2\sqrt{3}x - 9$$
$$= x^2 + 3\sqrt{3}x - \sqrt{3}x - 9 \quad \text{[using factorisation method]}$$
$$= x(x + 3\sqrt{3}) - \sqrt{3}(x + 3\sqrt{3})$$
$$= (x + 3\sqrt{3})(x - \sqrt{3})$$

The value of $x^2 + 2\sqrt{3}x - 9 = 0$, when

$$x + 3\sqrt{3} = 0 \text{ or } x - \sqrt{3} = 0$$
$$\Rightarrow \quad x = -3\sqrt{3} \text{ or } x = \sqrt{3}$$

Hence, the zeroes of $f(x)$ are $-3\sqrt{3}$ and $\sqrt{3}$.

(iv) Given that, $S = -\dfrac{3}{2\sqrt{5}}$ and $P = -\dfrac{1}{2}$

$\therefore$ Required quadratic polynomial,

$$f(x) = x^2 - Sx + P = x^2 + \frac{3}{2\sqrt{5}}x - \frac{1}{2} = 2\sqrt{5}x^2 + 3x - \sqrt{5}$$

Using factorisation method, $f(x) = 2\sqrt{5}\,x^2 + 5x - 2x - \sqrt{5}$

$$= \sqrt{5}x(2x + \sqrt{5}) - 1(2x + \sqrt{5}) = (2x + \sqrt{5})(\sqrt{5}x - 1)$$

The value of $2\sqrt{5}x^2 + 3x - \sqrt{5} = 0$, when

$$2x + \sqrt{5} = 0 \text{ or } \sqrt{5x} - 1 = 0$$
$$\Rightarrow \quad x = -\frac{\sqrt{5}}{2} \text{ or } x = \frac{1}{\sqrt{5}}$$

Hence, the zeroes of $f(x)$ are $-\dfrac{\sqrt{5}}{2}$ and $\dfrac{1}{\sqrt{5}}$.

***Q.2 Given that the zeroes of the cubic polynomial $x^3 - 6x^2 + 3x + 10$ are of the form a, $a + b$ and $a + 2b$ for some real numbers a and b, find the values of a and b as well as the zeroes of the given polynomial.**

- **Concept Insight** Using the following relations related to a cubic polynomial.

  (i) Sum of the zeroes $= -\dfrac{\text{Coefficient of } x^2}{\text{Coefficient of } x^3}$

  (ii) Sum of product of two zeroes at a time $= \dfrac{\text{Coefficient of } x}{\text{Coefficient of } x^3}$

Ans. Let $f(x) = x^3 - 6x^2 + 3x + 10$

Given that, a, $(a + b)$ and $(a + 2b)$ are the zeroes of $f(x)$, then

$$\text{Sum of the zeroes} = -\frac{(\text{Coefficient of of } x^2)}{(\text{Coefficient of } x^2)}$$

$$\Rightarrow \quad a + (a + b) + (a + 2b) = -\frac{(-6)}{1}$$
$$\Rightarrow \quad 3a + 3b = 6$$
$$\Rightarrow \quad a + b = 2 \qquad \text{...(i)}$$

$$\text{Sum of product of two zeroes at a time} = \left(\frac{\text{Coefficient of } x}{\text{Coefficient of } x^3}\right)$$

Note (✱) *Topics related to these question have been removed from latest NCERT.*

$$\Rightarrow \quad a(a+b)+(a+b)(a+2b)+a(a+2b)=\frac{3}{1}$$
$$\Rightarrow \quad a(a+b)+(a+b)\{(a+b)+b\}+a\{(a+b)+b\}=3$$
$$\Rightarrow \quad 2a+2(2+b)+a(2+b)=3 \quad \text{[using Eq. (i)]}$$
$$\Rightarrow \quad 2a+2(2+2-a)+a(2+2-a)=3 \quad \text{[using Eq. (i)]}$$
$$\Rightarrow \quad 2a+8-2a+4a-a^2=3$$
$$\Rightarrow \quad -a^2+8=3-4a$$
$$\Rightarrow \quad a^2-4a-5=0$$

Using factorisation method,

$$a^2-5a+a-5=0$$
$$\Rightarrow \quad a(a-5)+1(a-5)=0$$
$$\Rightarrow \quad (a-5)(a+1)=0$$
$$\Rightarrow \quad a=-1, 5$$

when $a=-1$, then $b=3$

when $a=5$, then $b=-3$ [using Eq. (i)]

$\therefore$ Required zeroes of $f(x)$ are

when $a=-1$ and $b=3$,

Then, $a, (a+b), (a+2b) = -1, (-1+3), (-1+6)$ or $-1, 2, 5$

when $a=5$ and $b=-3$, then

$$a, (a+b), (a+2b) = 5, (5-3), (5-6) \quad \text{or} \quad 5, 2, -1.$$

Hence, the required values are $a=-1$ and $b=3$ or $a=5$, $b=-3$ and the zeroes are -1, 2 and 5.

***Q.3** Given that $\sqrt{2}$ is a zero of the cubic polynomial $6x^3+\sqrt{2}x^2-10x-4\sqrt{2}$, find its other two zeroes.

Thinking Process Use division algorithm and get a quadratic polynomial. Further factorize the quadratic polynomial by factorisation method and get the other two required zeroes.

Ans. Let $f(x)=6x^3+\sqrt{2}x^2-10x-4\sqrt{2}$ and given that, $\sqrt{2}$ is one of the zeroes of $f(x)$ *i.e.*, $(x-\sqrt{2})$ is one of the factor of given cubic polynomial.

Now, using division algorithm,

$$\begin{array}{r|l} & 6x^2+7\sqrt{2}x+4 \\ (x-\sqrt{2}) & 6x^3+\sqrt{2}x^2-10x-4\sqrt{2} \\ & 6x^3-6\sqrt{2}x^2 \\ & - \quad + \\ \hline & 7\sqrt{2}x^2-10x-4\sqrt{2} \\ & 7\sqrt{2}x^2-14x \\ & - \quad + \\ \hline & 4x-4\sqrt{2} \\ & 4x-4\sqrt{2} \\ & - \quad + \\ \hline & \times \end{array}$$

Note (*) *Topics related to these question have been removed from latest NCERT.*

$\therefore\quad 6x^3 + \sqrt{2}x^2 - 10x - 4\sqrt{2} = (6x^2 + 7\sqrt{2}x + 4) \times (x - \sqrt{2}) + 0$

[$\because$ dividend = divisor × quotient + remainder]

$= (x - \sqrt{2})(6x^2 + 4\sqrt{2}x + 3\sqrt{2}x + 4)$

$= (x - \sqrt{2})\{\sqrt{2}x(3\sqrt{2}x + 4) + 1(3\sqrt{2}x + 4)\}$

$= (x - \sqrt{2})\{(3\sqrt{2}x + 4)(\sqrt{2}x + 1)\}$

$= (x - \sqrt{2})(\sqrt{2}x + 1)(3\sqrt{2}x + 4)$

The value of $6x^3 + \sqrt{2}x^2 - 10x - 4\sqrt{2} = 0$, when

$x - \sqrt{2} = 0$ or $\sqrt{2}x + 1 = 0$

or $\quad 3\sqrt{2}x + 4 = 0$

$\Rightarrow \quad x = \sqrt{2}$ or $x = -\dfrac{1}{\sqrt{2}}$

or $\quad x = -\dfrac{4}{3\sqrt{2}}$

So, its other zeroes are $-\dfrac{1}{\sqrt{2}}$ and $-\dfrac{4}{3\sqrt{2}}$.

***Q.4** Find k, so that $x^2 + 2x + k$ is a factor of $2x^4 + x^3 - 14x^2 + 5x + 6$. Also, find all the zeroes of the two polynomials.

Ans. Given that, $x^2 + 2x + k$ is a factor of $2x^4 + x^3 - 14x^2 + 5x + 6$, then we apply division algorithm,

$$\begin{array}{r|l} & 2x^2 - 3x + (-8 - 2k) \\ x^2 + 2x + k & 2x^4 + x^3 - 14x^2 + 5x + 6 \\ & \underline{\underset{-}{2x^4} + \underset{-}{4x^3} + \underset{-}{2kx^2}} \\ & -3x^3 - (2k + 14)x^2 + 5x + 6 \\ & \underline{\underset{+}{-3x^3} \underset{+}{- 6x^2} \quad \underset{+}{- 3kx}} \\ & (-8 - 2k)x^2 + (3k + 5)x + 6 \\ & \underline{\underset{-}{(-8 - 2k)x^2} + \underset{-}{2(-8 - 2k)x} + \underset{-}{k(-8 - 2k)}} \\ & (21 + 7k)x + (6 + 8k + 2k^2) \end{array}$$

Since, $(x^2 + 2x + k)$ is a factor of $2x^4 + x^3 - 14x^2 + 5x + 6$.

So, when we apply division algorithm remainder should be zero.

$\therefore \quad (7k + 21)x + (2k^2 + 8k + 6) = 0 \cdot x + 0$

$\Rightarrow \quad 7k + 21 = 0$ and $2k^2 + 8k + 6 = 0$

$\Rightarrow \quad k = -3$ or $k^2 + 4k + 3 = 0$

$\Rightarrow \quad k^2 + 3k + k + 3 = 0$ [by splitting middle term]

$\Rightarrow \quad k(k + 3) + 1(k + 3) = 0$

$\Rightarrow \quad (k + 1)(k + 3) = 0$

$\Rightarrow \quad k = -1$ or -3

Here, if we take $k = -3$, then remainder will be zero.

Note (*) *Topics related to these question have been removed from latest NCERT.*

Thus, the required value of k is -3.

Now, dividend = divisor × quotient + remainder

$\Rightarrow \quad 2x^4 + x^3 - 14x^2 + 5x + 16 = (x^2 + 2x - 3)(2x^2 - 3x - 2)$

Using factorisation method,

$$2x^4 + x^3 - 14x^2 + 5x + 16$$
$$= (x^2 + 3x - x - 3)(2x^2 - 4x + x - 2) \quad \text{[by splitting middle term]}$$
$$= \{x(x+3) - 1(x+3)\}\{2x(x-2) + 1(x-2)\}$$
$$= (x-1)(x+3)(x-2)(2x+1)$$

Hence, the zeroes of $x^2 + 2x - 3$ are 1, –3 and the zeroes of $2x^2 - 3x - 2$ are 2, $-\frac{1}{2}$.

Hence, the zeroes of $2x^4 + x^3 - 14x^2 + 5x + 6$ are 1, –3, 2, $\frac{-1}{2}$.

***Q. 5** Given that $x - \sqrt{5}$ is a factor of the cubic polynomial $x^3 - 3\sqrt{5}x^2 + 13x - 3\sqrt{5}$, find all the zeroes of the polynomial.

Ans. Let $f(x) = x^3 - 3\sqrt{5}x^2 + 13x - 3\sqrt{5}$ and given that, $(x - \sqrt{5})$ is a one of the factor of $f(x)$.

Now, using division algorithm,

$$\begin{array}{r|l} & x^2 - 2\sqrt{5}x + 3 \\ \hline x - \sqrt{5} & x^3 - 3\sqrt{5}x^2 + 13x - 3\sqrt{5} \\ & x^3 - \sqrt{5}x^2 \\ & \underline{- \quad +} \\ & -2\sqrt{5}x^2 + 13x - 3\sqrt{5} \\ & -2\sqrt{5}x^2 + 10x \\ & \underline{+ \quad -} \\ & 3x - 3\sqrt{5} \\ & 3x - 3\sqrt{5} \\ & \underline{- \quad +} \\ & 0 \end{array}$$

$\therefore x^3 - 3\sqrt{5}x^2 + 13x - 3\sqrt{5} = (x^2 - 2\sqrt{5}x + 3) \times (x - \sqrt{5})$

[$\because$ dividend = divisor × quotient + remainder]

$= (x - \sqrt{5})[x^2 - \{(\sqrt{5} + \sqrt{2}) + (\sqrt{5} - \sqrt{2})\}x + 3]$ [by splitting the middle term]

$= (x - \sqrt{5})[x^2 - (\sqrt{5} + \sqrt{2})x - (\sqrt{5} - \sqrt{2})x + (\sqrt{5} + \sqrt{2})(\sqrt{5} - \sqrt{2})]$

[$\because 3 = (\sqrt{5} + \sqrt{2})(\sqrt{5} - \sqrt{2})$]

$= (x - \sqrt{5})[x\{x - (\sqrt{5} + \sqrt{2})\} - (\sqrt{5} - \sqrt{2})\{x - (\sqrt{5} + \sqrt{2})\}]$

$= (x - \sqrt{5})\{x - (\sqrt{5} + \sqrt{2})\}\{x - (\sqrt{5} - \sqrt{2})\}$

Hence, all the zeroes of polynomial are $\sqrt{5}$, $(\sqrt{5} + \sqrt{2})$ and $(\sqrt{5} - \sqrt{2})$.

Note (*) *Topics related to these question have been removed from latest NCERT.*

***Q.6** For which values of a and b, are the zeroes of $q(x) = x^3 + 2x^2 + a$ also the zeroes of the polynomial $p(x) = x^5 - x^4 - 4x^3 + 3x^2 + 3x + b$? Which zeroes of $p(x)$ are not the zeroes of $q(x)$?

Thinking Process

(i) Firstly, we use the division algorithm to get the remainder. Since, $q(x)$ is a factor of $p(x)$. So, remainder should be zero.

(ii) Now, equating the like terms of x and get the values of 'a' and 'b'. After that factorise the quotient by splitting the middle term method.

(iii) Finally, we get two more zeroes, which are not the zeroes of $q(x)$.

Ans. Given that the zeroes of $q(x) = x^3 + 2x^2 + a$ are also the zeroes of the polynomial $p(x) = x^5 - x^4 - 4x^3 + 3x^2 + 3x + b$ *i.e.,* $q(x)$ is a factor of $p(x)$. Then, we use a division algorithm.

$$\begin{array}{r|l} & x^2 - 3x + 2 \\ x^3 + 2x^2 + a & x^5 - x^4 - 4x^3 + 3x^2 + 3x + b \\ & \underline{\overset{-}{x^5} \overset{-}{+ 2x^4} \quad \overset{-}{+ ax^2}} \\ & -3x^4 - 4x^3 + (3-a)x^2 + 3x + b \\ & \underline{\overset{+}{-3x^4} \overset{+}{- 6x^3} \quad \overset{+}{- 3ax}} \\ & 2x^3 + (3-a)x^2 + (3+3a)x + b \\ & \underline{\overset{-}{2x^3} \overset{-}{+ 4x^2} \quad \overset{-}{+ 2a}} \\ & -(1+a)x^2 + (3+3a)x + (b-2a) \end{array}$$

If $(x^3 + 2x^2 + a)$ is a factor of $(x^5 - x^4 - 4x^3 + 3x^2 + 3x + b)$, then remainder should be zero.

i.e., $-(1+a)x^2 + (3+3a)x + (b-2a) = 0 = 0 \cdot x^2 + 0 \cdot x + 0$

On comparing the coefficient of x and constant term, we get

$$a + 1 = 0$$

$\Rightarrow$ $$a = -1$$

and $$b - 2a = 0$$

$\Rightarrow$ $$b = 2a$$

$\Rightarrow$ $$b = 2(-1) = -2 \qquad [\because a = -1]$$

For $a = -1$ and $b = -2$, the zeroes of $q(x)$ are also the zeroes of the polynomial $p(x)$.

$\therefore$ $$q(x) = x^3 + 2x^2 - 1$$

and $$p(x) = x^5 - x^4 - 4x^3 + 3x^2 + 3x - 2$$

Now, dividend = divisor × quotient + remainder

$$p(x) = (x^3 + 2x^2 - 1)(x^2 - 3x + 2) + 0$$
$$= (x^3 + 2x^2 - 1)\{x^2 - 2x - x + 2\}$$
$$= (x^3 + 2x^2 - 1)(x - 2)(x - 1)$$

Hence, the zeroes of $p(x)$ are 1 and 2 which are not the zeroes of $q(x)$.

Note (*) *Topics related to these question have been removed from latest NCERT.*

Chapter
03

Pair of Linear Equations in Two Variables

Multiple Choice Questions (MCQs)

Choose the correct answer from the given four options in the following questions:

Q.1 Graphically, the pair of equations

$$6x - 3y + 10 = 0$$
$$2x - y + 9 = 0$$

represents two lines which are

(a) intersecting at exactly one point.
(b) intersecting exactly two points.
(c) coincident.
(d) parallel.

Ans. *(d)* We know that, the general form of the pair of linear equation is

$$a_1x + b_1y + c_1 = 0$$
$$a_2x + b_2y + c_2 = 0$$

Comparing the general form with the given pair of equations, we get

$$a_1 = 6, b_1 = -3, c_1 = 10$$
$$a_2 = 2, b_2 = -1, c_2 = 9$$

$\therefore$ $$\frac{a_1}{a_2} = \frac{6}{2} = \frac{3}{1}; \frac{b_1}{b_2} = \frac{-3}{-1} = \frac{3}{1}; \frac{c_1}{c_2} = \frac{10}{9}$$

$\therefore$ $$\frac{a_1}{a_2} = \frac{b_1}{b_2} \neq \frac{c_1}{c_2}$$

i.e., $$\frac{3}{1} = \frac{3}{1} \neq \frac{10}{9}$$

$\therefore$Lines representing the given equations can parallel.

Q.2 The pair of equations $x + 2y + 5 = 0$ and $-3x - 6y + 1 = 0$ have

(a) a unique solution
(b) exactly two solutions
(c) infinitely many solutions
(d) no solution

Ans. *(d)* Given, equations are $x + 2y + 5 = 0$ and $-3x - 6y + 1 = 0$

We know that the general form of the pair of linear equation is

$$a_1x + b_1y + c_1 = 0$$
$$a_2x + b_2y + c_2 = 0$$

So, comparing the general form with the given pair of equations, we get

Here, $a_1 = 1, b_1 = 2, c_1 = 5$ and $a_2 = -3, b_2 = -6, c_2 = 1$

$$\therefore \quad \frac{a_1}{a_2} = -\frac{1}{3}, \frac{b_1}{b_2} = -\frac{2}{6} = -\frac{1}{3}, \frac{c_1}{c_2} = \frac{5}{1}$$

$$\therefore \quad \frac{a_1}{a_2} = \frac{b_1}{b_2} \neq \frac{c_1}{c_2}$$

Hence, the pair of equations has no solution.

Q.3 If a pair of linear equations is consistent, then the lines will be

(a) parallel
(b) always coincident
(c) intersecting or coincident
(d) always intersecting

Ans. *(c)* Condition for a consistent pair of linear equations

$$\frac{a_1}{a_2} \neq \frac{b_1}{b_2}$$ [intersecting lines having unique solution]

and $$\frac{a_1}{a_2} = \frac{b_1}{b_2} = \frac{c_1}{c_2}$$ [coincident lines having infinitely many solutions]

Q. 4 The pair of equations $y = 0$ and $y = -7$ has

(a) one solution
(b) two solutions
(c) infinitely many solutions
(d) no solution

- **Concept Insight** Liner representing the equations $y = a$ or $y = -a$ if always parallel to X-axis.
  Line $y = 0$ always lie on the X-axis.

Ans. *(d)* The given pair of equations are $y = 0$ and $y = -7$.

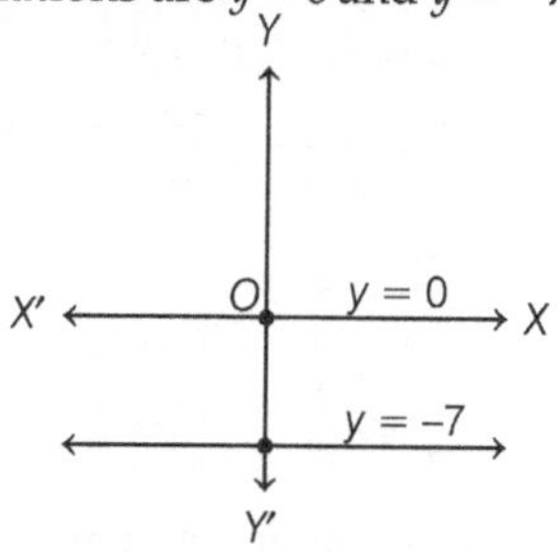

Graphically, we can observe that both lines are parallel. Lines have no solution.

Q.5 The pair of equations $x = a$ and $y = b$ graphically represents lines which are

(a) parallel
(b) intersecting at (b, a)
(c) coincident
(d) intersecting at (a, b)

- **Concept Insight** Graphically $x = a$ represents a line parallel to Y-axis at a distance of a unit, from Y-axis and $y = b$ represents a line parallel to X-axis at a distance of b unit from X-axis.

Ans. *(d)* By graphically in every condition, if $a, b > 0$; $a, b < 0$; $a > 0, b < 0$; $a < 0, b > 0$ but $a = b \neq 0$.

The pair of equations $x = a$ and $y = b$ graphically represents lines which are intersecting at (a, b).

If $a, b > 0$

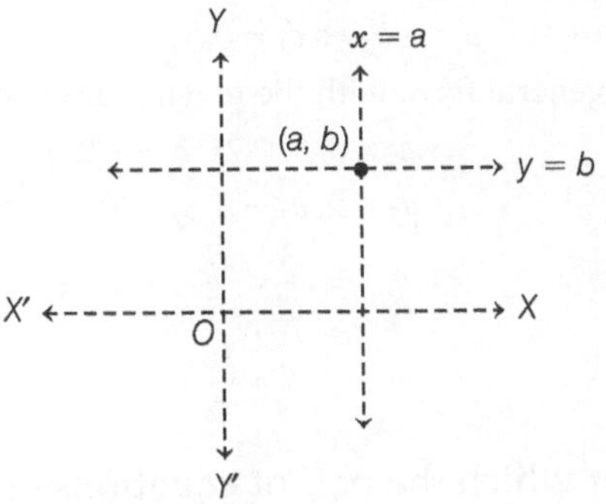

Similarly, in all cases two lines intersect at (a, b).

Q.6 For what value of k, do the equations $3x - y + 8 = 0$ and $6x - ky = -16$ represent coincident lines?

(a) $\frac{1}{2}$ (b) $-\frac{1}{2}$ (c) 2 (d) -2

Thinking Proces Apply the condition for coincident lines.

Ans. *(c)* Condition for coincident lines is

$$\frac{a_1}{a_2} = \frac{b_1}{b_2} = \frac{c_1}{c_2} \quad \text{...(i)}$$

Given lines, $3x - y + 8 = 0$

and $6x - ky + 16 = 0$

Here, $a_1 = 3, b_1 = -1, c_1 = 8$

and $a_2 = 6, b_2 = -k, c_2 = 16$

From Eq. (i), $\frac{3}{6} = \frac{-1}{-k} = \frac{8}{16}$

$\Rightarrow \frac{1}{k} = \frac{1}{2}$

$\therefore k = 2$

Q.7 If the lines given by $3x + 2ky = 2$ and $2x + 5y + 1 = 0$ are parallel, then the value of k is

(a) $-\frac{5}{4}$ (b) $\frac{2}{5}$

(c) $\frac{15}{4}$ (d) $\frac{3}{2}$

Ans. *(c)* Condition for parallel lines is

$$\frac{a_1}{a_2} = \frac{b_1}{b_2} \neq \frac{c_1}{c_2} \quad \ldots(i)$$

Given lines, $3x + 2ky - 2 = 0$

and $2x + 5y + 1 = 0$

We know, that the general form of the pair of linear equation is

$$a_1x + b_1y + c_1 = 0$$
$$a_2x + b_2y + c_2 = 0$$

On comparing the general form with the given pair of equations, we get

$$a_1 = 3, b_1 = 2k, c_1 = -2$$

and $a_2 = 2, b_2 = 5, c_2 = 1$

From Eq. (i), $\frac{3}{2} = \frac{2k}{5}$

$\therefore$ $k = \frac{15}{4}$

Q.8 The value of c for which the pair of equations $cx - y = 2$ and $6x - 2y = 3$ will have infinitely many solutions is

(a) 3 (b) -3 (c) -12 (d) no value

Ans. *(d)* Condition for infinitely many solutions is

$$\frac{a_1}{a_2} = \frac{b_1}{b_2} = \frac{c_1}{c_2} \quad \ldots(i)$$

The given lines are $cx - y = 2$ and $6x - 2y = 3$

We know, that the general form of the pair of linear equation is

$$a_1x + b_1y + c_1 = 0$$
$$a_2x + b_2y + c_2 = 0$$

On comparing the general form with the given pair of equations, we get

$$a_1 = c, b_1 = -1, c_1 = -2$$

and $a_2 = 6, b_2 = -2, c_2 = -3$

From Eq. (i), $\frac{c}{6} = \frac{-1}{-2} = \frac{-2}{-3}$

Here, $\frac{c}{6} = \frac{1}{2}$ and $\frac{c}{6} = \frac{2}{3}$

$\Rightarrow$ $c = 3$ and $c = 4$

Since, c has different values.

Hence, for no value of c the pair of linear equations will have infinitely many solutions.

Q.9 One equation of a pair of dependent linear equations is $-5x + 7y = 2$. The second equation can be

(a) $10x + 14y + 4 = 0$ (b) $-10x - 14y + 4 = 0$
(c) $-10x + 14y + 4 = 0$ (d) $10x - 14y = -4$

Thinking Process Condition for dependent linear equations is $\frac{a_1}{a_2} = \frac{b_1}{b_2} = \frac{c_1}{c_2} = \frac{1}{k}$.

Ans. *(d)* Given equation of line is, $-5x + 7y - 2 = 0$

Here, $a_1 = -5, b_1 = 7, c_1 = -2$

$\therefore$ $-\dfrac{5}{a_2} = \dfrac{7}{b_2} = -\dfrac{2}{c_2} = \dfrac{1}{k}$ [say]

$\Rightarrow$ $a_2 = -5k, b_2 = 7k, c_2 = -2k$

where, k is any arbitrary constant.

Putting $k = 2$, then $a_2 = -10, b_2 = 14$

and $c_2 = -4$

The required equation of line becomes

$$a_2x + b_2y + c_2 = 0$$

$$\Rightarrow \quad -10x + 14y - 4 = 0$$

$$\Rightarrow \quad 10x - 14y + 4 = 0$$

$$\Rightarrow \quad 10x - 14y = -4$$

Q. 10 A pair of linear equations which has a unique solution $x = 2, y = -3$ is

(a) $x + y = -1$ and $2x - 3y = -5$
(b) $2x + 5y = -11$ and $4x + 10y = -22$
(c) $2x - y = 1$ and $3x + 2y = 0$
(d) $x - 4y - 14 = 0$ and $5x - y - 13 = 0$

Thinking Process

(i) Use options, check the conditions for unique solution.
(ii) Substitute the value of x and y in the option that satisfy the condition of unique solution.

Ans. *(d)* From option (d) we have,

$$x - 4y - 14 = 0 \text{ and } 5x - y - 13 = 0$$

We known, that the general form of the pair of linear equation is

$$a_1x + b_1y + c_1 = 0$$

and $a_2x + b_2y + c_2 = 0$

On comparing the general form with the given equations, we get

$$a_1 = 1, b_1 = -4, c_1 = -1;$$

$$a_2 = 5, b_2 = -1, c_2 = -13$$

$\therefore$ $\dfrac{a_1}{a_2} = \dfrac{1}{5}; \dfrac{b_1}{b_2} = \dfrac{-4}{-1}$

$\therefore$ $\dfrac{a_1}{a_2} \neq \dfrac{b_1}{b_2}$

Thus, pair of linear equation have unique solution.

Now, for $x = 2, y = -3$

LHS $(2) - 4(-3) - 14 = 2 + 12 - 14 = \text{RHS}$

$5(2) - (-3) - 13 = 10 + 3 - 13 = 0 = \text{RHS}$

Q.11 If $x = a, y = b$ is the solution of the equations $x - y = 2$ and $x + y = 4$, then the values of a and b are, respectively

(a) 3 and 5 (b) 5 and 3 (c) 3 and 1 (d) -1 and -3

Ans. *(c)* Since, $x = a$ and $y = b$ is the solution of the equations $x - y = 2$ and $x + y = 4$, then these values will satisfy that equations

$$a - b = 2 \quad \dots(i)$$

and $$a + b = 4 \quad \dots(ii)$$

On adding Eqs. (i) and (ii), we get

$$2a = 6 \Rightarrow a = 3$$

On substituting value of a in Eq. (ii), we get

$$3 + b = 4 \Rightarrow b = 1$$

Q. 12 Aruna has only ₹ 1 and ₹ 2 coins with her. If the total number of coins that she has is 50 and the amount of money with her is ₹ 75, then the number of ₹ 1 and ₹ 2 coins are, respectively

(a) 35 and 15 (b) 35 and 20 (c) 15 and 35 (d) 25 and 25

- **Concept Insight** Use the concept, value of coins = Number of coins × Value of coin.

Ans. *(d)* Let number of ₹ 1 coins $= x$

and number of ₹ 2 coins $= y$

Now, by given conditions $$x + y = 50 \quad \dots(i)$$

Also, $$x \times 1 + y \times 2 = 75$$

$$\Rightarrow \quad x + 2y = 75 \quad \dots(ii)$$

On subtracting Eq. (i) from Eq. (ii), we get

$$(x + 2y) - (x + y) = 75 - 50$$

$$\Rightarrow \quad y = 25$$

When $y = 25$, then $x = 25$

Q.13 The father's age is six times his son's age. Four years hence, the age of the father will be four times his son's age. The present ages in years of the son and the father are, respectively

(a) 4 and 24 (b) 5 and 30 (c) 6 and 36 (d) 3 and 24

Ans. *(c)* Let x years be the present age of father and y years be the present age of son.

Four years hence, it has relation by given condition,

$$(x + 4) = 4(y + 4) \Rightarrow x + 4 = 4y + 16$$

$$\Rightarrow \quad x - 4y = 12 \quad \dots(i)$$

and $$x = 6y \quad \dots(ii)$$

On putting the value of x from Eq. (ii) in Eq. (i), we get

$$6y - 4y = 12 \Rightarrow 2y = 12$$

$$\Rightarrow \quad y = 6$$

When $y = 6$, then $x = 36$

Hence, present age of father is 36 years and age of son is 6 years.

Mistake Alert! *Students may incorrectly interprets the second condition as* $(x - 4) = 4(x - 4)$ *instead of* $(x + 4) = 4(x + 4)$

Short Answer Questions with Reasoning

Q.1 Do the following pair of linear equations have no solution? Justify your answer.

(i) $2x + 4y = 3$ and $12y + 6x = 6$

(ii) $x = 2y$ and $y = 2x$

(iii) $3x + y - 3 = 0$ and $2x + \frac{2}{3}y = 2$

Ans. We know, that the general form of the pair of linear equations is

$$a_1 x + b_1 y + c_1 = 0$$

and $$a_2 x + b_2 y + c_2 = 0$$

and the pair of linear equations have no solution, if

$$\frac{a_1}{a_2} = \frac{b_1}{b_2} \neq \frac{c_1}{c_2}$$

(i) *Yes*, given pair of linear equations is

$$2x + 4y = 3 \text{ and } 12y + 6x = 6$$

Here, $$a_1 = 2, b_1 = 4, c_1 = -3,$$

$$a_2 = 6, b_2 = 12, c_2 = -6$$

$$\therefore \quad \frac{a_1}{a_2} = \frac{2}{6} = \frac{1}{3}, \frac{b_1}{b_2} = \frac{4}{12} = \frac{1}{3}, \frac{c_1}{c_2} = \frac{-3}{-6} = \frac{1}{2}$$

$$\therefore \quad \frac{a_1}{a_2} = \frac{b_1}{b_2} \neq \frac{c_1}{c_2}$$

Hence, the given pair of linear equations has no solution.

(ii) *No*, given pair of linear equations is

$$x = 2y \text{ and } y = 2x$$

or $$x - 2y = 0 \text{ and } 2x - y = 0$$

Here, $$a_1 = 1, b_1 = -2, c_1 = 0;$$

$$a_2 = 2, b_2 = -1, c_2 = 0$$

$$\therefore \quad \frac{a_1}{a_2} = \frac{1}{2} \text{ and } \frac{b_1}{b_2} = \frac{2}{1}$$

$$\because \quad \frac{a_1}{a_2} \neq \frac{b_1}{b_2}$$

Hence, the given pair of linear equations has unique solution.

(iii) *No*, given pair of linear equations is

$$3x + y - 3 = 0 \text{ and } 2x + \frac{2}{3}y - 2 = 0$$

Here, $$a_1 = 3, b_1 = 1, c_1 = -3,$$

$$a_2 = 2, b_2 = \frac{2}{3}, c_2 = -2$$

$\therefore$ $$\frac{a_1}{a_2}=\frac{3}{2},\ \frac{b_1}{b_2}=\frac{1}{2/3}=\frac{3}{2},\ \frac{c_1}{c_2}=\frac{-3}{-2}=\frac{3}{2}$$

$\because$ $$\frac{a_1}{a_2}=\frac{b_1}{b_2}=\frac{c_1}{c_2}=\frac{3}{2}$$

Hence, the given pair of linear equations is coincident and having infinitely many solutions.

Q.2 Do the following equations represent a pair of coincident lines? Justify your answer.

(i) $3x+\frac{1}{7}y=3$ and $7x+3y=7$

(ii) $-2x-3y=1$ and $6y+4x=-2$

(iii) $\frac{x}{2}+y+\frac{2}{5}=0$ and $4x+8y+\frac{5}{16}=0$

Ans. We know that the general form of the pair of linear equation is

$$a_1x+b_1y+c_1=0$$

and $$a_2x+b_2y+c_2=0$$

and condition for coincident lines is

$$\frac{a_1}{a_2}=\frac{b_1}{b_2}=\frac{c_1}{c_2}$$

(i) *No*, given pair of linear equations is

$$3x+\frac{y}{7}-3=0$$

and $$7x+3y-7=0$$

where, $$a_1=3,\ b_1=\frac{1}{7},\ c_1=-3;$$

$$a_2=7,\ b_2=3,\ c_2=-7$$

Now, $$\frac{a_1}{a_2}=\frac{3}{7},\ \frac{b_1}{b_2}=\frac{1}{7}\div 3=\frac{1}{7}\times\frac{1}{3}=\frac{1}{21},\ \frac{c_1}{c_2}=\frac{-3}{-7}=\frac{3}{7}$$

$\because$ $$\frac{a_1}{a_2}\neq\frac{b_1}{b_2}$$

Hence, the given pair of linear equations has unique solution.

(ii) *Yes*, given pair of linear equations is

$$-2x-3y-1=0 \text{ and } 6y+4x+2=0$$

where, $$a_1=-2,\ b_1=-3,\ c_1=-1;$$

$$a_2=4,\ b_2=6,\ c_2=2$$

Now, $$\frac{a_1}{a_2}=-\frac{2}{4}=-\frac{1}{2},\ \frac{b_1}{b_2}=-\frac{3}{6}=-\frac{1}{2},\ \frac{c_1}{c_2}=-\frac{1}{2}$$

$\because$ $$\frac{a_1}{a_2}=\frac{b_1}{b_2}=\frac{c_1}{c_2}=-\frac{1}{2}$$

Hence, the given pair of linear equations is coincident.

(iii) *No*, the given pair of linear equations are

$$\frac{x}{2} + y + \frac{2}{5} = 0 \text{ and } 4x + 8y + \frac{5}{16} = 0$$

Here, $a_1 = \frac{1}{2}, b_1 = 1, c_1 = \frac{2}{5} \Rightarrow a_2 = 4, b_2 = 8, c_2 = \frac{5}{16}$

Now, $\frac{a_1}{a_2} = \frac{\frac{1}{2}}{4} = \frac{1}{8}, \frac{b_1}{b_2} = \frac{1}{8}, \frac{c_1}{c_2} = \frac{2}{5} \div \frac{5}{16} = \frac{2}{5} \times \frac{16}{5} = \frac{32}{25}$

$\because$ $\frac{a_1}{a_2} = \frac{b_1}{b_2} \neq \frac{c_1}{c_2}$

Hence, the given pair of linear equations has no solution.

Q.3 Are the following pair of linear equations consistent? Justify your answer.

(i) $-3x - 4y = 12$ and $4y + 3x = 12$

(ii) $\frac{3}{5}x - y = \frac{1}{2}$ and $\frac{1}{5}x - 3y = \frac{1}{6}$

(iii) $2ax + by = a$ and $4ax + 2by - 2a = 0$; $a, b \neq 0$

(iv) $x + 3y = 11$ and $2(2x + 6y) = 22$

Ans. Conditions for pair of linear equations are consistent

$$\frac{a_1}{a_2} \neq \frac{b_1}{b_2} \quad \text{[unique solution]}$$

and $$\frac{a_1}{a_2} = \frac{b_1}{b_2} = \frac{c_1}{c_2} \quad \text{[infinitely many solutions]}$$

(i) *No*, the given pair of linear equations is

$$-3x - 4y = 12 \text{ and } 3x + 4y = 12$$

$\Rightarrow$ $-3x - 4y - 12 = 0$ and $3x + 4y - 12 = 0$

Here, $a_1 = -3, b_1 = -4, c_1 = -12;$

$a_2 = 3, b_2 = 4, c_2 = -12$

Now, $\frac{a_1}{a_2} = -\frac{3}{3} = -1, \frac{b_1}{b_2} = -\frac{4}{4} = -1, \frac{c_1}{c_2} = \frac{-12}{-12} = 1$

$\because$ $\frac{a_1}{a_2} = \frac{b_1}{b_2} \neq \frac{c_1}{c_2}$

Hence, the pair of linear equations has no solution *i.e.*, inconsistent.

(ii) *Yes*, the given pair of linear equations is

$$\frac{3}{5}x - y = \frac{1}{2} \text{ and } \frac{1}{5}x - 3y = \frac{1}{6}$$

$\Rightarrow$ $\frac{3}{5}x - y - \frac{1}{2} = 0$ and $\frac{1}{5}x - 3y - \frac{1}{6} = 0$

Here, $a_1 = \frac{3}{5}, b_1 = -1, c_1 = -\frac{1}{2}$

and $a_2 = \frac{1}{5}, b_2 = -3, c_2 = -\frac{1}{6}$

Now, $$\frac{a_1}{a_2}=\frac{\frac{3}{5}}{\frac{1}{5}}=\frac{3}{1},\ \frac{b_1}{b_2}=\frac{-1}{-3}=\frac{1}{3},\ \frac{c_1}{c_2}=\frac{\frac{-1}{2}}{\frac{-1}{6}}=\frac{3}{1}$$

$\because$ $$\frac{a_1}{a_2}\neq\frac{b_1}{b_2}$$

Hence, the given pair of linear equations has unique solution *i.e.*, consistent.

(iii) *Yes*, the given pair of linear equations is

$$2ax+by-a=0 \text{ and } 4ax+2by-2a=0;\ a,b\neq 0$$

Here, $$a_1=2a,\ b_1=b,\ c_1=-a;$$
$$a_2=4a,\ b_2=2b,\ c_2=-2a$$

Now, $$\frac{a_1}{a_2}=\frac{2a}{4a}=\frac{1}{2},\ \frac{b_1}{b_2}=\frac{b}{2b}=\frac{1}{2},\ \frac{c_1}{c_2}=\frac{-a}{-2a}=\frac{1}{2}$$

$\because$ $$\frac{a_1}{a_2}=\frac{b_1}{b_2}=\frac{c_1}{c_2}=\frac{1}{2}$$

Hence, the given pair of linear equations has infinitely many solutions *i.e.*, consistent or dependent.

(iv) *No*, the given pair of linear equations is

$$x+3y=11 \text{ and } 2x+6y=11$$

$\Rightarrow$ $$x+3y-11=0 \text{ and } 2x+6y-11=0$$

Here, $$a_1=1,\ b_1=3,\ c_1=-11 \quad \ldots\text{(i)}$$
$$a_2=2,\ b_2=6,\ c_2=-11$$

Now, $$\frac{a_1}{a_2}=\frac{1}{2},\ \frac{b_1}{b_2}=\frac{3}{6}=\frac{1}{2},\ \frac{c_1}{c_2}=\frac{-11}{-11}=1$$

$\therefore$ $$\frac{a_1}{a_2}=\frac{b_1}{b_2}\neq\frac{c_1}{c_2}$$

Hence, the pair of linear equations has no solution *i.e.*, inconsistent.

Q.4 For the pair of equations $\lambda x+3y=-7$ and $2x+6y=14$ to have infinitely many solutions, the value of λ should be 1. Is the statement true? Give reasons.

Ans. *No*, the given pair of linear equations is

$$\lambda x+3y+7=0 \text{ and } 2x+6y-14=0$$

Here, $$a_1=\lambda,\ b_1=3,\ c_1=7;\ a_2=2,\ b_2=6,\ c_2=-14$$

If $\frac{a_1}{a_2}=\frac{b_1}{b_2}=\frac{c_1}{c_2}$, then the system linear equations has infinitely many solutions.

$\Rightarrow$ $$\frac{\lambda}{2}=\frac{3}{6}=-\frac{7}{14}$$

$\because$ $$\frac{\lambda}{2}=\frac{3}{6}\Rightarrow\lambda=1 \text{ and } \frac{\lambda}{2}=-\frac{7}{14}\Rightarrow\lambda=-1$$

Hence, $\lambda=-1$ does not have a unique value.

So, for no value of λ the given pair of linear equations has infinitely many solutions.

Q. 5 For all real values of c, the pair of equations $x - 2y = 8$ and $5x - 10y = c$ have a unique solution. Justify whether it is true or false.

Ans. *False,* the given pair of linear equations is

$$x - 2y - 8 = 0 \text{ and } 5x - 10y - c = 0$$

Here, $a_1 = 1, b_1 = -2, c_1 = -8$

$a_2 = 5, b_2 = -10, c_2 = -c$

Now, $\frac{a_1}{a_2} = \frac{1}{5}, \frac{b_1}{b_2} = \frac{-2}{-10} = \frac{1}{5}, \frac{c_1}{c_2} = \frac{-8}{-c} = \frac{8}{c}$

But if $c = 40$ (real value), then the ratio $\frac{c_1}{c_2}$ becomes $\frac{1}{5}$ and then the system of linear equations has an infinitely many solutions.

Also, if $c \neq 40, \frac{a_1}{a_2} = \frac{b_1}{b_2} \neq \frac{c_1}{c_2}$

Thus, for $c \neq 40$ the system of linear equations does not have any solution. Hence, for any value of c, the system of linear equations does not have a unique solution.

Q.6 The line represented by $x = 7$ is parallel to the X-axis. Justify whether the statement is true or not.

Ans. *Not true,* by graphically, we observe that $X = 7$ a line parallel to Y-axis and perpendicular to X-axis.

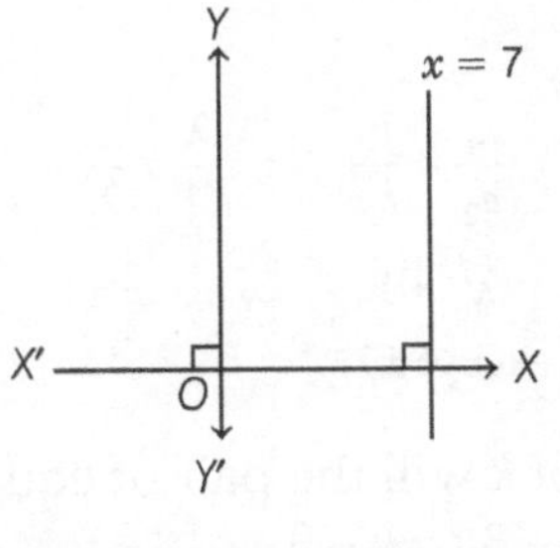

Short Answer Questions

Q.1 For which value(s) of λ, do the pair of linear equations $\lambda x + y = \lambda^2$ and $x + \lambda y = 1$ have

(i) no solution? (ii) infinitely many solutions?

(iii) a unique solution?

Ans. We know, the general form of the linear equation is

$$a_1x + b_1y + c_1 = 0 \text{ and } a_2x + b_2y + c_2 = 0$$

The given pair of linear equations is

$$\lambda x + y = \lambda^2 \text{ and } x + \lambda y = 1 \Rightarrow \lambda x + y - \lambda^2 = 0 \text{ and } x + \lambda y - 1 = 0$$

On comparing the given equation with the general form, we get

Here, $a_1 = \lambda, b_1 = 1, c_1 = -\lambda^2$

$a_2 = 1, b_2 = \lambda, c_2 = -1$

(i) For no solution,

$$\frac{a_1}{a_2} = \frac{b_1}{b_2} \neq \frac{c_1}{c_2}$$

$$\Rightarrow \quad \frac{\lambda}{1} = \frac{1}{\lambda} \neq \frac{-\lambda^2}{-1} \Rightarrow \frac{\lambda}{1} = \frac{1}{\lambda} \text{ and } \frac{\lambda}{1} \neq \frac{-\lambda^2}{-1}$$

$$\Rightarrow \quad \lambda^2 - 1 = 0 \text{ and } \lambda^2 - \lambda \neq 0$$

$$\Rightarrow \quad (\lambda - 1)(\lambda + 1) = 0 \text{ and } \lambda(\lambda - 1) \neq 0$$

$$\Rightarrow \quad \lambda = 1, -1 \text{ and } \lambda \neq 0, 1$$

So, $\lambda = -1$ the system of linear equations has no solution.

(ii) For infinitely many solutions,

$$\frac{a_1}{a_2} = \frac{b_1}{b_2} = \frac{c_1}{c_2}$$

$$\Rightarrow \quad \frac{\lambda}{1} = \frac{1}{\lambda} = \frac{\lambda^2}{1}$$

$$\Rightarrow \quad \frac{\lambda}{1} = \frac{\lambda^2}{1} \text{ and } \frac{\lambda}{1} = \frac{1}{\lambda}$$

$$\Rightarrow \quad \lambda^2 - \lambda = 0 \text{ and } \lambda^2 - 1 = 0$$

$$\Rightarrow \quad \lambda(\lambda - 1) = 0 \text{ and } (\lambda + 1)(\lambda - 1) = 0$$

$$\Rightarrow \quad \lambda = 0, 1 \text{ and } \lambda = 1, -1$$

So, $\lambda = 1$ system of linear equations has infinitely many solution $\lambda = 1, 0$ and $\lambda = 1, -1$.

(iii) For a unique solution,

$$\frac{a_1}{a_2} \neq \frac{b_1}{b_2} \Rightarrow \frac{\lambda}{1} \neq \frac{1}{\lambda}$$

$$\Rightarrow \quad \lambda^2 \neq 1 \quad \Rightarrow \lambda \neq \pm 1$$

So, all real values of λ except ± 1.

Q. 2 For which value (s) of k will the pair of equations

$$kx + 3y = k - 3,$$
$$12x + ky = k$$

has no solution?

Ans. Given pair of linear equations is

$$kx + 3y - (k - 3) = 0 \quad \ldots\text{(i)}$$

and

$$12x + ky - k = 0 \quad \ldots\text{(ii)}$$

On comparing with $ax + by + c = 0$, we get

$$a_1 = k, b_1 = 3 \text{ and } c_1 = -(k - 3) \quad \text{[from Eq. (i)]}$$

$$a_2 = 12, b_2 = k \text{ and } c_2 = -k \quad \text{[from Eq. (ii)]}$$

For no solution of the pair of linear equations,

$$\frac{a_1}{a_2} = \frac{b_1}{b_2} \neq \frac{c_1}{c_2}$$

$$\Rightarrow \quad \frac{k}{12} = \frac{3}{k} \neq \frac{-(k - 3)}{-k}$$

Taking first two parts, we get

$$\Rightarrow \quad \frac{k}{12} = \frac{3}{k}$$

$$\Rightarrow \quad k^2 = 36$$

$$\Rightarrow \quad k = \pm 6$$

Taking last two parts, we get

$$\frac{3}{k} \neq \frac{k-3}{k}$$

$$\Rightarrow \quad 3k \neq k(k-3)$$

$$\Rightarrow \quad 3k - k(k-3) \neq 0$$

$$\Rightarrow \quad k(3 - k + 3) \neq 0$$

$$\Rightarrow \quad k(6-k) \neq 0$$

$$\Rightarrow \quad k \neq 0 \text{ and } k \neq 6$$

Hence, required value of k for which the given pair of linear equations has no solution is – 6.

Q.3 For which values of a and b will the following pair of linear equations have infinitely many solutions?

$$x + 2y = 1$$

$$(a-b)x + (a+b)y = a + b - 2$$

Ans. Given pair of linear equations is

$$x + 2y - 1 = 0 \quad \text{...(i)}$$

and $$(a-b)x + (a+b)y - (a+b-2) = 0 \quad \text{...(ii)}$$

On comparing with $ax + by + c = 0$, we get

$$a_1 = 1, b_1 = 2 \text{ and } c_1 = -1 \quad \text{[from Eq. (i)]}$$

$$a_2 = (a-b), b_2 = (a+b) \quad \text{[from Eq. (ii)]}$$

and $$c_2 = -(a+b-2)$$

For infinitely many solutions of the the pairs of linear equations,

$$\frac{a_1}{a_2} = \frac{b_1}{b_2} = \frac{c_1}{c_2}$$

$$\Rightarrow \quad \frac{1}{a-b} = \frac{2}{a+b} = \frac{-1}{-(a+b-2)}$$

Taking first two parts,

$$\frac{1}{a-b} = \frac{2}{a+b} \Rightarrow a + b = 2a - 2b$$

$$\Rightarrow \quad 2a - a = 2b + b$$

$$\Rightarrow \quad a = 3b \quad \text{...(iii)}$$

Taking last two parts,

$$\frac{2}{a+b} = \frac{1}{(a+b-2)}$$

$$\Rightarrow \quad 2a + 2b - 4 = a + b$$

$$\Rightarrow \quad a + b = 4 \quad \text{...(iv)}$$

Now, put the value of a from Eq. (iii) in Eq. (iv), we get

$$3b + b = 4$$

$$\Rightarrow \quad 4b = 4$$

$$\Rightarrow \quad b = 1$$

Put the value of b in Eq. (iii), we get

$$a = 3 \times 1$$

$$\Rightarrow \quad a = 3$$

So, the values $(a, b) = (3, 1)$ satisfies all the parts.

Hence, required values of a and b are 3 and 1 respectively for which the given pair of linear equations has infinitely many solutions.

Q.4 Find the value(s) of p in (i) to (iv) and p and q in (v) for the following pair of equations

(i) $3x - y - 5 = 0$ and $6x - 2y - p = 0$, if the lines represented by these equations are parallel.

(ii) $-x + py = 1$ and $px - y = 1$, if the pair of equations has no solution.

(iii) $-3x + 5y = 7$ and $2px - 3y = 1$, if the lines represented by these equations are intersecting at a unique point.

(iv) $2x + 3y - 5 = 0$ and $px - 6y - 8 = 0$, if the pair of equations has a unique solution.

(v) $2x + 3y = 7$ and $2px + py = 28 - qy$, if the pair of equations have infinitely many solutions.

Ans. (i) Given pair of linear equations is

$$3x - y - 5 = 0 \quad \text{...(i)}$$

and $$6x - 2y - p = 0 \quad \text{...(ii)}$$

On comparing with $ax + by + c = 0$, we get

$$a_1 = 3, b_1 = -1 \text{ and } c_1 = -5 \quad \text{[from Eq. (i)]}$$

$$a_2 = 6, b_2 = -2 \text{ and } c_2 = -p \quad \text{[from Eq. (ii)]}$$

Since, the lines represented by these equations are parallel, then

$$\frac{a_1}{a_2} = \frac{b_1}{b_2} \neq \frac{c_1}{c_2}$$

$$\frac{3}{6} = \frac{-1}{-2} \neq \frac{-5}{-p}$$

Taking last two parts, we get $\dfrac{-1}{-2} \neq \dfrac{-5}{-p}$

$$\Rightarrow \quad \frac{1}{2} \neq \frac{5}{p}$$

$$\Rightarrow \quad p \neq 10$$

Hence, the given pair of linear equations are parallel for all real values of p except 10.

(ii) Given pair of linear equations is

$$-x + py - 1 = 0 \quad \text{...(i)}$$

and $$px - y - 1 = 0 \quad \text{...(ii)}$$

On comparing with $ax + by + c = 0$, we get

$a_1 = -1, b_1 = p$ and $c_1 = -1$ [from Eq. (i)]

$a_2 = p, b_2 = -1$ and $c_2 = -1$ [from Eq. (ii)]

Since, the pair of linear equations has no solution *i.e.*, both lines are parallel to each other.

$$\therefore \quad \frac{a_1}{a_2} = \frac{b_1}{b_2} \neq \frac{c_1}{c_2} \Rightarrow \frac{-1}{p} = \frac{p}{-1} \neq \frac{-1}{-1}$$

Taking last two parts, we get

$$\frac{p}{-1} \neq \frac{-1}{-1}$$

$$\Rightarrow \quad p \neq -1$$

Taking first two parts, we get

$$\frac{-1}{p} = \frac{p}{-1}$$

$$\Rightarrow \quad p^2 = 1$$

$$\Rightarrow \quad p = \pm 1$$

but $$p \neq -1$$

$$\therefore \quad p = 1$$

Hence, the given pair of linear equations has no solution for $p = 1$.

(iii) Given pair of linear equations is

$$-3x + 5y - 7 = 0 \quad \text{...(i)}$$

and $$2px - 3y - 1 = 0 \quad \text{...(ii)}$$

On comparing with $ax + by + c = 0$, we get

$a_1 = -3, b_1 = 5$ and $c_1 = -7$ [from Eq. (i)]

$a_2 = 2p, b_2 = -3$ and $c_2 = -1$ [from Eq. (ii)]

Since, the lines are intersecting at a unique point *i.e.*, it has a unique solution.

$$\therefore \quad \frac{a_1}{a_2} \neq \frac{b_1}{b_2}$$

$$\Rightarrow \quad \frac{-3}{2p} \neq \frac{5}{-3}$$

$$\Rightarrow \quad 9 \neq 10p$$

$$\Rightarrow \quad p \neq \frac{9}{10}.$$

Hence, the lines represented by these equations are intersecting at a unique point for all real values of p except $\frac{9}{10}$.

(iv) Given pair of linear equations is

$$2x + 3y - 5 = 0 \quad \ldots(i)$$

and $$px - 6y - 8 = 0 \quad \ldots(ii)$$

On comparing with $ax + by + c = 0$, we get

$$a_1 = 2, b_1 = 3 \text{ and } c_1 = -5 \quad \text{[from Eq. (i)]}$$

$$a_2 = p, \; b_2 = -6 \text{ and } c_2 = -8 \quad \text{[from Eq. (ii)]}$$

Since, the pair of linear equations has a unique solution.

$\therefore$ $$\frac{a_1}{a_2} \neq \frac{b_1}{b_2}$$

$\Rightarrow$ $$\frac{2}{p} \neq \frac{3}{-6}$$

$\Rightarrow$ $$p \neq -4$$

Hence, the pair of linear equations has a unique solution for all values of p except -4.

(v) Given pair of linear equations is

$$2x + 3y = 7 \Rightarrow 2x + 3y - 7 = 0 \quad \ldots(i)$$

and $$2px + py = 28 - qy$$

$\Rightarrow$ $$2px + (p + q)y - 28 = 0 \quad \ldots(ii)$$

On comparing with $ax + by + c = 0$, we get

$$a_1 = 2, b_1 = 3 \text{ and } c_1 = -7 \quad \text{[from Eq. (i)]}$$

$$a_2 = 2p, b_2 = (p + q) \text{ and } c_2 = -28 \quad \text{[from Eq. (ii)]}$$

Since, the pair of equations has infinitely many solutions *i.e.,* both lines are coincident.

$\therefore$ $$\frac{a_1}{a_2} = \frac{b_1}{b_2} = \frac{c_1}{c_2}$$

$\Rightarrow$ $$\frac{2}{2p} = \frac{3}{(p+q)} = \frac{-7}{-28}$$

Taking first and third parts, we get

$$\frac{2}{2p} = \frac{-7}{-28}$$

$\Rightarrow$ $$\frac{1}{p} = \frac{1}{4}$$

$\Rightarrow$ $$p = 4$$

Again, taking last two parts, we get

$$\frac{3}{p+q} = \frac{-7}{-28} \Rightarrow \frac{3}{p+q} = \frac{1}{4}$$

$\Rightarrow$ $$p + q = 12$$

$\Rightarrow$ $$4 + q = 12 \quad [\because p = 4]$$

$\therefore$ $$q = 8$$

Here, we see that the values of $p = 4$ and $q = 8$ satisfies all three parts.

Hence, the pair of equations has infinitely many solutions for the values of $p = 4$ and $q = 8$.

Q.5 Two straight paths are represented by the equations $x - 3y = 2$ and $-2x + 6y = 5$. Check whether the paths cross each other or not.

Ans. Given pair of linear equations is

$$x - 3y - 2 = 0 \quad \text{...(i)}$$

and

$$-2x + 6y - 5 = 0 \quad \text{...(ii)}$$

On comparing both the equations with $ax + by + c = 0$, we get

$$a_1 = 1, b_1 = -3 \text{ and } c_1 = -2 \quad \text{[from Eq. (i)]}$$

$$a_2 = -2, b_2 = 6 \text{ and } c_2 = -5 \quad \text{[from Eq. (ii)]}$$

Here,

$$\frac{a_1}{a_2} = \frac{1}{-2}$$

$$\frac{b_1}{b_2} = \frac{-3}{6} = -\frac{1}{2} \text{ and } \frac{c_1}{c_2} = \frac{-2}{-5} = \frac{2}{5}$$

i.e.,

$$\frac{a_1}{a_2} = \frac{b_1}{b_2} \neq \frac{c_1}{c_2} \quad \text{[parallel lines]}$$

Hence, two straight paths represented by the given equations never cross each other, because they are parallel to each other.

Q.6 Write a pair of linear equations which has the unique solution $x = -1, y = 3$. How many such pairs can you write?

Ans. Condition for the pair of linear equations to have unique solution

$$\frac{a_1}{a_2} \neq \frac{b_1}{b_2}$$

Let the equations are,

$$a_1x + b_1y + c_1 = 0$$

and

$$a_2x + b_2y + c_2 = 0$$

Since, $x = -1$ and $y = 3$ is the unique solution of these two equations, then

$$a_1(-1) + b_1(3) + c_1 = 0$$

$$\Rightarrow \quad -a_1 + 3b_1 + c_1 = 0 \quad \text{...(i)}$$

and

$$a_2(-1) + b_2(3) + c_2 = 0$$

$$\Rightarrow \quad -a_2 + 3b_2 + c_2 = 0 \quad \text{...(ii)}$$

So, the different values of a_1, a_2, b_1, b_2, c_1 and c_2 satisfy the Eqs. (i) and (ii).

Hence, infinitely many pairs of linear equations are possible.

Alternate Method

Infinite lines can pass through a point.

$\therefore$ These are infinitely many pair of linear equations, which passes though $(-1, 3)$.

Q.7 If $2x + y = 23$ and $4x - y = 19$, find the values of $5y - 2x$ and $\frac{y}{x} - 2$.

Thinking process If the coefficient of a variable are same, but opposite in sign, then add the pair of equations to get the value of one variable. Then, substitute that value of a variable in any pair of equation to find other variable.

Ans. Given pair of equations is

$$2x + y = 23 \quad \ldots\text{(i)}$$

and $$4x - y = 19 \quad \ldots\text{(ii)}$$

On adding Eq. (i) and (ii), we get

$$6x = 42 \Rightarrow x = 7$$

Put the value of x in Eq. (i), we get

$$2(7) + y = 23$$

$\Rightarrow$ $$14 + y = 23$$

$\Rightarrow$ $$y = 23 - 14$$

$\Rightarrow$ $$y = 9$$

We have, $$5y - 2x = 5 \times 9 - 2 \times 7$$

$$= 45 - 14 = 31$$

and $$\frac{y}{x} - 2 = \frac{9}{7} - 2 = \frac{9-14}{7} = -\frac{5}{7}$$

Hence, the values of $(5y - 2x)$ and $\left(\frac{y}{x} - 2\right)$ are 31 and $\frac{-5}{7}$ respectively.

Q.8 Find the values of x and y in the following rectangle.

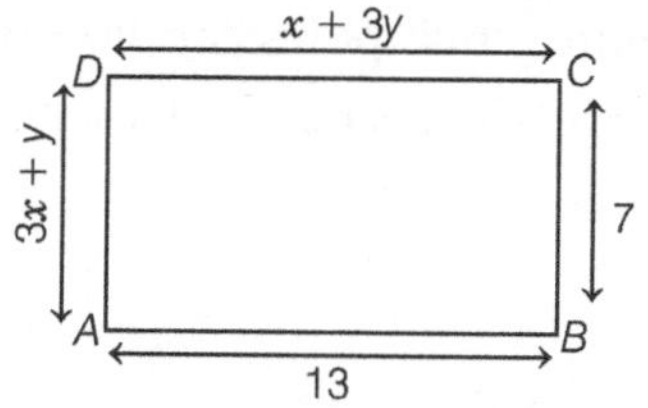

● **Concept Insight** Use the property of rectangle to form the pair of equations.

Ans. By property of rectangle,

Lengths are equal, *i.e.*, $$CD = AB$$

$\Rightarrow$ $$x + 3y = 13 \quad \ldots\text{(i)}$$

Breadths are equal, *i.e.*, $$AD = BC$$

$\Rightarrow$ $$3x + y = 7 \quad \ldots\text{(ii)}$$

On multiplying Eq. (ii) by 3 and then subtracting Eq. (i), we get

$$\begin{array}{r} 9x + 3y = 21 \\ x + 3y = 13 \\ - \quad - \quad\quad - \\ \hline 8x \qquad = 8 \end{array}$$

$$x = 1$$

On putting $x = 1$ in Eq. (i), we get

$$3y = 12 \Rightarrow y = 4$$

Hence, the required values of x and y are 1 and 4 respectively.

Mistake Alert! *Students often forget to change the sign, while using elimination method.*

Q.9 Solve the following pairs of equations.

(i) $x + y = 3.3,\quad \dfrac{0.6}{3x - 2y} = -1,\ 3x - 2y \neq 0$

(ii) $\dfrac{x}{3} + \dfrac{y}{4} = 4,\quad \dfrac{5x}{6} - \dfrac{y}{8} = 4$

*(iii) Solve the following pair of equations $4x + \dfrac{6}{y} = 15,\ 6x - \dfrac{8}{y} = 14,\ y \neq 0$

*(iv) Solve the following pair of equations $\dfrac{1}{2x} - \dfrac{1}{y} = -1,\ \dfrac{1}{x} + \dfrac{1}{2y} = 8,$ $x, y \neq 0$

(v) $43x + 67y = -24,\quad 67x + 43y = 24$

(vi) $\dfrac{x}{a} + \dfrac{y}{b} = a + b,\quad \dfrac{x}{a^2} + \dfrac{y}{b^2} = 2,\ a, b \neq 0$

*(vii) Solve the following pair of equations $\dfrac{2xy}{x+y} = \dfrac{3}{2},\ \dfrac{xy}{2x - y} = \dfrac{-3}{10},$ $x + y \neq 0,\ 2x - y \neq 0$

Ans. (i) Given pair of linear equations are

$$x + y = 3.3 \quad \text{...(i)}$$

and

$$\frac{0.6}{3x - 2y} = -1$$

$$\Rightarrow \quad 0.6 = -3x + 2y$$

$$\Rightarrow \quad 3x - 2y = -0.6 \quad \text{...(ii)}$$

Now, multiplying Eq. (i) by 2 and then adding with Eq. (ii), we get

$$2x + 2y = 6.6$$

$$\Rightarrow \quad 3x - 2y = -0.6$$

$$5x = 6 \Rightarrow x = \frac{6}{5} = 1.2$$

Now, put the value of x in Eq. (i), we get

$$1.2 + y = 3.3$$

$$\Rightarrow \quad y = 3.3 - 1.2$$

$$\Rightarrow \quad y = 2.1$$

Hence, the required values of x and y are 1.2 and 2.1 respectively.

(ii) Given pair of linear equations is

$$\frac{x}{3} + \frac{y}{4} = 4$$

On multiplying both sides by LCM (3, 4) = 12, we get

$$4x + 3y = 48 \quad \text{...(i)}$$

and

$$\frac{5x}{6} - \frac{y}{8} = 4$$

Note (*) *Topics related to these questions have been removed from latest NCERT.*

On multiplying both sides by LCM (6, 8) = 24, we get

$$20x - 3y = 96 \quad \text{...(ii)}$$

Now, adding Eqs. (i) and (ii), we get

$$24x = 144$$

$$\Rightarrow \quad x = 6$$

Now, put the value of x in Eq. (i), we get

$$4 \times 6 + 3y = 48$$

$$\Rightarrow \quad 3y = 48 - 24$$

$$\Rightarrow \quad 3y = 24 \Rightarrow y = 8$$

Hence, the required values of x and y are 6 and 8 respectively.

(iii) Given pair of linear equations is

$$4x + \frac{6}{y} = 15 \quad \text{...(i)}$$

and

$$6x - \frac{8}{y} = 14, y \neq 0 \quad \text{...(ii)}$$

Let $u = \frac{1}{y}$, then above equation becomes

$$4x + 6u = 15 \quad \text{...(iii)}$$

and

$$6x - 8u = 14 \quad \text{...(iv)}$$

On multiplying Eq. (iii) by 8 and Eq. (iv) by 6 and then adding both of them, we get

$$32x + 48u = 120$$

$$\underline{36x - 48u = 84}$$

$$68x = 204$$

$$\Rightarrow \quad x = 3$$

Now, put the value of x in Eq. (iii), we get

$$4 \times 3 + 6u = 15$$

$$\Rightarrow \quad 6u = 15 - 12 \Rightarrow 6u = 3$$

$$\Rightarrow \quad u = \frac{1}{2} \Rightarrow \frac{1}{y} = \frac{1}{2} \quad \left[\because u = \frac{1}{y}\right]$$

$$\Rightarrow \quad y = 2$$

Hence, the required values of x and y are 3 and 2 respectively.

(iv) Given pair of linear equations is

$$\frac{1}{2x} - \frac{1}{y} = -1 \quad \text{...(i)}$$

and

$$\frac{1}{x} + \frac{1}{2y} = 8, x, y \neq 0 \quad \text{...(ii)}$$

Let $u = \frac{1}{x}$ and $v = \frac{1}{y}$, then the above equations becomes

$$\frac{u}{2} - v = -1$$

$$\Rightarrow \quad u - 2v = -2 \quad \text{....(iii)}$$

and $$u + \frac{v}{2} = 8$$

$$\Rightarrow \quad 2u + v = 16 \quad \text{...(iv)}$$

On, multiplying Eq. (iv) by 2 and then adding with Eq. (iii), we get

$$\begin{array}{r} 4u + 2v = 32 \\ u - 2v = -2 \\ \hline 5u = 30 \end{array}$$

$$\Rightarrow \quad u = 6$$

Now, put the value of u in Eq. (iv), we get

$$2 \times 6 + v = 16$$

$$\Rightarrow \quad v = 16 - 12 = 4$$

$$\Rightarrow \quad v = 4$$

$$\therefore \quad x = \frac{1}{u} = \frac{1}{6} \text{ and } y = \frac{1}{v} = \frac{1}{4}$$

Hence, the required values of x and y are $\frac{1}{6}$ and $\frac{1}{4}$ respectively.

(v) We have

$$43x + 67y = -24 \quad \text{...(i)}$$

$$67x + 43y = 24 \quad \text{...(ii)}$$

On adding Eqs. (i) and (ii), we get

$$110x + 110y = 0$$

$$\Rightarrow \quad x + y = 0$$

$$\Rightarrow \quad x = -y \quad \text{...(iii)}$$

Now, subtracting Eq. (i) from Eq. (ii), we get

$$-24x + 24y = -48$$

$$\Rightarrow \quad -x + y = -2 \quad \text{...(iv)}$$

From Eqs. (iii) and (iv), we get

$$-(-y) + y = -2$$

$$\Rightarrow \quad -2y = -2 \Rightarrow y = 1$$

From Eqs. (iii), we get

$$x = -1$$

Hence, the required value of x and y are $-1, 1$ respectively.

(vi) Given pair of linear equations is

$$\frac{x}{a} + \frac{y}{b} = a + b \quad \text{...(i)}$$

and $$\frac{x}{a^2} + \frac{y}{b^2} = 2, a, b \neq 0 \quad \text{...(ii)}$$

On multiplying Eq. (i) by $\frac{1}{a}$ and then subtracting from Eq. (ii), we get

$$\frac{x}{a^2} + \frac{y}{b^2} = 2$$

$$\frac{x}{a^2}+\frac{y}{ab}=1+\frac{b}{a}$$

$$\underline{-\qquad -\qquad\quad -}$$

$$y\left(\frac{1}{b^2}-\frac{1}{ab}\right)=2-1-\frac{b}{a}$$

$\Rightarrow$ $$y\left(\frac{a-b}{ab^2}\right)=1-\frac{b}{a}=\left(\frac{a-b}{a}\right)$$

$\Rightarrow$ $$y=\frac{ab^2}{a}\Rightarrow y=b^2$$

Now, put the value of y in Eq. (ii), we get

$$\frac{x}{a^2}+\frac{b^2}{b^2}=2$$

$\Rightarrow$ $$\frac{x}{a^2}=2-1=1$$

$\Rightarrow$ $$x=a^2$$

Hence, the required values of x and y are a^2 and b^2 respectively.

(vii) Given pair of linear equations is

$$\frac{2xy}{x+y}=\frac{3}{2}, \text{ where } x+y\neq 0$$

$\Rightarrow$ $$\frac{x+y}{2xy}=\frac{2}{3}$$

$\Rightarrow$ $$\frac{x}{xy}+\frac{y}{xy}=\frac{4}{3}$$

$\Rightarrow$ $$\frac{1}{y}+\frac{1}{x}=\frac{4}{3} \qquad \text{...(i)}$$

and $$\frac{xy}{2x-y}=\frac{-3}{10}, \text{ where } 2x-y\neq 0$$

$\Rightarrow$ $$\frac{2x-y}{xy}=\frac{-10}{3}$$

$\Rightarrow$ $$\frac{2x}{xy}-\frac{y}{xy}=\frac{-10}{3}$$

$\Rightarrow$ $$\frac{2}{y}-\frac{1}{x}=\frac{-10}{3} \qquad \text{...(ii)}$$

Now, put $\frac{1}{x}=u$ and $\frac{1}{y}=v$, then the pair of equations becomes

$$v+u=\frac{4}{3} \qquad \text{...(iii)}$$

and $$2v-u=\frac{-10}{3} \qquad \text{...(iv)}$$

On adding Eqs (iii) and (iv) both equations, we get

$$3v=\frac{4}{3}-\frac{10}{3}=\frac{-6}{3}$$

$\Rightarrow$ $$3v=-2$$

$$\Rightarrow \quad v = \frac{-2}{3}$$

Now, put the value of v in Eq. (iii), we get

$$\frac{-2}{3} + u = \frac{4}{3}$$

$$\Rightarrow \quad u = \frac{4}{3} + \frac{2}{3} = \frac{6}{3} = 2$$

$$\therefore \quad x = \frac{1}{u} = \frac{1}{2}$$

and $$y = \frac{1}{v} = \frac{1}{(-2/3)} = \frac{-3}{2}$$

Hence, the required values of x and y are $\frac{1}{2}$ and $\frac{-3}{2}$ respectively.

Q.10 Find the solution of the pair of equations $\frac{x}{10} + \frac{y}{5} - 1 = 0$ and $\frac{x}{8} + \frac{y}{6} = 15$. Hence, find λ, if $y = \lambda x + 5$.

Ans. Given pair of linear equations is

$$\frac{x}{10} + \frac{y}{5} - 1 = 0 \quad \text{...(i)}$$

and $$\frac{x}{8} + \frac{y}{6} = 15 \quad \text{...(ii)}$$

Now, multiplying both sides of Eq. (i) by LCM (10, 5) = 10, we get

$$x + 2y - 10 = 0$$

$$\Rightarrow \quad x + 2y = 10 \quad \text{...(iii)}$$

Again, multiplying both sides of Eq. (iv) by LCM (8,6) = 24, we get

$$3x + 4y = 360 \quad \text{...(iv)}$$

On multiplying Eq. (iii) by 2 and then subtracting from Eq. (iv), we get

$$\begin{array}{r} 3x + 4y = 360 \\ \underline{\underset{-}{2x} + \underset{-}{4y} = \underset{-}{20}} \\ x = 340 \end{array}$$

Put the value of x in Eq. (iii), we get

$$340 + 2y = 10$$

$$\Rightarrow \quad 2y = 10 - 340 = -330$$

$$\Rightarrow \quad y = -165$$

Given that, the linear relation between x, y and λ is

$$y = \lambda x + 5$$

Now, put the values of x and y in above relation, we get

$$-165 = \lambda (340) + 5$$

$$\Rightarrow \quad 340\lambda = -170 \Rightarrow \lambda = -\frac{1}{2}$$

Hence, the solution of the pair of equations is $x = 340$, $y = -165$ and the required value of λ is $-\frac{1}{2}$.

Q. 11 By the graphical method, find whether the following pair of equations are consistent or not. If consistent, solve them.

(i) $3x+y+4=0, 6x-2y+4=0$

(ii) $x-2y=6, 3x-6y=0$

(iii) $x+y=3, 3x+3y=9$

Ans. (i) Given pair of linear equations is

$$3x + y + 4 = 0 \quad \text{...(i)}$$

and
$$6x - 2y + 4 = 0 \quad \text{...(ii)}$$

On comparing with $ax + by + c = 0$, we get

$$a_1 = 3, b_1 = 1 \text{ and } c_1 = 4 \quad \text{[from Eq. (i)]}$$

$$a_2 = 6, b_2 = -2 \text{ and } c_2 = 4 \quad \text{[from Eq. (ii)]}$$

Here,
$$\frac{a_1}{a_2} = \frac{3}{6} = \frac{1}{2}; \frac{b_1}{b_2} = \frac{1}{-2} \text{ and } \frac{c_1}{c_2} = \frac{4}{4} = \frac{1}{1}$$

$\because$
$$\frac{a_1}{a_2} \neq \frac{b_1}{b_2}$$

So, the given pair of linear equations are intersecting at one point, therefore these lines have unique solution.

Hence, given pair of linear equations is consistent.

We have,
$$3x + y + 4 = 0$$

$\Rightarrow$
$$y = -4 - 3x$$

When $x = 0$, then $y = -4$

When $x = -1$, then $y = -1$

When $x = -2$, then $y = 2$

x	0	-1	-2
y	-4	-1	2
Points	B	C	A

and
$$6x - 2y + 4 = 0$$

$\Rightarrow$
$$2y = 6x + 4$$

$\Rightarrow$
$$y = 3x + 2$$

When $x = 0$, then $y = 2$

When $x = -1$, then $y = -1$

When $x = 1$, then $y = 5$

x	-1	0	1
y	-1	2	5
Points	C	Q	P

Plotting the points $A(-2, 2)$ and $B(0, -4)$, we get the straight tine AB. Plotting the points $Q(0, 2)$ and $P(1, 5)$, we get the straight line PQ. The lines AB and PQ intersect at $C(-1, -1)$.

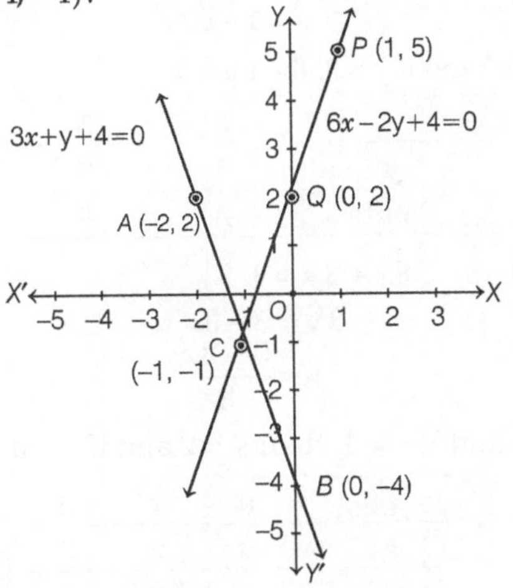

(ii) Given pair of linear equations is

$$x - 2y - 6 = 0 \quad \text{...(i)}$$

and $$3x - 6y = 0 \quad \text{...(ii)}$$

On comparing with $ax + by + c = 0$, we get

$$a_1 = 1, b_1 = -2 \text{ and } c_1 = -6 \quad \text{[from Eq. (i)]}$$

$$a_2 = 3, b_2 = -6 \text{ and } c_2 = 0 \quad \text{[from Eq. (ii)]}$$

Here, $$\frac{a_1}{a_2} = \frac{1}{3}, \frac{b_1}{b_2} = \frac{-2}{-6} = \frac{1}{3}$$

and $$\frac{c_1}{c_2} = \frac{-6}{0}$$

$\therefore$ $$\frac{a_1}{a_2} = \frac{b_1}{b_2} \neq \frac{c_1}{c_2}$$

Hence, the lines represented by the given equations are parallel. Therefore, it has no solution. So, the given pair of lines is inconsistent.

(iii) Given pair of linear equations is $x + y - 3 = 0$ ...(i)

and $$3x + 3y - 9 = 0 \quad \text{...(ii)}$$

On comparing with $ax + by + c = 0$, we get

$$a_1 = 1, b_1 = 1 \text{ and } c_1 = -3 \quad \text{[from Eq. (i)]}$$

$$a_2 = 3, b_2 = 3 \text{ and } c_2 = -9 \quad \text{[from Eq. (ii)]}$$

Here, $$\frac{a_1}{a_2} = \frac{1}{3}, \frac{b_1}{b_2} = \frac{1}{3}$$

and $$\frac{c_1}{c_2} = \frac{-3}{-9} = \frac{1}{3}$$

$\Rightarrow$ $$\frac{a_1}{a_2} = \frac{b_1}{b_2} = \frac{c_1}{c_2}$$

So, the given pair of lines is coincident. Therefore, these lines have infinitely many solutions. Hence, the given pair of linear equations is consistent.

Now, $$x + y = 3$$

$\Rightarrow$ $$y = 3 - x$$

If $x = 0$, then $y = 3$ and if $x = 3$, then $y = 0$.

x	0	3
y	3	0
Points	A	B

and $$3x + 3y = 9$$

$\Rightarrow$ $$3y = 9 - 3x$$

$\Rightarrow$ $$y = \frac{9 - 3x}{3}$$

If $x = 0$, then $y = 3$ and If $x = 1$, then $y = 2$ and if $x = 3$, then $y = 0$.

x	0	1	3
y	3	2	0
Points	C	D	E

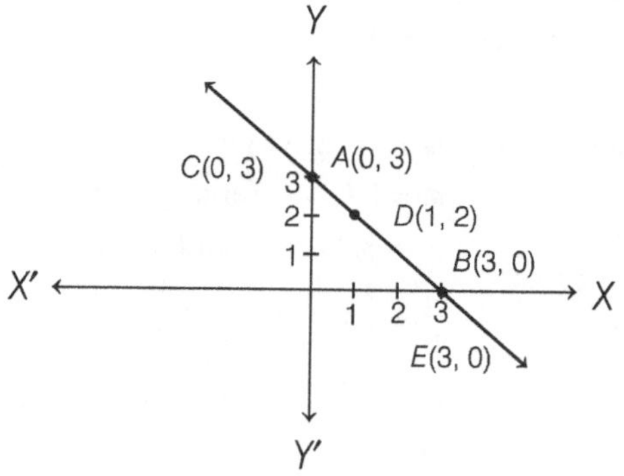

Plotting the points A (0,3) and B (3,0), we get the line AB. Again, plotting the points C (0,3) D (1, 2) and E (3,0), we get the line CDE.

We observe that the lines represented by equations (i) and (ii) are coincident.

***Q.12** Draw the graph of the pair of equations $2x + y = 4$ and $2x - y = 4$. Write the vertices of the triangle formed by these lines and the Y-axis. Also, find the area of this triangle?

Ans. The given pair of linear equations is

$$2x + y = 4 \text{ and } 2x - y = 4$$

Table for line $2x + y = 4$,

x	0	2
$y = 4 - 2x$	4	0
Points	A	B

Note (✱) *Topics related to these question have been removed from latest NCERT.*

and table for line $2x - y = 4$,

x	0	2
$y = 2x - 4$	-4	0
Points	C	B

Graphical representation of both lines are as follows

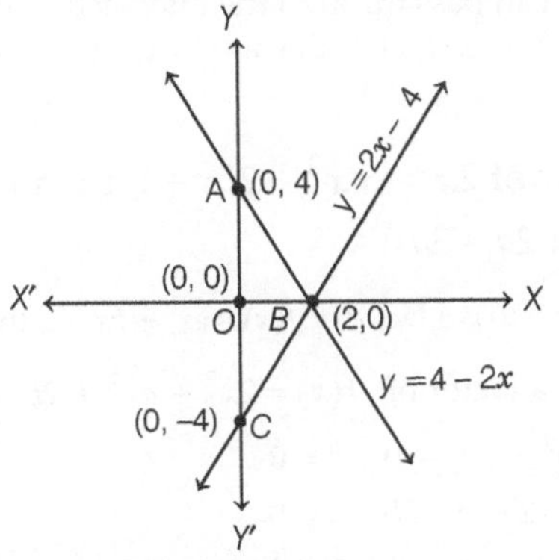

Here, both lines and Y-axis form a ΔABC.

Hence, the vertices of a ΔABC are $A(0, 4)$ $B(2, 0)$ and $C(0, -4)$.

$\therefore$ Required area of $\Delta ABC = 2 \times$ Area of ΔAOB

$$= 2 \times \frac{1}{2} \times 4 \times 2 = 8 \text{ sq. units}$$

Hence, the required area of the triangle is 8 sq. units.

Q.13 Write an equation of a line passing through the point representing solution of the pair of linear equations $x + y = 2$ and $2x - y = 1$. How many such lines can we find?

Ans. Given pair of linear equations is $x + y - 2 = 0$ ...(i)

and $2x - y - 1 = 0$ ...(ii)

On comparing with pair of linear equation *i.e,* $a_1x + b_1y + c_1 = 0$ and $a_2x + b_2y + c_2 = 0$, we get

$a_1 = 1, b_1 = 1$ and $c_1 = -2$ [from Eq. (i)]

$a_2 = 2, b_2 = -1$ and $c_2 = -1$ [from Eq. (ii)]

Here, $\frac{a_1}{a_2} = \frac{1}{2}, \frac{b_1}{b_2} = \frac{1}{-1} = -1$

and $\frac{c_1}{c_2} = \frac{-2}{-1} = \frac{2}{1} \Rightarrow \frac{a_1}{a_2} \neq \frac{b_1}{b_2}$

So, both lines intersect at a point. Therefore, the pair of equations has a unique solution. Hence, these equations are consistent.

Now, $x + y = 2 \Rightarrow y = 2 - x$

On substituting the value of $y = 2 - x$ in equation, we get

$$2x - y = 1$$

$$\Rightarrow \quad 2x - (2 - x) = 1$$

$\Rightarrow \quad 2x + x - 2 = 1$

$\Rightarrow \quad 3x = 3$

$\Rightarrow \quad x = 1$

On substituteing the value of $x = 1$ in $y = 2 - x$, we get

$\Rightarrow \quad y = 2 - 1 = 1$

Therefore, the given pair of lines have a unique solution *i.e.*, (1, 1).

Hence, infinite lines can pass through the intersection point of linear equations $x + y = 2$ and $2x - y = 1$ *i.e.*, E (1,1) like as $y = x$, $2x + y = 3$, $x + 2y = 3$ so on.

Q.14 If $(x + 1)$ is a factor of $2x^3 + ax^2 + 2bx + 1$, then find the values of a and b given that $2a - 3b = 4$.

- **Concept Insight** If $(x + \alpha)$ is a factor of $f(x) = ax^2 + bx + c$, then $f(-\alpha) = 0$.

Ans. Given that, $(x + 1)$ is a factor of $f(x) = 2x^3 + ax^2 + 2bx + 1$, then $f(-1) = 0$.

$\Rightarrow \quad 2(-1)^3 + a(-1)^2 + 2b(-1) + 1 = 0$

$\Rightarrow \quad -2 + a - 2b + 1 = 0$

$\Rightarrow \quad a - 2b - 1 = 0 \quad \text{...(i)}$

Also, $\quad 2a - 3b = 4$

$\Rightarrow \quad 3b = 2a - 4$

$\Rightarrow \quad b = \left(\dfrac{2a - 4}{3}\right)$

Now, put the value of b in Eq. (i), we get

$$a - 2\left(\frac{2a - 4}{3}\right) - 1 = 0$$

$\Rightarrow \quad 3a - 2(2a - 4) - 3 = 0$

$\Rightarrow \quad 3a - 4a + 8 - 3 = 0$

$\Rightarrow \quad -a + 5 = 0$

$\Rightarrow \quad a = 5$

Now, put the value of a in Eq. (i), we get

$$5 - 2b - 1 = 0$$

$\Rightarrow \quad 2b = 4$

$\Rightarrow \quad b = 2$

Hence, the required values of a and b are 5 and 2 respectively.

Q.15 The angles of a triangle are x, y and 40°. The difference between the two angles x and y is 30°. Find x and y.

- **Concept Insight** Sum of interior angle of a triangle is 180°.

Ans. Given that, x, y and 40° are the angles of a triangle.

$\therefore \quad x + y + 40° = 180°$

$\Rightarrow \quad x + y = 140° \quad \text{...(i)}$

Also, $\quad x - y = 30° \quad \text{...(ii)}$

On adding Eqs. (i) and (ii), we get

$$2x = 170°$$

$$\Rightarrow \quad x = 85°$$

On putting $x = 85°$ in Eq. (i), we get

$$85° + y = 140°$$

$$\Rightarrow \quad y = 55°$$

Hence, the required values of x and y are 85° and 55°, respectively.

Q.16 Two years ago, Salim was thrice as old as his daughter and six years later, he will be four years older than twice her age. How old are they now?

Ans. Let Salim and his daughter's present age be x years and y years, respectively.

Now, by first condition.

Two years ago, Salim was thrice as old as his daughter.

i.e., $$x - 2 = 3\,(y - 2) \Rightarrow x - 2 = 3y - 6$$

$$\Rightarrow \quad x - 3y = -4 \quad \text{...(i)}$$

and by second condition, six years later, Salim will be,four years older than twice her age.

i.e., $$x + 6 = 2\,(y + 6) + 4$$

$$\Rightarrow \quad x + 6 = 2y + 12 + 4$$

$$\Rightarrow \quad x - 2y = 16 - 6$$

$$\Rightarrow \quad x - 2y = 10 \quad \text{...(ii)}$$

On subtracting Eq. (i) from Eq. (ii), we get

$$\begin{array}{r} x - 2y = 10 \\ x - 3y = -4 \\ - \quad + \quad\quad + \\ \hline y = 14 \end{array}$$

On putting the value of y in Eq. (ii), we get

$$x - 2 \times 14 = 10$$

$$\Rightarrow \quad x = 10 + 28 \Rightarrow x = 38$$

Hence, Salim and his daughter's present age are 38 years and 14 years, respectively.

Q.17 The age of the father is twice the sum of the ages of his two children. After 20 years, his age will be equal to the sum of the ages of his children. Find the age of the father.

Ans. Let the present age of father and his two children be x years, y years and z years, respectively.

Now by given conditions, $$x = 2(y + z) \quad \text{...(i)}$$

and $$(x + 20) = (y + 20) + (z + 20)$$

$$\Rightarrow \quad y + z + 40 = x + 20$$

$$\Rightarrow \quad y + z = x - 20$$

On putting the value of $(y + z)$ in Eq. (i), we get

$$x = 2(x - 20)$$

$$\Rightarrow \quad x = 2x - 40 \Rightarrow x = 40$$

Hence, the father's age is 40 years.

Alternate Method

Let the age of the father be x years and the sum of the age of childrens be y years.

$$x = 2y \quad \text{(by given condition)}$$

After 20 years, $x + 20 = y + 40$ [$\because$ the age of each child will increase by 20 years]

$$\Rightarrow \quad x = y + 20 \quad \text{...(i)}$$

Substituting $x = 2y$ in Eq. (i), we get

$$2y - y = 20$$

$$\Rightarrow \quad y = 20$$

Father's age $= x = 2y = 2 \times 20 = 40$ years

Mistake Alert! *Students often increase the sum of age of both children by 20 after 20 years.*

Q.18 Two numbers are in the ratio 5 : 6. If 8 is subtracted from each of the numbers, the ratio becomes 4 : 5. Find the numbers.

Ans. Let the two numbers be x and y.

Then, by first condition, ratio of these two numbers $= 5 : 6$

$$x : y = 5 : 6$$

$$\Rightarrow \quad \frac{x}{y} = \frac{5}{6} \Rightarrow y = \frac{6x}{5} \quad \text{...(i)}$$

and by second condition, then 8 is subtracted from each of the numbers, then ratio becomes 4 : 5.

$$\frac{x - 8}{y - 8} = \frac{4}{5}$$

$$\Rightarrow \quad 5x - 40 = 4y - 32$$

$$\Rightarrow \quad 5x - 4y = 8 \quad \text{...(ii)}$$

Now, put the value of y from Eq. (i) in Eq. (ii), we get

$$5x - 4\left(\frac{6x}{5}\right) = 8$$

$$\Rightarrow \quad 25x - 24x = 40$$

$$\Rightarrow \quad x = 40$$

Put the value of x in Eq. (i), we get

$$y = \frac{6}{5} \times 40 = 6 \times 8 = 48$$

Hence, the required numbers are 40 and 48.

Q.19 There are some students in the two examination halls A and B. To make the number of students equal in each hall, 10 students are sent from A to B. But, if 20 students are sent from B to A, the number of students in A becomes double the number of students in B. Find the number of students in the two halls.

Ans. Let the number of students in halls A and B are x and y, respectively.

Now, by given condition, $x - 10 = y + 10$

$$\Rightarrow \quad x - y = 20 \quad \dots(i)$$

and $$(x + 20) = 2(y - 20) \Rightarrow x + 20 = 2y - 40$$

$$\Rightarrow \quad x - 2y = -60 \quad \dots(ii)$$

On subtracting Eq. (ii) from Eq. (i), we get

$$(x - y) - (x - 2y) = 20 + 60$$

$$x - y - x + 2y = 80 \Rightarrow y = 80$$

On putting $y = 80$ in Eq. (i), we get

$$x - 80 = 20 \Rightarrow x = 100$$

Hence, 100 students are in hall A and 80 students are in hall B.

Q.20 A shopkeeper gives books on rent for reading. She takes a fixed charge for the first two days and an additional charge for each day thereafter. Latika paid ₹ 22 for a book kept for six days, while Anand paid ₹ 16 for the book kept for four days. Find the fixed charges and the charge for each extra day.

Ans. Let fixed charge for the first two day is ₹ x and additional charge for each day thereafter is ₹ y.

Now by first condition.

Latika paid ₹ 22 for a book kept for six days *i.e.*,

$$x + 4y = 22 \quad \dots(i)$$

and by second condition,

Anand paid ₹ 16 for a book kept for four days *i.e.*,

$$x + 2y = 16 \quad \dots(ii)$$

Now, subtracting Eq. (ii) from Eq. (i), we get

$$2y = 6 \Rightarrow y = 3$$

On putting the value of y in Eq. (ii), we get

$$x + 2 \times 3 = 16$$

$$\therefore \quad x = 16 - 6 = 10$$

Hence, the fixed charge = ₹ 10

and the charge for each extra day = ₹ 3

Mistake Alert! *Students often multiply the additional charge by number of days books given for rent by ignoring the fixed charge for the first two days.*

Q.21 In a competitive examination, one mark is awarded for each correct answer while 1/2 mark is deducted for every wrong answer. Jayanti answered 120 questions and got 90 marks. How many questions did she answer correctly?

Ans. Let x be the number of correct answers of the questions and y be wrong answer of questions in a competitive examination.

Then, by given condition,

$$x + y = 120 \quad \ldots(i)$$

and $$x \times 1 - y \times \frac{1}{2} = 90$$

$\Rightarrow$ $$2x - y = 180 \quad \ldots(ii)$$

On adding Eqs. (i) and (ii), we get

$$3x = 300 \Rightarrow x = 100$$

Hence, Jayanti answered correctly 100 questions.

Q.22 The angles of a cyclic quadrilateral $ABCD$ are $\angle A = (6x + 10)°$, $\angle B = (5x)°$, $\angle C = (x + y)°$ and $\angle D = (3y - 10)°$.

Find x and y and hence the values of the four angles.

● **Concept Insight** Sum of the opposite angles of a cyclic quadrilateral is 180°.

Ans. We know that, by property of cyclic quadrilateral,

Sum of opposite angles = 180°

$$\angle A + \angle C = (6x + 10)° + (x + y)° = 180°$$

$$[\because \angle A = (6x + 10)°, \angle C = (x + y)°, \text{given}]$$

$\Rightarrow$ $$7x + y = 170° \quad \ldots(i)$$

and $$\angle B + \angle D = (5x)° + (3y - 10)° = 180°$$

$$[\because \angle B = (5x)°, \angle D = (3y - 10)°, \text{given}]$$

$\Rightarrow$ $$5x + 3y = 190° \quad \ldots(ii)$$

On multiplying Eq. (i) by 3 and then subtracting Eq. (ii) from Eq. (i), we get

$$3 \times (7x + y) - (5x + 3y) = 510° - 190°$$

$\Rightarrow$ $$21x + 3y - 5x - 3y = 320°$$

$\Rightarrow$ $$16x = 320°$$

$\therefore$ $$x = 20°$$

On putting $x = 20°$ in Eq. (i), we get

$$7 \times 20° + y = 170°$$

$\Rightarrow$ $$y = 170° - 140° \Rightarrow y = 30°$$

$\therefore$ $$\angle A = (6x + 10)° = 6 \times 20° + 10°$$

$$= 120° + 10° = 130°$$

$$\angle B = (5x)° = 5 \times 20° = 100°$$

$$\angle C = (x + y)° = 20° + 30° = 50°$$

$$\angle D = (3y - 10)° = 3 \times 30° - 10° = 90° - 10° = 80°$$

Hence, the required values of x and y are 20° and 30° respectively and the values of the four angles *i.e.*, $\angle A$, $\angle B$, $\angle C$ and $\angle D$ are 130°, 100°, 50° and 80° respectively.

Long Answer Questions

Q.1 Graphically, solve the following pair of equations

$$2x + y = 6 \text{ and } 2x - y + 2 = 0$$

Find the ratio of the areas of the two triangles formed by the lines representing these equations with the X-axis and the lines with the Y-axis.

Ans. Given equations are $2x + y = 6$ and $2x - y + 2 = 0$

Table for equation $2x + y = 6$,

x	0	3
y	6	0
Points	B	A

Table for equation $2x - y + 2 = 0$,

x	0	−1
y	2	0
Points	D	C

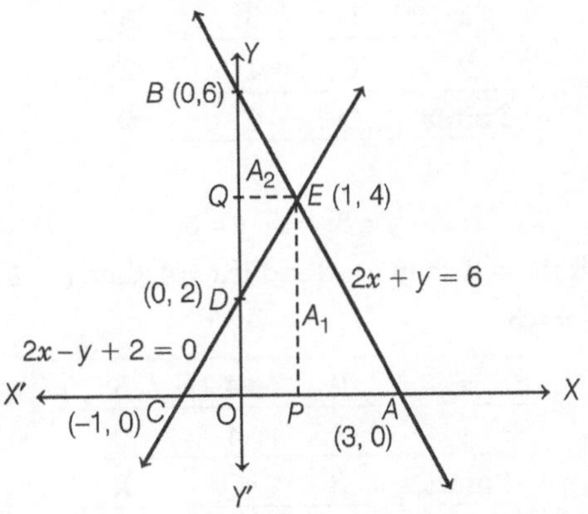

Hence, the pair of equations intersect graphically at point $E(1, 4)$, *i.e.*, $x = 1$ and $y = 4$.

Let A_1 and A_2 represent the areas of ΔACE and ΔBDE respectively.

Now, $\quad A_1 = \text{Area of } \Delta ACE = \frac{1}{2} \times AC \times PE$

$$= \frac{1}{2} \times 4 \times 4 = 8$$

and $\quad A_2 = \text{Area of } \Delta BDE = \frac{1}{2} \times BD \times QE$

$$= \frac{1}{2} \times 4 \times 1 = 2$$

$\therefore \quad A_1 : A_2 = 8 : 2 = 4 : 1$

Q.2 Determine, graphically, the vertices of the triangle formed by the lines $y = x$, $3y = x$ and $x + y = 8$

Ans. Given linear equations are

$$y = x \quad ...(i)$$

$$3y = x \quad ...(ii)$$

and $$x + y = 8 \quad ...(iii)$$

For equation $y = x$,

If $x = 1$, then $y = 1$

If $x = 0$, then $y = 0$

If $x = 2$, then $y = 2$

Table for line $y = x$,

x	0	1	2
y	0	1	2
Points	O	A	B

For equation $x = 3y$,

If $x = 0$, then $y = 0$; if $x = 3$, then $y = 1$ and if $x = 6$, then $y = 2$

Table for line $x = 3y$,

x	0	3	6
y	0	1	2
Points	O	C	D

For equation $x + y = 8 \Rightarrow y = 8 - x$

If $x = 0$, then $y = 8$; if $x = 8$, then $y = 0$ and if $x = 4$, then $y = 4$

Table for line $x + y = 8$.

x	0	4	8
y	8	4	0
Points	P	Q	R

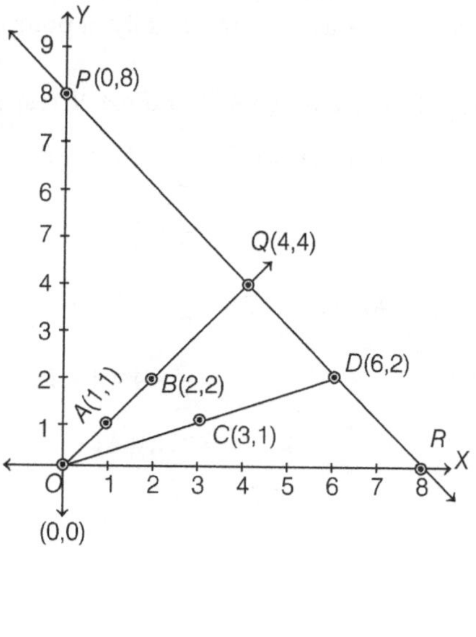

Plotting the points $A(1, 1)$ and $B(2, 2)$, we get the straight line AB. Plotting the points $C(3, 1)$ and $D(6, 2)$, we get the straight line CD. Plotting the points $P(0, 8)$, $Q(4, 4)$ and $R(8, 0)$, we get the straight line PQR. We see that lines AB and CD intersecting the line PR at Q and D, respectively.

So, ΔOQD is formed by these lines. Hence, the vertices of the ΔOQD are $O(0, 0)$, $Q(4, 4)$ and $D(6, 2)$.

Q.3 Draw the graphs of the equations $x = 3$, $x = 5$ and $2x - y - 4 = 0$. Also find the area of the quadrilateral formed by the lines and the X-axis.

Thinking Process

(i) Find the points for the given equations of gives and plot them to get lines on the graph.

(ii) Observe the quadrilateral formed by these lines.

(iii) Once you identify the quadrilateral find its area.

Ans. Given equation of lines $2x - y - 4 = 0$, $x = 3$ and $x = 5$

Table for line $2x - y - 4 = 0$,

x	0	2
$y = 2x - 4$	-4	0
Points	P	Q

Plot the points $P(0, -4)$ and $Q(2, 0)$ and join these points and form a line PQ also draw the lines $x = 3$ and $x = 5$.

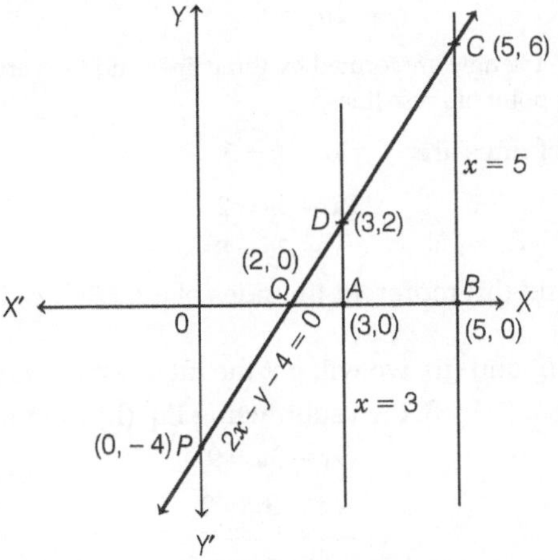

$\therefore$ Area of quadrilateral $ABCD = \frac{1}{2} \times$ distance between parallel lines

$\times$ (sum of parallel lines) [$\because$ quadrilateral $ABCD$ is a trapezium]

$$= \frac{1}{2} \times AB \times (AD + BC)$$

$$= \frac{1}{2} \times 2 \times (6 + 2)$$

[$\because AB = OB - OA = 5 - 3 = 2$, $AD = 2$ and $BC = 6$]

$= 8$ sq. units

Hence, the required area of the quadrilateral formed by the lines and the X-axis is 8 sq. units.

Q.4 The cost of 4 pens and 4 pencils boxes is ₹ 100. Three times the cost of a pen is ₹ 15 more than the cost of a pencil box. Form the pair of linear equations for the above situation. Find the cost of a pen and a pencil box.

Ans. Let the cost of a pen be ₹ x and the cost of a pencil box be ₹ y.

Then, by given condition,

$$4x + 4y = 100 \Rightarrow x + y = 25 \quad \text{...(i)}$$

and $$3x = y + 15$$

$\Rightarrow$ $$3x - y = 15 \quad \text{...(ii)}$$

On adding Eqs. (i) and (ii), we get

$$4x = 40$$

$\Rightarrow$ $$x = 10$$

On substituting $x = 10$ in Eq. (i), we get

$$y = 25 - 10 = 15$$

Hence, the cost of a pen and a pencil box are ₹ 10 and ₹ 15 respectively.

Q.5 Determine, algebraically, the vertices of the triangle formed by the lines

$$3x - y = 3$$
$$2x - 3y = 2$$
and $$x + 2y = 8$$

- **Concept Insight** Triangle are formed by three lines and the vertices of the triangle are the intersecting point of these lines.

Ans. Given equation of lines are $3x - y = 3$ ...(i)

$$2x - 3y = 2 \quad \text{...(ii)}$$

and $$x + 2y = 8 \quad \text{...(iii)}$$

Let lines (i), (ii) and (iii) represent the sides of a ΔABC *i.e.*, AB, BC and CA, respectively.

On solving lines (i) and (ii), we will get the intersecting point B.

On multiplying Eq. (i) by 3, then subtracting Eq. (ii) from it, we get

$$9x - 3y = 9$$
$$\underline{\underset{-}{2x} \underset{+}{- 3y} = \underset{-}{2}}$$
$$7x = 7 \Rightarrow x = 1$$

On putting the value of x in Eq. (i), we get

$$3 \times 1 - y = 3$$

$\Rightarrow$ $$y = 0$$

So, the coordinate of point or vertex B is $(1, 0)$.

On solving lines (ii) and (iii), we will get the intersecting point C.

On multiplying Eq. (iii) by 2 and then subtracting Eq. (ii) from it, we get

$$2x + 4y = 16$$
$$\underset{-\quad +\quad -}{2x - 3y = 2}$$
$$7y = 14$$
$$\Rightarrow \quad y = 2$$

On putting the value of y in Eq. (iii), we get

$$x + 2 \times 2 = 8$$
$$\Rightarrow \quad x = 8 - 4$$
$$\Rightarrow \quad x = 4$$

Hence, the coordinate of point or vertex C is (4, 2).

On solving lines (iii) and (i), we will get the intersecting point A.

On multiplying in Eq. (i) by 2 and then adding Eq. (iii), we get

$$6x - 2y = 6$$
$$\underline{x + 2y = 8}$$
$$7x = 14$$
$$\Rightarrow \quad x = 2$$

On putting the value of x in Eq. (i), we get

$$3 \times 2 - y = 3$$
$$\Rightarrow \quad y = 6 - 3$$
$$\Rightarrow \quad y = 3$$

So, the coordinate of point or vertex A is (2, 3).

Hence, the vertices of the ΔABC formed by the given lines are A (2, 3), B (1, 0) and C (4, 2).

***Q.6** Ankita travels 14 km to her home partly by rickshaw and partly by bus. She takes half an hour, if she travels 2 km by rickshaw and the remaining distance by bus. On the other hand, if she travels 4 km by rickshaw and the remaining distance by bus, she takes 9 minutes longer. Find the speed of the rickshaw and of the bus.

Ans. Let the speed of the rickshaw and the bus are x km/h and y km/h respectively.

Now, she has taken time to travel 2 km by rickshaw, $t_1 = \frac{2}{x}$ h. $\left[\because \text{speed} = \frac{\text{distance}}{\text{time}}\right]$

and she has taken time to travel remaining distance *i.e.*, (14 – 2) = 12 km by bus, $t_2 = \frac{12}{y}$ h.

By first condition, $\quad t_1 + t_2 = \frac{1}{2} \Rightarrow \frac{2}{x} + \frac{12}{y} = \frac{1}{2}$ ...(i)

Now, she has taken time to travel 4 km by rickshaw, $t_3 = \frac{4}{x}$ h

Note (*) *Topics related to these question have been removed from latest NCERT.*

and she has taken time to travel remaining distance *i.e.*, $(14-4)=10$ km by bus $= t_4 = \frac{10}{y}$ h.

By second condition, $t_3 + t_4 = \frac{1}{2} + \frac{9}{60} = \frac{1}{2} + \frac{3}{20}$

$$\Rightarrow \quad \frac{4}{x} + \frac{10}{y} = \frac{13}{20} \quad \text{...(ii)}$$

Let $\frac{1}{x} = u$ and $\frac{1}{y} = v$, then Eqs. (i) and (ii) becomes

$$2u + 12v = \frac{1}{2} \quad \text{...(iii)}$$

and

$$4u + 10v = \frac{13}{20} \quad \text{...(iv)}$$

On multiplying in Eq. (iii) by 2 and then subtracting, we get

$$4u + 24v = 1$$

$$\begin{array}{r} 4u + 10v = \frac{13}{20} \\ - \quad - \quad\quad - \end{array}$$

$$14v = 1 - \frac{13}{20} = \frac{7}{20} \Rightarrow 2v = \frac{1}{20} \Rightarrow v = \frac{1}{40}$$

Now, put the value of v in Eq. (iii), we get

$$2u + 12\left(\frac{1}{40}\right) = \frac{1}{2}$$

$$\Rightarrow \quad 2u = \frac{1}{2} - \frac{3}{10} = \frac{5-3}{10}$$

$$\Rightarrow \quad 2u = \frac{2}{10} \Rightarrow u = \frac{1}{10}$$

$$\therefore \quad \frac{1}{x} = u$$

$$\Rightarrow \quad \frac{1}{x} = \frac{1}{10} \Rightarrow x = 10 \text{ km/h}$$

and

$$\frac{1}{y} = v \Rightarrow \frac{1}{y} = \frac{1}{40}$$

$$\Rightarrow \quad y = 40 \text{ km/h}$$

Hence, the speed of rickshaw and the bus are 10 km/h and 40 km/h respectively.

*** Q.7** A person, rowing at the rate of 5 km/h in still water, takes thrice as much time in going 40 km upstream as in going 40 km downstream. Find the speed of the stream.

- **Concept Insight** Upstream refers to the direction against the flow of the current and downstream refers to the direction in the same direction as the flow of the current.

Ans. Let the speed of the stream be v km/h.

Given that, a person rowing in still water = 5 km/h

The speed of a person rowing in downstream = $(5 + v)$ km/h

and the speed of a person has rowing in upstream = $(5 - v)$ km/h

Note (*) *Topics related to these question have been removed from latest NCERT.*

Now, the person taken time to cover 40 km downstream,

$$t_1 = \frac{40}{5+v} \text{ h} \qquad \left[\because \text{speed} = \frac{\text{distance}}{\text{time}}\right]$$

and the person has taken time to cover 40 km upstream,

$$t_2 = \frac{40}{5-v} \text{ h.}$$

By condition, $t_2 = t_1 \times 3$

$\Rightarrow \quad \frac{40}{5-v} = \frac{40}{5+v} \times 3 \Rightarrow \frac{1}{5-v} = \frac{3}{5+v}$

$\Rightarrow \quad 5 + v = 15 - 3v \Rightarrow 4v = 10$

$\therefore \quad v = \frac{10}{4} = 2.5 \text{ km/h}$

Hence, the speed of the stream is 2.5 km/h.

***Q.8 A motorboat can travel 30 km upstream and 28 km downstream in 7 hours. It can travel 21 km upstream and return in 5 hours. Find the speed of the boat in still water and the speed of the stream.**

Ans. Let the speed of the motorboat in still water and the speed of the stream are u km/h and v km/h respectively.

Then, a motorboat's speed in downstream $= (u + v)$ km/h

and a motorboat's speed in upstream $= (u - v)$ km/h.

Motorboat has taken time to travel 30 km upstream,

$$t_1 = \frac{30}{u-v} \text{ h} \qquad \left[\because \text{Speed} = \frac{\text{Distance}}{\text{Time}}\right]$$

and motorboat has taken time to travel 28 km downstream,

$$t_2 = \frac{28}{u+v} \text{ h}$$

By first condition, a motorboat can travel 30 km upstream and 28 km downstream in 7 h

i.e., $t_1 + t_2 = 7\text{h}$

$\Rightarrow \quad \frac{30}{u-v} + \frac{28}{u+v} = 7 \qquad \text{...(i)}$

Now, motorboat has taken time to travel 21 km upstream and return *i.e.,* $t_3 = \frac{21}{u-v}$.

[for upstream]

and $t_4 = \frac{21}{u+v}$ [for downstream]

By second condition, $t_4 + t_3 = 5\text{h}$

$\Rightarrow \quad \frac{21}{u+v} + \frac{21}{u-v} = 5 \qquad \text{...(ii)}$

Let $x = \frac{1}{u+v}$ and $y = \frac{1}{u-v}$

Note (✱) *Topics related to these question have been removed from latest NCERT.*

Eqs. (i) and (ii) becomes $30x + 28y = 7$ ...(iii)

and $21x + 21y = 5$

$\Rightarrow \quad x + y = \frac{5}{21}$ ...(iv)

Now, multiplying in Eq. (iv) by 28 and then subtracting from Eq. (iii), we get

$$30x + 28y = 7$$
$$28x + 28y = \frac{140}{21}$$
$$- \quad - \quad -$$
$$2x = 7 - \frac{20}{3} = \frac{21-20}{3}$$

$\Rightarrow \quad 2x = \frac{1}{3} \Rightarrow x = \frac{1}{6}$

On putting the value of x in Eq. (iv), we get

$$\frac{1}{6} + y = \frac{5}{21}$$

$\Rightarrow \quad y = \frac{5}{21} - \frac{1}{6} = \frac{10-7}{42} = \frac{3}{42} \Rightarrow y = \frac{1}{14}$

$\therefore \quad x = \frac{1}{u+v} = \frac{1}{6} \Rightarrow u + v = 6$ ...(v)

and $y = \frac{1}{u-v} = \frac{1}{14}$

$\Rightarrow \quad u - v = 14$ ... (vi)

Now, adding Eqs. (v) and (vi), we get

$$2u = 20 \Rightarrow u = 10$$

On putting the value of u in Eq. (v), we get

$$10 + v = 6$$

$\Rightarrow \quad v = -4$

Hence, the speed of the motorboat in still water is 10 km/h and the speed of the stream is 4 km/h.

Mistake Alert ! *Students might leave their solution after getting the value of x and y whereas our aim is to get the value of u and v.*

Q.9 A two-digit number is obtained by either multiplying the sum of the digits by 8 and then subtracting 5 or by multiplying the difference of the digits by 16 and then adding 3. Find the number.

- **Concept Insight** Number formed by the digit is the sum of the product of each digit and its place value.

Ans. Let the two-digit number = $10x + y$

Case I Multiplying the sum of the digits by 8 and then subtracting 5 = two-digit number

$\Rightarrow \quad 8 \times (x + y) - 5 = 10x + y$

$\Rightarrow \quad 8x + 8y - 5 = 10x + y$

$\Rightarrow \quad 2x - 7y = -5$ ...(i)

***Case* II** Multiplying the difference of the digits by 16 and then adding 3 = two-digit number

$\Rightarrow \quad 16 \times (x - y) + 3 = 10x + y$

$\Rightarrow \quad 16x - 16y + 3 = 10x + y$

$\Rightarrow \quad 6x - 17y = -3 \quad \ldots\text{(ii)}$

Now, multiplying in Eq. (i) by 3 and then subtracting from Eq. (ii), we get

$$\begin{array}{r} 6x - 17y = -3 \\ 6x - 21y = -15 \\ \underline{- \quad + \quad\quad +} \\ 4y = 12 \Rightarrow y = 3 \end{array}$$

Now, puting the value of y in Eq. (i), we get

$$2x - 7 \times 3 = -5$$

$\Rightarrow \quad 2x = 21 - 5 = 16 \Rightarrow x = 8$

Hence, the required two-digit number

$$= 10x + y$$
$$= 10 \times 8 + 3 = 80 + 3 = 83$$

Mistake Alert! *Students often leave the solution after determing the value of x and y. But the main aim is to find the two digit number with the help of x and y.*

Q.10 A railway half ticket cost half the full fare but the reservation charges are the same on a half ticket as on a full ticket. One reserved first class ticket from the stations A to B costs ₹ 2530. Also, one reserved first class ticket and one reserved first class half ticket from A to B costs ₹ 3810. Find the full first class fare from stations A to B and also the reservation charges for a ticket.

Ans. Let the cost of full and half first class fare be ₹ x and ₹ $\frac{x}{2}$, respectively and reservation charges be ₹ y per ticket.

***Case* I** The cost of one reserved first class ticket from the stations A to B

$$= ₹\,2530$$

$\Rightarrow \quad x + y = 2530 \quad \ldots\text{(i)}$

***Case* II** The cost of one reserved first class ticket and one reserved first class half ticket from stations A to B = ₹ 3810

$\Rightarrow \quad x + y + \frac{x}{2} + y = 3810$

$\Rightarrow \quad \frac{3x}{2} + 2y = 3810$

$\Rightarrow \quad 3x + 4y = 7620 \quad \ldots\text{(ii)}$

Now, multiplying Eq. (i) by 4 and then subtracting from Eq. (ii), we get

$$\begin{array}{r} 3x + 4y = 7620 \\ 4x + 4y = 10120 \\ \underline{- \quad\quad - \quad\quad -} \\ -x = -2500 \end{array}$$

$\Rightarrow \quad x = 2500$

On putting the value of x in Eq. (i), we get

$$2500 + y = 2530$$

$$\Rightarrow \quad y = 2530 - 2500 \Rightarrow y = 30$$

Hence, full first class fare from stations A to B is ₹2500 and the reservation charge for a ticket is ₹30.

Mistake Alert! *Don't half the reservation charge while reserving half ticket as the reservation charge is same for half and full ticket.*

Q.11 A shopkeeper sells a saree at 8% profit and a sweater at 10% discount, thereby, getting a sum ₹1008. If she had sold the saree at 10% profit and the sweater at 8% discount, she would have got ₹1028. Find the cost price of the saree and the list price (price before discount) of the sweater.

Ans. Let the cost price of the saree and the list price of the sweater be ₹x and ₹y respectively.

Case I Sells a saree at 8% profit + Sells a sweater at 10% discount = ₹1008

$$\Rightarrow \quad (100 + 8)\% \text{ of } x + (100 - 10)\% \text{ of } y = 1008$$

$$\Rightarrow \quad 108\% \text{ of } x + 90\% \text{ of } y = 1008$$

$$\Rightarrow \quad 1.08x + 0.9y = 1008 \quad \text{...(i)}$$

Case II Sold the saree at 10% profit + Sold the sweater at 8% discount = ₹1028

$$\Rightarrow \quad (100 + 10)\% \text{ of } x + (100 - 8)\% \text{ of } y = 1028$$

$$\Rightarrow \quad 110\% \text{ of } x + 92\% \text{ of } y = 1028$$

$$\Rightarrow \quad 1.1\,x + 0.92y = 1028 \quad \text{...(ii)}$$

On putting the value of y from Eq. (i) into Eq. (ii), we get

$$1.1x + 0.92\left(\frac{1008 - 1.08x}{0.9}\right) = 1028$$

$$\Rightarrow \quad 1.1 \times 0.9x + 927.36 - 0.9936x = 1028 \times 0.9$$

$$\Rightarrow \quad 0.99x - 0.9936x = 925.2 - 927.36$$

$$\Rightarrow \quad -0.0036x = -2.16$$

$$\therefore \quad x = \frac{2.16}{0.0036} = 600$$

On putting the value of x in Eq. (i), we get

$$1.08 \times 600 + 0.9y = 1008$$

$$\Rightarrow \quad 108 \times 6 + 0.9y = 1008$$

$$\Rightarrow \quad 0.9y = 1008 - 648$$

$$\Rightarrow \quad 0.9y = 360$$

$$\Rightarrow \quad y = \frac{360}{0.9} = 400$$

Hence, the cost price of the saree and the list price (price before discount) of the sweater are ₹600 and ₹400, respectively.

Q.12 Susan invested certain amount of money in two schemes A and B, which offer interest at the rate of 8% per annum and 9% per annum, respectively. She received ₹ 1860 as annual interest. However, had she interchanged the amount of investments in the two schemes, she would have received ₹ 20 more as annual interest. How much money did she invest in each scheme?

Ans. Let the amount of investments in schemes A and B be ₹ x and ₹ y, respectively.

***Case* I** Interest at the rate of 8% per annum on scheme A+ Interest at the rate of 9% per annum on scheme B = Total annual interest

$$\Rightarrow \quad \frac{x \times 8 \times 1}{100} + \frac{y \times 9 \times 1}{100} = ₹\,1860 \quad \left[\because \text{ simple interest} = \frac{\text{principal} \times \text{rate} \times \text{time}}{100}\right]$$

$$\Rightarrow \quad 8x + 9y = 186000 \qquad \text{...(i)}$$

***Case* II** Interest at the rate of 9% per annum on scheme A + Interest at the rate of 8% per annum on scheme B = ₹ 20 more as annual interest

$$\Rightarrow \quad \frac{x \times 9 \times 1}{100} + \frac{y \times 8 \times 1}{100} = ₹\,20 + ₹\,1860$$

$$\Rightarrow \quad \frac{9x}{100} + \frac{8y}{100} = 1880 \qquad \text{...(ii)}$$

On multiplying Eq. (i) by 9 and Eq. (ii) by 8 and then subtracting them, we get

$$72x + 81y = 9 \times 186000$$
$$\underline{\underset{-}{72x} + \underset{-}{64y} = \underset{-}{8 \times 188000}}$$

$$\Rightarrow \quad 17y = 1000\,[(9 \times 186) - (8 \times 188)]$$
$$= 1000\,(1674 - 1504) = 1000 \times 170$$
$$\Rightarrow \quad 17y = 170000 \Rightarrow y = 10000$$

On putting the value of y in Eq. (i), we get

$$8x + 9 \times 10000 = 186000$$
$$\Rightarrow \quad 8x = 186000 - 90000$$
$$\Rightarrow \quad 8x = 96000$$
$$\Rightarrow \quad x = 12000$$

Hence, she invested ₹ 12000 and ₹ 10000 in two schemes A and B, respectively.

Q.13 Vijay had some bananas and he divided them into two lots A and B. He sold the first lot at the rate of ₹ 2 for 3 bananas and the second lot at the rate of ₹ 1 per banana and got a total of ₹ 400. If he had sold the first lot at the rate of ₹ 1 per banana and the second lot at the rate of ₹ 4 for 5 bananas, his total collection would have been ₹ 460. Find the total number of bananas he had.

Ans. Let the number of bananas in lots A and B be x and y respectively

***Case* I** Cost of the first lot at the rate of ₹ 2 for 3 bananas + Cost of the second lot at the rate of ₹ 1 per banana = Amount received

$$\Rightarrow \quad \frac{2}{3}x + y = 400$$

$$\Rightarrow \quad 2x + 3y = 1200 \quad \text{...(i)}$$

***Case* II** Cost of the first lot at the rate of ₹ 1 per banana + Cost of the second lot at the rate of ₹ 4 for 5 bananas = Amount received

$$\Rightarrow \quad x + \frac{4}{5}y = 460$$

$$\Rightarrow \quad 5x + 4y = 2300 \quad \text{...(ii)}$$

On multiplying in Eq. (i) by 4 and Eq. (ii) by 3 and then subtracting them, we get

$$\begin{array}{r} 8x + 12y = 4800 \\ 15x + 12y = 6900 \\ - \quad - \quad \quad \\ \hline -7x = -2100 \end{array}$$

$$\Rightarrow \quad x = 300$$

Now, put the value of x in Eq. (i), we get

$$2 \times 300 + 3y = 1200 \Rightarrow 600 + 3y = 1200$$

$$\Rightarrow \quad 3y = 1200 - 600 \Rightarrow 3y = 600$$

$$\Rightarrow \quad y = 200$$

$\therefore$ Total number of bananas = Number of bananas in lot A + Number of bananas in lot B

$$= x + y = 300 + 200 = 500$$

Hence, Vijay had 500 bananas.

Chapter

04

Quadratic Equations

Multiple Choice Questions (MCQs)

Choose the correct answer from the given four options in the following questions:

Q.1 Which of the following is a quadratic equation?

(a) $x^2 + 2x + 1 = (4 - x)^2 + 3$

(b) $-2x^2 = (5 - x)\left(2x - \frac{2}{5}\right)$

(c) $(k + 1)x^2 + \frac{3}{2}x = 7$, where $k = -1$

(d) $x^3 - x^2 = (x - 1)^3$

Thinking Process An equation which is of the form $ax^2 + bx + c = 0$ $a \neq 0$ is called a quadratic equation. So, simplify each option and check whether it is in the form of $ax^2 + bx + c = 0, a \neq 0$ or not.

Ans. *(d)*

(a) Given that, $x^2 + 2x + 1 = (4 - x)^2 + 3$

$$\Rightarrow \quad x^2 + 2x + 1 = 16 + x^2 - 8x + 3$$

$$\Rightarrow \quad 10x - 18 = 0$$

which is not of the form $ax^2 + bx + c, a \neq 0$. Thus, the equation is not a quadratic equation.

(b) Given that, $-2x^2 = (5 - x)\left(2x - \frac{2}{5}\right)$

$$\Rightarrow \quad -2x^2 = 10x - 2x^2 - 2 + \frac{2x}{5}$$

$$\Rightarrow \quad 50x + 2x - 10 = 0$$

$$\Rightarrow \quad 52x - 10 = 0$$

which is also not a quadratic equation.

(c) Given that, $x^2(k + 1) + \frac{3}{2}x = 7$

Given, $k = -1$

$$\Rightarrow \quad x^2(-1 + 1) + \frac{3}{2}x = 7$$

$$\Rightarrow \quad 3x - 14 = 0$$

which is also not a quadratic equation.

(d) Given that, $x^3 - x^2 = (x-1)^3$

$\Rightarrow$ $x^3 - x^2 = x^3 - 3x^2(1) + 3x(1)^2 - (1)^3$

$[\because (a-b)^3 = a^3 - b^3 - 3a^2b + 3ab^2]$

$\Rightarrow$ $x^3 - x^2 = x^3 - 3x^2 + 3x - 1$

$\Rightarrow$ $-x^2 + 3x^2 - 3x + 1 = 0$

$\Rightarrow$ $2x^2 - 3x + 1 = 0$

which represents a quadratic equation because it has the quadratic form $ax^2 + bx + c = 0, a \neq 0$.

Q.2 Which of the following is not a quadratic equation?

(a) $2(x-1)^2 = 4x^2 - 2x + 1$ (b) $2x - x^2 = x^2 + 5$

(c) $(\sqrt{2}x + \sqrt{3})^2 + x^2 = 3x^2 - 5x$ (d) $(x^2 + 2x)^2 = x^4 + 3 + 4x^3$

Ans. *(c)*

(a) Given that, $2(x-1)^2 = 4x^2 - 2x + 1$

$\Rightarrow$ $2(x^2 + 1 - 2x) = 4x^2 - 2x + 1$

$\Rightarrow$ $2x^2 + 2 - 4x = 4x^2 - 2x + 1$

$\Rightarrow$ $2x^2 + 2x - 1 = 0$

which represents a quadratic equation because it has the quadratic form $ax^2 + bx + c = 0, a \neq 0$.

(b) Given that, $2x - x^2 = x^2 + 5$

$\Rightarrow$ $2x^2 - 2x + 5 = 0$

which also represents a quadratic equation because it has the quadratic form $ax^2 + bx + c = 0, a \neq 0$.

(c) Given that, $(\sqrt{2}x + \sqrt{3})^2 + x^2 = 3x^2 - 5x$

$\Rightarrow$ $2x^2 + 3 + 2\sqrt{6}\cdot x + x^2 = 3x^2 - 5x$

$\Rightarrow$ $3 + 2\sqrt{6}x = -5x$

$(5 + 2\sqrt{6})x + 3 = 0$

which does not represent a quadratic equation because it has not the quadratic form $ax^2 + bx + c = 0, a \neq 0$.

(d) Given that, $(x^2 + 2x)^2 = x^4 + 3 + 4x^3$

$\Rightarrow$ $x^4 + 4x^2 + 4x^3 = x^4 + 3 + 4x^3$

$\Rightarrow$ $4x^2 - 3 = 0$

Which is of the form $ax^2 + bx + c, a \neq 0$. Thus, the equation is a quadratic.

Q.3 Which of the following equations has 2 as a root?

(a) $x^2 - 4x + 5 = 0$

(b) $x^2 + 3x - 12 = 0$

(c) $2x^2 - 7x + 6 = 0$

(d) $3x^2 - 6x - 2 = 0$

- **Concept Insight** If α is one of the root of any quadratic equation $ax^2 + bx + c = 0$, then $x = \alpha$ *i.e.*, α satisfies the equation $a\alpha^2 + b\alpha + c = 0$.

Ans. *(c)*

(a) Substituting $x = 2$ in $x^2 - 4x + 5$, we get $(2)^2 - 4(2) + 5$

$$= 4 - 8 + 5 = 1 \neq 0$$

So, $x = 2$ is not a root of $x^2 - 4x + 5 = 0$.

(b) Substituting $x = 2$ in $x^2 + 3x - 12$, we get

$$(2)^2 + 3(2) - 12 = 4 + 6 - 12 = -2 \neq 0$$

So, $x = 2$ is not a root of $x^2 + 3x - 12 = 0$.

(c) Substituting $x = 2$ in $2x^2 - 7x + 6$, we get

$$2(2)^2 - 7(2) + 6 = 2(4) - 14 + 6$$

$$= 8 - 14 + 6 = 14 - 14 = 0$$

So, $x = 2$ is a root of the equation $2x^2 - 7x + 6 = 0$.

(d) Substituting $x = 2$ in $3x^2 - 6x - 2$, we get

$$3(2)^2 - 6(2) - 2 = 12 - 12 - 2 = -2 \neq 0$$

So, $x = 2$ is not a root of $3x^2 - 6x - 2 = 0$.

Q.4 If $\frac{1}{2}$ is a root of the equation $x^2 + kx - \frac{5}{4} = 0$, then the value of k is

(a) 2 (b) -2 (c) $\frac{1}{4}$ (d) $\frac{1}{2}$

Thinking Process Since, $\frac{1}{2}$ is a root of the given equation, then put $x = \frac{1}{2}$ in given the equation and get the value of k. .

Ans. *(a)* Since, $\frac{1}{2}$ is a root of the quadratic equation $x^2 + kx - \frac{5}{4} = 0$.

Then, $$\left(\frac{1}{2}\right)^2 + k\left(\frac{1}{2}\right) - \frac{5}{4} = 0$$

$$\Rightarrow \quad \frac{1}{4} + \frac{k}{2} - \frac{5}{4} = 0 \Rightarrow \frac{1 + 2k - 5}{4} = 0$$

$$\Rightarrow \quad 2k - 4 = 0 \Rightarrow 2k = 4 \Rightarrow k = 2$$

Q.5 Which of the following equations has the sum of its roots as 3?

(a) $2x^2 - 3x + 6 = 0$ (b) $-x^2 + 3x - 3 = 0$

(c) $\sqrt{2}\,x^2 - \frac{3}{\sqrt{2}}x + 1 = 0$ (d) $3x^2 - 3x + 3 = 0$

Thinking Process If α and β are the roots of the quadratic equation $ax^2 + bx + c = 0, a \neq 0$, then sum of roots $= \alpha + \beta = -\frac{\text{Coefficient of } x}{\text{Coefficient of } x^2} = \frac{-b}{a}$

Ans. *(b)*

(a) Given that, $2x^2 - 3x + 6 = 0$

On comparing with $ax^2 + bx + c = 0$, we get

$$a = 2, b = -3 \text{ and } c = 6$$

$\therefore$ Sum of the roots $= \frac{-b}{a} = \frac{-(-3)}{2} = \frac{3}{2}$

So, sum of the roots of the quadratic equation $2x^2 - 3x + 6 = 0$ is not 3, so it is not the answer.

(b) Given that, $-x^2 + 3x - 3 = 0$

On compare with $ax^2 + bx + c = 0$, we get

$$a = -1, b = 3 \text{ and } c = -3$$

$\therefore$ Sum of the roots $= \dfrac{-b}{a} = \dfrac{-(3)}{-1} = 3$

So, sum of the roots of the quadratic equation $-x^2 + 3x - 3 = 0$ is 3, so it is the answer.

(c) Given that, $\sqrt{2}\,x^2 - \dfrac{3}{\sqrt{2}}x + 1 = 0$

$\Rightarrow$ $$2x^2 - 3x + \sqrt{2} = 0$$

On comparing with $ax^2 + bx + c = 0$, we get

$$a = 2, b = -3 \text{ and } c = \sqrt{2}$$

$\therefore$ Sum of the roots $= \dfrac{-b}{a} = \dfrac{-(-3)}{2} = \dfrac{3}{2}$

So, sum of the roots of the quadratic equation $\sqrt{2}x^2 - \dfrac{3}{\sqrt{2}}x + 1 = 0$ is not 3, so it is not the answer.

(d) Given that, $3x^2 - 3x + 3 = 0$

$\Rightarrow$ $$x^2 - x + 1 = 0$$

On comparing with $ax^2 + bx + c = 0$, we get

$$a = 1, b = -1 \text{ and } c = 1$$

$\therefore$ Sum of the roots $= \dfrac{-b}{a} = \dfrac{-(-1)}{1} = 1$

So, sum of the roots of the quadratic equation $3x^2 - 3x + 3 = 0$ is not 3, so it is not the answer.

Q.6 Value(s) of k for which the quadratic equation $2x^2 - kx + k = 0$ has equal roots is/are

(a) 0 (b) 4 (c) 8 (d) 0, 8

- **Concept Insight** If any quadratic equation *i.e.*, $ax^2 + bx + c = 0, a \neq 0$ has two equal real roots, then its discriminant should be equal to zero *i.e.*, $D = b^2 - 4ac = 0$

Ans. *(d)* Given equation is $2x^2 - kx + k = 0$

On comparing with $ax^2 + bx + c = 0$, we get

$$a = 2, b = -k \text{ and } c = k$$

For equal roots, the discriminant must be zero.

i.e., $$D = b^2 - 4ac = 0$$

$\Rightarrow$ $$(-k)^2 - 4(2)k = 0$$

$\Rightarrow$ $$k^2 - 8k = 0$$

$\Rightarrow$ $$k(k - 8) = 0$$

$\therefore$ $$k = 0, 8$$

Hence, the required values of k are 0 and 8.

Q.7 Which constant must be added and subtracted to solve the quadratic equation $9x^2 + \frac{3}{4}x - \sqrt{2} = 0$ by the method of completing the square?

(a) $\frac{1}{8}$ (b) $\frac{1}{64}$ (c) $\frac{1}{4}$ (d) $\frac{9}{64}$

Ans. *(b)* Given equation is $9x^2 + \frac{3}{4}x - \sqrt{2} = 0$.

$$(3x)^2 + \frac{1}{4}(3x) - \sqrt{2} = 0$$

On putting $3x = y$, we have $y^2 + \frac{1}{4}y - \sqrt{2} = 0$

$$\Rightarrow \quad y^2 + \frac{1}{4}y + \left(\frac{1}{8}\right)^2 - \left(\frac{1}{8}\right)^2 - \sqrt{2} = 0$$

$$\Rightarrow \quad \left(y + \frac{1}{8}\right)^2 = \frac{1}{64} + \sqrt{2}$$

$$\left(y + \frac{1}{8}\right)^2 = \frac{1 + 64\sqrt{2}}{64}$$

Thus, $\frac{1}{64}$ must be added and subtracted to solve the given equation.

Mistake Alert! *Students often struggle with adding and subtracting the correct term while using the method of completing the square.*

Q.8 The quadratic equation $2x^2 - \sqrt{5}x + 1 = 0$ has

(a) two distinct real roots (b) two equal real roots

(c) no real roots (d) more than 2 real roots

Thinking Process If a quadratic equation is in the from of $ax^2 + bx + c = 0$, $a \neq 0$, then

(i) If $D = b^2 - 4ac > 0$, then its roots are distinct and real.

(ii) If $D = b^2 - 4ac = 0$, then its roots are real and equal.

(iii) If $D = b^2 - 4ac < 0$, then its roots are not real or imaginary roots.

Any quadratic equation must have only two roots.

Ans. *(c)* Given equation is $2x^2 - \sqrt{5}x + 1 = 0$

On comparing with $ax^2 + bx + c = 0$, we get

$$a = 2, b = -\sqrt{5} \text{ and } c = 1$$

$\therefore$ Discriminant, $D = b^2 - 4ac = (-\sqrt{5})^2 - 4 \times (2) \times (1) = 5 - 8$

$$= -3 < 0$$

Since, discriminant is negative, therefore quadratic equation $2x^2 - \sqrt{5}x + 1 = 0$ has no real roots *i.e.*, imaginary roots.

Q.9 Which of the following equations has two distinct real roots?

(a) $2x^2 - 3\sqrt{2}\,x + \frac{9}{4} = 0$ (b) $x^2 + x - 5 = 0$

(c) $x^2 + 3x + 2\sqrt{2} = 0$ (d) $5x^2 - 3x + 1 = 0$

Ans. (b)

(a) Given equation is $2x^2 - 3\sqrt{2}x + \frac{9}{4} = 0$

On comparing with $ax^2 + bx + c = 0$

$$a = 2, b = -3\sqrt{2} \text{ and } c = \frac{9}{4}$$

Now, $D = b^2 - 4ac = (-3\sqrt{2})^2 - 4(2)\left(\frac{9}{4}\right) = 18 - 18 = 0$

Thus, the equation has real and equal roots.

(b) The given equation is $x^2 + x - 5 = 0$

On comparing with $ax^2 + bx + c = 0$, we get

$$a = 1, b = 1 \text{ and } c = -5$$

The discriminant of $x^2 + x - 5 = 0$ is

$$D = b^2 - 4ac = (1)^2 - 4(1)(-5) = 1 + 20 = 21$$

$\Rightarrow$ $b^2 - 4ac > 0$

So, $x^2 + x - 5 = 0$ has two distinct real roots.

(c) Given equation is $x^2 + 3x + 2\sqrt{2} = 0$

On comparing with $ax^2 + bx + c = 0$

$$a = 1, b = 3 \text{ and } c = 2\sqrt{2}$$

Now, $D = b^2 - 4ac = (3)^2 - 4(1)(2\sqrt{2}) = 9 - 8\sqrt{2} < 0$

$\therefore$ Roots of the equation are not real.

(d) Given equation is, $5x^2 - 3x + 1 = 0$

On comparing with $ax^2 + bx + c = 0$

$$a = 5, b = -3, c = 1$$

Now, $D = b^2 - 4ac = (-3)^2 - 4(5)(1) = 9 - 20 = -11 < 0$

Hence, roots of the equation are not real.

Q.10 Which of the following equations has no real roots?

(a) $x^2 - 4x + 3\sqrt{2} = 0$
(b) $x^2 + 4x - 3\sqrt{2} = 0$
(c) $x^2 - 4x - 3\sqrt{2} = 0$
(d) $3x^2 + 4\sqrt{3}x + 4 = 0$

- **Concept Insight** A quadratic equation is in the form of $ax^2 + bx + c = 0$, if $D = b^2 - 4ac < 0$, then the roots are not real.

Ans. (a)

(a) The given equation is $x^2 - 4x + 3\sqrt{2} = 0$.

On comparing with $ax^2 + bx + c = 0$, we get

$$a = 1, b = -4 \text{ and } c = 3\sqrt{2}$$

The discriminant of $x^2 - 4x + 3\sqrt{2} = 0$ is

$$D = b^2 - 4ac = (-4)^2 - 4(1)(3\sqrt{2}) = 16 - 12\sqrt{2} = 16 - 12 \times (1.41)$$
$$= 16 - 16.92 = -0.92 \Rightarrow b^2 - 4ac < 0$$

Hence, the equation has no real roots.

(b) The given equation is $x^2 + 4x - 3\sqrt{2} = 0$

On comparing the equation with $ax^2 + bx + c = 0$, we get

$$a = 1, b = 4 \text{ and } c = -3\sqrt{2}$$

Then, $D = b^2 - 4ac = (4)^2 - 4(1)(-3\sqrt{2}) = 16 + 12\sqrt{2} > 0$

Hence, the equation has real roots.

(c) Given equation is $x^2 - 4x - 3\sqrt{2} = 0$

On comparing the equation with $ax^2 + bx + c = 0$, we get

$$a = 1, b = -4 \text{ and } c = -3\sqrt{2}$$

Then, $D = b^2 - 4ac = (-4)^2 - 4(1)(-3\sqrt{2})$

$= 16 + 12\sqrt{2} > 0$

Hence, the equation has real roots.

(d) Given equation is $3x^2 + 4\sqrt{3}x + 4 = 0$.

On comparing the equation with $ax^2 + bx + c = 0$, we get

$$a = 3, b = 4\sqrt{3} \text{ and } c = 4$$

Then, $D = b^2 - 4ac = (4\sqrt{3})^2 - 4(3)(4) = 48 - 48 = 0$

Hence, the equation has real roots.

Q.11 $(x^2 + 1)^2 - x^2 = 0$ has

(a) four real roots (b) two real roots (c) no real roots (d) one real root

Ans. *(c)* Given equation is $(x^2 + 1)^2 - x^2 = 0$

$\Rightarrow$ $x^4 + 1 + 2x^2 - x^2 = 0$ $[\because (a+b)^2 = a^2 + b^2 + 2ab]$

$\Rightarrow$ $x^4 + x^2 + 1 = 0$

$\therefore$ $(x^2)^2 + x^2 + 1 = 0$

Let $x^2 = y$

$$y^2 + y + 1 = 0$$

On comparing with $ay^2 + by + c = 0$, we get

$$a = 1, b = 1 \text{ and } c = 1$$

Discriminant, $D = b^2 - 4ac$

$= (1)^2 - 4(1)(1) = 1 - 4 = -3$

Since, $D < 0$

$\therefore$ $y^2 + y + 1 = 0$ *i.e.*, $x^4 + x^2 + 1 = 0$ or $(x^2 + 1)^2 - x^2 = 0$ has no real roots.

Short Answer Questions with Reasoning

Q.1 State whether the following quadratic equations have two distinct real roots. Justify your answer.

(i) $x^2 - 3x + 4 = 0$

(ii) $2x^2 + x - 1 = 0$

(iii) $2x^2 - 6x + \frac{9}{2} = 0$

(iv) $3x^2 - 4x + 1 = 0$

(v) $(x + 4)^2 - 8x = 0$

(vi) $(x - \sqrt{2})^2 - 2(x + 1) = 0$

(vii) $\sqrt{2}x^2 - \frac{3}{\sqrt{2}}x + \frac{1}{\sqrt{2}} = 0$

(viii) $x(1 - x) - 2 = 0$

(ix) $(x - 1)(x + 2) + 2 = 0$

(x) $(x + 1)(x - 2) + x = 0$

Thinking Process If $ax^2 + bx + c = 0, a \neq 0$ be any quadratic equation and $D = b^2 - 4ac$ be its discriminant, then

(i) $D > 0$ *i.e.*, $b^2 - 4ac > 0 \Rightarrow$ Roots are real and distinct.

(ii) $D = 0$ *i.e.*, $b^2 - 4ac = 0 \Rightarrow$ Roots are real and equal.

(iii) $D < 0$ *i.e.*, $b^2 - 4ac < 0 \Rightarrow$ No reals roots *i.e.*, imaginary roots.

Ans. (i) Given equation is $x^2 - 3x + 4 = 0$

On comparing with $ax^2 + bx + c = 0$, we get

$$a = 1, b = -3 \text{ and } c = 4$$

$\therefore$ Discriminant, $D = b^2 - 4ac = (-3)^2 - 4(1)(4)$

$$= 9 - 16 = -7 < 0 \quad i.e., D < 0$$

Hence, the equation $x^2 - 3x + 4 = 0$ has no real roots.

(ii) Given equation is $2x^2 + x - 1 = 0$

On comparing with $ax^2 + bx + c = 0$, we get

$$a = 2, b = 1 \text{ and } c = -1$$

$\therefore$ Discriminant, $D = b^2 - 4ac = (1)^2 - 4(2)(-1)$

$$= 1 + 8 = 9 > 0 \quad i.e., D > 0$$

Hence, the equation $2x^2 + x - 1 = 0$ has two distinct real roots.

(iii) Given equation is $2x^2 - 6x + \frac{9}{2} = 0$

On comparing with $ax^2 + bx + c = 0$, we get

$$a = 2, b = -6 \text{ and } c = \frac{9}{2}$$

$\therefore$ Discriminant, $D = b^2 - 4ac$

$$= (-6)^2 - 4(2)\left(\frac{9}{2}\right) = 36 - 36 = 0 \quad i.e., D = 0$$

Hence, the equation $2x^2 - 6x + \frac{9}{2} = 0$ has equal and real roots.

(iv) Given equation is $3x^2 - 4x + 1 = 0$

On comparing with $ax^2 + bx + c = 0$, we get

$$a = 3, b = -4 \text{ and } c = 1$$

$\therefore$ Discriminant, $D = b^2 - 4ac = (-4)^2 - 4(3)(1)$

$$= 16 - 12 = 4 > 0 \quad i.e., D > 0$$

Hence, the equation $3x^2 - 4x + 1 = 0$ has two distinct real roots.

(v) Given equation is $(x + 4)^2 - 8x = 0$

$\Rightarrow \quad x^2 + 16 + 8x - 8x = 0 \quad [\because (a + b)^2 = a^2 + 2ab + b^2]$

$\Rightarrow \quad x^2 + 16 = 0$

$\Rightarrow \quad x^2 + 0 \cdot x + 16 = 0$

On comparing with $ax^2 + bx + c = 0$, we get

$$a = 1, b = 0 \text{ and } c = 16$$

$\therefore$ Discriminant, $D = b^2 - 4ac = (0)^2 - 4(1)(16) = -64 < 0 \quad i.e., D < 0$

Hence, the equation $(x + 4)^2 - 8x = 0$ has imaginary roots, *i.e.*, no real roots.

(vi) Given equation is $(x-\sqrt{2})^2 - 2(x+1) = 0$.

$\Rightarrow \quad x^2 + (\sqrt{2})^2 - 2x\sqrt{2} - 2x - 2 = 0 \quad [\because (a-b)^2 = a^2 - 2ab + b^2]$

$\Rightarrow \quad x^2 + 2 - 2\sqrt{2}x - 2x - 2 = 0$

$\Rightarrow \quad x^2 - (2\sqrt{2}+2)x + 0 = 0$

On comparing with $ax^2 + bx + c = 0$, we get

$$a = 1, b = -(2\sqrt{2}+2) \text{ and } c = 0$$

$\therefore$ Discriminant, $D = b^2 - 4ac$

$$= -(2\sqrt{2}+2) - 4(1)0$$

$$= (2\sqrt{2}+2) > 0 \text{ i.e., } D > 0$$

Hence, the equation $(x-\sqrt{2})^2 - 2(x+1) = 0$ has two distinct real roots.

(vii) Given, equation is $\sqrt{2}x^2 - \frac{3}{\sqrt{2}}x + \frac{1}{\sqrt{2}} = 0$

On comparing with $ax^2 + bx + c = 0$, we get

$$a = \sqrt{2}, b = -\frac{3}{\sqrt{2}} \text{ and } c = \frac{1}{\sqrt{2}}$$

$\therefore$ Discriminant, $D = b^2 - 4ac = \left(-\frac{3}{\sqrt{2}}\right)^2 - 4\sqrt{2}\left(\frac{1}{\sqrt{2}}\right)$

$$= \frac{9}{2} - 4 = \frac{9-8}{2} = \frac{1}{2} > 0 \text{ i.e., } D > 0$$

Hence, the equation $\sqrt{2}x^2 - \frac{3}{\sqrt{2}}x + \frac{1}{\sqrt{2}} = 0$ has two distinct real roots.

(viii) Given equation is $x(1-x) - 2 = 0$

$\Rightarrow \quad x - x^2 - 2 = 0$

$\Rightarrow \quad x^2 - x + 2 = 0$

On comparing with $ax^2 + bx + c = 0$, we get

$$a = 1, b = -1 \text{ and } c = 2$$

$\therefore$ Discriminant, $D = b^2 - 4ac$

$$= (-1)^2 - 4(1)(2) = 1 - 8 = -7 < 0 \text{ i.e., } D < 0$$

Hence, the equation $x(1-x) - 2 = 0$ has imaginary roots *i.e.*, no real roots.

(ix) Given equation is

$$(x-1)(x+2) + 2 = 0$$

$\Rightarrow \quad x^2 + x - 2 + 2 = 0$

$\Rightarrow \quad x^2 + x + 0 = 0$

On comparing the equation with $ax^2 + bx + c = 0$, We have

$$a = 1, b = 1 \text{ and } c = 0$$

$\therefore$ Discriminant, $\quad D = b^2 - 4ac$

$$= 1 - 4(1)(0) = 1 > 0 \text{ i.e., } D > 0$$

Hence, equation has two distinct real roots.

(x) Given equation is $(x+1)(x-2) + x = 0$

$\Rightarrow \quad x^2 + x - 2x - 2 + x = 0$

$\Rightarrow \quad x^2 - 2 = 0$

$\Rightarrow \quad x^2 + 0 \cdot x - 2 = 0$

On comparing with $ax^2 + bx + c = 0$, we get

$$a = 1, b = 0 \text{ and } c = -2$$

$\therefore$ Discriminant, $D = b^2 - 4ac = (0)^2 - 4(1)(-2) = 0 + 8 = 8 > 0$

Hence, the equation $(x + 1)(x - 2) + x = 0$ has two distinct real roots.

Q.2 Write whether the following statements are true or false. Justify your answers.

(i) Every quadratic equation has exactly one root.

(ii) Every quadratic equation has atleast one real root.

(iii) Every quadratic equation has atleast two roots.

(iv) Every quadratic equation has atmost two roots.

(v) If the coefficient of x^2 and the constant term of a quadratic equation have opposite signs, then the quadratic equation has real roots.

(vi) If the coefficient of x^2 and the constant term have the same sign and if the coefficient of x term is zero, then the quadratic equation has no real roots.

Ans. (i) *False*, since a quadratic equation has atmost two roots.

(ii) *False*, for example $x^2 + 4 = 0$ has no real root.

(iii) *False*, since a quadratic equation has atmost two roots.

(iv) *True*, because every quadratic equation has atmost two roots.

(v) *True*, since in this case discriminant is always positive, so it has always real roots, *i.e.*, $ac < 0$ and so, $b^2 - 4ac > 0$.

(vi) *True*, since in this case discriminant is always negative, so it has no real roots *i.e.*, if $b = 0$ and $ac > 0$, then $b^2 - 4ac \Rightarrow -4ac < 0$

Q.3 A quadratic equation with integral coefficient has integral roots. Justify your answer.

Ans. *No*, consider the quadratic equation $2x^2 + x - 6 = 0$ with integral coefficient. The roots of the given quadratic equation are -2 and $\frac{3}{2}$ which are not integers.

Q.4 Does there exist a quadratic equation whose coefficients are rational but both of its roots are irrational? Justify your answer.

Ans. *Yes*, consider the quadratic equation $2x^2 + x - 4 = 0$ with rational coefficient. The roots of the given quadratic equation are $\frac{-1+\sqrt{33}}{4}$ and $\frac{-1-\sqrt{33}}{4}$ which are irrational.

Mistake Alert! *Students may forget to consider both positive and negative square roots while applying the formula.*

Q.5 Does there exist a quadratic equation whose coefficient are all distinct irrationals but both the roots are rationals? why?

Ans. Yes, consider the quadratic equation with all distinct irrationals coefficients *i.e.*, $\sqrt{3}x^2 - 7\sqrt{3}x + 12\sqrt{3} = 0$. The roots of this quadratic equation are 3 and 4, which are rationals.

Q.6 Is 0.2 a root of the equation $x^2 - 0.4 = 0$? Justify your answer.

Ans. No, since 0.2 does not satisfy the quadratic equation *i.e.*, $(0.2)^2 - 0.4 = 0.04 - 0.4 = -0.36 \neq 0$.

Q.7 If $b = 0$, $c < 0$, is it true that the roots of $x^2 + bx + c = 0$ are numerically equal and opposite in sign? Justify

Ans. Given that, $b = 0$ and $c < 0$ and quadratic equation,

$$x^2 + bx + c = 0 \quad \text{...(i)}$$

Put $b = 0$ in Eq. (i), we get

$$x^2 + 0 + c = 0$$

$$\Rightarrow \quad x^2 = -c \quad \left[\begin{array}{l}\text{here } c < 0 \\ \therefore -c > 0\end{array}\right]$$

$$\therefore \quad x = \pm\sqrt{-c}$$

So, the roots of $x^2 + bx + c = 0$ are numerically equal and opposite in sign.

Short Answer Questions

Q.1 Find the roots of the quadratic equations by using the quadratic formula in each of the following.

(i) $2x^2 - 3x - 5 = 0$ (ii) $5x^2 + 13x + 8 = 0$

(iii) $-3x^2 + 5x + 12 = 0$ (iv) $-x^2 + 7x - 10 = 0$

(v) $x^2 + 2\sqrt{2}x - 6 = 0$ (vi) $x^2 - 3\sqrt{5}x + 10 = 0$

(vii) $\frac{1}{2}x^2 - \sqrt{11}x + 1 = 0$

Thinking Process Compare the given quadratic equation with $ax^2 + bx + c = 0$ and get the values of a, b and c. Now, use the quadratic formula for finding the roots of quadratic equation. *i.e.*, $x = \frac{-b \pm \sqrt{b^2 - 4ac}}{2a}$

Ans. (i) Given equation is $2x^2 - 3x - 5 = 0$

On comparing with $ax^2 + bx + c = 0$, we get

$$a = 2, b = -3 \text{ and } c = -5$$

By quadratic formula, $x = \frac{-b \pm \sqrt{b^2 - 4ac}}{2a}$

$$= \frac{-(-3) \pm \sqrt{(-3)^2 - 4(2)(-5)}}{2(2)} = \frac{3 \pm \sqrt{9 + 40}}{4}$$

$$= \frac{3 \pm \sqrt{49}}{4} = \frac{3 \pm 7}{4} = \frac{10}{4}, \frac{-4}{4} = \frac{5}{2}, -1$$

So, $\frac{5}{2}$ and -1 are the roots of the given equation.

(ii) Given equation is $5x^2 + 13x + 8 = 0$

On comparing with $ax^2 + bx + c = 0$, we get

$$a = 5, b = 13 \text{ and } c = 8$$

By quadratic formula, $x = \frac{-b \pm \sqrt{b^2 - 4ac}}{2a}$

$$= \frac{-(13) \pm \sqrt{(13)^2 - 4(5)(8)}}{2(5)}$$

$$= \frac{-13 \pm \sqrt{169 - 160}}{10} = \frac{-13 \pm \sqrt{9}}{10}$$

$$= \frac{-13 \pm 3}{10} = -\frac{10}{10}, -\frac{16}{10} = -1, -\frac{8}{5}$$

So, -1 and $-\frac{8}{5}$ are the roots of the given equation.

(iii) Given equation is $-3x^2 + 5x + 12 = 0$

On comparing with $ax^2 + bx + c = 0$, we get

$$a = -3, b = 5 \text{ and } c = 12$$

By quadratic formula, $x = \frac{-b \pm \sqrt{b^2 - 4ac}}{2a}$

$$= \frac{-(5) \pm \sqrt{(5)^2 - 4(-3)(12)}}{2(-3)}$$

$$= \frac{-5 \pm \sqrt{25 + 144}}{-6} = \frac{-5 \pm \sqrt{169}}{-6}$$

$$= \frac{-5 \pm 13}{-6} = \frac{8}{-6}, \frac{-18}{-6} = -\frac{4}{3}, 3$$

So, $-\frac{4}{3}$ and 3 are two roots of the given equation.

(iv) Given equation is $-x^2 + 7x - 10 = 0$

On comparing with $ax^2 + bx + c = 0$, we get

$$a = -1, b = 7 \text{ and } c = -10$$

By quadratic formula, $x = \frac{-b \pm \sqrt{b^2 - 4ac}}{2a}$

$$= \frac{-(7) \pm \sqrt{(7)^2 - 4(-1)(-10)}}{2(-1)} = \frac{-7 \pm \sqrt{49 - 40}}{-2}$$

$$= \frac{-7 \pm \sqrt{9}}{-2} = \frac{-7 \pm 3}{-2} = \frac{-4}{-2}, \frac{-10}{-2} = 2, 5$$

So, 2 and 5 are two roots of the given equation.

(v) Given equation is $x^2 + 2\sqrt{2}\,x - 6 = 0$

On comparing with $ax^2 + bx + c = 0$, we get

$$a = 1,\ b = 2\sqrt{2} \text{ and } c = -6$$

By quadratic formula, $x = \dfrac{-b \pm \sqrt{b^2 - 4ac}}{2a}$

$$= \frac{-(2\sqrt{2}) \pm \sqrt{(2\sqrt{2})^2 - 4(1)(-6)}}{2(1)} = \frac{-2\sqrt{2} \pm \sqrt{8+24}}{2}$$

$$= \frac{-2\sqrt{2} \pm \sqrt{32}}{2} = \frac{-2\sqrt{2} \pm 4\sqrt{2}}{2}$$

$$= \frac{-2\sqrt{2} + 4\sqrt{2}}{2}, \frac{-2\sqrt{2} - 4\sqrt{2}}{2} = \sqrt{2}, -3\sqrt{2}$$

So, $\sqrt{2}$ and $-3\sqrt{2}$ are the roots of the given equation.

(vi) Given equation is $x^2 - 3\sqrt{5}x + 10 = 0$

On comparing with $ax^2 + bx + c = 0$, we have

$$a = 1,\ b = -3\sqrt{5} \text{ and } c = 10$$

By quadratic formula, $x = \dfrac{-b \pm \sqrt{b^2 - 4ac}}{2a}$

$$= \frac{-(-3\sqrt{5}) \pm \sqrt{(-3\sqrt{5})^2 - 4(1)(10)}}{2(1)}$$

$$= \frac{3\sqrt{5} \pm \sqrt{45-40}}{2} = \frac{3\sqrt{5} \pm \sqrt{5}}{2}$$

$$= \frac{3\sqrt{5} + \sqrt{5}}{2}, \frac{3\sqrt{5} - \sqrt{5}}{2} = 2\sqrt{5}, \sqrt{5}$$

So, $2\sqrt{5}$ and $\sqrt{5}$ are the roots of the given equation.

(vii) Given equation is $\dfrac{1}{2}x^2 - \sqrt{11}x + 1 = 0$

On comparing with $ax^2 + bx + c = 0$, we get

$$a = \frac{1}{2},\ b = -\sqrt{11} \text{ and } c = 1$$

$\therefore$ By quadratic formula, $x = \dfrac{-b \pm \sqrt{b^2 - 4ac}}{2a}$

$$= \frac{-(-\sqrt{11}) \pm \sqrt{(-\sqrt{11})^2 - 4 \times \frac{1}{2} \times 1}}{2\left(\frac{1}{2}\right)}$$

$$= \frac{\sqrt{11} \pm \sqrt{11-2}}{1} = \sqrt{11} \pm \sqrt{9}$$

$$= \sqrt{11} \pm 3 = 3 + \sqrt{11}, \sqrt{11} - 3$$

So, $3 + \sqrt{11}$ and $\sqrt{11} - 3$ are the roots of the given equation.

Q.2 Find the roots of the following quadratic equations by the factorisation method.

(i) $2x^2 + \frac{5}{3}x - 2 = 0$ (ii) $\frac{2}{5}x^2 - x - \frac{3}{5} = 0$

(iii) $3\sqrt{2}x^2 - 5x - \sqrt{2} = 0$ (iv) $3x^2 + 5\sqrt{5}x - 10 = 0$

(v) $21x^2 - 2x + \frac{1}{21} = 0$

Thinking Process If any coefficient of the quadratic equation of the form $ax^2 + bx + c = 0$, is in fractional form, then make all the coefficients in integral form. Then, use the factorisation method *i.e.,* by splitting the middle term, we get the required roots of the given quadratic equation.

Ans. (i) Given equation is $2x^2 + \frac{5}{3}x - 2 = 0$

On multiplying by 3 on both sides, we get

$$6x^2 + 5x - 6 = 0$$

$\Rightarrow$ $6x^2 + (9x - 4x) - 6 = 0$ [by splitting the middle term]

$\Rightarrow$ $6x^2 + 9x - 4x - 6 = 0$

$\Rightarrow$ $3x(2x + 3) - 2(2x + 3) = 0$

$\Rightarrow$ $(2x + 3)(3x - 2) = 0$

Now, $2x + 3 = 0$

$\Rightarrow$ $x = -\frac{3}{2}$

and $3x - 2 = 0$

$\Rightarrow$ $x = \frac{2}{3}$

Hence, the roots of the equation $6x^2 + 5x - 6 = 0$ are $\frac{-3}{2}$ and $\frac{2}{3}$.

(ii) Given equation is $\frac{2}{5}x^2 - x - \frac{3}{5} = 0$.

On multiplying by 5 on both sides, we get

$\Rightarrow$ $2x^2 - 5x - 3 = 0$

$\Rightarrow$ $2x^2 - (6x - x) - 3 = 0$ [by splitting the middle term]

$\Rightarrow$ $2x^2 - 6x + x - 3 = 0$

$\Rightarrow$ $2x(x - 3) + 1(x - 3) = 0$

$\Rightarrow$ $(x - 3)(2x + 1) = 0$

Now, $x - 3 = 0 \Rightarrow x = 3$

and $2x + 1 = 0$

$\Rightarrow$ $x = -\frac{1}{2}$

Hence, the roots of the equation $2x^2 - 5x - 3 = 0$ are $-\frac{1}{2}$ and 3.

(iii) Given equation is $3\sqrt{2}\,x^2 - 5x - \sqrt{2} = 0$

$\Rightarrow \quad 3\sqrt{2}\,x^2 - (6x - x) - \sqrt{2} = 0$ [by splitting the middle term]

$\Rightarrow \quad 3\sqrt{2}x^2 - 6x + x - \sqrt{2} = 0$

$\Rightarrow \quad 3\sqrt{2}x^2 - 3\sqrt{2}\cdot\sqrt{2}x + x - \sqrt{2} = 0$

$\Rightarrow \quad 3\sqrt{2}\,x\,(x - \sqrt{2}) + 1(x - \sqrt{2}) = 0$

$\Rightarrow \quad (x - \sqrt{2})\,(3\sqrt{2}x + 1) = 0$

Now, $x - \sqrt{2} = 0 \Rightarrow x = \sqrt{2}$

and $3\sqrt{2}\,x + 1 = 0$

$\Rightarrow \quad x = -\dfrac{1}{3\sqrt{2}} = \dfrac{-\sqrt{2}}{6}$

Hence, the roots of the equation $3\sqrt{2}x^2 - 5x - \sqrt{2} = 0$ are $-\dfrac{\sqrt{2}}{6}$ and $\sqrt{2}$.

(iv) Given equation is $3x^2 + 5\sqrt{5}\,x - 10 = 0$

$\Rightarrow \quad 3x^2 + 6\sqrt{5}x - \sqrt{5}x - 2\sqrt{5}\cdot\sqrt{5} = 0$ [by splitting the middle term]

$\Rightarrow \quad 3x\,(x + 2\sqrt{5}) - \sqrt{5}\,(x + 2\sqrt{5}) = 0$

$\Rightarrow \quad (x + 2\sqrt{5})\,(3x - \sqrt{5}) = 0$

Now, $x + 2\sqrt{5} = 0$

$\Rightarrow \quad x = -2\sqrt{5}$ and $3x - \sqrt{5} = 0$

$\Rightarrow \quad x = \dfrac{\sqrt{5}}{3}$

Hence, the roots of the equation $3x^2 + 5\sqrt{5}\,x - 10 = 0$ are $-2\sqrt{5}$ and $\dfrac{\sqrt{5}}{3}$.

(v) Given equation is $21x^2 - 2x + \dfrac{1}{21} = 0$

On multiplying by 21 on both sides, we get

$441x^2 - 42x + 1 = 0$

$441x^2 - (21x + 21x) + 1 = 0$ [by splitting the middle term]

$\Rightarrow \quad 441x^2 - 21x - 21x + 1 = 0$

$\Rightarrow \quad 21x\,(21x - 1) - 1(21x - 1) = 0$

$\Rightarrow \quad (21x - 1)\,(21x - 1) = 0$

Now, $21x - 1 = 0 \Rightarrow x = \dfrac{1}{21}$ and $21x - 1 = 0$

$\therefore \quad x = \dfrac{1}{21}$

Hence, the roots of the equation $441x^2 - 42x + 1 = 0$ are $\dfrac{1}{21}$ and $\dfrac{1}{21}$.

Long Answer Questions

Q.1 Find whether the following equations have real roots. If real roots exist, find them.

(i) $8x^2 + 2x - 3 = 0$ (ii) $-2x^2 + 3x + 2 = 0$

(iii) $5x^2 - 2x - 10 = 0$ (iv) $\frac{1}{2x-3} + \frac{1}{x-5} = 1, x \neq \frac{3}{2}, 5$

(v) $x^2 + 5\sqrt{5}x - 70 = 0$

Thinking Process

(i) Firstly we will check the quadratic equation has real roots or not. For this, if discriminant, $D = b^2 - 4ac > 0$, then roots are real.

(ii) If roots are real, we may factorise the equation or use the quadratic formula to obtain the roots of the equation.

Ans. (i) Given equation is $8x^2 + 2x - 3 = 0$.

On comparing with $ax^2 + bx + c = 0$, we get

$$a = 8, b = 2 \text{ and } c = -3$$

$\therefore$ Discriminant, $D = b^2 - 4ac$

$$= (2)^2 - 4(8)(-3)$$
$$= 4 + 96 = 100 > 0$$

Therefore, the equation $8x^2 + 2x - 3 = 0$ has two distinct real roots because we know that, if the equation $ax^2 + bx + c = 0$ has discriminant greater than zero, then if has two distinct real roots.

Roots, $$x = \frac{-b \pm \sqrt{D}}{2a} = \frac{-2 \pm \sqrt{100}}{16} = \frac{-2 \pm 10}{16}$$
$$= \frac{-2+10}{16}, \frac{-2-10}{16}$$
$$= \frac{8}{16}, -\frac{12}{16} = \frac{1}{2}, -\frac{3}{4}$$

(ii) Given equation is $-2x^2 + 3x + 2 = 0$

On comparing with $ax^2 + bx + c = 0$, we get

$$a = -2, b = 3 \text{ and } c = 2$$

$\therefore$ Discriminant, $D = b^2 - 4ac$

$$= (3)^2 - 4(-2)(2)$$
$$= 9 + 16 = 25 > 0$$

Therefore, the equation $-2x^2 + 3x + 2 = 0$ has two distinct real roots because we know that if the equation $ax^2 + bx + c = 0$ has its discriminant greater than zero, then it has two distinct real roots.

Roots, $$x = \frac{-b \pm \sqrt{D}}{2a} = \frac{-3 \pm \sqrt{25}}{2(-2)}$$
$$= \frac{-3 \pm 5}{-4} = \frac{-3+5}{-4}, \frac{-3-5}{-4}$$
$$= \frac{2}{-4}, \frac{-8}{-4} = -\frac{1}{2}, 2$$

(iii) Given equation is $5x^2 - 2x - 10 = 0$.

On comparing with $ax^2 + bx + c = 0$, we get

$$a = 5, b = -2 \text{ and } c = -10$$

$\therefore$ Discriminant, $D = b^2 - 4ac$

$$= (-2)^2 - 4(5)(-10)$$

$$= 4 + 200 = 204 > 0$$

Therefore, the equation $5x^2 - 2x - 10 = 0$ has two distinct real roots.

$$\text{Roots, } x = \frac{-b \pm \sqrt{D}}{2a}$$

$$= \frac{-(-2) \pm \sqrt{204}}{2 \times 5} = \frac{2 \pm 2\sqrt{51}}{10}$$

$$= \frac{1 \pm \sqrt{51}}{5} = \frac{1 + \sqrt{51}}{5}, \frac{1 - \sqrt{51}}{5}$$

(iv) Given equation is $\frac{1}{2x-3} + \frac{1}{x-5} = 1, x \neq \frac{3}{2}, 5$

$$\Rightarrow \frac{x - 5 + 2x - 3}{(2x-3)(x-5)} = 1$$

$$\Rightarrow \frac{3x - 8}{2x^2 - 3x - 10x + 15} = 1$$

$$\Rightarrow \frac{3x - 8}{2x^2 - 13x + 15} = 1$$

$$\Rightarrow 3x - 8 = 2x^2 - 13x + 15$$

$$\Rightarrow 2x^2 - 13x + 15 - 3x + 8 = 0$$

$$\Rightarrow 2x^2 - 16x + 23 = 0$$

On comparing with $ax^2 + bx + c = 0$, we get

$$a = 2, b = -16 \text{ and } c = 23$$

$\therefore$ Discriminant, $D = b^2 - 4ac$

$$= (-16)^2 - 4 \times 2(23)$$

$$= 256 - 184 = 72 > 0$$

Therefore, the equation $2x^2 - 16x + 23 = 0$ has two distinct real roots.

$$\text{Roots, } x = \frac{-b \pm \sqrt{D}}{2a} = \frac{-(-16) \pm \sqrt{72}}{2(2)}$$

$$= \frac{16 \pm 6\sqrt{2}}{4} = \frac{8 \pm 3\sqrt{2}}{2}$$

$$= \frac{8 + 3\sqrt{2}}{2}, \frac{8 - 3\sqrt{2}}{2}$$

(v) Given equation is $x^2 + 5\sqrt{5}x - 70 = 0$

On comparing with $ax^2 + bx + c = 0$, we get

$$a = 1, b = 5\sqrt{5} \text{ and } c = -70$$

$\therefore$ Discriminant, $D = b^2 - 4ac = (5\sqrt{5})^2 - 4(1)(-70)$

$$= 125 + 280 = 405 > 0$$

Therefore, the equation $x^2 + 5\sqrt{5}x - 70 = 0$ has two distinct real roots.

$$\text{Roots, } x = \frac{-b \pm \sqrt{D}}{2a}$$

$$= \frac{-5\sqrt{5} \pm \sqrt{405}}{2(1)} = \frac{-5\sqrt{5} \pm 9\sqrt{5}}{2}$$

$$= \frac{-5\sqrt{5} + 9\sqrt{5}}{2}, \frac{-5\sqrt{5} - 9\sqrt{5}}{2}$$

$$= \frac{4\sqrt{5}}{2}, -\frac{14\sqrt{5}}{2} = 2\sqrt{5}, -7\sqrt{5}$$

Q.2 Find a natural number whose square diminished by 84 is equal to thrice of 8 more than the given number.

Thinking Process Firstly, we make a quadratic equation by using the given condition after that we solve the equation by factorisation equation. Finally, method to obtain the desired number.

Ans. Let n be a required natural number.

Square of a natural number diminished by 84 $= n^2 - 84$

and thrice of 8 more than the given number $= 3(n + 8)$

Now, by given condition,

$$n^2 - 84 = 3(n + 8)$$

$$\Rightarrow \quad n^2 - 84 = 3n + 24$$

$$\Rightarrow \quad n^2 - 3n - 108 = 0$$

$$\Rightarrow \quad n^2 - 12n + 9n - 108 = 0 \qquad \text{[by splitting the middle term]}$$

$$\Rightarrow \quad n(n - 12) + 9(n - 12) = 0$$

$$\Rightarrow \quad (n - 12)(n + 9) = 0$$

$$\Rightarrow \quad n = 12 \qquad [\because n \neq -9 \text{ because } n \text{ is a natural number}]$$

Hence, the required natural number is 12.

Q.3 A natural number, when increased by 12, equals 160 times its reciprocal. Find the number.

Ans. Let the natural number be x.

According to the question,

$$x + 12 = \frac{160}{x}$$

On multiplying by x on both sides, we get

$$\Rightarrow \quad x^2 + 12x - 160 = 0$$

$$x^2 + (20x - 8x) - 160 = 0$$

$$\Rightarrow \quad x^2 + 20x - 8x - 160 = 0 \qquad \text{[by factorisation method]}$$

$$\Rightarrow \quad x(x + 20) - 8(x + 20) = 0$$

$$\Rightarrow \quad (x + 20)(x - 8) = 0$$

Now, $x + 20 = 0 \Rightarrow x = -20$ which is not possible because natural number is always greater than zero and $x - 8 = 0 \Rightarrow x = 8$.

Hence, the required natural number is 8.

Q.4 A train, travelling at a uniform speed for 360 km, would have taken 48 minutes less to travel the same distance, if its speed were 5 km/h more. Find the original speed of the train.

Ans. Let the original speed of the train = x km/h

Then, the increased speed of the train = $(x + 5)$ km/h [by given condition]

and distance = 360 km

According to the question,

$$\frac{360}{x} - \frac{360}{x+5} = \frac{4}{5} \qquad \left[\because \text{time} = \frac{\text{Distance}}{\text{Speed}} \text{ and } 48 \text{ min} = \frac{48}{60}\text{ h} = \frac{4}{5}\text{ h}\right]$$

$$\Rightarrow \frac{360(x+5) - 360x}{x(x+5)} = \frac{4}{5}$$

$$\Rightarrow \frac{360x + 1800 - 360x}{x^2 + 5x} = \frac{4}{5}$$

$$\Rightarrow \frac{1800}{x^2 + 5x} = \frac{4}{5}$$

$$\Rightarrow x^2 + 5x = \frac{1800 \times 5}{4} = 2250$$

$$\Rightarrow x^2 + 5x - 2250 = 0$$

$$x^2 + (50x - 45x) - 2250 = 0$$

$$\Rightarrow x^2 + 50x - 45x - 2250 = 0 \qquad \text{[by factorisation method]}$$

$$\Rightarrow x(x + 50) - 45(x + 50) = 0$$

$$\Rightarrow (x + 50)(x - 45) = 0$$

Now, $x + 50 = 0 \Rightarrow x = -50$

which is not possible because speed cannot be negative and $x - 45 = 0 \Rightarrow x = 45$.

Hence, the original speed of the train = 45 km/h

Q.5 If Zeba were younger by 5 years than what she really is, then the square of her age (in years) would have been 11 more than five times her actual age. What is her age now?

Ans. Let the actual age of Zeba = x years

Her age when she was 5 years younger = $(x - 5)$ years.

Now, by given condition,

Square of her age = 11 more than five times her actual age

$$(x - 5)^2 = 5 \times \text{actual age} + 11$$

$$\Rightarrow (x - 5)^2 = 5x + 11$$

$$\Rightarrow x^2 + 25 - 10x = 5x + 11$$

$$\Rightarrow x^2 - 15x + 14 = 0$$

$$\Rightarrow x^2 - 14x - x + 14 = 0 \qquad \text{[by splitting the middle term]}$$

$$\Rightarrow \quad x(x-14)-1(x-14)=0$$
$$\Rightarrow \quad (x-1)(x-14)=0$$
$$\Rightarrow \quad x=14$$

[here, $x \neq 1$ because her age is $x-5$. So, $x-5=1-5=-4$
i.e., age cannot be negative]

Hence, required Zeba's age is 14 years.

Q.6 At present Asha's age (in years) is 2 more than the square of her daughter Nisha's age. When, Nisha grows to her mother's present age. Asha's age would be one year less than 10 times the present age of Nisha. Find the present ages of both Asha and Nisha.

Ans. Let Nisha's present age be x years.

Then, Asha's present age $=(x^2+2)$ [by given condition]

Now, when Nisha grows to her mother's present age *i.e.*, after $\{(x^2+2)-x\}$ years. Then, Asha's age also increased by $[(x^2+2)-x]$ years.

Again by given condition,

Age of Asha = One years less than 10 times the present age of Nisha

$$(x^2+2)+\{(x^2+2)-x\}=10x-1$$
$$\Rightarrow \quad 2x^2-x+4=10x-1$$
$$\Rightarrow \quad 2x^2-11x+5=0$$
$$\Rightarrow \quad 2x^2-10x-x+5=0$$
$$\Rightarrow \quad 2x(x-5)-1(x-5)=0$$
$$\Rightarrow \quad (x-5)(2x-1)=0$$
$$\therefore \quad x=5$$

[here, $x=\frac{1}{2}$ cannot be possible, because at $x=\frac{1}{2}$,
Asha's age is $2\frac{1}{4}$ years which is not possible]

Hence, required age of Nisha = 5 years
and required age of Asha $=x^2+2=(5)^2+2=25+2=27$ years

Q.7 In the centre of a rectangular lawn of dimensions 50 m × 40 m a rectangular pond has to be constructed, so that the area of the grass surrounding the pond would be 1184 m^2[see figure]. Find the length and breadth of the pond.

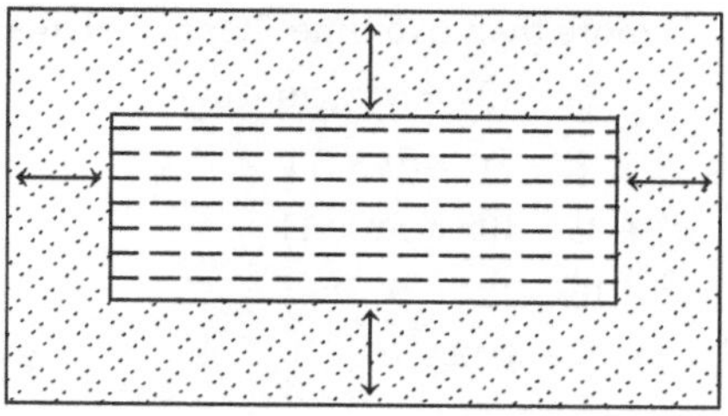

Ans. Given that a rectangular pond has to be constructed in the centre of a rectangular lawn of dimensions 50 m × 40 m, so the distance between pond and lawn would be same around the pond. Say x m.

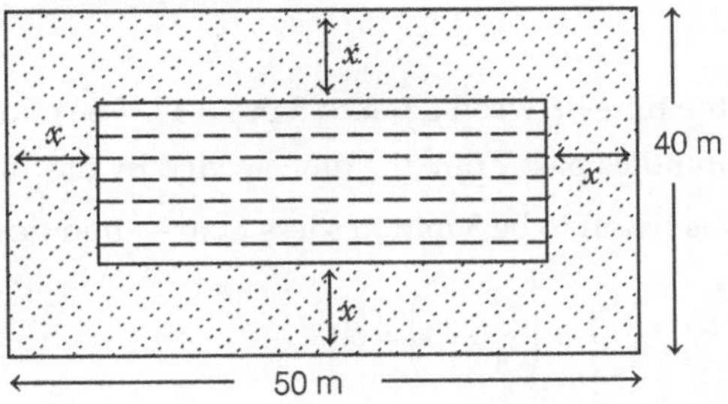

Now, length of rectangular lawn $(l_1) = 50$ m
and breadth of rectangular lawn $(b_1) = 40$ m
∴ Length of rectangular pond $(l_2) = 50 - (x + x) = 50 - 2x$
and breadth of rectangular pond $(b_2) = 40 - (x + x) = 40 - 2x$
Also, area of the grass surrounding the pond = 1184 m^2
∴ Area of rectangular lawn – Area of rectangular pond
= Area of grass surrounding the pond

$$l_1 \times b_1 - l_2 \times b_2 = 1184 \quad [\because \text{ area of rectangle} = \text{length} \times \text{breadth}]$$

$$\Rightarrow \quad 50 \times 40 - (50 - 2x)(40 - 2x) = 1184$$

$$\Rightarrow 2000 - (2000 - 80x - 100x + 4x^2) = 1184$$

$$\Rightarrow \quad 80x + 100x - 4x^2 = 1184$$

$$\Rightarrow \quad 4x^2 - 180x + 1184 = 0$$

$$\Rightarrow \quad x^2 - 45x + 296 = 0$$

$$\Rightarrow \quad x^2 - 37x - 8x + 296 = 0 \quad \text{[by splitting the middle term]}$$

$$\Rightarrow \quad x(x - 37) - 8(x - 37) = 0$$

$$\Rightarrow \quad (x - 37)(x - 8) = 0$$

$$\therefore \quad x = 8$$

[At $x = 37$, length and breadth of pond are –24 and –34 respectively but length and breadth cannot be negative. So, $x = 37$ cannot be possible]

∴ Length of pond $= 50 - 2x = 50 - 2(8) = 50 - 16 = 34$ m
and breadth of pond $= 40 - 2x = 40 - 2(8) = 40 - 16 = 24$ m
Hence, required length and breadth of pond are 34 m and 24 m respectively.

Q.8 At t minutes past 2 pm, the time needed by the minutes hand of a clock to show 3 pm was found to be 3 minutes less than $\frac{t^2}{4}$ minutes. Find t.

Ans. We know that, the time between 2 pm to 3 pm = 1h = 60 minuts

Given that, at t minutes past 2 pm, the time needed by the minutes and of a clock to show 3 pm was found to be 3 minutes less than $\frac{t^2}{4}$ minutes *i.e.,*

$$t + \left(\frac{t^2}{4} - 3\right) = 60$$

$$\Rightarrow \quad 4t + t^2 - 12 = 240$$

$$\Rightarrow \quad t^2 + 4t - 252 = 0$$

$$\Rightarrow \quad t^2 + 18t - 14t - 252 = 0 \quad \text{[by splitting the middle term]}$$

$$\Rightarrow \quad t(t + 18) - 14(t + 18) = 0$$

$$\Rightarrow \quad (t + 18)(t - 14) = 0$$

$$\therefore \quad t = 14 \text{ minutes}$$

[since, time cannot be negative, so $t \neq -18$]

Hence, the required value of t is 14 minutes.

Chapter 05

Arithmetic Progressions

Multiple Choice Questions (MCQs)

Choose the correct answer from the given four options in the following questions:

Q.1 In an AP, if $d = -4$, $n = 7$, $a_n = 4$, then a is

(a) 6 (b) 7 (c) 20 (d) 28

- **Concept Insight** In this question, we will use formula for nth term of A.P is given by $a_n = a + (n-1)d$.

Ans. *(d)* In an AP, $a_n = a + (n-1)d$

$\Rightarrow$ $4 = a + (7-1)(-4)$ [by given conditions]

$\Rightarrow$ $4 = a + 6(-4)$

$\Rightarrow$ $4 + 24 = a$

$\therefore$ $a = 28$

Q.2 In an AP, if $a = 3.5$, $d = 0$, $n = 101$, then a_n will be

(a) 0 (b) 3.5 (c) 103.5 (d) 104.5

Ans. *(b)* For an AP, $a_n = a + (n-1)d = 3.5 + (101-1) \times 0$ [by given conditions]

$\therefore$ $a_n = 3.5$

Q.3 The list of numbers $-10, -6, -2, 2, \ldots$ is

(a) an AP with $d = -16$ (b) an AP with $d = 4$

(c) an AP with $d = -4$ (d) not an AP

Ans. *(b)* The given numbers are $-10, -6, -2, 2, \ldots$

Here, $a_1 = -10$, $a_2 = -6$, $a_3 = -2$ and $a_4 = 2, \ldots$

Since, $a_2 - a_1 = -6 - (-10) = -6 + 10 = 4$

$a_3 - a_2 = -2 - (-6) = -2 + 6 = 4$

$a_4 - a_3 = 2 - (-2) = 2 + 2 = 4$

... ...

... ...

... ...

Each successive term of given list has same difference *i.e.,* 4.

So, the given list forms an AP with common difference, $d = 4$.

Mistake Alert ! *Students sometimes calculate incorrect common difference by calculating* $(a_1 - a_2)$ *or* $(a_2 - a_3)$ *i.e., incorrect - common difference* $(d) = -10 - (-6) = -6 - (-2) = -4$ *etc.*

Q.4 The 11th term of an AP $-5, \frac{-5}{2}, 0, \frac{5}{2}, \ldots$ is

(a) -20 (b) 20 (c) -30 (d) 30

Thinking process Firstly find first term and common difference of the AP. Then, calculate its 11th term by using the nth term formula of AP as $a_n = a + (n-1)d$

Ans. *(b)* Given AP, $-5, -\frac{5}{2}, 0, \frac{5}{2}$

Here, $a = -5, d = \frac{-5}{2} + 5 = \frac{5}{2}$

$$\therefore \quad a_{11} = a + (11-1)d \qquad [\because a_n = a + (n-1)d]$$

$$= -5 + (10) \times \frac{5}{2}$$

$$= -5 + 25 = 20$$

Q.5 The first four terms of an AP, whose first term is -2 and the common difference is -2 are

(a) $-2, 0, 2, 4$
(b) $-2, 4, -8, 16$
(c) $-2, -4, -6, -8$
(d) $-2, -4, -8, -16$

Ans. *(c)* Let the first four terms of an AP are $a, a+d, a+2d$ and $a+3d$.

Given, that first term, $a = -2$ and common difference, $d = -2$, then we have an AP as follows

$$-2, -2-2, -2+2(-2), -2+3(-2) = -2, -4, -6, -8$$

Q.6 The 21st term of an AP whose first two terms are -3 and 4, is

(a) 17 (b) 137 (c) 143 (d) -143

Ans. *(b)* Given, first two terms of an AP are $a = -3$ and $a + d = 4$.

$$\Rightarrow \quad -3 + d = 4$$

Common difference, $d = 7$

$$\therefore \quad a_{21} = a + (21-1)d \qquad [\because a_n = a + (n-1)d]$$

$$= -3 + (20)7$$

$$= -3 + 140 = 137$$

Mistake Alert! *Students may incorrectly calculate its* 21st term as $a_{21} = -3 + 21 \times 7 = 144$ instead of $a_{21} = -3 + 20 \times 7 = 137$.

Q.7 If the 2nd term of an AP is 13 and 5th term is 25, what is its 7th term?

(a) 30 (b) 33
(c) 37 (d) 38

Ans. *(b)* Given, $a_2 = 13$ and $a_5 = 25$

$\Rightarrow$ $a_2 = a + (2-1)\,d = 13$ $[\because a_n = a + (n-1)\,d]$

and $a_5 = a + (5-1)\,d = 25$

$\Rightarrow$ $a + d = 13$ ...(i)

and $a + 4\,d = 25$ ...(ii)

On subtracting Eq. (i) from Eq. (ii), we get

$$3d = 25 - 13 = 12 \Rightarrow d = 4$$

From Eq. (i), $a = 13 - 4 = 9$

$\therefore$ $a_7 = a + (7-1)\,d = 9 + 6 \times 4 = 9 + 24 = 33$

Q.8 Which term of the AP : 21, 42, 63, 84, ... is 210?

(a) 9th (b) 10th (c) 11th (d) 12th

Ans. *(b)* Let n^{th} term of the given AP be 210.

Here, first term, $a = 21$

and common difference, $d = 42 - 21 = 21$ and $a_n = 210$

$\because$ $a_n = a + (n-1)\,d$

$\Rightarrow$ $210 = 21 + (n-1)\,21$

$\Rightarrow$ $210 = 21 + 21n - 21$

$\Rightarrow$ $210 = 21n \Rightarrow n = 10$

Hence, the 10th term of the AP is 210.

Q.9 If the common difference of an AP is 5, then what is $a_{18} - a_{13}$?

(a) 5 (b) 20 (c) 25 (d) 30

Ans. *(c)* Given, the common difference of AP *i.e.*, $d = 5$

Now, $a_{18} - a_{13} = a + (18-1)\,d - [a + (13-1)\,d]$ $[\because a_n = a + (n-1)\,d]$

$= a + 17 \times 5 - a - 12 \times 5$

$= 85 - 60 = 25$

Q.10 What is the common difference of an AP in which $a_{18} - a_{14} = 32$?

(a) 8 (b) – 8 (c) – 4 (d) 4

Ans. *(a)* Given, $a_{18} - a_{14} = 32$

$\Rightarrow$ $a + (18-1)\,d - [a + (14-1)d] = 32$ $[\because a_n = a + (n-1)\,d]$

$\Rightarrow$ $a + 17d - a - 13d = 32$

$\Rightarrow$ $4d = 32$

$\Rightarrow$ $d = 8$

which is the required common difference of an AP.

Q.11 Two APs have the same common difference. The first term of one of these is – 1 and that of the other is – 8. The difference between their 4th terms is

(a) – 1 (b) – 8 (c) 7 (d) – 9

Ans. *(c)* Let the common difference of two APs are d_1 and d_2 respectively.

By condition, $d_1 = d_2 = d$ ...(i)

Let the first term of first AP $a = -1$

and the first term of second AP $a' = -8$

We know that, the nth term of an AP, $T_n = a + (n-1)d$

$\therefore$ 4th term of first AP, $T_4 = a + (4-1)d = -1 + 3d$

and 4th term of second AP, $T_4' = a' + (4-1)d = -8 + 3d$

Now, the difference between their 4th terms is *i.e.*,

$$|T_4 - T_4'| = (-1 + 3d) - (-8 + 3d)$$
$$= -1 + 3d + 8 - 3d = 7$$

Hence, the required difference is 7.

Q.12 If 7 times the 7th term of an AP is equal to 11 times its 11th term, then its 18th term will be

(a) 7 (b) 11 (c) 18 (d) 0

Ans. *(d)* According to the question,

$$7a_7 = 11a_{11}$$
$$\Rightarrow 7[a + (7-1)d] = 11[a + (11-1)d] \quad [\because a_n = a + (n-1)d]$$
$$\Rightarrow 7(a + 6d) = 11(a + 10d)$$
$$\Rightarrow 7a + 42d = 11a + 110d$$
$$\Rightarrow 4a + 68d = 0$$
$$\Rightarrow 4(a + 17d) = 0$$
$$\Rightarrow a + 17d = 0 \quad \text{...(i)}$$
$$\therefore \text{18th term of an AP, } a_{18} = a + (18-1)d$$
$$= a + 17d = 0 \quad \text{[from Eq. (i)]}$$

Q.13 The 4th term from the end of an AP $-11, -8, -5, \ldots, 49$ is

(a) 37 (b) 40 (c) 43 (d) 58

- **Concept Insight** The nth term of the A.P from the end is, $a_n = l - (n-1)d$, where l is the last term and d is the common difference.

Ans. *(b)* We know that, the nth term of an AP from the end is

$$a_n = l - (n-1)d \quad \text{...(i)}$$

Here, l = Last term and $l = 49$ [given]

Common difference, $d = -8 - (-11)$

$= -8 + 11 = 3$

From Eq. (i), $a_4 = 49 - (4-1)3 = 49 - 9 = 40$

Q. 14 The famous mathematician associated with finding the sum of the first 100 natural numbers is

(a) Pythagoras (b) Newton (c) Gauss (d) Euclid

Ans. *(c)* Gauss is the famous mathematician associated with finding the sum of the first 100 natural numbers *i.e.*, 1, 2, 3,...,100.

Q.15 If the first term of an AP is – 5 and the common difference is 2, then the sum of the first 6 terms is

(a) 0 (b) 5 (c) 6 (d) 15

- **Concept Insight** In this question, we will use the formula for sum of first n term of AP as $S_n = \frac{n}{2}[2a + (n-1)d]$

Ans. *(a)* Given, $a = -5$ and $d = 2$

$$\therefore \quad S_6 = \frac{6}{2}[2a + (6-1)d] \qquad \left[\because S_n = \frac{n}{2}\{2a + (n-1)d\}\right]$$

$$= 3[2(-5) + 5(2)]$$

$$= 3(-10 + 10) = 0$$

Q.16 The sum of first 16 terms of the AP 10, 6, 2, ... is

(a) – 320 (b) 320 (c) – 352 (d) – 400

Ans. *(a)* Given, AP is 10, 6, 2, ...

Here, first term, $a = 10$, common difference, $d = 6 - 10 = -4$

$$\therefore \quad S_{16} = \frac{16}{2}[2a + (16-1)d] \qquad \left[\because S_n = \frac{n}{2}\{2a + (n-1)d\}\right]$$

$$= 8[2 \times 10 + 15(-4)]$$

$$= 8(20 - 60) = 8(-40) = -320$$

Q.17 In an AP, if $a = 1$, $a_n = 20$ and $S_n = 399$, then n is

(a) 19 (b) 21 (c) 38 (d) 42

Ans. *(c)* Here, first term $a = 1$, $a_n = 20$ and $S_n = 399$

$$\Rightarrow \quad 399 = \frac{n}{2}[2 \times 1 + (n-1)d] \qquad \left[\because S_n = \frac{n}{2}[2a + (n-1)d]\right]$$

$$\Rightarrow \quad 798 = 2n + n(n-1)d \qquad \ldots(i)$$

and $a_n = 20$

$$\Rightarrow \quad a + (n-1)d = 20 \qquad [\because a_n = a + (n-1)d]$$

$$\Rightarrow \quad 1 + (n-1)d = 20 \Rightarrow (n-1)d = 19 \qquad \ldots(ii)$$

Using Eq. (ii) in Eq. (i), we get

$$798 = 2n + 19n$$

$$\Rightarrow \quad 798 = 21n \Rightarrow n = \frac{798}{21} = 38$$

Q.18 The sum of first five multiples of 3 is

(a) 45 (b) 55 (c) 65 (d) 75

Ans. *(a)* The first five multiples of 3 are 3, 6, 9, 12 and 15.

Here, first term, $a = 3$, common difference, $d = 6 - 3 = 3$ and number of terms, $n = 5$

$$\therefore \quad S_5 = \frac{5}{2}[2a + (5-1)d] \qquad \left[\because S_n = \frac{n}{2}\{2a + (n-1)d\}\right]$$

$$= \frac{5}{2}[2 \times 3 + 4 \times 3]$$

$$= \frac{5}{2}(6 + 12) = \frac{5}{2} \times 18 = 5 \times 9 = 45$$

Short Answer Questions with Reasoning

Q.1 Which of the following form of an AP ? Justify your answer.

(i) $-1, -1, -1, -1, \ldots$ (ii) $0, 2, 0, 2, \ldots$

(iii) $1, 1, 2, 2, 3, 3, \ldots$ (iv) $11, 22, 33, \ldots$

(v) $\frac{1}{2}, \frac{1}{3}, \frac{1}{4}, \ldots$ (vi) $2, 2^2, 2^3, 2^4, \ldots$

(vii) $\sqrt{3}, \sqrt{12}, \sqrt{27}, \sqrt{48}, \ldots$

Ans. (i) Here, $t_1 = -1, t_2 = -1, t_3 = -1$ and $t_4 = -1$

$$t_2 - t_1 = -1 + 1 = 0$$
$$t_3 - t_2 = -1 + 1 = 0$$
$$t_4 - t_3 = -1 + 1 = 0$$

Clearly, the difference of successive terms is same, therefore given list of numbers form an AP.

(ii) Here, $t_1 = 0, t_2 = 2, t_3 = 0$ and $t_4 = 2$

$$t_2 - t_1 = 2 - 0 = 2$$
$$t_3 - t_2 = 0 - 2 = -2$$
$$t_4 - t_3 = 2 - 0 = 2$$

Clearly, the difference of successive terms is not same, therefore given list of numbers does not form an AP.

(iii) Here, $t_1 = 1, t_2 = 1, t_3 = 2$ and $t_4 = 2$

$$t_2 - t_1 = 1 - 1 = 0$$
$$t_3 - t_2 = 2 - 1 = 1$$
$$t_4 - t_2 = 2 - 2 = 0$$

Clearly, the difference of successive terms is not same, therefore given list of numbers does not form an AP.

(iv) Here, $t_1 = 11, t_2 = 22$ and $t_3 = 33$

$$t_2 - t_1 = 22 - 11 = 11$$
$$t_3 - t_2 = 33 - 22 = 11$$

Clearly, the difference of successive terms is same, therefore given list of numbers form an AP.

(v) Here, $t_1 = \frac{1}{2}, t_2 = \frac{1}{3}$ and $t_3 = \frac{1}{4}$

$$t_2 - t_1 = \frac{1}{3} - \frac{1}{2} = \frac{2-3}{6} = -\frac{1}{6}$$
$$t_3 - t_2 = \frac{1}{4} - \frac{1}{3} = \frac{3-4}{12} = -\frac{1}{12}$$

Clearly, the difference of successive terms is not same, therefore given list of numbers does not form an AP.

(vi) $2, 2^2, 2^3, 2^4, \ldots$ *i.e.*, 2, 4, 8, 16, ...

Here, $t_1 = 2, t_2 = 4, t_3 = 8$ and $t_4 = 16$

$$t_2 - t_1 = 4 - 2 = 2$$
$$t_3 - t_2 = 8 - 4 = 4$$
$$t_4 - t_3 = 16 - 8 = 8$$

Clearly, the difference of successive terms is not same, therefore given list of numbers does not form an AP.

(vii) $\sqrt{3}, \sqrt{12}, \sqrt{27}, \sqrt{48}, \ldots$ *i.e.*, $\sqrt{3}, 2\sqrt{3}, 3\sqrt{3}, 4\sqrt{3}, \ldots$

Here, $t_1 = \sqrt{3}, t_2 = 2\sqrt{3}, t_3 = 3\sqrt{3}$ and $t_4 = 4\sqrt{3}$

$$t_2 - t_1 = 2\sqrt{3} - \sqrt{3} = \sqrt{3} \Rightarrow t_3 - t_2 = 3\sqrt{3} - 2\sqrt{3} = \sqrt{3}$$
$$t_4 - t_3 = 4\sqrt{3} - 3\sqrt{3} = \sqrt{3}$$

Clearly, the difference of successive terms is same, therefore given list of numbers form an AP.

Q.2 Justify whether it is true to say that $-1, \frac{-3}{2}, -2, \frac{5}{2}, \ldots$ forms an AP as $a_2 - a_1 = a_3 - a_2$.

Ans. *False*

Here, $a_1 = -1, a_2 = \frac{-3}{2}, a_3 = -2$

and $a_4 = \frac{5}{2}$

$$a_2 - a_1 = \frac{-3}{2} + 1 = -\frac{1}{2}$$
$$\Rightarrow \quad a_3 - a_2 = -2 + \frac{3}{2} = -\frac{1}{2}$$
$$a_4 - a_3 = \frac{5}{2} + 2 = \frac{9}{2}$$

Clearly, the difference of successive terms is not same, all though, $a_2 - a_1 = a_3 - a_2$ but $a_3 - a_2 \neq a_4 - a_3$, therefore it does not form an AP.

Q.3 For the AP $-3, -7, -11, \ldots$ can we find directly $a_{30} - a_{20}$ without actually finding a_{30} and a_{20}? Give reason for your answer.

Ans. *True*

$\because$ nth term of an AP, $a_n = a + (n-1)d$

$\therefore \quad a_{30} = a + (30 - 1)d = a + 29d$

and $\quad a_{20} = a + (20 - 1)d = a + 19d$ ...(i)

Now, $\quad a_{30} - a_{20} = (a + 29d) - (a + 19d) = 10d$

and from given AP, common difference, $d = -7 - (-3) = -7 + 3 = -4$

$\therefore \quad a_{30} - a_{20} = 10(-4) = -40$ [from Eq. (i)]

Q.4 Two AP's have the same common difference. The first term of one AP is 2 and that of the other is 7. The difference between their 10th terms is the same as the difference between their 21st terms, which is the same as the difference between any two corresponding terms? Why?

Ans. Let the same common difference of two AP's is d. Given that, the first term of first AP and second AP are 2 and 7 respectively, then the AP's are

$$2, 2+d, 2+2d, 2+3d, \ldots$$

and $$7, 7+d, 7+2d, 7+3d, \ldots$$

Now, 10th terms of first and second AP's are $2+9d$ and $7+9d$, respectively.

$$[\because a_{10} = a+(10-1)d]$$

So, their difference is $(7+9d)-(2+9d) = 7+9d-2-9d = 5$

Also, 21st terms of first and second AP's are $2+20d$ and $7+20d$, respectively.

$$[\because a_{21} = a+(21-1).d]$$

So, their difference is $(7+20d)-(2+20d) = 7+20d-2-20d = 5$

Also, if the a_n and b_n are the nth terms of first and second AP respectively.

Then, $b_n - a_n = [7+(n-1)d)] - [2+(n-1)d] = 7+(n-1)d-2-(n-1)d = 5$

Hence, the difference between any two corresponding terms of such AP's is the same as the difference between their first terms.

Q.5 Is 0 a term of the AP 31, 28, 25,...? Justify your answer.

Ans. Let 0 be the nth term of the given AP *i.e.*, $a_n = 0$.

Given that, first term $a = 31$, common difference, $d = 28-31 = -3$

The nth terms of an AP, is

$$a_n = a+(n-1)d$$

$$\Rightarrow \quad 0 = 31+(n-1)(-3)$$

$$\Rightarrow \quad 3(n-1) = 31 \Rightarrow n-1 = \frac{31}{3}$$

$$\therefore \quad n = \frac{31}{3}+1 = \frac{34}{3} = 11\frac{1}{3}$$

Since, n should be positive integer. So, 0 is not a term of the given AP.

Q.6 The taxi fare after each km, when the fare is ₹ 15 for the first km and ₹ 8 for each additional km, does not form an AP as the total fare (in ₹) after each km is 15, 8, 8, 8, … . Is the statement true? Give reasons.

Ans. *No*, because the total fare (in ₹) after each km is

$15, (15+8), (15+2\times 8), (15+3\times 8), \ldots = 15, 23, 31, 39, \ldots$

Let $\quad t_1 = 15, t_2 = 23, t_3 = 31$ and $t_4 = 39$

Now, $t_2 - t_1 = 23-15 = 8$

$t_3 - t_2 = 31-23 = 8$

$t_4 - t_3 = 39-31 = 8$

Since, all the successive terms of the given list have same difference *i.e.*, common difference = 8

Hence, the total fare after each km form an AP.

Q.7 In which of the following situations, do the lists of numbers involved form an AP? Give reasons for your answers.

(i) The fee charged from a student every month by a school for the whole session, when the monthly fee is ₹ 400.

(ii) The fee charged every month by a school from classes I to XII, When the monthly fee for class I is ₹ 250 and it increase by ₹ 50 for the next higher class.

(iii) The amount of money in the account of Varun at the end of every year when ₹ 1000 is deposited at simple interest of 10% per annum.

(iv) The number of bacteria in a certain food item after each second, when they double in every second.

Ans. (i) The fee charged from a student every month by a school for the whole session is

$$400, 400, 400, 400, \ldots$$

which form an AP, with common difference $(d) = 400 - 400 = 0$

(ii) The fee charged every month by a school from classes I to XII is

$$250, (250 + 50), (250 + 2 \times 50), (250 + 3 \times 50), \ldots$$

i.e., $250, 300, 350, 400, \ldots$

which form an AP, with common difference $(d) = 300 - 250 = 50$

(iii) $$\text{Simple interest} = \frac{\text{Principal} \times \text{Rate} \times \text{Time}}{100}$$

$$= \frac{1000 \times 10 \times 1}{100} = 100$$

So, the amount of money in the account of Varun at the end of every year is

$$1000, (1000 + 100 \times 1), (1000 + 100 \times 2), (1000 + 100 \times 3), \ldots$$

i.e., $1000, 1100, 1200, 1300, \ldots$

which form an AP, with common difference $(d) = 1100 - 1000 = 100$

(iv) Let the number of bacteria in a certain food $= x$

Since, they double in every second.

$$x, 2x, 2(2x), 2(2 \cdot 2 \cdot x), \ldots$$

i.e., $x, 2x, 4x, 8x, \ldots$

Now, let $t_1 = x, t_2 = 2x, t_3 = 4x$ and $t_4 = 8x$

$$t_2 - t_1 = 2x - x = x$$

$$t_3 - t_2 = 4x - 2x = 2x$$

$$t_4 - t_3 = 8x - 4x = 4x$$

Since, the difference between each successive term is not same. So, the list does not form an AP.

Q.8 Justify whether it is true to say that the following are the nth terms of an AP.

(i) $2n-3$ (ii) $3n^2+5$ (iii) $1+n+n^2$

Ans. (i) *Yes*, here $a_n = 2n-3$

Put $n=1$, $a_1 = 2(1)-3 = -1$

Put $n=2$, $a_2 = 2(2)-3 = 4-3 = 1$

Put $n=3$, $a_3 = 2(3)-3 = 6-3 = 3$

Put $n=4$, $a_4 = 2(4)-3 = 8-3 = 5$

$\therefore$ Terms of the sequence are $-1, 1, 3, \ldots$

Here, $a_2 - a_1 = 1-(-1) = 1+1 = 2$

$a_3 - a_2 = 3-1 = 2$

$a_4 - a_3 = 5-3 = 2$

$\because$ $a_2 - a_1 = a_3 - a_2 = a_4 - a_3 = \ldots$

Hence, $2n-3$ is the nth term of an AP.

(ii) *No*, here $a_n = 3n^2+5$

Put $n=1$, $a_1 = 3(1)^2 + 5 = 8$

Put $n=2$, $a_2 = 3(2)^2 + 5 = 3(4) + 5 = 12+5 = 17$

Put $n=3$, $a_3 = 3(3)^2 + 5 = 3(9) + 5 = 27 + 5 = 32$

$\therefore$ Terms of the sequence are 8, 17, 32, ...

Here, $a_2 - a_1 = 17-8 = 9$

$a_3 - a_2 = 32-17 = 15$

$\therefore$ $a_2 - a_1 \neq a_3 - a_2$

Since, the successive difference of the terms of the sequence not same. So, it does not form an AP.

(iii) *No*, here $a_n = 1+n+n^2$

Put $n=1$, $a_1 = 1+1+(1)^2 = 3$

Put $n=2$, $a_2 = 1+2+(2)^2 = 1+2+4 = 7$

Put $n=3$, $a_3 = 1+3+(3)^2 = 1+3+9 = 13$

$\therefore$ Terms of the sequence are 3, 7, 13,...

Here, $a_2 - a_1 = 7-3 = 4$

$a_3 - a_2 = 13-7 = 6$

$\therefore$ $a_2 - a_1 \neq a_3 - a_2$

Since, the successive difference of the terms of the sequence is not same. So, it does not form an AP.

Short Answer Questions

Q. 1 Match the AP's given in column A with suitable common differences given in column B.

	Column A		Column B
(A_1)	$2, -2, -6, -10, \ldots$	(B_1)	$\frac{2}{3}$
(A_2)	$a = -18, n = 10, a_n = 0$	(B_2)	-5
(A_3)	$a = 0, a_{10} = 6$	(B_3)	4
(A_4)	$a_2 = 13, a_4 = 3$	(B_4)	-4
		(B_5)	2
		(B_6)	$\frac{1}{2}$
		(B_7)	5

Ans. A_1. $2, -2, -6, -10, \ldots$

Here, common difference, $d = -2 - 2 = -4$

A_2. $\because \quad a_n = a + (n-1)d$

$\Rightarrow \quad 0 = -18 + (10-1)d$

$\Rightarrow \quad 18 = 9d$

$\therefore$ Common difference, $d = 2$

A_3. $\because \quad a_{10} = 6$

$\Rightarrow \quad a + (10-1)d = 6 \qquad [\because a_n = a + (n-1)d]$

$\Rightarrow \quad 0 + 9d = 6 \qquad [\because a = 0 \text{ (given)}]$

$\Rightarrow \quad 9d = 6 \Rightarrow d = \frac{2}{3}$

A_4. $\because \quad a_2 = 13$

$\Rightarrow \quad a + (2-1)d = 13 \qquad [\because a_n = a + (n-1)d]$

$\Rightarrow \quad a + d = 13 \qquad \ldots\text{(i)}$

and $\quad a_4 = 3 \Rightarrow a + (4-1)d = 3$

$\therefore \quad a + 3d = 3 \qquad \ldots\text{(ii)}$

On subtracting Eq. (i) from Eq. (ii), we get

$2d = -10$

$\Rightarrow \quad d = -5$

$\therefore (A_1) \rightarrow B_4, (A_2) \rightarrow B_5, (A_3) \rightarrow B_1$ and $(A_4) \rightarrow B_2$

Q. 2 Verify that each of the following is an AP and then write its next three terms.

(i) $0, \frac{1}{4}, \frac{1}{2}, \frac{3}{4}, \ldots$

(ii) $5, \frac{14}{3}, \frac{13}{3}, 4, \ldots$

(iii) $\sqrt{3}, 2\sqrt{3}, 3\sqrt{3}, \ldots$

(iv) $a + b, (a+1) + b, (a+1) + (b+1), \ldots$

(v) $a, 2a + 1, 3a + 2, 4a + 3, \ldots$

Ans. (i) Here, $a_1 = 0,\ a_2 = \frac{1}{4},\ a_3 = \frac{1}{2}$ and $a_4 = \frac{3}{4}$

$$a_2 - a_1 = \frac{1}{4} - 0 = \frac{1}{4},$$

$$a_3 - a_2 = \frac{2-1}{4} = \frac{1}{2} - \frac{1}{4} = \frac{1}{4}, \quad a_4 - a_3 = \frac{3}{4} - \frac{1}{2} = \frac{3-2}{4} = \frac{1}{4}$$

$\therefore \quad a_2 - a_1 = a_3 - a_2 = a_4 - a_3$

Since, the each successive term of the given list has the same difference. So, it forms an AP.

The next three terms are, $a_5 = a_1 + 4d$

$$= a + 4\left(\frac{1}{4}\right) = 0 + 1 = 1,\ a_6 = a_1 + 5d = a + 5\left(\frac{1}{4}\right) = 0 + \frac{5}{4} = \frac{5}{4}$$

$$a_7 = a + 6d = 0 + \frac{6}{4} = \frac{3}{2}$$

(ii) Here, $a_1 = 5,\ a_2 = \frac{14}{3},\ a_3 = \frac{13}{3}$ and $a_4 = 4$

$$a_2 - a_1 = \frac{14}{3} - 5 = \frac{14-15}{3} = \frac{-1}{3},\ a_3 - a_2 = \frac{13}{3} - \frac{14}{3} = -\frac{1}{3}$$

$$a_4 - a_3 = 4 - \frac{13}{3} = \frac{12-13}{3} = \frac{-1}{3}$$

$\because \quad a_2 - a_1 = a_3 - a_2 = a_4 - a_3$

Since, the each successive term of the given list has same difference.

So, it forms an AP.

The next three terms are,

$$a_5 = a_1 + 4d = 5 + 4\left(-\frac{1}{3}\right) = 5 - \frac{4}{3} = \frac{15-4}{3} = \frac{11}{3}$$

$$a_6 = a_1 + 5d = 5 + 5\left(-\frac{1}{3}\right) = 5 - \frac{5}{3} = \frac{15-5}{3} = \frac{10}{3}$$

$$a_7 = a_1 + 6d = 5 + 6\left(-\frac{1}{3}\right) = 5 - 2 = 3$$

(iii) Here, $a_1 = \sqrt{3},\ a_2 = 2\sqrt{3}$ and $a_3 = 3\sqrt{3}$

$$a_2 - a_1 = 2\sqrt{3} - \sqrt{3} = \sqrt{3},\ a_3 - a_2 = 3\sqrt{3} - 2\sqrt{3} = \sqrt{3}$$

$\because \quad a_2 - a_1 = a_3 - a_2 = \sqrt{3}$

Since, the each successive term of the given list has same difference.

So, it forms an AP.

The next three terms are,

$$a_4 = a_1 + 3d = \sqrt{3} + 3(\sqrt{3}) = 4\sqrt{3}$$

$$a_5 = a_1 + 4d = \sqrt{3} + 4\sqrt{3} = 5\sqrt{3}$$

$$a_6 = a_1 + 5d = \sqrt{3} + 5\sqrt{3} = 6\sqrt{3}$$

(iv) Here, $a_1 = a + b,\ a_2 = (a+1) + b,\ a_3 = (a+1) + (b+1)$

$$a_2 - a_1 = (a+1) + b - (a+b) = a + 1 + b - a - b = 1$$

$$a_3 - a_2 = (a+1) + (b+1) - [(a+1) + b]$$

$$= a + 1 + b + 1 - a - 1 - b = 1$$

$\because \quad a_2 - a_1 = a_3 - a_2 = 1$

Since, the each successive term of the given list has same difference.

So, it forms an AP.

The next three terms are,

$$a_4 = a_1 + 3d = a + b + 3(1) = (a+2) + (b+1)$$
$$a_5 = a_1 + 4d = a + b + 4(1) = (a+2) + (b+2)$$
$$a_6 = a_1 + 5d = a + b + 5(1) = (a+3) + (b+2)$$

(v) Here, $a_1 = a$, $a_2 = 2a + 1$, $a_3 = 3a + 2$ and $a_4 = 4a + 3$

$$a_2 - a_1 = 2a + 1 - a = a + 1$$
$$a_3 - a_2 = 3a + 2 - 2a - 1 = a + 1$$
$$a_4 - a_3 = 4a + 3 - 3a - 2 = a + 1$$
$$a_2 - a_1 = a_3 - a_2 = a_4 - a_3 = a + 1$$

Since, the each successive term of the given list has same difference.

So, it forms an AP.

The next three terms are,

$$a_5 = a_1 + 4d = a + 4(a+1) = a + 4a + 4 = 5a + 4$$
$$a_6 = a_1 + 5d = a + 5(a+1) = a + 5a + 5 = 6a + 5$$
$$a_7 = a_1 + 6d = a + 6(a+1) = a + 6a + 6 = 7a + 6$$

Q.3 Write the first three terms of the AP's, when a and d are as given below

(i) $a = \frac{1}{2}, d = -\frac{1}{6}$ (ii) $a = -5, d = -3$

(iii) $a = \sqrt{2}, d = \frac{1}{\sqrt{2}}$

Ans. (i) Given that, first term $(a) = \frac{1}{2}$ and common difference $(d) = -\frac{1}{6}$

$\because$ nth term of an AP, $T_n = a + (n-1)\,d$

$\therefore$ Second term of an AP, $T_2 = a + d = \frac{1}{2} - \frac{1}{6} = \frac{3-1}{6} = \frac{2}{6} = \frac{1}{3}$

and third term of an AP, $T_3 = a + 2d = \frac{1}{2} - \frac{2}{6} = \frac{1}{2} - \frac{1}{3} = \frac{3-2}{6} = \frac{1}{6}$

Hence, required three terms are $\frac{1}{2}, \frac{1}{3}, \frac{1}{6}$.

(ii) Given that, first term $(a) = -5$ and common difference $(d) = -3$

$\because$ nth term of an AP, $T_n = a + (n-1)\,d$

$\therefore$ Second term of an AP, $T_2 = a + d = -5 - 3 = -8$

and third term of an AP, $T_3 = a + 2d = -5 + 2(-3)$

$$= -5 - 6 = -11$$

Hence, required three terms are $-5, -8, -11$.

(iii) Given that, first term $(a) = \sqrt{2}$ and common difference $(d) = \frac{1}{\sqrt{2}}$

$\because$ nth term of an AP, $T_n = a + (n-1)\,d$

$\therefore$ Second term of an AP, $T_2 = a + d = \sqrt{2} + \frac{1}{\sqrt{2}} = \frac{2+1}{\sqrt{2}} = \frac{3}{\sqrt{2}}$

and third term of an AP, $T_3 = a + 2d = \sqrt{2} + \frac{2}{\sqrt{2}} = \frac{2+2}{\sqrt{2}} = \frac{4}{\sqrt{2}}$

Hence, required three terms are $\sqrt{2}, \frac{3}{\sqrt{2}}, \frac{4}{\sqrt{2}}$.

Q.4 Find a, b and c such that the following numbers are in AP $a, 7, b, 23$ and c.

Ans. Since, $a, 7, b, 23$ and c are in AP.

$$\therefore \quad \underset{\text{I}}{7 - a} = \underset{\text{II}}{b - 7} = \underset{\text{III}}{23 - b} = \underset{\text{IV}}{c - 23} = \text{Common difference}$$

Taking second and third terms, we get

$$b - 7 = 23 - b$$
$$\Rightarrow \quad 2b = 30$$
$$\Rightarrow \quad b = 15$$

Taking first and second terms, we get

$$7 - a = b - 7$$
$$\Rightarrow \quad 7 - a = 15 - 7 \quad [\because b = 15]$$
$$\Rightarrow \quad 7 - a = 8$$
$$\Rightarrow \quad a = -1$$

Taking third and fourth terms, we get

$$23 - b = c - 23$$
$$\Rightarrow \quad 23 - 15 = c - 23 \quad [\because b = 15]$$
$$\Rightarrow \quad 8 = c - 23$$
$$\Rightarrow \quad 8 + 23 = c \Rightarrow c = 31$$

Hence, $a = -1$, $b = 15$, $c = 31$

Q.5 Determine the AP whose fifth term is 19 and the difference of the eighth term from the thirteenth term is 20.

Ans. Let the first term of an AP be a and common difference d.

Given, $a_5 = 19$ and $a_{13} - a_8 = 20$ [given]

$$\therefore \quad a_5 = a + (5-1)d = 19 \text{ and } [a + (13-1)d] - [a + (8-1)d] = 20$$

$$[\because a_n = a + (n-1)d]$$

$$\Rightarrow \quad a + 4d = 19 \quad \text{...(i)}$$
$$\text{and} \quad a + 12d - a - 7d = 20 \Rightarrow 5d = 20$$
$$\therefore \quad d = 4$$

On putting $d = 4$ in Eq. (i), we get

$$a + 4(4) = 19 \Rightarrow a + 16 = 19$$
$$\Rightarrow \quad a = 19 - 16 = 3$$

So, required AP is $a, a+d, a+2d, a+3d, \ldots$ *i.e.*, $3, 3+4, 3+2(4), 3+3(4), \ldots$

i.e., $3, 7, 11, 15, \ldots$

Q.6 The 26th, 11th and the last term of an AP are, 0,3 and $-\frac{1}{5}$, respectively. Find the common difference and the number of terms.

Ans. Let the first term, common difference and number of terms of an AP are a, d and n, respectively.

We know that, if last term of an AP is known, then

$$l = a + (n-1)\,d \quad \text{...(i)}$$

and nth term of an AP is

$$T_n = a + (n-1)\,d \quad \text{...(ii)}$$

Given that, 26th term of an AP = 0

$$\Rightarrow \quad T_{26} = a + (26-1)\,d = 0 \quad \text{[from Eq. (ii)]}$$

$$\Rightarrow \quad a + 25\,d = 0 \quad \text{...(iii)}$$

11th term of an AP = 3

$$\Rightarrow \quad T_{11} = a + (11-1)\,d = 3 \quad \text{[from Eq. (ii)]}$$

$$\Rightarrow \quad a + 10d = 3 \quad \text{... (iv)}$$

and last term of an AP = $-1/5$

$$\Rightarrow \quad l = a + (n-1)\,d \quad \text{[from Eq. (i)]}$$

$$\Rightarrow \quad -1/5 = a + (n-1)\,d \quad \text{...(v)}$$

Now, subtracting Eq. (iv) from Eq. (iii), we get

$$\begin{array}{r} a + 25\,d = 0 \\ a + 10\,d = 3 \\ - \;\; - \qquad - \\ \hline 15d = -3 \end{array}$$

$$\Rightarrow \quad d = -\frac{1}{5}$$

Put the value of d in Eq. (iii), we get

$$a + 25\left(-\frac{1}{5}\right) = 0$$

$$\Rightarrow \quad a - 5 = 0 \Rightarrow a = 5$$

Now, put the value of a, d in Eq. (v), we get

$$-1/5 = 5 + (n-1)(-1/5)$$

$$\Rightarrow \quad -1 = 25 - (n-1)$$

$$\Rightarrow \quad -1 = 25 - n + 1$$

$$\Rightarrow \quad n = 25 + 2 = 27$$

Hence, the common difference and number of terms are $-1/5$ and 27 respectively.

Q.7 The sum of the 5th and the 7th terms of an AP is 52 and the 10th term is 46. Find the AP.

Ans. Let the first term and common difference of the AP are a and d respectively.

According to the question,

$$a_5 + a_7 = 52 \text{ and } a_{10} = 46$$

$$\Rightarrow \quad a + (5-1)\,d + a + (7-1)\,d = 52 \quad [\because a_n = a + (n-1)\,d]$$

and

$$a + (10-1)\,d = 46$$

$\Rightarrow \quad a + 4d + a + 6d = 52$

and $\quad a + 9d = 46$

$\Rightarrow \quad 2a + 10d = 52$

and $\quad a + 9d = 46$

$\Rightarrow \quad a + 5d = 26 \quad \text{...(i)}$

$a + 9d = 46 \quad \text{...(ii)}$

On subtracting Eq. (i) from Eq. (ii), we get

$$4d = 20 \Rightarrow d = 5$$

From Eq. (i), $\quad a = 26 - 5(5) = 26 - 25 = 1$

So, required AP is $a, a + d, a + 2d, a + 3d, \ldots$ *i.e.*, $1, 1 + 5, 1 + 2(5), 1 + 3(5), \ldots$ *i.e.*, $1, 6, 11, 16, \ldots$

Q.8 Find the 20th term of the AP whose 7th term is 24 less than the 11th term, first term being 12.

Ans. Let the first term, common difference and number of terms of an AP are a, d and n, respectively.

Given that, first term $(a) = 12$

Now by condition,

$$\text{7th term } (T_7) = \text{11th term } (T_{11}) - 24$$

[$\because$ nth term of an AP, $T_n = a + (n - 1)d$]

$\Rightarrow \quad a + (7 - 1)d = a + (11 - 1)d - 24$

$\Rightarrow \quad a + 6d = a + 10d - 24$

$\Rightarrow \quad 24 = 4d \Rightarrow d = 6$

$\therefore \quad$ 20th term of AP, $T_{20} = a + (20 - 1)d$

$= 12 + 19 \times 6 = 12 + 114 = 126 \quad [\because d = 6]$

Hence, the required 20th term of an *AP* is 126.

Q.9 If the 9th term of an AP is zero, prove that its 29th term is twice its 19th term.

Ans. Let the first term, common difference and number of terms of an AP are a, d and n respectively.

Given that, 9th term of an AP, $T_9 = 0$

$\Rightarrow \quad a + (9 - 1)d = 0 \quad$ [$\because$ nth term of an AP, $T_n = a + (n - 1)d$]

$\Rightarrow \quad a + 8d = 0 \Rightarrow a = -8d \quad \text{... (i)}$

Now, its 19th term, $T_{19} = a + (19 - 1)d$

$= -8d + 18d \quad$ [from Eq. (i)]

$T_{19} = 10d \quad \text{... (ii)}$

and its 29th term, $T_{29} = a + (29 - 1)d$

$= -8d + 28d \quad$ [from Eq. (i)]

$= 20d = 2 \times (10d)$

$\Rightarrow \quad T_{29} = 2 \times T_{19} \quad$ [from Eq. (ii)]

Hence, its 29th term is twice its 19th term. **Hence proved.**

Q.10 Find whether 55 is a term of the AP: 7, 10, 13, ... or not. If yes, find which term it is.

Ans. *Yes*, let the first term, common difference and the number of terms of an AP are a, d and n respectively.

Let the nth term of an AP be 55. *i.e.*, $T_n = 55$.

We know that, the nth term of an AP, $T_n = a + (n-1)d$ ...(i)

Given that, first term $(a) = 7$ and common difference $(d) = 10 - 7 = 3$

From Eq. (i), $55 = 7 + (n-1) \times 3$

$\Rightarrow \quad 55 = 7 + 3n - 3 \Rightarrow 55 = 4 + 3n \Rightarrow 3n = 51$

$\therefore \quad n = 17$

Since, n is a positive integer. So, 55 is a term of the AP.

Now, put the values of a, d and n in Eq. (i),

$$T_{17} = 7 + (17-1)(3)$$
$$= 7 + 16 \times 3 = 7 + 48 = 55$$

Hence, 17th term of an AP is 55.

Q.11 Determine k, so that $k^2 + 4k + 8$, $2k^2 + 3k + 6$, $3k^2 + 4k + 4$ are three consecutive terms of an AP.

Ans. Since, $k^2 + 4k + 8$, $2k^2 + 3k + 6$ and $3k^2 + 4k + 4$ are consecutive terms of an AP.

$\therefore 2k^2 + 3k + 6 - (k^2 + 4k + 8) = 3k^2 + 4k + 4 - (2k^2 + 3k + 6) =$ Common difference

$\Rightarrow \quad 2k^2 + 3k + 6 - k^2 - 4k - 8 = 3k^2 + 4k + 4 - 2k^2 - 3k - 6$

$\Rightarrow \quad k^2 - k - 2 = k^2 + k - 2$

$\Rightarrow \quad -k = k \Rightarrow 2k = 0 \Rightarrow k = 0$

Q.12 Split 207 into three parts such that these are in AP and the product of the two smaller parts is 4623.

Ans. Let the three parts of the number 207 are $(a-d)$, a and $(a+d)$, which are in AP.

Now, by given condition,

$\Rightarrow \quad$ Sum of these parts = 207

$\Rightarrow \quad a - d + a + a + d = 207$

$\Rightarrow \quad 3a = 207 \Rightarrow a = 69$ ...(i)

Given that, product of the two smaller parts = 4623

$\Rightarrow \quad a(a-d) = 4623$

$\Rightarrow \quad 69 \cdot (69 - d) = 4623$ [from Eq. (i)]

$\Rightarrow \quad 69 - d = 67$

$\Rightarrow \quad d = 69 - 67 = 2$

So, first part $= a - d = 69 - 2 = 67$,

second part $= a = 69$

and third part $= a + d = 69 + 2 = 71$,

Hence, required three parts are 67, 69, 71.

Q.13 The angles of a triangle are in AP. The greatest angle is twice the least. Find all the angles of the triangle.

- **Concept Insight** (i) Sum of angles of a triangle is 180°.
  (ii) if a, b, c are in AP, then $b = \frac{a+c}{2}$ and b is called as arithmetic mean of a and c.

Ans. Given that, the angles of a triangle are in AP.

Let A, B and C are angles of a ΔABC, which are in A.P.

$$\therefore \quad B = \frac{A+C}{2}$$

$$\Rightarrow \quad 2B = A + C \quad \text{...(i)}$$

We know that, sum of all interior angles of a $\Delta ABC = 180°$

$$A + B + C = 180°$$

$$\Rightarrow \quad 2B + B = 180° \quad \text{[from Eq. (i)]}$$

$$\Rightarrow \quad 3B = 180° \Rightarrow B = 60°$$

Let the greatest and least angles are A and C respectively.

$$A = 2C \quad \text{[by condition] ... (ii)}$$

Now, put the values of B and A in Eq. (i), we get

$$2 \times 60° = 2C + C$$

$$\Rightarrow \quad 120° = 3C \Rightarrow C = 40°$$

Put the value of C in Eq. (ii), we get

$$A = 2 \times 40° \Rightarrow A = 80°$$

Hence, the required angles of triangle are 80°, 60° and 40°.

Q.14 If the nth terms of the two AP's: 9, 7, 5, ... and 24, 21, 18, ... are the same, find the value of n. Also, find that term.

Ans. Let the first term, common difference and number of terms of the AP 9, 7, 5, ... are a_1, d_1 and n_1, respectively.

i.e., first term $(a_1) = 9$ and common difference $(d_1) = 7 - 9 = -2$.

$$\therefore \text{ Its } n\text{th term,} \quad T'_{n_1} = a_1 + (n_1 - 1)\, d_1$$

$$\Rightarrow \quad T'_{n_1} = 9 + (n_1 - 1)(-2)$$

$$\Rightarrow \quad T'_{n_1} = 9 - 2n_1 + 2$$

$$\Rightarrow \quad T'_{n_1} = 11 - 2n_1 \quad [\because n\text{th term of an AP, } T_n = a + (n-1)\, d] \text{...(i)}$$

Let the first term, common difference and the number of terms of the AP 24, 21, 18, ... are a_2, d_2 and n_2 respectively.

i.e., first term, $(a_2) = 24$ and common difference $(d_2) = 21 - 24 = -3$.

$$\therefore \text{ Its } n\text{th term,} \quad T''_{n_2} = a_2 + (n_2 - 1)\, d_2$$

$$\Rightarrow \quad T''_{n_2} = 24 + (n_2 - 1)(-3)$$

$$\Rightarrow \quad T''_{n_2} = 24 - 3n_2 + 3$$

$$\Rightarrow \quad T''_{n_2} = 27 - 3n_2 \quad \text{...(ii)}$$

Now, by given condition,

nth terms of the both APs are same *i.e.*, $T'_{n_1} = T''_{n_1}$

$$11 - 2n_1 = 27 - 3n_2 \quad \text{[from Eqs. (i) and (ii)]}$$

$$\Rightarrow \quad n = 16 \quad [\because n_1 = n_2 = n]$$

$\therefore$ nth term of first AP, $T'n_1 = 11 - 2n_1 = 11 - 2(16)$

$= 11 - 32 = -21$

and nth term of second AP, $T''n_2 = 27 - 3n_2 = 27 - 3(16)$

$= 27 - 48 = -21$

Hence, the value of n is 16 and that term *i.e.*, nth term is –21.

Q.15 **If sum of the 3rd and the 8th terms of an AP is 7 and the sum of the 7th and 14th terms is –3, find the 10th term.**

Ans. Let the first term and common difference of an AP are a and d respectively.

According to the question,

$$a_3 + a_8 = 7 \text{ and } a_7 + a_{14} = -3$$

$\Rightarrow$ $a + (3-1)d + a + (8-1)d = 7$ $[\because a_n = a + (n-1)d]$

and $a + (7-1)d + a + (14-1)d = -3$

$a + 2d + a + 7d = 7$

and $a + 6d + a + 13d = -3$

$\Rightarrow$ $2a + 9d = 7$ ...(i)

and $2a + 19d = -3$ ...(ii)

On subtracting Eq. (i) from Eq. (ii), we get

$$10d = -10 \Rightarrow d = -1$$

$2a + 9(-1) = 7$

$\Rightarrow$ $2a - 9 = 7$ [from Eq. (i)]

$\Rightarrow$ $2a = 16 \Rightarrow a = 8$

$\therefore$ $a_{10} = a + (10-1)d$

$= 8 + 9(-1)$

$= 8 - 9 = -1$

Q.16 **Find the 12th term from the end of the AP – 2, – 4, – 6, ..., – 100.**

Ans. Given AP, –2, – 4, – 6,..., – 100

Here, first term $(a) = -2$, common difference $(d) = -4 - (-2) = -2$ and the last term $(l) = -100$.

$\therefore n$th term from the end, $a_n = l - (n-1)d$

$\therefore$ 12th term from the end,

$a_{12} = -100 - (12-1)(-2)$ $[\because a_n = l - (n-1)d]$

$= -100 + (11)(2) = -100 + 22 = -78.$

Hence, the 12th term from the end is –78.

Alternate Method

For finding 12th term from the end, we write the AP in reverse order *i.e.*, –100, –98, –96,..., –6, –4, –2.

Here, first $(a) = -100$, common difference $(d) = -98 - (-100) = 2$

nth term $= a_n = a + (n-1)d$

$\Rightarrow$ $a_{12} = -100 + (12-1)2 = -100 + 22 = -78$

Hence, the 12th term from the end is –78.

Q.17 Which term of the AP: 53, 48, 43, ... is the first negative term?

Ans. Given AP is 53, 48, 43, ...

Whose, first term $(a) = 53$ and common difference $(d) = 48 - 53 = -5$

Let nth term of the AP be the first negative term.

i.e., $T_n < 0$

$(a + (n-1)d) < 0$ $\quad$ [$\because$ nth term of an AP, $T_n = a + (n-1)d$]

$\Rightarrow 53 + (n-1)(-5) < 0$

$\Rightarrow 53 - 5n + 5 < 0$

$\Rightarrow 58 - 5n < 0 \Rightarrow 5n > 58$

$\Rightarrow n > 11.6 \Rightarrow n = 12$

i.e., 12th term is the first negative term of the given AP.

$\therefore T_{12} = a + (12-1)d = 53 + 11(-5)$

$= 53 - 55 = -2 < 0$

Q.18 How many numbers lie between 10 and 300, which when divided by 4 leave a remainder 3?

Ans. Here, the first number is 11, which divided by 4 leave remainder 3 between 10 and 300. Last term before 300 is 299, which divided by 4 leave remainder 3.

$\therefore$ 11, 15, 19, 23,..., 299

Here, first term $(a) = 11$, common difference $d = 15 - 11 = 4$ and last term $l = 299$

$\because$ nth term, $a_n = a + (n-1)d = l$

$\Rightarrow 299 = 11 + (n-1)4$

$\Rightarrow 299 - 11 = (n-1)4$

$\Rightarrow 4(n-1) = 288$

$\Rightarrow (n-1) = 72$

$\therefore n = 73$

Q.19 Find the sum of the two middle most terms of an AP $-\frac{4}{3}, -1, -\frac{2}{3}, \ldots, 4\frac{1}{3}$.

- **Concept Insight** If 'n' is even, then the two middle terms $\left(\frac{n}{2}\right)$th and $\left(\frac{n}{2}+1\right)$th will be middle terms of an arithmetic progression.

Ans. Here, first term $(a) = -\frac{4}{3}$, common difference $(d) = -1 + \frac{4}{3} = \frac{1}{3}$

and the last term $(l) = 4\frac{1}{3} = \frac{13}{3}$

$\because$ nth term of an AP, $l = a_n = a + (n-1)d$

$\Rightarrow \frac{13}{3} = -\frac{4}{3} + (n-1)\frac{1}{3}$

$\Rightarrow 13 = -4 + (n-1)$

$\Rightarrow n - 1 = 17$

$\Rightarrow n = 18$ $\quad$ [even]

So, the two middle most terms are $\left(\frac{n}{2}\right)$th and $\left(\frac{n}{2}+1\right)$th. *i.e.,* $\left(\frac{18}{2}\right)$th and $\left(\frac{18}{2}+1\right)$th terms

i.e., 9th and 10th terms.

$\therefore \quad a_9 = a + 8d = -\frac{4}{3} + 8\left(\frac{1}{3}\right) = \frac{8-4}{3} = \frac{4}{3}$

and $\quad a_{10} = a + 9d = \frac{-4}{3} + 9\left(\frac{1}{3}\right) = \frac{9-4}{3} = \frac{5}{3}$

So, sum of the two middle most terms $= a_9 + a_{10} = \frac{4}{3} + \frac{5}{3} = \frac{9}{3} = 3$

Q.20 The first term of an AP is – 5 and the last term is 45. If the sum of the terms of the AP is 120, then find the number of terms and the common difference.

- **Concept Insight** If a is the first term and l is the last term of the finite AP, then the sum of all n terms of the AP is $S_n = \frac{n}{2}(a+l)$.

Ans. Let the first term, common difference and the number of terms of an AP are a, d and n respectively.

Given that, first term $(a) = -5$ and last term $(l) = 45$

Sum of the terms of the AP $= 120 \Rightarrow S_n = 120$

We know that, if last term of an AP is known, then sum of n terms of an AP is,

$$S_n = \frac{n}{2}(a+l) \Rightarrow 120 = \frac{n}{2}(-5+45) \Rightarrow 120 \times 2 = 40 \times n$$

$$\Rightarrow \quad n = 3 \times 2 \Rightarrow n = 6$$

$\therefore$ If the number of terms of an AP is known, then the nth term of an AP is,

$$l = a + (n-1)d \Rightarrow 45 = -5 + (6-1)d$$

$$\Rightarrow \quad 50 = 5d \Rightarrow d = 10$$

So, the common difference is 10.

Hence, number of terms and the common difference of an AP are 6 and 10 respectively.

Q.21 Find the sum

(i) $1 + (-2) + (-5) + (-8) + \ldots + (-236)$

(ii) $\left(4 - \frac{1}{n}\right) + \left(4 - \frac{2}{n}\right) + \left(4 - \frac{3}{n}\right) + \ldots$ upto n terms.

(iii) $\frac{a-b}{a+b} + \frac{3a-2b}{a+b} + \frac{5a-3b}{a+b} + \ldots$ to 11 terms.

Ans. (i) Here, first term $(a) = 1$ and common difference $(d) = (-2) - 1 = -3$

$\because$ Sum of n terms of an AP, $S_n = \frac{n}{2}[2a + (n-1)d]$

$$\Rightarrow \quad S_n = \frac{n}{2}[2 \times 1 + (n-1) \times (-3)]$$

$$\Rightarrow \quad S_n = \frac{n}{2}(2 - 3n + 3) \Rightarrow S_n = \frac{n}{2}(5 - 3n) \quad \ldots(i)$$

We know that, if the last term (l) of an AP is known, then

$$l = a + (n-1)\,d$$

$\Rightarrow$ $-236 = 1 + (n-1)(-3)$ $\quad$ [$\because l = -236$, (given)]

$\Rightarrow$ $-237 = -(n-1) \times 3$

$\Rightarrow$ $n - 1 = 79 \Rightarrow n = 80$

Now, put the value of n in Eq. (i), we get

$$S_n = \frac{80}{2}[5 - 3 \times 80] = 40\,(5 - 240)$$

$$= 40 \times (-235) = -9400$$

Hence, the required sum is -9400.

Alternate Method

Given, $\quad a = 1, d = -3$ and $l = -236$

$\therefore$ Sum of n terms of an AP, $S_n = \frac{n}{2}[a + l]$

$$= \frac{80}{2}(1 + (-236)) \quad [\because n = 80]$$

$$= 40 \times (-235) = -9400$$

(ii) Here, first term, $a = 4 - \frac{1}{n}$

Common difference, $d = \left(4 - \frac{2}{n}\right) - \left(4 - \frac{1}{n}\right) = \frac{-2}{n} + \frac{1}{n} = \frac{-1}{n}$

$\because$ Sum of n terms of an AP, $S_n = \frac{n}{2}[2a + (n-1)\,d]$

$\Rightarrow$

$$S_n = \frac{n}{2}\left[2\left(4 - \frac{1}{n}\right) + (n-1)\left(\frac{-1}{n}\right)\right] = \frac{n}{2}\left\{8 - \frac{2}{n} - 1 + \frac{1}{n}\right\}$$

$$= \frac{n}{2}\left(7 - \frac{1}{n}\right) = \frac{n}{2} \times \left(\frac{7n-1}{n}\right) = \frac{7n-1}{2}$$

(iii) Here, first term $a = \frac{a-b}{a+b}$

and common difference, $d = \frac{3a-2b}{a+b} - \frac{a-b}{a+b} = \frac{3a-2b-a+b}{a+b} = \frac{2a-b}{a+b}$

$\because$ Sum of n terms of an AP, $S_n = \frac{n}{2}[2a + (n-1)d]$

$\Rightarrow$

$$S_n = \frac{n}{2}\left\{2\frac{(a-b)}{(a+b)} + (n-1)\frac{(2a-b)}{(a+b)}\right\}$$

$$= \frac{n}{2}\left\{\frac{2a - 2b + 2an - 2a - bn + b}{a+b}\right\} = \frac{n}{2}\left(\frac{2an - bn - b}{a+b}\right)$$

$\therefore$

$$S_{11} = \frac{11}{2}\left\{\frac{2a\,(11) - b\,(11) - b}{a+b}\right\}$$

$$= \frac{11}{2}\left(\frac{22a - 12b}{a+b}\right) = \frac{11\,(11a - 6b)}{a+b}$$

Q.22 Which term of the AP: $-2, -7, -12, \ldots$ will be -77 ? Find the sum of this AP upto the term -77.

Ans. Given, AP $-2, -7, -12, \ldots$

Let the nth term of an AP is -77.

Then, first term $(a) = -2$ and common difference $(d) = -7-(-2) = -7+2 = -5$.

$\because$ nth term of an AP, $T_n = a + (n-1)d$

$$\Rightarrow \quad -77 = -2 + (n-1)(-5)$$

$$\Rightarrow \quad -75 = -(n-1) \times 5$$

$$\Rightarrow \quad (n-1) = 15 \Rightarrow n = 16.$$

So, the 16th term of the given AP will be -77.

Now, the sum of n terms of an AP is

$$S_n = \frac{n}{2}[2a + (n-1)d]$$

So, sum of 16 terms *i.e.,* upto the term -77.

i.e.,
$$S_{16} = \frac{16}{2}[2 \times (-2) + (16-1)(-5)]$$
$$= 8(-4-75)$$
$$= 8 \times (-79) = -632$$

Hence, the sum of this AP upto the term -77 is -632.

Q.23 If $a_n = 3 - 4n$, show that $a_1, a_2, a_3, \ldots$ form an AP. Also, find S_{20}.

Ans. Given that, nth term of the series is $a_n = 3 - 4n$...(i)

Put $n = 1$, $\quad a_1 = 3 - 4(1) = 3 - 4 = -1$

Put $n = 2$, $\quad a_2 = 3 - 4(2) = 3 - 8 = -5$

Put $n = 3$, $\quad a_3 = 3 - 4(3) = 3 - 12 = -9$

Put $n = 4$, $\quad a_4 = 3 - 4(4) = 3 - 16 = -13$

So, the series becomes $-1, -5, -9, -13, \ldots$

We see that,

$$a_2 - a_1 = -5 - (-1) = -5 + 1 = -4,$$
$$a_3 - a_2 = -9 - (-5) = -9 + 5 = -4,$$
$$a_4 - a_3 = -13 - (-9) = -13 + 9 = -4$$

i.e.,
$$a_2 - a_1 = a_3 - a_2 = a_4 - a_3 = \ldots = -4$$

Since, the each successive term of the series has the same difference. So, it forms an AP. We know that, sum of n terms of an AP, $S_n = \frac{n}{2}[2a + (n-1)d]$

$\therefore$ Sum of 20 terms of the AP, $S_{20} = \frac{20}{2}[2(-1) + (20-1)(-4)]$

$$= 10(-2 + (19)(-4)) = 10(-2-76)$$
$$= 10 \times -78 = -780$$

Hence, the required sum of 20 terms *i.e.,* S_{20} is -780.

Q.24 In an AP, if $S_n = n(4n+1)$, find the AP.

- **Concept Insight** In an AP, if S_n is the sum of n terms and S_{n-1} is the sum of $(n-1)$ terms, then the nth term is $a_n = s_n - s_{n-1}$

Ans. We know that, the nth term of an AP is

$$a_n = S_n - S_{n-1}$$

$$a_n = n(4n+1) - (n-1)\{4(n-1)+1\} \quad [\because S_n = n(4n+1)]$$

$$\Rightarrow a_n = 4n^2 + n - (n-1)(4n-4+1) = 4n^2 + n - (n-1)(4n-3)$$

$$= 4n^2 + n - 4n^2 + 3n + 4n - 3 = 8n - 3$$

Put $n = 1$, $\quad a_1 = 8(1) - 3 = 5$

Put $n = 2$, $\quad a_2 = 8(2) - 3 = 16 - 3 = 13$

Put $n = 3$, $\quad a_3 = 8(3) - 3 = 24 - 3 = 21$

Hence, the required AP is 5, 13, 21, ...

Q.25 In an AP, if $S_n = 3n^2 + 5n$ and $a_k = 164$, find the value of k.

Ans. $\because$ nth term of an AP,

$$a_n = S_n - S_{n-1}$$

$$= 3n^2 + 5n - 3(n-1)^2 - 5(n-1) \quad [\because S_n = 3n^2 + 5n \text{ (given)}]$$

$$= 3n^2 + 5n - 3(n^2 + 1 - 2n) - 5n + 5$$

$$= 3n^2 - 3n^2 - 3 + 6n + 5$$

$$a_n = 6n + 2 \quad \text{...(i)}$$

or $\quad a_k = 6k + 2 = 164 \quad [\because a_k = 164 \text{ (given)}]$

$\Rightarrow \quad 6k = 164 - 2 = 162$

$\therefore \quad k = 27$

Q. 26 If S_n denotes the sum of first n terms of an AP, prove that $S_{12} = 3(S_8 - S_4)$.

Ans. $\because$ Sum of n terms of an AP, $S_n = \frac{n}{2}[2a + (n-1)d]$ ...(i)

$\therefore \quad S_8 = \frac{8}{2}[2a + (8-1)d] = 4(2a + 7d) = 8a + 28d$

and $\quad S_4 = \frac{4}{2}[2a + (4-1)d] = 2(2a + 3d) = 4a + 6d$

Now, $\quad S_8 - S_4 = 8a + 28d - 4a - 6d = 4a + 22d$ ...(ii)

and $\quad S_{12} = \frac{12}{2}[2a + (12-1)d] = 6(2a + 11d)$

$$= 3(4a + 22d) = 3(S_8 - S_4) \quad \text{[from Eq. (ii)]}$$

$\therefore \quad S_{12} = 3(S_8 - S_4)$ **Hence proved.**

Q.27 Find the sum of first 17 terms of an AP whose 4th and 9th terms are -15 and -30 respectively.

Thinking process Firstly, find first term and common difference of the A.P. by the given condition using the formula for nth term of an A.P. as $a_n = a + (n-1)d$. Then find sum of first 17 terms of the A.P. using the following formula, $S_n = \frac{n}{2}[(2a + (n-1)d]$

Ans. Let the first term, common difference and the number of terms in an AP are a, d and n, respectively.

We know that, the nth term of an AP, $T_n = a + (n-1)d$ ... (i)

$\therefore$ 4th term of an AP, $T_4 = a + (4-1)d = -15$ [given]

$\Rightarrow$ $a + 3d = -15$ ...(ii)

and 9th term of an AP, $T_9 = a + (9-1)d = -30$ [given]

$\Rightarrow$ $a + 8d = -30$ ...(iii)

Now, subtract Eq. (ii) from Eq. (iii), we get

$$\begin{array}{r} a + 8d = -30 \\ a + 3d = -15 \\ - \quad - \quad\quad + \\ \hline 5d = -15 \end{array}$$

$\Rightarrow$ $d = -3$

Put the value of d in Eq. (ii), we get

$$a + 3(-3) = -15 \Rightarrow a - 9 = -15$$

$\Rightarrow$ $a = -15 + 9 \Rightarrow a = -6$

$\because$ Sum of first n terms of an AP, $S_n = \frac{n}{2}[2a + (n-1)d]$

$\therefore$ Sum of first 17 terms of an AP, $S_{17} = \frac{17}{2}[2 \times (-6) + (17-1)(-3)]$

$$= \frac{17}{2}[-12 + (16)(-3)]$$

$$= \frac{17}{2}(-12 - 48) = \frac{17}{2} \times (-60)$$

$$= 17 \times (-30) = -510$$

Hence, the required sum of first 17 terms of an AP is -510.

Q.28 **If sum of first 6 terms of an AP is 36 and that of the first 16 terms is 256, find the sum of first 10 terms.**

Ans. Let a and d be the first term and common difference respectively of an AP.

$\because$ Sum of n terms of an AP, $S_n = \frac{n}{2}[2a + (n-1)d]$ ...(i)

Now, $S_6 = 36$ [given]

$\Rightarrow$ $\frac{6}{2}[2a + (6-1)d] = 36 \Rightarrow 3(2a + 5d) = 36$

$\Rightarrow$ $2a + 5d = 12$ ...(ii)

and $S_{16} = 256$

$\Rightarrow$ $\frac{16}{2}[2a + (16-1)d] = 256 \Rightarrow 8(2a + 15d) = 256$

$\Rightarrow$ $2a + 15d = 32$ ...(iii)

On subtracting Eq. (ii) from Eq. (iii), we get

$$10d = 20 \Rightarrow d = 2$$

From Eq. (ii), $2a + 5(2) = 12$

$\Rightarrow$ $2a = 12 - 10 = 2$

$\Rightarrow \quad a = 1$

$$\therefore \quad S_{10} = \frac{10}{2}[2a + (10-1)d]$$
$$= 5[2(1) + 9(2)] = 5(2 + 18)$$
$$= 5 \times 20 = 100$$

Hence, the required sum of first 10 terms is 100.

Q.29 Find the sum of all the 11 terms of an AP whose middle most term is 30.

- **Concept Insight** In an AP, if the total number of terms (n) is odd, then the middle most term is $\left(\frac{n+1}{2}\right)$th term.

Ans. Since, the total number of terms $(n) = 11$ [odd]

$\therefore$ Middle most term $= \left(\frac{(n+1)}{2}\right)$th term $= \left(\frac{11+1}{2}\right)$th term $= 6$th term

Given that, $a_6 = 30$

$\Rightarrow \quad a + (6-1)d = 30$

$\Rightarrow \quad a + 5d = 30 \quad$ ...(i)

$\because$ Sum of n terms of an AP, $S_n = \frac{n}{2}[2a + (n-1)d]$

$$\therefore \quad S_{11} = \frac{11}{2}[2a + (11-1)d] = \frac{11}{2}(2a + 10d) = 11(a + 5d)$$
$$= 11 \times 30 = 330 \quad \text{[from Eq. (i)]}$$

Q.30 Find the sum of last ten terms of the AP: 8, 10, 12,..., 126.

Ans. For finding, the sum of last ten terms, we write the given AP in reverse order.

i.e., 126, 124, 122, ..., 12, 10, 8

Here, first term $(a) = 126$, common difference, $(d) = 124 - 126 = -2$

$$\therefore \quad S_{10} = \frac{10}{2}[2a + (10-1)d] \quad \left[\because S_n = \frac{n}{2}[2a + (n-1)d]\right]$$
$$= 5\{2(126) + 9(-2)\} = 5(252 - 18) = 5 \times 234 = 1170$$

Mistake Alert! *Students may incorrectly calculate the value of d as* $10 - 8 = 2$ *instead of* $124 - 126 = -2$.

Q.31 Find the sum of first seven numbers which are multiples of 2 as well as of 9.

Ans. For finding, the sum of first seven numbers which are multiples of 2 as well as of 9. Take LCM of 2 and 9 which is 18.

So, the series becomes 18, 36, 54,...

Here, first term $(a) = 18$, common difference $(d) = 36 - 18 = 18$

$$\therefore \quad S_7 = \frac{7}{2}[2(18) + (7-1)18] \quad \left[\because S_n = \frac{n}{2}[2a + (n-1)d]\right]$$
$$= \frac{7}{2}[36 + 6 \times 18] = 7(18 + 3 \times 18)$$
$$= 7(18 + 54) = 7 \times 72 = 504$$

Q.32 How many terms of the AP $-15, -13, -11, \ldots$ are needed to make the sum -55? Explain the reason for double answer.

Ans. Let n be the number of terms are needed to make the sum -55.

Here, first term $(a) = -15$, common difference $(d) = -13 + 15 = 2$

$\because$ Sum of n terms of an AP, $S_n = \frac{n}{2}[2a + (n-1)d]$

$\Rightarrow \quad -55 = \frac{n}{2}[2(-15) + (n-1)2] \quad [\because S_n = -55 \text{ (given)}]$

$\Rightarrow \quad -55 = -15n + n(n-1) \Rightarrow -55 = -15n + n^2 - n$

$\Rightarrow \quad n^2 - 16n + 55 = 0$

$\Rightarrow \quad n^2 - 11n - 5n + 55 = 0$ [by factorisation method]

$\Rightarrow \quad n(n-11) - 5(n-11) = 0$

$\Rightarrow \quad (n-11)(n-5) = 0$

$\therefore \quad n = 5, 11$

Hence, either 5 or 11 terms are needed to make the sum -55.

When $n = 5$, AP will be $-15, -13, -11, -9, -7$. So, resulting sum will be -55

When $n = 11$, AP will be $-15, -13, -11, -9, -7, -5, -3, -1, 1, 3, 5$

So, the resulting sum will be -55 because the sum of 6th to 11th terms is 0.

Q.33 The sum of the first n terms of an AP whose first term is 8 and the common difference is 20 is equal to the sum of first $2n$ terms of another AP whose first term is -30 and the common difference is 8. Find n.

Ans. Given that, first term of the first AP $(a) = 8$

and common difference of the first AP $(d) = 20$

Let the number of terms in first AP be n.

$\because$ Sum of first n terms of an AP, $S_n = \frac{n}{2}[2a + (n-1)d]$

$\therefore \quad S_n = \frac{n}{2}[2 \times 8 + (n-1)20]$

$\Rightarrow \quad S_n = \frac{n}{2}(16 + 20n - 20)$

$\Rightarrow \quad S_n = \frac{n}{2}(20n - 4)$

$\therefore \quad S_n = n(10n - 2) \quad \ldots\text{(i)}$

Now, first term of the second AP $(a') = -30$

and common difference of the second AP $(d') = 8$

$\therefore$ Sum of first $2n$ terms of second AP, $S_{2n} = \frac{2n}{2}[2a' + (2n-1)d']$

$\Rightarrow \quad S_{2n} = n[2(-30) + (2n-1)(8)]$

$\Rightarrow \quad S_{2n} = n[-60 + 16n - 8)]$

$\Rightarrow \quad S_{2n} = n[16n - 68] \quad \ldots\text{(ii)}$

Now, by given condition,

Sum of first n terms of the first AP = Sum of first $2n$ terms of the second AP

$\Rightarrow \quad S_n = S_{2n}$ [from Eqs. (i) and (ii)]

$\Rightarrow \quad n(10n-2) = n(16n-68)$

$\Rightarrow \quad n[(16n-68)-(10n-2)] = 0$

$\Rightarrow \quad n(16n-68-10n+2) = 0$

$\Rightarrow \quad n(6n-66) = 0$

$\therefore \quad n = 11$ $[\because n \neq 0]$

Hence, the required value of n is 11.

Q.34 **Kanika was given her pocket money on Jan 1th, 2008. She puts ₹ 1 on day 1, ₹ 2 on day 2, ₹ 3 on day 3 and continued doing so till the end of the month, from this money into her piggy bank she also spent ₹ 204 of her pocket money, and found that at the end of the month she still had ₹ 100 with her. How much was her pocket money for the month?**

Ans. Let her pocket money be ₹ x.

Now, she puts ₹ 1 on day 1, ₹ 2 on day 2, ₹ 3 on day 3 and so on till the end of the month, from this money into her piggy bank.

i.e., $\quad 1+2+3+4+\ldots+31$

which form an AP in which number of terms are 31 and first term $(a) = 1$, common difference $(d) = 2-1 = 1$

$\therefore$ Sum of first 31 terms $= S_{31}$

Sum of n terms, $\quad S_n = \frac{n}{2}[2a+(n-1)d]$

$$\therefore \quad S_{31} = \frac{31}{2}[2\times 1+(31-1)\times 1]$$

$$= \frac{31}{2}(2+30) = \frac{31\times 32}{2}$$

$$= 31\times 16 = 496$$

So, Kanika puts ₹ 496 till the end of the month from this money into her piggy bank.

Also, she spent ₹ 204 of her pocket money and found that at the end of the month she still has ₹ 100 with her.

Now, according to the condition,

$$(x-496)-204 = 100$$

$$\Rightarrow \quad x-700 = 100$$

$$\therefore \quad x = ₹\,800$$

Hence, ₹ 800 was her pocket money for the month.

Q.35 **Yasmeen saves ₹ 32 during the first month, ₹ 36 in the second month and ₹ 40 in the third month. If she continues to save in this manner, in how many months will she save ₹ 2000?**

Ans. Given that,

Yasmeen, during the first month, saves = ₹ 32

During the second month, saves = ₹ 36

During the third month, saves = ₹ 40

Let Yasmeen saves ₹ 2000 during the n months.

Here, we have arithmetic progression 32, 36, 40, ...

First term (a) = 32, common difference (d) = 36 − 32 = 4

and she saves total money, *i.e.*, S_n = ₹ 2000

We know that, sum of first n terms of an AP is,

$$S_n = \frac{n}{2}[2a + (n-1)d]$$

$$\Rightarrow \quad 2000 = \frac{n}{2}[2 \times 32 + (n-1) \times 4]$$

$$\Rightarrow \quad 2000 = n[32 + (n-1)2]$$

$$\Rightarrow \quad 2000 = n(32 + 2n - 2)$$

$$\Rightarrow \quad 2000 = n(30 + 2n)$$

$$\Rightarrow \quad 1000 = n(15 + n)$$

$$\Rightarrow \quad 1000 = 15n + n^2$$

$$\Rightarrow \quad n^2 + 15n - 1000 = 0$$

$$\Rightarrow \quad n^2 + 40n - 25n - 1000 = 0$$

$$\Rightarrow \quad n(n + 40) - 25(n + 40) = 0 \Rightarrow (n + 40)(n - 25) = 0$$

$$\therefore \quad n = 25 \; [\because n \neq -40] \quad [\because \text{months cannot be negative}]$$

Hence, she will save ₹2000 in 25 months.

Long Answer Questions

Q.1 **The sum of the first five terms of an AP and the sum of the first seven terms of the same AP is 167. If the sum of the first ten terms of this AP is 235, find the sum of its first twenty terms.**

Ans. Let the first term, common difference and the number of terms of an AP are a, d and n respectively.

$\because$ Sum of first n terms of an AP, $S_n = \frac{n}{2}[2a + (n-1)d]$ ...(i)

$\therefore$ Sum of first five terms of an AP, $S_5 = \frac{5}{2}[2a + (5-1)d]$ [from Eq.(i)]

$$= \frac{5}{2}(2a + 4d) = 5(a + 2d)$$

$$\Rightarrow \quad S_5 = 5a + 10d \quad \text{...(ii)}$$

and sum of first seven terms of an AP, $S_7 = \frac{7}{2}[2a + (7-1)d]$ [from Eq. (i)]

$$= \frac{7}{2}[2a + 6d] = 7(a + 3d)$$

$$\Rightarrow \quad S_7 = 7a + 21d \quad \text{...(iii)}$$

Now, by given condition,

$$S_5 + S_7 = 167$$

$\Rightarrow \quad 5a + 10d + 7a + 21d = 167$

$\Rightarrow \quad 12a + 31d = 167$ ...(iv)

Given that, sum of first ten terms of this AP is 235.

$\therefore \quad S_{10} = 235$

$\Rightarrow \quad \frac{10}{2}[2a + (10-1)d] = 235$

$\Rightarrow \quad 5(2a + 9d) = 235$

$\Rightarrow \quad 2a + 9d = 47$ ...(v)

On multiplying Eq. (v) by 6 and then subtracting Eq. (iv) from it, we get

$$12a + 54d = 282$$
$$12a + 31d = 167$$
$$- \quad - \quad -$$
$$23d = 115$$

$\Rightarrow \quad d = 5$

Now, put the value of d in Eq. (v), we get

$$2a + 9(5) = 47 \Rightarrow 2a + 45 = 47$$

$\Rightarrow \quad 2a = 47 - 45 = 2 \Rightarrow a = 1$

Sum of first twenty terms of this AP, $S_{20} = \frac{20}{2}[2a + (20-1)d]$

$$= 10[2 \times (1) + 19 \times (5)] = 10(2 + 95)$$
$$= 10 \times 97 = 970$$

Hence, the required sum of its first twenty terms is 970.

Q.2 Find the

(i) sum of those integers between 1 and 500 which are multiples of 2 as well as of 5.

(ii) sum of those integers from 1 to 500 which are multiples of 2 as well as of 5.

(iii) sum of those integers from 1 to 500 which are multiples of 2 or 5.

Ans. (i) Since, multiples of 2 as well as of 5 = LCM of (2, 5) = 10

$\therefore$ Multiples of 2 as well as of 5 between 1 and 500 is 10, 20, 30,..., 490 which form an AP with first term $(a) = 10$ and common difference $(d) = 20 - 10 = 10$

$$n\text{th term } a_n = \text{Last term } (l) = 490$$

$\therefore$ Sum of n terms between 1 and 500, is $S_n = \frac{n}{2}[a + l]$ ...(i)

Now, first find the value of n by using the formula $l = a + (n-1)d$.

$\Rightarrow \quad 10 + (n-1)10 = 490$

$\Rightarrow \quad (n-1)10 = 480$

$\Rightarrow \quad n - 1 = 48$

$\Rightarrow \quad n = 49$

From Eq. (i), we get $S_{49} = \frac{49}{2}(10 + 490) = \frac{49}{2} \times 500$

$= 49 \times 250 = 12250$

(ii) Same as part (i),

but multiples of 2 as well as of 5 from 1 to 500 is 10, 20, 30, ..., 500.

$\therefore \quad a = 10, d = 10, a_n = l = 500$

$\because \quad a_n = a + (n-1)d = l$

$\Rightarrow \quad 500 = 10 + (n-1)10$

$\Rightarrow \quad 490 = (n-1)10$

$\Rightarrow \quad n - 1 = 49 \Rightarrow n = 50$

$\because \quad S_n = \frac{n}{2}(a + l)$

$\Rightarrow \quad S_{50} = \frac{50}{2}(10 + 500) = \frac{50}{2} \times 510$

$= 50 \times 255 = 12750$

(iii) Since, multiples of 2 or 5 = Multiple of 2 + Multiple of 5 – Multiples of 2 as well as of 5 *i.e.*, LCM (2, 5) = 10

$\therefore$ Multiples of 2 or 5 from 1 to 500

= List of multiple of 2 from 1 to 500 + List of multiple of 5 from 1 to 500 – List of multiple of 10 from 1 to 500

$= (2, 4, 6, ..., 500) + (5, 10, 15, ..., 500) - (10, 20, ..., 500)$ ...(i)

All of these list form an AP.

Let n_1, n_2 and n_3 are the first term of first list, second list and third list respectively.

Now, number of terms in first list,

$500 = 2 + (n_1 - 1)2 \Rightarrow 498 = (n_1 - 1)2$ $[\because a_n = a + (n-1)d]$

$\Rightarrow \quad n_1 - 1 = 249 \Rightarrow n_1 = 250$

Number of terms in second list,

$500 = 5 + (n_2 - 1)5 \Rightarrow 495 = (n_2 - 1)5$

$\Rightarrow \quad 99 = (n_2 - 1) \Rightarrow n_2 = 100$

and number of terms in third list,

$500 = 10 + (n_3 - 1)10 \Rightarrow 490 = (n_3 - 1)10$

$\Rightarrow \quad n_3 - 1 = 49 \Rightarrow n_3 = 50$

From Eq. (i), we get sum of multiples of 2 or 5 from 1 to 500

= Sum of (2, 4, 6, ..., 500) + Sum of (5, 10, ..., 500) – Sum of (10, 20, ..., 500)

$= \frac{n_1}{2}[2 + 500] + \frac{n_2}{2}[5 + 500] - \frac{n_3}{2}[10 + 500]$ $\left[\because S_n = \frac{n}{2}(a + l)\right]$

$= \frac{250}{2} \times 502 + \frac{100}{2} \times 505 - \frac{50}{2} \times 510$

$= 250 \times 251 + 505 \times 50 - 25 \times 510 = 62750 + 25250 - 12750$

$= 88000 - 12750 = 75250$

Q.3 The eighth term of an AP is half of its second term and the eleventh term exceeds one-third of its fourth term by 1. Find the 15th term.

Ans. Let a and d be the first term and common difference of an AP respectively.

Now, by given condition, $a_8 = \frac{1}{2} a_2$

$\Rightarrow \quad a + 7d = \frac{1}{2}(a + d) \quad [\because a_n = a + (n-1)d]$

$\Rightarrow \quad 2a + 14d = a + d$

$\Rightarrow \quad a + 13d = 0 \quad \ldots(i)$

and $a_{11} = \frac{1}{3} a_4 + 1$

$\Rightarrow \quad a + 10d = \frac{1}{3}[a + 3d] + 1$

$\Rightarrow \quad 3a + 30d = a + 3d + 3$

$\Rightarrow \quad 2a + 27d = 3 \quad \ldots(ii)$

From Eqs. (i) and (ii), we get

$2(-13d) + 27d = 3 \quad [\because a = -13d]$

$\Rightarrow \quad -26d + 27d = 3$

$\Rightarrow \quad d = 3$

From Eq. (i), we get

$a + 13(3) = 0$

$\Rightarrow \quad a = -39$

$\therefore \quad a_{15} = a + 14d = -39 + 14(3)$

$= -39 + 42 = 3$

Q.4 An AP consists of 37 terms. The sum of the three middle most terms is 225 and the sum of the last three terms is 429. Find the AP.

Ans. Since, total number of terms $(n) = 37$ [odd]

$\therefore$ Middle term $= \left(\frac{37+1}{2}\right)$th term $= 19$th term

So, the three middle most terms = 18th, 19th and 20th.

By given condition,

Sum of the three middle most terms = 225

$a_{18} + a_{19} + a_{20} = 225$

$\Rightarrow \quad (a + 17d) + (a + 18d) + (a + 19d) = 225$

$\Rightarrow \quad 3a + 54d = 225$

$\Rightarrow \quad a + 18d = 75 \quad \ldots(i)$

and sum of the last three terms = 429

$\Rightarrow \quad a_{35} + a_{36} + a_{37} = 429$

$\Rightarrow \quad (a + 34d) + (a + 35d) + (a + 36d) = 429$

$\Rightarrow \quad 3a + 105d = 429$

$\Rightarrow \quad a + 35d = 143 \quad \ldots(ii)$

On subtracting Eq. (i) from Eq. (ii), we get

$$17d = 68 \Rightarrow d = 4$$

From Eq. (i), we get $a + 18(4) = 75$

$\Rightarrow$ $a = 75 - 72 \Rightarrow a = 3$

$\therefore$ Required AP is $a, a + d, a + 2d, a + 3d, \ldots$

i.e., $3, 3 + 4, 3 + 2(4), 3 + 3(4), \ldots$

i.e., $3, 7, 3 + 8, 3 + 12, \ldots$

i.e., $3, 7, 11, 15, \ldots$

Q.5 Find the sum of the integers between 100 and 200 that are

(i) divisible by 9 (ii) not divisible by 9

Ans.

(i) The numbers (integers) between 100 and 200 which is divisible by 9 are 108, 117, 126, ... 198.

Let n be the number of terms between 100 and 200 which is divisible by 9.

Here, $a = 108, d = 117 - 108 = 9$ and $a_n = l = 198$

$\because$ $a_n = l = a + (n - 1)d$

$\Rightarrow$ $198 = 108 + (n - 1)9$

$\Rightarrow$ $90 = (n - 1)9 \Rightarrow n - 1 = 10$

$\Rightarrow$ $n = 11$

$\therefore$ Sum of terms between 100 and 200 which is divisible by 9,

$$S_n = \frac{n}{2}[2a + (n - 1)d]$$

$\Rightarrow$ $S_{11} = \frac{11}{2}[2(108) + (11 - 1)9] = \frac{11}{2}[216 + 90]$

$$= \frac{11}{2} \times 306 = 11 \times 153 = 1683$$

Hence, required sum of the integers between 100 and 200 that are divisible by 9 is 1683.

(ii) The sum of the integers between 100 and 200 which is not divisible by 9 = (sum of total numbers between 100 and 200) – (sum of total numbers between 100 and 200 which is divisible by 9). ...(i)

The integers between 100 and 200 are

101, 102, 103, ...199

Let n be the number of integers between 100 and 200.

Here, $a = 101, d = 102 - 101 = 1$ and $a_n = l = 199$

$\because$ $a_n = l = a + (n - 1)d \Rightarrow 199 = 101 + (n - 1)1$

$\Rightarrow$ $(n - 1) = 98 \Rightarrow n = 99$

$\therefore$ Sum of terms between 100 and 200, $S_n = \frac{n}{2}[2a + (n - 1)d]$

$\Rightarrow$ $S_{99} = \frac{99}{2}[2(101) + (99 - 1)1] = \frac{99}{2}[202 + 98]$

$$= \frac{99}{2} \times 300 = 99 \times 150 = 14850$$

From Eq. (i), sum of the integers between 100 and 200 which is not divisible by 9

$= 14850 - 1683$ [from part (i)]

$= 13167$

Hence, the required sum is 13167.

Q.6 The ratio of the 11th term to the 18th term of an AP is 2 : 3. Find the ratio of the 5th term to the 21st term and also the ratio of the sum of the first five terms to the sum of the first 21 terms.

Ans. Let a and d be the first term and common difference of an AP.

Given that, $a_{11} : a_{18} = 2 : 3 \Rightarrow \dfrac{a + 10d}{a + 17d} = \dfrac{2}{3}$ $[\because a_n = a + (n-1)d]$

$\Rightarrow$ $3a + 30d = 2a + 34d$

$\Rightarrow$ $a = 4d$ ...(i)

Now, $a_5 = a + 4d = 4d + 4d = 8d$ [from Eq. (i)]

and $a_{21} = a + 20d = 4d + 20d = 24d$ [from Eq. (i)]

$\therefore$ $a_5 : a_{21} = 8d : 24d = 1 : 3$

Now, sum of the first five terms, $S_5 = \dfrac{5}{2}[2a + (5-1)d]$ $\left[\because S_n = \dfrac{n}{2}[2a + (n-1)d]\right]$

$= \dfrac{5}{2}[2(4d) + 4d]$ [from Eq. (i)]

$= \dfrac{5}{2}(8d + 4d) = \dfrac{5}{2} \times 12d = 30d$

and sum of the first 21 terms, $S_{21} = \dfrac{21}{2}[2a + (21-1)d]$

$= \dfrac{21}{2}[2(4d) + 20d]$ [from Eq. (i)]

$= \dfrac{21}{2}(28d) = 294d$

So, ratio of the sum of the first five terms to the sum of the first 21 terms

$S_5 : S_{21} = 30d : 294d = 5 : 49$

Q.7 Show that the sum of an AP whose first term is a, the second term b and the last term c, is equal to $\dfrac{(a+c)(b+c-2a)}{2(b-a)}$.

Ans. Given that, the AP is $a, b, \ldots, c$.

Here, first term $= a$, common difference $= b - a$

and last term, $l = a_n = c$

$\because$ $a_n = l = a + (n-1)d$

$\Rightarrow$ $c = a + (n-1)(b-a) \Rightarrow c - a = (n-1)(b-a)$

$\Rightarrow$ $(n-1) = \dfrac{c-a}{b-a} \Rightarrow n = \dfrac{c-a}{b-a} + 1$

$\Rightarrow$ $n = \dfrac{c - a + b - a}{b-a} = \dfrac{c + b - 2a}{b-a}$ ...(i)

$\therefore$ Sum of an AP, $S_n = \frac{n}{2}[2a + (n-1)d]$

$$= \frac{(b+c-2a)}{2(b-a)}\left[2a + \left\{\frac{b+c-2a}{b-a} - 1\right\}(b-a)\right]$$

$$= \frac{b+c-2a}{2(b-a)}\left[2a + \left\{\frac{b+c-2a-b+a}{b-a}\right\}(b-a)\right]$$

$$= \frac{(b+c-2a)}{2(b-a)}\left[2a + \frac{c-a}{b-a}\cdot(b-a)\right]$$

$$= \frac{(b+c-2a)}{2(b-a)}(2a+c-a) = \frac{(b+c-2a)\cdot(a+c)}{2(b-a)}$$ **Hence proved.**

Q.8 Solve the equation $-4 + (-1) + 2 + \ldots + x = 437$.

Ans. Given equation is, $-4 - 1 + 2 + \ldots + x = 437$ ...(i)

Here, $-4 - 1 + 2 + \ldots + x$ forms an AP with first term $(a) = -4$, common difference $(d) = -1 + 4 = 3$, $a_n = l = x$

$\because$ n^{th} term of an AP, $a_n = l = a + (n-1)d$

$\Rightarrow$ $x = -4 + (n-1)3 \Rightarrow x + 4 = (n-1)3$

$\Rightarrow$ $\frac{x+4}{3} = n - 1 \Rightarrow n = \frac{x+4}{3} + 1 \Rightarrow n = \frac{x+7}{3}$ ...(ii)

$\therefore$ Sum of an AP, $S_n = \frac{n}{2}[2a + (n-1)d]$

$$S_n = \frac{x+7}{2\times 3}\left[2(-4) + \left(\frac{x+4}{3}\right)\cdot 3\right]$$

$$= \frac{x+7}{2\times 3}(-8 + x + 4) = \frac{(x+7)(x-4)}{2\times 3}$$

From Eq. (i), we get

$$S_n = 437 \Rightarrow \frac{(x+7)(x-4)}{2\times 3} = 437$$

$\Rightarrow$ $x^2 + 7x - 4x - 28 = 437 \times 2 \times 3 = 2622$

$\Rightarrow$ $x^2 + 3x - 2650 = 0$

$$x = \frac{-3 \pm \sqrt{(3)^2 - 4(1)(-2650)}}{2\times 1}$$ [by quadratic formula]

$$= \frac{-3 \pm \sqrt{9 + 10600}}{2} = \frac{-3 \pm \sqrt{10609}}{2} = \frac{-3 \pm 103}{2} = \frac{100}{2}, \frac{-106}{2}$$

$$= 50, -53$$

Here, x cannot be negative *i.e.*, $x \neq -53$.

Also for $x = -53$, n will be negative which is not possible.

Hence, the required value of x is 50.

Q.9 Jaspal Singh repays his total loan of ₹ 118000 by paying every month starting with the first instalment of ₹ 1000. If he increases the instalment by ₹ 100 every month, what amount will be paid by him in the 30th instalment? What amount of loan does he still have to pay after the 30th instalment?

Ans. Given that,

Jaspal singh takes total loan = ₹ 118000

He repays his total loan by paying every month.

His first instalment = ₹ 1000

Second instalment = ₹ 1000 + ₹ 100 = ₹ 1100

Third instalment = ₹ 1100 + ₹ 100 = ₹ 1200 and so on

Let its 30th instalment be n.

Thus, we have 1000, 1100, 1200, ... which form an AP, with first term $(a) = 1000$ and common difference $(d) = 1100 - 1000 = 100$

$\because$ nth term of an AP, $T_n = a + (n-1)\,d$

For 30th instalment, $T_{30} = 1000 + (30-1)\,100$

$= 1000 + 29 \times 100$

$= 1000 + 2900 = 3900$

So, ₹ 3900 will be paid by him in the 30th instalment.

He paid total amount upto 30 instalments in the following form

$$1000 + 1100 + 1200 + \ldots + 3900$$

First term $(a) = 1000$ and last term $(l) = 3900$

$\therefore$ Sum of 30 instalments, $S_{30} = \dfrac{30}{2}[1000 + 3900]$

$\left[\because \text{ sum of first } n \text{ terms of an AP is, } S_n = \dfrac{n}{2}[a + l], \text{ where } l = \text{last term}\right]$

$S_{30} = 15 \times 4900 =$ ₹ 73500

$\therefore$ Total amount he still have to pay after the 30th instalment

= (Amount of loan) − (Sum of 30 instalments)

= ₹ 118000 − ₹ 73500 = ₹ 44500

Hence, ₹ 44500 still have to pay after the 30th instalment.

Q.10 The students of a school decided to beautify the school on the annual day by fixing colourful flags on the straight passage of the school. They have 27 flags to be fixed at intervals of every 2 m. The flags are stored at the position of the middle most flag. Ruchi was given the responsibility of placing the flags. Ruchi kept her books where the flags were stored. She could carry only one flag at a time. How much distance she did cover in completing this job and returning back to collect her books? What is the maximum distance she travelled carrying a flag?

Ans. Given that, the students of a school decided to beautify the school on the annual day by fixing colourful flags on the straight passage of the school.

Given that, the number of flags = 27 and distance between each flag = 2 m. Also, the flags are stored at the position of the middle most flag *i.e.,* 14th flag and Ruchi was given the responsibility of placing the flags. Ruchi kept her books, where the flags were stored *i.e.,* 14th flag and she could carry only one flag at a time.

Let she placed 13 flags into her left position from middle most flag *i.e.,* 14th flag. For placing second flag and return his initial position distance travelled

$= 2 + 2 = 4$ m.

Similarly, for placing third flag and return his initial position, distance travelled $= 4 + 4 = 8$ m

For placing fourth flag and return his initial position, distance travelled

$= 6 + 6 = 12$ m.

For placing fourteenth flag and return his initial position, distance travelled

$= 26 + 26 = 52$ m

Proceed same manner into her right position from middle most flag *i.e.,* 14th flag.

Total distance travelled in that case = 52 m

Also, when Ruchi placed the last flag she return his middle most position and collect her books. This distance also included in placed the last flag.

So, these distances form a series.

$$4 + 8 + 12 + 16 + \dots + 52 \qquad \text{[for left]}$$

and

$$4 + 8 + 12 + 16 + \dots + 52 \qquad \text{[for right]}$$

$\therefore$ Total distance covered by Ruchi for placing these flags

$$= 2 \times (4 + 8 + 12 + \dots + 52)$$

$$= 2 \times \left[\frac{13}{2}\{2 \times 4 + (13 - 1) \times (8 - 4)\}\right] \qquad \left\{\begin{array}{l}\because \text{Sum of } n \text{ terms of an AP} \\ S_n = \frac{n}{2}[2a + (n-1)d]\end{array}\right\}$$

$$= 2 \times \left[\frac{13}{2}(8 + 12 \times 4)\right]$$

[$\because$ number of flags on both sides of Ruchi *i.e.,* $n = 13$]

$$= 2 \times [13(4 + 12 \times 2)] = 2 \times 13(4 + 24)$$

$$= 2 \times 13 \times 28 = 728 \text{ m}$$

Hence, the required distance is 728 m in which she did cover in completing this job and returning back to collect her books.

Now, the maximum distance she travelled carrying a flag = Distance travelled by Ruchi during placing the 14th flag in her left position or 27th flag in her right position

$$= (2 + 2 + 2 + \dots + 13 \text{ times})$$

$$= 2 \times 13 = 26 \text{ m}$$

Hence, the required maximum distance she travelled carrying a flag is 26 m.

Chapter

06 Triangles

Multiple Choice Questions (MCQs)

Choose the correct answer from the given four options in the following questions:

Q.1 In figure, if $\angle BAC = 90°$ and $AD \perp BC$. Then,

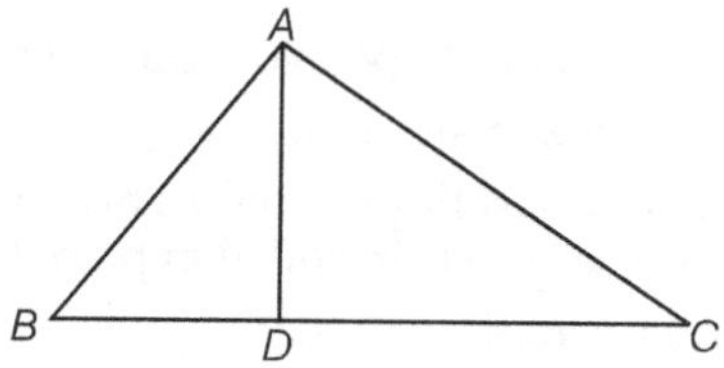

(a) $BD \cdot CD = BC^2$
(b) $AB \cdot AC = BC^2$
(c) $BD \cdot CD = AD^2$
(d) $AB \cdot AC = AD^2$

Ans. *(c)* In ΔABC,

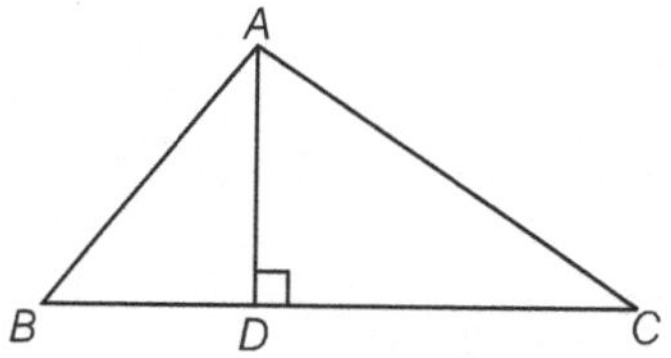

$\angle ABC + \angle ACB + \angle BAC = 180°$ (by angle sum property)

$\Rightarrow \angle ABC + \angle ACB + 90° = 180°$ ($\because \angle BAC = 90°$, given)

$\Rightarrow \angle ABC = 180° - 90° - \angle ACB$

$\Rightarrow \angle ABC = 90° - \angle ACB$

Similarly, in ΔADC, $\angle DAC = 90° - \angle ACD$

$\because \angle ACD = \angle ACB$ (common angle)

$\therefore \angle DAC = 90° - \angle ACB$

In ΔADB and ΔADC,

$\angle ADB = \angle ADC = 90°$

$\angle DBA = \angle DAC$ [each equal to $90° - \angle ACB$]

$\therefore \Delta ADB \sim \Delta CDA$ [by AA similarity criterion]

$\therefore \dfrac{BD}{AD} = \dfrac{AD}{CD}$

$\Rightarrow BD \cdot CD = AD^2$

***Q.2** The lengths of the diagonals of rhombus are 16 cm and 12 cm. Then, the length of the sides of the rhombus is

(a) 9 cm (b) 10 cm (c) 8 cm (d) 20 cm

Ans. *(b)* We know that, the diagonals of a rhombus are perpendicular bisector of each other.

Let $AC = 16\text{ cm and } BD = 12\text{ cm}$

$\therefore$ $AO = 8\text{ cm}, BO = 6\text{ cm}$

and $\angle AOB = 90^\circ$

In right angled ΔAOB,

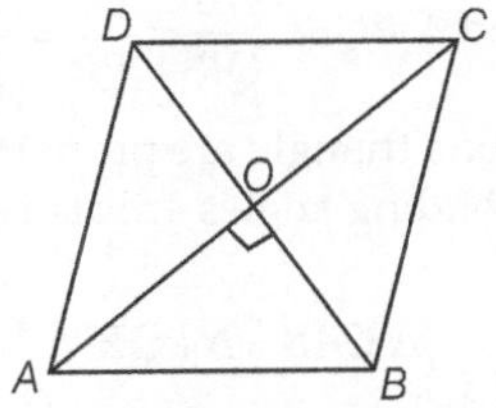

$$AB^2 = AO^2 + OB^2 \quad \text{[by Pythagoras theorem]}$$

$$\Rightarrow AB^2 = 8^2 + 6^2 = 64 + 36 = 100$$

$$\therefore AB = 10\text{ cm}$$

Q.3 If $\Delta ABC \sim \Delta EDF$ and ΔABC is not similar to ΔDEF, then which of the following is not true?

(a) $BC \cdot EF = AC \cdot FD$ (b) $AB \cdot EF = AC \cdot DE$

(c) $BC \cdot DE = AB \cdot EF$ (d) $BC \cdot DE = AB \cdot FD$

Ans. *(c)*

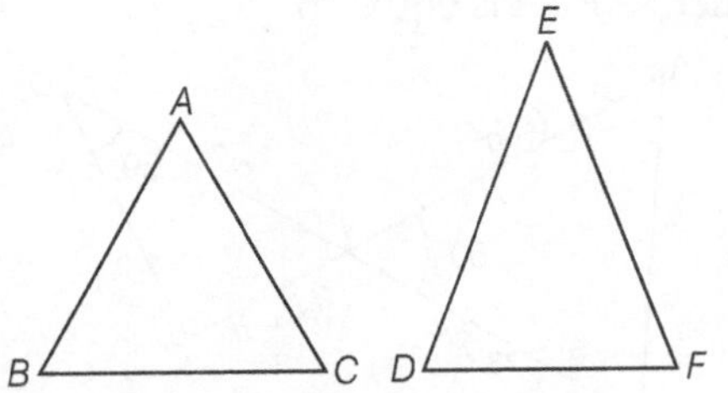

Given, $\Delta ABC \sim \Delta EDF$

$$\therefore \frac{AB}{ED} = \frac{BC}{DF} = \frac{AC}{EF}$$

Taking first two terms, we get

$$\frac{AB}{ED} = \frac{BC}{DF} \Rightarrow AB \cdot DF = ED \cdot BC$$

or $BC \cdot DE = AB \cdot DF$

So, option (d) is true.

Taking last two terms, we get

$$\frac{BC}{DF} = \frac{AC}{EF} \Rightarrow BC \cdot EF = AC \cdot DF$$

So, option (a) is also true.

Note (*) *Topics related to these question have been removed from latest NCERT.*

Taking first and last terms, we get

$$\frac{AB}{ED} = \frac{AC}{EF} \Rightarrow AB \cdot EF = ED \cdot AC$$

Hence, option (b) is true.

Q.4 If in two ΔABC and ΔPQR, $\frac{AB}{QR} = \frac{BC}{PR} = \frac{CA}{PQ}$, then

(a) $\Delta PQR \sim \Delta CAB$
(b) $\Delta PQR \sim \Delta ABC$
(c) $\Delta CBA \sim \Delta PQR$
(d) $\Delta BCA \sim \Delta PQR$

Ans. ***(a)*** Given, in two ΔABC and ΔPQR, $\frac{AB}{QR} = \frac{BC}{PR} = \frac{CA}{PQ}$

which shows that sides of one triangle are proportional to the side of the other triangle, then their corresponding angles are also equal, so by SSS similarity, triangles are similar.

i.e., $\Delta CAB \sim \Delta PQR$

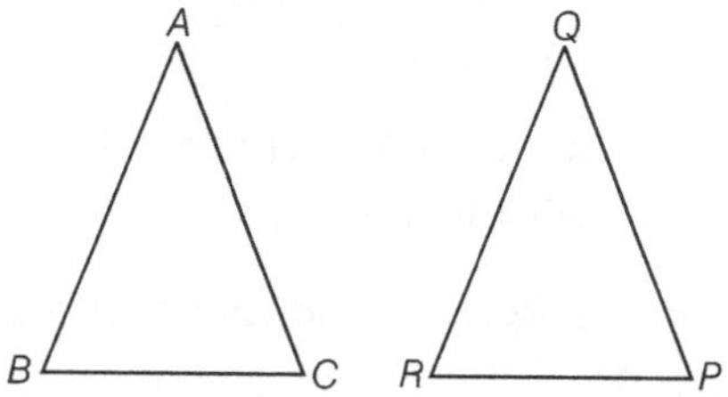

Q.5 In figure, two line segments AC and BD intersect each other at the point P such that $PA = 6$ cm, $PB = 3$ cm, $PC = 2.5$ cm, $PD = 5$ cm, $\angle APB = 50°$ and $\angle CDP = 30°$. Then, $\angle PBA$ is equal to

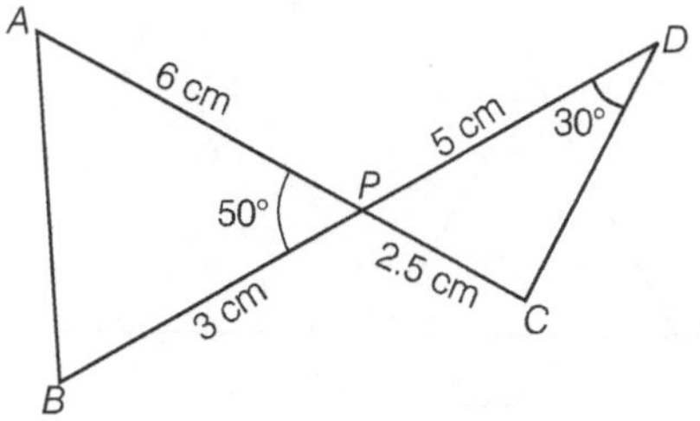

(a) 50°
(b) 30°
(c) 60°
(d) 100°

Ans. ***(d)*** In ΔAPB and ΔCPD, $\angle APB = \angle CPD = 50°$ [vertically opposite angles]

$$\frac{AP}{PD} = \frac{6}{5} \quad ...(i)$$

and

$$\frac{BP}{CP} = \frac{3}{2.5} = \frac{6}{5} \quad ...(ii)$$

From Eqs. (i) and (ii)

$$\frac{AP}{PD} = \frac{BP}{CP}$$

$\therefore$ $\Delta APB \sim \Delta DPC$ [by SAS similarity criterion]

$\therefore$ $\angle A = \angle D = 30°$ [corresponding angles of similar triangles]

In ΔAPB, $\quad \angle A + \angle B + \angle APB = 180°$ [sum of angles of a triangle = 180°]

$\Rightarrow \quad 30° + \angle B + 50° = 180°$

$\therefore \quad \angle B = 180° - (50° + 30°) = 100°$

i.e., $\quad \angle PBA = 100°$

Q.6 If in two triangles DEF and triangles PQR, $\angle D = \angle Q$ and $\angle R = \angle E$, then which of the following is not true?

(a) $\frac{EF}{PR} = \frac{DF}{PQ}$ (b) $\frac{DE}{PQ} = \frac{EF}{RP}$ (c) $\frac{DE}{QR} = \frac{DF}{PQ}$ (d) $\frac{EF}{RP} = \frac{DE}{QR}$

Ans. ***(b)*** Given, in ΔDEF and ΔPQR, $\angle D = \angle Q$, $\angle R = \angle E$

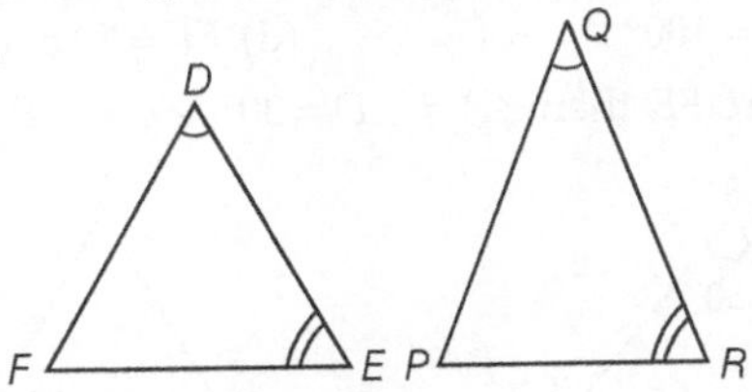

$\therefore \quad \Delta DEF \sim \Delta QRP$ [by AA similarity criterion]

$\Rightarrow \quad \angle F = \angle P$ [corresponding angles of similar triangles]

$\therefore \quad \frac{DF}{QP} = \frac{ED}{RQ} = \frac{FE}{PR}$

Q.7 In triangle ABC and triangle DEF, $\angle B = \angle E$, $\angle F = \angle C$ and $AB = 3DE$. Then, the two triangles are

(a) congruent but not similar (b) similar but not congruent

(c) neither congruent nor similar (d) congruent as well as similar

Ans. ***(b)*** In ΔABC and ΔDEF, $\angle B = \angle E$, $\angle F = \angle C$ and $AB = 3DE$

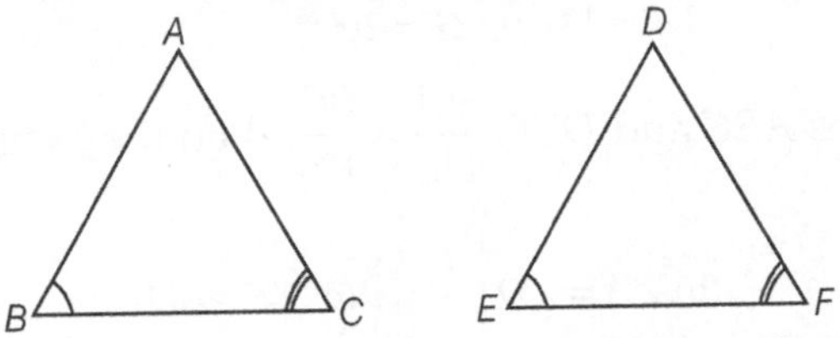

We know that, if in two triangles corresponding two angles are same, then they are similar by AA similarity criterion. Also, ΔABC and ΔDEF do not satisfy any rule of congruency, (SAS, ASA, SSS), so both triangles are not congruent.

***Q.8** It is given that $\Delta ABC \sim \Delta PQR$ with $\frac{BC}{QR} = \frac{1}{3}$, then $\frac{ar(\Delta PRQ)}{ar(\Delta BCA)}$ is equal to

(a) 9 (b) 3 (c) $\frac{1}{3}$ (d) $\frac{1}{9}$

Thinking Process Use the property of area of similar triangle.

Note (✱) *Topics related to these question have been removed from latest NCERT.*

Ans. *(a)* Given, $\Delta ABC \sim \Delta PQR$ and $\frac{BC}{QR} = \frac{1}{3} \Rightarrow \frac{QR}{BC} = \frac{3}{1}$

We know that, the ratio of the areas of two similar triangles is equal to square of the ratio of their corresponding sides.

$$\therefore \quad \frac{\text{ar}\,(\Delta PRQ)}{\text{ar}\,(\Delta BCA)} = \frac{(QR)^2}{(BC)^2} = \left(\frac{QR}{BC}\right)^2 = \left(\frac{3}{1}\right)^2 = \frac{9}{1} = 9$$

Q.9 It is given that $\Delta ABC \sim \Delta DFE$, $\angle A = 30°$, $\angle C = 50°$, $AB = 5$ cm, $AC = 8$ cm and $DF = 7.5$ cm. Then, which of the following is true?

(a) $DE = 12$ cm, $\angle F = 50°$
(b) $DE = 12$ cm, $\angle F = 100°$
(c) $EF = 12$ cm, $\angle D = 100°$
(d) $EF = 12$ cm, $\angle D = 30°$

Ans. *(b)* Given, $\Delta ABC \sim \Delta DFE$, then $\angle A = \angle D = 30°$, $\angle C = \angle E = 50°$

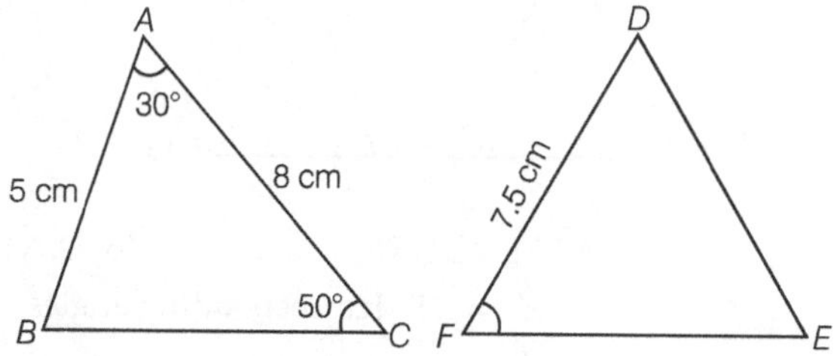

$\therefore \quad \angle B = \angle F = 180° - (30° + 50°) = 100°$ $[\because \angle B = 180° - (\angle A + \angle C)]$

Also, $AB = 5$ cm, $AC = 8$ cm and $DF = 7.5$ cm

$\therefore \quad \frac{AB}{DF} = \frac{AC}{DE}$

$\Rightarrow \quad \frac{5}{7.5} = \frac{8}{DE}$

$\therefore \quad DE = \frac{8 \times 7.5}{5} = 12$ cm

Hence, $DE = 12$ cm, $\angle F = 100°$

Q.10 If in triangles ABC and DEF, $\frac{AB}{DE} = \frac{BC}{FD}$, then they will be similar, when

(a) $\angle B = \angle E$
(b) $\angle A = \angle D$
(c) $\angle B = \angle D$
(d) $\angle A = \angle F$

Ans. *(c)* Given, in ΔABC and ΔEDF,

$$\frac{AB}{DE} = \frac{BC}{FD}$$

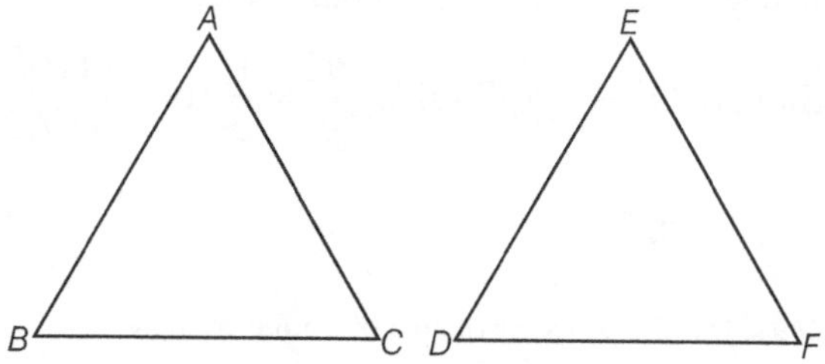

So, $\Delta ABC \sim \Delta EDF$ when $\angle B = \angle D$

***Q.11** If $\Delta ABC \sim \Delta QRP$, $\dfrac{ar(\Delta ABC)}{ar(\Delta PQR)} = \dfrac{9}{4}$, $AB = 18$ cm and $BC = 15$ cm, then PR is equal to

(a) 10 cm (b) 12 cm (c) $\dfrac{20}{3}$ cm (d) 8 cm

Ans. *(a)* Given, $\Delta ABC \sim \Delta QRP$, $AB = 18$ cm and $BC = 15$ cm.

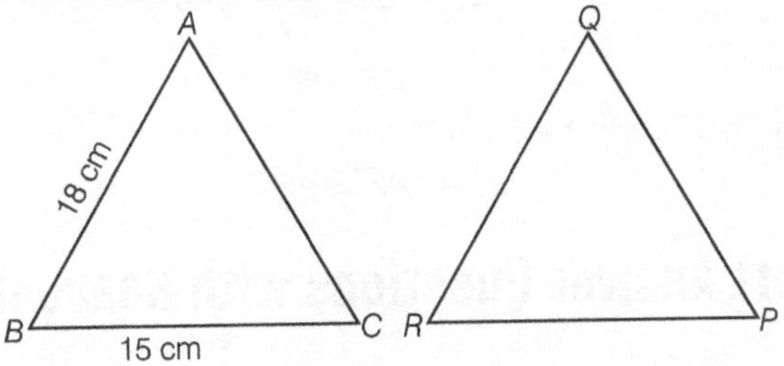

We know that, the ratio of area of two similar triangles is equal to the ratio of square of their corresponding sides.

$$\therefore \quad \frac{ar(\Delta ABC)}{ar(\Delta QRP)} = \frac{(BC)^2}{(RP)^2}$$

But given, $$\frac{ar(\Delta ABC)}{ar(\Delta PQR)} = \frac{9}{4}$$

$$\Rightarrow \quad \frac{(15)^2}{(RP)^2} = \frac{9}{4} \qquad [\because BC = 15 \text{ cm}, \text{ given}]$$

$$\Rightarrow \quad (RP)^2 = \frac{225 \times 4}{9} = 100$$

$$\therefore \quad RP = 10 \text{ cm}$$

***Q.12** If S is a point on side PQ of a ΔPQR such that $PS = QS = RS$, then

(a) $PR \cdot QR = RS^2$ (b) $QS^2 + RS^2 = QR^2$
(c) $PR^2 + QR^2 = PQ^2$ (d) $PS^2 + RS^2 = PR^2$

Ans. *(c)* Given, in ΔPQR,

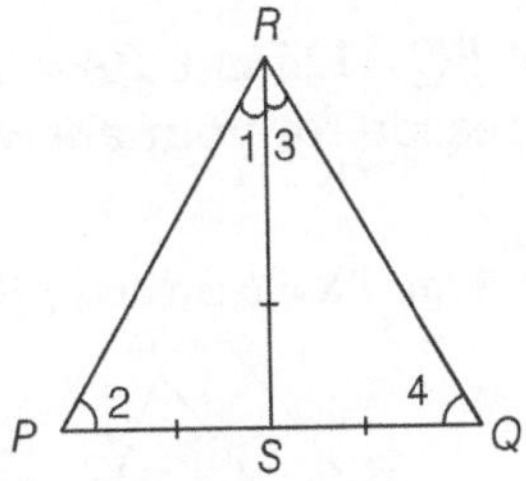

$$PS = QS = RS \qquad \text{...(i)}$$

In ΔPSR, $$PS = RS \qquad \text{[from Eq. (i)]}$$

$$\Rightarrow \quad \angle 1 = \angle 2 \qquad \text{...(ii)}$$

Similarly, in ΔRSQ,

$$\Rightarrow \quad \angle 3 = \angle 4 \qquad \text{...(iii)}$$

[corresponding angles of equal sides are equal]

Note (*) *Topics related to these question have been removed from latest NCERT.*

Now, in ΔPQR, sum of angles = 180°

$\Rightarrow \quad \angle P + \angle Q + \angle R = 180°$

$\Rightarrow \quad \angle 2 + \angle 4 + \angle 1 + \angle 3 = 180°$

$\Rightarrow \quad \angle 1 + \angle 3 + \angle 1 + \angle 3 = 180°$ [using Eqs. (ii) and (iii)]

$\Rightarrow \quad 2(\angle 1 + \angle 3) = 180°$

$\Rightarrow \quad \angle 1 + \angle 3 = \frac{180°}{2} = 90°$

$\therefore \quad \angle R = 90°$

$\therefore$ In ΔPQR, by Pythagoras theorem,

$$PR^2 + QR^2 = PQ^2$$

Short Answer Questions with Reasoning

***Q.1** Is the triangle with sides 25 cm, 5 cm and 24 cm a right triangle? Give reason for your answer.

- **Concept Insight** If the sum of square of two sides of a triangle is equal to the square of its third side, then the triangle is a right triangle.

Ans. *False*

Let $a = 25$ cm, $b = 5$ cm and $c = 24$ cm

Now, $\quad b^2 + c^2 = (5)^2 + (24)^2 = 25 + 576 = 601 \neq (25)^2$

Hence, given sides do not make a right triangle because it does not satisfy the property of Pythagoras theorem.

Q.2 It is given that $\Delta DEF \sim \Delta RPQ$. Is it true to say that $\angle D = \angle R$ and $\angle F = \angle P$? Why?

Ans. *False*

We know that, if two triangles are similar, then their corresponding angles are equal.

$\therefore \quad \angle D = \angle R, \angle E = \angle P$ and $\angle F = \angle Q$

Q.3 A and B are respectively the points on the sides PQ and PR of a triangle PQR such that $PQ = 12.5$ cm, $PA = 5$ cm, $BR = 6$ cm and $PB = 4$ cm. Is $AB \parallel QR$? Give reason for your answer.

Ans. *True*

Given, $PQ = 12.5$ cm, $PA = 5$ cm, $BR = 6$ cm and $PB = 4$ cm

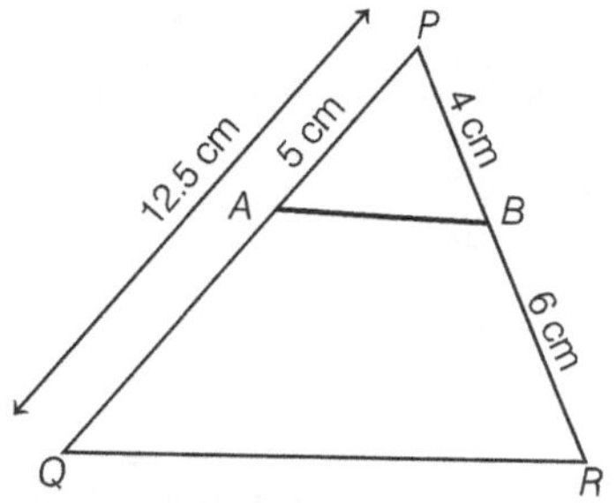

Note (*) *Topics related to these question have been removed from latest NCERT.*

Then, $QA = QP - PA = 12.5 - 5 = 7.5$ cm

Now, $\frac{PA}{AQ} = \frac{5}{7.5} = \frac{50}{75} = \frac{2}{3}$ ...(i)

and $\frac{PB}{BR} = \frac{4}{6} = \frac{2}{3}$ ...(ii)

From Eqs. (i) and (ii), we get $\frac{PA}{AQ} = \frac{PB}{BR}$

By converse of basic proportionality theorem,

$AB \parallel QR$

Q.4 In figure, BD and CE intersect each other at the point P. Is $\Delta PBC \sim \Delta PDE$? Why?

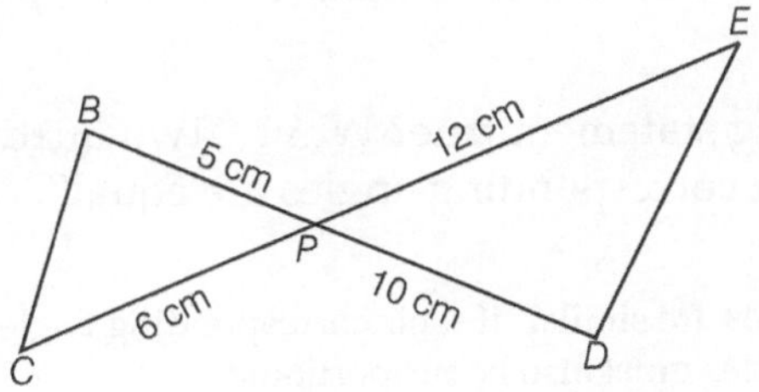

Ans. *True*

In ΔPBC and ΔPDE,

$\angle BPC = \angle EPD$ [vertically opposite angles]

Now, $\frac{PB}{PD} = \frac{5}{10} = \frac{1}{2}$ ...(i)

and $\frac{PC}{PE} = \frac{6}{12} = \frac{1}{2}$ ...(ii)

From Eqs. (i) and (ii), we get $\frac{PB}{PD} = \frac{PC}{PE}$

Since, one angle of ΔPBC is equal to one angle of ΔPDE and the sides including these angles are proportional, so both triangles are similar.

Hence, $\Delta PBC \sim \Delta PDE$, by SAS similarity criterion.

Q.5 In triangles PQR and MST, $\angle P = 55°$, $\angle Q = 25°$, $\angle M = 100°$ and $\angle S = 25°$. Is $\Delta QPR \sim \Delta TSM$? Why?

Ans. *False*

We know that, the sum of three angles of a triangle is 180°.

In ΔPQR, $\angle P + \angle Q + \angle R = 180°$

$\Rightarrow$ $55° + 25° + \angle R = 180°$

$\Rightarrow$ $\angle R = 180° - (55° + 25°) = 180° - 80° = 100°$

In ΔTSM, $\angle T + \angle S + \angle M = 180°$

$\Rightarrow$ $\angle T + \angle 25° + 100° = 180°$

$\Rightarrow \quad \angle T = 180° - (25° + 100°)$

$= 180° - 125° = 55°$

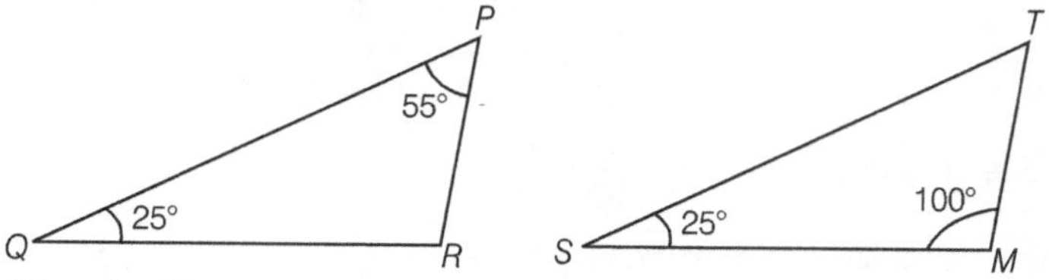

In ΔPQR and ΔTSM,

$$\angle P = \angle T, \angle Q = \angle S \text{ and } \angle R = \angle M$$

$\therefore \quad \Delta PQR \sim \Delta TSM$ [since, all corresponding angles are equal]

Hence, ΔQPR is not similar to ΔTSM, since correct correspondence is $P \leftrightarrow T$, $Q \leftrightarrow S$ and $R \leftrightarrow M$.

Q.6 Is the following statement true? Why? "Two quadrilaterals are similar, if their corresponding angles are equal".

Ans. *False*

Two quadrilaterals are similar, if their corresponding angles are equal and corresponding sides must also be proportional.

*** Q.7** Two sides and the perimeter of one triangle are respectively three times the corresponding sides and the perimeter of the other triangle. Are the two triangles similar? Why?

Ans. *True*

Here, the corresponding two sides and the perimeters of two triangles are proportional, then third side of both triangles will also in proportion.

Q.8 If in two right triangles, one of the acute angles of one triangle is equal to an acute angle of the other triangle, can you say that two triangles will be similar? Why?

Ans. *True*

Let two right angled triangles be ΔABC and ΔPQR.

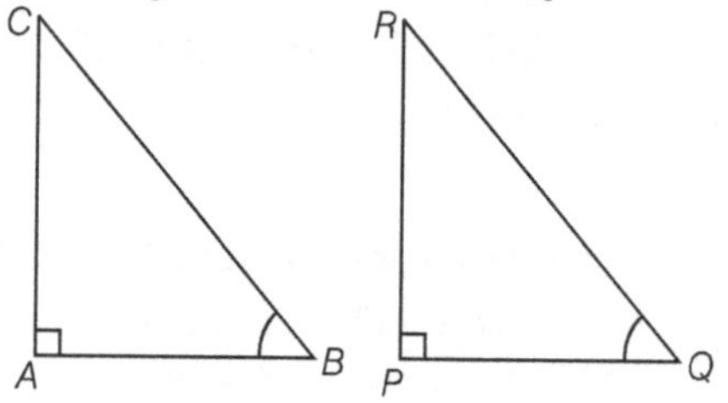

In which $\quad \angle A = \angle P = 90°$

and $\quad \angle B = \angle Q =$ acute angle

Then, by AA similarity criterion, $\Delta ABC \sim \Delta PQR$

Note (*) *Topics related to these question have been removed from latest NCERT.*

***Q.9** The ratio of the corresponding altitudes of two similar triangles is $\frac{3}{5}$. Is it correct to say that ratio of their areas is $\frac{6}{5}$? Why?

Ans. *False,* By the property of area of two similar triangles,

$$\left(\frac{\text{Area}_1}{\text{Area}_2}\right)=\left(\frac{\text{Altitude}_1}{\text{Altitude}_2}\right)^2$$

$$\Rightarrow \quad \left(\frac{\text{Area}_1}{\text{Area}_2}\right)=\left(\frac{3}{5}\right)^2 \qquad \left[\because \frac{\text{altitude}_1}{\text{altitude}_2}=\frac{3}{5}, \text{(given)}\right]$$

$$=\frac{9}{25}\neq\frac{6}{5}$$

So, given statement is not correct.

Mistake Alert ! *Students may miscalculate the ratio of areas based on side lengths, especially when they confuse side ratios with area ratios.*

Q.10 D is a point on side QR of ΔPQR such that $PD \perp QR$. Will it be correct to say that $\Delta PQD \sim \Delta RPD$? Why?

Ans. *False*

In ΔPQD and ΔRPD,

$PD = PD$ [common side]

$\angle PDQ = \angle PDR$ [each 90°]

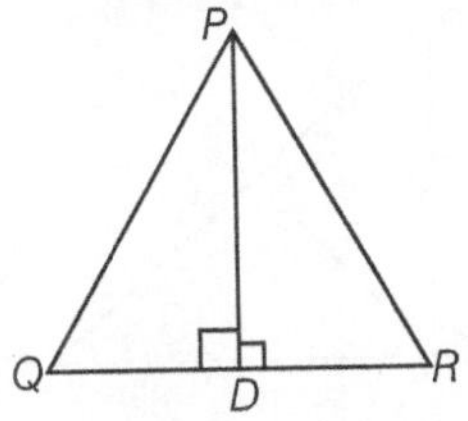

Here, no other sides or angles are equal, so we can say that ΔPQD is not similar to ΔRPD.

Q.11 In figure, if $\angle D = \angle C$, then it is true that $\Delta ADE \sim \Delta ACB$? Why?

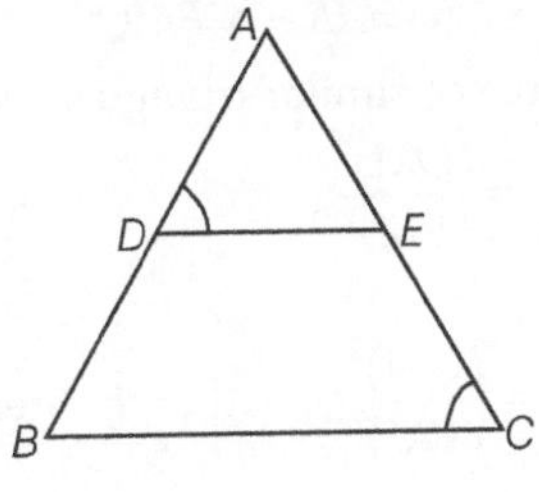

Ans. *True*

In ΔADE and ΔACB,

$\angle A = \angle A$ [common angle]

$\angle D = \angle C$ [given]

$\therefore \quad \Delta ADE \sim \Delta ACB$ [by AA similarity criterion]

Note (*) *Topics related to these question have been removed from latest NCERT.*

Q.12 Is it true to say that, if in two triangles, an angle of one triangle is equal to an angle of another triangle and two sides of one triangle are proportional to the two sides of the other triangle, then the triangles are similar? Give reason for your answer.

Ans. *False*

Because, according to SAS similarity criterion, if one angle of a triangle is equal to one angle of the other triangle and the sides including these angles are proportional, then the two triangles are similar.

Here, one angle and two sides of two triangles are equal but these sides not including equal angle, so given statement is not correct.

Short Answer Questions

* **Q.1** In a ΔPQR, $PR^2 - PQ^2 = QR^2$ and M is a point on side PR such that $QM \perp PR$. Prove that $QM^2 = PM \times MR$.

Ans. **Given** In ΔPQR, $PR^2 - PQ^2 = QR^2$ and $QM \perp PR$

To prove $QM^2 = PM \times MR$

Proof Since, $PR^2 - PQ^2 = QR^2$

$\Rightarrow$ $PR^2 = PQ^2 + QR^2$

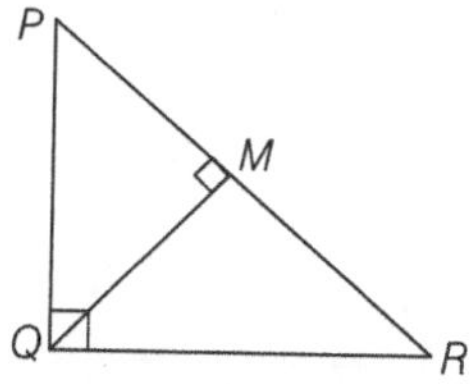

So, ΔPQR is right angled triangle at Q.

In ΔQMR and ΔPMQ, $\angle M = \angle M$ [each 90°]

$\angle MQR = \angle QPM$ [each equal to $90° - \angle R$]

$\therefore$ $\Delta QMR \sim \Delta PMQ$ [by AA similarity criterion]

Now, using property of area of similar triangles, we get

$$\frac{\text{ar}(\Delta QMR)}{\text{ar}(\Delta PMQ)} = \frac{(QM)^2}{(PM)^2}$$

$$\Rightarrow \quad \frac{\frac{1}{2} \times RM \times QM}{\frac{1}{2} \times PM \times QM} = \frac{(QM)^2}{(PM)^2} \quad \left[\because \text{area of triangle} = \frac{1}{2} \times \text{base} \times \text{height}\right]$$

$$\Rightarrow \quad \frac{RM \times (PM)^2}{PM} = QM^2$$

$\Rightarrow$ $QM^2 = PM \times RM$ **Hence proved.**

Note (*) *Topics related to these question have been removed from latest NCERT.*

Q.2 Find the value of x for which $DE \parallel AB$ in given figure.

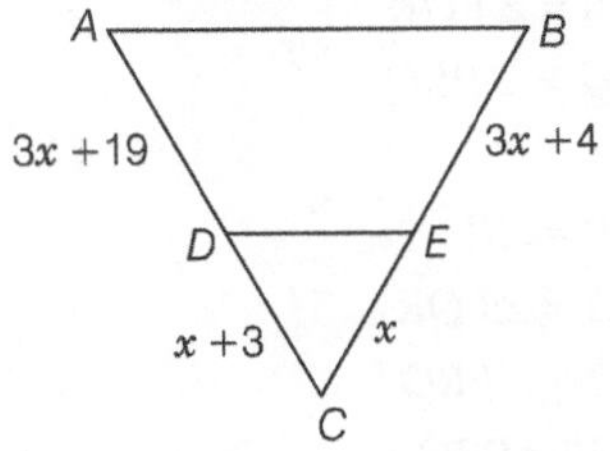

Thinking Process Use the basic proportionality theorem to get required value of x.

i.e., $$\frac{CD}{AD} = \frac{CE}{BE}$$

Ans. Given, $$DE \parallel AB$$

$\therefore$ $$\frac{CD}{AD} = \frac{CE}{BE} \quad \text{[by basic proportionality theorem]}$$

$\Rightarrow$ $$\frac{x+3}{3x+19} = \frac{x}{3x+4}$$

$\Rightarrow$ $$(x+3)(3x+4) = x(3x+19)$$

$\Rightarrow$ $$3x^2 + 4x + 9x + 12 = 3x^2 + 19x$$

$\Rightarrow$ $$19x - 13x = 12$$

$\Rightarrow$ $$6x = 12$$

$\therefore$ $$x = \frac{12}{6} = 2$$

Hence, the required value of x is 2.

Q.3 In figure, if $\angle 1 = \angle 2$ and $\Delta NSQ \cong \Delta MTR$, then prove that $\Delta PTS \sim \Delta PRQ$.

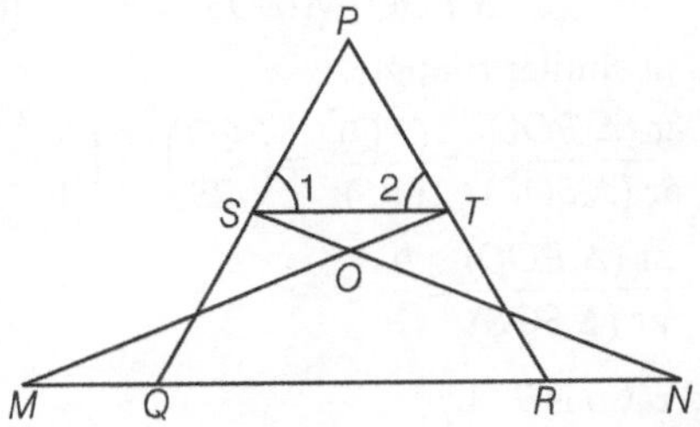

Thinking Process Firstly, show that $ST \parallel QR$ with the help of given information, then use AAA similarity criterion to prove required result.

Ans. Given $\Delta NSQ \cong \Delta MTR$ and $\angle 1 = \angle 2$

To prove $\Delta PTS \sim \Delta PRQ$

Proof Since, $\Delta NSQ \cong \Delta MTR$

So, $SQ = TR$ ...(i)

Also, $\angle 1 = \angle 2 \Rightarrow PT = PS$ ...(ii)

[since, sides opposite to equal angles are also equal]

From Eqs. (i) and (ii), we get $\frac{PS}{SQ} = \frac{PT}{TR}$

$\Rightarrow \quad ST \parallel QR$ [by converse of basic proportionality theorem]

$\therefore \quad \angle 1 = \angle PQR$ [corresponding angles]

and $\quad \angle 2 = \angle PRQ$ [corresponding angle]

In ΔPTS and ΔPRQ,

$\angle P = \angle P$ [common angles]

$\angle 1 = \angle PQR$

$\angle 2 = \angle PRQ$

$\therefore \quad \Delta PTS \sim \Delta PRQ$ [by AAA similarity criterion]

Hence proved.

***Q.4** Diagonals of a trapezium $PQRS$ intersect each other at the point O, $PQ \parallel RS$ and $PQ = 3\,RS$. Find the ratio of the areas of triangles POQ and ROS.

Thinking Process Firstly, show that $\Delta\, POQ$ and $\Delta\, ROS$ are similar by AA similarity, then use property of area of similar triangle to get required ratio.

Ans. Given $PQRS$ is a trapezium in which $PQ \parallel RS$ and $PQ = 3\,RS$

$$\Rightarrow \quad \frac{PQ}{RS} = \frac{3}{1} \quad \ldots(i)$$

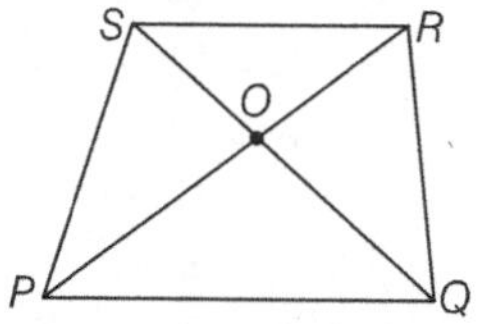

In ΔPOQ and ΔROS, $\angle\, SOR = \angle\, QOP$ [vertically opposite angles]

$\angle\, SRP = \angle\, RPQ$ [alternate angles]

$\therefore \quad \Delta\, POQ \sim \Delta\, ROS$ [by AA similarity criterion]

By property of area of similar triangle,

$$\frac{\text{ar}(\Delta\, POQ)}{\text{ar}(\Delta\, SOR)} = \frac{(PQ)^2}{(RS)^2} = \left(\frac{PQ}{RS}\right)^2 = \left(\frac{3}{1}\right)^2 \quad \text{[from Eq. (i)]}$$

$$\Rightarrow \quad \frac{\text{ar}(\Delta\, POQ)}{\text{ar}(\Delta\, SOR)} = \frac{9}{1}$$

Hence, the required ratio is 9 : 1.

Q.5 In figure, if $AB \parallel DC$ and AC and PQ intersect each other at the point O, prove that $OA \cdot CQ = OC \cdot AP$.

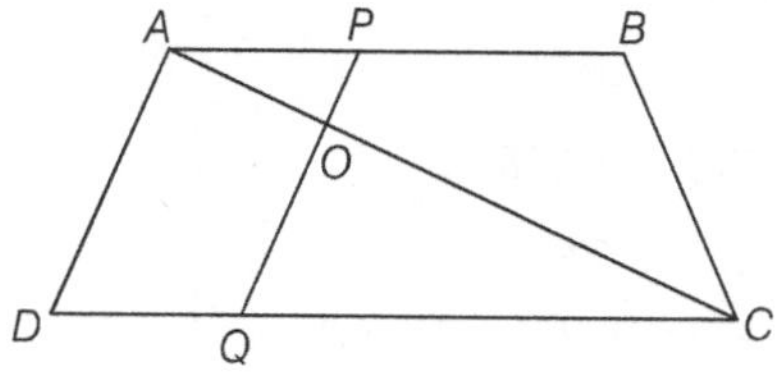

Note (*) *Topics related to these question have been removed from latest NCERT.*

Ans. **Given** AC and PQ intersect each other at the point O and $AB \parallel DC$.

To prove $OA \cdot CQ = OC \cdot AP$

Proof In ΔAOP and ΔCOQ, $\angle AOP = \angle COQ$ [vertically opposite angles]

$\angle APO = \angle CQO$

[since, $AB \parallel DC$ and PQ is transversal, so alternate angles]

$\therefore$ $\Delta AOP \sim \Delta COQ$ [by AA similarity criterion]

Then, $\frac{OA}{OC} = \frac{AP}{CQ}$ [since, corresponding sides are proportional]

$\Rightarrow$ $OA \cdot CQ = OC \cdot AP$ **Hence proved.**

***Q.6** Find the altitude of an equilateral triangle of side 8 cm.

Ans. Let ABC be an equilateral triangle of side 8 cm *i.e.,* $AB = BC = CA = 8$ cm.

Draw altitude AD which is perpendicular to BC. Then, D is the mid-point of BC.

$\therefore$ $BD = CD = \frac{1}{2} BC = \frac{8}{2} = 4$ cm

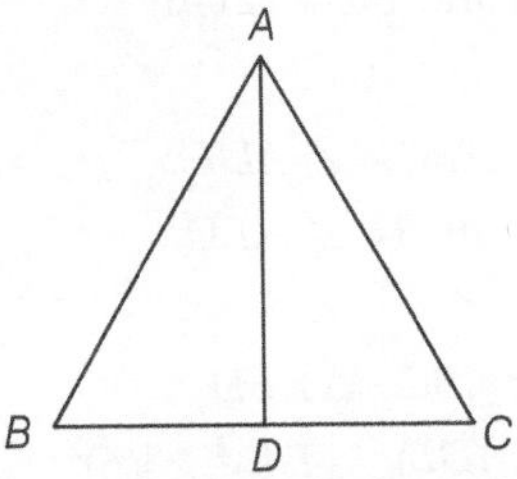

Now, $AB^2 = AD^2 + BD^2$ [by Pythagoras theorem]

$\Rightarrow$ $(8)^2 = AD^2 + (4)^2$

$\Rightarrow$ $64 = AD^2 + 16$

$\Rightarrow$ $AD^2 = 64 - 16 = 48$

$\Rightarrow$ $AD = \sqrt{48} = 4\sqrt{3}$ cm.

Hence, altitude of the given equilateral triangle is $4\sqrt{3}$ cm.

Q.7 If $\Delta ABC \sim \Delta DEF$, $AB = 4$ cm, $DE = 6$, $EF = 9$ cm and $FD = 12$ cm, find the perimeter of ΔABC.

Ans. Given $AB = 4$ cm, $DE = 6$ cm and $EF = 9$ cm and $FD = 12$ cm

Also, $\Delta ABC \sim \Delta DEF$

$\therefore$ $\frac{AB}{ED} = \frac{BC}{EF} = \frac{AC}{DF} \Rightarrow \frac{4}{6} = \frac{BC}{9} = \frac{AC}{12}$

On taking first two terms, we get

$$\frac{4}{6} = \frac{BC}{9}$$

$\Rightarrow$ $BC = \frac{4 \times 9}{6} = 6$ cm

Note (*) *Topics related to these question have been removed from latest NCERT.*

On taking last two terms, we get

$$\frac{BC}{9} = \frac{AC}{12}$$

$$\Rightarrow \quad \frac{6}{9} = \frac{AC}{12} \Rightarrow AC = \frac{6 \times 12}{9} = 8 \text{ cm}$$

Now, perimeter of $\Delta ABC = AB + BC + AC$

$$= 4 + 6 + 8 = 18 \text{ cm}$$

***Q.8** In figure, if $DE \parallel BC$, find the ratio of ar (ΔADE) and ar $(DECB)$.

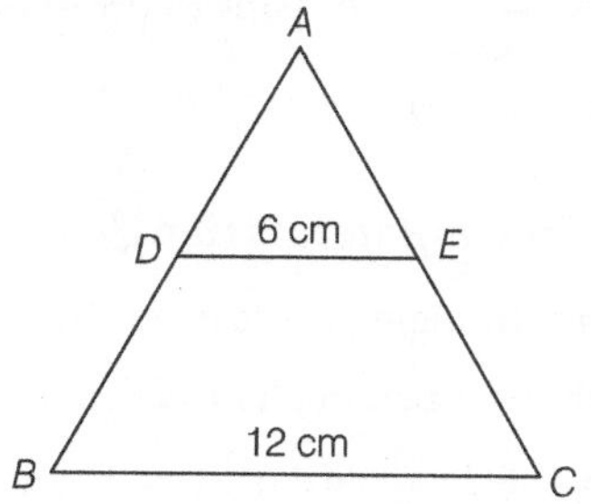

Ans. Given, $DE \parallel BC$, $DE = 6$ cm and $BC = 12$ cm

In ΔABC and ΔADE,

$\angle ABC = \angle ADE$ [corresponding angle]

$\angle ACB = \angle AED$ [corresponding angle]

and $\angle A = \angle A$ [common angle]

$\therefore$ $\Delta ABC \sim \Delta AED$ [by AAA similarity criterion]

Then, $$\frac{\text{ar}(\Delta ADE)}{\text{ar}(\Delta ABC)} = \frac{(DE)^2}{(BC)^2} = \frac{(6)^2}{(12)^2} = \left(\frac{1}{2}\right)^2$$

$$\Rightarrow \quad \frac{\text{ar}(\Delta ADE)}{\text{ar}(\Delta ABC)} = \left(\frac{1}{2}\right)^2 = \frac{1}{4}$$

Let ar $(\Delta ADE) = k$, then ar $(\Delta ABC) = 4k$

Now, ar $(DECB)$ = ar (ABC) − ar $(ADE) = 4k - k = 3k$

$\therefore$ Required ratio = ar (ADE) : ar $(DECB) = k : 3k = 1 : 3$

Q.9 $ABCD$ is a trapezium in which $AB \parallel DC$ and P and Q are points on AD and BC respectively, such that $PQ \parallel DC$. If $PD = 18$ cm, $BQ = 35$ cm and $QC = 15$ cm, find AD.

Ans. Given, a trapezium $ABCD$ in which $AB \parallel DC$. P and Q are points on AD and BC, respectively such that $PQ \parallel DC$. Thus, $AB \parallel PQ \parallel DC$.

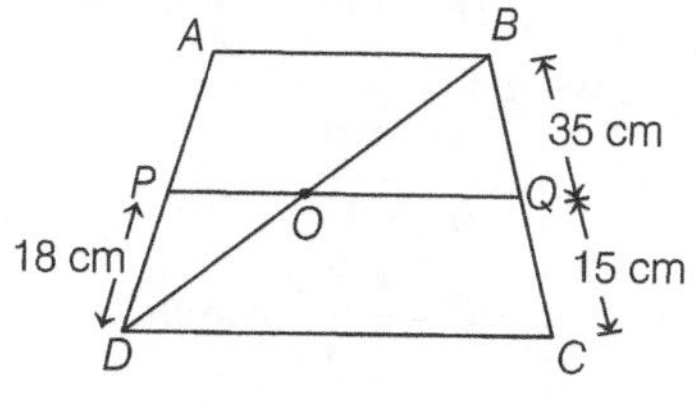

Note (✱) *Topics related to these question have been removed from latest NCERT.*

Join BD.

In ΔABD, $PO \parallel AB$ [$\because PQ \parallel AB$]

By basic proportionality theorem, $\frac{DP}{AP} = \frac{DO}{OB}$ ...(i)

In ΔBDC, $OQ \parallel DC$ [$\because PQ \parallel DC$]

By basic proportionality theorem,

$$\frac{BQ}{QC} = \frac{OB}{OD}$$

$\Rightarrow$ $\frac{QC}{BQ} = \frac{OD}{OB}$ ...(ii)

From Eqs. (i) and (ii), we get $\frac{DP}{AP} = \frac{QC}{BQ}$

$\Rightarrow$ $\frac{18}{AP} = \frac{15}{35} \Rightarrow AP = \frac{18 \times 35}{15} = 42$

$\therefore$ $AD = AP + DP = 42 + 18 = 60$ cm

***Q.10** Corresponding sides of two similar triangles are in the ratio of 2 : 3. If the area of the smaller triangle is 48 cm^2, find the area of the larger triangle.

Thinking Process Use the property area of similar triangle to get required area.

Ans. Given, ratio of corresponding sides of two similar triangles = 2 : 3 or $\frac{2}{3}$

Area of smaller triangle = 48 cm^2

By the property of area of two similar triangle,

Ratio of area of both triangles = (Ratio of their corresponding sides)^2

i.e., $\frac{\text{ar (smaller triangle)}}{\text{ar (larger triangle)}} = \left(\frac{2}{3}\right)^2$

$\Rightarrow$ $\frac{48}{\text{ar (larger triangle)}} = \frac{4}{9}$

$\Rightarrow$ $\text{ar (larger triangle)} = \frac{48 \times 9}{4} = 12 \times 9 = 108 \text{ cm}^2$

Q.11 In a triangle PQR, N is a point on PR, such that $QN \perp PR$. If $PN \cdot NR = QN^2$, prove that $\angle PQR = 90°$.

Ans. **Given** ΔPQR, N is a point on PR, such that $QN \perp PR$

and $PN \cdot NR = QN^2$

To prove $\angle PQR = 90°$

Proof We have, $PN \cdot NR = QN^2$

$\Rightarrow$ $PN \cdot NR = QN \cdot QN$

$\Rightarrow$ $\frac{PN}{QN} = \frac{QN}{NR}$ ...(i)

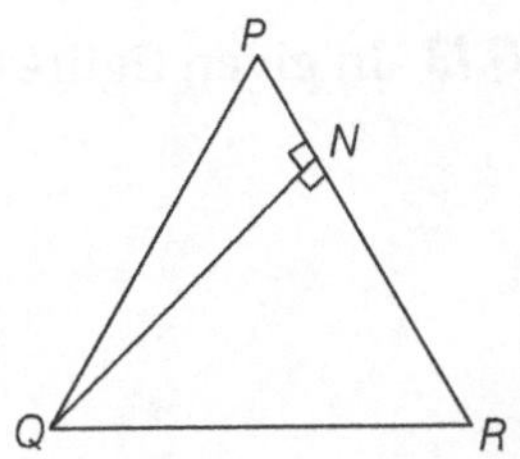

In ΔQNP and ΔRNQ, $\frac{PN}{QN} = \frac{QN}{NR}$

Note (*) *Topics related to these question have been removed from latest NCERT.*

and $\angle PNQ = \angle RNQ$ [each equal to 90°]

$\therefore$ $\Delta QNP \sim \Delta RNQ$ [by SAS similarity criterion]

$\therefore$ $\angle PQN = \angle QRN$ ...(iii)

$\angle RQN = \angle QPN$ ...(iv)

On adding Eqs. (iii) and (iv), we get

$$\angle PQN + \angle RQN = \angle QRN + \angle QPN$$

$\Rightarrow$ $\angle PQR = \angle QRN + \angle QPN$ ...(v)

We know that, sum of angles of a triangle = 180°

In ΔPQR, $\angle PQR + \angle QPR + \angle QRP = 180°$

$\Rightarrow$ $\angle PQR + \angle QPN + \angle QRN = 180°$ [$\because \angle QPR = \angle QPN$ and $\angle QRP = \angle QRN$]

$\Rightarrow$ $\angle PQR + \angle PQR = 180°$ [by using Eq. (i)]

$\Rightarrow$ $2\angle PQR = 180°$

$\Rightarrow$ $\angle PQR = \dfrac{180°}{2} = 90°$

$\therefore$ $\angle PQR = 90°$ **Hence proved.**

***Q.12** Areas of two similar triangles are 36 cm^2 and 100 cm^2. If the length of a side of the larger triangle is 20 cm, find the length of the corresponding side of the smaller triangle.

- **Concept Insight** In this question, we will use concept of area of similar triangle.

Ans. Given, area of smaller triangle = 36 cm^2 and area of larger triangle = 100 cm^2

Also, length of a side of the larger triangle = 20 cm

Let length of the corresponding side of the smaller triangle = x cm

By property of area of similar triangle,

$$\frac{\text{ar (larger triangle)}}{\text{ar (smaller triangle)}} = \frac{(\text{Side of larger triangle})^2}{\text{Side of smaller triangle}^2}$$

$\Rightarrow$ $\dfrac{100}{36} = \dfrac{(20)^2}{x^2}$

$\Rightarrow$ $x^2 = \dfrac{(20)^2 \times 36}{100}$

$\Rightarrow$ $x^2 = \dfrac{400 \times 36}{100} = 144$

$\therefore$ $x = \sqrt{144} = 12$ cm

Hence, the length of corresponding side of the smaller triangle is 12 cm.

Q.13 In given figure, if $\angle ACB = \angle CDA$, $AC = 8$ cm and $AD = 3$ cm, find BD.

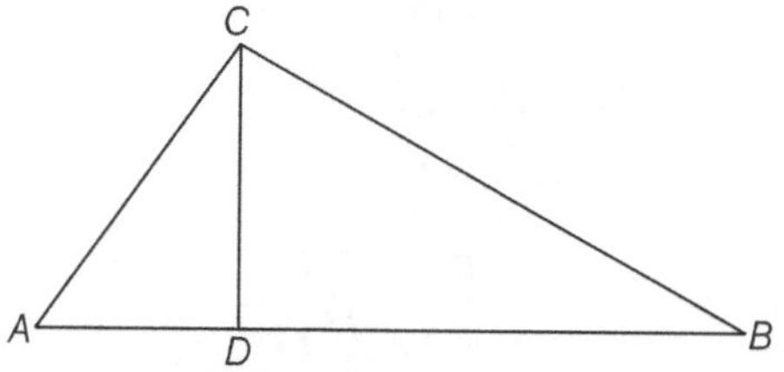

Note (*) *Topics related to these question have been removed from latest NCERT.*

Ans. Given, $AC = 8$ cm, $AD = 3$ cm and $\angle ACB = \angle CDA$

In ΔADC and ΔACB,

$$\angle A = \angle A \quad \text{[common angle]}$$

$$\angle ACB = \angle CDA \quad \text{[given]}$$

$$\therefore \quad \Delta ADC \sim \Delta ACB \quad \text{[by AA similarity criterion]}$$

$$\Rightarrow \quad \frac{AC}{AD} = \frac{AB}{AC} \quad \text{[corresponding sides are proportional]}$$

$$\Rightarrow \quad \frac{8}{3} = \frac{AB}{8}$$

$$\Rightarrow \quad AB = \frac{8 \times 8}{3}$$

$$\Rightarrow \quad AB = \frac{64}{3} \text{ cm}$$

$$\therefore \quad BD = AB - AD = \frac{64}{3} - 3 = \frac{64 - 9}{3} = \frac{55}{3} \text{ cm}$$

Q.14 A 15 m high tower casts a shadow 24 m long at a certain time and at the same time, a telephone pole casts a shadow 16 m long. Find the height of the telephone pole.

Thinking Process Firstly, draw the figure according to given conditions, then show that both triangles are similar by AA similarity criterion and then use ratio of sides of both triangles to get required length.

Ans. Let $BC = 15$ m be the tower and its shadow AB is 24 m. At that time $\angle CAB = \theta$. Again, let $EF = h$ be a telephone pole and its shadow $DE = 16$ m. At the same time $\angle EDF = \theta$.

Here, ΔABC and ΔDEF both are right angled triangles.

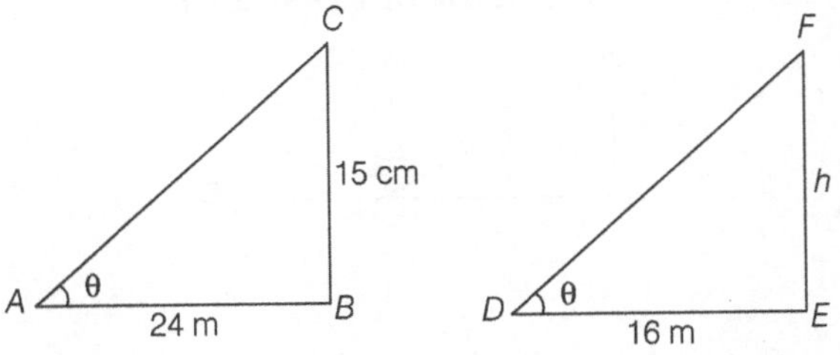

In ΔABC and ΔDEF,

$$\angle CAB = \angle EDF = \theta$$

$$\angle B = \angle E \quad \text{[each 90°]}$$

$$\therefore \quad \Delta ABC \sim \Delta DEF \quad \text{[by AA similarity criterion]}$$

$$\text{Then,} \quad \frac{AB}{DE} = \frac{BC}{EF} \quad \text{[corresponding sides are proportional]}$$

$$\Rightarrow \quad \frac{24}{16} = \frac{15}{h}$$

$$\therefore \quad h = \frac{15 \times 16}{24} = 10$$

Hence, the height of the telephone pole is 10 m.

*** Q.15** Foot of a 10 m long ladder leaning against a vertical wall is 6 m away from the base of the wall. Find the height of the point on the wall where the top of the ladder reaches.

Thinking Process Firstly, draw the figure according to given conditions and then apply Pythagoras theorem to get required height.

Ans. Let AB be a vertical wall and $AC = 10$ m is a ladder. The top of the ladder reaches to A and distance of ladder from the base of the wall BC is 6 m.

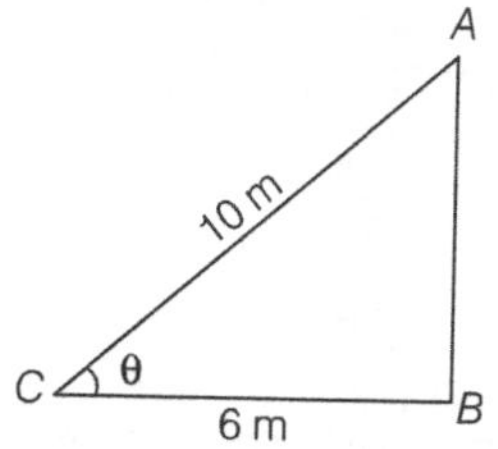

In right angled ΔABC, $AC^2 = AB^2 + BC^2$ [by Pythagoras theorem]

$\Rightarrow (10)^2 = AB^2 + (6)^2$

$\Rightarrow 100 = AB^2 + 36$

$\Rightarrow AB^2 = 100 - 36 = 64$

$\therefore AB = \sqrt{64} = 8$ cm

Hence, the height of the point on the wall where the top of the ladder reaches is 8 cm.

Long Answer Questions

Q.1 In given figure, if $\angle A = \angle C$, $AB = 6$ cm, $BP = 15$ cm, $AP = 12$ cm and $CP = 4$ cm, then find the lengths of PD and CD.

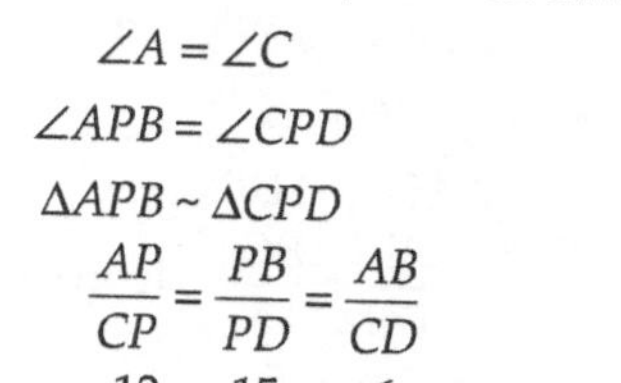

Ans. Given, $\angle A = \angle C$, $AB = 6$ cm, $BP = 15$ cm, $AP = 12$ cm and $CP = 4$ cm

In ΔAPB and ΔCPD, $\angle A = \angle C$ [given]

$\angle APB = \angle CPD$ [vertically opposite angles]

$\therefore \Delta APB \sim \Delta CPD$ [by AA similarity criterion]

$$\Rightarrow \frac{AP}{CP} = \frac{PB}{PD} = \frac{AB}{CD}$$

$$\Rightarrow \frac{12}{4} = \frac{15}{PD} = \frac{6}{CD}$$

On taking first two terms, we get

$$\frac{12}{4} = \frac{15}{PD}$$

Note (*) *Topics related to these question have been removed from latest NCERT.*

$$\Rightarrow \qquad PD = \frac{15 \times 4}{12} = 5 \text{ cm}$$

On taking first and last term, we get

$$\frac{12}{4} = \frac{6}{CD}$$

$$\Rightarrow \qquad CD = \frac{6 \times 4}{12} = 2 \text{ cm}$$

Hence, length of $PD = 5$ cm and length of $CD = 2$ cm.

Q.2 It is given that $\Delta ABC \sim \Delta EDF$ such that $AB = 5$ cm, $AC = 7$ cm, $DF = 15$ cm and $DE = 12$ cm. Find the lengths of the remaining sides of the triangles.

Thinking Process Use the property of similar triangles *i.e.*, the corresponding sides are in the same ratio and then simplify.

Ans. Given, $\Delta ABC \sim \Delta EDF$, so the corresponding sides of ΔABC and ΔEDF are in the same ratio.

i.e.,
$$\frac{AB}{ED} = \frac{AC}{EF} = \frac{BC}{DF} \qquad \text{...(i)}$$

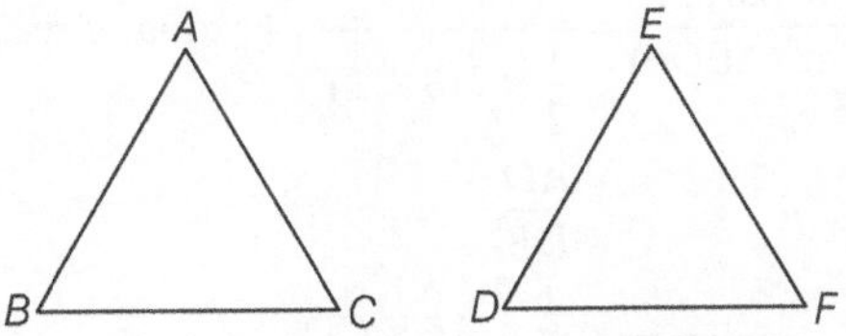

Also, $AB = 5$ cm, $AC = 7$ cm,
$DF = 15$ cm and $DE = 12$ cm

On putting these values in Eq. (i), we get

$$\frac{5}{12} = \frac{7}{EF} = \frac{BC}{15}$$

On taking first and second terms, we get

$$\frac{5}{12} = \frac{7}{EF}$$

$$\Rightarrow \qquad EF = \frac{7 \times 12}{5} = 16.8 \text{ cm}$$

On taking first and third terms, we get

$$\frac{5}{12} = \frac{BC}{15}$$

$$\Rightarrow \qquad BC = \frac{5 \times 15}{12} = 6.25 \text{ cm}$$

Hence, lengths of the remaining sides of the triangles are $EF = 16.8$ cm and $BC = 6.25$ cm.

Q.3 Prove that, if a line is drawn parallel to one side of a triangle to intersect the other two sides, then the two sides are divided in the same ratio.

Ans. Let a ΔABC in which a line DE parallel to BC intersects AB at D and AC at E.

To prove DE divides the two sides in the same ratio.

i.e., $$\frac{AD}{DB} = \frac{AE}{EC}$$

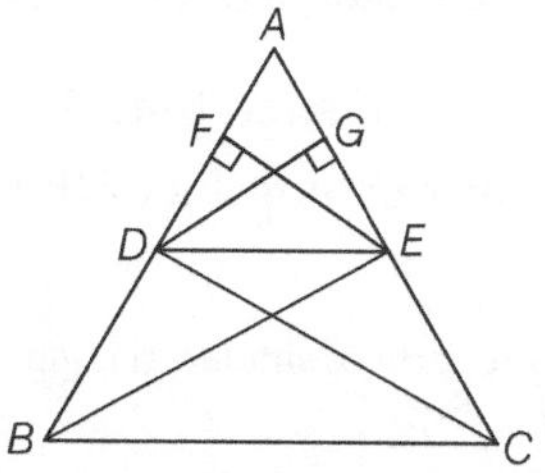

Construction Join BE, CD and draw $EF \perp AB$ and $DG \perp AC$.

Proof Here, $$\frac{\text{ar}(\Delta ADE)}{\text{ar}(\Delta BDE)} = \frac{\frac{1}{2} \times AD \times EF}{\frac{1}{2} \times DB \times EF} \quad \left[\because \text{area of triangle} = \frac{1}{2} \times \text{base} \times \text{height}\right]$$

$$= \frac{AD}{DB} \quad \text{...(i)}$$

Similarly, $$\frac{\text{ar}(\Delta ADE)}{\text{ar}(\Delta DEC)} = \frac{\frac{1}{2} \times AE \times GD}{\frac{1}{2} \times EC \times GD} = \frac{AE}{EC} \quad \text{...(ii)}$$

Now, since, ΔBDE and ΔDEC lie between the same parallel lines DE and BC and on the same base DE.

So, $$\text{ar}(\Delta BDE) = \text{ar}(\Delta DEC) \quad \text{...(iii)}$$

From Eqs. (i), (ii) and (iii), we get

$$\frac{AD}{DB} = \frac{AE}{EC}$$ **Hence proved.**

Q.4 In the given figure, if $PQRS$ is a parallelogram and $AB \parallel PS$, then prove that $OC \parallel SR$.

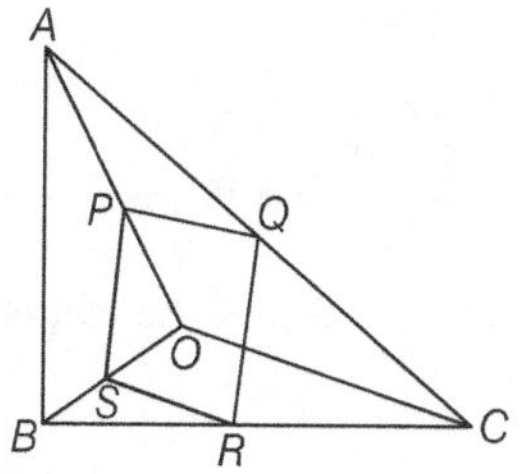

Ans. Given $PQRS$ is a parallelogram, so $PQ \parallel SR$ and $PS \parallel QR$. Also, $AB \parallel PS$.

To prove $OC \parallel SR$

Proof in ΔOPS and ΔOAB, $PS \parallel AB$

$$\angle POS = \angle AOB \quad \text{[common angle]}$$

$$\angle OSP = \angle OBA \quad \text{[corresponding angles]}$$

$$\therefore \quad \Delta OPS \sim \Delta OAB \quad \text{[by AA similarity criterion]}$$

Then,

$$\frac{PS}{AB} = \frac{OS}{OB} \quad \text{...(i)}$$

In ΔCQR and ΔCAB, $QR \parallel PS \parallel AB$

$$\angle QCR = \angle ACB \quad \text{[common angle]}$$

$$\angle CRQ = \angle CBA \quad \text{[corresponding angles]}$$

$$\therefore \quad \Delta CQR \sim \Delta CAB \quad \text{[by AA similarity criterion]}$$

Then,

$$\frac{QR}{AB} = \frac{CR}{CB}$$

$$\Rightarrow \quad \frac{PS}{AB} = \frac{CR}{CB} \quad \text{...(ii)}$$

[$\because$ $PQRS$ is a parallelogram, so $PS = QR$]

From Eqs. (i) and (ii), we get

$$\frac{OS}{OB} = \frac{CR}{CB} \text{ or } \frac{OB}{OS} = \frac{CB}{CR}$$

On subtracting 1 from both sides, we get

$$\frac{OB}{OS} - 1 = \frac{CB}{CR} - 1$$

$$\Rightarrow \quad \frac{OB - OS}{OS} = \frac{CB - CR}{CR}$$

$$\Rightarrow \quad \frac{BS}{OS} = \frac{BR}{CR}$$

By converse of basic proportionality theorem,

$$SR \parallel OC$$

Hence proved.

*** *Q.5*** **A 5m long ladder is placed leaning towards a vertical wall such that it reaches the wall at a point 4 m high. If the foot of the ladder is moved 1.6 m towards the wall, then find the distance by which the top of the ladder would slide upwards on the wall.**

Ans. Let AC be the ladder of length 5 m and $BC = 4$ m be the height of the wall, which ladder is placed. If the foot of the ladder is moved 1.6 m towards the wall *i.e*, $AD = 1.6$ m, then the ladder is slide upward *i.e.*, $CE = x$ m.

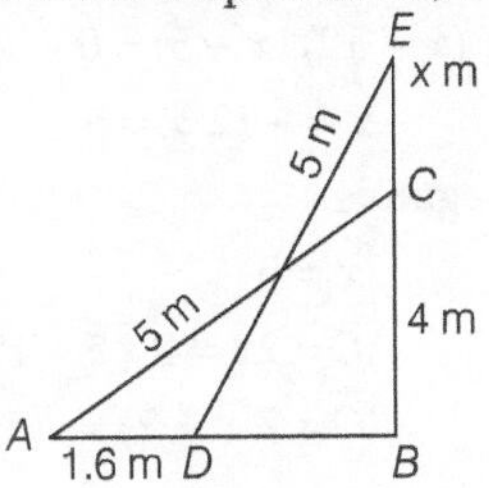

Note (✱) *Topics related to these question have been removed from latest NCERT.*

In right angled ΔABC,

$$AC^2 = AB^2 + BC^2 \quad \text{[by Pythagoras theorem]}$$
$$\Rightarrow \quad (5)^2 = (AB)^2 + (4)^2$$
$$\Rightarrow \quad AB^2 = 25 - 16 = 9 \Rightarrow AB = 3\text{ m}$$
$$\therefore \quad DB = AB - AD = 3 - 1.6 = 1.4\text{ m}$$

In right angled ΔEBD, $ED^2 = EB^2 + BD^2$ [by Pythagoras theorem]

$$\Rightarrow \quad (5)^2 = (EB)^2 + (1.4)^2 \quad [\because BD = 1.4\text{ m}]$$
$$\Rightarrow \quad 25 = (EB)^2 + 1.96$$
$$\Rightarrow \quad (EB)^2 = 25 - 1.96 = 23.04$$
$$\Rightarrow \quad EB = \sqrt{23.04} = 4.8$$

Now, $EC = EB - BC = 4.8 - 4 = 0.8$

Hence, the top of the ladder would slide upwards on the wall at distance 0.8 m.

***Q.6** For going to a city B from city A, there is a route via city C such that $AC \perp CB$, $AC = 2x$ km and $CB = 2(x+7)$ km. It is proposed to construct a 26 km highway which directly connects the two cities A and B. Find how much distance will be saved in reaching city B from city A after the construction of the highway.

Thinking Process Firstly draw the figure according to the given conditions and use Pythagoras theorem to find the value of x. Then, required saved distance will be equal to the difference of $(AC + BC)$ and 26.

Ans. Given, $AC \perp CB$, km, $CB = 2(x + 7)$ km and $AB = 26$ km

On drawing the figure, we get the right angled $\Delta\, ACB$ right angled at C.

Now, In ΔACB, by Pythagoras theorem,

$$AB^2 = AC^2 + BC^2$$
$$\Rightarrow \quad (26)^2 = (2x)^2 + \{2(x + 7)\}^2$$
$$\Rightarrow \quad 676 = 4x^2 + 4(x^2 + 49 + 14x)$$
$$\Rightarrow \quad 676 = 4x^2 + 4x^2 + 196 + 56x$$
$$\Rightarrow \quad 676 = 8x^2 + 56x + 196$$
$$\Rightarrow \quad 8x^2 + 56x - 480 = 0$$

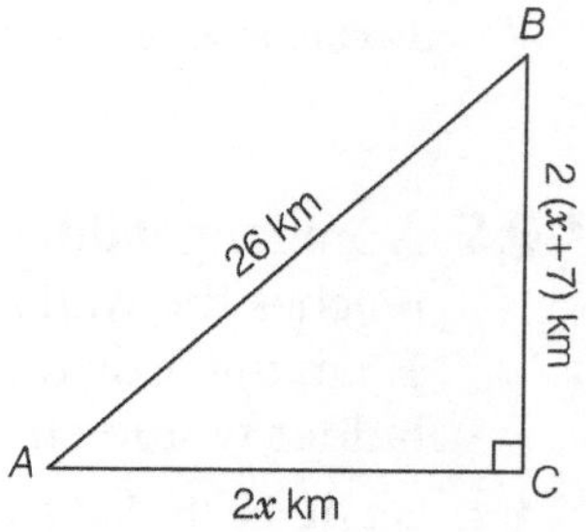

On dividing by 8, we get $x^2 + 7x - 60 = 0$

$$\Rightarrow \quad x^2 + 12x - 5x - 60 = 0$$
$$\Rightarrow \quad x(x + 12) - 5(x + 12) = 0$$
$$\Rightarrow \quad (x + 12)(x - 5) = 0$$
$$\therefore \quad x = -12, x = 5$$

Since, distance cannot be negative.

$$\therefore \quad x = 5 \quad [\because x \neq -12]$$

Now, $AC = 2x = 2 \times 5 = 10$ km

and $BC = 2(x + 7) = 2(5 + 7) = 2 \times 12 = 24$ km

Note (*) *Topics related to these question have been removed from latest NCERT.*

The distance covered to reach city B from city A *via* city C

$$= AC + BC = 10 + 24 = 34 \text{ km}$$

Distance covered to reach city B from city A after the construction of the highway

$$= BA = 26 \text{ km}$$

Hence, the required saved distance is $34 - 26$ *i.e.*, 8 km.

*** Q.7** A flag pole 18 m high casts a shadow 9.6 m long. Find the distance of the top of the pole from the far end of the shadow.

Ans. Let $BC = 18$ m be the flag pole and its shadow be $AB = 9.6$ m. The distance of the top of the pole, C from the far end *i.e.*, A of the shadow is AC.

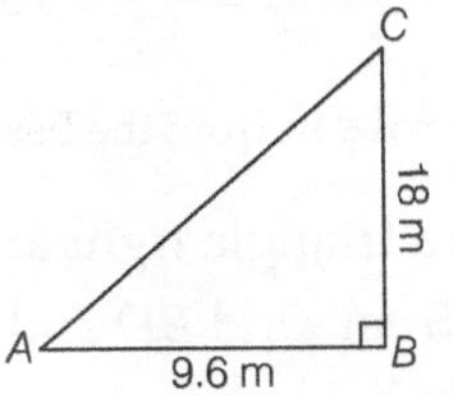

In right angled ΔABC, $AC^2 = AB^2 + BC^2$ [by Pythagoras theorem]

$\Rightarrow$ $AC^2 = (9.6)^2 + (18)^2$

$AC^2 = 92.16 + 324$

$\Rightarrow$ $AC^2 = 416.16$

$\therefore$ $AC = \sqrt{416.16} = 20.4$ m

Hence, the required distance is 20.4 m.

Q.8 A street light bulb is fixed on a pole 6 m above the level of the street. If a woman of height 1.5 m casts a shadow of 3 m, find how far she is away from the base of the pole.

Thinking Process Firstly, draw the figure according to the question and get two triangles. Then, show both triangles are similar by AA similarity criterion and then by using basic proportionality theorem calculate required distance.

Ans. Let A be the position of the street bulb fixed on a pole $AB = 6$ m and $CD = 1.5$ m be the height of a woman and her shadow be $ED = 3$ m. Let distance between pole and woman be x m.

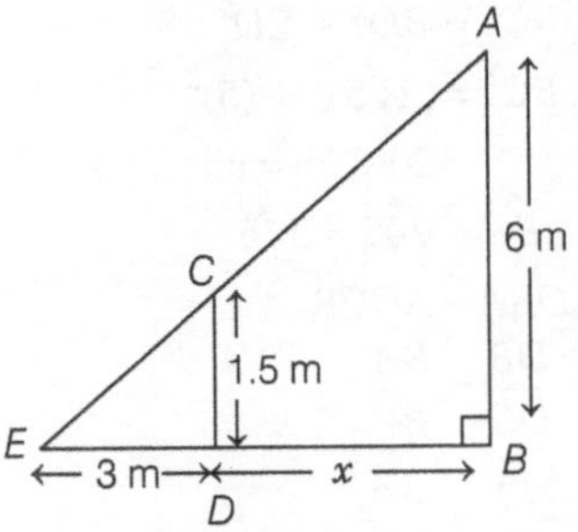

Here, woman and pole both are standing vertically.

So, $CD \parallel AB$

Note (*) *Topics related to these question have been removed from latest NCERT.*

In ΔCDE and ΔABE, $\angle E = \angle E$ [common angle]

$\angle ABE = \angle CDE$ [each equal to 90°]

$\therefore$ $\Delta CDE \sim \Delta ABE$ [by AA similarity criterion]

Then, $\frac{ED}{EB} = \frac{CD}{AB}$

$\Rightarrow$ $\frac{3}{3+x} = \frac{1.5}{6} \Rightarrow 3 \times 6 = 1.5(3+x)$

$\Rightarrow$ $18 = 1.5 \times 3 + 1.5x$

$\Rightarrow$ $1.5x = 18 - 4.5 = 13.5$

$\therefore$ $x = \frac{13.5}{1.5} = 9\,\text{m}$

Hence, she is at the distance of 9 m from the base of the pole.

Q.9 In given figure, ABC is a triangle right angled at B and $BD \perp AC$. If $AD = 4$ cm and $CD = 5$ cm, find BD and AB.

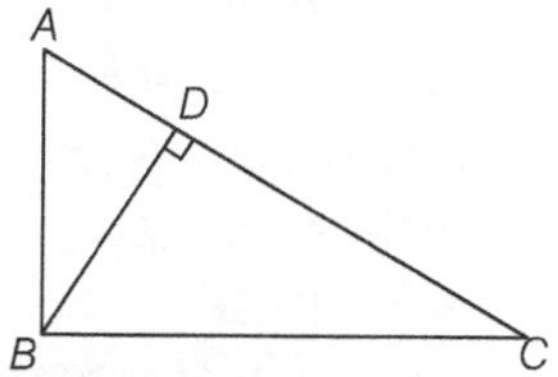

Ans. Given, ΔABC in which $\angle B = 90°$ and $BD \perp AC$

Also, $AD = 4\,\text{cm}$ and $CD = 5\,\text{cm}$

In ΔADB and ΔCDB, $\angle ADB = \angle CDB$ [each equal to 90°]

and $\angle BAD = \angle DBC$ [each equal to $90° - \angle C$]

$\therefore$ $\Delta DBA \sim \Delta DCB$ [by AA similarity criterion]

Then, $\frac{DB}{DA} = \frac{DC}{DB}$

$\Rightarrow$ $DB^2 = DA \times DC$

$\Rightarrow$ $DB^2 = 4 \times 5 = 20$

$\Rightarrow$ $DB = 2\sqrt{5}\,\text{cm}$

In right angled ΔBDC, $BC^2 = BD^2 + CD^2$ [by Pythagoras theorem]

$\Rightarrow$ $BC^2 = (2\sqrt{5})^2 + (5)^2$

$= 20 + 25 = 45$

$\Rightarrow$ $BC = \sqrt{45} = 3\sqrt{5}$

Again, $\Delta DBA \sim \Delta DCB$,

$\therefore$ $\frac{DB}{DC} = \frac{BA}{BC}$

$\Rightarrow$ $\frac{2\sqrt{5}}{5} = \frac{BA}{3\sqrt{5}}$

$\therefore$ $BA = \frac{2\sqrt{5} \times 3\sqrt{5}}{5} = 6\,\text{cm}$

Hence, $BD = 2\sqrt{5}$ cm and $AB = 6$ cm

Q.10 In given figure PQR is a right triangle, right angled at Q and $QS \perp PR$. If $PQ = 6$ cm and $PS = 4$ cm, find QS, RS and QR.

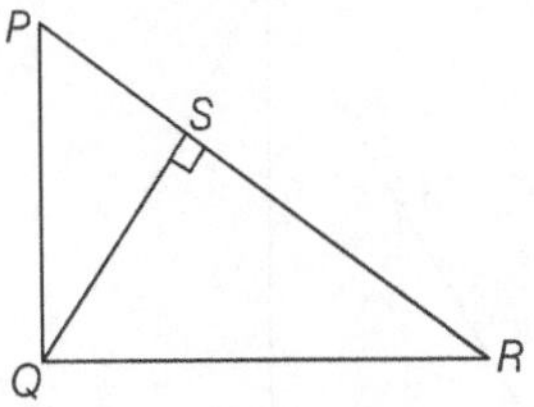

Ans. Given, ΔPQR in which $\angle Q = 90°$, $QS \perp PR$ and $PQ = 6$ cm, $PS = 4$ cm

In ΔSQP and ΔSRQ,

$$\angle PSQ = \angle RSQ \quad \text{[each equal to 90°]}$$

$$\angle SPQ = \angle SQR \quad \text{[each equal to 90° − ∠R]}$$

$$\therefore \quad \Delta SQP \sim \Delta SRQ \quad \text{[by AA similarity criterion]}$$

Then, $$\frac{SQ}{PS} = \frac{SR}{SQ}$$

$$\Rightarrow \quad SQ^2 = PS \times SR \quad \ldots\text{(i)}$$

In right angled ΔPSQ, $$PQ^2 = PS^2 + QS^2 \quad \text{[by Pythagoras theorem]}$$

$$\Rightarrow \quad (6)^2 = (4)^2 + QS^2$$

$$\Rightarrow \quad 36 = 16 + QS^2$$

$$\Rightarrow \quad QS^2 = 36 - 16 = 20$$

$$\therefore \quad QS = \sqrt{20} = 2\sqrt{5} \text{ cm}$$

On putting the value of QS in Eq. (i), we get

$$(2\sqrt{5})^2 = 4 \times SR \Rightarrow 20 = 4 \times SR$$

$$\Rightarrow \quad SR = \frac{20}{4} = 5 \text{ cm}$$

In right angled ΔQSR, $$QR^2 = QS^2 + SR^2$$

$$\Rightarrow \quad QR^2 = (2\sqrt{5})^2 + (5)^2$$

$$\Rightarrow \quad QR^2 = 20 + 25$$

$$\therefore \quad QR = \sqrt{45} = 3\sqrt{5} \text{ cm}$$

Hence, $QS = 2\sqrt{5}$ cm, $RS = 5$ cm and $QR = 3\sqrt{5}$ cm

***Q.11** In ΔPQR, $PD \perp QR$ such that D lies on QR. If $PQ = a$, $PR = b$, $QD = c$ and $DR = d$, prove that $(a+b)(a-b) = (c+d)(c-d)$.

Thinking Process Apply the Pythagoras theorem in both ΔPDQ and ΔPDR to get two equations and then equate them to prove the required result.

Ans. Given In ΔPQR, $PD \perp QR$, $PQ = a$, $PR = b$, $QD = c$ and $DR = d$

To prove $(a+b)(a-b) = (c+d)(c-d)$

Proof In right angled ΔPDQ,

$$PQ^2 = PD^2 + QD^2 \quad \text{[by Pythagoras theorem]}$$

$$\Rightarrow \quad a^2 = PD^2 + c^2$$

Note (*) *Topics related to these question have been removed from latest NCERT.*

$\Rightarrow \quad PD^2 = a^2 - c^2 \quad \ldots(i)$

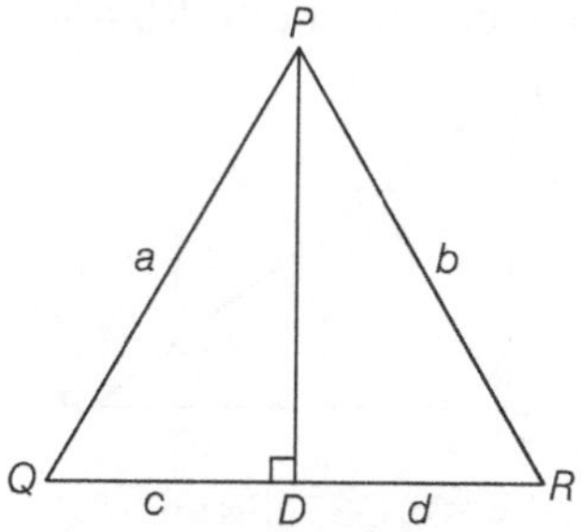

In right angled ΔPDR, $PR^2 = PD^2 + DR^2$ [by Pythagoras theorem]

$\Rightarrow \quad b^2 = PD^2 + d^2$

$\Rightarrow \quad PD^2 = b^2 - d^2 \quad \ldots(ii)$

From Eqs. (i) and (ii),

$$a^2 - c^2 = b^2 - d^2$$

$\Rightarrow \quad a^2 - b^2 = c^2 - d^2$

$\Rightarrow \quad (a-b)(a+b) = (c-d)(c+d)$ **Hence proved.**

***Q.12** In a quadrilateral $ABCD$, $\angle A + \angle D = 90°$. Prove that

$$AC^2 + BD^2 = AD^2 + BC^2.$$

Thinking Process Firstly, produce AB and DC and show that $\angle E = 90°$. Then, apply Pythagoras theorem in different right triangles made with E and show the required result.

Ans. Given Quadrilateral $ABCD$, in which $\angle A + \angle D = 90°$

To prove $AC^2 + BD^2 = AD^2 + BC^2$

Construct Produce AB and CD to meet at E.

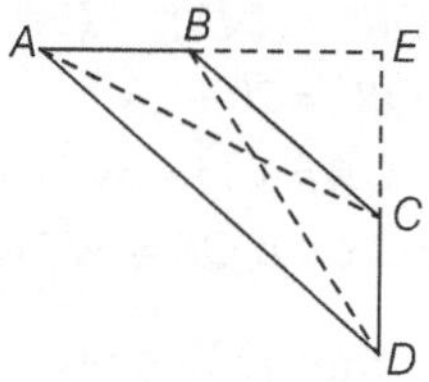

Also, join AC and BD.

Proof In ΔAED, $\angle A + \angle D = 90°$ [given]

$\therefore \quad \angle E = 180° - (\angle A + \angle D) = 90°$

[$\because$ sum of angles of a triangle = 180°]

Then, by Pythagoras theorem, $AD^2 = AE^2 + DE^2$

In ΔBEC, by Pythagoras theorem, $BC^2 = BE^2 + EF^2$

On adding both equations, we get

$$AD^2 + BC^2 = AE^2 + DE^2 + BE^2 + CE^2 \quad \ldots(i)$$

Note (*) *Topics related to these question have been removed from latest NCERT.*

In ΔAEC, by Pythagoras theorem,

$$AC^2 = AE^2 + CE^2 \quad \text{...(ii)}$$

and in ΔBED, by Pythagoras theorem,

$$BD^2 = BE^2 + DE^2 \quad \text{...(iii)}$$

On adding Eqs. (ii) and (iii), we get

$$AC^2 + BD^2 = AE^2 + CE^2 + BE^2 + DE^2 \quad \text{...(iv)}$$

From Eqs. (i) and (iv), we get

$$AC^2 + BD^2 = AD^2 + BC^2$$

Hence proved.

Q.13 In given figure, $l \parallel m$ and line segments AB, CD and EF are concurrent at point P. Prove that $\frac{AE}{BF} = \frac{AC}{BD} = \frac{CE}{FD}$.

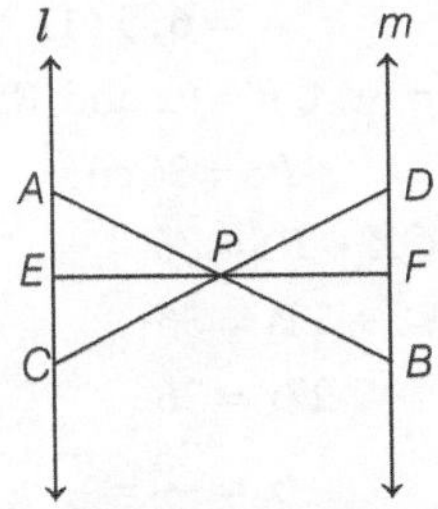

Ans. Given $l \parallel m$ and line segments AB, CD and EF are concurrent at point P.

To prove $\frac{AE}{BF} = \frac{AC}{BD} = \frac{CE}{FD}$

Proof In ΔAPC and ΔBPD, $\angle APC = \angle BPD$ [vertically opposite angles]

$\angle PAC = \angle PBD$ [alternate angles]

$\therefore$ $\Delta APC \sim \Delta BPD$ [by AA similarity criterion]

Then, $\frac{AP}{PB} = \frac{AC}{BD} = \frac{PC}{PD}$ ...(i)

In ΔAPE and ΔBPF, $\angle APE = \angle BPF$ [vertically opposite angles]

$\angle PAE = \angle PBF$ [alternate angles]

$\therefore$ $\Delta APE \sim \Delta BPF$ [by AA similarity criterion]

Then, $\frac{AP}{PB} = \frac{AE}{BF} = \frac{PE}{PF}$ ...(ii)

In ΔPEC and ΔPFD, $\angle EPC = \angle FPD$ [vertically opposite angles]

$\angle PCE = \angle PDF$ [alternate angles]

$\therefore$ $\Delta PEC \sim \Delta PFD$ [by AA similarity criterion]

Then, $\frac{PE}{PF} = \frac{PC}{PD} = \frac{EC}{FD}$ ...(iii)

From Eqs. (i), (ii) and (iii), we get

$$\frac{AP}{PB} = \frac{AC}{BD} = \frac{AE}{BF} = \frac{PE}{PF} = \frac{EC}{FD}$$

$\therefore$ $\frac{AE}{BF} = \frac{AC}{BD} = \frac{CE}{FD}$ **Hence proved.**

Q. 14 In figure, PA, QB, RC and SD are all perpendiculars to a line l, $AB = 6$ cm, $BC = 9$ cm, $CD = 12$ cm and $SP = 36$ cm. Find PQ, QR and RS.

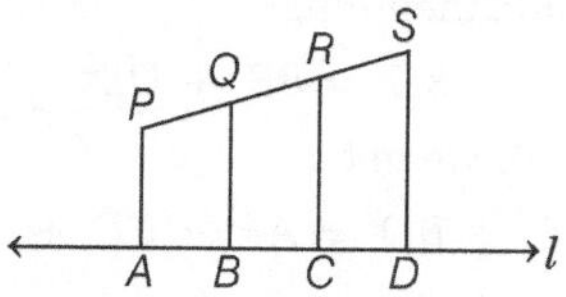

Ans. Given, $AB = 6$ cm, $BC = 9$ cm, $CD = 12$ cm and $SP = 36$ cm

Also, PA, QB, RC and SD are all perpendiculars to line l.

$\therefore \quad PA \parallel QB \parallel RC \parallel SD$

By basic proportionality theorem,

$$PQ : QR : RS = AB : BC : CD$$
$$= 6 : 9 : 12$$

Let $\quad PQ = 6x$, $QR = 9x$ and $RS = 12x$

Since, length of $\quad PS = 36$ cm

$\therefore \quad PQ + QR + RS = 36$

$\Rightarrow \quad 6x + 9x + 12x = 36$

$\Rightarrow \quad 27x = 36$

$\therefore \quad x = \frac{36}{27} = \frac{4}{3}$

Now, $\quad PQ = 6x = 6 \times \frac{4}{3} = 8$ cm

$QR = 9x = 9 \times \frac{4}{3} = 12$ cm

and $\quad RS = 12x = 12 \times \frac{4}{3} = 16$ cm

Q. 15 O is the point of intersection of the diagonals AC and BD of a trapezium $ABCD$ with $AB \parallel DC$. Through O, a line segment PQ is drawn parallel to AB meeting AD in P and BC in Q. Prove that $PO = QO$.

Ans. Given $ABCD$ is a trapezium. Diagonals AC and BD are intersect at O.

$PQ \parallel AB \parallel DC$.

To prove $\quad PO = QO$

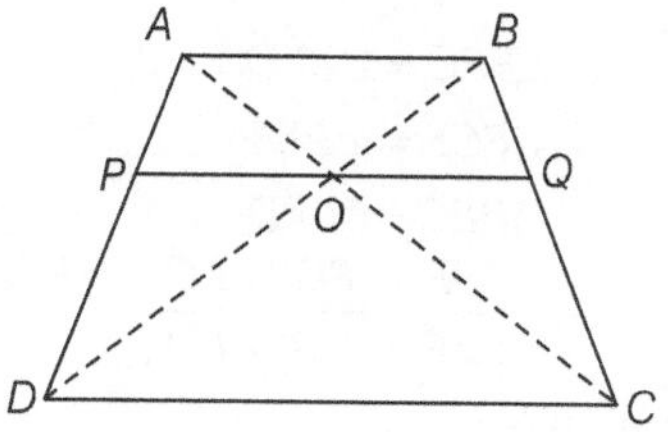

Proof In ΔABD and ΔPOD, $\quad PO \parallel AB \quad [\because PQ \parallel AB]$

$\angle D = \angle D \quad$ [common angle]

$\angle ABD = \angle POD \quad$ [corresponding angles]

$\therefore$ $\Delta ABD \sim \Delta POD$ [by AA similarity criterion]

Then, $\dfrac{OP}{AB} = \dfrac{PD}{AD}$ ...(i)

In ΔABC and ΔOQC, $OQ \parallel AB$ [$\because PQ \parallel AB$]

$\angle C = \angle C$ [common angle]

$\angle BAC = \angle QOC$ [corresponding angle]

$\therefore$ $\Delta ABC \sim \Delta OQC$ [by AA similarity criterion]

Then, $\dfrac{OQ}{AB} = \dfrac{QC}{BC}$ ...(ii)

Now, in ΔADC, $OP \parallel DC$ [$\because PQ \parallel DC$]

$\therefore$ $\dfrac{AP}{PD} = \dfrac{OA}{OC}$ [by basic proportionality theorem]...(iii)

In ΔABC, $OQ \parallel AB$ [$\because PQ \parallel AB$]

$\therefore$ $\dfrac{BQ}{QC} = \dfrac{OA}{OC}$ [by basic proportionality theorem]...(iv)

From Eqs. (iii) and (iv),

$$\frac{AP}{PD} = \frac{BQ}{QC}$$

Adding 1 on both sides, we get

$$\frac{AP}{PD} + 1 = \frac{BQ}{QC} + 1$$

$$\Rightarrow \quad \frac{AP + PD}{PD} = \frac{BQ + QC}{QC}$$

$$\Rightarrow \quad \frac{AD}{PD} = \frac{BC}{QC}$$

$$\Rightarrow \quad \frac{PD}{AD} = \frac{QC}{BC}$$

From Eqs. (i) and (ii), we get

$$\frac{OP}{AB} = \frac{OQ}{AB}$$

$\Rightarrow$ $OP = OQ$ **Hence proved.**

Q.16 In figure, line segment DF intersects the side AC of a ΔABC at the point E such that E is the mid-point of CA and $\angle AEF = \angle AFE$. Prove that $\dfrac{BD}{CD} = \dfrac{BF}{CE}$.

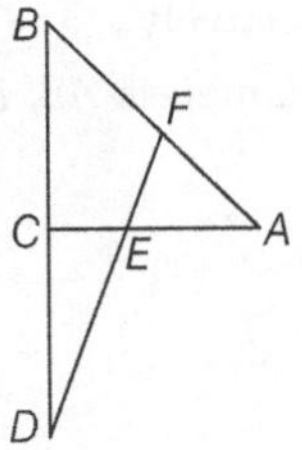

Ans. **Given** ΔABC, E is the mid-point of CA and $\angle AEF = \angle AFE$

To prove $$\frac{BD}{CD} = \frac{BF}{CE}$$

Construction Take a point G on AB such that $CG \parallel EF$.

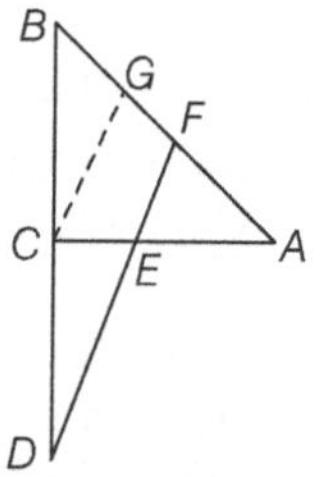

Proof Since, E is the mid-point of CA.

$\therefore$ $$CE = AE \quad \text{...(i)}$$

In ΔACG, $CG \parallel EF$ and E is mid-point of CA.

So, $$CE = GF \quad \text{[by mid-point theorem]...(ii)}$$

Now, in ΔBCG and ΔBDF, $CG \parallel EF$

$\therefore$ $$\frac{BC}{CD} = \frac{BG}{GF} \quad \text{[by basic proportionality theorem]}$$

$\Rightarrow$ $$\frac{BC}{CD} = \frac{BF - GF}{GF} \Rightarrow \frac{BC}{CD} = \frac{BF}{GF} - 1$$

$\Rightarrow$ $$\frac{BC}{CD} + 1 = \frac{BF}{GF}$$

$\Rightarrow$ $$\frac{BC}{CD} + 1 = \frac{BF}{CE} \quad \text{[from Eq. (ii)]}$$

$\Rightarrow$ $$\frac{BC + CD}{CD} = \frac{BF}{CE} \Rightarrow \frac{BD}{CD} = \frac{BF}{CE}$$ **Hence proved.**

***Q.17** Prove that the area of the semi-circle drawn on the hypotenuse of a right angled triangle is equal to the sum of the areas of the semi-circles drawn on the other two sides of the triangle.

Thinking Process Firstly, draw these semi-circles on three sides of right triangle taking each side as diameter. Then, find area of each semi-circle by using formula area of semi-circle $= \frac{\pi r^2}{2}$ and then proceed required result.

Ans. Let ABC be a right triangle, right angled at B and $AB = y$, $BC = x$.

Three semi-circles are drawn on the sides AB, BC and AC, respectively with diameters AB, BC and AC, respectively.

Again, let area of circles with diameters AB, BC and AC are respectively A_1, A_2 and A_3.

Note (✱) *Topics related to these question have been removed from latest NCERT.*

To prove $A_3 = A_1 + A_2$

Proof In ΔABC, by Pythagoras theorem,

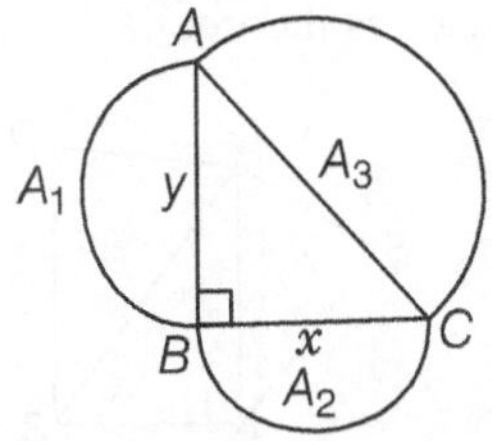

$$AC^2 = AB^2 + BC^2 \Rightarrow AC^2 = y^2 + x^2$$

$$\Rightarrow \quad AC = \sqrt{y^2 + x^2}$$

We know that, area of a semi-circle with radius, $r = \dfrac{\pi r^2}{2}$

$\therefore$ Area of semi-circle drawn on AC, $A_3 = \dfrac{\pi}{2}\left(\dfrac{AC}{2}\right)^2 = \dfrac{\pi}{2}\left(\dfrac{\sqrt{y^2 + x^2}}{2}\right)^2$

$$\Rightarrow \quad A_3 = \frac{\pi(y^2 + x^2)}{8} \qquad \text{...(i)}$$

Now, area of semi-circle drawn on AB, $A_1 = \dfrac{\pi}{2}\left(\dfrac{AB}{2}\right)^2$

$$\Rightarrow \quad A_1 = \frac{\pi}{2}\left(\frac{y}{2}\right)^2 \Rightarrow A_1 = \frac{\pi y^2}{8} \qquad \text{...(ii)}$$

and area of semi-circle drawn on BC, $A_2 = \dfrac{\pi}{2}\left(\dfrac{BC}{2}\right)^2 = \dfrac{\pi}{2}\left(\dfrac{x}{2}\right)^2$

$$\Rightarrow \quad A_2 = \frac{\pi x^2}{8}$$

On adding Eqs. (ii) and (iii), we get $A_1 + A_2 = \dfrac{\pi y^2}{8} + \dfrac{\pi x^2}{8}$

$$= \frac{\pi(y^2 + x^2)}{8} = A_3 \qquad \text{[from Eq. (i)]}$$

$$\therefore \quad A_1 + A_2 = A_3$$

Hence proved.

Q.18 Prove that the area of the equilateral triangle drawn on the hypotenuse of a right angled triangle is equal to the sum of the areas of the equilateral triangle drawn on the other two sides of the triangle.

Thinking Process Firstly draw equilateral triangles on each side of right angled ΔABC and then find the area of each equilateral triangle by using the formula, area of equilateral triangle $= \dfrac{\sqrt{3}}{4}(\text{Side})^2$ and prove the required result.

Ans. Let a right triangle BAC in which $\angle A$ is right angle and $AC = y$, $AB = x$.

Three equilateral triangles ΔAEC, ΔAFB and ΔCBD are drawn on the three sides of ΔABC.

Again, let area of triangles made on AC, AB and BC are A_1, A_2 and A_3, respectively.

To prove $A_3 = A_1 + A_2$

Proof In ΔCAB, by Pythagoras theorem,

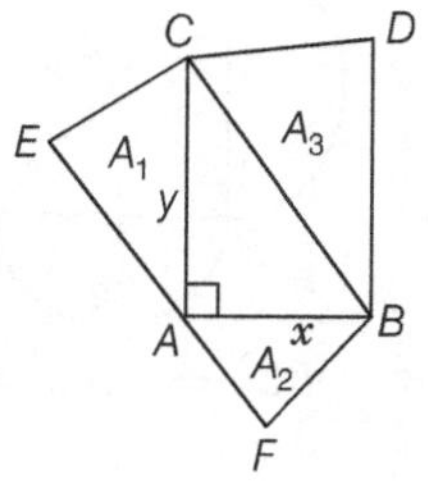

$$BC^2 = AC^2 + AB^2$$

$$\Rightarrow \quad BC^2 = y^2 + x^2$$

$$\Rightarrow \quad BC = \sqrt{y^2 + x^2}$$

We know that, area of an equilateral triangle $= \frac{\sqrt{3}}{4}(\text{Side})^2$

$\therefore$ Area of equilateral ΔAEC, $A_1 = \frac{\sqrt{3}}{4}(AC)^2$

$$\Rightarrow \quad A_1 = \frac{\sqrt{3}}{4}y^2 \qquad \text{....(i)}$$

Area of equitateral ΔAFB, $A_2 = \frac{\sqrt{3}}{4}(AB)^2 = \frac{\sqrt{3}}{4}x^2$ ...(ii)

and area of equilateral ΔCBD, $A_3 = \frac{\sqrt{3}}{4}(CB)^2 = \frac{\sqrt{3}}{4}[\sqrt{(y^2 + x^2)}]^2$

$$= \frac{\sqrt{3}}{4}(y^2 + x^2) = \frac{\sqrt{3}}{4}y^2 + \frac{\sqrt{3}}{4}x^2$$

From Eqs. (i) and (ii), we get $A_3 = A_1 + A_2$ **Hence proved.**

Chapter

07

Coordinate Geometry

Multiple Choice Questions (MCQs)

Choose the correct answer from the given four options in the following questions:

Q.1 The distance of the point $P(2, 3)$ from the X-axis is

(a) 2 (b) 3
(c) 1 (d) 5

Ans. *(b)* We know that, if (x, y) is any point on the cartesian plane in first quadrant.

Then, $x =$ Perpendicular distance from Y-axis

and $y =$ Perpendicular distance from X-axis

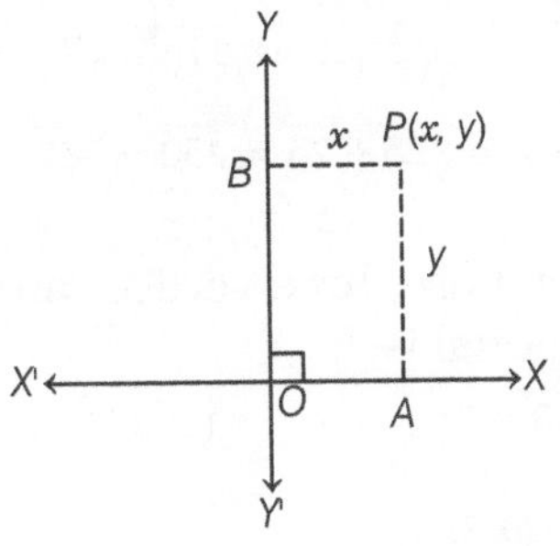

Distance of the point $P(2, 3)$ from the X-axis = Ordinate of a point $P(2, 3) = 3$.

Q.2 The distance between the points $A(0, 6)$ and $B(0, -2)$ is

(a) 6 (b) 8 (c) 4 (d) 2

● **Concept Insight** The distance between two points (x_1, y_1) and (x_2, y_2) is $\sqrt{(x_2 - x_1)^2 + (y_2 - y_1)^2}$. Use this formula and simplify it.

Ans. *(b)* $\because$ Distance between the points (x_1, y_1) and (x_2, y_2),

$$d = \sqrt{(x_2 - x_1)^2 + (y_2 - y_1)^2}$$

Here, $x_1 = 0, y_1 = 6$ and $x_2 = 0, y_2 = -2$

$\therefore$ Distance between $A(0, 6)$ and $B(0, -2)$,

$$AB = \sqrt{(0 - 0)^2 + (-2 - 6)^2}$$

$$= \sqrt{0 + (-8)^2} = \sqrt{8^2} = 8$$

Q.3 The distance of the point $P(-6, 8)$ from the origin is

(a) 8 (b) $2\sqrt{7}$ (c) 10 (d) 6

Thinking Process Coordinate of origin is (0, 0).

Ans. *(c)* $\because$ Distance between the points (x_1, y_1) and (x_2, y_2),

$$d = \sqrt{(x_2 - x_1)^2 + (y_2 - y_1)^2}$$

Here, $x_1 = -6, y_1 = 8$ and $x_2 = 0, y_2 = 0$

$\therefore$ Distance between $P(-6, 8)$ and origin *i.e.*, $O(0, 0)$,

$$PO = \sqrt{[0-(-6)]^2 + (0-8)^2}$$
$$= \sqrt{(6)^2 + (-8)^2}$$
$$= \sqrt{36 + 64} = \sqrt{100} = 10$$

Q.4 The distance between the points (0, 5) and (– 5, 0) is

(a) 5 (b) $5\sqrt{2}$ (c) $2\sqrt{5}$ (d) 10

Ans. *(b)* $\because$ Distance between the points (x_1, y_1) and (x_2, y_2),

$$d = \sqrt{(x_2 - x_1)^2 + (y_2 - y_1)^2}$$

Here, $x_1 = 0, y_1 = 5$ and $x_2 = -5, y_2 = 0$

$\therefore$ Distance between the points (0, 5) and (–5, 0)

$$= \sqrt{(-5-0)^2 + (0-5)^2}$$
$$= \sqrt{25 + 25} = \sqrt{50} = 5\sqrt{2}$$

Q.5 $AOBC$ is a rectangle whose three vertices are $A(0, 3)$, $O(0, 0)$ and $B(5, 0)$. The length of its diagonal is

(a) 5 (b) 3 (c) $\sqrt{34}$ (d) 4

Ans. *(c)*

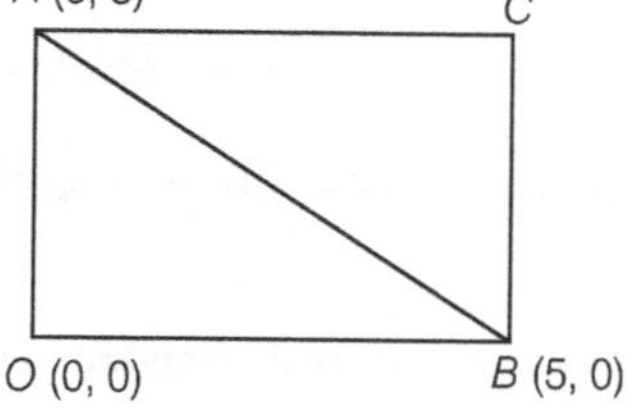

Now, length of the diagonal AB = Distance between the points $A(0, 3)$ and $B(5, 0)$.

$\because$ Distance between the points (x_1, y_1) and (x_2, y_2),

$$d = \sqrt{(x_2 - x_1)^2 + (y_2 - y_1)^2}$$

Here, $x_1 = 0, y_1 = 3$ and $x_2 = 5, y_2 = 0$

$\therefore$ Distance between the points $A(0, 3)$ and $B(5, 0)$

$$AB = \sqrt{(5-0)^2 + (0-3)^2}$$
$$= \sqrt{25 + 9} = \sqrt{34}$$

Hence, the required length of its diagonal is $\sqrt{34}$.

Q.6 The perimeter of a triangle with vertices (0, 4), (0, 0) and (3, 0) is

(a) 5 (b) 12 (c) 11 (d) $7+\sqrt{5}$

Thinking Process

(i) Firstly, plot the given points on a graph paper and join them to get a triangle.

(ii) Secondly, determine the length of the each sides by using the distance formula, $\sqrt{(x_2-x_1)^2+(y_2-y_1)^2}$

(iii) Further, adding all the distance of a triangle to get the perimeter of a triangle.

Ans. *(b)* We plot the vertices of the triangle *i.e.*, (0, 4), (0, 0) and (3, 0) on the paper shown as given below

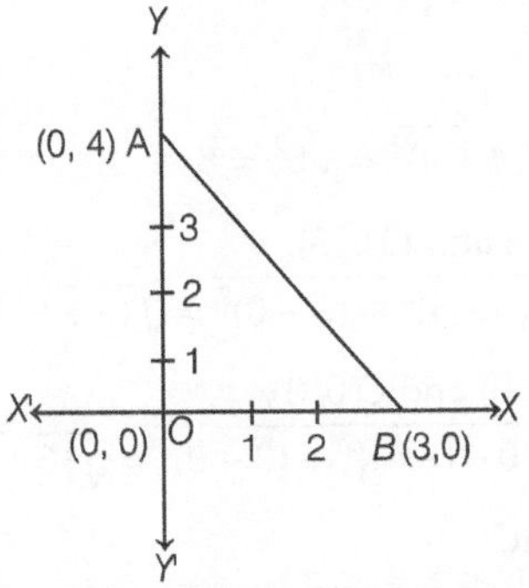

Now, perimeter of ΔAOB = Sum of the length of all its sides

$$= d(AO)+d(OB)+d(AB)$$

= Distance between $A(0, 4)$ and $O(0, 0)$ + Distance between $O(0, 0)$ and $B(3, 0)$ + Distance between $A(0, 4)$ and $B(3, 0)$

$$=\sqrt{(0-0)^2+(0-4)^2}+\sqrt{(3-0)^2+(0-0)^2}+\sqrt{(3-0)^2+(0-4)^2}$$

$$\left[\because d=\sqrt{(x_2-x_1)^2+(y_2-y_1)^2}\right]$$

$$=\sqrt{0+16}+\sqrt{9+0}+\sqrt{(3)^2+(4)^2}=4+3+\sqrt{9+16}=7+\sqrt{25}=7+5=12$$

Hence, the required perimeter of the triangle is 12.

*** Q.7** The area of a triangle with vertices $A(3, 0)$, $B(7, 0)$ and $C(8, 4)$ is

(a) 14 (b) 28 (c) 8 (d) 6

Thinking Process The area of triangle, whose vertices are $A(x_1, y_1)$, $B(x_2, y_2)$ and $C(x_3, y_3)$ is given by mode $\left|\frac{1}{2}[x_1(y_2-y_3)+x_2(y_3-y_1)+x_3(y_1-y_2)]\right|$. Use this formula and simplify it to get the result.

Ans. *(c)* Area of ΔABC whose Vertices $A=(x_1, y_1)$, $B=(x_2, y_2)$ and $C=(x_3, y_3)$ are given by

$$\Delta=\left|\frac{1}{2}[x_1(y_2-y_3)+x_2(y_3-y_1)+x_3(y_1-y_2)]\right|$$

Here, $x_1=3, y_1=0, x_2=7, y_2=0, x_3=8$ and $y_3=4$

$$\therefore \quad \Delta=\left|\frac{1}{2}[3(0-4)+7(4-0)+8(0-0)]\right|=\left|\frac{1}{2}(-12+28+0)\right|=\left|\frac{1}{2}(16)\right|=8$$

Hence, the required area of ΔABC is 8.

Note (*) *Topics related to these question have been removed from latest NCERT.*

Q.8 The points (– 4, 0), (4, 0) and (0, 3) are the vertices of a

(a) right triangle
(b) isosceles triangle
(c) equilateral triangle
(d) scalene triangle

Ans. *(b)* Let $A(-4, 0)$, $B(4, 0)$, $C(0, 3)$ are the given vertices.

Now, distance between $A(-4, 0)$ and $B(4, 0)$,

$$AB = \sqrt{[4-(-4)]^2 + (0-0)^2}$$

$\left[\because \text{distance between two points } (x_1, y_1) \text{ and } (x_2, y_2),\ d = \sqrt{(x_2 - x_1)^2 + (y_2 - y_1)^2}\right]$

$$= \sqrt{(4+4)^2} = \sqrt{8^2} = 8$$

Distance between $B(4, 0)$ and $C(0, 3)$,

$$BC = \sqrt{(0-4)^2 + (3-0)^2} = \sqrt{16+9} = \sqrt{25} = 5$$

Distance between $A(-4, 0)$ and $C(0, 3)$,

$$AC = \sqrt{[0-(-4)]^2 + (3-0)^2} = \sqrt{16+9} = \sqrt{25} = 5$$

$\because \quad BC = AC$

Hence, ΔABC is an isosceles triangle because an isosceles triangle has two sides equal.

Q.9 The point which divides the line segment joining the points (7, – 6) and (3, 4) in ratio 1 : 2 internally lies in the

(a) I quadrant (b) II quadrant (c) III quadrant (d) IV quadrant

● **Concept Insight** If $P(x, y)$ divides the line segment joining $A(x_1, y_1)$ and $B(x_2, y_2)$ internally in the ratio $m:n$, then $x = \dfrac{mx_2 + nx_1}{m+n}$ and $y = \dfrac{my_2 + ny_1}{m+n}$

Ans. *(d)* Given that, $x_1 = 7, y_1 = -6,\ x_2 = 3, y_2 = 4,\ m = 1$ and $n = 2$

$\therefore \quad x = \dfrac{1(3) + 2(7)}{1+2}, y = \dfrac{1(4) + 2(-6)}{1+2}$ [by section formula]

$\Rightarrow \quad x = \dfrac{3+14}{3}, y = \dfrac{4-12}{3} \Rightarrow x = \dfrac{17}{3}, y = -\dfrac{8}{3}$

So, $(x, y) = \left(\dfrac{17}{3}, -\dfrac{8}{3}\right)$ lies in IV quadrant.

[since, in IV quadrant, x-coordinate is positive and y-coordinate is negative]

Q.10 The point which lies on the perpendicular bisector of the line segment joining the points $A(-2, -5)$ and $B(2, 5)$ is

(a) (0, 0) (b) (0, 2) (c) (2, 0) (d) (–2, 0)

● **Concept Insight** Mid-point of any line segment which end points are (x_1, y_1) and $(x_2, y_2) = \left(\dfrac{x_1 + x_2}{2}, \dfrac{y_1 + y_2}{2}\right)$.

Ans. *(a)* We know that, the perpendicular bisector of the any line segment divides the line segment into two equal parts *i.e.*, the perpendicular bisector of the line segment always passes through the mid-point of the line segment.

$\therefore$ Mid-point of the line segment joining the points $A(-2, -5)$ and $B(2, 5)$

$$= \left(\frac{-2+2}{2}, \frac{-5+5}{2} \right) = (0, 0) \quad \text{[by mid-point formula]}$$

Hence, (0, 0) is the required point lies on the perpendicular bisector of the lines segment.

Mistake Alert ! *Students may get confused in applying the mid-point formula as* $\left(\frac{x_1+y_1}{2}, \frac{x_2+y_2}{2} \right)$ *instead of* $\left(\frac{x_1+x_2}{2}, \frac{y_1+y_2}{2} \right)$.

Q.11 The fourth vertex D of a parallelogram $ABCD$ whose three vertices are $A(-2, 3)$, $B(6, 7)$ and $C(8, 3)$ is

(a) (0, 1) (b) (0, – 1) (c) (– 1, 0) (d) (1, 0)

Thinking Process

(i) Firstly, consider the fourth vertex of a parallelogram be $D(x_4, y_4)$.

(ii) Secondly, determine the mid-points of diagonals by using the mid-point formula.

(iii) Further, equate both points and get the required coordinate of fourth vertex.

Ans. *(b)* Let the fourth vertex of parallelogram, $D \equiv (x_4, y_4)$ and L, M be the mid-points of AC and BD, respectively.

Then, $$L \equiv \left(\frac{-2+8}{2}, \frac{3+3}{2} \right) \equiv (3, 3)$$

$\left[\because \text{mid - point of a line segment having end points } (x_1, y_1) \text{ and } (x_2, y_2) = \left(\frac{x_1+x_2}{2}, \frac{y_1+y_2}{2} \right) \right]$

and $$M \equiv \left(\frac{6+x_4}{2}, \frac{7+y_4}{2} \right)$$

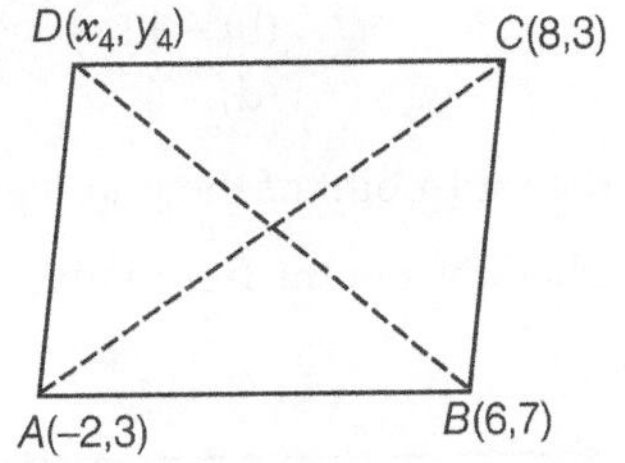

Since, $ABCD$ is a parallelogram, therefore diagonals AC and BD will bisect each other. Hence, L and M are the same points.

$$\therefore \quad 3 = \frac{6+x_4}{2} \text{ and } 3 = \frac{7+y_4}{2}$$

$$\Rightarrow \quad 6 = 6 + x_4 \text{ and } 6 = 7 + y_4$$

$$\Rightarrow \quad x_4 = 6 - 6 \text{ and } y_4 = 6 - 7$$

$$\therefore \quad x_4 = 0 \text{ and } y_4 = -1$$

Hence, the fourth vertex of parallelogram is $D \equiv (x_4, y_4) \equiv (0, -1)$.

Q.12 If the point $P(2, 1)$ lies on the line segment joining points $A(4, 2)$ and $B(8, 4)$, then

(a) $AP = \frac{1}{3} AB$ (b) $AP = PB$ (c) $PB = \frac{1}{3} AB$ (d) $AP = \frac{1}{2} AB$

Ans. ***(d)*** Given that, the point $P(2, 1)$ lies on the line segment joining the points $A(4, 2)$ and $B(8, 4)$, which shows in the figure below:

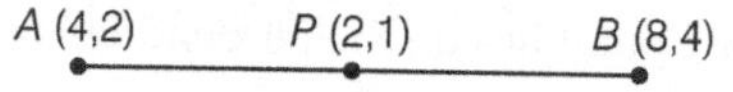

Now, distance between $A(4, 2)$ and $P(2, 1)$, $AP = \sqrt{(2-4)^2 + (1-2)^2}$

$\left[\because \text{distance between two points } (x_1, y_1) \text{ and } (x_2, y_2),\ d = \sqrt{(x_2 - x_1)^2 + (y_2 - y_1)^2}\right]$

$$= \sqrt{(-2)^2 + (-1)^2} = \sqrt{4 + 1} = \sqrt{5}$$

Distance between $A(4, 2)$ and $B(8, 4)$,

$$AB = \sqrt{(8-4)^2 + (4-2)^2}$$

$$= \sqrt{(4)^2 + (2)^2} = \sqrt{16 + 4} = \sqrt{20} = 2\sqrt{5}$$

Distance between $B(8, 4)$ and $P(2, 1)$, $BP = \sqrt{(8-2)^2 + (4-1)^2}$

$$= \sqrt{6^2 + 3^2} = \sqrt{36 + 9} = \sqrt{45} = 3\sqrt{5}$$

Here, $AB = 2\sqrt{5} = 2AP \Rightarrow AP = \frac{AB}{2}$

Hence, required condition is $AP = \frac{AB}{2}$.

Q.13 If $P\left(\frac{a}{3}, 4\right)$ is the mid-point of the line segment joining the points $Q(-6, 5)$ and $R(-2, 3)$, then the value of a is

(a) -4 (b) -12

(c) 12 (d) -6

Ans. ***(b)*** Given that, $P\left(\frac{a}{3}, 4\right)$ is the mid-point of the line segment joining the points $Q(-6, 5)$ and $R(-2, 3)$, which shows in the figure given below

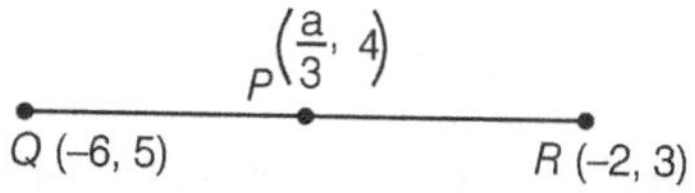

$\therefore$ Mid-point of $QR = P\left(\frac{-6-2}{2}, \frac{5+3}{2}\right) = P(-4, 4)$

$\left[\because \text{mid-point of line segment having end points } (x_1, y_1) \text{ and } (x_2, y_2) = \left(\frac{(x_1 + x_2)}{2}, \frac{(y_1 + y_2)}{2}\right)\right]$

But mid-point $P\left(\frac{a}{3}, 4\right)$ is given.

$$\therefore \quad \left(\frac{a}{3}, 4\right) = (-4, 4)$$

On comparing the mid-point coordinates, we get

$$\frac{a}{3} = -4$$

$$\therefore \quad a = -12$$

Hence, the required value of a is −12.

Q.14 The perpendicular bisector of the line segment joining the points $A(1, 5)$ and $B(4, 6)$ cuts the Y-axis at

(a) (0, 13) (b) (0, −13)

(c) (0, 12) (d) (13, 0)

Ans. *(a)* Let line q be the perpendicular bisector of AB.

Also, let line q meets the Y-axis at a point C.

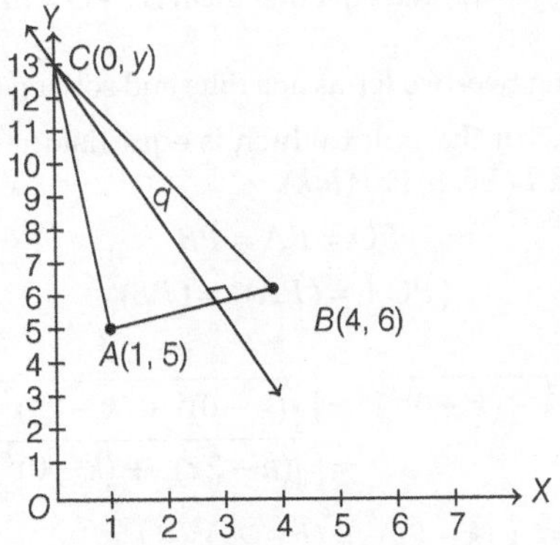

∴ coordinates of C is $(0, y)$.

As, point C is equidistant from AB.

$$\therefore \quad AC = BC$$

$$\sqrt{(0-1)^2 + (y-5)^2} = \sqrt{(0-4)^2 + (y-6)^2}$$

$$[\because \text{Distance formula} = \sqrt{(x_2 - x_1)^2 + (y_2 - y_1)^2}]$$

$$\Rightarrow \quad \sqrt{1 + (y-5)^2} = \sqrt{16 + (y-6)^2}$$

On squaring both sides, we get

$$1 + (y-5)^2 = 16 + (y-6)^2$$

$$\Rightarrow \quad y^2 + 25 - 10y + 1 = 16 + y^2 + 36 - 12y$$

$$\Rightarrow \quad 26 - 10y = 52 - 12y$$

$$\Rightarrow \quad 2y = 26$$

$$\Rightarrow \quad y = 13$$

∴ Required coordinate of C is $(0, 13)$.

Q.15 The coordinates of the point which is equidistant from the three vertices of the ΔAOB as shown in the figure is

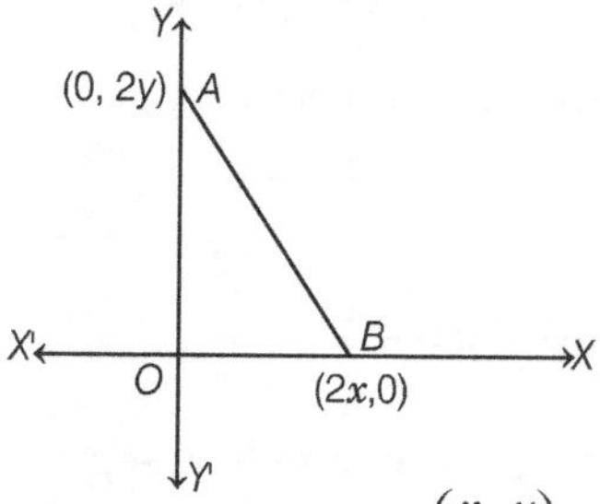

(a) (x, y) (b) (y, x) (c) $\left(\frac{x}{2}, \frac{y}{2}\right)$ (d) $\left(\frac{y}{2}, \frac{x}{2}\right)$

Thinking Process

(i) Firstly, consider the new point be $P(h, k)$.

(ii) Secondly, determine the distance PO, PA and PB by using the distance formula, $\sqrt{(x_2 - x_1)^2 + (y_2 - y_1)^2}$ and equating them *i.e.*, $PO = PA = PB$.

(iii) Further, solving two-two terms at a time and solving them to get required point.

Ans. *(a)* Let the coordinate of the point which is equidistant from the three vertices $O(0, 0)$, $A(0, 2y)$ and $B(2x, 0)$ is $P(h,k)$.

Then, $$PO = PA = PB$$

$\Rightarrow$ $$(PO)^2 = (PA)^2 = (PB)^2 \quad \text{... (i)}$$

By distance formula,

$$[\sqrt{(h-0)^2 + (k-0)^2}]^2 = [\sqrt{(h-0)^2 + (k-2y)^2}]^2$$
$$= [\sqrt{(h-2x)^2 + (k-0)^2}]^2$$

$\Rightarrow$ $$h^2 + k^2 = h^2 + (k-2y)^2 = (h-2x)^2 + k^2 \quad \text{... (ii)}$$

Taking first two terms, we get

$$h^2 + k^2 = h^2 + (k-2y)^2$$

$\Rightarrow$ $$k^2 = k^2 + 4y^2 - 4yk \Rightarrow 4y(y-k) = 0$$

$\Rightarrow$ $$y = k \quad [\because y \neq 0]$$

Taking first and third terms, we get

$$h^2 + k^2 = (h-2x)^2 + k^2$$

$\Rightarrow$ $$h^2 = h^2 + 4x^2 - 4xh$$

$\Rightarrow$ $$4x(x-h) = 0 \Rightarrow x - h = 0 \Rightarrow x = h \quad [\because x \neq 0]$$

$\therefore$ Required points $= (h, k) = (x, y)$

Q.16 A circle drawn with origin as the centre, passes through $\left(\frac{13}{2}, 0\right)$.

The point which does not lie in the interior of the circle is

(a) $\left(\frac{-3}{4}, 1\right)$ (b) $\left(2, \frac{7}{3}\right)$

(c) $\left(5, \frac{-1}{2}\right)$ (d) $\left(-6, \frac{5}{2}\right)$

Ans. ***(d)*** It is given that, centre of circle is (0,0) and passes through the point $\left(\frac{13}{2}, 0\right)$.

$\therefore$ Radius of circle = Distance between (0, 0) and $\left(\frac{13}{2}, 0\right)$

$$= \sqrt{\left(\frac{13}{2} - 0\right)^2 + (0 - 0)^2} = \sqrt{\left(\frac{13}{2}\right)^2} = \frac{13}{2} = 6.5$$

The distance of a point (*d*) from the centre of a circle determines whether the point is inside, outside or on the circle.

If $d > r$ the point is outside the circle, if $d = r$, then the point is on the circle and if $d < r$, then the point is inside the circle.

Now, to get the correct option we have to check the option one by one.

(a) Distance between (0,0) and $\left(\frac{-3}{4}, 1\right) = \sqrt{\left(\frac{-3}{4} - 0\right)^2 + (1 - 0)^2}$

$$= \sqrt{\frac{9}{16} + 1} = \sqrt{\frac{25}{16}} = \frac{5}{4} = 1.25 < 6.5$$

So, the point $\left(-\frac{3}{4}, 1\right)$ lies inside to the circle.

(b) Distance between (0,0) and $\left(2, \frac{7}{3}\right) = \sqrt{(2 - 0)^2 + \left(\frac{7}{3} - 0\right)^2}$

$$= \sqrt{4 + \frac{49}{9}} = \sqrt{\frac{36 + 49}{9}}$$

$$= \sqrt{\frac{85}{9}} = \frac{9.22}{3} = 3.07 < 6.5$$

So, the point $\left(2, \frac{7}{3}\right)$ lies inside the circle.

(c) Distance between (0,0) and $\left(5, \frac{-1}{2}\right) = \sqrt{(5 - 0)^2 + \left(-\frac{1}{2} - 0\right)^2}$

$$= \sqrt{25 + \frac{1}{4}} = \sqrt{\frac{101}{4}} = \frac{10.05}{2}$$

$$\Rightarrow \quad = 5.025 < 6.5$$

So, the point $\left(5, -\frac{1}{2}\right)$ lies inside the circle.

(d) Distance between (0,0) and $\left(-6, \frac{5}{2}\right) = \sqrt{(-6 - 0)^2 + \left(\frac{5}{2} - 0\right)^2}$

$$= \sqrt{36 + \frac{25}{4}} = \sqrt{\frac{144 + 25}{4}}$$

$$= \sqrt{\frac{169}{4}} = \frac{13}{2} = 6.5$$

So, the point $\left(-6, \frac{5}{2}\right)$ lis on the circle *i.e.*, does not lie inside to the circle.

Q.17 A line intersects the Y-axis and X-axis at the points P and Q, respectively. If $(2, -5)$ is the mid-point of PQ, then the coordinates of P and Q are, respectively

(a) $(0, -5)$ and $(2, 0)$
(b) $(0, 10)$ and $(-4, 0)$
(c) $(0, 4)$ and $(-10, 0)$
(d) $(0, -10)$ and $(4, 0)$

Ans. ***(d)*** Let the coordinates of P and Q are $(0, y)$ and $(x, 0)$, respectively.

So, the mid-point of $P(0, y)$ and $Q(x, 0)$ is $M\left(\frac{0+x}{2}, \frac{y+0}{2}\right)$.

$\left[\because \text{ mid-point of a line segment having end points } (x_1, y_1) \text{ and } (x_2, y_2) = \left(\frac{x_1+x_2}{2}, \frac{y_1+y_2}{2}\right)\right]$

But it is given that, mid-point of PQ is $(2, -5)$.

$$\therefore \quad 2 = \frac{x+0}{2}$$

$$\text{and} \quad -5 = \frac{y+0}{2}$$

$$\Rightarrow \quad x = 4 \text{ and } y = -10$$

So, the coordinates of P and Q are $(0, -10)$ and $(4, 0)$, respectively.

***Q.18** The area of a triangle with vertices $(a, b+c)$, $(b, c+a)$ and $(c, a+b)$ is

(a) $(a+b+c)^2$
(b) 0
(c) $(a+b+c)$
(d) abc

Ans. ***(b)*** Let the vertices of a triangle are, $A = (x_1, y_1) = (a, b+c)$

$B = (x_2, y_2) = (b, c+a)$ and $C = (x_3, y_3) = (c, a+b)$

$$\because \text{ Area of } \Delta ABC = \Delta = \left|\frac{1}{2}[x_1(y_2 - y_3) + x_2(y_3 - y_1) + x_3(y_1 - y_2)]\right|$$

$$\therefore \quad \Delta = \left|\frac{1}{2}[a(c+a-a-b) + b(a+b-b-c) + c(b+c-c-a)]\right|$$

$$= \left|\frac{1}{2}[a(c-b) + b(a-c) + c(b-a)]\right|$$

$$= \left|\frac{1}{2}(ac - ab + ab - bc + bc - ac)\right| = \left|\frac{1}{2}(0)\right| = 0$$

Hence, the required area of triangle is 0.

Q.19 If the distance between the points $(4, p)$ and $(1, 0)$ is 5, then the value of p is

(a) 4 only
(b) ± 4
(c) -4 only
(d) 0

Note (*) *Topics related to these question have been removed from latest NCERT.*

Ans. ***(b)*** According to the question, the distance between the points $(4, p)$ and $(1, 0) = 5$

i.e., $\sqrt{(1-4)^2 + (0-p)^2} = 5$ $\left[\because \text{distance between the points } (x_1, y_1) \text{ and } (x_2, y_2), \; d = \sqrt{(x_2 - x_1)^2 + (y_2 - y_1)^2}\right]$

$\Rightarrow \quad \sqrt{(-3)^2 + p^2} = 5$

$\Rightarrow \quad \sqrt{9 + p^2} = 5$

On squaring both the sides, we get

$9 + p^2 = 25$

$\Rightarrow \quad p^2 = 16$

$\Rightarrow \quad p = \pm 4$

Hence, the required value of p is ± 4.

Mistake Alert! *Students may get confused between $p^2 = 16$ and $p = \sqrt{16}$. If $p^2 = 16$, then $p = \pm 4$, if $p = \sqrt{16}$, then $p = 4$.*

****Q.20*** If the points $A(1, 2)$, $B(0, 0)$ and $C(a, b)$ are collinear, then

(a) $a = b$
(b) $a = 2b$
(c) $2a = b$
(d) $a = -b$

Ans. ***(c)*** Let the given points are $A = (x_1, y_1) = (1, 2)$, $B = (x_2, y_2) = (0, 0)$ and $C = (x_3, y_3) = (a, b)$.

$\because$ Area of ΔABC $\Delta = \left|\frac{1}{2}[x_1(y_2 - y_3) + x_2(y_3 - y_1) + x_3(y_1 - y_2)]\right|$

$$\therefore \quad \Delta = \left|\frac{1}{2}[1(0-b) + 0(b-2) + a(2-0)]\right|$$

$$= \left|\frac{1}{2}(-b + 0 + 2a)\right|$$

$$= \left|\frac{1}{2}(2a - b)\right|$$

Since, the points $A(1, 2)$, $B(0, 0)$ and $C(a, b)$ are collinear, then area of ΔABC should be equal to zero.

i.e., area of $\Delta ABC = 0$

$\Rightarrow \quad \left|\frac{1}{2}(2a - b)\right| = 0$

$\Rightarrow \quad 2a - b = 0$

$\Rightarrow \quad 2a = b$

Hence, the required relation is $2a = b$.

Note (✱) *Topics related to these question have been removed from latest NCERT.*

Short Answer Questions with Reasoning

State whether the following statements are true or false. Justify your answer.

Q.1 ΔABC with vertices $A(-2, 0)$, $B(2, 0)$ and $C(0,2)$ is similar to ΔDEF with vertices $D(-4, 0)$, $E(4, 0)$ and $F(0, 4)$.

- **Concept Insight** In this question, we will use the concept of similarity of two triangles.

Ans. *True*

Distance between $A(-2,0)$ and $B(2, 0)$, $AB = \sqrt{[2-(-2)]^2 + (0-0)^2} = \sqrt{(4)^2} = 4$

[$\because$ distance between the points (x_1, y_1) and (x_2, y_2), $d = \sqrt{(x_2 - x_1)^2 + (y_2 - y_1)^2}$]

Similarly, distance between $B(2, 0)$ and $C(0, 2)$,

$$BC = \sqrt{(0-2)^2 + (2-0)^2} = \sqrt{4+4} = \sqrt{8} = 2\sqrt{2}$$

Distance between $C(0, 2)$ and $A(-2, 0)$,

$$CA = \sqrt{(-2-0)^2 + (0-2)^2} = \sqrt{(-2)^2 + (-2)^2} = \sqrt{4+4} = \sqrt{8} = 2\sqrt{2}$$

Distance between $F(0, 4)$ and $D(-4, 0)$, $FD = \sqrt{(-4-0)^2 + (0-4)^2}$

$$= \sqrt{(-4)^2 + (-4)^2} = \sqrt{16+16} = \sqrt{32} = 4\sqrt{2}$$

Distance between $F(0, 4)$ and $E(4, 0)$, $FE = \sqrt{(4-0)^2 + (0-4)^2}$

$$= \sqrt{4^2 + 4^2} = \sqrt{16+16} = \sqrt{32} = 4\sqrt{2}$$

and distance between $E(4, 0)$ and $D(-4, 0)$,

$$ED = \sqrt{[-4-4]^2 + (0)^2} = \sqrt{(-8)^2} = \sqrt{64} = \sqrt{8} = 8$$

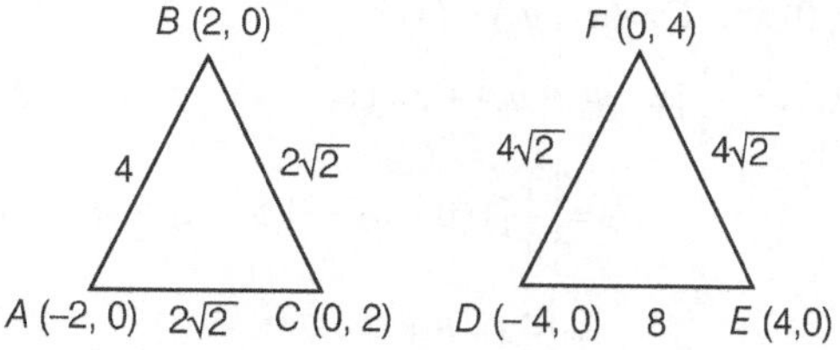

Now,
$$\frac{AB}{DE} = \frac{4}{8} = \frac{1}{2}$$

$$\frac{AC}{DF} = \frac{2\sqrt{2}}{4\sqrt{2}} = \frac{1}{2}$$

$$\frac{BC}{EF} = \frac{2\sqrt{2}}{4\sqrt{2}} = \frac{1}{2}$$

$\therefore$
$$\frac{AB}{DE} = \frac{AC}{DF} = \frac{BC}{EF} = \frac{1}{2}$$

Here, we see that sides of ΔABC and ΔDEF are propotional.

Hence, both the triangles are similar. [by SSS rule]

Q.2 Point $P(-4, 2)$ lies on the line segment joining the points $A(-4, 6)$ and $B(-4, -6)$.

Ans. *True*

We plot all the points $P(-4, 2)$, $A(-4, 6)$ and $B(-4, -6)$ on the graph paper.

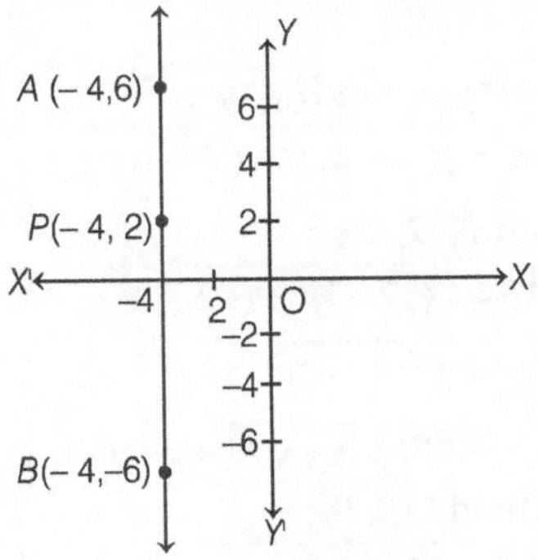

From the figure, point $P(-4, 2)$ lies on the line segment joining the points $A(-4, 6)$ and $B(-4, -6)$.

***Q.3** The points (0, 5), (0, –9) and (3, 6) are collinear.

Ans. *False*

If the area of triangle formed by the points (0, 5), (0 – 9) and (3, 6) is zero, then the points are collinear.

Here, $x_1 = 0, x_2 = 0, x_3 = 3$ and $y_1 = 5, y_2 = -9, y_3 = 6$

$\because$ Area of triangle, $\Delta = \left|\frac{1}{2}[x_1(y_2 - y_3) + x_2(y_3 - y_1) + x_3(y_1 - y_2)]\right|$

$$\therefore \quad \Delta = \left|\frac{1}{2}[0(-9-6) + 0(6-5) + 3(5+9)]\right|$$

$$= \left|\frac{1}{2}(0 + 0 + 3 \times 14)\right| = 21 \neq 0$$

Hence, the points are non-collinear.

Q.4 Point $P(0, 2)$ is the point of intersection of y-axis and perpendicular bisector of line segment joining the points $A(-1, 1)$ and $B(3, 3)$.

Ans. *False*

We know that, the points lies on perpendicular bisector of the line segment joining the two points is equidistant from these two points.

$$\therefore \quad PA = \sqrt{(-1-0)^2 + (1-2)^2}$$

$$= \sqrt{1+1} = \sqrt{2}$$

$$PB = \sqrt{(3-0)^2 + (3-2)^2} = \sqrt{9+1} = \sqrt{10}$$

$$\because \quad PA \neq PB$$

So, the point P does not lie on the perpendicular bisctor of AB.

Note (*) *Topics related to these question have been removed from latest NCERT.*

Q.5 Points $A(3, 1)$, $B(12, -2)$ and $C(0, 2)$ cannot be the vertices of a triangle.

- **Concept Insight** From triangle inequality theorem the sum of any two sides of a triangle is always greater than the third side.

Ans. *True*

We know that,

Distance between the points (x_1, y_1) and (x_2, y_2)

$$d = \sqrt{(x_2 - x_1)^2 + (y_2 - y_1)^2}$$

Distance between $A(3,1)$ and $B(12,-2)$,

$$AB = \sqrt{(12-3)^2 + (-2-1)^2}$$
$$= \sqrt{9^2 + (-3)^2}$$
$$= \sqrt{81+9} = \sqrt{90} = 9.486$$

Distance between $B(12,-2)$ and $C(0,2)$,

$$BC = \sqrt{(0-12)^2 + [2-(-2)]^2} = \sqrt{(-12)^2 + 4^2}$$
$$= \sqrt{144+16} = \sqrt{160} = 12.649$$

Distance between $A(3,1)$ and $C(0,2)$

$$AC = \sqrt{(0-3)^2 + (2-1)^2}$$
$$= \sqrt{(-3)^2 + (1)^2} = \sqrt{9+1}$$
$$= \sqrt{10} = 3.162$$

Since, the sum of AB and AC is equal to BC.

So, the points $A(3,1)$, $B(12,-2)$ and $C(0,2)$ cannot be the vertices of a triangle.

Q.6 Points $A(4, 3)$, $B(6, 4)$, $C(5, -6)$ and $D(-3, 5)$ are vertices of a parallelogram.

Ans. *False*

Distance between $A(4, 3)$ and $B(6, 4)$, $AB = \sqrt{(6-4)^2 + (4-3)^2}$

$$= \sqrt{2^2 + 1^2} = \sqrt{4+1} = \sqrt{5}$$

[$\because$ distance between the points (x_1, y_1) and (x_2, y_2), $d = \sqrt{(x_2 - x_1)^2 + (y_2 - y_1)^2}$]

Distance between $B(6,4)$ and $C(5,-6)$, $BC = \sqrt{(5-6)^2 + (-6-4)^2}$

$$= \sqrt{(-1)^2 + (-10)^2}$$
$$= \sqrt{1+100} = \sqrt{101}$$

Distance between $C(5,-6)$ and $D(-3,5)$, $CD = \sqrt{(-3-5)^2 + (5-(-6))^2}$

$$= \sqrt{(-8)^2 + 11^2} = \sqrt{64+121} = \sqrt{185}$$

Distance between $D(-3,5)$ and $A(4,3)$, $DA = \sqrt{[4-(-3)]^2 + (3-5)^2}$

$$= \sqrt{7^2 + (-2)^2} = \sqrt{49+4} = \sqrt{53}$$

In parallelogram, opposite sides are equal.

Here, we see that all sides AB, BC, CD and DA are different.

Hence, given vertices are not the vertices of a parallelogram.

Q.7 A circle has its centre at the origin and a point P (5, 0) lies on it. The point Q (6, 8) lies outside the circle.

Thinking Process Firstly, we find the distance between $Q(6, 8)$ and origin $O(0, 0)$ by distance formula and check OQ is greater than the length of radius, *i.e.*, OP or not.

Ans. *True*

First, we draw a circle and a point from the given information.

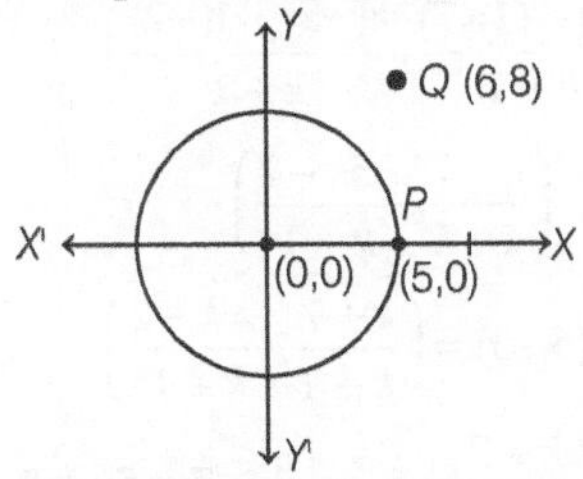

Now, distance between origin *i.e.*, $O(0, 0)$ and $P(5, 0)$, $OP = \sqrt{(5-0)^2 + (0-0)^2}$

$\left[\because \text{Distance between two points } (x_1, y_1) \text{ and } (x_2, y_2),\ d = \sqrt{(x_2 - x_1)^2 + (y_2 - y_1)^2}\right]$

$= \sqrt{5^2 + 0^2} = 5 =$ Radius of circle

and distance between origin $O(0, 0)$ and $Q(6, 8)$, $OQ = \sqrt{(6-0)^2 + (8-0)^2}$

$= \sqrt{6^2 + 8^2} = \sqrt{36 + 64} = \sqrt{100} = 10$

We know that, if the distance of any point from the centre is less than, equal to or more than the radius, then the point is inside, on or outside the circle, respectively.

Here, we see that, $OQ > OP$

Hence, it is true that point Q (6, 8), lies outside the circle.

Mistake Alert! *Students may mistakenly consider OP as diameter instead of radius.*

Q.8 The point A (2, 7) lies on the perpendicular bisector of line segment joining the points P (6, 5) and Q (0, – 4).

Ans. *False*

If A (2,7) lies on perpendicular bisector of $P(6, 5)$ and Q (0, – 4), then $AP = AQ$

$$\therefore \quad AP = \sqrt{(6-2)^2 + (5-7)^2}$$
$$= \sqrt{(4)^2 + (-2)^2}$$
$$= \sqrt{16+4} = \sqrt{20}$$

and
$$AQ = \sqrt{(0-2)^2 + (-4-7)^2}$$
$$= \sqrt{(-2)^2 + (-11)^2}$$
$$= \sqrt{4+121} = \sqrt{125}$$
$$\because \quad AP \neq AQ$$

So, A does not lie on the perpendicular bisector of PQ.

Q.9 Point $P(5, -3)$ is one of the two points of trisection of line segment joining the points $A(7, -2)$ and $B(1, -5)$.

Ans. *True*

Let P (5,–3) divides the line segment joining the points A (7,–2) and B (1,–5) in the ratio $k : 1$ internally.

By section formula, the coordinate of point P will be

$$\left(\frac{k(1)+(1)(7)}{k+1}, \frac{k(-5)+1(-2)}{k+1}\right)$$

i.e.,
$$\left(\frac{k+7}{k+1}, \frac{-5k-2}{k+1}\right)$$

Now,
$$(5,-3) = \left(\frac{k+7}{k+1}, \frac{-5k-2}{k+1}\right)$$

$$\Rightarrow \quad \frac{k+7}{k+1} = 5 \Rightarrow k+7 = 5k+5$$

$$\Rightarrow \quad -4k = -2$$

$$\therefore \quad k = \frac{1}{2}$$

So, the point P divides the line segment AB in ratio 1: 2.

Hence, point P is one of the two points of trisection of AB.

***Q.10** Points $A(-6, 10)$, $B(-4, 6)$ and $C(3, -8)$ are collinear such that $AB = \frac{2}{9}AC$.

- **Concept Insight** If the area of triangle formed by the points (x_1, y_1), (x_2, y_2) and (x_3, y_3) is zero, then the points are collinear.

Ans. *True*

Here, $x_1 = -6, x_2 = -4, x_3 = 3$ and $y_1 = 10, y_2 = 6, y_3 = -8$

$$\because \text{Area of triangle} = \left|\frac{1}{2}[x_1(y_2 - y_3) + x_2(y_3 - y_1) + x_3(y_1 - y_2)]\right|$$

$$\therefore \quad \text{Area of } \Delta ABC = \left|\frac{1}{2}[-6\{6-(-8)\} + (-4)(-8-10) + 3(10-6)]\right|$$

$$= \left|\frac{1}{2}[-6(14) + (-4)(-18) + 3(4)]\right|$$

$$= \left|\frac{1}{2}(-84 + 72 + 12)\right| = 0$$

So, given points are collinear.

Now, distance between $A(-6, 10)$ and $B(-4, 6)$, $AB = \sqrt{(-4+6)^2 + (6-10)^2}$

$$= \sqrt{2^2 + 4^2} = \sqrt{4+16} = \sqrt{20} = 2\sqrt{5}$$

$$\left[\because \text{distance between the points } (x_1, y_1) \text{ and } (x_2, y_2),\ d = \sqrt{(x_2 - x_1)^2 + (y_2 - y_1)^2}\right]$$

Note (*) *Topics related to these question have been removed from latest NCERT.*

Distance between $A(-6, 10)$ and $C(3, -8)$, $AC = \sqrt{(3+6)^2 + (-8-10)^2}$

$$= \sqrt{9^2 + (-18)^2} = \sqrt{81 + 324} = \sqrt{405} = \sqrt{81 \times 5} = 9\sqrt{5}$$

$$AB = 2\sqrt{5} = \frac{2}{9} \times 9\sqrt{5} = \frac{2}{9} AC$$

$\therefore$ $$AB = \frac{2}{9} AC$$

which is the required relation.

Q.11 The point $P(-2, 4)$ lies on a circle of radius 6 and centre $(3, 5)$.

Ans. *False*

If the distance between the centre and any point is equal to the radius, then we say that point lie on the circle.

Now, distance between $P(-2, 4)$ and centre $(3, 5)$

$$= \sqrt{(3+2)^2 + (5-4)^2}$$

$$= \sqrt{5^2 + 1^2}$$

$$= \sqrt{25 + 1} = \sqrt{26} = 5.099$$

$\left[\because \text{distance between the points } (x_1, y_1) \text{ and } (x_2, y_2),\ d = \sqrt{(x_2 - x_1)^2 + (y_2 - y_1)^2}\right]$

which is not equal to the radius of the circle.

Hence, the point $P(-2, 4)$ does not lie on the circle.

Q.12 The points $A(-1, -2)$, $B(4, 3)$, $C(2, 5)$ and $D(-3, 0)$ in that order form a rectangle.

Ans. *True*

Distance between $A(-1, -2)$ and $B(4, 3)$,

$$AB = \sqrt{(4+1)^2 + (3+2)^2}$$

$\left[\because \text{distance between the points } (x_1, y_1) \text{ and } (x_2, y_2),\ d = \sqrt{(x_2 - x_1)^2 + (y_2 - y_1)^2}\right]$

$$= \sqrt{5^2 + 5^2} = \sqrt{25 + 25} = \sqrt{50} = 5\sqrt{2}$$

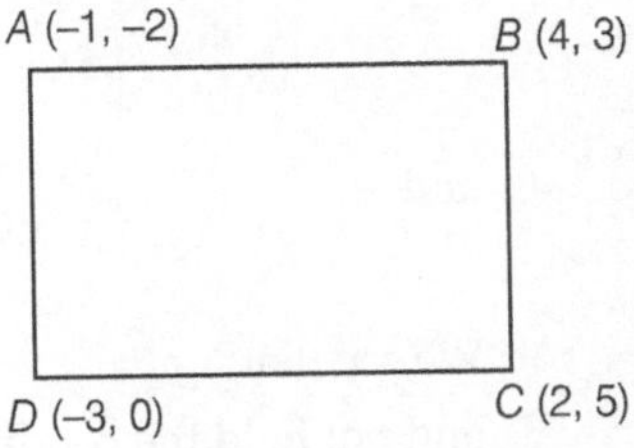

Distance between $C(2, 5)$ and $D(-3, 0)$,

$$CD = \sqrt{(-3-2)^2 + (0-5)^2}$$

$$= \sqrt{(-5)^2 + (-5)^2}$$

$$= \sqrt{25 + 25} = \sqrt{50} = 5\sqrt{2}$$

Distance between $A(-1, -2)$ and $D(-3, 0)$,

$$AD = \sqrt{(-3+1)^2 + (0+2)^2} = \sqrt{(-2)^2 + 2^2} = \sqrt{4 + 4} = \sqrt{8} = 2\sqrt{2}$$

and distance between $B(4, 3)$ and $C(2, 5)$, $BC = \sqrt{(4-2)^2 + (3-5)^2}$

$$= \sqrt{2^2 + (-2)^2} = \sqrt{4+4} = \sqrt{8} = 2\sqrt{2}$$

also, distance between $A(-1, -2)$ and $C(2, 5)$, $AC = \sqrt{(2+1)^2 + (5+2)^2}$

$$= \sqrt{3^2 + 7^2} = \sqrt{9+49} = \sqrt{58}$$

and distance between $D(-3, 0)$ and $B(4, 3)$, $DB = \sqrt{(4+3)^2 + (3-0)^2}$

$$= \sqrt{7^2 + 3^2} = \sqrt{49+9} = \sqrt{58}$$

We know that, in a rectangle, opposite sides and diagonals are equal.

Since, $AB = CD$ and $AD = BC$

And diagonals AC and BD are equal.

Hence, the points $A(-1, -2)$, $B(4, 3)$, $C(2, 5)$ and $D(-3, 0)$ form a rectangle.

Short Answer Questions

Q.1 Name the type of triangle formed by the points $A(-5, 6)$, $B(-4, -2)$ and $C(7, 5)$.

Thinking Process

(i) Firstly, determine the distances AB, BC and CA by using the distance formula, $\sqrt{(x_2 - x_1)^2 + (y_2 - y_1)^2}$

(ii) Secondly, check the condition for types of a triangles

(a) If any two sides are equal, then it is an isosceles triangle.

(b) If sides of a triangle satisfy the Pythagoras theorem, then it is a right angled triangle.

(c) If all three sides of a triangle are equal, then it is an equilateral triangle.

(d) If none of the side of a triangle are equal, then it is an scalene triangle.

Ans. To find the type of triangle, first we determine the length of all three sides and see whatever condition of triangle is satisfied by these sides.

Now, using distance formula between two points,

$$AB = \sqrt{(-4+5)^2 + (-2-6)^2} \quad [\because d = \sqrt{(x_2 - x_1) + (y_2 - y_1)^2}]$$

$$= \sqrt{(1)^2 + (-8)^2}$$

$$= \sqrt{1+64} = \sqrt{65}$$

$$BC = \sqrt{(7+4)^2 + (5+2)^2} = \sqrt{(11)^2 + (7)^2}$$

$$= \sqrt{121+49} = \sqrt{170}$$

and $$CA = \sqrt{(-5-7)^2 + (6-5)^2} = \sqrt{(-12)^2 + (1)^2}$$

$$= \sqrt{144+1} = \sqrt{145}$$

We see that, $AB \neq BC \neq CA$

and not hold the condition of Pythagoras in ΔABC.

i.e., $(\text{Hypotenuse})^2 = (\text{Base})^2 + (\text{Perpendicular})^2$

Hence, the required triangle is a scalene triangle.

Q.2 Find the points on the x-axis which are at a distance of $2\sqrt{5}$ from the point (7, −4). How many such points are there?

Ans. We know that, every point on the x-axis is in the form $(x, 0)$.

Let $P(x, 0)$ be the point on the x-axis have $2\sqrt{5}$ distance from the point $Q(7, -4)$.

By given condition, $PQ = 2\sqrt{5}$

$\Rightarrow \quad (PQ)^2 = (2\sqrt{5})^2$ [$\because$ distance formula $= \sqrt{(x_2 - x_1)^2 + (y_2 - y_1)^2}$]

$\Rightarrow \quad (\sqrt{((x-7)^2 + (0+4)^2})^2 = 20$

$\Rightarrow \quad [(x-7)^2 + (4)^2] = 20$

$\Rightarrow \quad x^2 + 49 - 14x + 16 = 20$

$\Rightarrow \quad x^2 - 14x + 65 - 20 = 0$

$\Rightarrow \quad x^2 - 14x + 45 = 0$

$\Rightarrow \quad x^2 - 9x - 5x + 45 = 0$ [by factorisation method]

$\Rightarrow \quad x(x-9) - 5(x-9) = 0$

$\Rightarrow \quad (x-9)(x-5) = 0$

$\therefore \quad x = 5, 9$

Hence, there are two points lies on the x-axis, which are (5, 0) and (9, 0), have $2\sqrt{5}$ distance from the point (7, − 4).

Q.3 What type of a quadrilateral do the points $A(2, -2)$, $B(7, 3)$, $C(11, -1)$ and $D(6, -6)$ taken in that order form?

Thinking Process

(i) Firstly, determine the distances AB, BC, CD, DA, AC and BD by using the distance formula $= \sqrt{(x_2 - x_1)^2 + (y_2 - y_1)^2}$.

(ii) Secondly, check the condition for types of a quadrilaterals

(a) If all four sides and also diagonals are equal, then quadrilateral is a square.

(b) If all four sides are equal but diagonal are not equal, then quadrilateral is a rhombus.

(c) If opposite sides of a quadrilateral are equal and diagonals are also equal, then quadrilateral is a rectangle.

Ans. To find the type of quadrilateral, we find the length of all four sides as well as two diagonals and see whatever condition of quadrilateral is satisfied by these sides as well as diagonals.

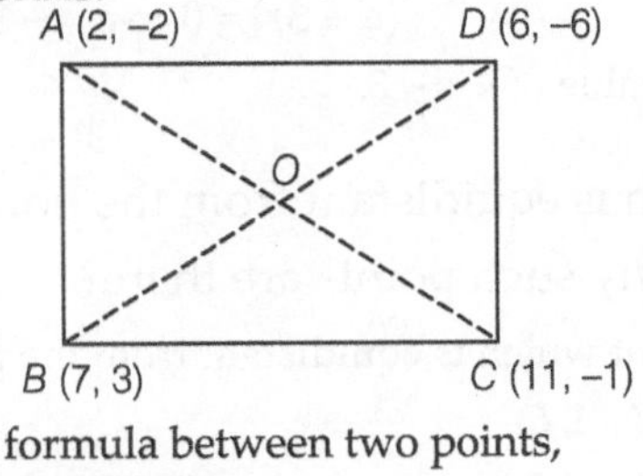

Now, using distance formula between two points,

side, $AB = \sqrt{(7-2)^2 + (3+2)^2}$

$\left[\because \text{distance between two points } (x_1, y_1) \text{ and } (x_2, y_2) = \sqrt{(x_2 - x_1) + (y_2 - y_1)^2}\right]$

$$= \sqrt{(5)^2 + (5)^2} = \sqrt{25 + 25}$$
$$= \sqrt{50} = 5\sqrt{2}$$
$$BC = \sqrt{(11 - 7)^2 + (-1 - 3)^2} = \sqrt{(4)^2 + (-4)^2}$$
$$= \sqrt{16 + 16} = \sqrt{32} = 4\sqrt{2}$$
$$CD = \sqrt{(6 - 11)^2 + (-6 + 1)^2}$$
$$= \sqrt{(-5)^2 + (-5)^2}$$
$$= \sqrt{25 + 25} = \sqrt{50} = 5\sqrt{2}$$

and $$DA = \sqrt{(2 - 6)^2 + (-2 + 6)^2}$$
$$= \sqrt{(-4)^2 + (4)^2} = \sqrt{16 + 16}$$
$$= \sqrt{32} = 4\sqrt{2}$$

Diagonals, $$AC = \sqrt{(11 - 2)^2 + (-1 + 2)^2}$$
$$= \sqrt{(9)^2 + (1)^2} = \sqrt{81 + 1} = \sqrt{82}$$

and $$BD = \sqrt{(6 - 7)^2 + (-6 - 3)^2} = \sqrt{(-1)^2 + (-9)^2}$$
$$= \sqrt{1 + 81} = \sqrt{82}$$

Here, we see that the sides $AB = CD$ and $BC = DA$

Also, diagonals are equal *i.e.*, $AC = BD$

which shows that the quadrilateral is a rectangle.

Q.4 Find the value of a, if the distance between the points $A(-3, -14)$ and $B(a, -5)$ is 9 units.

Ans. According to the question,

Distance between $A(-3, -14)$ and $B(a, -5)$, $AB = 9$ units.

$$\Rightarrow \quad \sqrt{(a + 3)^2 + (-5 + 14)^2} = 9 \quad [\because d = \sqrt{(x_2 - x_1)^2 + (y_2 - y_1)^2}]$$
$$\Rightarrow \quad \sqrt{(a + 3)^2 + (9)^2} = 9$$

On squaring both the sides, we get

$$(a + 3)^2 + 81 = 81$$
$$\Rightarrow \quad (a + 3)^2 = 0 \Rightarrow a = -3$$

Hence, the required value of a is -3.

Q.5 Find a point which is equidistant from the points $A(-5, 4)$ and $B(-1, 6)$. How many such points are there?

Ans. Let $P(h, k)$ be the point which is equidistant from the points $A(-5, 4)$ and $B(-1, 6)$.

$$\therefore \quad PA = PB$$
$$\Rightarrow \quad (PA)^2 = (PB)^2 \quad [\because \text{distance} = \sqrt{(x_2 - x_1)^2 + (y_2 - y_1)^2}]$$
$$\Rightarrow \quad (-5 - h)^2 + (4 - k)^2 = (-1 - h)^2 + (6 - k)^2$$

$$\Rightarrow \quad 25 + h^2 + 10h + 16 + k^2 - 8k = 1 + h^2 + 2h + 36 + k^2 - 12k$$

$$\Rightarrow \quad 25 + 10h + 16 - 8k = 1 + 2h + 36 - 12k$$

$$\Rightarrow \quad 8h + 4k + 41 - 37 = 0$$

$$\Rightarrow \quad 8h + 4k + 4 = 0$$

$$\Rightarrow \quad 2h + k + 1 = 0 \quad \text{...(i)}$$

$$\text{Mid-point of } AB = \left(\frac{-5-1}{2}, \frac{4+6}{2}\right) = (-3, 5)$$

$$\left[\because \text{ mid-point} = \left(\frac{x_1 + x_2}{2}, \frac{y_1 + y_2}{2}\right)\right]$$

At point (– 3, 5), LHS of Eq. (i),

$$2h + k + 1 = 2(-3) + 5 + 1 = -6 + 5 + 1 = 0$$

So, the mid-point of AB satisfy the Eq. (i). Hence, infinite number of points, in fact all points which are solution of the equation $2h + k + 1 = 0$, are equidistant from the points A and B.

Q.6 Find the coordinates of the point Q on the x-axis which lies on the perpendicular bisector of the line segment joining the points $A(-5, -2)$ and $B(4, -2)$. Name the type of triangle formed by the point Q, A and B.

Ans. Firstly, we plot the points of the line segment on the paper and join them.

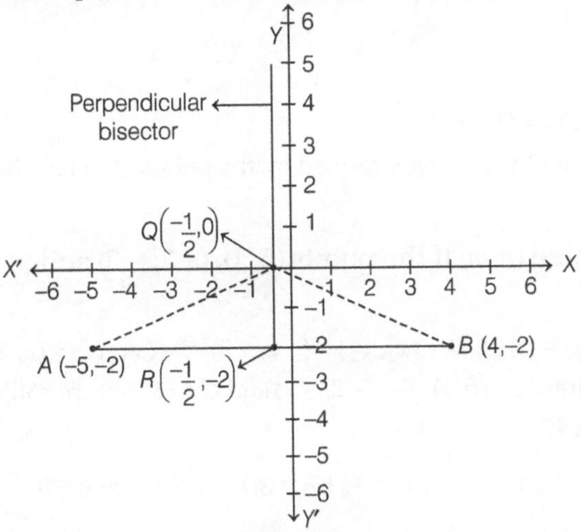

We know that, the perpendicular bisector of the line segment AB bisect the segment AB, *i.e.*, perpendicular bisector of the line segment AB passes through the mid-point of AB.

$$\therefore \quad \text{Mid-point of } AB = \left(\frac{-5+4}{2}, \frac{-2-2}{2}\right)$$

$$\Rightarrow \quad R = \left(-\frac{1}{2}, -2\right)$$

[$\because$ mid-point of a line segment having end points (x_1, y_1) and (x_2, y_2) is $\left(\frac{x_1 + x_2}{2}, \frac{y_1 + y_2}{2}\right)$]

Now, we draw a straight line on paper passes through the mid-point R which is perpendicular to AB. We see that perpendicular bisector cuts the x-axis at the point $Q\left(-\frac{1}{2}, 0\right)$.

Hence, the required coordinates of $Q = \left(-\frac{1}{2}, 0\right)$

To know the type of triangle formed by the points Q, A and B. We find the length of all three sides and see whatever condition of triangle is satisfied by these sides.

Now, using distance formula between two points,

$$\Rightarrow \quad AB = \sqrt{(4+5)^2 + (-2+2)^2} = \sqrt{(9)^2 + 0} = 9$$

[$\because$ distance between two points (x_1, y_1) and $(x_2, y_2) = \sqrt{(x_2 - x_1)^2 + (y_2 - y_1)^2}$]

$$\Rightarrow \quad BQ = \sqrt{\left(\frac{-1}{2} - 4\right)^2 + (0+2)^2}$$

$$= \sqrt{\left(\frac{-9}{2}\right)^2 + (2)^2} = \sqrt{\frac{81}{4} + 4} = \sqrt{\frac{97}{4}} = \frac{\sqrt{97}}{2}$$

and

$$QA = \sqrt{\left(-5 + \frac{1}{2}\right)^2 + (-2-0)^2} = \sqrt{\left(\frac{-9}{2}\right)^2 + (2)^2}$$

$$= \sqrt{\frac{81}{4} + 4} = \sqrt{\frac{97}{4}} = \frac{\sqrt{97}}{2}$$

We see that, $BQ = QA \neq AB$

which shows that the triangle formed by the points Q, A and B is an isosceles triangle.

*** Q.7 Find the value of m, if the points (5, 1), (− 2, − 3) and (8, 2m) are collinear.**

Ans. Let $A = (x_1, y_1) = (5, 1)$, $B = (x_2, y_2) = (-2, -3)$, $C = (x_3, y_3) = (8, 2m)$

Since, the points $A = (5, 1)$, $B = (-2, -3)$ and $C = (8, 2m)$ are collinear.

$\therefore$ Area of $\Delta ABC = 0$

$$\Rightarrow \quad \frac{1}{2}[x_1(y_2 - y_3) + x_2(y_3 - y_1) + x_3(y_1 - y_2)] = 0$$

$$\Rightarrow \quad \frac{1}{2}[5(-3-2m) + (-2)(2m-1) + 8\{1-(-3)\}] = 0$$

$$\Rightarrow \quad \frac{1}{2}(-15 - 10m - 4m + 2 + 32) = 0$$

$$\Rightarrow \quad \frac{1}{2}(-14m + 19) = 0 \Rightarrow -14m + 19 = 0 \Rightarrow m = \frac{19}{14}$$

Hence, the required value of m is $\frac{19}{14}$.

Note (✱) *Topics related to these question have been removed from latest NCERT.*

Q.8 If the point $A(2, -4)$ is equidistant from $P(3, 8)$ and $Q(-10, y)$, find the values of y. Also, find distance PQ.

Ans. According to the question,

$A(2, -4)$ is equidistant from $P(3, 8)$ and $Q(-10, y)$

i.e., $$PA = QA$$

$$\Rightarrow \sqrt{(2-3)^2 + (-4-8)^2} = \sqrt{(2+10)^2 + (-4-y)^2}$$

[$\because$ distance between two points (x_1, y_1) and (x_2, y_2), $d = \sqrt{(x_2 - x_1)^2 + (y_2 - y_1)^2}$]

$$\Rightarrow \sqrt{(-1)^2 + (-12)^2} = \sqrt{(12)^2 + (4+y)^2}$$

$$\Rightarrow \sqrt{1 + 144} = \sqrt{144 + 16 + y^2 + 8y}$$

$$\Rightarrow \sqrt{145} = \sqrt{160 + y^2 + 8y}$$

On squaring both the sides, we get

$$145 = 160 + y^2 + 8y$$

$$\Rightarrow y^2 + 8y + 160 - 145 = 0$$

$$\Rightarrow y^2 + 8y + 15 = 0$$

$$\Rightarrow y^2 + 5y + 3y + 15 = 0$$

$$\Rightarrow y(y+5) + 3(y+5) = 0$$

$$(y+5)(y+3) = 0$$

If $y + 5 = 0$, then $y = -5$

or if $y + 3 = 0$, then $y = -3$

$$\therefore \quad y = -3, -5$$

Now, distance between $P(3, 8)$ and $Q(-10, y)$,

$$PQ = \sqrt{(-10-3)^2 + (y-8)^2}$$

$$\Rightarrow \quad = \sqrt{(-13)^2 + (-3-8)^2} \quad \text{[putting } y = -3\text{]}$$

$$= \sqrt{169 + 121} = \sqrt{290}$$

Again, distance between $P(3, 8)$ and $(-10, y)$, $PQ = \sqrt{(-13)^2 + (-5-8)^2}$

[putting $y = -5$]

$$= \sqrt{169 + 169} = \sqrt{338}$$

Hence, the values of y are -3, -5 and corresponding values of PQ are $\sqrt{290}$ and $\sqrt{338} = 13\sqrt{2}$, respectively.

***Q.9** Find the area of the triangle whose vertices are $(-8, 4)$, $(-6, 6)$ and $(-3, 9)$.

Ans. Given that, the vertices of triangles are $(-8,4)$,$(-6, 6)$ and $(-3, 9)$.

Here, $x_1 = -8$, $x_2 = -6$, $x_3 = -3$ and $y_1 = 4$, $y_2 = 6$, $y_3 = 9$

We know that, the area of triangle with vertices (x_1, y_1), (x_2, y_2) and (x_3, y_3)

$$\Delta = \left| \frac{1}{2}[x_1(y_2 - y_3) + x_2(y_3 - y_1) + x_3(y_1 - y_2)] \right|$$

Note (*) *Topics related to these question have been removed from latest NCERT.*

$$\therefore \quad = \left|\frac{1}{2}[-8(6-9)-6(9-4)+(-3)(4-6)]\right|$$

$$= \left|\frac{1}{2}[-8(-3)-6(5)-3(-2)] = \frac{1}{2}(24-30+6)\right|$$

$$= \left|\frac{1}{2}(30-30) = \frac{1}{2}(0)\right| = 0$$

Hence, the required area of triangle is 0.

Q.10 In what ratio does the X-axis divide the line segment joining the points $(-4, -6)$ and $(-1, 7)$? Find the coordinates of the points of division.

- **Concept Insight** Assume the required ratio to be $k:1$ and apply the section formula *i.e.*, $\left(\frac{mx_2+nx_1}{m+n}, \frac{my_2+ny_1}{m+n}\right)$.

Ans. Let the required ratio be $k:1$. So, the coordinates of the point M of division $A(-4,-6)$ and $B(-1,7)$ are

$$\left(\frac{kx_2+1\cdot x_1}{k+1}, \frac{ky_2+1\cdot y_1}{k+1}\right)$$

Here, $\quad x_1=-4,\ x_2=-1$ and $y_1=-6,\ y_2=7$

i.e., $\quad \left(\frac{k(-1)+1(-4)}{k+1}, \frac{k(7)+1\cdot(-6)}{k+1}\right) = \left(\frac{-k-4}{k+1}, \frac{7k-6}{k+1}\right)$

But according to the question, line segment joining $A(-4,-6)$ and $B(-1,7)$ is divided by the x-axis. So, y-coordinate must be zero.

$$\therefore \quad \frac{7k-6}{k+1} = 0$$

$$\Rightarrow \quad 7k-6=0$$

$$\therefore \quad K = \frac{6}{7}$$

So, the required ratio is $6:7$ and the point of division is $\left(\frac{-\frac{6}{7}-4}{\frac{6}{7}+1}, \frac{7\times\frac{6}{7}-6}{\frac{6}{7}+1}\right)$

i.e., $\quad \left(\frac{\frac{-34}{7}}{\frac{13}{7}}, \frac{6-6}{\frac{13}{7}}\right)$ *i.e.*, $\left(\frac{-34}{13}, 0\right)$.

Hence, the required point of division is $\left(\frac{-34}{13}, 0\right)$.

Q.11 Find the ratio in which the point $P\left(\frac{3}{4}, \frac{5}{12}\right)$ divides the line segment joining the points $A\left(\frac{1}{2}, \frac{3}{2}\right)$ and $B(2,-5)$.

Ans. Let point p divides the line segment AB in the ratio $k : 1$.

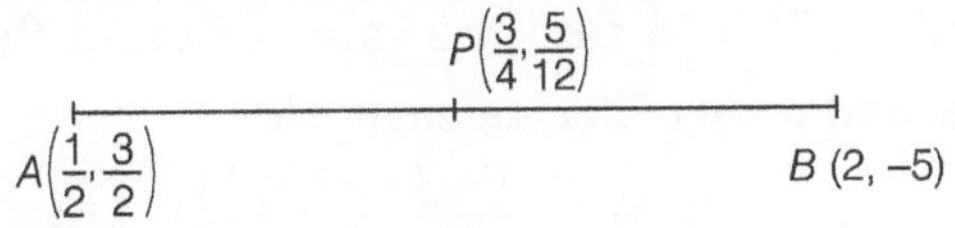

Using section formula,

$$(x, y) = \left(\frac{mx_2 + nx_1}{m+n}, \frac{my_2 + ny_1}{m+n}\right)$$

$$\therefore \quad \frac{3}{4} = \frac{k(2) + (1)\left(\frac{1}{2}\right)}{k+1} \Rightarrow \frac{3}{4} = \frac{2k + \frac{1}{2}}{k+1}$$

$$\Rightarrow \quad 3(k+1) = 4\left(2k + \frac{1}{2}\right)$$

$$\Rightarrow \quad 3k + 3 = 8k + 2$$

$$\Rightarrow \quad 5k = 1$$

$$\Rightarrow \quad k = \frac{1}{5}$$

$\therefore$Required ratio $= \frac{1}{5} : 1 = 1 : 5$

Q.12 If $P(9a - 2, -b)$ divides line segment joining $A(3a + 1, -3)$ and $B(8a, 5)$ in the ratio 3 : 1, find the values of a and b.

Ans. Let $P(9a - 2, -b)$ divides AB internally in the ratio 3 : 1.

By section formula,

$$9a - 2 = \frac{3(8a) + 1(3a + 1)}{3 + 1}$$

and $$-b = \frac{3(5) + 1(-3)}{3 + 1}$$

$$\Rightarrow \quad 9a - 2 = \frac{24a + 3a + 1}{4}$$

and $$-b = \frac{15 - 3}{4}$$

$$\Rightarrow \quad 9a - 2 = \frac{27a + 1}{4}$$

and $$-b = \frac{12}{4}$$

$$\Rightarrow \quad 36a - 8 = 27a + 1$$

and $$b = -3$$

$$\Rightarrow \quad 36a - 27a = 1 + 8$$

$$\Rightarrow \quad 9a = 9$$

$$\therefore \quad a = 1$$

Hence, the required values of a and b are 1 and – 3, respectively.

Q.13 If (a, b) is the mid-point of the line segment joining the points $A(10, -6)$ and $B(k, 4)$ and $a - 2b = 18$, find the value of k and the distance AB.

Ans. Since, (a, b) is the mid-point of line segment AB.

$$\therefore \quad (a, b) = \left(\frac{10 + k}{2}, \frac{-6 + 4}{2}\right)$$

$\left[\because \text{ mid-point of a line segment having end points } (x_1, y_1) \text{ and } (x_2, y_2) = \left(\frac{x_1 + x_2}{2}, \frac{y_1 + y_2}{2}\right)\right]$

$$\Rightarrow \quad (a, b) = \left(\frac{10 + k}{2}, -1\right)$$

Now, equating coordinates on both sides, we get

$$\therefore \quad a = \frac{10 + k}{2} \quad \ldots \text{(i)}$$

and $\quad b = -1 \quad \ldots$(ii)

Given, $\quad a - 2b = 18$

$\Rightarrow \quad a - 2(-1) = 18 \quad$ [from Eq. (ii)]

$\Rightarrow \quad a + 2 = 18 \Rightarrow a = 16$

From Eq. (i), we get $\quad 16 = \dfrac{10 + k}{2} \Rightarrow 32 = 10 + k \Rightarrow k = 22$

Hence, the required value of k is 22.

$\therefore \quad A = (10, -6), B = (22, 4)$

Now, distance between $A(10, -6)$ and $B(22, 4)$,

$$AB = \sqrt{(22 - 10)^2 + (4 + 6)^2}$$

[$\because$ distance between the points (x_1, y_1) and (x_2, y_2), $d = \sqrt{(x_2 - x_1)^2 + (y_2 - y_1)^2}$]

$$= \sqrt{(12)^2 + (10)^2} = \sqrt{144 + 100} = \sqrt{244} = 2\sqrt{61}$$

Hence, the required distance of AB is $2\sqrt{61}$.

Q.14 The centre of a circle is $(2a, a - 7)$. Find the values of a, if the circle passes through the point $(11, -9)$ and has diameter $10\sqrt{2}$ units.

Thinking Process

(i) Firstly, determine the distance between centre and point on the circle by using the distance formula $\sqrt{(x_2 - x_1)^2 + (y_2 - y_1)^2}$, which is equal to the radius of circle.

(ii) Further, using the given condition and simplify it.

Ans. By given condition,

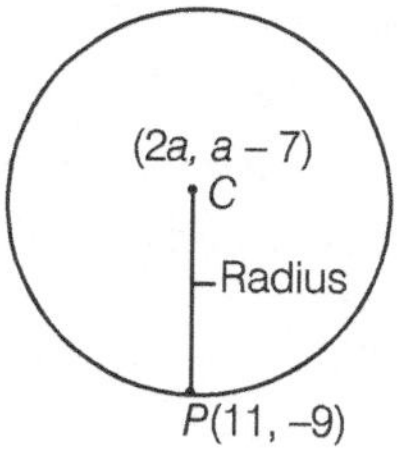

Distance between the centre $C(2a, a-7)$ and the point $P(11, -9)$, which lie on the circle = Radius of circle

$\therefore$ Radius of circle $= \sqrt{(11-2a)^2 + (-9-a+7)^2}$ ...(i)

[$\because$ distance between two points (x_1, y_1) and $(x_2, y_2) = \sqrt{(x_2-x_1)^2 + (y_2-y_1)^2}$]

Given that, length of diameter $= 10\sqrt{2}$ units

$$\therefore \quad \text{Length of radius} = \frac{\text{Length of diameter}}{2} = \frac{10\sqrt{2}}{2} = 5\sqrt{2}$$

Put this value in Eq. (i), we get

$$5\sqrt{2} = \sqrt{(11-2a)^2 + (-2-a)^2}$$

On squaring both sides, we get

$$50 = (11-2a)^2 + (2+a)^2$$
$$\Rightarrow \quad 50 = 121 + 4a^2 - 44a + 4 + a^2 + 4a$$
$$\Rightarrow \quad 5a^2 - 40a + 125 - 50 = 0$$
$$\Rightarrow \quad 5a^2 - 40a + 75 = 0$$
$$\Rightarrow \quad a^2 - 8a + 15 = 0$$
$$\Rightarrow \quad a^2 - 5a - 3a + 15 = 0 \quad \text{[by factorisation method]}$$
$$\Rightarrow \quad a(a-5) - 3(a-5) = 0$$
$$\Rightarrow \quad (a-5)(a-3) = 0$$
$$\therefore \quad a = 3, 5$$

Hence, the required values of a are 5 and 3.

Q.15 The line segment joining the points $A(3, 2)$ and $B(5, 1)$ is divided at the point P in the ratio $1:2$ and it lies on the line $3x - 18y + k = 0$. Find the value of k.

Ans. Given that, the line segment joining the points $A(3, 2)$ and $B(5, 1)$ is divided at the point P in the ratio $1:2$.

$$\therefore \text{Coordinates of point } P = \left\{\frac{5(1)+3(2)}{1+2}, \frac{1(1)+2(2)}{1+2}\right\}$$
$$= \left(\frac{5+6}{3}, \frac{1+4}{3}\right) = \left(\frac{11}{3}, \frac{5}{3}\right)$$

$$\left[\because \text{section formula for internal ratio} \equiv \left(\frac{m_1x_2 + m_2x_1}{m_1+m_2}, \frac{m_1y_2 + m_2y_1}{m_1+m_2}\right)\right]$$

But the point $P\left(\frac{11}{3}, \frac{5}{3}\right)$ lies on the line $3x - 18y + k = 0$. [given]

$$\therefore \quad 3\left(\frac{11}{3}\right) - 18\left(\frac{5}{3}\right) + k = 0 \Rightarrow 11 - 30 + k = 0$$
$$\Rightarrow \quad k - 19 = 0 \Rightarrow k = 19$$

Hence, the required value of k is 19.

***Q.16** If $D\left(-\frac{1}{2}, \frac{5}{2}\right)$, $E(7, 3)$ and $F\left(\frac{7}{2}, \frac{7}{2}\right)$ are the mid-points of sides of ΔABC, find the area of the ΔABC.

Thinking Process

(i) Firstly, consider the vertices of of ΔABC be $A(x_1\ y_1)$, $B(x_2, y_2)$ and $C(x_3, y_3)$.

(ii) With the help of mid-point formula form the equations in terms of x_1, y_1, x_2, y_2, x_3 and y_3 and solve them to get the values of vertices.

(iii) Further, determine the area of triangle by using the formula,
$$\left|\frac{1}{2}[x_1(y_2 - y_3) + x_2(y_3 - y_1) + x_3(y_1 - y_2)]\right|$$

Ans. Let $A = (x_1, y_1)$, $B = (x_2, y_2)$ and $C = (x_3, y_3)$ are the vertices of the ΔABC and $D\left(-\frac{1}{2}, \frac{5}{2}\right)$, $E(7, 3)$ and $F\left(\frac{7}{2}, \frac{7}{2}\right)$ be the mid-points of the sides BC, CA and AB, respectively.

Since, $D\left(-\frac{1}{2}, \frac{5}{2}\right)$ is the mid-point of BC.

$$\therefore \quad \frac{x_2 + x_3}{2} = -\frac{1}{2}$$

$\left[\because \text{mid-point of a line segment having end points } (x_1, y_1) \text{ and } (x_2, y_2) \text{ is } \left(\frac{x_1 + x_2}{2}, \frac{y_1 + y_2}{2}\right)\right]$

$$\text{and} \quad \frac{y_2 + y_3}{2} = \frac{5}{2}$$

$$\Rightarrow \quad x_2 + x_3 = -1 \quad \text{...(i)}$$

$$\text{and} \quad y_2 + y_3 = 5 \quad \text{...(ii)}$$

As $E(7, 3)$ is the mid-point of CA.

$$\therefore \quad \frac{x_3 + x_1}{2} = 7$$

$$\text{and} \quad \frac{y_3 + y_1}{2} = 3$$

$$\Rightarrow \quad x_3 + x_1 = 14 \quad \text{...(iii)}$$

$$\text{and} \quad y_3 + y_1 = 6 \quad \text{...(iv)}$$

Also, $F\left(\frac{7}{2}, \frac{7}{2}\right)$ is the mid-point of AB.

$$\therefore \quad \frac{x_1 + x_2}{2} = \frac{7}{2}$$

$$\text{and} \quad \frac{y_1 + y_2}{2} = \frac{7}{2}$$

$$\Rightarrow \quad x_1 + x_2 = 7 \quad \text{...(v)}$$

$$\text{and} \quad y_1 + y_2 = 7 \quad \text{...(vi)}$$

On adding Eqs. (i), (iii) and (v), we get

$$2(x_1 + x_2 + x_3) = 20$$

Note (*) *Topics related to these question have been removed from latest NCERT.*

$$\Rightarrow \quad x_1 + x_2 + x_3 = 10 \quad \text{...(vii)}$$

On subtracting Eqs. (i), (iii) and (v) from Eq. (vii) respectively, we get

$$x_1 = 11, x_2 = -4, x_3 = 3$$

On adding Eqs. (ii), (iv) and (vi), we get

$$2(y_1 + y_2 + y_3) = 18$$

$$\Rightarrow \quad y_1 + y_2 + y_3 = 9 \quad \text{...(viii)}$$

On subtracting Eqs. (ii), (iv) and (vi) from Eq. (viii) respectively, we get

$$y_1 = 4, y_2 = 3, y_3 = 2$$

Hence, the vertices of ΔABC are $A(11, 4)$, $B(-4, 3)$ and $C(3, 2)$.

$$\because \quad \text{Area of } \Delta ABC = \Delta = \left|\frac{1}{2}[x_1(y_2 - y_3) + x_2(y_3 - y_1) + x_3(y_1 - y_2)]\right|$$

$$\therefore \quad \Delta = \frac{1}{2}[11(3-2) + (-4)(2-4) + 3(4-3)]$$

$$= \frac{1}{2}[11 \times 1 + (-4)(-2) + 3(1)] = \frac{1}{2}(11 + 8 + 3) = \frac{22}{2} = 11$$

$\therefore$ Required area of $\Delta ABC = 11$ sq. units.

***Q.17** The points $A(2, 9)$, $B(a, 5)$ and $C(5, 5)$ are the vertices of a ΔABC right angled at B. Find the values of a and hence the area of ΔABC.

Ans. Given, Vertices of right angles triangle ABC are $A(2, 9)$, $B(a, 5)$ and $C(5, 5)$

By Pythagoras theorem, $AC^2 = AB^2 + BC^2$ ...(i)

Now, by distance formula, $AB = \sqrt{(a-2)^2 + (5-9)^2}$

$$\left[\because \text{distance between two points } (x_1, y_1) \text{ and } (x_2, y_2) = \sqrt{(x_2 - x_1)^2 + (y_2 - y_1)^2}\right]$$

$$= \sqrt{a^2 + 4 - 4a + 16} = \sqrt{a^2 - 4a + 20}$$

$$BC = \sqrt{(5-a)^2 + (5-5)^2}$$

$$= \sqrt{(5-a)^2 + 0} = 5 - a$$

and

$$AC = \sqrt{(2-5)^2 + (9-5)^2}$$

$$= \sqrt{(-3)^2 + (4)^2} = \sqrt{9 + 16} = \sqrt{25} = 5$$

Put the values of AB, BC and AC in Eq. (i), we get

$$(5)^2 = (\sqrt{a^2 - 4a + 20})^2 + (5-a)^2$$

$$\Rightarrow \quad 25 = a^2 - 4a + 20 + 25 + a^2 - 10a$$

$$\Rightarrow \quad 2a^2 - 14a + 45 - 25 = 0$$

$$\Rightarrow \quad 2a^2 - 14a + 20 = 0$$

$$\Rightarrow \quad a^2 - 7a + 10 = 0$$

$$\Rightarrow \quad a^2 - 2a - 5a + 10 = 0 \quad \text{[by factorisation method]}$$

$$\Rightarrow \quad a(a-2) - 5(a-2) = 0$$

$$\Rightarrow \quad (a-2)(a-5) = 0$$

Note (*) *Topics related to these question have been removed from latest NCERT.*

$\therefore \qquad a = 2, 5$

Here, $a \neq 5$, since at $a = 5$, the length of $BC = 0$. It is not possible because the sides AB, BC and CA form a right angled triangle.

So, $\qquad a = 2$

Now, the coordinate of A, B and C becomes (2, 9), (2, 5) and (5, 5), respectively.

$$\because \quad \text{Area of } \Delta\, ABC = \left|\frac{1}{2}[x_1(y_2 - y_3) + x_2(y_3 - y_1) + x_3(y_1 - y_2)]\right|$$

$$\therefore \quad \Delta = \left|\frac{1}{2}[2(5-5) + 2(5-9) + 5(9-5)]\right|$$

$$= \left|\frac{1}{2}[2 \times 0 + 2(-4) + 5(4)]\right|$$

$$= \left|\frac{1}{2}(0 - 8 + 20)\right| = \left|\frac{1}{2} \times 12\right| = 6$$

Hence, the required area of ΔABC is 6 sq. units.

Q.18 Find the coordinates of the point R on the line segment joining the points $P(-1, 3)$ and $Q(2, 5)$ such that $PR = \frac{3}{5} PQ$.

Ans. According to the question,

Given that, $\qquad PR = \frac{3}{5} PQ$

$$\Rightarrow \quad \frac{PQ}{PR} = \frac{5}{3} \Rightarrow \frac{PR + RQ}{PR} = \frac{5}{3}$$

$$\Rightarrow \quad 1 + \frac{RQ}{PR} = \frac{5}{3}$$

$$\Rightarrow \quad \frac{RQ}{PR} = \frac{5}{3} - 1 = \frac{2}{3}$$

$\therefore \qquad RQ : PR = 2 : 3$

or $\qquad PR : RQ = 3 : 2$

Suppose, $R(x, y)$ be the point which divides the line segment joining the points $P(-1, 3)$ and $Q(2, 5)$ in the ratio 3 : 2.

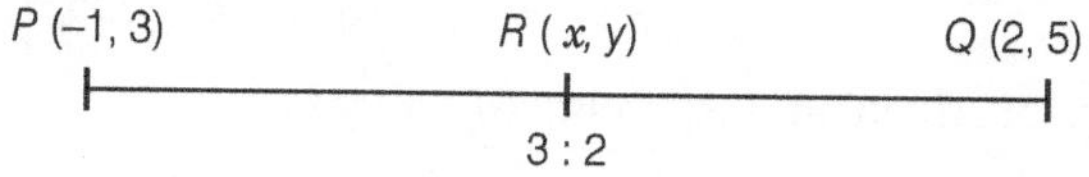

$$\therefore \quad (x, y) = \left\{\frac{3(2) + 2(-1)}{3+2}, \frac{3(5) + 2(3)}{3+2}\right\}$$

$$\left[\because \text{internal section formula}, = \left\{\frac{m_1x_2 + m_2x_1}{m_1 + m_2}, \frac{m_1y_2 + m_2y_1}{m_1 + m_2}\right\}\right]$$

$$= \left(\frac{6-2}{5}, \frac{15+6}{5}\right) = \left(\frac{4}{5}, \frac{21}{5}\right)$$

Hence, the required coordinates of the point R is $\left(\frac{4}{5}, \frac{21}{5}\right)$.

***Q.19** Find the values of k, if the points $A(k+1, 2k)$, $B(3k, 2k+3)$ and $C(5k-1, 5k)$ are collinear.

Ans. We know that, if three points are collinear, then the area of triangle formed by these points is zero.

Since, the points $A(k+1, 2k)$, $B(3k, 2k+3)$ and $C(5k-1, 5k)$ are collinear.

Then, area of $\Delta ABC = 0$

$$\Rightarrow \quad \frac{1}{2}[x_1(y_2 - y_3) + x_2(y_3 - y_1) + x_3(y_1 - y_2)] = 0$$

Here, $x_1 = k+1, x_2 = 3k, x_3 = 5k-1$ and $y_1 = 2k, y_2 = 2k+3, y_3 = 5k$

$$\Rightarrow \frac{1}{2}[(k+1)(2k+3-5k) + 3k(5k-2k) + (5k-1)(2k-(2k+3))] = 0$$

$$\Rightarrow \quad \frac{1}{2}[(k+1)(-3k+3) + 3k(3k) + (5k-1)(2k-2k-3)] = 0$$

$$\Rightarrow \quad \frac{1}{2}[-3k^2 + 3k - 3k + 3 + 9k^2 - 15k + 3] = 0$$

$$\Rightarrow \quad \frac{1}{2}(6k^2 - 15k + 6) = 0$$

$$\Rightarrow \quad 6k^2 - 15k + 6 = 0 \quad \text{[multiply by 2]}$$

$$\Rightarrow \quad 2k^2 - 5k + 2 = 0 \quad \text{[divide by 3]}$$

$$\Rightarrow \quad 2k^2 - 4k - k + 2 = 0 \quad \text{[by factorisation method]}$$

$$\Rightarrow \quad 2k(k-2) - 1(k-2) = 0$$

$$\Rightarrow \quad (k-2)(2k-1) = 0$$

If $k - 2 = 0$, then $k = 2$

If $2k - 1 = 0$, then $k = \frac{1}{2}$

$$\therefore \quad k = 2, \frac{1}{2}$$

Hence, the required values of k are 2 and $\frac{1}{2}$.

Q.20 Find the ratio in which the line $2x + 3y - 5 = 0$ divides the line segment joining the points $(8, -9)$ and $(2, 1)$. Also find the coordinates of the point of division.

Ans. Let the line $2x + 3y - 5 = 0$ divides the line joining the points $(8, -9)$ and $(2, 1)$ in $k : 1$.

Again, let coordinates of the point is $(p, q) = \left[\frac{2k+8}{k+1}, \frac{k-9}{k+1}\right]$

$\because$ Point (p, q) also lie on the line.

$$\therefore \quad 2\left(\frac{2k+8}{k+1}\right) + 3\left(\frac{k-9}{k+1}\right) - 5 = 0$$

$$\Rightarrow \quad \frac{4k+16}{k+1} + \frac{3k-27}{k+1} = 5$$

Note (*) *Topics related to these question have been removed from latest NCERT.*

$$\Rightarrow \quad 7k - 11 = 5k + 5$$

$$\Rightarrow \quad 2k = 16 \Rightarrow k = 8$$

Hence, the ratio is 8 : 1.

and the coordinates of the point (p, q)

$$= \left(\frac{16+8}{8+1}, \frac{8-9}{8+1}\right)$$

$$= \left(\frac{24}{9}, \frac{-1}{9}\right)$$

$$= \left(\frac{8}{3}, \frac{-1}{9}\right)$$

Long Answer Type Questions

Q.1 If $(-4, 3)$ and $(4, 3)$ are two vertices of an equilateral triangle, find the coordinates of the third vertex, given that the origin lies in the interior of the triangle.

Ans. Let the third vertex of an equilateral triangle be (x, y). Let three vertices of triangle are $A(-4, 3)$, $B(4, 3)$ and $C(x, y)$.

We know that, in equilateral triangle the angle between two adjacent side is 60° and all three sides are equal.

$$\therefore \quad AB = BC = CA$$

$$\Rightarrow \quad AB^2 = BC^2 = CA^2 \quad \text{...(i)}$$

Now, taking first two parts.

$$AB^2 = BC^2$$

$$\Rightarrow \quad (4+4)^2 + (3-3)^2 = (x-4)^2 + (y-3)^2$$

$$\Rightarrow \quad 64 + 0 = x^2 + 16 - 8x + y^2 + 9 - 6y$$

$$\Rightarrow \quad x^2 + y^2 - 8x - 6y = 64 - (16+9) = 39 \quad \text{...(ii)}$$

Now, taking first and third parts,

$$AB^2 = CA^2$$

$$\Rightarrow \quad (4+4)^2 + (3-3)^2 = (-4-x)^2 + (3-y)^2$$

$$\Rightarrow \quad 64 + 0 = 16 + x^2 + 8x + 9 + y^2 - 6y$$

$$\Rightarrow \quad x^2 + y^2 + 8x - 6y = 64 - (16+9) = 39 \quad \text{...(iii)}$$

On subtracting Eq. (ii) from Eq. (iii), we get

$$\begin{array}{r} x^2 + y^2 + 8x - 6y = 39 \\ x^2 + y^2 - 8x - 6y = 39 \\ - \quad - \quad + \quad + \quad - \\ \hline 16x = 0 \end{array}$$

$$\Rightarrow \quad x = 0$$

Now, put the value of x in Eq. (ii), we get

$$0 + y^2 - 0 - 6y = 39$$

$$\Rightarrow \quad y^2 - 6y - 39 = 0$$

$$\therefore \qquad y = \frac{6 \pm \sqrt{(-6)^2 - 4(1)(-39)}}{2 \times 1}$$

$$\left[\because \text{ solution of } ax^2 + bx + c = 0 \text{ is } x = \frac{-b \pm \sqrt{b^2 - 4ac}}{2a}\right]$$

$$\Rightarrow \qquad y = \frac{6 \pm \sqrt{36 + 156}}{2}$$

$$\Rightarrow \qquad y = \frac{6 \pm \sqrt{192}}{2}$$

$$\Rightarrow \qquad y = \frac{6 \pm 2\sqrt{48}}{2} = 3 \pm \sqrt{48}$$

$$\Rightarrow \qquad y = 3 \pm 4\sqrt{3}$$

$$\Rightarrow \qquad y = 3 + 4\sqrt{3} \text{ or } 3 - 4\sqrt{3}$$

So, the points of third vertex are $(0, 3 + 4\sqrt{3})$ or $(0, 3 - 4\sqrt{3})$

But given that, the origin lies in the interior of the ΔABC and the x-coordinate of third vertex is zero. Then, y-coordinate of third vertex should be negative.

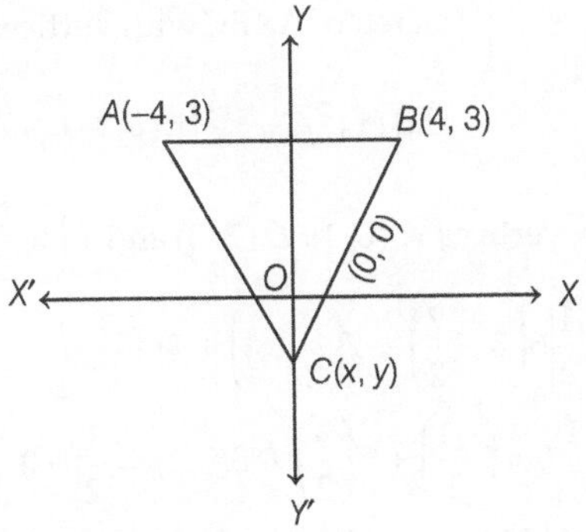

Hence, the required coordinate of third vertex, $C = (0, 3 - 4\sqrt{3})$. $[\because c \neq (0, 3 + 4\sqrt{3})]$

***Q.2** $A(6, 1)$, $B(8, 2)$ and $C(9, 4)$ are three vertices of a parallelogram $ABCD$. If E is the mid-point of DC, find the area of ΔADE.

Ans. Given that, $A(6, 1)$, $B(8, 2)$ and $C(9, 4)$ are three vertices of a parallelogram $ABCD$.

Let the fourth vertex of parallelogram be $D(x, y)$.

We know that, the diagonals of a parallelogram bisect each other.

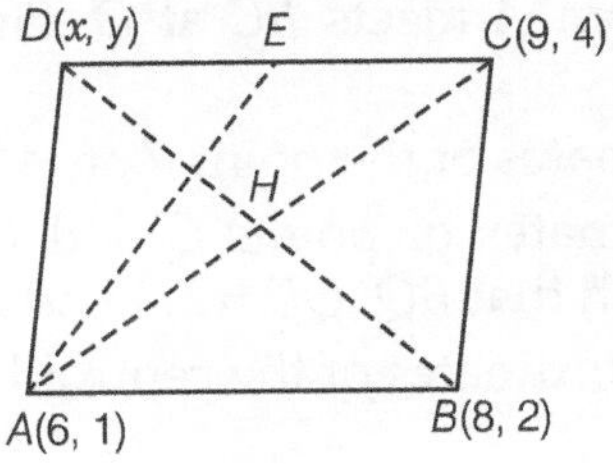

Note (✱) *Topics related to these question have been removed from latest NCERT.*

$\therefore$ Mid-point of BD = Mid-point of AC

$$\Rightarrow \left(\frac{8+x}{2}, \frac{2+y}{2}\right) = \left(\frac{6+9}{2}, \frac{1+4}{2}\right)$$

[$\because$ mid-point of a line segment joining the points (x_1, y_1) and $(x_2, y_2) = \left(\frac{x_1+x_2}{2}, \frac{y_1+y_2}{2}\right)$]

$$\Rightarrow \left(\frac{8+x}{2}, \frac{2+y}{2}\right) = \left(\frac{15}{2}, \frac{5}{2}\right)$$

$$\therefore \frac{8+x}{2} = \frac{15}{2} \Rightarrow 8+x = 15 \Rightarrow x = 7 \text{ and } \frac{2+y}{2} = \frac{5}{2} \Rightarrow 2+y=5 \Rightarrow y=3$$

So, fourth vertex of a parallelogram is $D(7, 3)$.

Now, mid-point of side $DC = \left(\frac{7+9}{2}, \frac{3+4}{2}\right)$

$$\Rightarrow E = \left(8, \frac{7}{2}\right)$$

[$\because$ area of ΔABC with vertices (x_1, y_1), (x_2, y_2) and $(x_3, y_3) = \frac{1}{2}|x_1(y_2-y_3)+x_2(y_3-y_1)+x_3(y_1-y_2)|$]

$\therefore$ Area of ΔADE with vertices $A(6, 1)$, $D(7, 3)$ and $E\left(8, \frac{7}{2}\right)$,

$$\Delta = \frac{1}{2}\left|6\left(3-\frac{7}{2}\right)+7\left(\frac{7}{2}-1\right)+8(1-3)\right|$$

$$\frac{1}{2}\left|6\times\left(\frac{-1}{2}\right)+7\left(\frac{5}{2}\right)+8(-2)\right| = \frac{1}{2}\left|-3+\frac{35}{2}-16\right|$$

$$= \frac{1}{2}\left|\frac{35}{2}-19\right| = \frac{1}{2}\left|\frac{-3}{2}\right| = \frac{3}{4}$$

Hence, the required area of ΔADE is $\frac{3}{4}$ sq. units.

Mistake Alert ! *Students might find the area using the formula but forget to apply the absolute value.*

Q.3 The points $A(x_1, y_1)$, $B(x_2, y_2)$ and $C(x_3, y_3)$ are the vertices of ΔABC.

(i) The median from A meets BC at D. Find the coordinates of the point D.

(ii) Find the coordinates of the point P on AD such that $AP:PD = 2:1$.

(iii) Find the coordinates of points Q and R on medians BE and CF, respectively such that $BQ:QE = 2:1$ and $CR:RF = 2:1$.

(iv) What are the coordinates of the centroid of the ΔABC?

Ans. Given that, the points $A(x_1, y_1)$, $B(x_2, y_2)$ and $C(x_3, y_3)$ are the vertices of ΔABC.

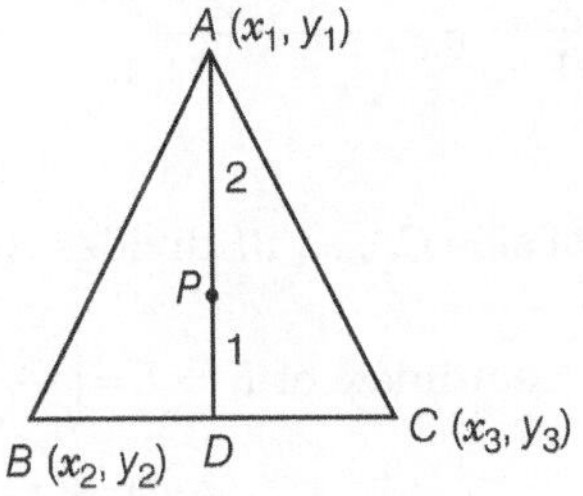

(i) We know that, the median bisect the line segment into two equal parts *i.e.*, here D is the mid-point of BC.

$\therefore$ Coordinate of mid-point of BC, $D = \left(\frac{x_2 + x_3}{2}, \frac{y_2 + y_3}{2}\right)$

(ii) Let the coordinates of a point P be (x, y).

Given that, the point $P(x, y)$ divide the line joining $A(x_1, y_1)$ and $D\left(\frac{x_2 + x_3}{2}, \frac{y_2 + y_3}{2}\right)$ in the ratio 2 : 1, then the coordinates of P

$$= \left(\frac{2\cdot\left(\frac{x_2 + x_3}{2}\right) + 1\cdot x_1}{2+1}, \frac{2\cdot\left(\frac{y_2 + y_3}{2}\right) + 1\cdot y_1}{2+1}\right)$$

$$\left[\because \text{internal section formula} = \left(\frac{m_1x_2 + m_2x_1}{m_1 + m_2}, \frac{m_1y_2 + m_2y_1}{m_1 + m_2}\right)\right]$$

$$= \left(\frac{x_2 + x_3 + x_1}{3}, \frac{y_2 + y_3 + y_1}{3}\right)$$

$\therefore$ So, required coordinates of point $P = \left(\frac{x_1 + x_2 + x_3}{3}, \frac{y_1 + y_2 + y_3}{3}\right)$

(iii) Let the coordinates of a point Q be (p, q).

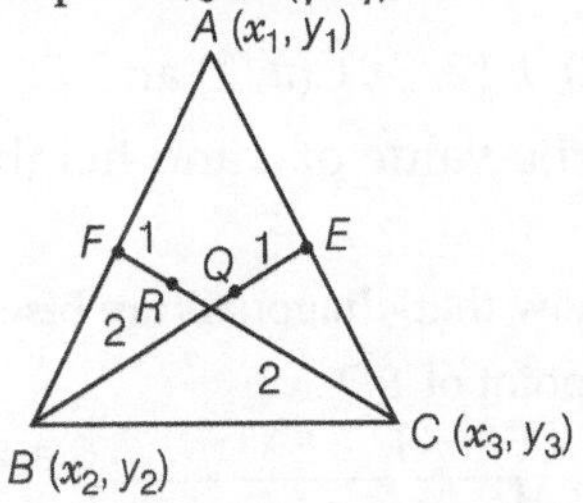

Given that, the point $Q(p, q)$ divide the line joining $B(x_2, y_2)$ and $E\left(\frac{x_1 + x_3}{2}, \frac{y_1 + y_3}{2}\right)$ in the ratio 2 : 1, then the coordinates of Q

$$=\left(\frac{2\cdot\left(\frac{x_1+x_3}{2}\right)+1\cdot x_2}{2+1},\frac{2\cdot\left(\frac{y_1+y_3}{2}\right)+1\cdot y_2}{2+1}\right)=\left(\frac{x_1+x_2+x_3}{3},\frac{y_1+y_2+y_3}{3}\right)$$

[$\because$ *BE* is the median of side *CA*, so *BE* divides *AC* in to two equal parts.

$\therefore$ mid-point of AC = Coordinate of $E \Rightarrow E=\left(\frac{x_1+x_3}{2},\frac{y_1+y_3}{2}\right)$]

So, the required coordinate of point $Q=\left(\frac{x_1+x_2+x_3}{3},\frac{y_1+y_2+y_3}{3}\right)$

Now, let the coordinates of a point R be (α,β). Given that, the point $R(\alpha,\beta)$ divide the line joining $C(x_3, y_3)$ and $F\left(\frac{x_1+x_2}{2},\frac{y_1+y_2}{2}\right)$ in the ratio 2 : 1, then the coordinates of R

$$\equiv\left[\frac{2\cdot\left(\frac{x_1+x_2}{2}\right)+1\cdot x_3}{2+1},\frac{2\cdot\left(\frac{y_1+y_2}{2}\right)+1\cdot y_3}{2+1}\right]=\left(\frac{x_1+x_2+x_3}{3},\frac{y_1+y_2+y_3}{3}\right)$$

[$\because$ *CF* is the median of side *AB*. So, *CF* divides *AB* in to two equal parts.

$\therefore$mid-point of AB = coordinate of $F \Rightarrow F=\left(\frac{x_1+x_2}{2},\frac{y_1+y_2}{2}\right)$]

So, the required coordinate of point $R=\left(\frac{x_1+x_2+x_3}{3},\frac{y_1+y_2+y_3}{3}\right)$

(iv) Coordinate of the centroid of the ΔABC

$$=\left(\frac{\text{Sum of abscissa of all vertices}}{3},\frac{\text{Sum of ordinate of all vertices}}{3}\right)$$

$$=\left(\frac{x_1+x_2+x_3}{3},\frac{y_1+y_2+y_3}{3}\right)$$

Q.4 If the points $A(1,-2)$, $B(2,3)$, $C(a,2)$ and $D(-4,-3)$ form a parallelogram, find the value of a and height of the parallelogram taking AB as base.

Ans. In parallelogram, we know that, diagonals are bisects each other *i.e.*, mid-point of AC = mid-point of BD

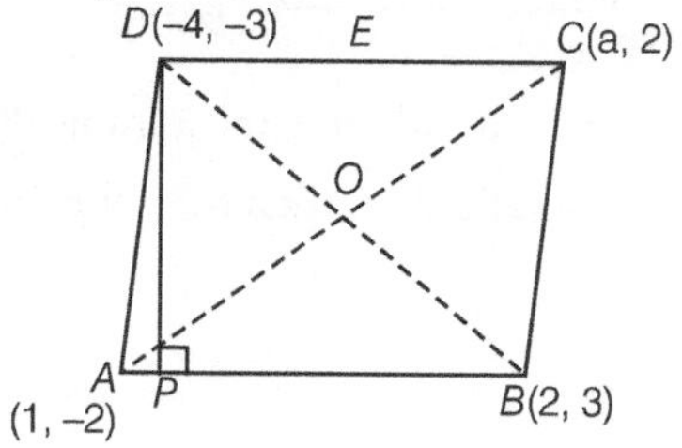

$$\Rightarrow \quad \left(\frac{1+a}{2}, \frac{-2+2}{2}\right) = \left(\frac{2-4}{2}, \frac{3-3}{2}\right)$$

$$\left[\because \text{mid-point of a line segment having end points } (x_1, y_1) \text{ and } (x_2, y_2) \text{ is } \left(\frac{x_1+x_2}{2}, \frac{y_1+y_2}{2}\right)\right]$$

$$\Rightarrow \quad \frac{1+a}{2} = \frac{2-4}{2} = \frac{-2}{2} = -1$$

$$\Rightarrow \quad 1+a = -2$$

$$\Rightarrow \quad a = -3$$

So, the required value of a is -3.

Given that, AB as base of a parallelogram and drawn a perpendicular from D to AB which meet AB at P. So, DP is a height of a parallelogram.

Now, Area of $\Delta ABC = \frac{1}{2}[x_1(y_2 - y_3) + x_2(y_3 - y_1) + x_3(y_1 - y_2)]$

Here, $x_1 = 1, x_2 = 2, x_3 = -3$

and $y_1 = -2, y_2 = 3, y_3 = 2$

$$\therefore \text{Area of } \Delta ABC = \frac{1}{2}[1(3-2) + 2(2+2) + (-3)(-2-3)] = \frac{1}{2}[1 + 2(4) - 3(-5)]$$

$$= \frac{1}{2}[1 + 8 + 15] = \frac{1}{2} \times 24 = 12 \text{ sq units.}$$

Since, $ABCD$ is a parallelogram and we know that, diagonal of parallelogram divides it into two congruent triangles.

$\therefore$ Area of ΔACD = Area of ΔABC = 12 units

Area of parallelogram $ABCD$ = Area of ΔABC + Area of ΔACD

$$= 12 + 12 = 24 \text{ sq. units} \qquad \ldots(i)$$

Now,
$$AB = \sqrt{(2-1)^2 + [3-(-2)]^2}$$

[by distance formula $d = \sqrt{(x_2 - x_1)^2 + (y_2 - y_1)^2}$]

$$= \sqrt{(1)^2 + (5)^2}$$

$$= \sqrt{1+25} = \sqrt{26}$$

Now area of parallelogram $ABCD$

$$AB \times DP = 24$$

$$\Rightarrow \quad \sqrt{26} \times DP = 24$$

$$\Rightarrow \quad DP = \frac{24}{\sqrt{26}}$$

$$= \frac{24 \times \sqrt{26}}{26} = \frac{12\sqrt{26}}{13}$$

$\therefore$ Height of the parallelogram $ABCD$ is $\frac{12\sqrt{26}}{13}$ units.

Q.5 Students of a school are standing in rows and columns in their playground for a drill practice. A, B, C and D are the positions of four students as shown in figure. Is it possible to place Jaspal in the drill in such a way that he is equidistant from each of the four students A, B, C and D? If so, what should be his position?

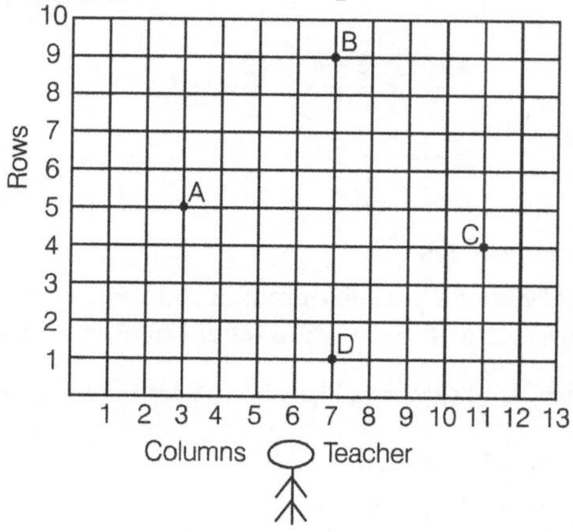

Thinking Process Firstly, find the distance between the points and if the distance is equal, then find the mid-point of AC to get the coordinates of point P.

Ans. Yes, from the figure we observe that the positions of four students A, B, C and D are (3, 5), (7, 9), (11, 5) and (7, 1) respectively *i.e.*, these are four vertices of a quadrilateral. Now, we will find the type of this quadrilateral. For this, we will find all its sides.

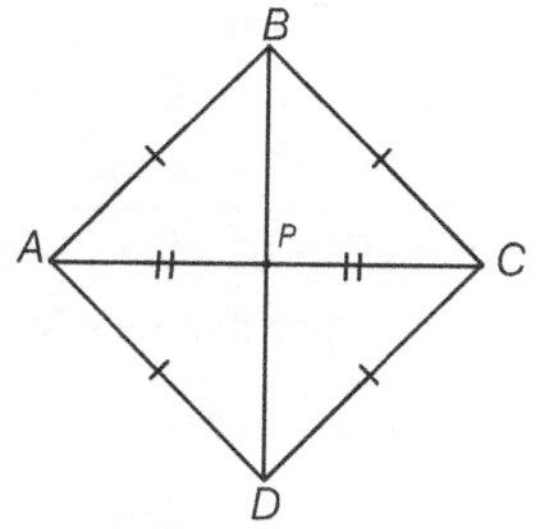

Now, $$AB = \sqrt{(7-3)^2 + (9-5)^2}$$

$$\left[\text{by distance formula, } d = \sqrt{(x_2 - x_1)^2 + (y_2 - y_1)^2}\right]$$

$$\Rightarrow \quad AB = \sqrt{(4)^2 + (4)^2} = \sqrt{16+16} = \sqrt{32}$$

$$\Rightarrow \quad AB = 4\sqrt{2}$$

$$BC = \sqrt{(11-7)^2 + (5-9)^2} = \sqrt{(4)^2 + (-4)^2}$$

$$= \sqrt{16+16} = \sqrt{32} = 4\sqrt{2}$$

$$CD = \sqrt{(7-11)^2 + (1-5)^2} = \sqrt{(-4)^2 + (-4)^2}$$

$$= \sqrt{16+16} = \sqrt{32} = 4\sqrt{2}$$

and $$DA = \sqrt{(3-7)^2 + (5-1)^2} = \sqrt{(-4)^2 + (4)^2}$$
$$= \sqrt{16+16} = \sqrt{32} = 4\sqrt{2}$$

We see that, $AB = BC = CD = DA$ *i.e.*, all sides are equal.

Now, we find length of both diagonals.

$$AC = \sqrt{(11-3)^2 + (5-5)^2} = \sqrt{(8)^2 + 0} = 8$$

and $$BD = \sqrt{(7-7)^2 + (1-9)^2} = \sqrt{0 + (-8)^2} = 8$$

Here, $AC = BD$

Since, $AB = BC = CD = DA$ and $AC = BD$

which represent a square. Also, known the diagonals of a square bisect each other. So, P be position of Jaspal in which he is equidistant from each of the four students A, B, C and D.

$\therefore$ Coordinates of point P = Mid-point of AC

$$= \left(\frac{3+11}{2}, \frac{5+5}{2}\right) = \left(\frac{14}{2}, \frac{10}{2}\right) = (7, 5)$$

$\left[\because \text{ mid-point of a line segment having end points } (x_1, y_1) \text{ and } (x_2, y_2) = \left(\frac{x_1+x_2}{2}, \frac{y_1+y_2}{2}\right)\right]$

Hence, the required position of Jaspal is (7, 5).

Q.6 Ayush starts walking from his house to office. Instead of going to the office directly, he goes to a bank first, from there to his daughter's school and then reaches the office. What is the extra distance travelled by Ayush in reaching his office? (Assume that all distance covered are in straight lines).
If the house is situated at (2, 4), bank at (5, 8), school at (13, 14) and office at (13, 26) and coordinates are in km.

Ans. By given condition, we drawn a figure in which every place are indicated with his coordinates and direction also.

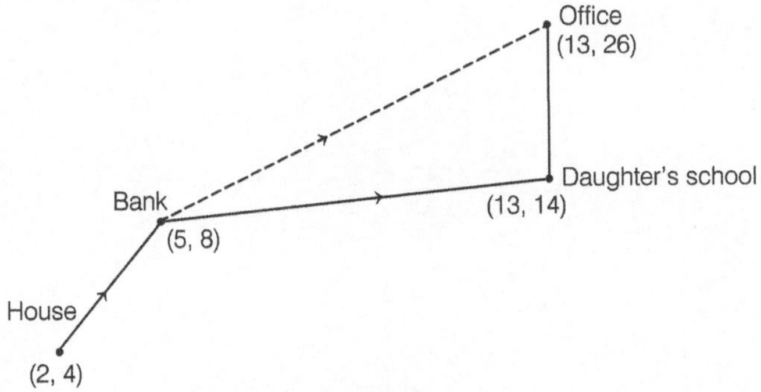

We know that, distance between two points (x_1, y_1) and (x_2, y_2),

$$d = \sqrt{(x_2 - x_1)^2 + (y_2 - y_1)^2}$$

Now, distance between house and bank

$$= \sqrt{(5-2)^2 + (8-4)^2}$$

$$= \sqrt{(3)^2 + (4)^2}$$

$$= \sqrt{9+16} = \sqrt{25} = 5\,\text{km}$$

Distance between bank and daughter's school

$$= \sqrt{(13-5)^2 + (14-8)^2} = \sqrt{(8)^2 + (6)^2}$$

$$= \sqrt{64+36} = \sqrt{100} = 10 \text{ km}$$

Distance between daughter's school and office $= \sqrt{(13-13)^2 + (26-14)^2}$

$$= \sqrt{0 + (12)^2} = 12\,\text{km}$$

Total distance (House + Bank + School + Office) travelled = 5 + 10 + 12 = 27 km

Distance between house to offices $= \sqrt{(13-2)^2 + (26-4)^2}$

$$= \sqrt{(11)^2 + (22)^2} = \sqrt{121 + 484}$$

$$= \sqrt{605} = 24.59 \approx 24.6\,\text{km}$$

So, extra distance travelled by Ayush in reaching his office = 27 – 24.6 = 2.4 km

Chapter

08

Introduction to Trigonometry and its Applications

Multiple Choice Questions (MCQs)

Choose the correct answer from the given four options in the following questions:

Q.1 If $\cos A = \frac{4}{5}$, then the value of $\tan A$ is

(a) $\frac{3}{5}$ (b) $\frac{3}{4}$ (c) $\frac{4}{3}$ (d) $\frac{5}{3}$

Thinking Process

(i) First, we use the formula $\sin\theta = \sqrt{1-\cos^2\theta}$ to get the value of $\sin\theta$.

(ii) Second, we use the formula $\tan\theta = \frac{\sin\theta}{\cos\theta}$ to get the value of $\tan\theta$.

Ans. ***(b)*** Given, $\cos A = \frac{4}{5}$

$\therefore \quad \sin A = \sqrt{1-\cos^2 A}$ $\quad \left[\because \sin^2 A + \cos^2 A = 1 \quad \therefore \sin A = \sqrt{1-\cos^2 A}\right]$

$$= \sqrt{1-\left(\frac{4}{5}\right)^2} = \sqrt{1-\frac{16}{25}} = \sqrt{\frac{9}{25}} = \frac{3}{5}$$

Now, $\tan A = \frac{\sin A}{\cos A} = \frac{\frac{3}{5}}{\frac{4}{5}} = \frac{3}{4}$

Hence, the required value of $\tan A$ is $\frac{3}{4}$.

Q. 2 If $\sin A = \frac{1}{2}$, then the value of $\cot A$ is

(a) $\sqrt{3}$ (b) $\frac{1}{\sqrt{3}}$ (c) $\frac{\sqrt{3}}{2}$ (d) 1

Thinking Process

(i) First, we use the formula $\cos\theta = \sqrt{1-\sin^2\theta}$ to get the value of $\cos\theta$.

(ii) Now, we use the trigonometric ratio $\cot\theta = \frac{\cos\theta}{\sin\theta}$ to get the value of $\cot\theta$.

Ans. ***(a)*** Given, $\sin A = \frac{1}{2}$

$$\therefore \quad \cos A = \sqrt{1-\sin^2 A} = \sqrt{1-\left(\frac{1}{2}\right)^2} \quad [\because \sin^2 A + \cos^2 = 1 \Rightarrow \cos A = \sqrt{1-\sin^2 A}]$$

$$= \sqrt{1-\frac{1}{4}} = \sqrt{\frac{3}{4}} = \frac{\sqrt{3}}{2}$$

Now, $$\cot A = \frac{\cos A}{\sin A} = \frac{\frac{\sqrt{3}}{2}}{\frac{1}{2}} = \sqrt{3}$$

Hence, the required value of $\cot A$ is $\sqrt{3}$.

***Q.3** The value of the expression
$\operatorname{cosec}(75° + \theta) - \sec(15° - \theta) - \tan(55° + \theta) + \cot(35° - \theta)$ is

(a) -1 (b) 0 (c) 1 (d) $\frac{3}{2}$

Thinking Process We see that, the given trigonometric angle of the ratio are the reciprocal in the sense of sign. Then, use the following formulae

(i) $\operatorname{cosec}(90° - \theta) = \sec\theta$ (ii) $\cot(90° - \theta) = \tan\theta$

Ans. ***(b)*** Given, $\operatorname{cosec}(75° + \theta) - \sec(15° - \theta) - \tan(55° + \theta) + \cot(35° - \theta)$

$$= \operatorname{cosec}[90° - (15° - \theta)] - \sec(15° - \theta) - \tan(55° + \theta) + \cot\{90° - (55° + \theta)\}$$

$$= \sec(15° - \theta) - \sec(15° - \theta) - \tan(55° + \theta) + \tan(55° + \theta)$$

$$[\because \operatorname{cosec}(90° - \theta) = \sec\theta \text{ and } \cot(90° - \theta) = \tan\theta]$$

$$= 0$$

Hence, the required value of the given expression is 0.

Mistake Alert! *Students may forget to use the transformation* $\operatorname{cosec}(90° - \theta) = \sec\theta$ *and* $\tan(90° - \theta) = \cot\theta$.

Q.4 Given that $\sin\theta = \frac{a}{b}$, then $\cos\theta$ is equal to

(a) $\frac{b}{\sqrt{b^2 - a^2}}$ (b) $\frac{b}{a}$

(c) $\frac{\sqrt{b^2 - a^2}}{b}$ (d) $\frac{a}{\sqrt{b^2 - a^2}}$

Ans. ***(c)*** Given, $\sin\theta = \frac{a}{b}$ $\quad [\because \sin^2\theta + \cos^2\theta = 1 \Rightarrow \cos\theta = \sqrt{1-\sin^2\theta}]$

$$\therefore \quad \cos\theta = \sqrt{1-\sin^2\theta}$$

$$= \sqrt{1-\left(\frac{a}{b}\right)^2} = \sqrt{1-\frac{a^2}{b^2}} = \frac{\sqrt{b^2 - a^2}}{b}$$

Mistake Alert! *Students may applied the wrong identity as* $\cos\theta = 1 - \sin^2\theta$ *instead of* $\cos\theta = \sqrt{1-\sin^2\theta}$.

Note (*) *Topics related to these question have been removed from latest NCERT.*

***Q.5** If $\cos(\alpha+\beta)=0$, then $\sin(\alpha-\beta)$ can be reduced to

(a) $\cos\beta$ (b) $\cos 2\beta$
(c) $\sin\alpha$ (d) $\sin 2\alpha$

Ans. ***(b)*** Given, $\cos(\alpha+\beta)=0=\cos 90°$ $[\because \cos 90°=0]$

$\Rightarrow \alpha+\beta=90°$

$\Rightarrow \alpha=90°-\beta$ ...(i)

Now, $\sin(\alpha-\beta)=\sin(90°-\beta-\beta)$ [put the value from Eq. (i)]

$=\sin(90°-2\beta)$

$=\cos 2\beta$ $[\because \sin(90°-\theta)=\cos\theta]$

Hence, $\sin(\alpha-\beta)$ can be reduced to $\cos 2\beta$.

***Q.6** The value of $(\tan 1° \tan 2° \tan 3° \dots \tan 89°)$ is

(a) 0 (b) 1
(c) 2 (d) $\frac{1}{2}$

Ans. ***(b)*** $\tan 1°\cdot\tan 2°\cdot\tan 3° \dots \tan 89°$

$=\tan 1°\cdot\tan 2°\cdot\tan 3°\dots \tan 44°\cdot\tan 45°\cdot\tan 46°\dots\tan 87°\cdot\tan 88°\cdot\tan 89°$

$=\tan 1°\cdot\tan 2°\cdot\tan 3°\dots\tan 44°\cdot(1)\cdot\tan(90°-44°)\dots\tan(90°-3°)\cdot$
$\tan(90°-2°)\cdot\tan(90°-1°)$ $[(\because \tan 45°=1)]$

$=\tan 1°\cdot\tan 2°\cdot\tan 3° \dots \tan 44°\cdot(1)\cdot\cot 44° \dots \cot 3°\cdot\cot 2°\cdot\cot 1°$
$[\because \tan(90°-\theta)=\cot\theta]$

$=\tan 1°.\tan 2°.\tan 3°\dots\tan 44°(1).\frac{1}{\tan 44°}\dots\frac{1}{\tan 30°}.\frac{1}{\tan 2°}.\frac{1}{\tan 1°}$

$=1$ $\left[\because \cot\theta=\frac{1}{\tan\theta}\right]$

***Q.7** If $\cos 9\alpha=\sin\alpha$ and $9\alpha<90°$, then the value of $\tan 5\alpha$ is

(a) $\frac{1}{\sqrt{3}}$ (b) $\sqrt{3}$
(c) 1 (d) 0

Ans. ***(c)*** Given, $\cos 9\alpha=\sin\alpha$ and $9\alpha<90°$ *i.e.*, acute angle.

$\Rightarrow \sin(90°-9\alpha)=\sin\alpha$ $[\because \cos A=\sin(90°-A)]$

$\Rightarrow 90°-9\alpha=\alpha$

$\Rightarrow 10\alpha=90°$

$\Rightarrow \alpha=9°$

$\therefore \tan 5\alpha=\tan(5\times 9°)=\tan 45°=1$ $[\because \tan 45°=1]$

Q.8 If ΔABC is right angled at C, then the value of $\cos(A+B)$ is

(a) 0 (b) 1
(c) $\frac{1}{2}$ (d) $\frac{\sqrt{3}}{2}$

Note (*) *Topics related to these question have been removed from latest NCERT.*

Ans. *(a)* We know that, in ΔABC, sum of three angles = 180°

i.e., $\angle A + \angle B + \angle C = 180°$

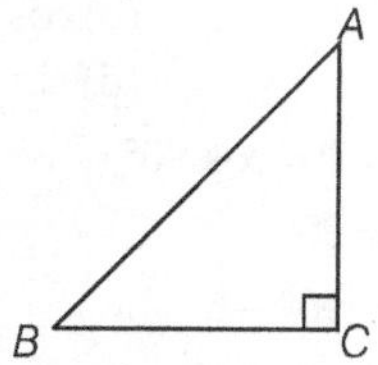

But right angled at C *i.e.,* $\angle C = 90°$ [given]

$$\angle A + \angle B + 90° = 180°$$

$\Rightarrow$ $A + B = 90°$

$\therefore$ $\cos(A + B) = \cos 90° = 0$ $[\because \cos 90° = 0]$

Q.9 If $\sin A + \sin^2 A = 1$, then the value of the expression $(\cos^2 A + \cos^4 A)$ is

(a) 1 (b) $\frac{1}{2}$ (c) 2 (d) 3

Ans. *(a)* Given, $\sin A + \sin^2 A = 1$

$\Rightarrow$ $\sin A = 1 - \sin^2 A = \cos^2 A$ $[\because \sin^2\theta + \cos^2\theta = 1]$

On squaring both sides, we get

$$\sin^2 A = \cos^4 A \Rightarrow 1 - \cos^2 A = \cos^4 A$$

$\Rightarrow$ $\cos^2 A + \cos^4 A = 1$

Q.10 Given that $\sin\alpha = \frac{1}{2}$ and $\cos\beta = \frac{1}{2}$, then the value of $(\alpha + \beta)$ is

(a) 0° (b) 30° (c) 60° (d) 90°

Ans. *(d)* Given, $\sin\alpha = \frac{1}{2} = \sin 30°$ $\left[\because \sin 30° = \frac{1}{2}\right]$

$\Rightarrow$ $\alpha = 30°$

and $\cos\beta = \frac{1}{2} = \cos 60°$ $\left[\because \cos 60° = \frac{1}{2}\right]$

$\Rightarrow$ $\beta = 60°$

$\therefore$ $\alpha + \beta = 30° + 60° = 90°$

***Q.11** The value of the expression

$$\left(\frac{\sin^2 22° + \sin^2 68°}{\cos^2 22° + \cos^2 68°} + \sin^2 63° + \cos 63° \sin 27°\right) \text{ is}$$

(a) 3 (b) 2 (c) 1 (d) 0

● **Concept Insight** In this question, we will use, $\sin(90° - \theta) = \cos\theta$ and $\cos(90° - \theta) = \sin\theta$.

Ans. *(b)* Given expression, $\dfrac{\sin^2 22° + \sin^2 68°}{\cos^2 22° + \cos^2 68°} + \sin^2 63° + \cos 63° \sin 27°$

$$= \frac{\sin^2 22° + \sin^2(90° - 22°)}{\cos^2(90° - 68°) + \cos^2 68°} + \sin^2 63° + \cos 63° \sin(90° - 63°)$$

Note (*) *Topics related to these question have been removed from latest NCERT.*

$$= \frac{\sin^2 22° + \cos^2 22°}{\sin^2 68° + \cos^2 68°} + \sin^2 63° + \cos 63° \cdot \cos 63° \quad \left[\begin{array}{l} \because \sin(90° - \theta) = \cos\theta \\ \text{and } \cos(90° - \theta) = \sin\theta \end{array}\right]$$

$$= \frac{1}{1} + (\sin^2 63° + \cos^2 63°) \quad [\because \sin^2\theta + \cos^2\theta = 1]$$

$$= 1 + 1 = 2$$

Q.12 If $4\tan\theta = 3$, then $\left(\frac{4\sin\theta - \cos\theta}{4\sin\theta + \cos\theta}\right)$ is equal to

(a) $\frac{2}{3}$ (b) $\frac{1}{3}$ (c) $\frac{1}{2}$ (d) $\frac{3}{4}$

Ans. *(c)* Given, $4\tan\theta = 3$ ...(i)

$$\therefore \quad \frac{4\sin\theta - \cos\theta}{4\sin\theta + \cos\theta} = \frac{4\frac{\sin\theta}{\cos\theta} - 1}{4\frac{\sin\theta}{\cos\theta} + 1}$$

[divide by $\cos\theta$ in both numerator and denominator]

$$= \frac{4\tan\theta - 1}{4\tan\theta + 1} \quad \left[\because \tan\theta = \frac{\sin\theta}{\cos\theta}\right]$$

$$= \frac{3-1}{3+1} = \frac{2}{4} = \frac{1}{2} \quad \text{[put the value from Eq. (i)]}$$

Q.13 If $\sin\theta - \cos\theta = 0$, then the value of $(\sin^4\theta + \cos^4\theta)$ is

(a) 1 (b) $\frac{3}{4}$ (c) $\frac{1}{2}$ (d) $\frac{1}{4}$

Ans. *(c)* Given, $\sin\theta - \cos\theta = 0$

$$\Rightarrow \quad \sin\theta = \cos\theta \Rightarrow \frac{\sin\theta}{\cos\theta} = 1$$

$$\Rightarrow \quad \tan\theta = 1 \quad \left[\because \tan\theta = \frac{\sin\theta}{\cos\theta}\right]$$

$$\Rightarrow \quad \tan\theta = \tan 45° \quad [\because \tan 45° = 1]$$

$$\therefore \quad \theta = 45°$$

Now, $\sin^4\theta + \cos^4\theta = \sin^4 45° + \cos^4 45°$

$$= \left(\frac{1}{\sqrt{2}}\right)^4 + \left(\frac{1}{\sqrt{2}}\right)^4 \quad \left[\because \sin 45° = \cos 45° = \frac{1}{\sqrt{2}}\right]$$

$$= \frac{1}{4} + \frac{1}{4} = \frac{2}{4} = \frac{1}{2}$$

*** Q.14** $\sin(45° + \theta) - \cos(45° - \theta)$ is equal to

(a) $2\cos\theta$ (b) 0 (c) $2\sin\theta$ (d) 1

Ans. *(b)* $\sin(45° + \theta) - \cos(45° - \theta) = \cos[90° - (45° + \theta)] - \cos(45° - \theta)$

$[\because \cos(90° - \theta) = \sin\theta]$

$$= \cos(45° - \theta) - \cos(45° - \theta) = 0$$

Note (*) *Topics related to these question have been removed from latest NCERT.*

Q.15 If a pole 6 m high casts a shadow $2\sqrt{3}$ m long on the ground, then the Sun's elevation is

(a) 60° (b) 45° (c) 30° (d) 90°

Ans. *(a)* Let $BC = 6$ m be the height of the pole and $AB = 2\sqrt{3}$ m be the length of the shadow on the ground.

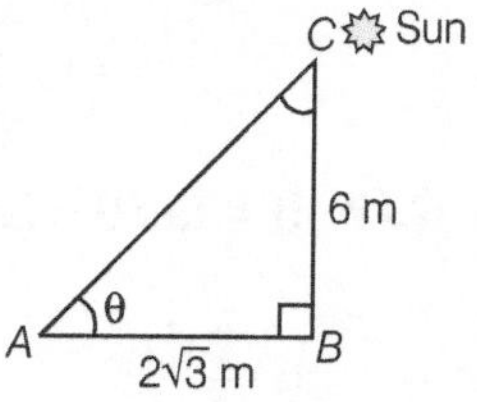

Let the Sun makes an angle θ on the ground.

Now, in ΔBAC, $\tan\theta = \dfrac{BC}{AB}$

$\Rightarrow \quad \tan\theta = \dfrac{6}{2\sqrt{3}} = \dfrac{3}{\sqrt{3}} \cdot \dfrac{\sqrt{3}}{\sqrt{3}}$

$\Rightarrow \quad \tan\theta = \dfrac{3\sqrt{3}}{3} = \sqrt{3} = \tan 60^\circ$ $[\because \tan 60^\circ = \sqrt{3}]$

$\therefore \quad \theta = 60^\circ$

Hence, the Sun's elevation is 60°.

Mistake Alert! *Student may incorrectly consider* $\tan\theta = \dfrac{AB}{BC}$ *instead of* $\tan\theta = \dfrac{BC}{AB}$.

Short Answer Questions with Reasoning

Write True or False and justify your answer in each of the following.

*** Q.1** $\dfrac{\tan 47^\circ}{\cot 43^\circ} = 1$

Ans. *True*

$$\frac{\tan 47^\circ}{\cot 43^\circ} = \frac{\tan(90^\circ - 43^\circ)}{\cot 43^\circ} = \frac{\cot 43^\circ}{\cot 43^\circ} = 1 \quad [\because \tan(90^\circ - \theta) = \cot\theta]$$

***Q.2** The value of the expression $(\cos^2 23^\circ - \sin^2 67^\circ)$ is positive.

Ans. *False*

$$\cos^2 23^\circ - \sin^2 67^\circ = (\cos 23^\circ - \sin 67^\circ)(\cos 23^\circ + \sin 67^\circ) \quad [\because (a^2 - b^2) = (a-b)(a+b)]$$
$$= [\cos 23^\circ - \sin(90^\circ - 23^\circ)](\cos 23^\circ + \sin 67^\circ)$$
$$= (\cos 23^\circ - \cos 23^\circ)(\cos 23^\circ + \sin 67^\circ) \quad [\because \sin(90^\circ - \theta) = \cos\theta]$$
$$= 0 \cdot (\cos 23^\circ + \sin 67^\circ) = 0$$

which neither be either positive or negative.

Alternate method

$$\cos^2 23^\circ - \sin^2 67^\circ = \cos^2 23^\circ - [\sin^2(90^\circ - 23^\circ)]$$
$$= \cos^2 23^\circ - \cos^2 23^\circ \quad [\because \sin(90^\circ - \theta) = \cos\theta]$$
$$= 0$$

Which neither positive or negative.

Note (✱) *Topics related to these question have been removed from latest NCERT.*

Q.3 The value of the expression (sin 80° – cos 80°) is negative.

Ans. *False*

We know that, $\sin\theta$ is increasing when, $0° \le \theta \le 90°$ and $\cos\theta$ is decreasing when, $0° \le \theta \le 90°$.

$\therefore \quad \sin 80° - \cos 80° > 0 \quad$ [positive]

Q.4 $\sqrt{(1-\cos^2\theta)\sec^2\theta} = \tan\theta$

Ans. *True*

$$\sqrt{(1-\cos^2\theta)\sec^2\theta} = \sqrt{\sin^2\theta \cdot \sec^2\theta} \quad [\because \sin^2\theta + \cos^2\theta = 1]$$

$$= \sqrt{\sin^2\theta \cdot \frac{1}{\cos^2\theta}} = \sqrt{\tan^2\theta} = \tan\theta \quad \left[\because \sec\theta = \frac{1}{\cos\theta}, \tan\theta = \frac{\sin\theta}{\cos\theta}\right]$$

Q.5 If $\cos A + \cos^2 A = 1$, then $\sin^2 A + \sin^4 A = 1$

Ans. *True*

$\because \quad \cos A + \cos^2 A = 1$

$\Rightarrow \quad \cos A = 1 - \cos^2 A = \sin^2 A \quad [\because \sin^2 A + \cos^2 A = 1]$

On squaring both sides, we get

$\cos^2 A = \sin^4 A$

$\Rightarrow \quad 1 - \sin^2 A = \sin^4 A \quad [\because \cos^2 A = 1 - \sin^2 A]$

$\Rightarrow \quad \sin^2 A + \sin^4 A = 1$

Q.6 $(\tan\theta + 2)(2\tan\theta + 1) = 5\tan\theta + \sec^2\theta$

Ans. *False*

$$\text{LHS} = (\tan\theta + 2)(2\tan\theta + 1)$$
$$= 2\tan^2\theta + 4\tan\theta + \tan\theta + 2$$
$$= 2(\sec^2\theta - 1) + 5\tan\theta + 2 \quad [\because \sec^2\theta - 1 = \tan^2\theta]$$
$$= 2\sec^2\theta - 2 + 5\tan\theta + 2$$
$$= 2\sec^2\theta + 5\tan\theta \ne \text{RHS}$$

Mistake Alert! *Students may applies wrong identity as* $\tan^2\theta = \sec^2\theta + 1$ *instead of* $\tan^2\theta = \sec^2\theta - 1$.

Q.7 If the length of the shadow of a tower is increasing, then the angle of elevation of the Sun is also increasing.

Ans. *False*

To understand the fact of this question, consider the following example

(i) A tower $2\sqrt{3}$ m high casts a shadow 2 m long on the ground, then the Sun's elevation is 60°.

In ΔACB, $\quad \tan\theta = \dfrac{BC}{AB} = \dfrac{2\sqrt{3}}{2}$

$\Rightarrow \quad \tan\theta = \sqrt{3} = \tan 60°$

$\therefore \quad \theta = 60°$

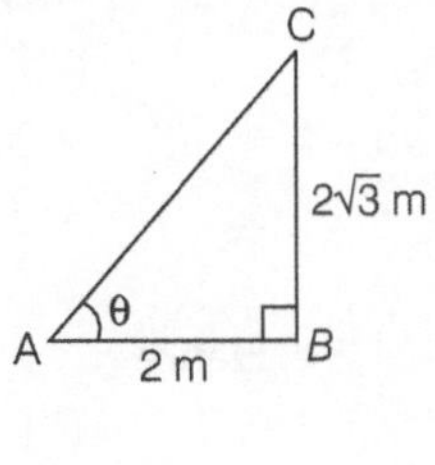

(ii) A same height of tower casts a shadow 4 m more from preceding point, then the Sun's elevation is 30°.

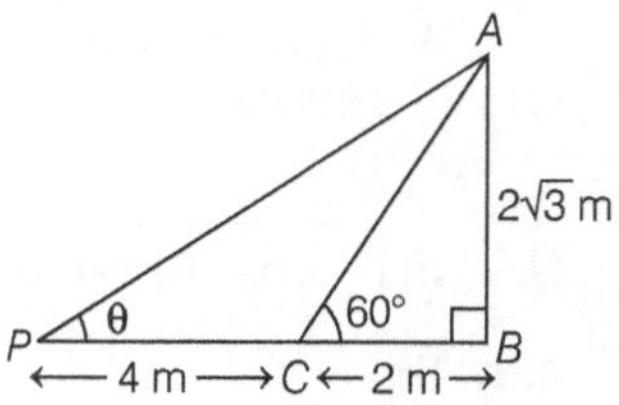

In ΔAPB, $\tan\theta = \frac{AB}{PB} = \frac{AB}{PC + CB}$

$\Rightarrow$ $\tan\theta = \frac{2\sqrt{3}}{4+2} = \frac{2\sqrt{3}}{6}$

$\Rightarrow$ $\tan\theta = \frac{\sqrt{3}}{3} \cdot \frac{\sqrt{3}}{\sqrt{3}} = \frac{3}{3\sqrt{3}}$

$\Rightarrow$ $\tan\theta = \frac{1}{\sqrt{3}} = \tan 30°$

$\therefore$ $\theta = 30°$

Hence, we conclude from above two examples that if the length of the shadow of a tower is increasing, then the angle of elevation of the Sun is decreasing.

Alternate Method

We know that, if the angle of elevation moves towards the tower, then it increases and if the angle of elevation moves away the tower, then it decreases. Hence, if the shadow of a tower is increasing, then the angle of elevation of a Sun is not increasing.

Q.8 If a man standing on a plat form 3m above the surface of a lake observes a cloud and its reflection in the lake, then the angle of elevation of the cloud is equal to the angle of depression of its reflection.

Ans. *False*

From figure, we observe that, a man standing on a platform at point P, 3 m above the surface of a lake observes a cloud at point C. Let the height of the cloud from the surface of the platform is h and angle of elevation of the cloud is θ_1.

Now, at same point P a man observes a cloud reflection in the lake at point P and the height of reflection of cloud in lake is $(h + 3)$ because in lake platform height is also added to reflection of cloud. So, angle of depression is different in the lake from the angle of elevation of the cloud above the surface of a lake.

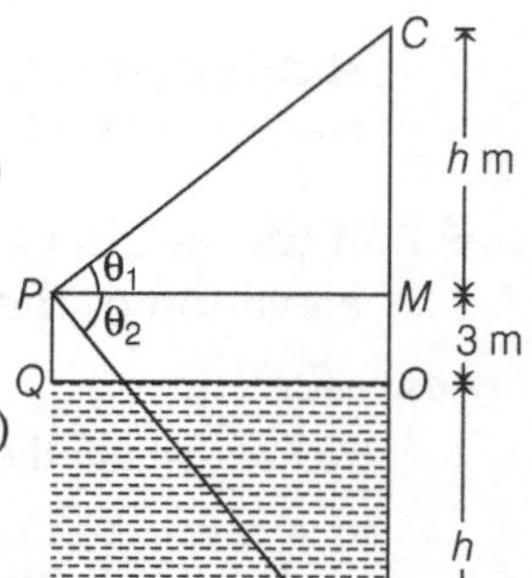

In ΔMPC, $\tan\theta_1 = \frac{CM}{PM} = \frac{h}{PM}$

$\Rightarrow$ $\frac{\tan\theta_1}{h} = \frac{1}{PM}$ ...(i)

In ΔDPM, $\tan\theta_2 = \frac{DM}{PM} = \frac{OD + OM}{PM} = \frac{h+3}{PM}$

$\Rightarrow$ $\frac{\tan\theta_2}{h+3} = \frac{1}{PM}$ ...(ii)

From Eqs. (i) and (ii), we get

$$\frac{\tan\theta_1}{h} = \frac{\tan\theta_2}{h+3}$$

$\Rightarrow$ $\tan\theta_2 = \left(\frac{h+3}{h}\right)\tan\theta_1$

Hence, $\theta_1 \neq \theta_2$

Alternate Method

We know that, if P is a point above the lake at a distance d, then the reflection of the point in the lake would be at the same distance d. Also, the angle of elevation and depression from the surface of the lake is same.

Here, the man is standing on a platform 3 m above the surface, so its angle of elevation to the cloud and angle of depression to the reflection of the cloud is not same.

Mistake Alert! *Students may confuse angles of elevation and depression resulting in errors when setting up their equations.*

Q.9 The value of $2\sin\theta$ can be $a+\frac{1}{a}$, where a is a positive number and $a \neq 1$.

Ans. *False*

Let $a = 3$, then $a+\frac{1}{a} = 3+\frac{1}{3} = \frac{10}{3}$ ...(i)

If $2\sin\theta = a+\frac{1}{a}$, then

$$2\sin\theta = \frac{10}{3} \quad \text{[from Eq. (i)]}$$

$$\Rightarrow \sin\theta = \frac{5}{3}$$

$$\Rightarrow \sin\theta = 1.67$$

which is not possible. $[\because \sin\theta \le 1]$

Q.10 $\cos\theta = \frac{a^2+b^2}{2ab}$, where a and b are two distinct numbers such that $ab > 0$.

Ans. *False*

Given, a and b are two distinct numbers such that $ab > 0$.

Using, $AM > GM$

[since, AM and GM of two number a and b are $\frac{a+b}{2}$ and $\sqrt{ab}$, respectively]

$$\Rightarrow \frac{a^2+b^2}{2} > \sqrt{a^2 \cdot b^2}$$

$$\Rightarrow a^2+b^2 > 2ab$$

$$\Rightarrow \frac{a^2+b^2}{2ab} > 1$$

$$\Rightarrow \cos\theta > 1 \quad \left[\because \cos\theta = \frac{a^2+b^2}{2ab}\right]$$

which is not possible.

Hence, $\cos\theta \neq \frac{a^2+b^2}{2ab}$ $[\because -1 \le \cos\theta \le 1]$

Q.11 The angle of elevation of the top of a tower is 30°. If the height of the tower is doubled, then the angle of elevation of its top will also be doubled.

Thinking Process

(i) Firstly, we find relation between height and distance of the point of observation from its foot x by putting angle of elevation is 30° in case I.

(ii) After that we take double height and taking angle of elevation is θ. Now, use the relation (i) and get the desired result.

Ans. *False*

***Case* I** Let the height of the tower is h m and $BC = x$ m

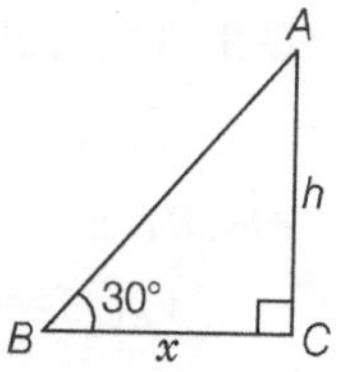

In ΔABC,

$$\tan 30° = \frac{AC}{BC} = \frac{h}{x}$$

$$\Rightarrow \quad \frac{1}{\sqrt{3}} = \frac{h}{x} \quad \text{....(i)}$$

***Case* II** By condition, the height of the tower is doubled. *i.e.,* $PQ = 2h$.

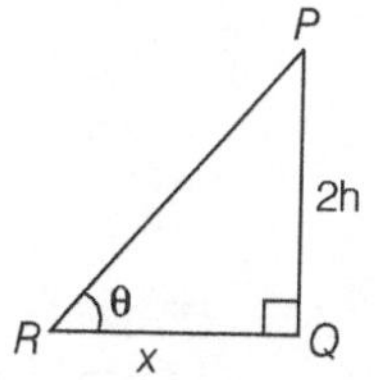

In ΔPQR, $$\tan \theta = \frac{PQ}{QR} = \frac{2h}{x}$$

$$\Rightarrow \quad \tan \theta = \frac{2}{\sqrt{3}} \quad [\because \text{ from Eq. (i)}]$$

$$\Rightarrow \quad \tan \theta = 1.15$$

$$\therefore \quad \theta < 60°$$

Hence, the required angle is not doubled.

Q.12 If the height of a tower and the distance of the point of observation from its foot, both are increased by 10%, then the angle of elevation of its top remains unchanged.

Ans. *True*

***Case* I** Let the height of a tower be h and the distance of the point ofobservation from its foot is x.

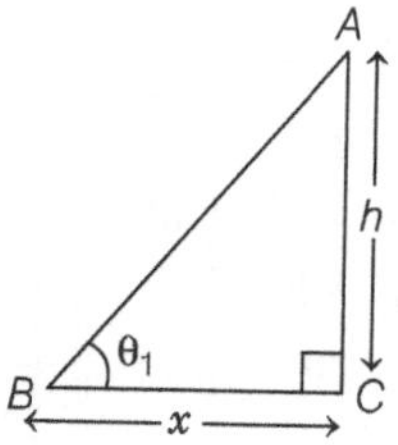

In ΔABC,

$$\tan \theta_1 = \frac{AC}{BC} = \frac{h}{x} \quad \text{...(i)}$$

***Case* II** Now, the height of a tower increased by 10% $= h +$ 10% of $h = h + h \times \frac{10}{100} = \frac{11h}{10}$

and the distance of the point of observation from its foot = x + 10% of x

$$= x + x \times \frac{10}{100} = \frac{11x}{10}$$

In ΔPQR, $\tan \theta_2 = \frac{PR}{QR} = \frac{\left(\frac{11h}{10}\right)}{\left(\frac{11x}{10}\right)}$

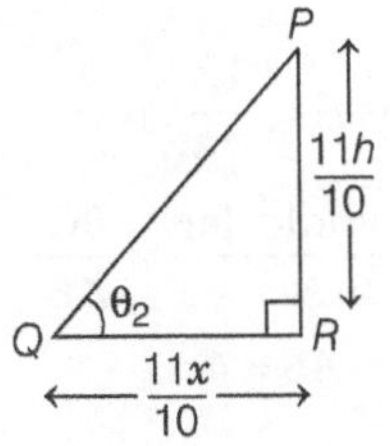

$\Rightarrow$ $\tan \theta_2 = \frac{h}{x}$ ...(ii)

From Eqs. (i) and (ii), we get

$$\theta_1 = \theta_2$$

Hence, the required angle of elevation of its top remains unchanged.

Short Answer Questions

Prove the following (Q1 to Q7).

Q.1 $\frac{\sin\theta}{1+\cos\theta} + \frac{1+\cos\theta}{\sin\theta} = 2\,\text{cosec}\theta$

Ans. LHS $= \frac{\sin\theta}{1+\cos\theta} + \frac{1+\cos\theta}{\sin\theta} = \frac{\sin^2\theta + (1+\cos\theta)^2}{\sin\theta\,(1+\cos\theta)}$

$= \frac{\sin^2\theta + 1 + \cos^2\theta + 2\cos\theta}{\sin\theta\,(1+\cos\theta)}$ $[\because (a+b)^2 = a^2 + b^2 + 2ab]$

$= \frac{1 + 1 + 2\cos\theta}{\sin\theta\,(1+\cos\theta)}$ $[\because \sin^2\theta + \cos^2\theta = 1]$

$= \frac{2(1+\cos\theta)}{\sin\theta\,(1+\cos\theta)} = \frac{2}{\sin\theta}$

$= 2\,\text{cosec}\,\theta = \text{RHS}$ $\left[\because \text{cosec}\theta = \frac{1}{\sin\theta}\right]$

Q.2 $\frac{\tan A}{1+\sec A} - \frac{\tan A}{1-\sec A} = 2\,\text{cosec}\,A$

Ans. LHS $= \frac{\tan A}{1+\sec A} - \frac{\tan A}{1-\sec A}$

$= \frac{\tan A(1-\sec A) - \tan A(1+\sec A)}{(1+\sec A)(1-\sec A)} = \frac{\tan A\,(1-\sec A - 1 - \sec A)}{(1+\sec A)\,(1-\sec A)}$

$= \frac{\tan A\,(-2\sec A)}{(1-\sec^2 A)} = \frac{2\tan A \cdot \sec A}{(\sec^2 A - 1)}$ $[\because (a+b)(a-b) = a^2 - b^2]$

$$= \frac{2 \tan A \cdot \sec A}{\tan^2 A} \quad [\because \sec^2 A - \tan^2 A = 1]$$

$$= \frac{2 \sec A}{\tan A} = \frac{2}{\sin A} \quad \left[\because \sec \theta = \frac{1}{\cos \theta} \text{ and } \tan \theta = \frac{\sin \theta}{\cos \theta}\right]$$

$$= 2 \operatorname{cosec} A = \text{RHS} \quad \left[\because \operatorname{cosec} \theta = \frac{1}{\sin \theta}\right]$$

Q.3 If $\tan A = \frac{3}{4}$, then $\sin A \cos A = \frac{12}{25}$.

Ans. Given, $\tan A = \frac{3}{4} = \frac{\text{Perpendicular}}{\text{Base}} = \frac{BC}{AB}$

Let $BC = 3k$ and $AB = 4k$

By Pythagoras theorem,

$$AC^2 = BC^2 + AB^2 = (3k)^2 + (4k)^2$$
$$= 9k^2 + 16k^2 = 25k^2$$

$\Rightarrow$ $AC = 5k$ [$\because$ side cannot be negative]

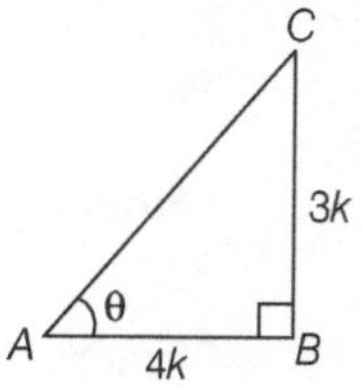

$\therefore$ $\sin A = \frac{BC}{AC} = \frac{3k}{5k} = \frac{3}{5}$

and $\cos A = \frac{AB}{AC} = \frac{4k}{5k} = \frac{4}{5}$

Now, $\sin A \cos A = \frac{3}{5} \cdot \frac{4}{5} = \frac{12}{25}$ **Hence proved.**

Q.4 $(\sin\alpha + \cos\alpha)(\tan\alpha + \cot\alpha) = \sec\alpha + \operatorname{cosec}\alpha$

Ans. LHS $= (\sin \alpha + \cos \alpha)(\tan \alpha + \cot \alpha)$

$$= (\sin \alpha + \cos \alpha)\left(\frac{\sin \alpha}{\cos \alpha} + \frac{\cos \alpha}{\sin \alpha}\right) \quad \left[\because \tan \theta = \frac{\sin \theta}{\cos \theta} \text{ and } \cot \theta = \frac{\cos \theta}{\sin \theta}\right]$$

$$= (\sin \alpha + \cos \alpha)\left(\frac{\sin^2 \alpha + \cos^2 \alpha}{\sin \alpha \cdot \cos \alpha}\right)$$

$$= (\sin \alpha + \cos \alpha) \cdot \frac{1}{(\sin \alpha \cdot \cos \alpha)} \quad [\because \sin^2 \theta + \cos^2 \theta = 1]$$

$$= \frac{1}{\cos \alpha} + \frac{1}{\sin \alpha}$$

$$= \sec \alpha + \operatorname{cosec} \alpha = \text{RHS} \quad \left[\because \sec \theta = \frac{1}{\cos\theta} \text{ and } \operatorname{cosec} \theta = \frac{1}{\sin \theta}\right]$$ **Hence proved.**

Mistake Alert! *Student may not convert the value of tan α and cot α in the form of sin α and cos α.*

Q.5 $(\sqrt{3}+1)(3-\cot 30^\circ) = \tan^3 60^\circ - 2\sin 60^\circ$

Ans. $\text{RHS} = \tan^3 60^\circ - 2\sin 60^\circ = (\sqrt{3})^3 - 2\times\frac{\sqrt{3}}{2} = 3\sqrt{3}-\sqrt{3} = 2\sqrt{3}$

$\text{LHS} = (\sqrt{3}+1)(3-\cot 30^\circ) = (\sqrt{3}+1)(3-\sqrt{3})$

$\left[\because \tan 60^\circ = \sqrt{3},\ \sin 60^\circ = \frac{\sqrt{3}}{2} \text{ and } \cot 30^\circ = \sqrt{3}\right]$

$= (\sqrt{3}+1)\sqrt{3}(\sqrt{3}-1) = \sqrt{3}((\sqrt{3})^2-1) = \sqrt{3}(3-1) = 2\sqrt{3}$

$\therefore$ LHS = RHS **Hence proved.**

Q.6 $1+\frac{\cot^2\alpha}{1+\text{cosec}\,\alpha} = \text{cosec}\,\alpha$

Ans. $\text{LHS} = 1+\frac{\cot^2\alpha}{1+\text{cosec}\,\alpha} = 1+\frac{\cos^2\alpha/\sin^2\alpha}{1+1/\sin\alpha}$ $\left[\because \cot\theta = \frac{\cos\theta}{\sin\theta} \text{ and cosec}\,\theta = \frac{1}{\sin\theta}\right]$

$= 1+\frac{\cos^2\alpha}{\sin\alpha(1+\sin\alpha)} = \frac{\sin\alpha(1+\sin\alpha)+\cos^2\alpha}{\sin\alpha(1+\sin\alpha)}$

$= \frac{\sin\alpha + (\sin^2\alpha+\cos^2\alpha)}{\sin\alpha(1+\sin\alpha)}$ $[\because \sin^2\theta+\cos^2\theta = 1]$

$= \frac{(\sin\alpha+1)}{\sin\alpha(\sin\alpha+1)} = \frac{1}{\sin\alpha}$ $\left[\because \text{cosec}\,\theta = \frac{1}{\sin\theta}\right]$

$= \text{cosec}\,\alpha = \text{RHS}$

***Q.7** $\tan\theta + \tan(90^\circ-\theta) = \sec\theta\sec(90^\circ-\theta)$

Ans. $\text{LHS} = \tan\theta + \tan(90^\circ-\theta)$

$= \tan\theta + \cot\theta$ $[\because \tan(90^\circ-\theta) = \cot\theta]$

$= \frac{\sin\theta}{\cos\theta}+\frac{\cos\theta}{\sin\theta} = \frac{\sin^2\theta+\cos^2\theta}{\sin\theta\cos\theta}$ $\left[\because \tan\theta = \frac{\sin\theta}{\cos\theta} \text{ and } \cot\theta = \frac{\cos\theta}{\sin\theta}\right]$

$= \frac{1}{\sin\theta\cos\theta}$ $[\because \sin^2\theta+\cos^2\theta = 1]$

$= \sec\theta\,\text{cosec}\,\theta$ $\left[\because \sec\theta = \frac{1}{\cos\theta} \text{ and coseco}\,\theta = \frac{1}{\sin\theta}\right]$

$= \sec\theta\sec(90^\circ-\theta) = \text{RHS}$ $[\because \sec(90^\circ-\theta) = \text{cosec}\,\theta]$

Q.8 Find the angle of elevation of the Sun when the shadow of a pole h m high is $\sqrt{3}\,h$ m long.

Ans. Let the angle of elevation of the Sun is θ.

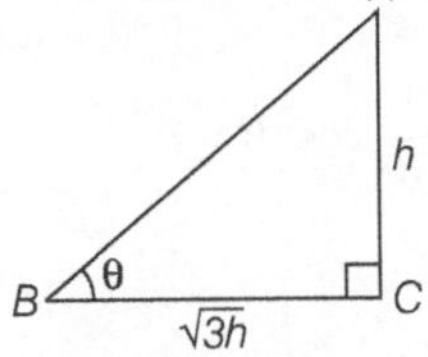

Note (*) *Topics related to these question have been removed from latest NCERT.*

Given, height of pole = h

Now, in ΔABC,

$$\tan\theta = \frac{AC}{BC} = \frac{h}{\sqrt{3}h}$$

$$\Rightarrow \quad \tan\theta = \frac{1}{\sqrt{3}} = \tan 30^\circ \Rightarrow \theta = 30^\circ$$

Hence, the angle of elevation of the Sun is 30°.

Q.9 If $\sqrt{3}\tan\theta = 1$, then find the value of $\sin^2\theta - \cos^2\theta$.

Thinking Process From the given equation, get the value of θ and put the value of θ in the given expression, we get the required value.

Ans. Given that, $\sqrt{3}\tan\theta = 1$

$$\Rightarrow \quad \tan\theta = \frac{1}{\sqrt{3}} = \tan 30^\circ$$

$$\Rightarrow \quad \theta = 30^\circ$$

Now,

$$\sin^2\theta - \cos^2\theta = \sin^2 30^\circ - \cos^2 30^\circ$$

$$= \left(\frac{1}{2}\right)^2 - \left(\frac{\sqrt{3}}{2}\right)^2$$

$$= \frac{1}{4} - \frac{3}{4} = \frac{1-3}{4} = -\frac{2}{4} = -\frac{1}{2}$$

Q.10 A ladder 15 m long just reaches the top of a vertical wall. If the ladder makes an angle of 60° with the wall, find the height of the wall.

Ans. Given that, the height of the ladder = 15 m

Let the height of the vertical wall = h

and the ladder makes an angle of elevation 60° with the wall *i.e.*, $\theta = 60^\circ$.

In ΔQPR,

$$\cos 60^\circ = \frac{PR}{PQ} = \frac{h}{15}$$

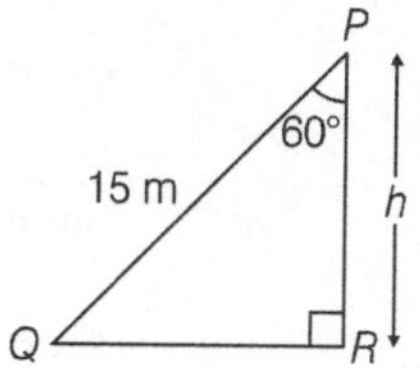

$$\Rightarrow \quad \frac{1}{2} = \frac{h}{15}$$

$$\Rightarrow \quad h = \frac{15}{2}\text{ m}$$

Hence, the required height of the wall $\frac{15}{2}$ m.

Q.11 Simplify $(1+\tan^2\theta)(1-\sin\theta)(1+\sin\theta)$.

Ans. $(1+\tan^2\theta)(1-\sin\theta)(1+\sin\theta) = (1+\tan^2\theta)(1-\sin^2\theta)$ $[\because (a-b)(a+b) = a^2 - b^2]$

$$= \sec^2\theta \cdot \cos^2\theta$$

$[\because 1+\tan^2\theta = \sec^2\theta \text{ and } \cos^2\theta + \sin^2\theta = 1]$

$$= \frac{1}{\cos^2\theta}\cdot\cos^2\theta = 1 \quad \left[\because \sec\theta = \frac{1}{\cos\theta}\right]$$

Q.12 If $2\sin^2\theta - \cos^2\theta = 2$, then find the value of θ.

Ans. Given, $2\sin^2\theta - \cos^2\theta = 2$

$\Rightarrow 2\sin^2\theta - (1 - \sin^2\theta) = 2$ $[\because \sin^2\theta + \cos^2\theta = 1]$

$\Rightarrow 2\sin^2\theta + \sin^2\theta - 1 = 2$

$\Rightarrow 3\sin^2\theta = 3 \Rightarrow \sin^2\theta = 1$

$\Rightarrow \sin\theta = 1 = \sin 90°$ $[\because \sin 90° = 1]$

$\therefore \theta = 90°$

***Q.13** Show that $\dfrac{\cos^2(45°+\theta) + \cos^2(45°-\theta)}{\tan(60°+\theta)\tan(30°-\theta)} = 1$

Ans. $\text{LHS} = \dfrac{\cos^2(45°+\theta) + \cos^2(45°-\theta)}{\tan(60°+\theta)\cdot\tan(30°-\theta)} = \dfrac{\cos^2(45°+\theta) + [\sin\{90°-(45°-\theta)\}]^2}{\tan(60°+\theta)\cdot\cot\{90°-(30°-\theta)\}}$

$[\because \sin(90°-\theta) = \cos\theta \text{ and } \cot(90°-\theta) = \tan\theta]$

$= \dfrac{\cos^2(45°+\theta) + \sin^2(45°+\theta)}{\tan(60°+\theta)\cdot\cot(60°+\theta)}$

$= \dfrac{1}{\tan(60°+\theta)\cdot\dfrac{1}{\tan(60°+\theta)}} = 1 = \text{RHS}$ $[\because \sin^2\theta + \cos^2\theta = 1 \text{ and } \cot\theta = 1/\tan\theta]$

Q.14 An observer 1.5 metres tall is 20.5 m away from a tower 22 m high. Determine the angle of elevation of the top of the tower from the eye of the observer.

Ans. Let the angle of elevation of the top of the tower from the eye of the observer is θ

Given that, $AB = 22\text{ m}, PQ = 1.5\text{ m} = MB$

and $QB = PM = 20.5\text{ m}$

$\Rightarrow AM = AB - MB$

$= 22 - 1.5 = 20.5\text{ m}$

Now, in ΔAPM, $\tan\theta = \dfrac{AM}{PM} = \dfrac{20.5}{20.5} = 1$

$\Rightarrow \tan\theta = \tan 45°$

$\therefore \theta = 45°$

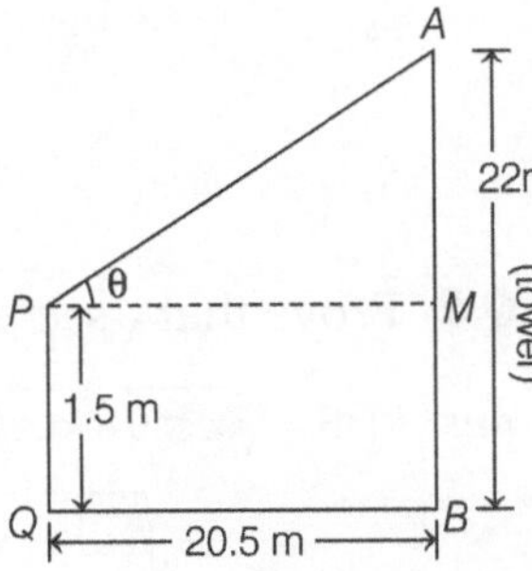

Hence, required angle of elevation of the top of the tower from the eye of the observer is 45°.

Q.15 Show that $\tan^4\theta + \tan^2\theta = \sec^4\theta - \sec^2\theta$.

Ans. $\text{LHS} = \tan^4\theta + \tan^2\theta = \tan^2\theta(\tan^2\theta + 1)$

$= \tan^2\theta\cdot\sec^2\theta$ $[\because \sec^2\theta = \tan^2\theta + 1]$

$= (\sec^2\theta - 1)\cdot\sec^2\theta$ $[\because \tan^2\theta = \sec^2\theta - 1]$

$= \sec^4\theta - \sec^2\theta = \text{RHS}$

Note (*) *Topics related to these question have been removed from latest NCERT.*

Long Answer Questions

Q.1 If $\operatorname{cosec}\theta + \cot\theta = p$, then prove that $\cos\theta = \dfrac{p^2-1}{p^2+1}$.

Thinking Process Reduce the given equation into $\sin\theta$ and $\cos\theta$ and simplify it.
In simplification form, we use the componendo and dividendo rule to get the desired result.

Ans. Given, $\operatorname{cosec}\theta + \cot\theta = p$

$$\Rightarrow \frac{1}{\sin\theta} + \frac{\cos\theta}{\sin\theta} = p \qquad \left[\because \operatorname{cosec}\theta = \frac{1}{\sin\theta} \text{ and } \cot\theta = \frac{\cos\theta}{\sin\theta}\right]$$

$$\Rightarrow \frac{1+\cos\theta}{\sin\theta} = \frac{p}{1}$$

$$\Rightarrow \frac{(1+\cos\theta)^2}{\sin^2\theta} = \frac{p^2}{1} \qquad \text{[take square on both sides]}$$

$$\Rightarrow \frac{1+\cos^2\theta + 2\cos\theta}{\sin^2\theta} = \frac{p^2}{1}$$

Using componendo and dividendo rule, we get

$$\frac{(1+\cos^2\theta + 2\cos\theta) - \sin^2\theta}{(1+\cos^2\theta + 2\cos\theta) + \sin^2\theta} = \frac{p^2-1}{p^2+1}$$

$$\Rightarrow \frac{1+\cos^2\theta + 2\cos\theta - (1-\cos^2\theta)}{1+2\cos\theta + (\cos^2\theta + \sin^2\theta)} = \frac{p^2-1}{p^2+1}$$

$$\Rightarrow \frac{2\cos^2\theta + 2\cos\theta}{2+2\cos\theta} = \frac{p^2-1}{p^2+1} \qquad [\because \sin^2\theta + \cos^2\theta = 1]$$

$$\Rightarrow \frac{2\cos\theta\,(\cos\theta + 1)}{2\,(\cos\theta + 1)} = \frac{p^2-1}{p^2+1}$$

$$\therefore \cos\theta = \frac{p^2-1}{p^2+1}$$

Hence proved.

Q.2 Prove that $\sqrt{\sec^2\theta + \operatorname{cosec}^2\theta} = \tan\theta + \cot\theta$.

Ans. LHS $= \sqrt{\sec^2\theta + \operatorname{cosec}^2\theta}$

$$= \sqrt{\frac{1}{\cos^2\theta} + \frac{1}{\sin^2\theta}} \qquad \left[\because \sec\theta = \frac{1}{\cos\theta} \text{ and } \operatorname{cosec}\theta = \frac{1}{\sin\theta}\right]$$

$$= \sqrt{\frac{\sin^2\theta + \cos^2\theta}{\sin^2\theta\cdot\cos^2\theta}} = \sqrt{\frac{1}{\sin^2\theta\cdot\cos^2\theta}} \qquad [\because \sin^2\theta + \cos^2\theta = 1]$$

$$= \frac{1}{\sin\theta\cdot\cos\theta} = \frac{\sin^2\theta + \cos^2\theta}{\sin\theta\cdot\cos\theta}$$

$$= \frac{\sin^2\theta}{\sin\theta\cdot\cos\theta} + \frac{\cos^2\theta}{\sin\theta\cdot\cos\theta} = \frac{\sin\theta}{\cos\theta} + \frac{\cos\theta}{\sin\theta}$$

$$= \tan\theta + \cot\theta = \text{RHS} \qquad \left[\because \tan\theta = \frac{\sin\theta}{\cos\theta} \text{ and } \cot\theta = \frac{\cos\theta}{\sin\theta}\right]$$

Hence proved.

Q.3 The angle of elevation of the top of a tower from certain point is 30°. If the observer moves 20 m towards the tower, the angle of elevation of the top increases by 15°. Find the height of the tower.

Ans. Let the height of the tower be h.

also, $SR = x$ m, $\angle PSR = \theta$

Given that, $QS = 20$ m

and $\angle PQR = 30°$

Now, in ΔPSR,

$$\tan\theta = \frac{PR}{SR} = \frac{h}{x}$$

$$\Rightarrow \quad x = \frac{h}{\tan\theta} \quad \text{...(i)}$$

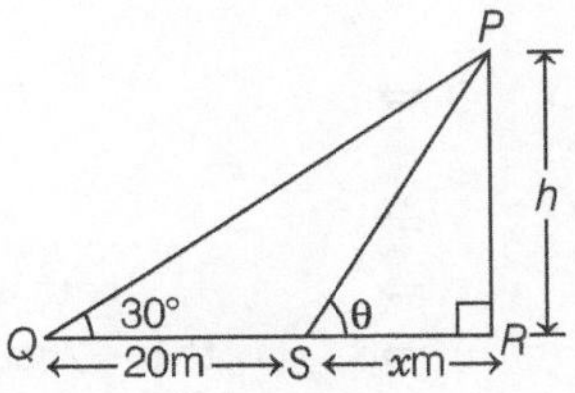

Now, in ΔPQR,

$$\tan 30° = \frac{PR}{QR} = \frac{PR}{QS + SR}$$

$$\Rightarrow \quad \frac{1}{\sqrt{3}} = \frac{h}{20 + x}$$

$$\Rightarrow \quad 20 + x = h\sqrt{3}$$

$$\Rightarrow \quad 20 + \frac{h}{\tan\theta} = h\sqrt{3} \quad \text{[from Eq. (i)]...(ii)}$$

Since, after moving 20 m towards the tower the angle of elevation of the top increases by 15°.

i.e., $\angle PSR = \theta = \angle PQR + 15°$

$$\Rightarrow \quad \theta = 30° + 15 = 45°$$

$$\therefore \quad 20 + \frac{h}{\tan 45°} = h\sqrt{3} \quad \text{[from Eq. (i)]}$$

$$\Rightarrow \quad 20 + \frac{h}{1} = h\sqrt{3}$$

$$\Rightarrow \quad 20 = h\sqrt{3} - h$$

$$\Rightarrow \quad h(\sqrt{3} - 1) = 20$$

$$\therefore \quad h = \frac{20}{\sqrt{3} - 1} \cdot \frac{\sqrt{3} + 1}{\sqrt{3} + 1} \quad \text{[by rationalisation]}$$

$$\Rightarrow \quad = \frac{20(\sqrt{3} + 1)}{3 - 1} = \frac{20(\sqrt{3} + 1)}{2} \quad [\because (a+b)(a-b) = a^2 - b^2]$$

$$\Rightarrow \quad = 10(\sqrt{3} + 1) \text{ m}$$

Hence, the required height of tower is $10(\sqrt{3} + 1)$ m.

Q.4 If $1+\sin^2\theta = 3\sin\theta\cos\theta$, then prove that $\tan\theta = 1$ or $\frac{1}{2}$.

Thinking Process

(i) First we reduce the given equation, with the help of trigonometric ratio and identities in the form of $\cot\theta$.

(ii) Now, factorise the quadratic equation in $\cot\theta$ by splitting the middle term and get the desired result.

Ans. Given, $1+\sin^2\theta = 3\sin\theta\cdot\cos\theta$

On dividing by $\sin^2\theta$ on both sides, we get

$$\frac{1}{\sin^2\theta}+1 = 3\cot\theta \qquad \left[\because \cot\theta = \frac{\cos\theta}{\sin\theta}\right]$$

$$\Rightarrow \quad \operatorname{cosec}^2\theta + 1 = 3\cot\theta \qquad \left[\operatorname{cosec}\theta = \frac{1}{\sin\theta}\right]$$

$$\Rightarrow \quad 1+\cot^2\theta + 1 = 3\cot\theta \qquad [\because \operatorname{cosec}^2\theta - \cot^2\theta = 1]$$

$$\Rightarrow \quad \cot^2\theta - 3\cot\theta + 2 = 0$$

$$\Rightarrow \quad \cot^2\theta - 2\cot\theta - \cot\theta + 2 = 0 \qquad \text{[by splitting the middle term]}$$

$$\Rightarrow \quad \cot\theta(\cot\theta - 2) - 1(\cot\theta - 2) = 0$$

$$\Rightarrow \quad (\cot\theta - 2)(\cot\theta - 1) = 0 \Rightarrow \cot\theta = 1 \text{ or } 2$$

$$\Rightarrow \quad \tan\theta = 1 \text{ or } \frac{1}{2} \qquad \left[\because \tan\theta = \frac{1}{\cot\theta}\right]$$

Hence proved.

Q.5 Given that $\sin\theta + 2\cos\theta = 1$, then prove that $2\sin\theta - \cos\theta = 2$.

Ans. Given, $\sin\theta + 2\cos\theta = 1$

On squaring both sides, we get

$$(\sin\theta + 2\cos\theta)^2 = (1)^2$$

$$\Rightarrow \quad \sin^2\theta + 4\cos^2\theta + 4\sin\theta\cdot\cos\theta = 1$$

$$\Rightarrow \quad (1-\cos^2\theta) + 4(1-\sin^2\theta) + 4\sin\theta\cdot\cos\theta = 1 \qquad [\because \sin^2\theta + \cos^2\theta = 1]$$

$$\Rightarrow \quad 1-\cos^2\theta + 4 - 4\sin^2\theta + 4\sin\theta\cos\theta = 1$$

$$\Rightarrow \quad -\cos^2\theta - 4\sin^2\theta + 4\sin\theta\cdot\cos\theta = -4$$

$$\Rightarrow \quad 4\sin^2\theta + \cos^2\theta - 4\sin\theta\cdot\cos\theta = 4$$

$$\Rightarrow \quad (2\sin\theta - \cos\theta)^2 = 4 \qquad [\because a^2 + b^2 - 2ab = (a-b)^2]$$

$$\Rightarrow \quad 2\sin\theta - \cos\theta = 2$$

Hence proved.

***Q.6** The angle of elevation of the top of a tower from two points distant s and t from its foot are complementary. Prove that the height of the tower is $\sqrt{st}$.

Thinking Process Use the concept of complementary angles in the angle of elevation *i.e.,* if two anlges α and β are complementary to each other, then the sum of both angles is equal to 90°.

$$\Rightarrow \quad \alpha + \beta = 90^\circ$$

where, $\quad \alpha = \theta$ and $\beta = (90^\circ - \theta)$

Note (*) *Topics related to these question have been removed from latest NCERT.*

Ans. Let the height of the tower is h.

and $\angle ABC = \theta$

Given that, $BC = s,\ PC = t$

and angle of elevation on both positions are complementary.

i.e., $\angle APC = 90^\circ - \theta$

[if two angles are complementary to each other, then the sum of both angles is equal to 90°.]

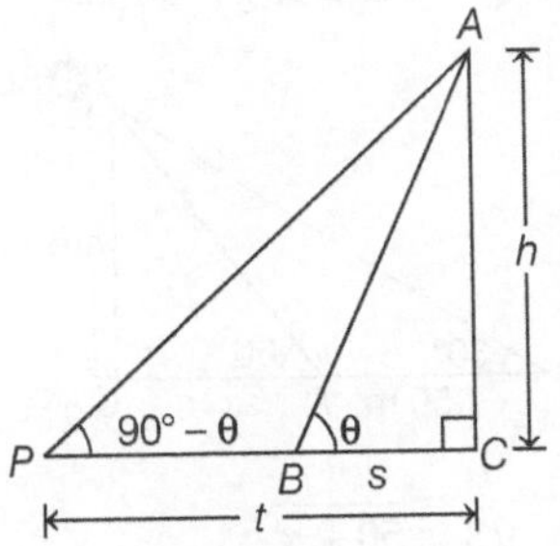

Now in ΔABC, $$\tan\theta = \frac{AC}{BC} = \frac{h}{s} \quad \text{...(i)}$$

and in ΔAPC

$$\tan(90^\circ - \theta) = \frac{AC}{PC}$$

$$\Rightarrow \quad \cot\theta = \frac{h}{t} \qquad [\because \tan(90^\circ - \theta) = \cot\theta]$$

$$\Rightarrow \quad \frac{1}{\tan\theta} = \frac{h}{t} \qquad \left[\because \cot\theta = \frac{1}{\tan\theta}\right] \text{...(ii)}$$

On, multiplying Eqs. (i) and (ii), we get

$$\tan\theta \cdot \frac{1}{\tan\theta} = \frac{h}{s} \cdot \frac{h}{t}$$

$$\Rightarrow \quad \frac{h^2}{st} = 1$$

$$\Rightarrow \quad h^2 = st$$

$$\Rightarrow \quad h = \sqrt{st}$$

So, the required height of the tower is $\sqrt{st}$. **Hence proved.**

Q.7 The shadow of a tower standing on a level plane is found to be 50 m longer when Sun's elevation is 30° than when it is 60°. Find the height of the tower.

Thinking Process Consider the shadow of the tower be x m when the angle of elevation in that position is 60°, when angle of elevation is 30°, then the distance becomes $(50 + x)$ m. Now, apply suitable trigonometric ratios in the triangle and get the desired result.

Ans. Let the height of the tower be h and $RQ = x$ m

Given that, $\angle SPQ = 30°$, $\angle SRQ = 60°$

Now, in ΔSRQ, $\tan 60° = \dfrac{SQ}{RQ}$

$$\Rightarrow \quad \sqrt{3} = \frac{h}{x} \Rightarrow x = \frac{h}{\sqrt{3}} \quad \text{...(i)}$$

and in ΔSPQ, $\tan 30° = \dfrac{SQ}{PQ} = \dfrac{SQ}{PR + RQ} = \dfrac{h}{50 + x}$

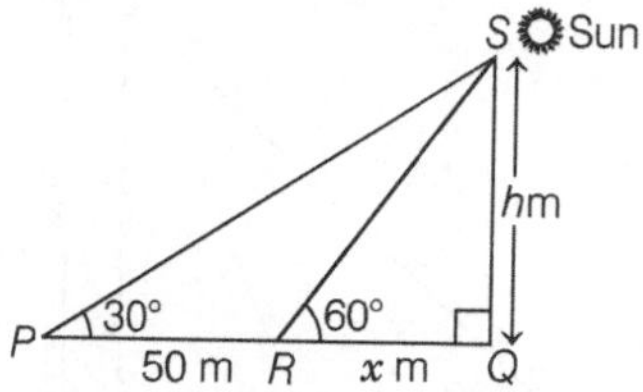

$$\Rightarrow \quad \frac{1}{\sqrt{3}} = \frac{h}{50 + x}$$

$$\Rightarrow \quad \sqrt{3} \cdot h = 50 + x$$

$$\Rightarrow \quad \sqrt{3} \cdot h = 50 + \frac{h}{\sqrt{3}} \quad \text{[from Eq. (i)]}$$

$$\Rightarrow \quad \left(\sqrt{3} - \frac{1}{\sqrt{3}}\right) h = 50$$

$$\Rightarrow \quad \frac{(3-1)}{\sqrt{3}} h = 50$$

$$\therefore \quad h = \frac{50\sqrt{3}}{2}$$

$$h = 25\sqrt{3} \text{ m}$$

Hence, the required height of tower is $25\sqrt{3}$ m.

Q.8 A vertical tower stands on a horizontal plane and is surmounted by a vertical flag staff of height h. At a point on the plane, the angles of elevation of the bottom and the top of the flag staff are α and β respectively. Prove that the height of the tower is $\left(\dfrac{h \tan \alpha}{\tan \beta - \tan \alpha}\right)$.

Ans. Let the height of the tower be H and $OR = x$

Given that, height of flag staff $= h = FP$ and $\angle PRO = \alpha$, $\angle FRO = \beta$

Now, in ΔPRO, $\tan \alpha = \dfrac{PO}{RO} = \dfrac{H}{x}$

$$\Rightarrow \quad x = \frac{H}{\tan \alpha} \quad \text{...(i)}$$

and in ΔFRO, $\tan \beta = \dfrac{FO}{RO} = \dfrac{FP + PO}{RO}$

$$\tan\beta = \frac{h+H}{x}$$

$$\Rightarrow \quad x = \frac{h+H}{\tan\beta} \quad \ldots\text{(ii)}$$

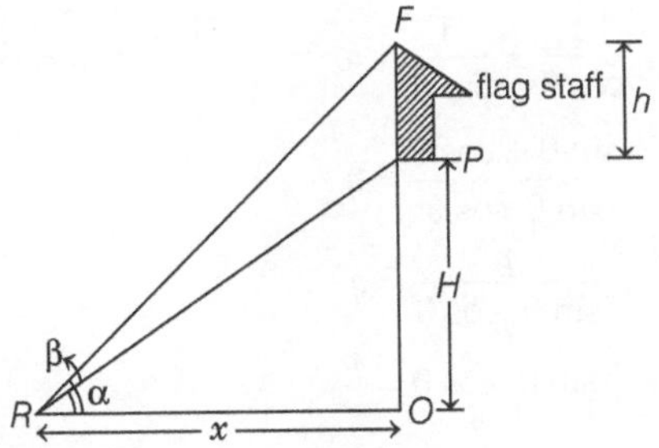

From Eqs. (i) and (ii), we get

$$\frac{H}{\tan\alpha} = \frac{h+H}{\tan\beta}$$

$$\Rightarrow \quad H\tan\beta = h\tan\alpha + H\tan\alpha$$

$$\Rightarrow H\tan\beta - H\tan\alpha = h\tan\alpha$$

$$\Rightarrow \quad H(\tan\beta - \tan\alpha) = h\tan\alpha \quad \Rightarrow \quad H = \frac{h\tan\alpha}{\tan\beta - \tan\alpha}$$

Hence, the required height of tower is $\frac{h\tan\alpha}{\tan\beta - \tan\alpha}$ **Hence proved.**

Q.9 If $\tan\theta + \sec\theta = l$, then prove that $\sec\theta = \frac{l^2+1}{2l}$.

Thinking Process Firstly, we find the value of $(\sec\theta - \tan\theta)$. By using identity $\sec^2\theta - \tan^2\theta = 1$ and get the desired result. If $\sec\theta + \tan\theta = a$, then $\sec\theta - \tan\theta = \frac{1}{a}$.

Ans. Given, $\tan\theta + \sec\theta = l$ ...(i)

[multiply by $(\sec\theta - \tan\theta)$ on numerator and denominator LHS]

$$\Rightarrow \quad \frac{(\tan\theta + \sec\theta)(\sec\theta - \tan\theta)}{(\sec\theta - \tan\theta)} = l \quad \Rightarrow \quad \frac{(\sec^2\theta - \tan^2\theta)}{(\sec\theta - \tan\theta)} = l$$

$$\Rightarrow \quad \frac{1}{\sec\theta - \tan\theta} = l \quad [\because \sec^2\theta - \tan^2\theta = 1]$$

$$\Rightarrow \quad \sec\theta - \tan\theta = \frac{1}{l} \quad \ldots\text{(ii)}$$

On adding Eqs. (i) and (ii), we get

$$2\sec\theta = l + \frac{1}{l}$$

$$\Rightarrow \quad \sec\theta = \frac{l^2+1}{2l}$$

Hence proved.

Q.10 If $\sin\theta + \cos\theta = p$ and $\sec\theta + \text{cosec}\,\theta = q$, then prove that $q(p^2 - 1) = 2p$.

Ans. Given that, $\sin\theta + \cos\theta = p$ ...(i)

and $\sec\theta + \text{cosec}\,\theta = q$

$\Rightarrow \dfrac{1}{\cos\theta} + \dfrac{1}{\sin\theta} = q$ $\left[\because \sec\theta = \dfrac{1}{\cos\theta} \text{ and } \text{cosec}\,\theta = \dfrac{1}{\sin\theta}\right]$

$\Rightarrow \dfrac{\sin\theta + \cos\theta}{\sin\theta.\cos\theta} = q$

$\Rightarrow \dfrac{p}{\sin\theta\cdot\cos\theta} = q$ [from Eq. (i)]

$\Rightarrow \sin\theta\cdot\cos\theta = \dfrac{p}{q}$ [from Eq. (i)]...(ii)

Now, $\sin\theta + \cos\theta = p$ [given]

On squaring both sides, we get

$(\sin\theta + \cos\theta)^2 = p^2$

$\Rightarrow (\sin^2\theta + \cos^2\theta) + 2\sin\theta.\cos\theta = p^2$ $[\because (a+b)^2 = a^2 + 2ab + b^2]$

$\Rightarrow 1 + 2\sin\theta\cdot\cos\theta = p^2$ $[\because \sin^2\theta + \cos^2\theta = 1]$

$\Rightarrow 1 + 2\cdot\dfrac{p}{q} = p^2$ [from Eq. (ii)]

$\Rightarrow q + 2p = p^2q \Rightarrow 2p = p^2q - q$

$\Rightarrow q(p^2 - 1) = 2p$ **Hence proved.**

Q.11 If $a\sin\theta + b\cos\theta = c$, then prove that $a\cos\theta - b\sin\theta = \sqrt{a^2 + b^2 - c^2}$.

Ans. Given that, $a\sin\theta + b\cos\theta = c$

On squaring both sides,

$(a\cdot\sin\theta + \cos\theta\cdot b)^2 = c^2$

$\Rightarrow a^2\sin^2\theta + b^2\cos^2\theta + 2ab\sin\theta\cdot\cos\theta = c^2$ $[\because (x+y)^2 = x^2 + 2xy + y^2]$

$\Rightarrow a^2(1 - \cos^2\theta) + b^2(1 - \sin^2\theta) + 2ab\sin\theta\cdot\cos\theta = c^2$ $[\because \sin^2\theta + \cos^2\theta = 1]$

$\Rightarrow a^2 - a^2\cos^2\theta + b^2 - b^2\sin^2\theta + 2ab\sin\theta\cdot\cos\theta = c^2$

$\Rightarrow a^2 + b^2 - c^2 = a^2\cos^2\theta + b^2\sin^2\theta - 2ab\sin\theta\cdot\cos\theta$

$\Rightarrow (a^2 + b^2 - c^2) = (a\cos\theta - b\sin\theta)^2$ $[\because a^2 + b^2 - 2ab = (a-b)^2]$

$\Rightarrow a\cos\theta - b\sin\theta = \sqrt{a^2 + b^2 - c^2}$ **Hence proved.**

Q.12 Prove that $\dfrac{1 + \sec\theta - \tan\theta}{1 + \sec\theta + \tan\theta} = \dfrac{1 - \sin\theta}{\cos\theta}$

Ans. LHS $= \dfrac{1 + \sec\theta - \tan\theta}{1 + \sec\theta + \tan\theta}$

$= \left(\dfrac{1 + \sec\theta - \tan\theta}{1 + (\sec\theta + \tan\theta)}\right) \times \dfrac{(\sec\theta - \tan\theta)}{(\sec\theta - \tan\theta)}$

[multiply by $(\sec\theta - \tan\theta)$ on both numerator and denominator]

$$= \frac{(1+\sec\theta - \tan\theta)(\sec\theta - \tan\theta)}{(\sec\theta - \tan\theta)+(\sec\theta + \tan\theta)(\sec\theta - \tan\theta)}$$

$$= \frac{(1+\sec\theta - \tan\theta)(\sec\theta - \tan\theta)}{(\sec\theta - \tan\theta)+(\sec^2\theta - \tan^2\theta)}$$

$$= \frac{(1+\sec\theta - \tan\theta)(\sec\theta - \tan\theta)}{(\sec\theta - \tan\theta + 1)} \qquad [\because 1+\tan^2\theta = \sec^2\theta]$$

$$= \sec\theta - \tan\theta = \frac{1}{\cos\theta} - \frac{\sin\theta}{\cos\theta} \qquad \left[\because \sec\theta = \frac{1}{\cos\theta} \text{ and } \tan\theta = \frac{\sin\theta}{\cos\theta}\right]$$

$$= \frac{1-\sin\theta}{\cos\theta} = \text{RHS}$$

Hence proved.

Q.13 The angle of elevation of the top of a tower 30 m high from the foot of another tower in the same plane is 60° and the angle of elevation of the top of the second tower from the foot of the first tower is 30°. Find the distance between the two towers and also the height of the tower.

Ans. Let distance between the two towers $= AB = 'x'$ m

and height of the other tower $= PA = 'h'$ m

Given that, height of the tower $= QB = 30$ m, $\angle QAB = 60°$ and $\angle PBA = 30°$

Now, in ΔQAB, $\tan 60° = \frac{QB}{AB} = \frac{30}{x}$

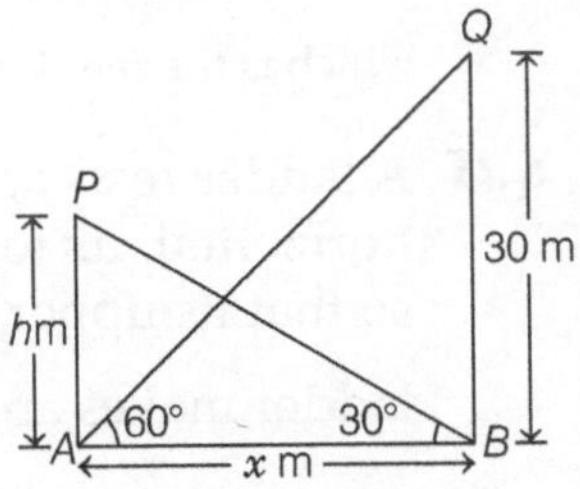

$\Rightarrow \quad \sqrt{3} = \frac{30}{x}$

$\therefore \quad x = \frac{30}{\sqrt{3}} \cdot \frac{\sqrt{3}}{\sqrt{3}} = \frac{30\sqrt{3}}{3} = 10\sqrt{3}$ m

and in ΔPBA,

$\tan 30° = \frac{PA}{AB} = \frac{h}{x}$

$\Rightarrow \quad \frac{1}{\sqrt{3}} = \frac{h}{10\sqrt{3}} \qquad [\because x = 10\sqrt{3} \text{ m}]$

$\Rightarrow \quad h = 10$ m

Hence, the required distance and height are $10\sqrt{3}$ m and 10 m, respectively.

Q.14 From the top of a tower h m high, the angles of depression of two objects, which are in line with the foot of the tower are α and β $(\beta > \alpha)$. Find the distance between the two objects.

Ans. Let the distance between two objects is $'x'$ m.

and $CD = 'y'$ m.

Given that, $\angle BAX = \alpha = \angle ABD$, [alternate angle]

$\angle CAX = \beta = \angle ACD$ [alternate angle]

and the height of tower, $AD = 'h'$ m

Now, in ΔACD,

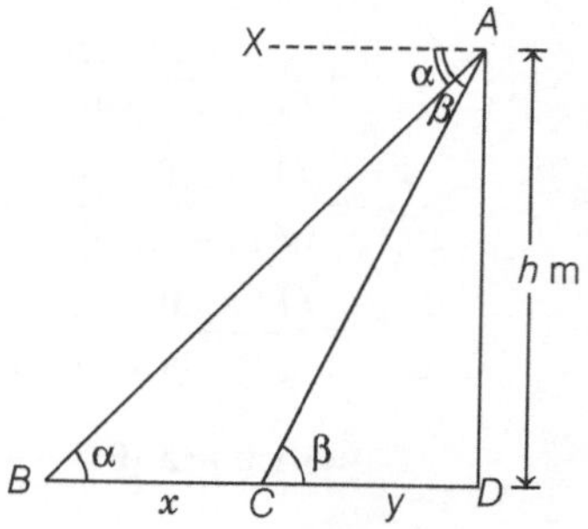

$$\tan \beta = \frac{AD}{CD} = \frac{h}{y}$$

$$\Rightarrow \quad y = \frac{h}{\tan \beta} \quad \ldots(i)$$

and in ΔABD,

$$\tan \alpha = \frac{AD}{BD} \Rightarrow = \frac{AD}{BC + CD}$$

$$\Rightarrow \quad \tan \alpha = \frac{h}{x+y} \Rightarrow x + y = \frac{h}{\tan \alpha}$$

$$\Rightarrow \quad y = \frac{h}{\tan \alpha} - x \quad \ldots(ii)$$

From Eqs. (i) and (ii), we get

$$\frac{h}{\tan \beta} = \frac{h}{\tan \alpha} - x$$

$$\therefore \quad x = \frac{h}{\tan\alpha} - \frac{h}{\tan\beta} = h\left(\frac{1}{\tan\alpha} - \frac{1}{\tan\beta}\right) = h(\cot\alpha - \cot\beta) \quad \left[\because \cot\theta = \frac{1}{\tan\theta}\right]$$

which is the required distance between the two objects.

Q.15 A ladder rests against a vertical wall at an inclination α to the horizontal. Its foot is pulled away from the wall through a distance p, so that its upper end slides a distance q down the wall and then the ladder makes an angle β to the horizontal. Show that $\frac{p}{q} = \frac{\cos\beta - \cos\alpha}{\sin\alpha - \sin\beta}$.

Ans. Let $OQ = x$ and $OA = y$

Given that, $BQ = q$, $SA = p$ and $AB = SQ =$ Length of ladder

Also, $\angle BAO = \alpha$ and $\angle QSO = \beta$

Now, in ΔBAO,

$$\cos \alpha = \frac{OA}{AB} \Rightarrow \cos \alpha = \frac{y}{AB}$$

$$\Rightarrow \quad y = AB \cos \alpha = OA \quad \ldots(i)$$

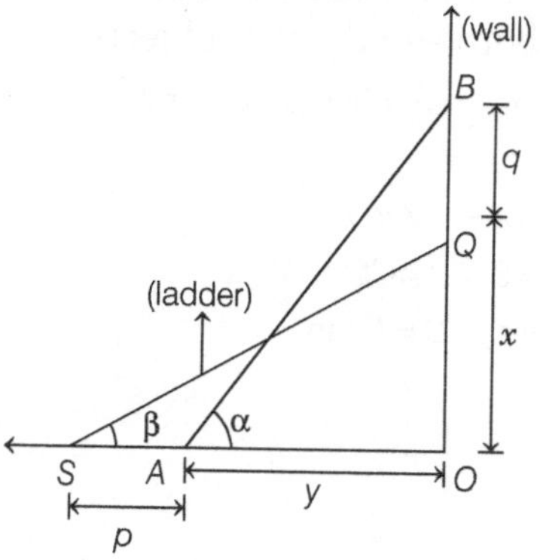

and $\sin\alpha = \dfrac{OB}{AB}$

$\Rightarrow \quad OB = BA\sin\alpha$ ...(ii)

Now, in ΔQSO

$$\cos\beta = \frac{OS}{SQ}$$

$\Rightarrow \quad OS = SQ\cos\beta = AB\cos\beta$ [$\because AB = SQ$]...(iii)

and $\sin\beta = \dfrac{OQ}{SQ}$

$\Rightarrow \quad OQ = SQ\sin\beta = AB\sin\beta$ [$\because AB = SQ$]...(iv)

Now, $SA = OS - AO$

$\Rightarrow \quad p = AB\cos\beta - AB\cos\alpha$ [from Eqs. (i) and (iii)]

$\Rightarrow \quad p = AB(\cos\beta - \cos\alpha)$ ...(v)

and $BQ = BO - QO$

$\Rightarrow \quad q = BA\sin\alpha - AB\sin\beta$ [from Eqs. (ii) and (iv)]

$\Rightarrow \quad q = AB(\sin\alpha - \sin\beta)$ ...(vi)

Eq. (v) divided by Eq. (vi), we get

$$\frac{p}{q} = \frac{AB(\cos\beta - \cos\alpha)}{AB(\sin\alpha - \sin\beta)}$$

$\Rightarrow \quad \dfrac{p}{q} = \dfrac{\cos\beta - \cos\alpha}{\sin\alpha - \sin\beta}$ **Hence proved.**

Q.16 The angle of elevation of the top of a vertical tower from a point on the ground is 60°. From another point 10 m vertically above the first, its angle of elevation is 45°. Find the height of the tower.

Ans. Let the height of the vertical tower be $OT = H$

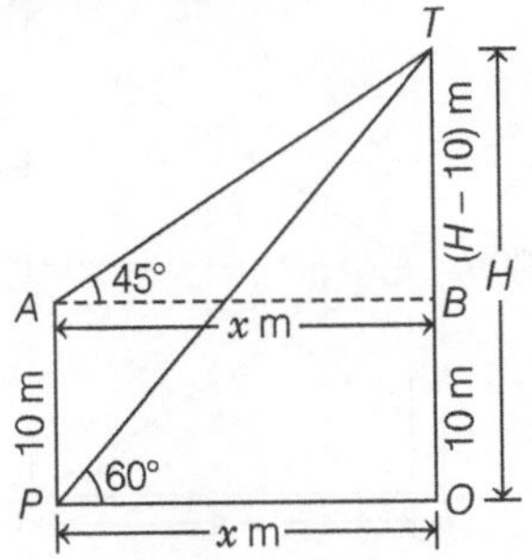

and $OP = AB = x$ m

Given that, $AP = 10$ m

and $\angle TPO = 60°, \angle TAB = 45°$

Now, in ΔTPO, $\tan 60° = \dfrac{OT}{OP} = \dfrac{H}{x}$

$\Rightarrow \quad \sqrt{3} = \dfrac{H}{x}$

$\Rightarrow \quad x = \dfrac{H}{\sqrt{3}}$ ...(i)

and in ΔTAB, $\tan 45° = \frac{TB}{AB} = \frac{H-10}{x}$

$\Rightarrow$ $1 = \frac{H-10}{x} \Rightarrow x = H - 10$

$\Rightarrow$ $\frac{H}{\sqrt{3}} = H - 10$ [from Eq. (i)]

$\Rightarrow$ $H - \frac{H}{\sqrt{3}} = 10 \Rightarrow H\left(1 - \frac{1}{\sqrt{3}}\right) = 10$

$\Rightarrow$ $H\left(\frac{\sqrt{3}-1}{\sqrt{3}}\right) = 10 \Rightarrow H = \frac{10\sqrt{3}}{\sqrt{3}-1}$

$\therefore$ $H = \frac{10\sqrt{3}}{\sqrt{3}-1} \cdot \frac{\sqrt{3}+1}{\sqrt{3}+1}$ [by rationalisation]

$= \frac{10\sqrt{3}(\sqrt{3}+1)}{3-1} = \frac{10\sqrt{3}(\sqrt{3}+1)}{2}$

$\Rightarrow$ $= 5\sqrt{3}(\sqrt{3}+1) = 5(\sqrt{3}+3)$ m.

Hence, the required height of the tower is $5(\sqrt{3}+3)$ m.

Q.17 A window of a house is h m above the ground. From the window, the angles of elevation and depression of the top and the bottom of another house situated on the opposite side of the lane are found to be α and β, respectively. Prove that the height of the other house is $h(1 + \tan\alpha \cot\beta)$ metres.

Ans. Let the height of the other house $= OQ = H$

and $OB = MW = x$ m

Given that, height of the first house $= WB = h = MO$

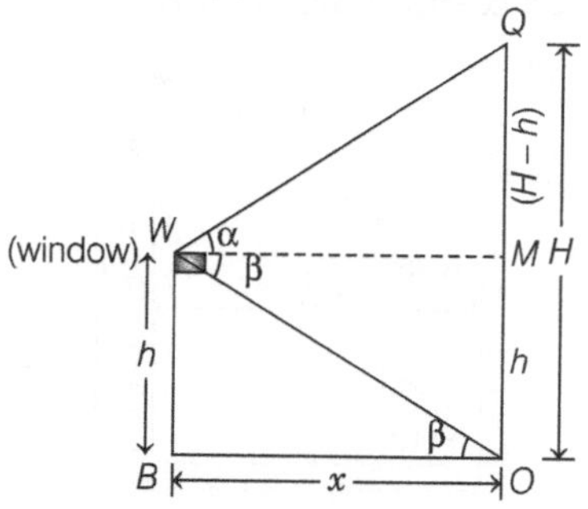

and $\angle QWM = \alpha$, $\angle OWM = \beta = \angle WOB$ [alternate angle]

Now, in ΔWOB, $\tan\beta = \frac{WB}{OB} = \frac{h}{x}$

$\Rightarrow$ $x = \frac{h}{\tan\beta}$ ...(i)

and in ΔQWM, $\tan\alpha = \dfrac{QM}{WM} = \dfrac{OQ - MO}{WM}$

$$\Rightarrow \quad \tan\alpha = \frac{H-h}{x}$$

$$\Rightarrow \quad x = \frac{H-h}{\tan\alpha} \quad \text{...(ii)}$$

From Eqs. (i) and (ii), we get

$$\frac{h}{\tan\beta} = \frac{H-h}{\tan\alpha}$$

$$\Rightarrow \quad h\tan\alpha = (H-h)\tan\beta$$

$$\Rightarrow \quad h\tan\alpha = H\tan\beta - h\tan\beta$$

$$\Rightarrow \quad H\tan\beta = h(\tan\alpha + \tan\beta)$$

$$\therefore \quad H = h\left(\frac{\tan\alpha + \tan\beta}{\tan\beta}\right)$$

$$= h\left(1 + \tan\alpha \cdot \frac{1}{\tan\beta}\right) = h(1 + \tan\alpha \cdot \cot\beta)$$

$$\left[\because \cot\theta = \frac{1}{\tan\theta}\right]$$

Hence, the required height of the other house is $h(1 + \tan\alpha \cdot \cot\beta)$ **Hence proved.**

Q.18 The lower window of a house is at a height of 2 m above the ground and its upper window is 4 m vertically above the lower window. At certain instant the angles of elevation of a balloon from these windows are observed to be 60° and 30°, respectively. Find the height of the balloon above the ground.

Ans. Let the height of the balloon from above the ground is H.

and $OP = w_2R = w_1Q = x$

Given that, height of lower window from the ground $= w_2P = 2\text{ m} = OR$

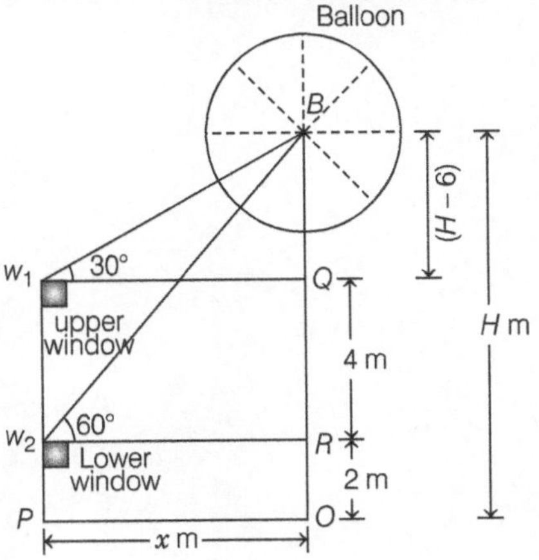

Height of upper window from the lower window = $w_1 w_2 = 4$ m = QR

$$\therefore \quad BQ = OB - (QR + RO)$$
$$= H - (4 + 2) = H - 6$$

and $\angle Bw_1 Q = 30°$

$\Rightarrow \angle Bw_2 R = 60°$

Now, in $\Delta Bw_2 R$,

$$\tan 60° = \frac{BR}{w_2 R} = \frac{BQ + QR}{x}$$

$$\Rightarrow \quad \sqrt{3} = \frac{(H-6)+4}{x}$$

$$\Rightarrow \quad x = \frac{H-2}{\sqrt{3}} \quad \text{...(i)}$$

and in $\Delta Bw_1 Q$,

$$\tan 30° = \frac{BQ}{w_1 Q} \Rightarrow \tan 30° = \frac{H-6}{x} = \frac{1}{\sqrt{3}}$$

$$\Rightarrow \quad x = \sqrt{3}(H-6) \quad \text{...(ii)}$$

From Eqs. (i) and (ii), we get

$$\sqrt{3}(H-6) = \frac{(H-2)}{\sqrt{3}}$$

$$3(H-6) = H-2 \Rightarrow 3H - 18 = H - 2$$

$$\Rightarrow \quad 2H = 16 \Rightarrow H = 8$$

So, the required height is 8 m.

Hence, the required height of the balloon from the ground is 8 m.

Chapter

09 Circles

Multiple Choice Questions (MCQs)

Choose the correct answer from the given four options in the following questions:

Q.1 If radii of two concentric circles are 4 cm and 5 cm, then length of each chord of one circle which is tangent to the other circle, is

(a) 3 cm (b) 6 cm (c) 9 cm (d) 1 cm

- **Concept Insight** In this question, we will use Pythagoras theorem.

Ans. ***(b)*** Let O be the centre of two concentric circles C_1 and C_2, whose radii are $r_1 = 4$ cm and $r_2 = 5$ cm. Now, we draw a chord AC of circle C_2, which touches the circle C_1 at B. Also, join OB, which is perpendicular to AC.

[Tangent at any point of circle is perpendicular to radius throughly the point of contact]

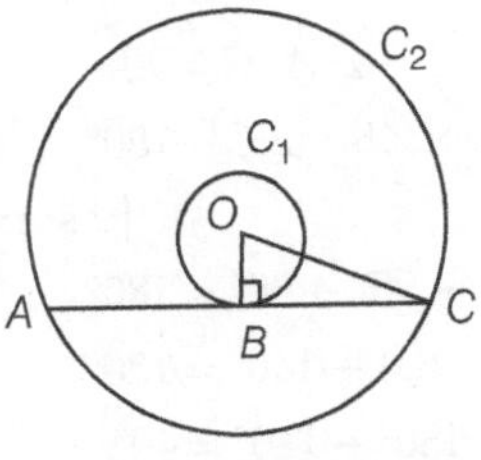

Now, in right angled ΔOBC, by using Pythagoras theorem,

$$OC^2 = BC^2 + BO^2$$

[$\because$ (hypotenuse)^2 = (base)^2 + (perpendicular)^2]

$\Rightarrow$ $$5^2 = BC^2 + 4^2$$

$\Rightarrow$ $$BC^2 = 25 - 16 = 9 \Rightarrow BC = 3 \text{ cm}$$

$\therefore$ Length of chord $AC = 2\ BC = 2 \times 3 = 6$ cm

Q.2 In figure, if $\angle AOB = 125°$, then $\angle COD$ is equal to

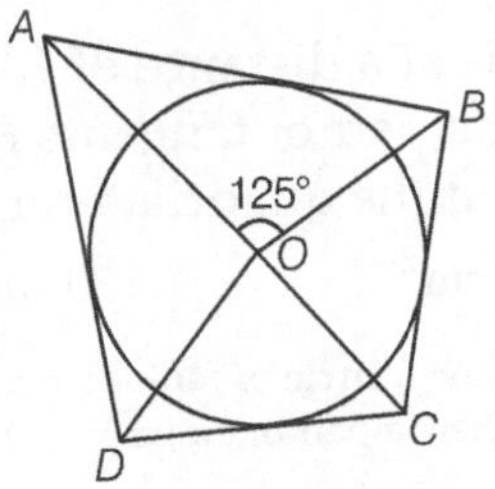

(a) 62.5° (b) 45° (c) 35° (d) 55°

Ans. *(d)* We know that, the opposite sides of a quadrilateral circumscribing a circle subtend supplementary angles at the centre of the circle.

i.e., $\angle AOB + \angle COD = 180°$

$\Rightarrow \angle COD = 180° - \angle AOB$

$= 180° - 125° = 55°$

Mistake Alert ! *Students may assume that AOC and DOB are intersecting lines, so the result will be incorrect.*

Q.3 In figure, AB is a chord of the circle and AOC is its diameter such that $\angle ACB = 50°$. If AT is the tangent to the circle at the point A, then $\angle BAT$ is equal to

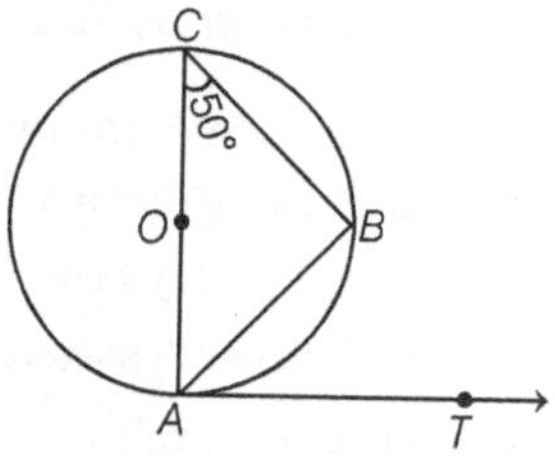

(a) 65° (b) 60° (c) 50° (d) 40°

Thinking process The diameter of a circle subtends an angle 90° at the circle.

Ans. *(c)* In figure, AOC is a diameter of the circle. We know that, diameter subtends an angle 90° at the circle.

So, $\angle ABC = 90°$

In ΔACB, $\angle A + \angle B + \angle C = 180°$

[$\because$ sum of all angles of a triangle is 180°]

$\Rightarrow \angle A + 90° + 50° = 180°$

$\Rightarrow \angle A + 140° = 180°$

$\Rightarrow \angle A = 180° - 140° = 40°$

$\angle A$ or $\angle OAB = 40°$

Now, AT is the tangent to the circle at point A. So, OA is perpendicular to AT.

$\therefore \angle OAT = 90°$

$\Rightarrow \angle OAB + \angle BAT = 90°$

On putting $\angle OAB = 40°$, we get

$\Rightarrow \angle BAT = 90° - 40° = 50°$

Hence, the value of $\angle BAT$ is 50°.

Q.4 From a point P which is at a distance of 13 cm from the centre O of a circle of radius 5 cm, the pair of tangents PQ and PR to the circle is drawn. Then, the area of the quadrilateral $PQOR$ is

(a) 60 cm^2 (b) 65 cm^2 (c) 30 cm^2 (d) 32.5 cm^2

Thinking Process Firstly, draw a circle of radius 5 cm having centre O. P is a point at a distance of 13 cm from O. Then, a pair of tangents PQ and PR are drawn.

Ans. *(a)* From the given information, we draw the following figure make proper right angle (90°).

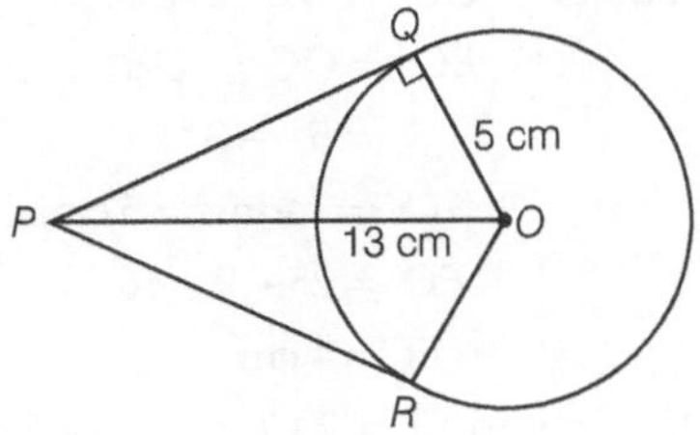

Thus, quadrilateral *PQOR* is formed.

$\because$ $OQ \perp QP$ [$\because$ *QP* is a tangent line]

In right angled ΔPQO, $OP^2 = OQ^2 + QP^2$

$\Rightarrow$ $13^2 = 5^2 + QP^2$

$\Rightarrow$ $QP^2 = 169 - 25 = 144$

$\Rightarrow$ $QP = 12$ cm

Now, Area of $\Delta OQP = \frac{1}{2} \times QP \times QO$

$= \frac{1}{2} \times 12 \times 5 = 30 \text{ cm}^2$

$\therefore$ Area of quadrilateral $QORP = 2\, \Delta OQP$

$= 2 \times 30 = 60 \text{ cm}^2$

Q.5 At one end *A* of a diameter *AB* of a circle of radius 5 cm, tangent *XAY* is drawn to the circle. The length of the chord *CD* parallel to *XY* and at a distance 8 cm from *A*, is

(a) 4 cm (b) 5 cm

(c) 6 cm (d) 8 cm

Ans. *(d)* First, draw a circle of radius 5 cm having centre *O*. A tangent *XY* is drawn at point *A*.

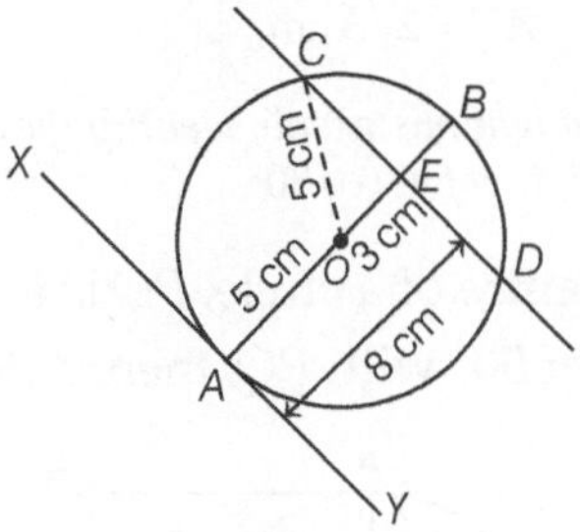

A chord *CD* is drawn which is parallel to *XY* and at a distance of 8 cm from *A*.

Now, $\angle OAY = 90°$

[Tangent at any point of a circle is perpendicular to the radius through the point of contact]

$\Delta OAY + \Delta OED = 180°$ [$\because$ sum of co-interior is 180°]

$\Rightarrow$ $\Delta OED = 180° - 90° = 90°$

Also, $AE = 8$ cm.

Join OC.

Now, in right angled ΔOEC, $OC^2 = OE^2 + EC^2$

$\Rightarrow$ $EC^2 = OC^2 - OE^2$ [by Pythagoras theorem]

$= 5^2 - 3^2$

[$\because$ OC = radius = 5 cm, $OE = AE - AO = 8 - 5 = 3$ cm]

$\Rightarrow$ $EC^2 = 25 - 9 = 16$

$\Rightarrow$ $EC = 4$ cm

Hence, length of chord $CD = 2\,CE = 2 \times 4 = 8$ cm

[$\because$ perpendicular from centre to the chord bisects the chord]

Q.6 In figure, AT is a tangent to the circle with centre O such that $OT = 4$ cm and $\angle OTA = 30°$. Then, AT is equal to

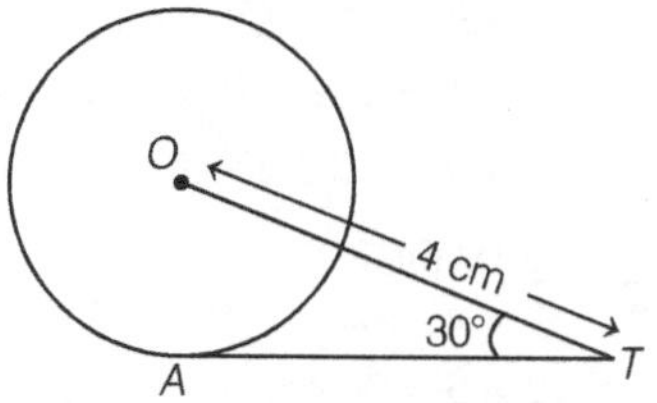

(a) 4 cm (b) 2 cm

(c) $2\sqrt{3}$ cm (d) $4\sqrt{3}$ cm

Ans. *(c)* Join OA.

We know that, the tangent at any point of a circle is perpendicular to the radius through the point of contact.

$\therefore$ $\angle OAT = 90°$

In ΔOAT, $\cos 30° = \dfrac{AT}{OT}$

$\Rightarrow$ $\dfrac{\sqrt{3}}{2} = \dfrac{AT}{4}$

$\Rightarrow$ $AT = 2\sqrt{3}$ cm

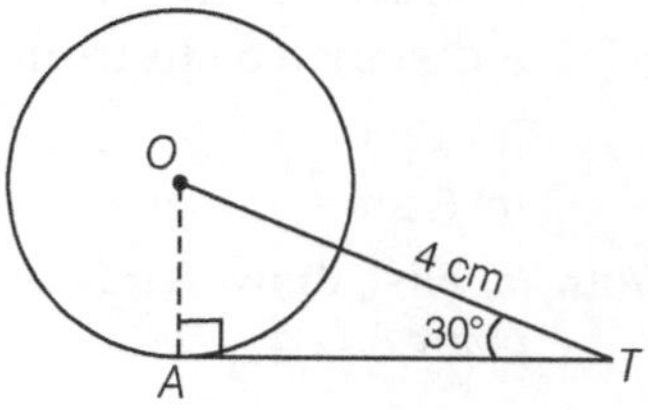

Mistake Alert! *Students might mistakenly identify the adjacent side as the opposite side, leading to incorrect calculation for* $\cos 30°$.

Q.7 In figure, if O is the centre of a circle, PQ is a chord and the tangent PR at P makes an angle of 50° with PQ, then $\angle POQ$ is equal to

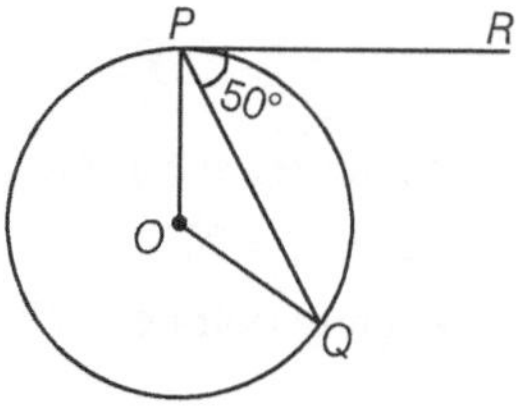

(a) 100° (b) 80°

(c) 90° (d) 75°

Ans. *(a)* Given, $\angle QPR = 50°$

We know that, the tangent at any point of a circle is perpendicular to the radius through the point of contact.

$\therefore \quad \angle OPR = 90°$

$\Rightarrow \quad \angle OPQ + \angle QPR = 90°$

$\Rightarrow \quad \angle OPQ = 90° - 50° = 40° \quad [\because \angle QPR = 50°]$

Now, $\quad OP = OQ =$ Radius of circle

$\therefore \quad \angle OQP = \angle OPQ = 40°$

[$\because$ angles opposite to equal sides are equal]

In ΔOPQ, $\quad \angle POQ + \angle OPQ + \angle OQP = 180°$

[$\because$ sum of angles of a triangle = 180°]

$\Rightarrow \quad \angle POQ = 180° - (40° + 40°) \quad [\because \angle OPQ = 40° = \angle OQP]$

$= 180° - 80° = 100°$

Q.8 In figure, if PA and PB are tangents to the circle with centre O such that $\angle APB = 50°$, then $\angle OAB$ is equal to

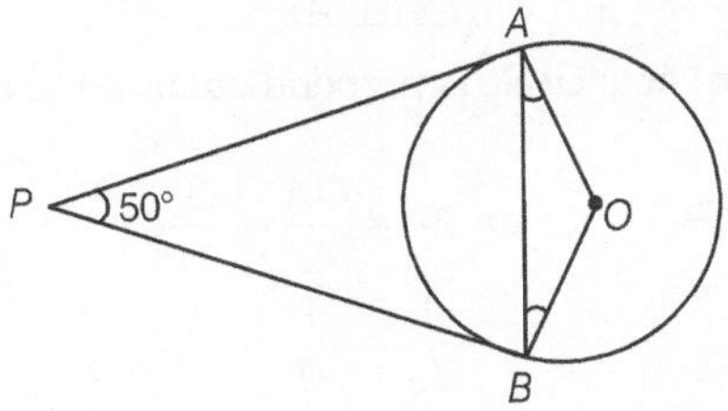

(a) 25° (b) 30° (c) 40° (d) 50°

Ans. *(a)* Given, PA and PB are tangent lines.

$\therefore \quad PA = PB$

[since, the length of tangents drawn from an external point to a circle is equal]

$\Rightarrow \quad \angle PBA = \angle PAB = \theta$ [say]

In ΔPAB,

$\angle APB + \angle PAB + \angle PBA = 180°$

[$\because$ sum of angles of a triangle = 180°]

$\Rightarrow \quad 50° + \theta + \theta = 180°$

$\Rightarrow \quad 2\theta = 180° - 50° = 130°$

$\Rightarrow \quad \theta = 65°$

Also, $\quad OA \perp PA$

[since, tangent at any point of a circle is perpendicular to the radius through the point of contact]

$\therefore \quad \angle PAO = 90°$

$\Rightarrow \quad \angle PAB + \angle OAB = 90°$

$\Rightarrow \quad 65° + \angle OAB = 90°$

$\Rightarrow \quad \angle OAB = 90° - 65° = 25°$

Q.9 If two tangents inclined at an angle 60° are drawn to a circle of radius 3 cm, then the length of each tangent is

(a) $\frac{3}{2}\sqrt{3}$ cm (b) 6 cm (c) 3 cm (d) $3\sqrt{3}$ cm

Ans. *(d)* Let P be an external point and a pair of tangents is drawn from point P and angle between these two tangents is 60°.

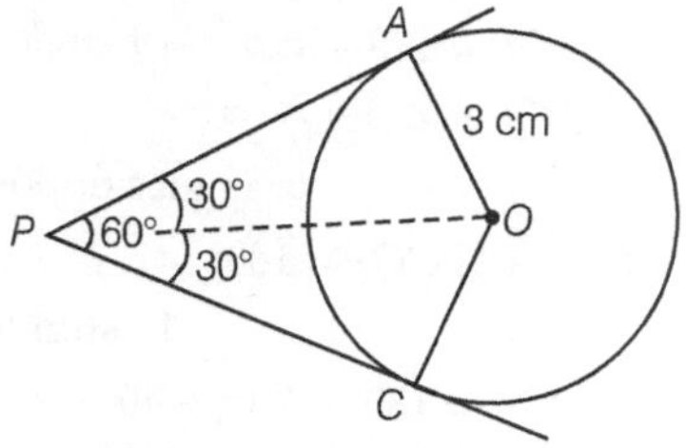

Join OA and OP.

Also, OP is a bisector line of $\angle APC$.

$\therefore$ $\angle APO = \angle CPO = 30°$

Also, $OA \perp AP$

[Tangent at any point of a circle is perpendicular to the radius through the point of contact.]

In right angled ΔOAP, $\tan 30° = \frac{OA}{AP} = \frac{3}{AP}$

$\Rightarrow$ $\frac{1}{\sqrt{3}} = \frac{3}{AP}$

$\Rightarrow$ $AP = 3\sqrt{3}$ cm

Hence, the length of each tangent is $3\sqrt{3}$ cm.

Q.10 In figure, if PQR is the tangent to a circle at Q whose centre is O, AB is a chord parallel to PR and $\angle BQR = 70°$, then $\angle AQB$ is equal to

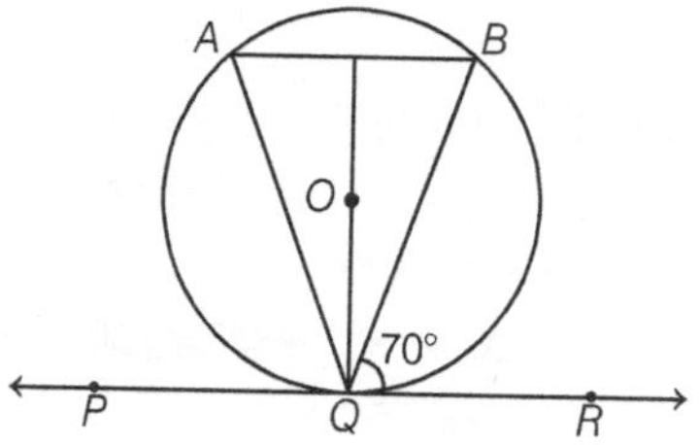

(a) 20° (b) 40° (c) 35° (d) 45°

Ans. *(b)* Given, $AB \parallel PR$

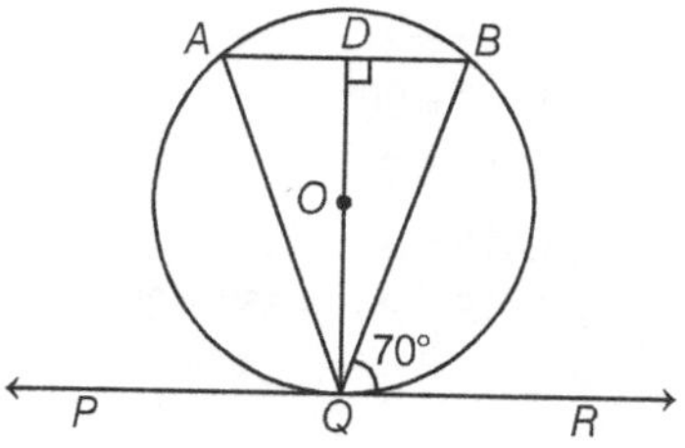

$\therefore \quad \angle ABQ = \angle BQR = 70°$ [alternate angles]

Also, QD is perpendicular to AB and QD bisects AB.

In ΔQDA and ΔQDB, $\angle QDA = \angle QDB$ [each 90°]

$AD = BD$

$QD = QD$ [common side]

$\therefore \quad \Delta ADQ \cong \Delta BDQ$ [by SAS congruency]

Then, $\angle QAD = \angle QBD$ [CPCT] ...(i)

Also $\angle ABQ = \angle BQR$ [alternate interior angle]

$\therefore \quad \angle ABQ = 70°$ [$\because \angle BQR = 70°$]

Hence, $\angle QAB = 70°$ [from Eq. (i)]

Now, in ΔABQ, $\angle QAB + \angle ABQ + \angle AQB = 180°$

$\Rightarrow \quad \angle AQB = 180° - (70° + 70°) = 40°$

Short Answer Questions with Reasoning

Write 'true' or 'false' and justify your answer in each of the following.

Q.1 If a chord AB subtends an angle of 60° at the centre of a circle, then angle between the tangents at A and B is also 60°.

Ans. *False*

Since, a chord AB subtends an angle of 60° at the centre of a circle.

i.e., $\angle AOB = 60°$

As $OA = OB =$ Radius of the circle

$\therefore \quad \angle OAB = \angle OBA = 60°$

The tangent at points A and B is drawn, which intersect at C.

We know, $OA \perp AC$ and $OB \perp BC$.

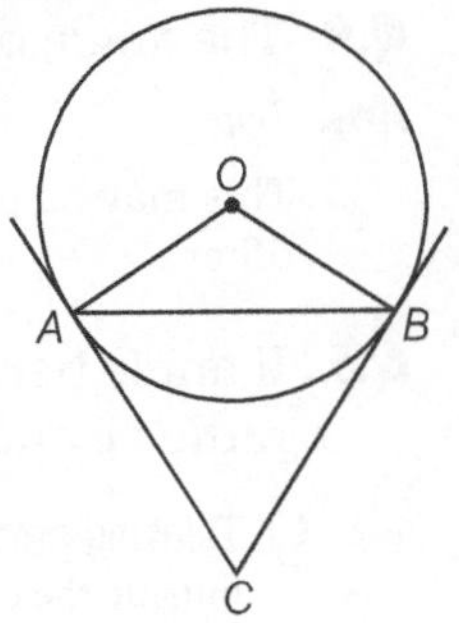

$\therefore \quad \angle OAC = 90°, \angle OBC = 90°$

$\Rightarrow \quad \angle OAB + \angle BAC = 90°$

and $\angle OBA + \angle ABC = 90°$

$\Rightarrow \quad \angle BAC = 90° - 60° = 30°$

and $\angle ABC = 90° - 60° = 30°$

In ΔABC, $\angle BAC + \angle CBA + \angle ACB = 180°$

[since, sum of all interior angles of a triangle is 180°.]

$\Rightarrow \quad \angle ACB = 180° - (30° + 30°) = 120°$

Alternate method

Since, a chord AB subtends an angle of 60° at the centre of the circle *i.e,*. $\angle AOB = 60°$

We know that, tangent at any point of a circle is perpendicular to the radius through the point of contact.

$\therefore \quad \angle OAC = \angle OBC = 90°$

In quadrilateral $OACB$,

$\angle AOB + \angle OAC + \angle ACB + \angle OBC = 360°$ [by angle sum property of quadrilateral]

$\Rightarrow \quad 60° + 90° + \angle ACB + 90° = 360°$

$\Rightarrow \quad \angle ACB + 240° = 360°$

$\Rightarrow \quad \angle ACB = 360° - 240° = 120°$

Q.2 The length of tangent from an external point on a circle is always greater than the radius of the circle.

Ans. *False*

Because the length of tangent from an external point on a circle may or may not be greater than the radius of the circle.

Mistake Alert! *Students might forget that the tangent is always perpendicular to the radius at the point of contact.*

Q.3 The length of tangent from an external point P on a circle with centre O is always less than OP.

Ans. *True*

PT is a tangent drawn from external point P.
Join OT.

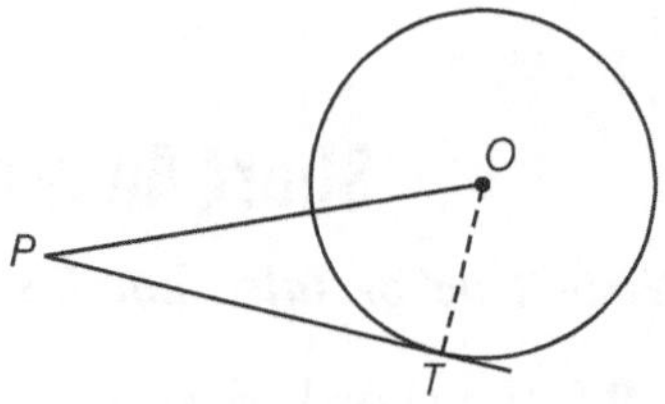

$\because \quad OT \perp PT$

So, OPT is a right angled triangle formed.

In right angled triangle, hypotenuse is always greater than any of the two sides of the triangle.

$\therefore \quad OP > PT$

or $\quad PT < OP$

Q.4 The angle between two tangents to a circle may be 0°.

Ans. *True*

This may be possible only when both tangent lines coincide or are parallel to each other.

Q.5 If angle between two tangents drawn from a point P to a circle of radius a and centre O is 90°, then $OP = a\sqrt{2}$.

Thinking process Firstly, draw a circle of radius 'a' with centre O and take P is any point outside the circle. Then, a pair of tangent PT and PR are drawn.

Ans. *True*

From point P, two tangents are drawn.

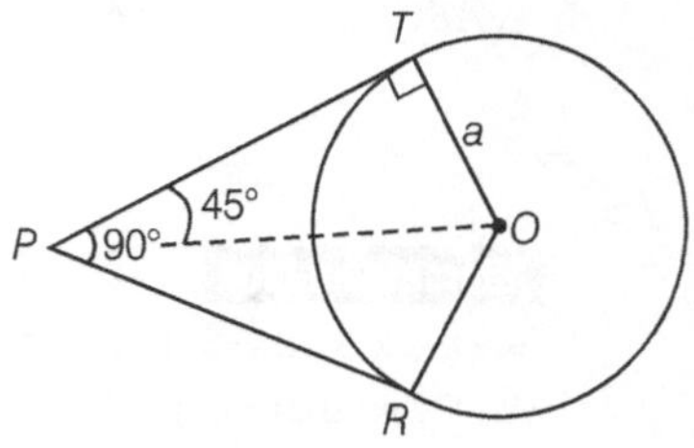

Given, $\quad OT = a$

Also, line OP bisects the $\angle RPT$.

$\therefore \quad \angle TPO = \angle RPO = 45°$

Also, $\quad OT \perp PT$

$\therefore \quad \angle PTO = 90°$

In right angled ΔOTP, $\sin 45° = \dfrac{OT}{OP}$

$\Rightarrow \quad \dfrac{1}{\sqrt{2}} = \dfrac{a}{OP}$

$\Rightarrow \quad OP = a\sqrt{2}$

Q.6 If angle between two tangents drawn from a point P to a circle of radius a and centre O is $60°$, then $OP = a\sqrt{3}$.

Ans. *False*

From point P, two tangents are drawn.

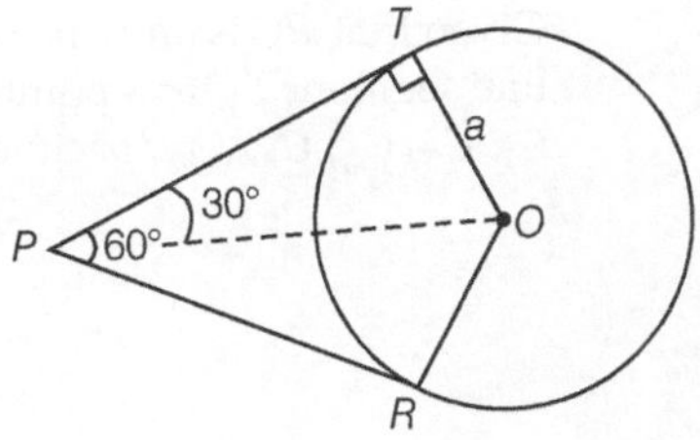

Given, $OT = a$

Also, line OP bisects the $\angle RPT$.

$\therefore$ $\angle TPO = \angle RPO = 30°$

Also, $OT \perp PT$

In right angled ΔOTP,

$$\sin 30° = \frac{OT}{OP}$$

$$\Rightarrow \quad \frac{1}{2} = \frac{a}{OP}$$

$$\Rightarrow \quad OP = 2a$$

Q.7 The tangent to the circumcircle of an isosceles ΔABC at A, in which $AB = AC$, is parallel to BC.

Ans. *True*

Let EAF be tangent to the circumcircle of ΔABC.

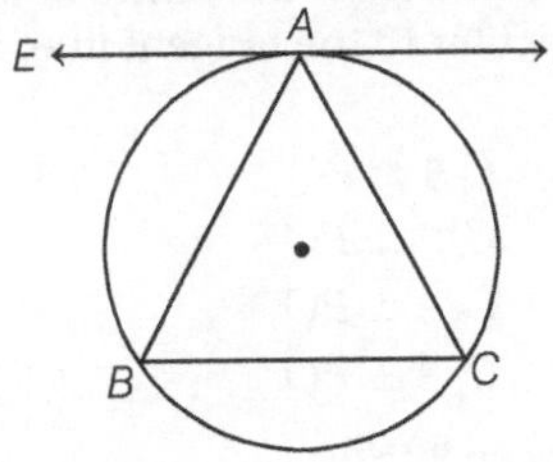

To prove $EAF \parallel BC$

Here, $AB = AC$

$\Rightarrow$ $\angle ABC = \angle ACB$ ...(i)

$\therefore$ Also, $\angle EAB = \angle BCA$ ...(ii)

[angle between tangent and chord is equal to angle made by chord in the alternate segment]

From Eqs. (i) and (ii), we get

$$\angle EAB = \angle ABC$$

$\Rightarrow$ $EAF \parallel BC$ [$\because$ alternate angles are equal]

Q.8 If a number of circles touch a given line segment PQ at a point A, then their centres lie on the perpendicular bisector of PQ.

Ans. *False*

Given that PQ is any line segment and $S_1, S_2, S_3, S_4, \ldots$ are circles which touch a line segment PQ at a point A. Let the centres of the circles $S_1, S_2, S_3, S_4, \ldots$ be $C_1, C_2, C_3, C_4, \ldots$ respectively.

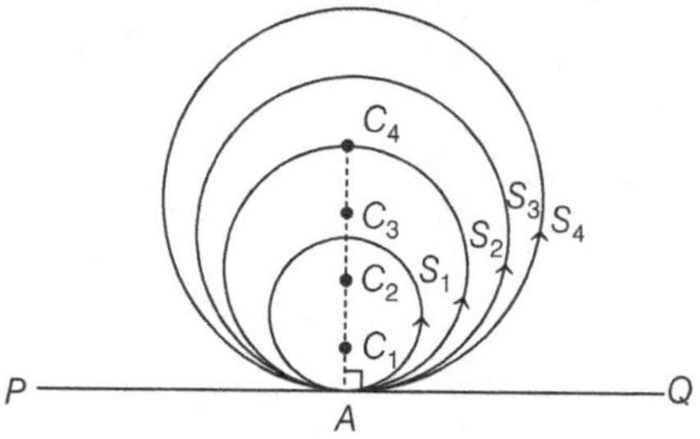

To prove Centres of these circles lie on the perpendicular bisector of PQ.

Now, joining each centre of the circles to the point A on the line segment PQ by a line segment *i.e.*, $C_1A, C_2A, C_3A, C_4A, \ldots$ so on.

We know that, if we draw a line from the centre of a circle to its tangent line, then the line is always perpendicular to the tangent line. But it not bisect the line segment PQ.

So,
$$C_1A \perp PQ \quad \text{[for } S_1]$$
$$C_2A \perp PQ \quad \text{[for } S_2]$$
$$C_3A \perp PQ \quad \text{[for } S_3]$$
$$C_4A \perp PQ \quad \text{[for } S_4]$$
... so on.

Since, each circle is passing through a point A. Therefore, all the line segments $C_1A, C_2A, C_3A, C_4A, \ldots$, so on are coincident.

So, centre of each circle lies on the perpendicular line of PQ but they do not lie on the perpendicular bisector of PQ.

Hence, a number of circles touch a given line segment PQ at a point A, then their centres lie on the perpendicular of PQ but not on the perpendicular bisector of PQ.

Q.9 If a number of circles pass through the end points P and Q of a line segment PQ, then their centres lie on the perpendicular bisector of PQ.

Ans. *True*

Let draw three circles with centres C_1, C_2 and C_3 passing through the end points P and Q of a line segment PQ. We know, that perpendicular bisectors of a chord of a circle always passes through the centre of circle.

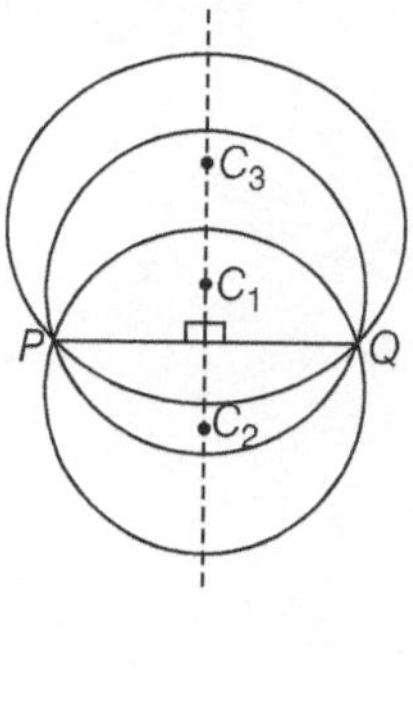

Thus, perpendicular bisector of PQ passes through C_1, C_2 and C_3. Similarly, all the circle passing through PQ will have their centre on perpendiculars bisectors of PQ.

Q.10 AB is a diameter of a circle and AC is its chord such that $\angle BAC = 30°$. If the tangent at C intersects AB extended at D, then $BC = BD$.

Ans. *True*

To Prove, $BC = BD$

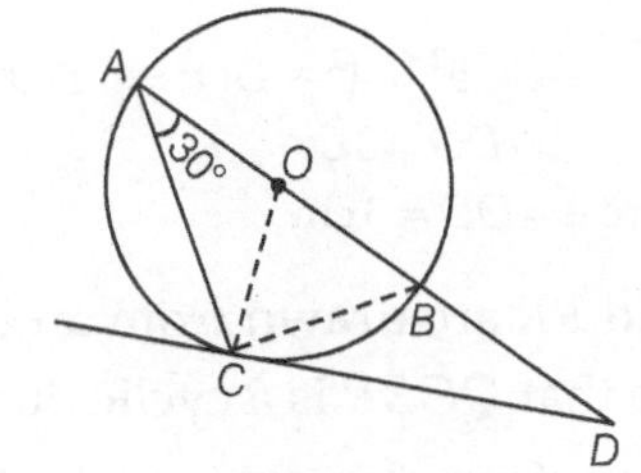

Join BC and OC.

Given, $\angle BAC = 30°$

$\Rightarrow \angle BCD = 30°$

[angle between tangent and chord is equal to angle made by chord in the alternate segment]

$\therefore \angle ACD = \angle ACO + \angle OCD = 30° + 90° = 120°$

[$\because OC \perp CD$ and $OA = OC$ = radius $\Rightarrow \angle OAC = \angle OCA = 30°$]

In ΔACD, $\angle CAD + \angle ACD + \angle ADC = 180°$

[since, sum of all interior angles of a triangle is 180°]

$\Rightarrow 30° + 120° + \angle ADC = 180°$

$\Rightarrow \angle ADC = 180° - (30° + 120°) = 30°$

Now, in ΔBCD,

$\angle BCD = \angle BDC = 30°$

$\Rightarrow BC = BD$

[since, sides opposite to equal angles are equal]

Short Answer Questions

Q.1 Out of the two concentric circles, the radius of the outer circle is 5 cm and the chord AC of length 8 cm is a tangent to the inner circle. Find the radius of the inner circle.

- **Concept Insight** In this question, we will use Pythagoras theorem to find the radius of the inner circle.

Ans. Let C_1 and C_2 be the two circles having same centre O. AC is a chord which touches the C_1 at point D.

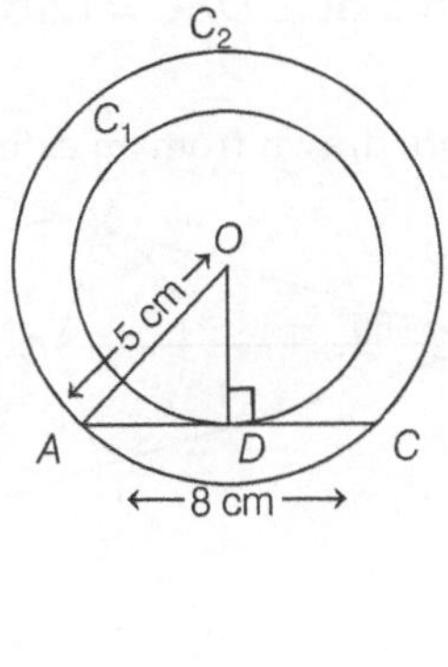

Join OD.

Also, $OD \perp AC$

$\therefore$ $AD = DC = 4$ cm [perpendicular line OD bisects the chord AC]

In right angled ΔAOD, $OA^2 = AD^2 + DO^2$

[by Pythagoras theorem]

$\Rightarrow$ $5^2 = 4^2 + DO^2 \Rightarrow DO^2 = 5^2 - 4^2 = 25 - 16 = 9$

$\Rightarrow$ $DO = 3$ cm

$\therefore$ Radius of the inner circle = $OD = 3$ cm

Q.2 Two tangents PQ and PR are drawn from an external point to a circle with centre O. Prove that $QORP$ is a cyclic quadrilateral.

- **Concept Insight** If the sum of opposite angles in quadrilateral is 180°, then the quadrilateral is cyclic.

Ans. Given, Two tangents PQ and PR are drawn from an external point P to a circle with centre O.

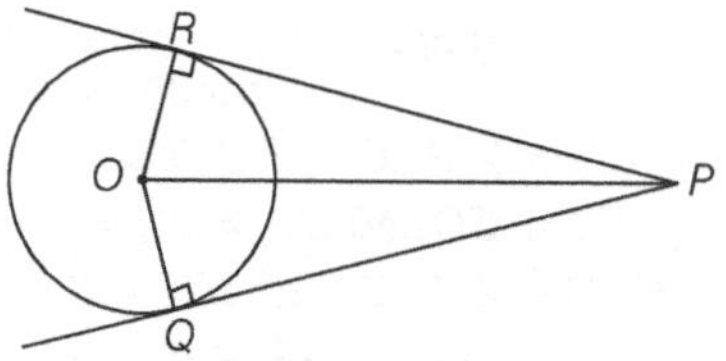

To prove $QORP$ is a cyclic quadrilateral.

proof Since, PR and PQ are tangents.

So, $OR \perp PR$ and $OQ \perp PQ$

[since, if we drawn a line from centre of a circle to its tangent line, then the line always perpendicular to the tangent line]

$\therefore$ $\angle ORP = \angle OQP = 90°$

Hence, $\angle ORP + \angle OQP = 180°$ ...(i)

Now, in quadrilateral $PROQ$,

$\angle ORP + \angle OQR + \angle ROQ + \angle RPQ = 360°$

[by angle sum property of a quadrilateral]

$\Rightarrow$ $180° + \angle ROQ + \angle RPQ = 360°$

$\Rightarrow$ $\angle ROQ + \angle RPQ = 360° - 180° = 180°$

So, $QORP$ is cyclic quadrilateral.

[If sum of opposite angles in quadrilateral is 180°, then the quadrilateral is cyclic]

Hence proved.

Q.3 If from an external point B of a circle with centre O, two tangents BC and BD are drawn such that $\angle DBC = 120°$, prove that $BC + BD = BO$ i.e., $BO = 2BC$.

Ans. Two tangents BD and BC are drawn from an external point B.

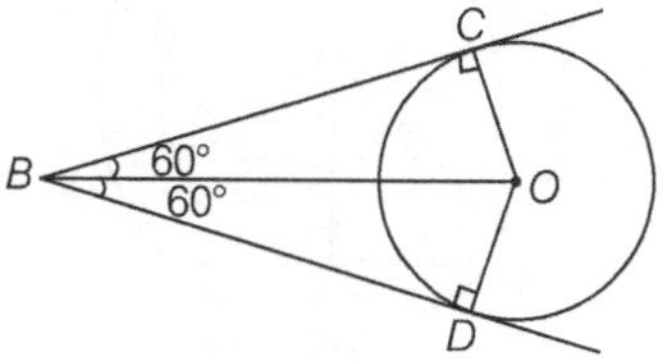

To prove

$$BO = 2BC$$

Given, $\angle DBC = 120°$

Join OC, OD and BO.

Since, BC and BD are tangents.

$\therefore$ $OC \perp BC$ and $OD \perp BD$

We know, OB is a angle bisector of $\angle DBC$.

$\therefore$ $\angle OBC = \angle DBO = 60°$

In right angled ΔOBC, $\cos 60° = \dfrac{BC}{OB}$

$\Rightarrow$ $\dfrac{1}{2} = \dfrac{BC}{OB}$

$\Rightarrow$ $OB = 2BC$ ...(i)

Also, $BC = BD$ ...(ii)

[tangent drawn from external point to circle are equal]

$\therefore$ $OB = BC + BC$ [from Eq. (i)]

$\Rightarrow$ $OB = BC + BD$ [from Eq. (ii)]

Hence proved.

Q.4 Prove that the centre of a circle touching two intersecting lines lies on the angle bisector of the lines.

Ans. **Given** Two tangents PQ and PR are drawn from an external point P to a circle with centre O.

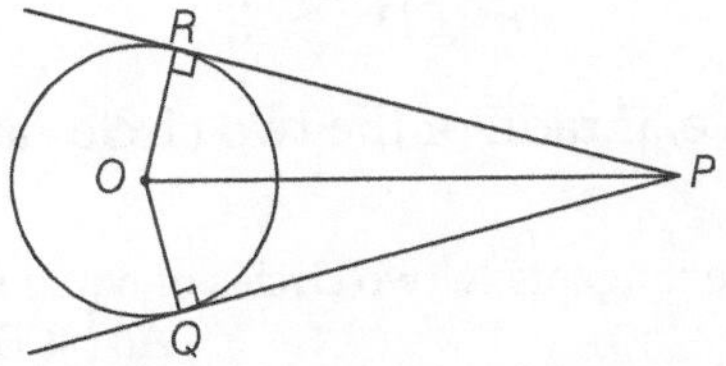

To prove Centre of a circle touching two intersecting lines lies on the angle bisector of the lines.

Construction Join OR, and OQ.

In ΔPOR and ΔPOQ

$$\angle PRO = \angle PQO = 90°$$

[tangent at any point of a circle is perpendicular to the radius through the point of contact]

$OR = OQ$ [radii of same circle]

Since, OP is common.

$\therefore$ $\Delta PRO \cong \Delta PQO$ [by RHS congruency]

Hence, $\angle RPO = \angle QPO$ [by CPCT]

Thus, O lies on angle bisecter of PR and PQ. **Hence proved.**

Q.5 In figure, AB and CD are common tangents to two circles of unequal radii. Prove that $AB = CD$

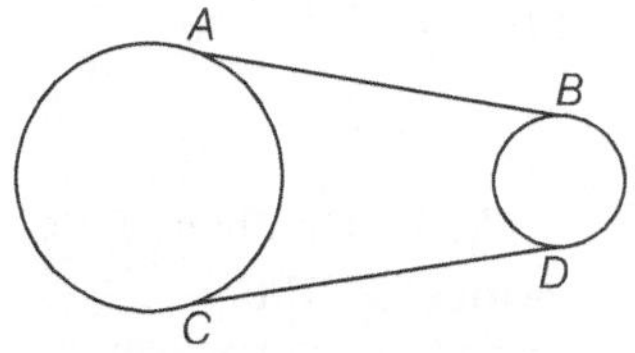

Ans. Given AB and CD are common tangent to two circles of unequal radius

To prove $AB = CD$

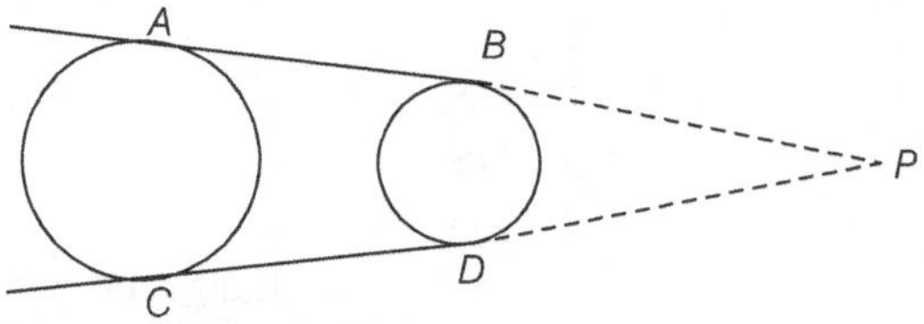

Construction Produce AB and CD, to intersect at P.

Proof $PA = PC$ ...(i)

[the length of tangents drawn from an external point to a circle are equal]

Also, $PB = PD$ ...(ii)

[the lengths of tangents drawn from an external point to a circle are equal]

From Eq. (i), we get

$PA - PB = PC - PB$ [subtracting PB on both sides]

$\Rightarrow$ $PA - PB = PC - PD$ [from Eq. (ii)]

$AB = CD$ **Hence proved.**

Q.6 In question 5 above, if radii of the two circles are equal prove that $AB = CD$.

Ans. Given AB and CD are tangents to two circles of equal radii.

To prove $AB = CD$

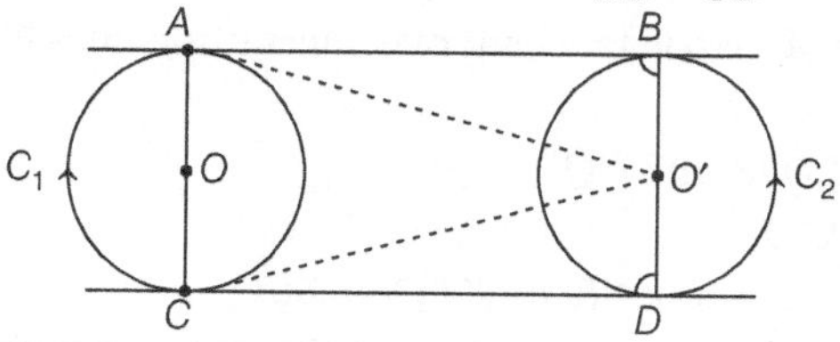

Construction Join OA, OC, $O'B$ and $O'D$

Proof Now, $\angle OAB = \angle OCD = 90°$

[tangent at any point of a circle is perpendicular to radius through the point of contact]

Thus, AC is a straight line.

Also, $\angle OAB + \angle OCD = 90° + 90° = 180°$

$\therefore$ $AB \parallel CD$

Similarly, BD is a straight line

and $\angle O'BA = \angle O'DC = 90°$

Also, $AC = BD$

[radii of two circles are equal, so its diameter are also equal]

In quadrilateral $ABCD$, $\angle A = \angle B = \angle C = \angle D = 90°$
and $AC = BD$
$\therefore$ $ABCD$ is a rectangle,
Hence, $AB = CD$ [opposite sides of rectangle are equal]

Q.7 In figure, common tangents AB and CD to circles intersect at E. Prove that $AB = CD$.

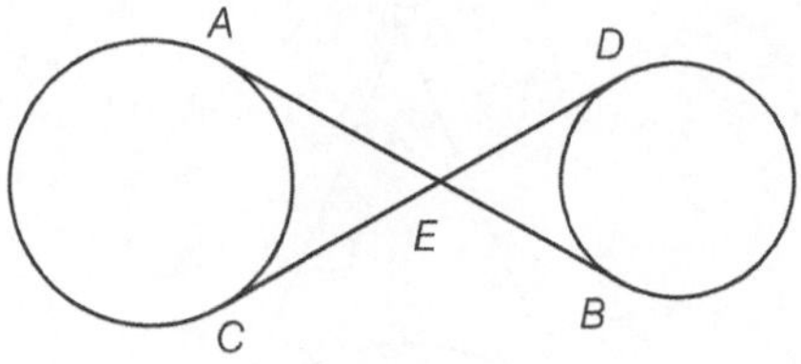

Ans. **Given** Common tangents AB and CD to two circles intersecting at E.
To prove $AB = CD$

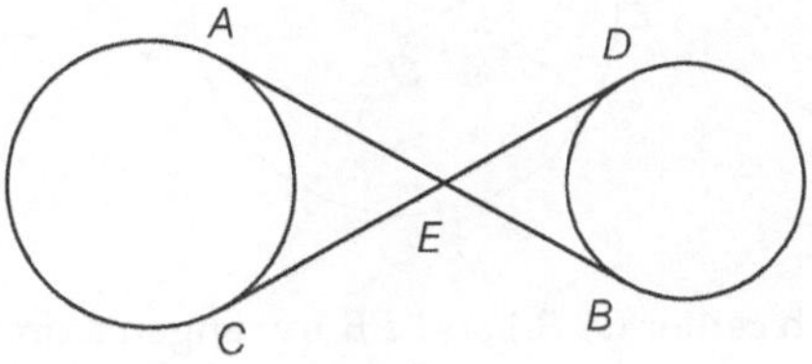

Proof $EA = EC$ ...(i)
[the lengths of tangents drawn from an external point to a circle are equal]
Similarly, $EB = ED$ ...(ii)
On adding Eqs. (i) and (ii), we get
$$EA + EB = EC + ED$$
$\Rightarrow$ $AB = CD$ **Hence proved.**

Q.8 A chord PQ of a circle is parallel to the tangent drawn at a point R of the circle. Prove that R bisects the arc PRQ.

Ans. **Given** Chord PQ is parallel to tangent at R.
To prove R bisects the arc PRQ

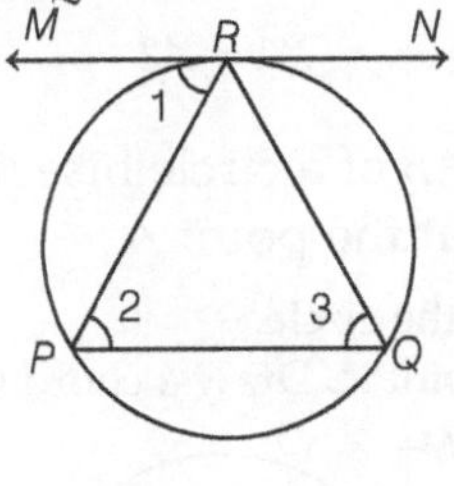

Proof $\angle 1 = \angle 2$ [alternate interior angles]
$\angle 1 = \angle 3$
[angle between tangent and chord is equal to angle made by chord in alternate segment]
$\therefore$ $\angle 2 = \angle 3$

$\Rightarrow$ $PR = QR$ [sides opposite to equal angles are equal]

$\Rightarrow$ arc PR = arc QR

So, R bisects the arc PRQ.

Q.9 Prove that the tangents drawn at the ends of a chord of a circle make equal angles with the chord.

Ans.

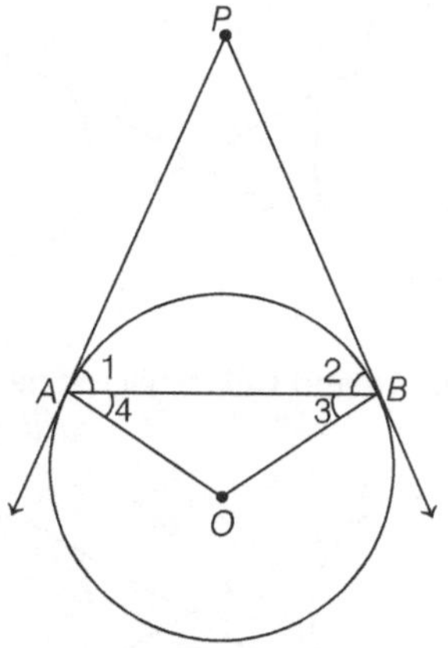

Given A circle with center O, PA and PB are tangents drawn at ends A and B on chord AB.

To prove $\angle PAB = \angle PBA$ or $\angle 1 = \angle 2$

In ΔAOB,

we have $OA = OB$ (radius)

$\angle OAB = \angle OBA$ ..(i)

(angles opposite to equal sides are equal)

$\angle OAP = \angle OBP = 90°$ ($\because$ radius $\perp$ tangent)

$\Rightarrow$ $\angle OAB + \angle PAB = \angle OBA + \angle PBA$

$\Rightarrow$ $\angle OAB + \angle PAB = \angle OAB + \angle PBA$ [from Eq. (i)]

$\Rightarrow$ $\angle PAB = \angle PBA$

$\Rightarrow$ $\angle 1 = \angle 2$ **Hence proved.**

Q.10 Prove that a diameter AB of a circle bisects all those chords which are parallel to the tangent at the point A.

Ans. Given, AB is a diameter of the circle.

A tangent is drawn from point A. Draw a chord CD parallel to the tangent MAN.

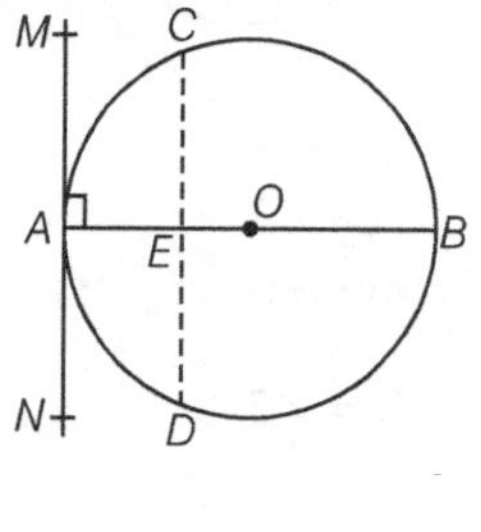

So, CD is a chord of the circle and OA is a radius of the circle.

$\therefore \quad \angle MAO = 90°$

[tangent at any point of a circle is perpendicular to the radius through the point of contact]

$\angle CEO = \angle MAO$ [corresponding angles]

$\therefore \quad \angle CEO = 90°$

Thus, OE bisects CD, [perpendicular drawn from centre of circle to chord bisects the chord]

Similarly, the diameter AB bisects all chords which are parallel to the tangent at the point A.

Long Answer Questions

Q.1 If a hexagon $ABCDEF$ circumscribe a circle, prove that

$$AB + CD + EF = BC + DE + FA.$$

Ans. Given A hexagon $ABCDEF$ circumscribe a circle.

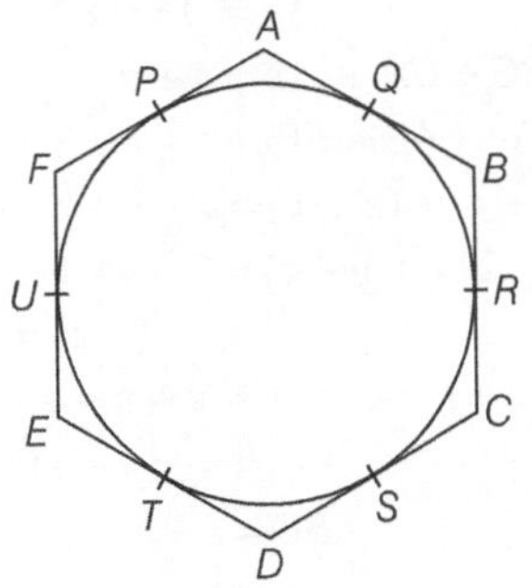

To prove $AB + CD + EF = BC + DE + FA$

Proof $\because$
$$AQ = AP$$
$$QB = BR$$
$$CS = CR$$
$$DS = DT$$
$$EU = ET$$
$$UF = FP$$

[tangents drawn from an external point to a circle are equal]

$\therefore \quad AB + CD + EF = (AQ + QB) + (CS + SD) + (EU + UF)$

$= AP + BR + CR + DT + ET + FP$

$= (AP + FP) + (BR + CR) + (DT + ET)$

$\Rightarrow AB + CD + EF = AF + BC + DE$ **Hence proved.**

Q.2 Let s denotes the semi-perimeter of a ΔABC in which $BC = a$, $CA = b$ and $AB = c$. If a circle touches the sides BC, CA, AB at D, E, F, respectively, prove that $BD = s - b$.

Ans. A circle is inscribed in the ΔABC, which touches the BC, CA and AB.

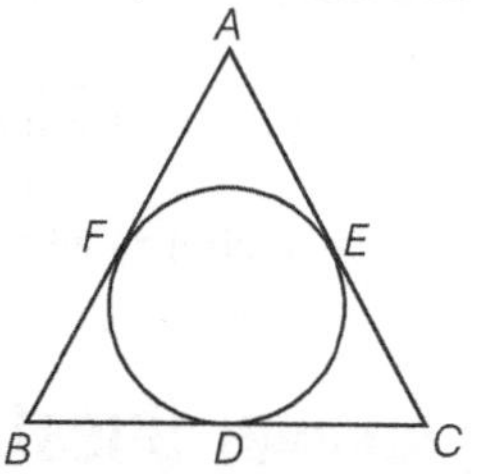

Given, $BC = a$, $CA = b$ and $AB = c$

By using the property, tangents are drawn from an external point to the circle are equal in length.

$\therefore$ $BD = BF = x$ [say]

$DC = CE = y$ [say]

and $AE = AF = z$ [say]

Now, $BC + CA + AB = a + b + c$

$\Rightarrow (BD + DC) + (CE + EA) + (AF + FB) = a + b + c$

$\Rightarrow$ $(x + y) + (y + z) + (z + x) = a + b + c$

$\Rightarrow$ $2(x + y + z) = 2s$

[$\because 2s = a + b + c =$ perimeter of ΔABC]

$\Rightarrow$ $s = x + y + z$

$\Rightarrow$ $x = s - (y + z)$

$\Rightarrow$ $BD = s - b$ [$\because b = AE + EC = z + y$]

Hence proved.

Q.3 From an external point P, two tangents, PA and PB are drawn to a circle with centre O. At one point E on the circle tangent is drawn which intersects PA and PB at C and D, respectively. If $PA = 10$ cm, find the perimeter of the trianlge PCD.

Ans. Two tangents PA and PB are drawn to a circle with centre O from an external point P.

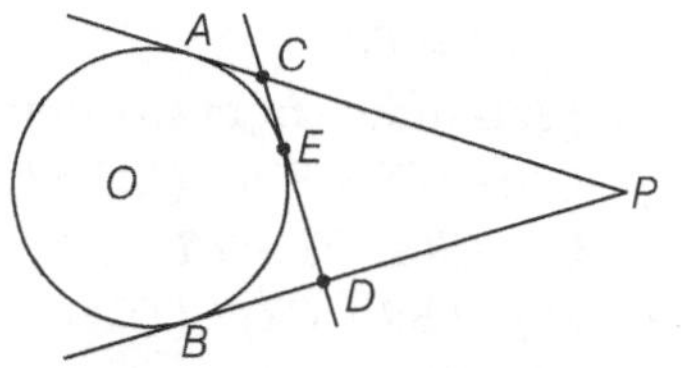

Perimeter of $\Delta PCD = PC + CD + PD$

$= PC + CE + ED + PD$

$= PC + CA + DB + PD$ [$\because CE = CA$, $DE = DB$]

$= PA + PB$

$= 2PA = 2(10)$

[$\because PA = PB$, tangents from external point to a circle are equal]

$= 20$ cm

Q.4 If AB is a chord of a circle with centre O, AOC is a diameter and AT is the tangent at A as shown in figure. Prove that $\angle BAT = \angle ACB$.

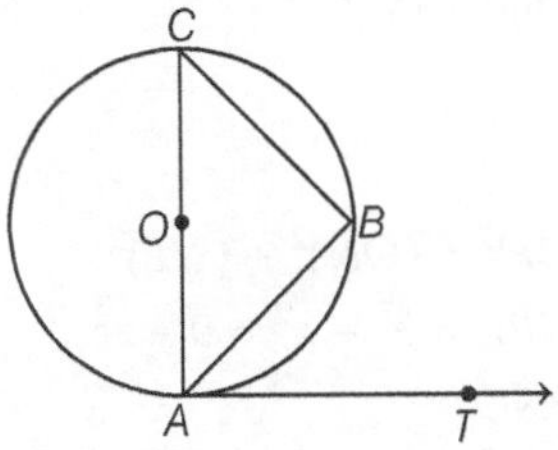

Thinking Process Angle in semi-circle is right angle.

Ans. Since, AC is a diameter line, so angle in semi-circle makes an angle 90°.

$\therefore$ $$\angle ABC = 90°$$

In ΔABC,

$$\angle CAB + \angle ABC + \angle ACB = 180°$$

[$\because$ sum of all interior angles of any triangle is 180°]

$\Rightarrow$ $$\angle CAB + \angle ACB = 180° - 90° = 90° \quad \ldots(i)$$

Since, diameter of a circle is perpendicular to the tangent.

i.e., $$CA \perp AT$$

$\therefore$ $$\angle CAT = 90°$$

$\Rightarrow$ $$\angle CAB + \angle BAT = 90° \quad \ldots(ii)$$

From Eqs. (i) and (ii), we get

$$\angle CAB + \angle ACB = \angle CAB + \angle BAT$$

$\Rightarrow$ $$\angle ACB = \angle BAT$$ **Hence proved.**

Q.5 Two circles with centres O and O' of radii 3 cm and 4 cm, respectively intersect at two points P and Q, such that OP and $O'P$ are tangents to the two circles. Find the length of the common chord PQ.

Ans. Here, two circles are of radii $OP = 3$ cm and $PO' = 4$ cm.
These two circles intersect at P and Q.

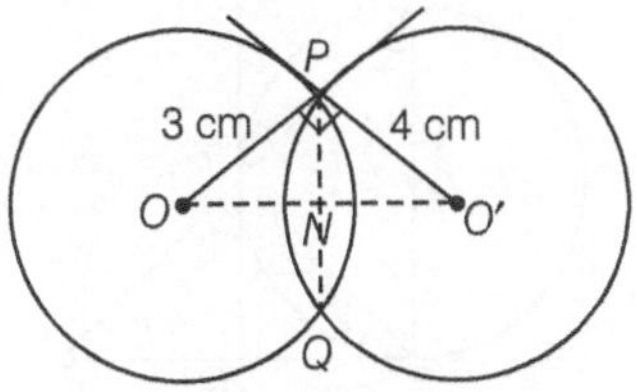

Here, OP and PO' are two tangents drawn at point P.

$$\angle OPO' = 90°$$

[tangent at any point of circle is perpendicular to radius through the point of contact]

Join OO' and PN.
In right angled $\Delta OPO'$,

$$(OO')^2 = (OP)^2 + (PO')^2 \quad \text{[by Pythagoras theorem]}$$

$\Rightarrow \quad (OO')^2 = (3)^2 + (4)^2 = 25$

$\Rightarrow \quad OO' = 5\,\text{cm}$

Also, $\quad PN \perp OO'$

Let $ON = x$, then $NO' = 5 - x$

In right angled ΔOPN,

$(OP)^2 = (ON)^2 + (NP)^2$ [by Pythagoras theorem]

$\Rightarrow \quad (NP)^2 = 3^2 - x^2 = 9 - x^2$ ...(i)

Again in right angled $\Delta PNO'$,

$(PO')^2 = (PN)^2 + (NO')^2$ [by Pythagoras theorem]

$\Rightarrow \quad (4)^2 = (PN)^2 + (5 - x)^2$

$\Rightarrow \quad (PN)^2 = 16 - (5 - x)^2$ ...(ii)

From Eqs. (i) and (ii),

$9 - x^2 = 16 - (5 - x)^2$

$\Rightarrow \quad 7 + x^2 - (25 + x^2 - 10x) = 0 \Rightarrow 7 + x^2 - 25 - x^2 + 10x = 0$

$\Rightarrow \quad 10x = 18$

$\therefore \quad x = 1.8$

Again, in right angled ΔOPN,

$OP^2 = (ON)^2 + (NP)^2$ [by Pythagoras theorem]

$\Rightarrow \quad 3^2 = (1.8)^2 + (NP)^2$

$\Rightarrow \quad (NP)^2 = 9 - 3.24 = 5.76$

$\therefore \quad (NP) = 2.4$ cm

$\therefore$ Length of common chord, $PQ = 2\,PN = 2 \times 2.4 = 4.8\,\text{cm}$

Q.6 In a right triangle ABC is which $\angle B = 90°$, a circle is drawn with AB as diameter intersecting the hypotenuse AC at P. Prove that the tangent to the circle at P bisects BC.

Ans. Let O be the centre of the given circle. Suppose, the tangent at P meets BC at Q. Join BP.

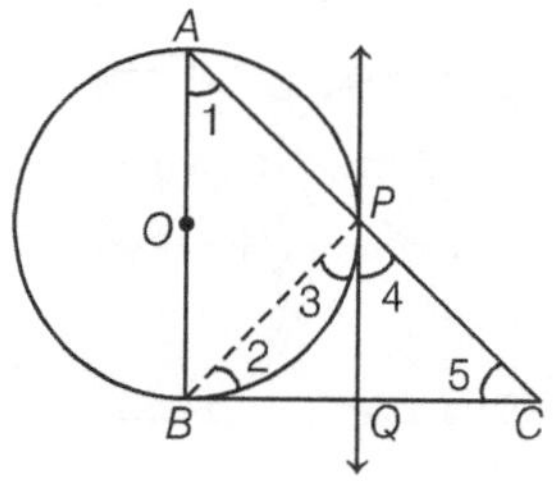

To prove $\quad BQ = QC$

Proof $\quad \angle ABC = 90°$

[tangent at any point of circle is perpendicular to radius through the point of contact]

$\therefore$ In ΔABC, $\quad \angle 1 + \angle 5 = 90°$ [angle sum property, $\angle ABC = 90°$]

$\angle 3 = \angle 1$

[angle between tangent and the chord equals angle made by the chord in alternate segment]

$\therefore$ $\angle 3 + \angle 5 = 90°$ ...(i)

Also, $\angle APB = 90°$ [angle in semi-circle]

$\Rightarrow$ $\angle 3 + \angle 4 = 90°$ [$\angle APB + \angle BPC = 180°$, linear pair]...(ii)

From Eqs. (i) and (ii), we get

$$\angle 3 + \angle 5 = \angle 3 + \angle 4$$

$\Rightarrow$ $\angle 5 = \angle 4$

$\Rightarrow$ $PQ = QC$ [sides opposite to equal angles are equal]

Also, $QP = QB$

[tangents drawn from an external point to a circle are equal]

$\Rightarrow$ $QB = QC$ **Hence proved.**

Q.7 In figure, tangents PQ and PR are drawn to a circle such that $\angle RPQ = 30°$. A chord RS is drawn parallel to the tangent PQ. Find the $\angle RQS$.

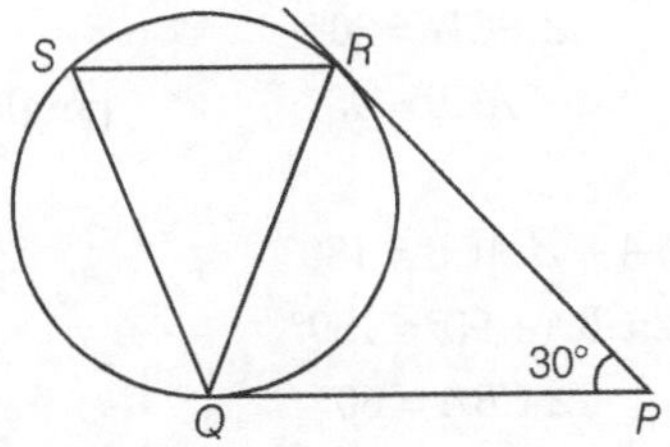

Ans. PQ and PR are two tangents drawn from an external point P.

$\therefore$ $PQ = PR$

[the lengths of tangents drawn from an external point to a circle are equal]

$\Rightarrow$ $\angle PQR = \angle QRP$

[angles opposite to equal sides are equal]

Now, in ΔPQR

$$\angle PQR + \angle QRP + \angle RPQ = 180°$$

[sum of all interior angles of any triangle is 180°]

$\Rightarrow$ $\angle PQR + \angle PQR + 30° = 180°$

$\Rightarrow$ $2\angle PQR = 180° - 30° = 150°$

$\Rightarrow$ $\angle PQR = 75°$

Since, $SR \parallel QP$

$\therefore$ $\angle SRQ = \angle RQP = 75°$ [alternate interior angles]

Also, $\angle PQR = \angle QSR = 75°$ [by alternate segment theorem]

In ΔQRS,

$$\angle RQS + \angle SRQ + \angle QSR = 180°$$

[$\because$ sum of all interior angles of any triangle is 180°]

$\Rightarrow$ $\angle RQS = 180° - (75° + 75°) = 30°$

Q.8 *AB* is a diameter and *AC* is a chord of a circle with centre *O* such that $\angle BAC = 30°$. The tangent at *C* intersects extended *AB* at a point *D*. Prove that $BC = BD$.

Ans. **Given** *AB* is *a* diameter and *AC* is a chord of circle with certer *O*, $\angle BAC = 30°$.

To prove $BC = BD$

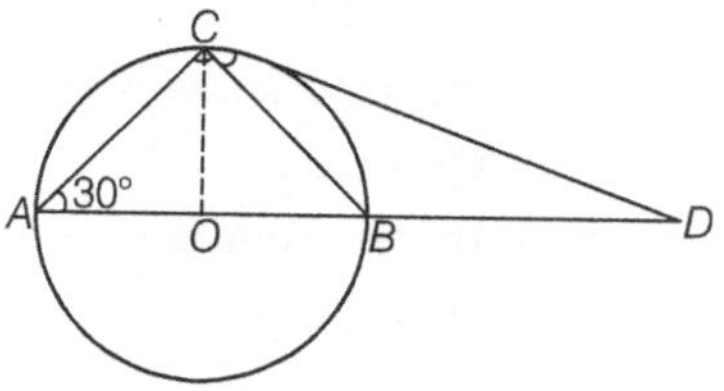

Proof $\angle BCD = \angle CAB$ [alternate segment theorem]

$\angle CAB = 30°$ [given]

$\angle BCD = 30°$ ...(i)

$\angle ACB = 90°$ [angle in semi-circle is right angle]

In ΔABC,

$\angle BAC + \angle CBA + \angle ACB = 180°$ [$\because$ by angle sum property]

$30° + \angle CBA + 90° = 180°$

$\Rightarrow \angle CBA = 60°$

Also, $\angle CBA + \angle CBD = 180°$ [linear pair]

$\Rightarrow \angle CBD = 180° - 60° = 120°$ [$\because \angle CBA = 60°$]

Now, in ΔCBD

$\angle CBD + \angle BDC + \angle DCB = 180°$ [$\because$ by angle sum property]

$\Rightarrow 120° + \angle BDC + 30° = 180°$ [fromEq.(i)]

$\Rightarrow \angle BDC = 180° - 150° = 30°$ ...(ii)

From Eqs. (i) and (ii), we get

$\angle BCD = \angle BDC$

$\therefore BC = BD$

[sides opposite to equal angles are equal]

Q.9 Prove that the tangent drawn at the mid-point of an arc of a circle is parallel to the chord joining the end points of the arc.

Ans. Let mid-point of an arc *AMB* be *M* and *TMT'* be the tangent to the circle. Join *AB*, *AM* and *MB*.

Since, arc AM = arc MB

$\Rightarrow$ Chord AM = Chord MB

In ΔAMB, $AM = MB$

$\Rightarrow \angle MAB = \angle MBA$ ...(i)

[angle opposite to equal sides are equal]

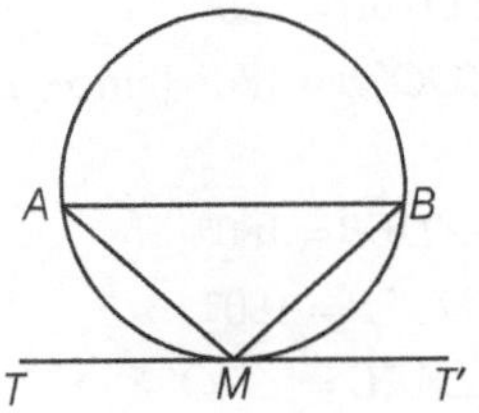

Since, TMT' is a tangent line.

$\therefore \quad \angle AMT = \angle MBA$

[angles in alternate segments are equal]

$\Rightarrow \quad \angle AMT = \angle MAB$ [from Eq. (i)]

But $\angle AMT$ and $\angle MAB$ are alternate angles, which is possible only when

$$AB \parallel TMT'$$

Hence, the tangent drawn at the mid-point of an arc of a circle is parallel to the chord joining the end points of the arc. **Hence proved.**

Q.10 In given figure, the common tangents, AB and CD to two circles with centres O and O' intersect at E. Prove that the points O, E and O' are collinear.

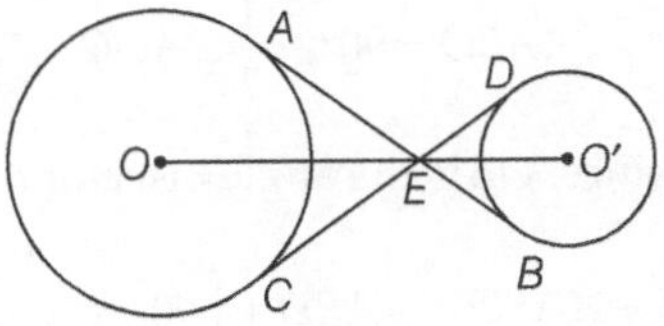

Ans. Join AO, OC and $O'D$, $O'B$.

Now, in $\Delta EO'D$ and $\Delta EO'B$,

$O'D = O'B$ [radii of same circle]

$O'E = O'E$ [common side]

$ED = EB$

[since, tangents drawn from an external point to the circle are equal in length]

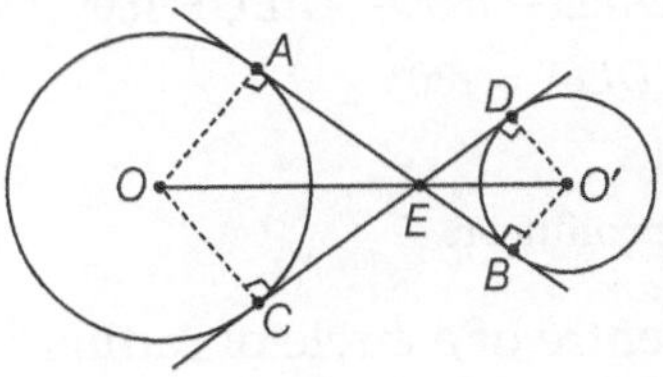

$\therefore \quad \Delta EO'D \cong \Delta EO'B$ [by SSS congruence rule]

$\Rightarrow \quad \angle O'ED = \angle O'EB$

$O'E$ is the angle bisector of $\angle DEB$. ...(i)

Similarly, OE is the angle bisector of $\angle AEC$.

Now, in quadrilateral $DEBO'$,

$$\angle O'DE = \angle O'BE = 90°$$

[since, CED is a tangent to the circle and $O'D$ is the radius *i.e.*, $O'D \perp CED$]

$\Rightarrow \quad \angle O'DE + \angle O'BE = 180°$

$\therefore \quad \angle DEB + \angle DO'B = 180°$ [since, $DEBO'$ is cyclic quadrilateral] ...(ii)

Since, AB is a straight line.

$\therefore \quad \angle AED + \angle DEB = 180°$

$\Rightarrow \quad \angle AED + 180° - \angle DO'B = 180°$ [from Eq. (ii)]

$\Rightarrow \quad \angle AED = \angle DO'B$ ...(iii)

Similarly, $\angle AED = \angle AOC$ ...(iv)

Again from Eq. (ii), we get $\angle DEB = 180° - \angle DO'B$

Divided by 2 on both sides, we get

$$\frac{1}{2}\angle DEB = 90° - \frac{1}{2}\angle DO'B$$

$\Rightarrow \quad \angle DEO' = 90° - \frac{1}{2}\angle DO'B$ ...(v)

[since, $O'E$ is the angle bisector of $\angle DEB$ *i.e.*, $\frac{1}{2}\angle DEB = \angle DEO'$]

Similarly, $\angle AEC = 180° - \angle AOC$

On divided by 2 on both sides, we get

$$\frac{1}{2}\angle AEC = 90° - \frac{1}{2}\angle AOC$$

$\Rightarrow \quad \angle AEO = 90° - \frac{1}{2}\angle AOC$ ...(vi)

[since, OE is the angle bisector of $\angle AEC$ *i.e.*, $\frac{1}{2}\angle AEC = \angle AEO$]

Now, $\angle AED + \angle DEO' + \angle AEO = \angle AED + \left(90° - \frac{1}{2}\angle DO'B\right) + \left(90° - \frac{1}{2}\angle AOC\right)$

$= \angle AED + 180° - \frac{1}{2}(\angle DO'B + \angle AOC)$

$= \angle AED + 180° - \frac{1}{2}(\angle AED + \angle AED)$ [from Eqs. (iii) and (iv)]

$= \angle AED + 180° - \frac{1}{2}(2 \times \angle AED)$

$= \angle AED + 180° - \angle AED = 180°$

$\therefore \angle AEO + \angle AED + \angle DEO' = 180°$

So, OEO' is straight line.

Hence, O, E and O' are collinear. **Hence proved.**

Q.11 In figure, O is the centre of a circle of radius 5 cm, T is a point such that $OT = 13$ and OT intersects the circle at E. If AB is the tangent to the circle at E, find the length of AB.

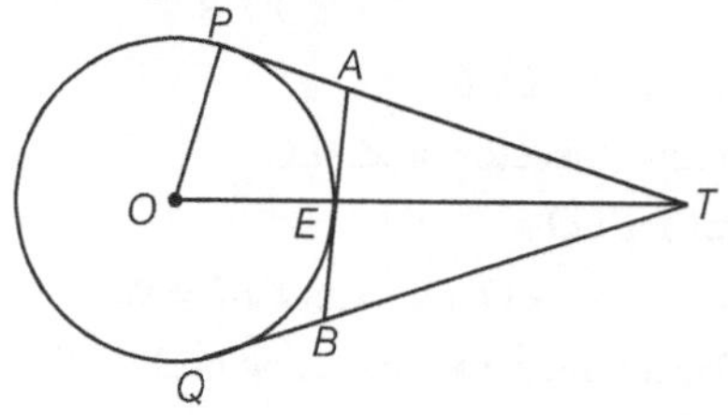

Ans. Given, $OT = 13$ cm and $OP = 5$ cm

Since, if we drawn a line from the centre to the tangent of the circle, then it is always perpendicular to the tangent *i.e.*, $OP \perp PT$.

In right angled ΔOPT,

$$OT^2 = OP^2 + PT^2 \quad \text{[by Pythagoras theorem]}$$

$$\Rightarrow \quad PT^2 = (13)^2 - (5)^2 = 169 - 25 = 144$$

$$\Rightarrow \quad PT = 12 \text{ cm}$$

Since, the length of pair of tangents from an external point T is equal.

$$\therefore \quad QT = 12 \text{ cm}$$

Now, $$TA = PT - PA$$

$$\Rightarrow \quad TA = 12 - PA \quad \text{...(i)}$$

Similarly, $$TB = QT - QB$$

$$\Rightarrow \quad TB = 12 - QB \quad \text{...(ii)}$$

Again, using the property,length of pair of tangents from an external point is equal.

$$\therefore \quad PA = AE \text{ and } QB = EB \quad \text{...(iii)}$$

$$\because \quad OT = 13 \text{ cm} \quad \text{[given]}$$

$$\therefore \quad ET = OT - OE \quad [\because OE = 5 \text{ cm} = \text{radius}]$$

$$\Rightarrow \quad ET = 13 - 5$$

$$\Rightarrow \quad ET = 8 \text{ cm}$$

Since, AB is a tangent and OE is the radius.

$$\therefore \quad OE \perp AB$$

$$\Rightarrow \quad \angle OEA = 90^\circ$$

$$\therefore \quad \angle AET = 180^\circ - \angle OEA \quad \text{[linear pair]}$$

$$\Rightarrow \quad \angle AET = 90^\circ$$

Now, in right angled ΔAET,

$$(AT)^2 = (AE)^2 + (ET)^2 \quad \text{[by Pythagoras theorem]}$$

$$\Rightarrow \quad (PT - PA)^2 = (AE)^2 + (8)^2$$

$$\Rightarrow \quad (12 - PA)^2 = (PA)^2 + (8)^2 \quad \text{[from Eq. (iii)]}$$

$$\Rightarrow \quad 144 + (PA)^2 - 24 \cdot PA = (PA)^2 + 64$$

$$\Rightarrow \quad 24 \cdot PA = 80$$

$$\Rightarrow \quad PA = \frac{10}{3} \text{ cm}$$

$$\therefore \quad AE = \frac{10}{3} \text{ cm} \quad \text{[from Eq. (iii)]}$$

Similarly $$BE = \frac{10}{3} \text{cm}$$

Hence, $$AB = AE + EB$$

$$= \frac{10}{3} + \frac{10}{3} = \frac{20}{3} \text{ cm}$$

Hence,the required length of AB is $\frac{20}{3}$ cm.

Q.12 The tangent at a point C of a circle and a diameter AB when extended intersect at P. If $\angle PCA = 110°$, find $\angle CBA$.

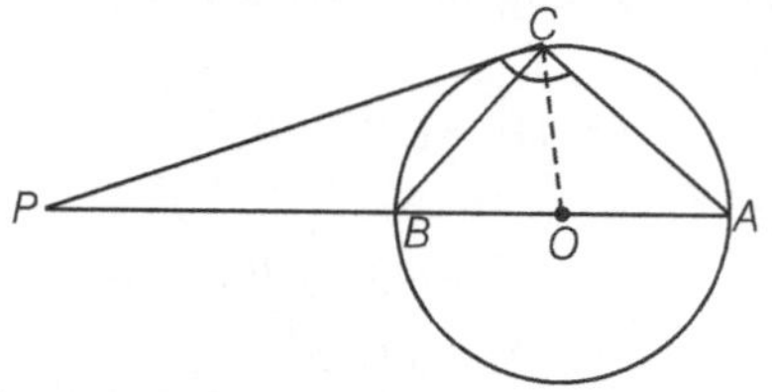

Ans. Here, AB is a diameter of the circle and from point C a tangent is drawn which meets at a point P. When AB extended.

Here, OC is radius.

Since, tangent at any point of a circle is perpendicular to the radius through point of contact circle.

$\therefore \quad OC \perp PC$

Now, $\quad \angle PCA = 110°$ [given]

$\Rightarrow \quad \angle PCO + \angle OCA = 110°$

$\Rightarrow \quad 90° + \angle OCA = 110°$

$\Rightarrow \quad \angle OCA = 20°$

$\therefore \quad OC = OA = \text{Radius of circle}$

$\Rightarrow \quad \angle OCA = \angle OAC = 20°$

[since, two sides are equal, then their opposite angles are equal]

Since, PC is a tangent, so $\quad \angle BCP = \angle CAB = 20°$

[angles in a alternate segment are equal]

In ΔPCA, $\quad \angle APC + \angle ACP + \angle PAC = 180°$ [by angle sum property]

$\Rightarrow \quad \angle APC = 180° - (\angle ACP + \angle PAC)$

$= 180° - (110° + 20°)$

$= 180° - 130° = 50°$

In ΔPBC, $\quad \angle BPC + \angle PCB + \angle PBC = 180°$

[sum of all interior angles of any triangle is 180°]

$\Rightarrow \quad 50° + 20° + \angle PBC = 180°$

$\Rightarrow \quad \angle PBC = 180° - 70°$

$\Rightarrow \quad \angle PBC = 110°$

Since, ABP is a straight line.

$\therefore \quad \angle PBC + \angle CBA = 180°$

$\Rightarrow \quad \angle CBA = 180° - 110° = 70°$

Q.13 If an isosceles triangle ABC in which $AB = AC = 6$ cm, is inscribed in a circle of radius 9 cm, find the area of the triangle.

Ans. In a circle, ΔABC is inscribed.

Join OB, OC and OA.

Conside ΔABO and ΔACO

$$AB = AC \qquad \text{[given]}$$
$$BO = CO \qquad \text{[radii of same circle]}$$

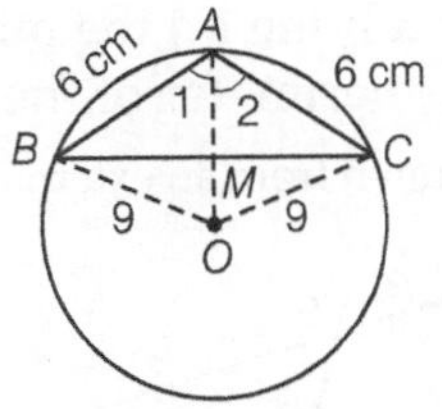

$$OA = AO \qquad \text{[common]}$$

$\therefore \quad \Delta ABO \cong \Delta ACO$ [by SSS congruence rule]

$\Rightarrow \quad \angle 1 = \angle 2$ [CPCT]

Now, in ΔABM and ΔACM,

$$AB = AC \qquad \text{[given]}$$
$$\angle 1 = \angle 2 \qquad \text{[proved above]}$$

AM is common.

$\therefore \quad \Delta AMB \cong \Delta AMC$ [by SAS congruence rule]

$\Rightarrow \quad \angle AMB = \angle AMC$ [CPCT]

Also, $\quad \angle AMB + \angle AMC = 180°$ [linear pair]

$\Rightarrow \quad \angle AMB = 90°$

We know that a perpendicular from centre of circle bisects the chord.

So, OA is perpendicular bisector of BC.

Let $AM = x$, then $OM = 9 - x$ [$\because OA$ = radius = 9 cm]

In right angled ΔAMC, $\quad AC^2 = AM^2 + MC^2$ [by Pythagoras theorem]

$\Rightarrow \quad MC^2 = 6^2 - x^2$ ...(i)

and in right ΔOMC, $\quad OC^2 = OM^2 + MC^2$ [by Pythagoras theorem]

$\Rightarrow \quad MC^2 = 9^2 - (9 - x)^2$ ...(ii)

From Eqs. (i) and (ii), we get $6^2 - x^2 = 9^2 - (9 - x)^2$

$\Rightarrow \quad 36 - x^2 = 81 - (81 + x^2 - 18x)$

$\Rightarrow \quad 36 - x^2 = 81 - 81 - x^2 + 18x$

$\Rightarrow \quad 36 = 18x \Rightarrow x = 2$

$\therefore \quad AM = x = 2$

In right angled ΔABM, $\quad AB^2 = BM^2 + AM^2$ [by Pythagoras theorem]

$$6^2 = BM^2 + 2^2$$

$\Rightarrow \quad BM^2 = 36 - 4 = 32$

$\Rightarrow \quad BM = 4\sqrt{2}$

$\therefore \quad BC = 2\,BM = 8\sqrt{2}$ cm

$\therefore \quad$ Are of $\Delta ABC = \dfrac{1}{2} \times \text{Base} \times \text{Height}$

$$= \frac{1}{2} \times BC \times AM = \frac{1}{2} \times 8\sqrt{2} \times 2 = 8\sqrt{2}\text{ cm}^2$$

Hence, the required area of ΔABC is $8\sqrt{2}$ cm^2.

Q.14 A is a point at a distance 13 cm from the centre O of a circle of radius 5 cm. AP and AQ are the tangents to the circle at P and Q. If a tangent BC is drawn at a point R lying on the minor arc PQ to intersect AP at B and AQ at C, find the perimeter of the ΔABC.

Ans. Given Two tangents are drawn from an external point A to the circle with centre O,

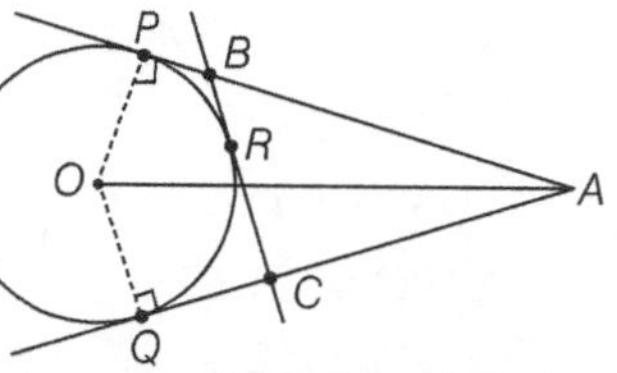

Tangent BC is drawn at a point R, radius of circle equals 5 cm and $OA = 13$ cm .

To find perimeter of ΔABC.

Proof $\angle OPA = 90°$

[tangent at any point of a circle is perpendicular to the radius through the point of contact]

In ΔAPO

$\therefore$ $OA^2 = OP^2 + PA^2$ [by Pythagoras theorm]

$\Rightarrow$ $(13)^2 = 5^2 + PA^2$

$\Rightarrow$ $PA^2 = 169 - 25$

$\Rightarrow$ $PA^2 = 144 = 12^2$

$\Rightarrow$ $PA = 12$ cm

Now, perimeter of $\Delta ABC = AB + BC + CA$

$= (AB + BR) + (RC + CA)$ [$\because BC = BR + RC$]

$= (AB + BP) + (CQ + CA)$

[$\because BR = BP, RC = CQ$ *i.e.*, tangents from external point to a circle are equal]

$\Rightarrow$ Perimeter of ΔABC $= AP + AQ$

$= 2AP$

$= 2(12)$

$= 24$ cm

[$AP = AQ$ *i.e.*, tangent from external point to a circle are equal]

Hence, the perimeter of $\Delta ABC = 24$ cm.

Chapter

10 Constructions*

Multiple Choice Questions (MCQs)

Choose the correct answer from the given four options in the following questions:

Q.1 To divide a line segment AB in the ratio 5 : 7, first a ray AX is drawn, so that $\angle BAX$ is an acute angle and then at equal distances points are marked on the ray AX such that the minimum number of these points is

(a) 8 (b) 10 (c) 11 (d) 12

Ans. *(d)* We know that, to divide a line segment AB in the ratio $m:n$, first draw a ray AX which makes an acute angle $\angle BAX$, then marked $m+n$ points at equal distance.

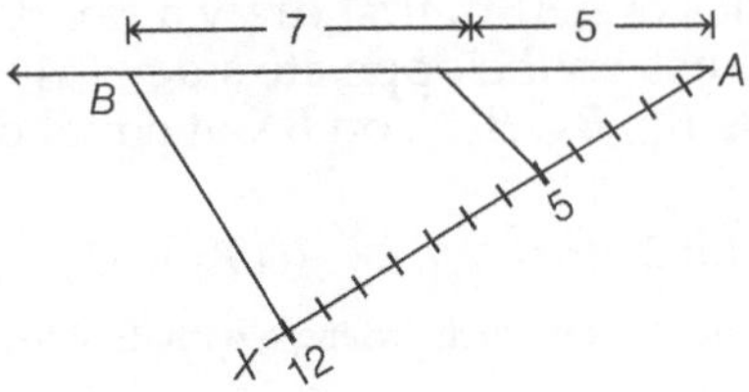

Here, $m = 5, n = 7$

So, minimum number of these points $= m + n = 5 + 7 = 12$

Mistake Alert! *Students may mistakenly identify the minimum number of points on the ray AX as 5 instead of 12.*

Q.2 To divide a line segment AB in the ratio 4 : 7, a ray AX is drawn first such that $\angle BAX$ is an acute angle and then points $A_1, A_2, A_3, \ldots$ are located at equal distances on the ray AX and the point B is joined to

(a) A_{12} (b) A_{11} (c) A_{10} (d) A_9

Ans. *(b)* Here, minimum $4 + 7 = 11$ points are located at equal distances on the ray AX, and then B is joined to last point is A_{11}.

Q.3 To divide a line segment AB in the ratio 5 : 6, draw a ray AX such that $\angle BAX$ is an acute angle, then draw a ray BY parallel to AX and the points $A_1, A_2, A_3, \ldots$ and $B_1, B_2, B_3, \ldots$ are located to equal distances on ray AX and BY, respectively. Then, the points joined are

(a) A_5 and B_6 (b) A_6 and B_5 (c) A_4 and B_5 (d) A_5 and B_4

Note (*) *This chepter has been deleted* from latest NCERT.

Ans. *(a)* Given, a line segment AB and we have to divide it in the ratio 5 : 6.

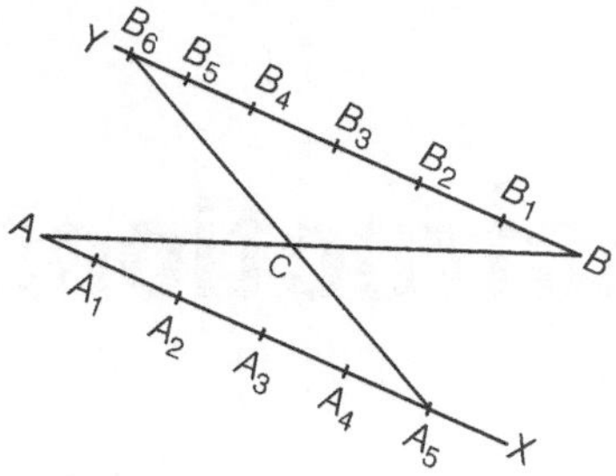

Steps of construction

1. Draw a ray AX making an acute $\angle BAX$.
2. Draw a ray BY parallel to AX by making $\angle ABY$ equal to $\angle BAX$.
3. Now, locate the points A_1, A_2, A_3, A_4 and A_5 $(m = 5)$ on AX and B_1, B_2, B_3, B_4, B_5 and B_6 $(n = 6)$ such that all the points are at equal distance from each other.
4. Join B_6A_5. Let it intersects AB at a point C.

   Then, $AC : BC = 5 : 6$.

Q.4 To construct a triangle similar to a given ΔABC with its sides $\frac{3}{7}$ of the corresponding sides of ΔABC, first draw a ray BX such that $\angle CBX$ is an acute angle and X lies on the opposite side of A with respect to BC. Then, locate points $B_1, B_2, B_3, \ldots$ on BX at equal distances and next step is to join

(a) B_{10} to C (b) B_3 to C (c) B_7 to C (d) B_4 to C

- **Concept Insight** In order to construct a triangle with its sides $\frac{m}{n}$ of the corresponding sides of the triangle, the mininum number of points to be located at equal distance on the ray is m or n, whichever is greater.

Ans. *(c)* Here, we locate points $B_1, B_2, B_3, B_4, B_5, B_6$ and B_7 on BX at equal distance and in next step join the last points is B_7 to C. $[\because n > m]$

Q.5 To construct a triangle similar to a given ΔABC with its sides $\frac{8}{5}$ of the corresponding sides of ΔABC draw a ray BX such that $\angle CBX$ is an acute angle and X is on the opposite side of A with respect to BC. The minimum number of points to be located at equal distances on ray BX is

(a) 5 (b) 8 (c) 13 (d) 3

Ans. *(b)* To construct a triangle similar to a given triangle, with its sides $\frac{m}{n}$ of the corresponding sides of given triangle the minimum number of points to be located at equal distance is equal to the greater of m and n in $\frac{m}{n}$.

Here, $$\frac{m}{n} = \frac{8}{5}$$

So, the minimum number of point to be located at equal distance on ray BX is 8.

Mistake Alert! *Students may incorrectly take the minimum number of points on the ray BX as 5 instead of 8.*

Q.6 To draw a pair of tangents to a circle which are inclined to each other at an angle of 60°, it is required to draw tangents at end points of those two radii of the circle, the angle between them should be

(a) 135° (b) 90° (c) 60° (d) 120°

Ans. *(d)* The angle between them should be 120° because in that case the figure formed by the intersection point of pair of tangent, the two end points of those two radii (at which tangents are drawn) and the centre of the circle is a quadrilateral.

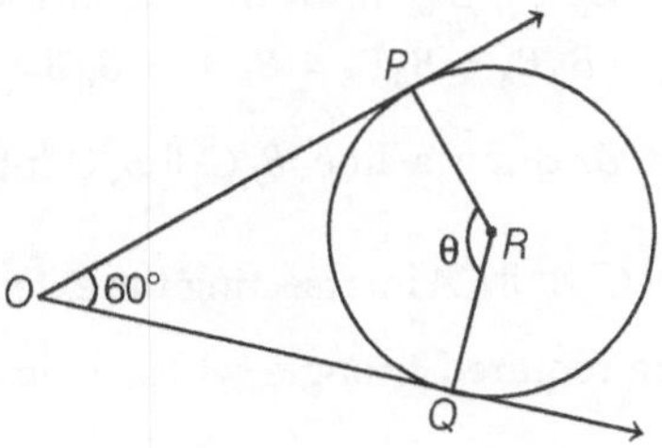

From figure it is quadrilateral,

$$\angle POQ + \angle PRQ = 180° \quad [\because \text{ sum of opposite angles are } 180°]$$

$$60° + \theta = 180°$$

$$\therefore \quad \theta = 120°$$

Hence, the required angle between them is 120°.

Short Answer Questions with Reasoning

Write True or false and give reasons for your answer in each of the following.

Q.1 By geometrical construction, it is possible to divide a line segment in the ratio $\sqrt{3} : \frac{1}{\sqrt{3}}$.

Ans. *True*

Given, $$\text{ratio} = \sqrt{3} : \frac{1}{\sqrt{3}}$$

$$\therefore \quad \text{Required ratio} = 3 : 1 \quad [\text{multiply } \sqrt{3} \text{ in each term}]$$

So, $\sqrt{3} : \frac{1}{\sqrt{3}}$ can be simplified as 3 : 1 and 3 as well as 1 both are positive integer.

Hence, the geometrical construction is possible to divide a line segment in the ratio 3 : 1.

Q.2 To construct a triangle similar to a given ΔABC with its sides $\frac{7}{3}$ of the corresponding sides of ΔABC, draw a ray BX making acute angle with BC and X lies on the opposite side of A with respect of BC. The points $B_1, B_2, \ldots, B_7$ are located at equal distances on BX, B_3 is joined to C and then a line segment B_6C' is drawn parallel to B_3C, where C' lines on BC produced. Finally, line segment $A'C'$ is drawn parallel to AC.

Ans. *False*

Steps of construction

1. Draw a line segment BC with suitable length.
2. Taking B and C as centres draw two arcs of suitable radii intersecting each other at A.
3. Join BA and CA. ΔABC is the required triangle.
4. From B draw any ray BX downwards making an acute angle CBX.
5. Locate seven points $B_1, B_2, B_3, \ldots, B_7$ on BX, such that
   $BB_1 = B_1B_2 = B_2B_3 = B_3B_4 = B_4B_5 = B_5B_6 = B_6B_7$.
6. Join B_3C and from B_7 draw a line $B_7C' \parallel B_3C$ intersecting the extended line segment BC at C'.
7. From point C' draw $C'A' \parallel CA$ intersecting the extended line segment BA at A'.

   Then, $\Delta A'BC'$ is the required triangle whose sides are $\frac{7}{3}$ of the corresponding sides of ΔABC.

   Given that, segment B_6C' is drawn parallel to B_3C. But from our construction is never possible that segment B_6C' is parallel to B_3C because the similar triangle $A'BC'$ has its sides $\frac{7}{3}$ of the corresponding sides of triangle ABC. So, B_7C' is parallel to B_3C.

Q.3 A pair of tangents can be constructed from a point P to a circle of radius 3.5 cm situated at a distance of 3 cm from the centre.

Thinking Process Let r = radius of circle and d = distance of a point from the centre.

(i) If $r = d$, then point lies on the circle *i.e.*, only one tangent is possible

(ii) If $r < d$, then point lies outside the circle *i.e.*, a pair of tangent is possible.

(iii) If $r > d$, then point lies inside the circle *i.e.*, no tangent is possible.

Ans. *False*

Since, the radius of the circle is 3.5 cm *i.e.*, $r = 3.5$ cm and a point P situated at a distance of 3 cm from the centre *i.e.*, $d = 3$ cm

We see that, $r > d$

i.e., a point P lies inside the circle. So, no tangent can be drawn to a circle from a point lying inside it.

Q.4 A pair of tangents can be constructed to a circle inclined at an angle of 170°.

Thinking Process If the angle between pair of tangents is greater than 180°, then a pair of tangent never constructed to a circle.

Ans. **True**

If the angle between the pair of tangents is always greater than 0° or less than 180°, then we can construct a pair of tangents to a circle.

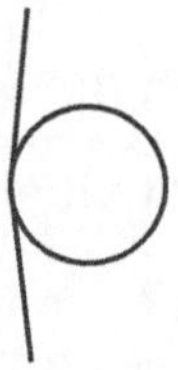

Hence, we can draw a pair of tangents to a circle inclined at an angle of 170°.

Short Answer Questions

Q.1 Draw a line segment of length 7 cm. Find a point P on it which divides it in the ratio 3 : 5.

Ans. **Steps of construction**

1. Draw a line segment $AB = 7$ cm.
2. Draw a ray AX, making an acute $\angle BAX$.
3. Along AX, mark $3 + 5 = 8$ points
   $A_1, A_2, A_3, A_4, A_5, A_6, A_7, A_8$ such that
   $AA_1 = A_1A_2 = A_2A_3 = A_3A_4 = A_4A_5 = A_5A_6 = A_6A_7 = A_7A_8$
4. Join A_8B.
5. From A_3, draw $A_3P \parallel A_8B$ meeting AB at P.

[by making an angle equal to $\angle BA_8A$ at A_3]

Then, P is the point on AB which divides it in the ratio 3 : 5.

Thus, $AP : PB = 3 : 5$

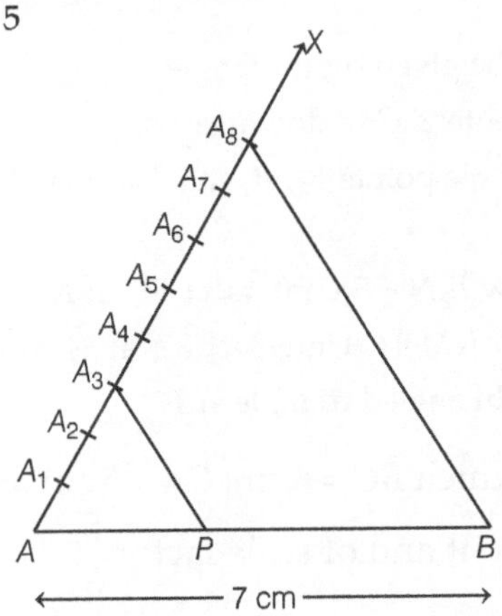

Justification

Let $AA_1 = A_1A_2 = A_2A_3 = A_3A_4 = ... = A_7A_8 = x$

In ΔABA_8, we have

$A_3P \parallel A_8B$

$$\therefore \quad \frac{AP}{PB} = \frac{AA_3}{A_3A_8} = \frac{3x}{5x} = \frac{3}{5}$$

Hence, $AP : PB = 3 : 5$

Q.2 Draw a right ΔABC in which $BC = 12$ cm, $AB = 5$ cm and $\angle B = 90°$. Construct a triangle similar to it and of scale factor $\frac{2}{3}$. Is the new triangle also a right triangle?

- **Concept Insight** Here, scale factor $\frac{m}{n} = \frac{2}{3}$ *i.e.*, $m < n$, then the triangle to be constructed is smaller than the given triangle. Use this concept and then construct the required triangle.

Ans. **Steps of construction**

1. Draw a line segment $BC = 12$ cm.
2. From B draw a line $AB = 5$ cm which makes right angle at B.

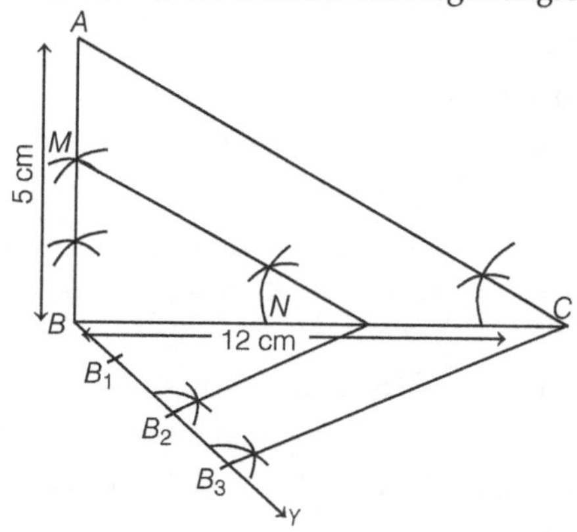

3. Join AC, ΔABC is the given right triangle.
4. From B draw an acute $\angle CBY$ downwards.
5. On ray BY, mark three points B_1, B_2 and B_3, such that $BB_1 = B_1B_2 = B_2B_3$.
6. Join B_3C.
7. From point B_2 draw $B_2N \parallel B_3C$ intersect BC at N.
8. From point N draw $NM \parallel CA$ intersect BA at M. ΔMBN is the required triangle. ΔMBN is also a right angled triangle at B.

Q.3 Draw a ΔABC in which $BC = 6$ cm, $CA = 5$ cm and $AB = 4$ cm. Construct a triangle similar to it and of scale factor $\frac{5}{3}$.

- **Concept Insight** Here, scale factor $\frac{m}{n} = \frac{5}{3}$ *i.e.*, $m > n$, then the triangle to be constructed is larger than the given triangle. Use this concept and then construct the required triangle.

Ans. **Steps of construction**

1. Draw a line segment $BC = 6$ cm.
2. Taking B and C as centres, draw two arcs of radii 4 cm and 5 cm intersecting each other at A.
3. Join BA and CA. ΔABC is the required triangle.
4. From B, draw any ray BX downwards making an acute angle.
5. Mark five points B_1, B_2, B_3, B_4 and B_5 on BX, such that $BB_1 = B_1B_2 = B_2B_3 = B_3B_4 = B_4B_5$.

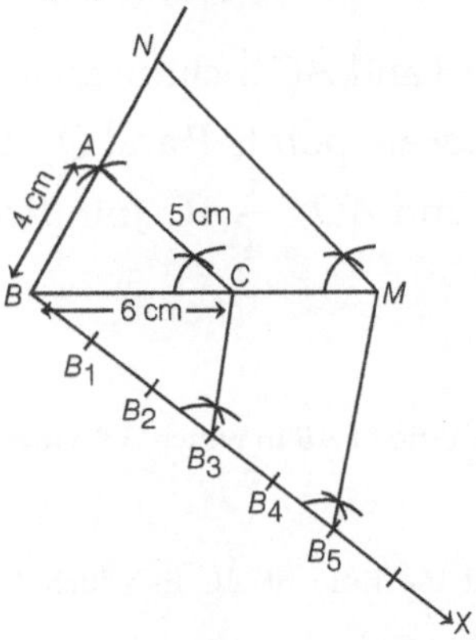

6. Join B_3C and from B_5 draw $B_5M \parallel B_3C$ intersecting the extended line segment BC at M.
7. From point M draw $MN \parallel CA$ intersecting the extended line segment BA at N.

Then, ΔNBM is the required triangle whose sides is equal to $\frac{5}{3}$ of the corresponding sides of the ΔABC.

Hence, ΔNBM is the required triangle.

Q.4 Construct a tangent to a circle of radius 4 cm from a point which is at a distance of 6 cm from its centre.

Thinking Process

(i) Firstly taking the perpendicular bisector of the distance from the centre to the external point. After that taking one half of bisector as radius and draw a circle.

(ii) Drawing a circle that intersects the given circle at two points. Now, join these intersecting points to an external point and get the required tangents.

Ans. Given, a point M' is at a distance of 6 cm from the centre of a circle of radius 4 cm.

Steps of construction

1. Draw a circle of radius 4 cm. Let centre of this circle is O.

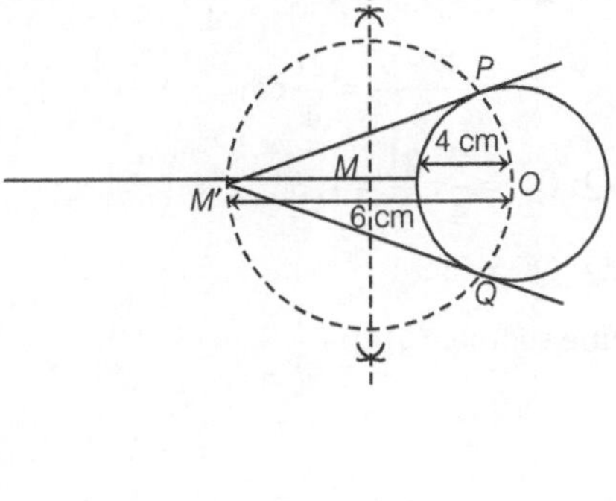

2. Join OM' and bisect it. Let M be mid-point of OM'.
3. Taking M as centre and MO as radius draw a circle to intersect circle (0, 4) at two points, P and Q.
4. Join PM' and QM'. PM' and QM' are the required tangents from M' to circle $C(0, 4)$.

Long Answer Questions

Q.1 Two line segments AB and AC include an angle of 60°, where $AB = 5$ cm and $AC = 7$ cm. Locate points P and Q on AB and AC, respectively such that $AP = \frac{3}{4}AB$ and $AQ = \frac{1}{4}AC$. Join P and Q and measure the length PQ.

Thinking Process

(i) Firstly, we find the ratio of AB in which P divides it with the help of the relation $AP = \frac{3}{4}AB$.

(ii) Secondly, we find the ratio of AC in which Q divides it with the help of the relation $AQ = \frac{1}{4}AC$.

(iii) Now, construct the line segment AB and AC in which P and Q respectively divides it in the ratio from step (i) and (ii), respectively.

(iv) Finally, get the point P and Q. After that join PQ and get the required measurement of PQ.

Ans. Given that, $AB = 5$ cm and $AC = 7$ cm

Also, $$AP = \frac{3}{4}AB \text{ and } AQ = \frac{1}{4}AC \quad \text{...(i)}$$

From Eq. (i), $$AP = \frac{3}{4}\cdot AB = \frac{3}{4}\times 5 = \frac{15}{4} \text{ cm}$$

Then, $$PB = AB - AP = 5 - \frac{15}{4} = \frac{20-15}{4} = \frac{5}{4} \text{ cm} \quad [\because P \text{ is any point on the } AB]$$

$$\therefore \quad AP : PB = \frac{15}{4} : \frac{5}{4} \Rightarrow AP : PB = 3 : 1$$

i.e., scale factor of line segment AB is $\frac{3}{1}$.

Again from Eq. (i), $$AQ = \frac{1}{4}AC = \frac{1}{4}\times 7 = \frac{7}{4} \text{ cm}$$

Then, $$QC = AC - AQ = 7 - \frac{7}{4}$$

$$= \frac{28-7}{4} = \frac{21}{4} \text{ cm} \quad [\because Q \text{ is any point on the } AC]$$

$$\therefore \quad AQ : QC = \frac{7}{4} : \frac{21}{4} = 1 : 3$$

$$\Rightarrow \quad AQ : QC = 1 : 3$$

i.e., scale factor of line segment AQ is $\frac{1}{3}$.

Steps of construction

1. Draw a line segment $AB = 5$ cm.
2. Now, draw a ray AZ making an acute $\angle BAZ = 60°$.
3. With A as centre and radius equal to 7 cm draw an arc cutting the line AZ at C.
4. Draw a ray AX, making an acute $\angle BAX$.
5. Along AX, mark $1 + 3 = 4$ points A_1, A_2, A_3, and A_4
   Such that $AA_1 = A_1A_2 = A_2A_3 = A_3A_4$
6. Join A_4B
7. From A_3 draw $A_3P \parallel A_4B$ meeting AB at P. [by making an angle equal to $\angle AA_4B$]
   Then, P is the point on AB which divides it in the ratio 3 : 1.
   So, $AP : PB = 3 : 1$
8. Draw a ray AY, making an acute $\angle CAY$.

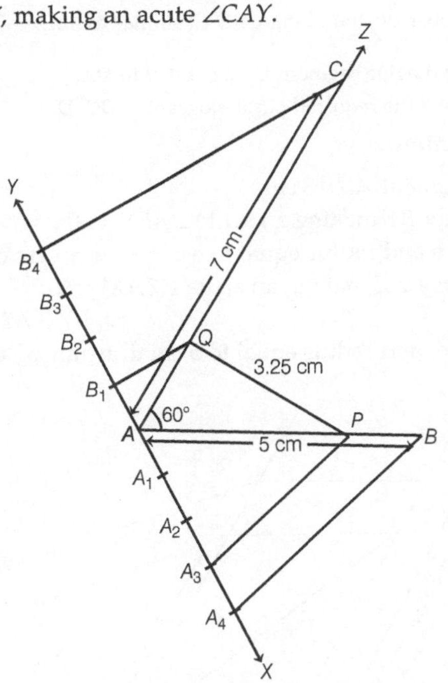

9. Along AY, mark $3 + 1 = 4$ points B_1, B_2, B_3 and B_4.
   Such that $AB_1 = B_1B_2 = B_2B_3 = B_3B_4$
10. Join B_4C.
11. From B_1 draw $B_1Q \parallel B_4C$ meeting AC at Q. [by making an angle equal to $\angle AB_4C$]
    Then, Q is the point on AC which divides it in the ratio 1 : 3.
    So, $AQ : QC = 1 : 3$
12. Finally, join PQ and its measurment is 3.25 cm.

Q.2 Draw a parallelogram $ABCD$ in which $BC = 5$ cm, $AB = 3$ cm and $\angle ABC = 60°$, divide it into triangles BCD and ABD by the diagonal BD.

Construct the triangle $BD'C'$ similar to ΔBDC with scale factor $\frac{4}{3}$.

Draw the line segment $D'A'$ parallel to DA, where A' lies on extended side BA. Is $A'BC'D'$ a parallelogram?

Thinking Process

(i) Firstly, we draw a line segment, then either of one end of the line segment with length 5 cm and make an angle 60° with this end. We know that in parallelogram both opposite sides are equal and parallel, then again draw a line with 5 cm making an angle with 60° from other end of line segment. Now, join both parallel line by a line segment whose measurement is 3 cm, we get a parallelogram. After that we draw a diagonal and get a triangle BOC.

(ii) Now, we construct the triangle $BD'C'$ similar to ΔBDC with scale factor $\frac{4}{3}$.

(iii) Now, draw the line segment $D'A'$ parallel to DA.

(iv) Finaly, we get the required parallelogram $A'BC'D$.

Ans. **Steps of construction**

1. Draw a line segment $AB = 3$ cm.
2. Now, draw a ray BY making an acute $\angle ABY = 60°$.
3. With B as centre and radius equal to 5 cm draw an arc cut the point C on BY.
4. Again draw a ray AZ making an acute $\angle ZAX' = 60°$.

$[\because BY \parallel AZ, \therefore \angle YBX' = ZAX' = 60°]$

5. With A as centre and radius equal to 5 cm draw an arc cut the point D on AZ.

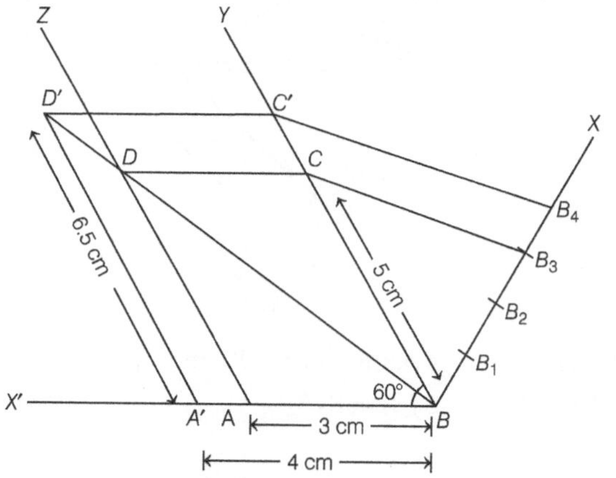

6. Now, join CD and finally make a parallelogram $ABCD$.
7. Join BD, which is a diagonal of parallelogram $ABCD$.
8. From B draw any ray BX downwards making an acute $\angle CBX$.
9. Locate 4 points B_1, B_2, B_3, B_4 on BX, such that $BB_1 = B_1B_2 = B_2B_3 = B_3B_4$.
10. Join B_4C' and from B_3C draw a line $B_4C' \parallel B_3C$ intersecting the extended line segment BC at C'.

11. From point C' draw $C'D' \parallel CD$ intersecting the extended line segment BD at D'. Then, $\Delta D'BC'$ is the required triangle whose sides are $\frac{4}{3}$ of the corresponding sides of ΔDBC.
12. Now draw a line segment $D'A'$ parallel to DA, where A' lies on extended side BA *i.e.*, a ray BX'.
13. Finally, we observe that $A'BC'D'$ is a parallelogram in which $A'D' = 6.5$ cm $A'B = 4$ cm and $\angle A'BD' = 60°$ divide it into triangles $BC'D'$ and $A'BD'$ by the diagonal BD'.

Q.3 **Draw two concentric circles of radii 3 cm and 5 cm. Taking a point on outer circle construct the pair of tangents to the other. Measure the length of a tangent and verify it by actual calculation.**

Ans. Given, two concentric circles of radii 3 cm and 5 cm with centre O. We have to draw pair of tangents from point P on outer circle to the other.

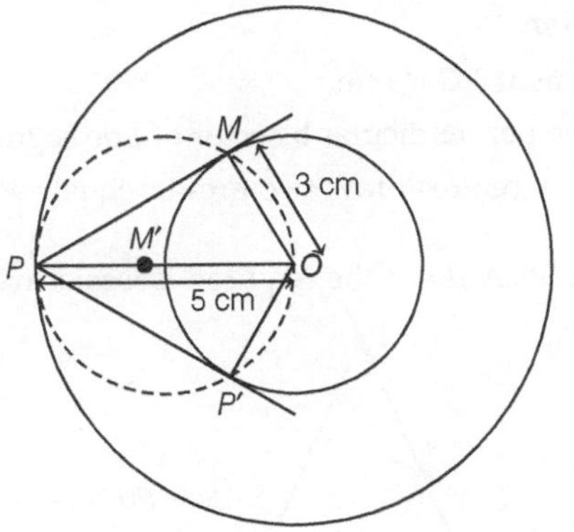

Steps of construction

1. Draw two concentric circles with centre O and radii 3 cm and 5 cm.
2. Taking any point P on outer circle. Join OP.
3. Bisect OP, let M' be the mid-point of OP.
   Taking M' as centre and OM' as radius draw a dotted circle which cuts the inner circle at M and P'.
4. Join PM and PP'. Thus, PM and PP' are the required tangents.
5. On measuring PM and PP', we find that $PM = PP' = 4$ cm.

Actual calculation

In right angle ΔOMP, $\angle PMO = 90°$

$\therefore$ $PM^2 = OP^2 - OM^2$

[by Pythagoras theorem *i.e.*, $(\text{hypotenuse})^2 = (\text{base})^2 + (\text{perpendicular})^2$]

$\Rightarrow$ $PM^2 = (5)^2 - (3)^2 = 25 - 9 = 16$

$\Rightarrow$ $PM = 4$ cm

Hence, the length of both tangents is 4 cm.

Q.4 Draw an isosceles triangle ABC in which $AB = AC = 6$ cm and $BC = 5$ cm. Construct a triangle PQR similar to ΔABC in which $PQ = 8$ cm. Also justify the construction.

Thinking Process

(i) Here, for making two similar triangles with one vertex at the same point on the base. We assume that,

In ΔABC and ΔPQR; vertex B = vertex Q

So, we get the required scale factor.

(ii) Now, construct a ΔABC and then a ΔPBR, similar to ΔABC whose sides are $\frac{PQ}{AB}$ of the corresponding sides of the ΔABC.

Ans. Let ΔPQR and ΔABC are similar triangles, then its scale factor between the corresponding sides is $\frac{PQ}{AB} = \frac{8}{6} = \frac{4}{3}$.

Steps of construction

1. Draw a line segment $BC = 5$ cm.
2. Construct OQ the perpendicular bisector of line segment BC meeting BC at P'.
3. Taking B and C as centres draw two arcs of equal radius 6 cm intersecting each other at A.
4. Join BA and CA. So, ΔABC is the required isosceles triangle.

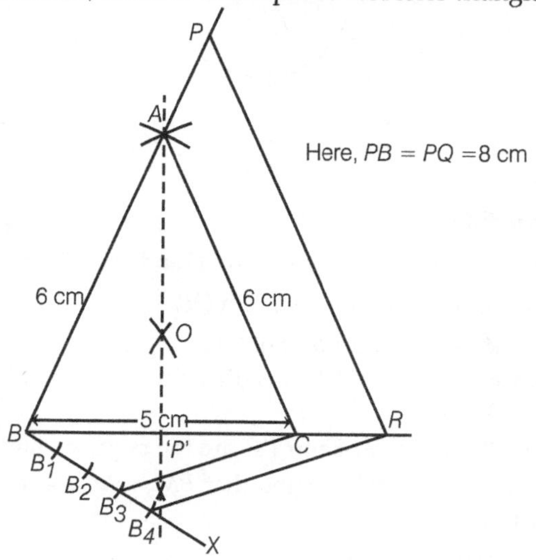

5. From B, draw any ray BX making an acute $\angle CBX$.
6. Locate four points B_1, B_2, B_3 and B_4 on BX such that $BB_1 = B_1B_2 = B_2B_3 = B_3B_4$.
7. Join B_3C and from B_4 draw a line $B_4R \parallel B_3C$ intersecting the extended line segment BC at R.
8. From point R, draw $RP \parallel CA$ meeting BA produced at P.

Then, ΔPBR is the required triangle.

Justification

$\because \quad B_4R \parallel B_3C$ (by construction)

$$\therefore \quad \frac{BC}{CR} = \frac{3}{1}$$

Now,
$$\frac{BR}{BC} = \frac{BC + CR}{BC}$$
$$= 1 + \frac{CR}{BC} = 1 + \frac{1}{3} = \frac{4}{3}$$

Also, $RP \parallel CA$

$$\therefore \quad \Delta ABC \sim \Delta PBR$$

and
$$\frac{PB}{AB} = \frac{RP}{CA} = \frac{BR}{BC} = \frac{4}{3}$$

Hence, the new triangle is similar to the given triangle which sides are $\frac{4}{3}$ times of the corresponding sides of the isosceles ΔABC.

Q.5 Draw a ΔABC in which $AB = 5$ cm, $BC = 6$ cm and $\angle ABC = 60°$. Construct a triangle similar to ΔABC with scale factor $\frac{5}{7}$. Justify the construction.

Ans. **Steps of construction**

1. Draw a line segment $AB = 5$ cm.
2. From point B, draw $\angle ABY = 60°$ on which take $BC = 6$ cm.
3. Join AC, ΔABC is the required triangle.
4. From A, draw any ray AX downwards making an acute angle.
5. Mark 7 points $B_1, B_2, B_3, B_4, B_5, B_6$ and B_7 on AX, such that $AB_1 = B_1B_2 = B_2B_3$ $= B_3B_4 = B_4B_5 = B_5B_6 = B_6B_7$.
6. Join B_7B and from B_5 draw $B_5M \parallel B_7B$ intersecting AB at M.
7. From point M draw $MN \parallel BC$ intersecting AC at N.

   Then, ΔAMN is the required triangle whose sides are equal to $\frac{5}{7}$ of the corresponding sides of the ΔABC.

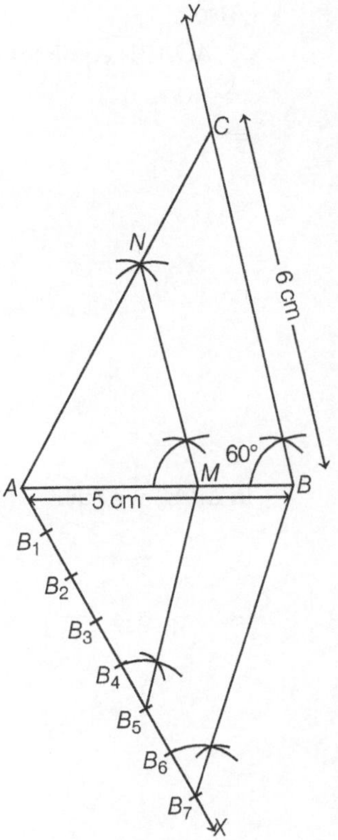

Justification

Here, $B_5M \parallel B_7B$ (by construction)

$$\therefore \quad \frac{AM}{MB} = \frac{5}{2}$$

Now,
$$\frac{AB}{AM} = \frac{AM + MB}{AM}$$

$$= 1 + \frac{MB}{AM} = 1 + \frac{2}{5} = \frac{7}{5}$$

Also, $MN \parallel BC$

$\therefore$ $\Delta AMN \sim \Delta ABC$

Therefore, $\frac{AM}{AB} = \frac{AN}{AC} = \frac{NM}{BC} = \frac{5}{7}$

Q.6 Draw a circle of radius 4 cm. Construct a pair of tangents to it, the angle between which is 60°. Also justify the construction. Measure the distance between the centre of the circle and the point of intersection of tangents.

Ans. In order to draw the pair of tangents, we follow the following steps;

Steps of construction

1. Take a point O on the plane of the paper and draw a circle of radius $OA = 4$ cm.
2. Produce OA to B such that $OA = AB = 4$ cm.
3. Take A as the centre draw a circle of radius $AO = AB = 4$ cm.
   Suppose it cuts the circle drawn in step 1 at P and Q.
4. Join BP and BQ to get desired tangents.

Justification In ΔOAP, we have

$OA = OP = 4$ cm (∵ radius)

Also, $AP = 4$ cm (∵ radius of circle with centre A)

$\therefore$ ΔOAP is equilateral

$\Rightarrow$ $\angle PAO = 60°$

$\Rightarrow$ $\angle BAP = 120°$

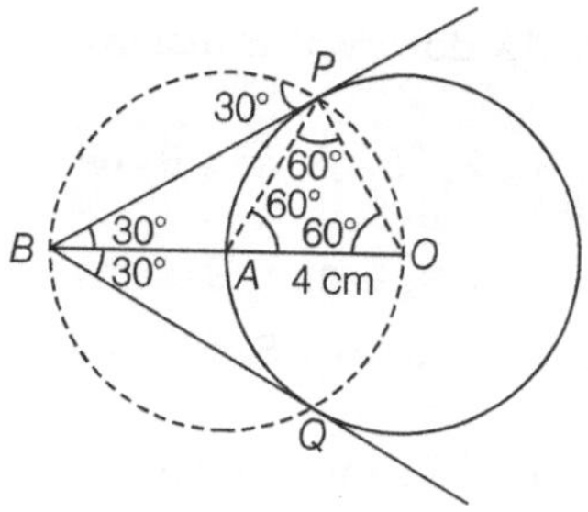

In ΔBAP, we have

$BA = AP$ and $\angle BAP = 120°$

$\therefore$ $\angle ABP = \angle APB = 30°$

$\Rightarrow$ $\angle PBQ = 60°$

Alternate Method

Steps of construction

1. Take a point O on the plane of the paper and draw a circle with centre O and radius $OA = 4$ cm.
2. At O construct radii OA and OB such that to $\angle AOB$ equal 120° *i.e.*, supplement of the angle between the tangents.
3. Draw perpendiculars to OA and OB at A and B, respectively. Suppose these perpendiculars intersect at P. Then, PA and PB are required tangents.

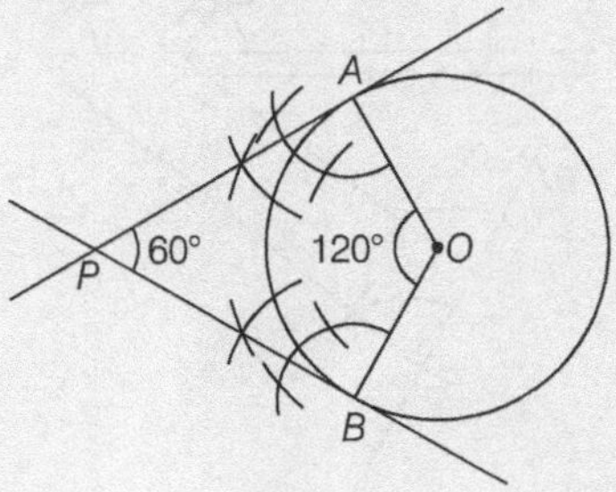

Justification

In quadrilateral $OAPB$, we have

$$\angle OAP = \angle OBP = 90^\circ$$

and $$\angle AOB = 120^\circ$$

$\therefore$ $\angle OAP + \angle OBP + \angle AOB + \angle APB = 360^\circ$

$\Rightarrow$ $90^\circ + 90^\circ + 120^\circ + \angle APB = 360^\circ$

$\therefore$ $\angle APB = 360^\circ - (90^\circ + 90^\circ + 120^\circ)$

$= 360^\circ - 300^\circ = 60^\circ$

Q.7 **Draw a ΔABC in which $AB = 4$ cm, $BC = 6$ cm and $AC = 9$ cm. Construct a triangle similar to ΔABC with scale factor $\frac{3}{2}$. Justify the construction. Are the two triangles congruent? Note that, all the three angles and two sides of the two triangles are equal.**

Thinking Process Triangles are congruent when all corresponding sides and interior angles are congruent. The triangles will have the same shape and size, but one may be a mirror image of the other. So, first we construct a triangle similar to $\Delta\ ABC$ with scale factor 3/2 and use the above concept to check the triangles are congruent or not.

Ans. **Steps of construction**

1. Draw a line segment $BC = 6$ cm.
2. Taking B and C as centres, draw two arcs of radii 4 cm and 9 cm respectively intersecting each other at A.
3. Join BA and CA. ΔABC is the required triangle.
4. From B, draw any ray BX downwards making an acute angle.
5. Mark three points B_1, B_2, B_3 on BX, such that $BB_1 = B_1B_2 = B_2B_3$.

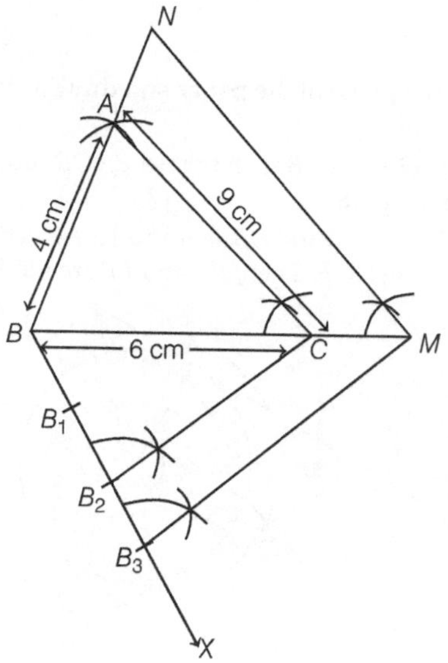

6. Join B_2C and from B_3 draw $B_3M \parallel B_2C$ intersecting the extended line segment BC at M.
7. From point M, draw $MN \parallel CA$ intersecting the extended line segment BA to N.

   Then, ΔNBM is the required triangle whose sides are equal to $\frac{3}{2}$ of the corresponding sides of the ΔABC.

Justification

Here, $$B_3M \parallel B_2C$$

$\therefore$ $$\frac{BC}{CM} = \frac{2}{1}$$

Now, $$\frac{BM}{BC} = \frac{BC + CM}{BC}$$

$$= 1 + \frac{CM}{BC} = 1 + \frac{1}{2} = \frac{3}{2}$$

Also, $$MN \parallel CA$$

$\therefore$ $$\Delta ABC \sim \Delta NBM$$

Therefore, $$\frac{NB}{AB} = \frac{NM}{AC} = \frac{BM}{BC} = \frac{3}{2}$$

The two triangles are not congruent because, if two triangles are congruent, then they have same shape and same size. Here, all the three angles are same but three sides are not same *i.e.*, one side is different.

Chapter

11

Areas Related to Circles

Multiple Choice Questions (MCQS)

Choose the correct answer from the given four options in the following questions:

***Q.1** If the sum of the areas of two circles with radii R_1 and R_2 is equal to the area of a circle of radius R, then

(a) $R_1 + R_2 = R$ (b) $R_1^2 + R_2^2 = R^2$

(c) $R_1 + R_2 < R$ (d) $R_1^2 + R_2^2 < R^2$

Ans. ***(b)*** According to the given condition,

Area of circle = Area of first circle + Area of second circle

$\therefore \quad \pi R^2 = \pi R_1^2 + \pi R_2^2$

$\Rightarrow \quad R^2 = R_1^2 + R_2^2$

***Q.2** If the sum of the circumferences of two circles with radii R_1 and R_2 is equal to the circumference of a circle of radius R, then

(a) $R_1 + R_2 = R$

(b) $R_1 + R_2 > R$

(c) $R_1 + R_2 < R$

(d) Nothing definite can be said about the relation among R_1, R_2 and R.

Ans. ***(a)*** According to the given condition,

Circumference of circle = Circumference of first circle + Circumference of second circle

$\therefore \quad 2\pi R = 2\pi R_1 + 2\pi R_2$

$\Rightarrow \quad R = R_1 + R_2$

***Q.3** If the circumference of a circle and the perimeter of a square are equal, then

(a) Area of the circle = Area of the square

(b) Area of the circle > Area of the square

(c) Area of the circle < Area of the square

(d) Nothing definite can be said about the relation between the areas of the circle and square

Note (*) *Topics related to these question have been removed from latest NCERT.*

Ans. ***(b)*** According to the given condition,

Circumference of a circle = Perimeter of square

$$2\pi r = 4a$$

[where, r and a are radius of circle and side of square, respectively]

$$\Rightarrow \quad \frac{22}{7} r = 2a \Rightarrow 11r = 7a$$

$$\Rightarrow \quad a = \frac{11}{7} r \Rightarrow r = \frac{7a}{11} \quad \text{...(i)}$$

Now, Area of circle, $A_1 = \pi r^2$

$$= \pi \left(\frac{7a}{11}\right)^2 = \frac{22}{7} \times \frac{49a^2}{121} \quad \text{[from Eq. (i)]}$$

$$= \frac{14a^2}{11} \quad \text{...(ii)}$$

and Area of square, $A_2 = (a)^2$ ...(iii)

From Eqs. (ii) and (iii), we get $A_1 = \frac{14}{11} A_2$

$\therefore \quad A_1 > A_2$

Hence, Area of the circle > Area of the square.

***Q.4** Area of the largest triangle that can be inscribed in a semi-circle of radius r units is

(a) r^2 sq. units (b) $\frac{1}{2} r^2$ sq. units (c) $2r^2$ sq. units (d) $\sqrt{2}\, r^2$ sq. units

Thinking process The angle on the circumference of the semi-circle is 90°.

Ans. ***(a)*** Take a point C on the circumference of the semi-circle and join it by the end points of diameter A and B.

$\therefore \quad \angle C = 90°$

[$\because$ the angle on the circumference of the semi-circle is 90°]

So, ΔABC is right angled triangle.

The largest triangle that can be inscribed in a semi-circle will have a base equal to the diameter and hight equal to the radius of the semi-circle.

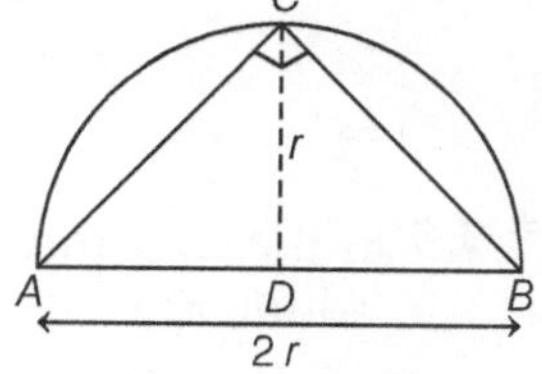

$\therefore$ Area of largest $\Delta ABC = \frac{1}{2} \times AB \times CD$

$$= \frac{1}{2} \times 2r \times r$$

$$= r^2 \text{ sq. units}$$

***Q.5** If the perimeter of a circle is equal to that of a square, then the ratio of their areas is

(a) 22 : 7 (b) 14 : 11 (c) 7 : 22 (d) 11 : 14

Ans. ***(b)*** Let radius of circle be r and side of a square be a.

According to the given condition,

Perimeter of a circle = Perimeter of a square

Note (*) *Topics related to these question have been removed from latest NCERT.*

$\therefore \qquad 2\pi r = 4a \Rightarrow a = \dfrac{\pi r}{2}$ ...(i)

Now, $\dfrac{\text{Area of circle}}{\text{Area of square}} = \dfrac{\pi r^2}{(a)^2} = \dfrac{\pi r^2}{\left(\dfrac{\pi r}{2}\right)^2}$ [from Eq. (i)]

$$= \frac{\pi r^2}{\pi^2 r^2 / 4} = \frac{4}{\pi} = \frac{4}{22/7} = \frac{28}{22} = \frac{14}{11}$$

So, the required ratio is 14 : 11.

***Q.6** It is proposed to build a single circular park equal in area to the sum of areas of two circular parks of diameters 16 m and 12 m in a locality. The radius of the new park would be

(a) 10 m (b) 15 m (c) 20 m (d) 24 m

Ans. *(a)* Area of first circular park, whose diameter is 16 m

$$= \pi r^2 = \pi \left(\frac{16}{2}\right)^2 = (8)^2 \pi = 64\pi \text{ m}^2 \qquad \left[\because r = \frac{d}{2} = \frac{16}{2} = 8 \text{ m}\right]$$

Area of second circular park, whose diameter is 12 m

$$= \pi \left(\frac{12}{2}\right)^2 = \pi (6)^2 = 36\pi \text{ m}^2 \qquad \left[\because r = \frac{d}{2} = \frac{12}{2} = 6 \text{ m}\right]$$

According to the given condition,

Area of single circular park = Area of first circular park + Area of second circular park

$\pi R^2 = 64\pi + 36\pi$ [$\because R$ be the radius of single circular park]

$\Rightarrow \quad \pi R^2 = 100\pi \Rightarrow R^2 = 100$

$\therefore \quad R = 10$ m

***Q.7** The area of the circle that can be inscribed in a square of side 6 cm is

(a) 36π cm^2 (b) 18π cm^2 (c) 12π cm^2 (d) 9π cm^2

Thinking process If a circle is inscribed in a square, then the diameter of the circle is equal to the side of the square.

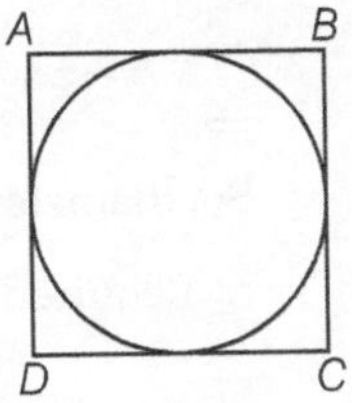

Ans. *(d)* Given, side of square = 6 cm

$\therefore$ Diameter of a circle, (d) = Side of square = 6 cm

$\therefore \quad$ Radius of a circle $(r) = \dfrac{d}{2} = \dfrac{6}{2} = 3$ cm

$\therefore \quad$ Area of circle $= \pi (r)^2$

$= \pi (3)^2 = 9\pi$ cm^2

***Q.8** The area of the square that can be inscribed in a circle of radius 8 cm is

(a) 256 cm^2 (b) 128 cm^2 (c) $64\sqrt{2}$ cm^2 (d) 64 cm^2

Ans. *(b)* Given, radius of circle, $r = OC = 8$ cm.

$\therefore$ Diameter of the circle $= AC = 2 \times OC = 2 \times 8 = 16$ cm

Note (*) *Topics related to these question have been removed from latest NCERT.*

which is equal to the diagonal of a square.

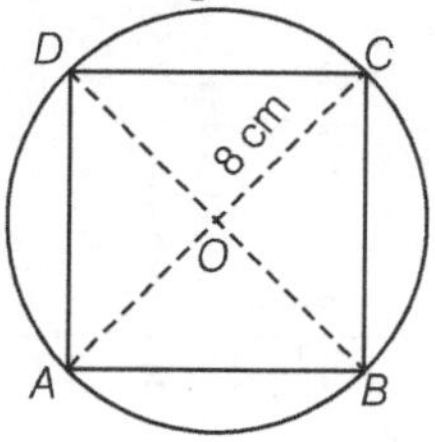

Let side of square be x.

In right angled ΔABC, $AC^2 = AB^2 + BC^2$ [by Pythagoras theorem]

$\Rightarrow$ $(16)^2 = x^2 + x^2$

$\Rightarrow$ $256 = 2x^2$

$\Rightarrow$ $x^2 = 128$

$\therefore$ Area of square $= x^2 = 128 \text{ cm}^2$

Alternate Method

Radius of circle $(r) = 8$ cm

Diameter of circle $(d) = 2r = 2 \times 8 = 16$ cm

Since, square inscribed in circle.

$\therefore$ Diagonal of the squre = Diameter of the circle

Now, area of the square $= \dfrac{(\text{Diagonal})^2}{2} = \dfrac{(16)^2}{2} = \dfrac{256}{2} = 128 \text{ cm}^2$

***Q.9** The radius of a circle whose circumference is equal to the sum of the circumferences of the two circles of diameters 36 cm and 20 cm is

(a) 56 cm (b) 42 cm (c) 28 cm (d) 16 cm

Ans. *(c)* $\because$ Circumference of first circle $= \pi d_1 = 36\pi$ cm [given, $d_1 = 36$ cm]

and circumference of second circle $= \pi d_2 = 20\pi$ cm [given, $d_2 = 20$ cm]

According to the given condition,

Circumference of circle = Circumference of first circle + Circumference of second circle

$\Rightarrow$ $\pi D = 36\pi + 20\pi$ [where, D is diameter of a circle]

$\Rightarrow$ $D = 56$ cm

So, diameter of a circle is 56 cm.

$\therefore$ Required radius of circle $= \dfrac{56}{2} = 28$ cm

Mistake Alert! *Students may assume that the radius of the circle is 56 cm instead of 28 cm.*

***Q.10** The diameter of a circle whose area is equal to the sum of the areas of the two circles of radii 24 cm and 7 cm is

(a) 31 cm (b) 25 cm

(c) 62 cm (d) 50 cm

Note (*) *Topics related to these question have been removed from latest NCERT.*

Ans. *(d)* Let $r_1 = 24$ cm and $r_2 = 7$ cm

$\therefore$ Area of first circle $= \pi r_1^2 = \pi (24)^2 = 576\pi \text{ cm}^2$

and area of second circle $= \pi r_2^2 = \pi (7)^2 = 49\pi \text{ cm}^2$

According to the given condition,

Area of circle = Area of first circle + Area of second circle

$\therefore \quad \pi R^2 = 576\pi + 49\pi$ [where, R be the radius of the circle]

$\Rightarrow \quad R^2 = 625 \Rightarrow R = 25$ cm

$\therefore$ Diameter of a circle $= 2R = 2 \times 25 = 50$ cm

Short Answer Questions with Reasoning

* **Q.1** Is the area of the circle inscribed in a square of side a cm, is $\pi a^2 \text{ cm}^2$? Give reasons for your answer.

Ans. *No*

Let $ABCD$ be a square of side a cm.

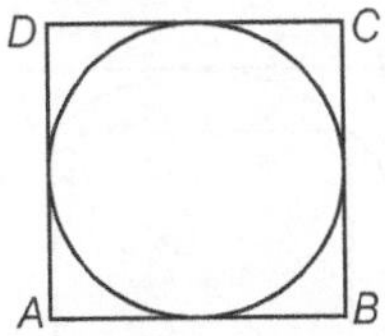

$\therefore$ Diameter of circle = Side of square = a

$\therefore$ Radius of circle $= \dfrac{a}{2}$

$\therefore$ Area of circle $= \pi \text{ (Radius)}^2 = \pi \left(\dfrac{a}{2}\right)^2 = \dfrac{\pi a^2}{4}$

Hence, area of the circle is $\dfrac{\pi a^2}{4} \text{ cm}^2$.

***Q.2** Will it be true to say that the perimeter of a square circumscribing a circle of radius a cm is $8a$ cm? Give reason for your answer.

Thinking process Firstly, find diameter of the circle, which is equal to the side of square. Then, find perimeter of the square using formula, perimeter = 4 × side

Ans. *Yes*

Given, radius of circle, $r = a$ cm

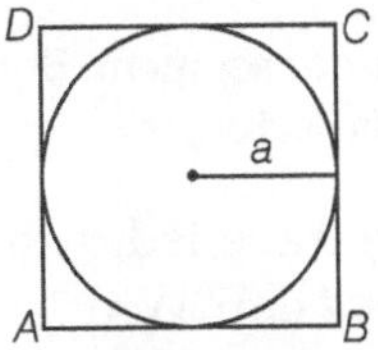

$\therefore$ Diameter of circle, $d = 2 \times \text{Radius} = 2a$ cm

$\therefore$ Side of a square = Diameter of circle $= 2a$ cm

$\therefore$ Perimeter of a square $= 4 \times \text{(Side)} = 4 \times 2a = 8a$ cm

Note (*) *Topics related to these question have been removed from latest NCERT.*

***Q.3** In figure, a square is inscribed in a circle of diameter d and another square is circumscribing the circle. Is the area of the outer square four times the area of the inner square? Give reason for your answer.

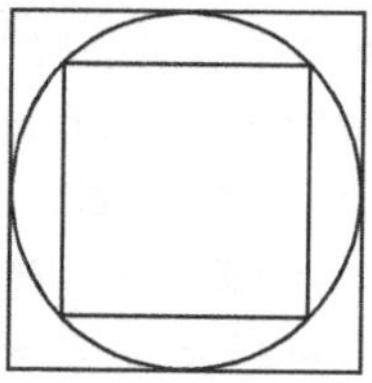

Ans. *No*

Given, diameter of circle is d.

$\therefore$ Diagonal of inner square $EFGH$ = Diameter of circle = d

Let side of inner square $EFGH$ be x.

$\therefore$ In right angled ΔEFG,

$$EG^2 = EF^2 + FG^2 \quad \text{[by Pythagoras theorem]}$$

$$\Rightarrow \quad d^2 = x^2 + x^2$$

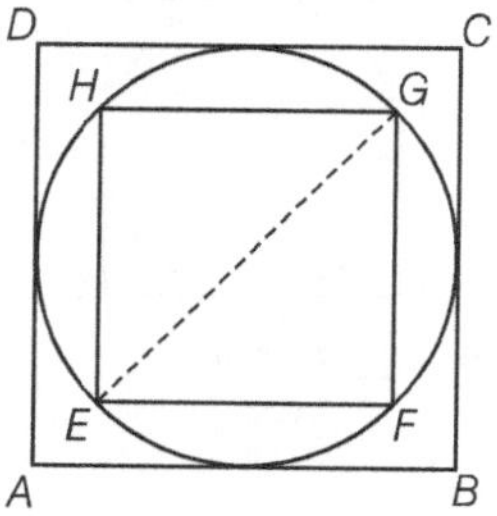

$$\Rightarrow \quad d^2 = 2x^2 \Rightarrow x^2 = \frac{d^2}{2}$$

$\therefore$ Area of inner square $EFGH = (\text{Side})^2 = x^2 = \dfrac{d^2}{2}$

But side of the outer square $ABCD$ = Diameter of circle = d

$\therefore$ Area of outer square $ABCD = d^2$

Hence, area of outer square is not equal to four times the area of the inner square.

Q.4 Is it true to say that area of segment of a circle is less than the area of its corresponding sector? Why?

Ans. *No*

It is true only in the case of minor segment. But in case of major segment area is always greater than the area of sector.

***Q.5** Is it true that the distance travelled by a circular wheel of diameter d cm in one revolution is $2\pi d$ cm? Why?

Ans. *No*, Because the distance travelled by the wheel in one revolution is equal to its circumference *i.e.*, πd.

$$\Rightarrow \quad \pi(2r) = 2\pi r = \text{Circumference of wheel} \quad [\because d = 2r]$$

Note (✱) *Topics related to these question have been removed from latest NCERT.*

***Q.6** In covering a distance s metres, a circular wheel of radius r metres makes $\frac{s}{2\pi r}$ revolution. Is this statement true? Why?

Ans. *Yes*

The distance covered in one revolution is $2\pi r$ *i.e.,* its circumference.

$\therefore$ Number of revolutions made in covering a distance of s metres $= \frac{s}{2\pi r}$

***Q.7** The numerical value of the area of a circle is greater than the numerical value of its circumference. Is this statement true? Why?

Ans. *No*

If $0 < r < 2$, then numerical value of circumference is greater than numerical value of area of circle and if $r > 2$, numerical value of area is greater than circumference.

Q.8 If the length of an arc of a circle of radius r is equal to that of an arc of a circle of radius $2r$, then the angle of the corresponding sector of the first circle is double the angle of the corresponding sector of the other circle. Is this statement false? Why?

Ans. *No*

Let two circles C_1 and C_2 of radius r and $2r$ with centres O and O', respectively.

It is given that the arc length $\widehat{AB}$ of C_1 is equal to arc length $\widehat{CD}$ of C_2 *i.e.,* $\widehat{AB} = \widehat{CD} = l$ (say)

Now, let θ_1 be the angle subtended by arc $\widehat{AB}$ and θ_2 be the angle subtended by arc $\widehat{CD}$ at the centre.

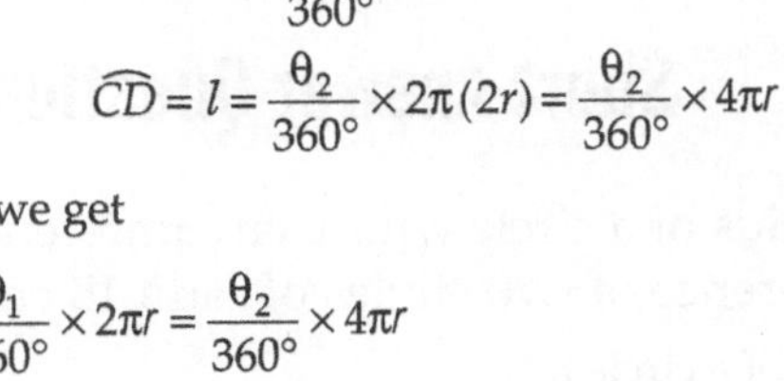

$\therefore$ $$3\widehat{AB} = l = \frac{\theta_1}{360^\circ} \times 2\pi r \quad \ldots(i)$$

and $$\widehat{CD} = l = \frac{\theta_2}{360^\circ} \times 2\pi(2r) = \frac{\theta_2}{360^\circ} \times 4\pi r \quad \ldots(ii)$$

From Eqs. (i) and (ii), we get

$$\frac{\theta_1}{360^\circ} \times 2\pi r = \frac{\theta_2}{360^\circ} \times 4\pi r$$

$\Rightarrow$ $$\theta_1 = 2\theta_2$$

i.e., angle of the corresponding sector of C_1 is double the angle of the corresponding sector of C_2. It is true statement.

Q.9 The areas of two sectors of two different circles with equal corresponding arc lengths are equal. Is this statement true? Why?

Ans. *No*

It is true for arcs of the same circle. But in different circle, it is not possible.

Note (*) *Topics related to these question have been removed from latest NCERT.*

Q.10 The areas of two sectors of two different circles are equal. Is it necessary that their corresponding arc lengths are equal? Why?

Ans. *No*

It is true for arcs of the same circle. But in different circle, it is not possible.

***Q.11** Is the area of the largest circle that can be drawn inside a rectangle of length a cm and breadth b cm $(a > b)$ is πb^2 cm? Why?

Ans. *No*

The area of the largest circle that can be drawn inside, a rectangle is $\pi \left(\frac{b}{2}\right)^2$ cm, where $\left(\frac{b}{2}\right)$ is the radius of the circle.

***Q.12** Circumference of two circles are equal. Is it necessary that their areas be equal? Why?

Ans. *Yes*

If circumference of two circles are equal, then their corresponding radii are equal. So, their areas will be equal.

***Q.13** Areas of two circles are equal. Is it necessary that their circumferences are equal? Why?

Ans. *Yes*

If areas of two circles are equal, then their corresponding radii are equal. So, their circumference will be equal.

***Q.14** Is it true to say that area of a square inscribed in a circle of diameter p cm is p^2 cm^2? Why?

Ans. *No*

When the square is inscribed in the circle, the diameter of a circle is equal to the diagonal of a square but not the side of the square.

Short Answer Questions

***Q.1** Find the radius of a circle whose circumference is equal to the sum of the circumference of two circles of radii 15 cm and 18 cm.

Ans. Let the radius of a circle be r.

$\therefore$ Circumference of a circle $= 2\pi r$

Let the radii of two circles are r_1 and r_2 whose values are 15 cm and 18 cm, respectively.

i.e., $r_1 = 15$ cm and $r_2 = 18$ cm

Now, by given condition,

Circumference of circle = Circumference of first circle + Circumference of second circle

Note (*) *Topics related to these question have been removed from latest NCERT.*

$$\Rightarrow \quad 2\pi r = 2\pi r_1 + 2\pi r_2$$

$$\Rightarrow \quad r = r_1 + r_2 \Rightarrow r = 15 + 18$$

$$\therefore \quad r = 33 \text{ cm}$$

Hence, required radius of a circle is 33 cm.

***Q.2** In figure, a square of diagonal 8 cm is inscribed in a circle. Find the area of the shaded region.

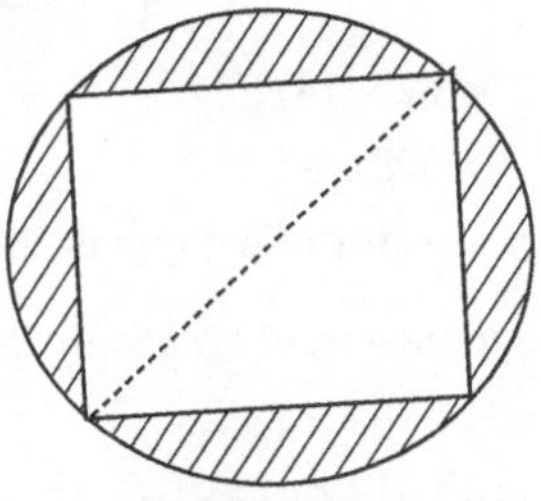

Ans. Let the side of a square be a and the radius of circle be r.

Given that length of diagonal of square = 8 cm

$$\Rightarrow \quad a\sqrt{2} = 8$$

$$\Rightarrow \quad a = 4\sqrt{2} \text{ cm}$$

Now, Diagonal of a square = Diameter of a circle

$$\Rightarrow \quad \text{Diameter of circle} = 8$$

$$\Rightarrow \quad \text{Radius of circle} = r = \frac{\text{Diameter}}{2}$$

$$\Rightarrow \quad r = \frac{8}{2} = 4 \text{ cm}$$

$$\therefore \quad \text{Area of circle} = \pi r^2 = \pi(4)^2 = 16\pi \text{ cm}^2$$

and $\quad \text{Area of square} = a^2 = (4\sqrt{2})^2 = 32 \text{ cm}^2$

So, the area of the shaded region = Area of circle – Area of square

$$= (16\pi - 32) \text{ cm}^2$$

Hence, the required area of the shaded region is $(16\pi - 32) \text{ cm}^2$.

Q.3 Find the area of a sector of a circle of radius 28 cm and central angle 45°.

Ans. Given that, radius of a circle, $r = 28$ cm

and measure of central angle, $\theta = 45°$

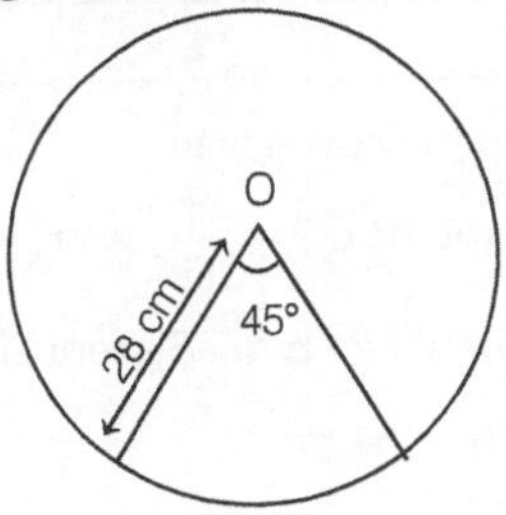

Note (*) *Topics related to these question have been removed from latest NCERT.*

$\therefore$ Area of a sector of a circle $= \dfrac{\pi r^2}{360°} \times \theta$

$$= \frac{22}{7} \times \frac{(28)^2}{360°} \times 45°$$
$$= \frac{22 \times 28 \times 28}{7} \times \frac{45°}{360°}$$
$$= 22 \times 4 \times 28 \times \frac{1}{8}$$
$$= 22 \times 14$$
$$= 308 \text{ cm}^2$$

Hence, the required area of a sector of a circle is 308 cm^2.

Mistake Alert ! *Students might mistakenly calculate the area of the whole circle instead of area of sector.*

***Q.4** The wheel of a motor cycle is of radius 35 cm. How many revolutions per minute must the wheel make, so as to keep a speed of 66 km/h?

Ans. Given, radius of wheel, $r = 35$ cm

Circumference of the wheel $= 2\pi r = 2 \times \dfrac{22}{7} \times 35 = 220$ cm

But speed of the wheel $= 66 \text{ kmh}^{-1} = \dfrac{66 \times 1000}{60}$ m / min

$$= 1100 \times 100 \text{ cm min}^{-1} = 110000 \text{ cm min}^{-1}$$

$\therefore$ Number of revolutions in 1 min $= \dfrac{110000}{220} = 500$

Hence, required number of revolutions per minute is 500.

Q.5 A cow is tied with a rope of length 14 m at the corner of a rectangular field of dimensions 20 m × 16 m. Find the area of the field in which the cow can graze.

Ans. Let $ABCD$ be a rectangular field of dimensions 20 m × 16 m. Suppose, a cow is tied at a point A. Let length of rope be $AE = 14 \text{ m} = r$ (say).

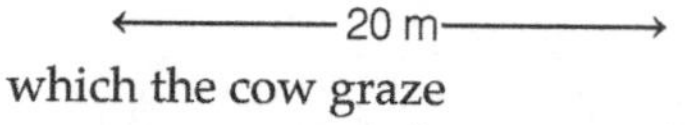

$\therefore$ Area of the field in which the cow graze

$$= \text{Area of sector } AFEG = \frac{\theta}{360°} \times \pi r^2 = \frac{90°}{360°} \times \pi (14)^2$$

[$\because$ the angle between two adjacent sides of a rectangle is $90° = \theta$ (say)]

$$= \frac{1}{4} \times \frac{22}{7} \times 196 = 154 \text{ m}^2$$

Note (*) *Topics related to these question have been removed from latest NCERT.*

***Q.6** Find the area of the flower bed (with semi-circular ends) shown in the figure.

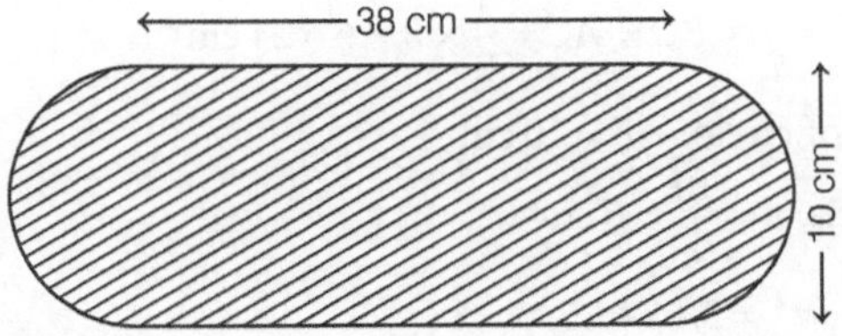

Ans. Area of the flower made = Area of rectangle + 2 × Area of semicircle

$\therefore$ Area of rectangle $ACDF$ = Length × Breadth = $38 \times 10 = 380\ \text{cm}^2$

[given, length = 38 cm and breadth = 10 cm]

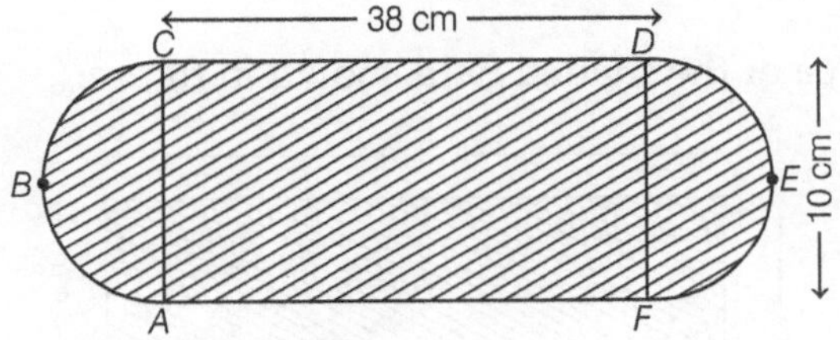

Both ends of flower bed are semi-circles.

$\therefore$ Radius of semi-circle $= \dfrac{DF}{2} = \dfrac{10}{2} = 5$ cm

$\therefore$ Area of one semi-circles $= \dfrac{\pi r^2}{2} = \dfrac{\pi}{2}(5)^2 = \dfrac{25\pi}{2}\ \text{cm}^2$

$\therefore$ Area of two semi-circles $= 2 \times \dfrac{25}{2}\pi = 25\pi\ \text{cm}^2$

$\therefore$ Total area of flower bed = Area of rectangle $ACDF$ + Area of two semi-circles

$= (380 + 25\pi)\ \text{cm}^2$

***Q.7** In figure, AB is a diameter of the circle, $AC = 6$ cm and $BC = 8$ cm. Find the area of the shaded region. (use $\pi = 3.14$)

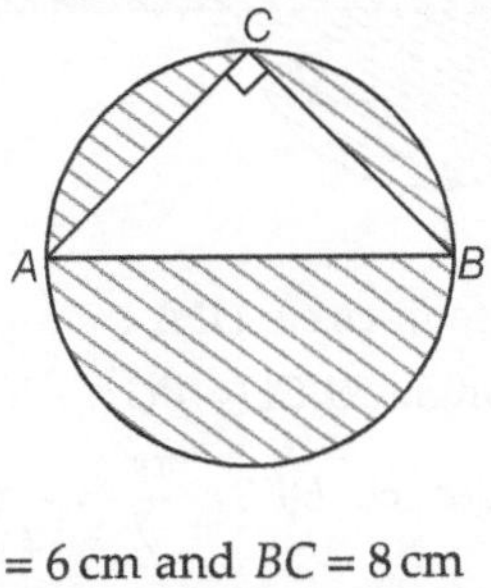

Ans. Given, $AC = 6$ cm and $BC = 8$ cm

We know that the angle at the circumfrence in a semi-circle is 90°.

$\therefore$ $\angle C = 90°$

In right angled ΔACB, by Pythagoras theorem,

$\therefore$ $AB^2 = AC^2 + CB^2$

$\Rightarrow$ $AB^2 = 6^2 + 8^2 = 36 + 64$

Note (*) *Topics related to these question have been removed from latest NCERT.*

$$\Rightarrow \qquad AB^2 = 100$$

$$\Rightarrow \qquad AB = 10 \text{ cm} \qquad [\because \text{ side cannot be negative}]$$

$\therefore$ Area of $\Delta ABC = \frac{1}{2} \times BC \times AC = \frac{1}{2} \times 8 \times 6 = 24 \text{ cm}^2$

Here, diameter of circle, $AB = 10$ cm

$\therefore$ Radius of circle, $r = \frac{10}{2} = 5$ cm

Area of circle $= \pi r^2 = 3.14 \times (5)^2$

$= 3.14 \times 25 = 78.5 \text{cm}^2$

$\therefore$ Area of the shaded region = Area of circle – Area of ΔABC

$= 78.5 - 24 = 54.5 \text{ cm}^2$

***Q.8** Find the area of the shaded field shown in figure.

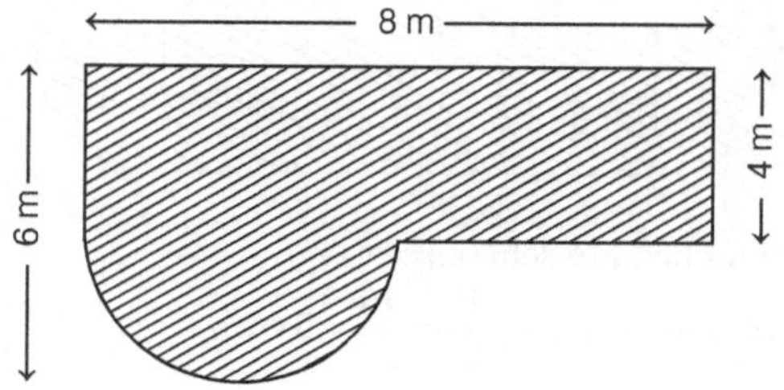

- **Concept Insight** In this question, we will use formula for area of rectangle as length × breadth and formula for area of semi-circle as $\frac{\pi(R)^2}{2}$.

Ans. In the given figure, join ED

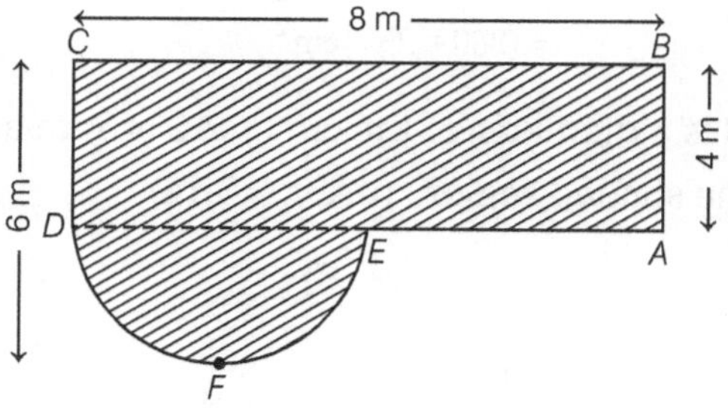

From the figure, radius of semi-circle DFE, $r = 6 - 4 = 2$ m

Now, area of rectangle $ABCD = BC \times AB = 8 \times 4 = 32 \text{ m}^2$

and area of semi-circle $DFE = \frac{\pi r^2}{2} = \frac{\pi}{2}(2)^2 = 2\pi \text{ m}^2$

$\therefore$ Area of shaded region = Area of rectangle $ABCD$ + Area of semi-circle DFE

$= (32 + 2\pi) \text{ m}^2$

Note (✱) *Topics related to these question have been removed from latest NCERT.*

***Q.9** Find the area of the shaded region in figure.

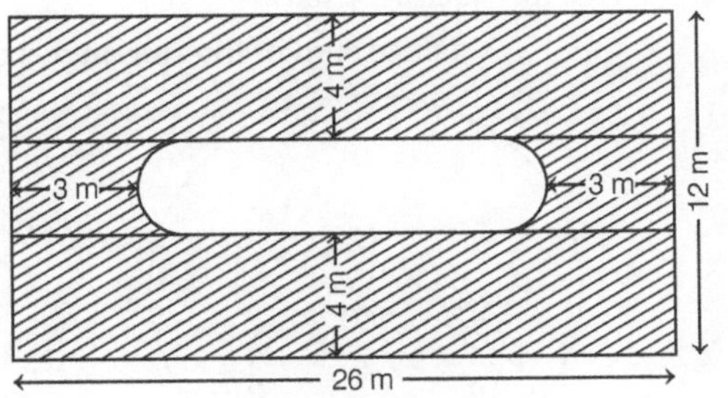

Ans. Join GH and FE.

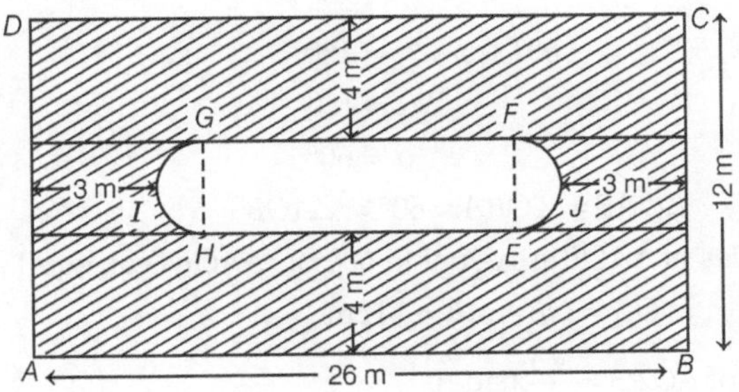

Here, breadth of the rectangle $BC = 12\text{ m}$

$\therefore$ Breadth of the inner rectangle $EFGH = 12 - (4 + 4) = 4\text{ m}$

which is equal to the diameter of the semi-circle EJF and GIH, $d = 4\text{ m}$

$\therefore$ Radius of semi-circle EJF and GIH, $r = 2\text{ m}$

$\therefore$ Length of inner rectangle $EFGH = 26 - (5 + 5) = 16\text{ m}$

$\therefore$ Area of two semi-circles EJF and $HIG = 2\left(\dfrac{\pi r^2}{2}\right) = 2 \times \pi \dfrac{(2)^2}{2} = 4\pi$ m.

Now, Area of inner rectangle $EFGH = EH \times FE = 16 \times 4 = 64\text{ m}^2$

and Area of outer rectangle $ABCD = 26 \times 12 = 312\text{ m}^2$

$\therefore$ Area of shaded region = Area of outer rectangle – (Area of two semi-circles + Area of inner rectangle)

$$= 312 - (64 + 4\pi) = (248 - 4\pi)\text{ m}^2$$

Q.10 Find the area of the minor segment of a circle of radius 14 cm, when the angle of the corresponding sector is 60°.

Ans. Given that, radius of circle $(r) = 14$ cm

and angle of the corresponding sector *i.e.*, central angle $(\theta) = 60°$

Since, in ΔAOB, $OA = OB$ = Radius of circle *i.e.*, ΔAOB is isosceles.

$\Rightarrow$ $\angle OAB = \angle OBA = \alpha$

Note (*) *Topics related to these question have been removed from latest NCERT.*

Now, in ΔOAB

$$\angle AOB + \angle OAB + \angle OBA = 180^\circ$$

[since sum of interior angles of any triangle is 180°]

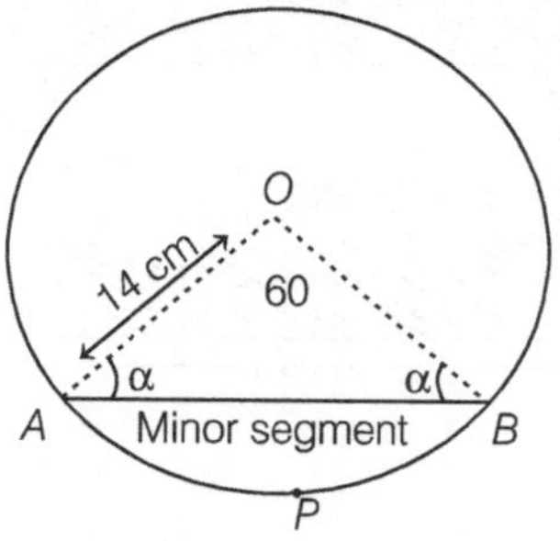

$\Rightarrow \quad 60^\circ + \alpha + \alpha = 180^\circ$ [given, $\angle AOB = 60^\circ$]

$\Rightarrow \quad 2\alpha = 120^\circ$

$\Rightarrow \quad \alpha = 60^\circ$

i.e., $\angle OAB = \angle OBA = 60^\circ = \angle AOB$

Since, all angles of ΔAOB are equal to 60° *i.e.*, ΔAOB is an equilateral triangle.

Also, $OA = OB = AB = 14\text{ cm}$

So, area of $\Delta OAB = \dfrac{\sqrt{3}}{4}(\text{side})^2$

$= \dfrac{\sqrt{3}}{4} \times (14)^2$ [$\because$ area of an equilateral triangle $= \dfrac{\sqrt{3}}{4}(\text{side})^2$]

$= \dfrac{\sqrt{3}}{4} \times 196 = 49\sqrt{3}\text{ cm}^2$

and area of sector $OBPA = \dfrac{\pi r^2}{360^\circ} \times \theta$

$= \dfrac{22}{7} \times \dfrac{14 \times 14}{360^\circ} \times 60^\circ$

$= \dfrac{22 \times 2 \times 14}{6}$

$= \dfrac{22 \times 14}{3} = \dfrac{308}{3}\text{ cm}^2$

$\therefore$ Area of minor segment = Area of sector $OBPA$ – Area of ΔOAB

$= \left(\dfrac{308}{3} - 49\sqrt{3}\right)\text{cm}^2$

Hence, the required area of the minor segment is $\left(\dfrac{308}{3} - 49\sqrt{3}\right)\text{cm}^2$.

Mistake Alert! *Students may forget to subtract the area of the triangle from the area of the sector to find the area of the minor segment.*

***Q.11** Find the area of the shaded region in figure, where arcs drawn with centres A, B, C and D intersect in pairs at mid-point P, Q, R and S of the sides AB, BC, CD and DA, respectively of a square $ABCD$. (use $\pi = 3.14$)

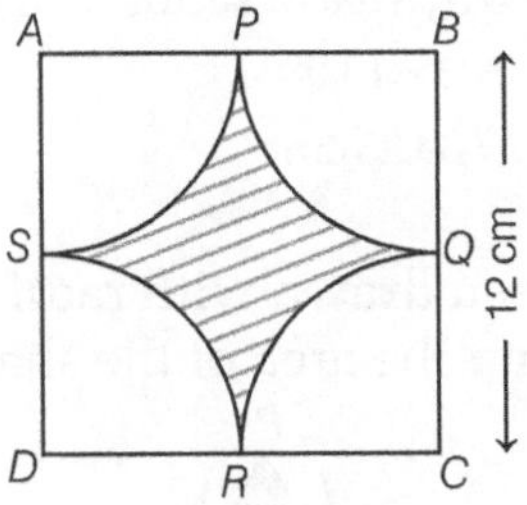

Ans. Given, side of a square $BC = 12$ cm

Since, Q is a mid-point of BC.

$\therefore$ $$\text{Radius} = BQ = \frac{12}{2} = 6 \text{ cm}$$

Now, $$\text{Area of quadrant } BPQ = \frac{\pi r^2}{4} = \frac{3.14 \times (6)^2}{4} = \frac{113.04}{4} \text{cm}^2$$

$$\text{Area of four quadrants} = \frac{4 \times 113.04}{4} = 113.04 \text{ cm}^2$$

Now, $$\text{Area of square } ABCD = (12)^2 = 144 \text{ cm}^2$$

$\therefore$ Area of the shaded region = Area of square – Area of four quadrants

$$= 144 - 113.04 = 30.96 \text{ cm}^2$$

Q.12 In figure, arcs are drawn by taking vertices A, B and C of an equilateral triangle of side 10 cm to intersect the sides BC, CA and AB at their, respective mid-points D, E and F. Find the area of the shaded region. (use $\pi = 3.14$)

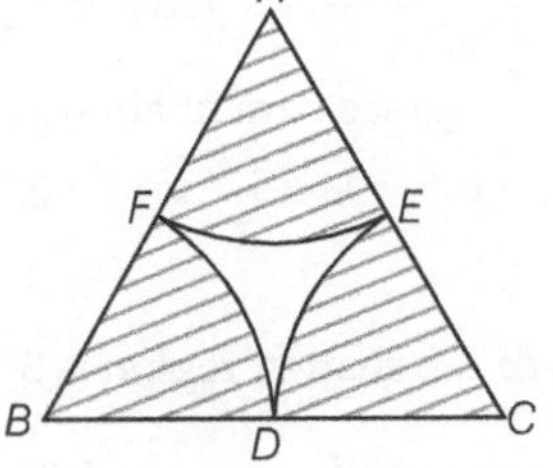

Ans. Since, ABC is an equilateral triangle.

$\therefore$ $$\angle A = \angle B = \angle C = 60° = \theta \quad \text{(say)}$$

and $$AB = BC = AC = 10 \text{ cm}$$

$\because$ E, F and D are mid-points of the sides.

$\therefore$ $$AE = EC = CD$$
$$= BD = BF = FA = 5 \text{ cm}$$

Note (*) *Topics related to these question have been removed from latest NCERT.*

Now, area of sector $CDE = \frac{\theta \pi r^2}{360°} = \frac{60° \times 3.14}{360°} (5)^2$

$= \frac{3.14 \times 25}{6} = \frac{78.5}{6} = 13.0833 \text{ cm}^2$

$\therefore$ Area of shaded region = 3 (Area of sector CDE)

$= 3 \times 13.0833$

$= 39.25 \text{ cm}^2$

Q.13 In figure, arcs have been drawn with radii 14 cm each and with centres P, Q and R. Find the area of the shaded region.

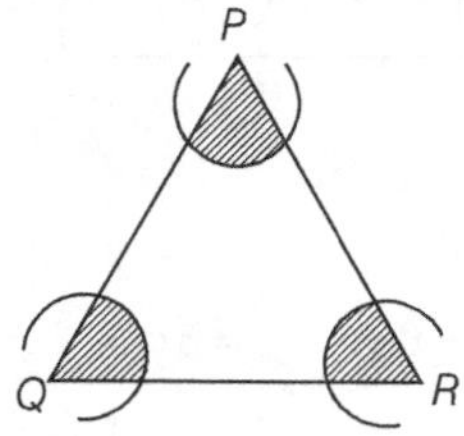

Ans. Given that radii of each arc $(r) = 14$ cm

Now, area of the sector with central angle $P = \frac{\angle P}{360°} \times \pi r^2 = \frac{\angle P}{360°} \times \pi \times (14)^2 \text{ cm}^2$

[$\because$ area of any sector with central angle θ and radius $r = \frac{\pi r^2}{360°} \times \theta$]

Area of the sector with central angle $Q = \frac{\angle Q}{360°} \times \pi r^2 = \frac{\angle Q}{360°} \times \pi \times (14)^2 \text{ cm}^2$

and area of the sector with central angle $R = \frac{\angle R}{360°} \times \pi r^2 = \frac{\angle R}{360°} \times \pi \times (14)^2 \text{ cm}^2$

Therefore, sum of the areas (in cm^2) of three sectors

$= \frac{\angle P}{360°} \times \pi \times (14)^2 + \frac{\angle Q}{360°} \times \pi \times (14)^2 + \frac{\angle R}{360°} \times \pi \times (14)^2$

$= \frac{(\angle P + \angle Q + \angle R)}{360°} \times 196 \times \pi = \frac{180°}{360°} \times 196\pi$

[since sum of all interior angles in any triangle is 180°]

$= 98\, \pi \text{ cm}^2 = 98 \times \frac{22}{7} = 14 \times 22 = 308 \text{ cm}^2$

Hence, the required area of the shaded region is 308 cm^2.

***Q.14** A circular park is surrounded by a road 21 m wide. If the radius of the park is 105 m, find the area of the road.

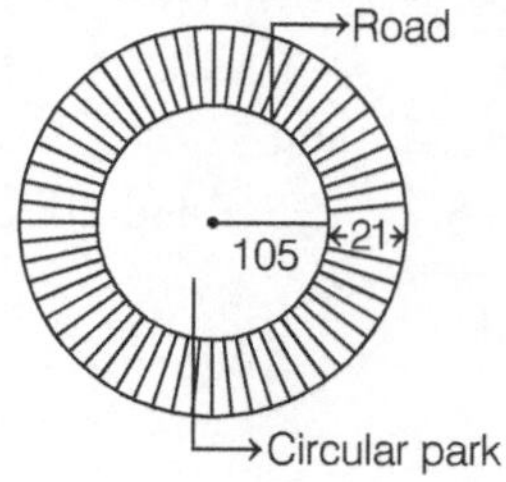

Ans. Given that, a circular park is surrounded by a road.

Width of the road = 21 m

Radius of the park $(r_i) = 105$ m

$\therefore$ Radius of whole circular portion (park + road),

$r_e = 105 + 21 = 126$ m

Note (✱) *Topics related to these question have been removed from latest NCERT.*

Now, area of road = Area of whole circular portion – Area of circular park

$= \pi r_e^2 - \pi r_i^2$ [∵ area of circle $= \pi r^2$]

$= \pi(r_e^2 - r_i^2)$

$= \pi(126^2 - 105^2)$

$= \frac{22}{7} \times (126 + 105)(126 - 105)$ [∵ $(a^2 - b^2) = (a - b)(a + b)$]

$= \frac{22}{7} \times 231 \times 21$

$= 66 \times 231$

$= 15246\ m^2$

Hence, the area of the road is 15246 m^2.

Q.15 In figure, arcs have been drawn of radius 21 cm each with vertices *A, B, C* and *D* of quadrilateral *ABCD* as centres. Find the area of the shaded region.

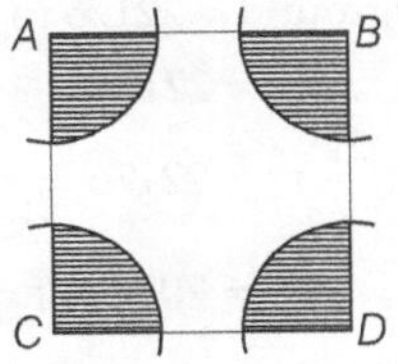

Ans. Given that, radius of each arc $(r) = 21\ cm$

Area of sector with $\angle A = \frac{\angle A}{360°} \times \pi r^2 = \frac{\angle A}{360°} \times \pi \times (21)^2\ cm^2$

[∵ area of any sector with central angle θ and radius $r = \frac{\pi r^2}{360°} \times \theta$]

Area of sector with $\angle B = \frac{\angle B}{360°} \times \pi r^2 = \frac{\angle B}{360°} \times \pi \times (21)^2\ cm^2$

Area of sector with $\angle C = \frac{\angle C}{360°} \times \pi r^2 = \frac{\angle C}{360°} \times \pi \times (21)^2\ cm^2$

and area of sector with $\angle D = \frac{\angle D}{360°} \times \pi r^2 = \frac{\angle D}{360°} \times \pi \times (21)^2 cm^2$

Therefore, sum of the areas (in cm^2) of the four sectors

$= \frac{\angle A}{360°} \times \pi \times (21)^2 + \frac{\angle B}{360°} \times \pi \times (21)^2 + \frac{\angle C}{360°} \times \pi \times (21)^2 + \frac{\angle D}{360°} \times \pi \times (21)^2$

$= \frac{(\angle A + \angle B + \angle C + \angle D)}{360°} \times \pi \times (21)^2 = \frac{360°}{360°} \times \frac{22}{7} \times 21 \times 21$

[∵ sum of all interior angles in any quadrilateral = 360°]

$= 22 \times 3 \times 21 = 1386\ cm^2$

Hence, required area of the shaded region is 1386 cm^2.

Q.16 A piece of wire 20 cm long is bent into the from of an arc of a circle, subtending an angle of 60° at its centre. Find the radius of the circle.

Ans. Length of arc of circle = 20 cm

Here, central angle, $\theta = 60°$

$\therefore$ Length of arc $= \dfrac{\theta}{360°} \times 2\pi r$

$\Rightarrow$ $20 = \dfrac{60°}{360°} \times 2\pi r \Rightarrow \dfrac{20 \times 6}{2\pi} = r$

$\therefore$ $r = \dfrac{60}{\pi} = \dfrac{60}{\frac{22}{7}} = \dfrac{210}{11}$ cm

Hence, the radius of circle is $\dfrac{210}{11}$ cm.

Long Answer Questions

***Q.1** The area of a circular playground is 22176 m^2. Find the cost of fencing this ground at the rate of ₹ 50 per m.

Ans. Let r be the radius of the circle.

Given, area of a circular playground = 22176 m^2

$\therefore$ $\pi r^2 = 22176$ [$\because$ area of circle $= \pi r^2$]

$\Rightarrow$ $\dfrac{22}{7} r^2 = 22176 \Rightarrow r^2 = 1008 \times 7$

$\Rightarrow$ $r^2 = 7056 \Rightarrow r = 84$ m

$\therefore$ Circumference of the circular play ground $= 2\pi r = 2 \times \dfrac{22}{7} \times 84$

$= 44 \times 12 = 528$ m

$\therefore$ Cost of fencing this ground $= 528 \times 50 =$ ₹ 26400

***Q.2** The diameters of front and rear wheels of a tractor are 80 cm and 2m, respectively. Find the number of revolutions that rear wheel will make in covering a distance in which the front wheel makes 1400 revolutions.

Ans. Given, diameter of front wheels, $d_1 = 80$ cm

and diameter of rear wheels, $d_2 = 2$ m $= 200$ cm

$\therefore$ Radius of front wheel $(r_1) = \dfrac{80}{2} = 40$ cm

and radius of rear wheel $(r_2) = \dfrac{200}{2} = 100$ cm

$\therefore$ Circumference of the front wheel $= 2\pi r_1 = \dfrac{2 \times 22}{7} \times 40 = \dfrac{1760}{7}$

$\therefore$ Total distance covered by front wheel in 1400 revolutions

$= 1400 \times \dfrac{1760}{7} = 200 \times 1760 = 352000$ cm

Number of revolutions by rear wheel $= \dfrac{\text{Distance coverd}}{\text{Circumference}}$

$= \dfrac{352000}{2 \times \frac{22}{7} \times 100} = \dfrac{7 \times 3520}{2 \times 22} = \dfrac{24640}{44} = 560$

Note (*) *Topics related to these question have been removed from latest NCERT.*

Q.3 Sides of a triangular field are 15 m, 16m and 17m. With the three corners of the field a cow, a buffalo and a horse are tied separately with ropes of length 7m each to graze in the field.
Find the area of the field which cannot be grazed by the three animals.

Ans. Given that, a triangular field with the three corners of the field a cow, a buffalo and a horse are tied separately with ropes. So, each animal grazed the field in each corner of triangular field as a sectorial form.

Given, radius of each sector $(r) = 7\text{m}$

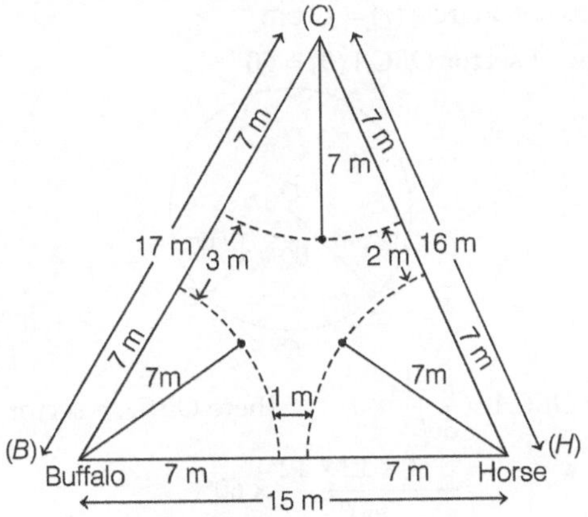

Now, area of sector with $\angle C = \dfrac{\angle C}{360°} \times \pi r^2 = \dfrac{\angle C}{360°} \times \pi \times (7)^2 \text{m}^2$

Area of the sector with $\angle B = \dfrac{\angle B}{360°} \times \pi r^2 = \dfrac{\angle B}{360°} \times \pi \times (7)^2 \text{m}^2$

and area of the sector with $\angle H = \dfrac{\angle H}{360°} \times \pi r^2 = \dfrac{\angle H}{360°} \times \pi \times (7)^2 \text{m}^2$

Therefore, sum of the areas (in cm^2) of the three sectors

$$= \frac{\angle C}{360°} \times \pi \times (7)^2 + \frac{\angle B}{360°} \times \pi \times (7)^2 + \frac{\angle H}{360°} \times \pi \times (7)^2$$

$$= \frac{(\angle C + \angle B + \angle H)}{360°} \times \pi \times 49.$$

$$= \frac{180°}{360°} \times \frac{22}{7} \times 49 = 11 \times 7 = 77 \text{ cm}^2$$

Given that, sides of triangle are $a = 15$, $b = 16$ and $c = 17$

Now, semi-perimeter of triangle, $s = \dfrac{a + b + c}{2}$

$$\Rightarrow \quad = \frac{15 + 16 + 17}{2} = \frac{48}{2} = 24 \text{ m}$$

$\therefore$ Area of triangular field $= \sqrt{s(s-a)(s-b)(s-c)}$ [by Heron's formula]

$$= \sqrt{24(24-15)(24-16)(24-17)}$$

$$= \sqrt{24 \cdot 9 \cdot 8 \cdot 7}$$

$$= \sqrt{64 \cdot 9 \cdot 21}$$

$$= 8 \times 3\sqrt{21} = 24\sqrt{21} \text{ m}^2$$

So, area of the field which cannot be grazed by the three animals

= Area of triangular field – Total area grazed by all three animals

$= (24\sqrt{21} - 77)\ m^2$

Hence, the required area of the field which can not be grazed by the three animals is $(24\sqrt{21} - 77) m^2$.

Q.4 Find the area of the segment of a circle of radius 12 cm whose corresponding sector has a central angle of 60°. (use $\pi = 3.14$)

Ans. Given that, radius of a circle $(r) = 12$ cm

and central angle of sector $OBCA\ (\theta) = 60^\circ$

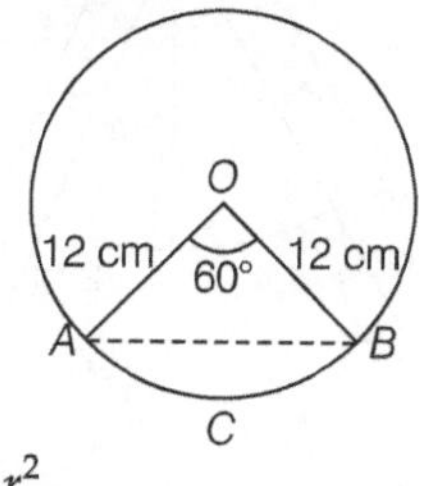

$\therefore$ Area of sector $OBCA = \dfrac{\pi r^2}{360^\circ} \times \theta$ [here $OBCA$ = sector and $ABCA$ = segment]

$= \dfrac{3.14 \times 12 \times 12}{360^\circ} \times 60^\circ$

$= 3.14 \times 2 \times 12$

$= 3.14 \times 24 = 75.36\ cm^2$

Since, ΔOAB is an isosceles triangle.

Let $\angle OAB = \angle OBA = \theta_1$

[angles opposite to equal sides are also equal]

and $\angle AOB = \theta = 60^\circ$

$\therefore \quad \angle OAB + \angle OBA + \angle AOB = 180^\circ$

[$\because$ sum of all interior angles of a triangle is 180°]

$\Rightarrow \quad \theta_1 + \theta_1 + 60^\circ = 180^\circ$

$\Rightarrow \quad 2\theta_1 = 120^\circ$

$\Rightarrow \quad \theta_1 = 60^\circ$

$\therefore \quad \theta_1 = \theta = 60^\circ$

So, ΔAOB is an equilateral triangle.

Now, area of $\Delta AOB = \dfrac{\sqrt{3}}{4} (\text{side})^2 = \dfrac{\sqrt{3}}{4} (12)^2$

$= \dfrac{\sqrt{3}}{4} \times 12 \times 12 = 36\sqrt{3}\ cm^2$

Now, area of the segment of a circle

i.e., $ABCA$ = Area of sector $OBCA$ – Area of ΔAOB

$= (75.36 - 36\sqrt{3})\ cm^2$

Hence, the required area of segment of the circle is $(75.36 - 36\sqrt{3})\ cm^2$.

***Q.5** A circular pond is 17.5 m is of diameter. It is surrounded by a 2m wide path. Find the cost of constructing the path at the rate of ₹ 25 Per m^2?

Ans. Given that, a circular pond is surrounded by a wide path.

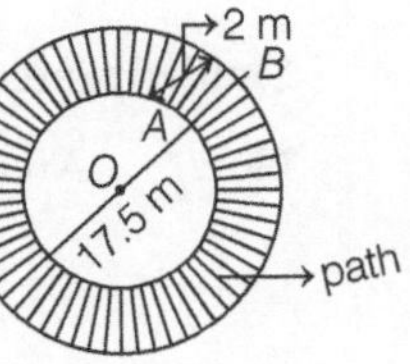

The diameter of circular pond = 17.5 m

$\therefore$ Radius of circular pond $(r_i) = \frac{\text{Diameter}}{2}$

i.e., $OA = r_i = \frac{17.5}{2} = 8.75\,\text{m}$

and the width of the path = 2 m

i.e., $AB = 2\,\text{m}$

Now, length of $OB(r_e) = OA + AB = r_i + AB = 8.75 + 2 = 10.75$ m

So, area of circular path = Area of outer circle *i.e.,* (circular pond + path) – Area of circular pond

$$= \pi r_e^2 - \pi r_i^2 \quad [\because \text{area of circle} = \pi r^2]$$
$$= \pi(r_e^2 - r_i^2)$$
$$= \pi\{(10.75)^2 - (8.75)^2\}$$
$$= \pi\{(10.75 + 8.75)(10.75 - 8.75)\}$$
$$= 3.14 \times 19.5 \times 2 = 122.46\,\text{m}^2$$

Now, cost of constructing the path per square metre = ₹ 25

$\therefore$ Cost constructing the path = $122.46 \times 25 =$ ₹ 3061 . 50

Hence, required cost of constructing the path at the rate of ₹ 25 per m^2 is ₹ 3061.50.

***Q.6** In figure, *ABCD* is a trapezium with $AB \parallel DC$. $AB = 18$ cm, $DC = 32$ cm and distance between *AB* and *DC* = 14 cm. If arcs of equal radii 7 cm with centres *A*, *B*, *C* and *D* have been drawn, then find the area of the shaded region of the figure.

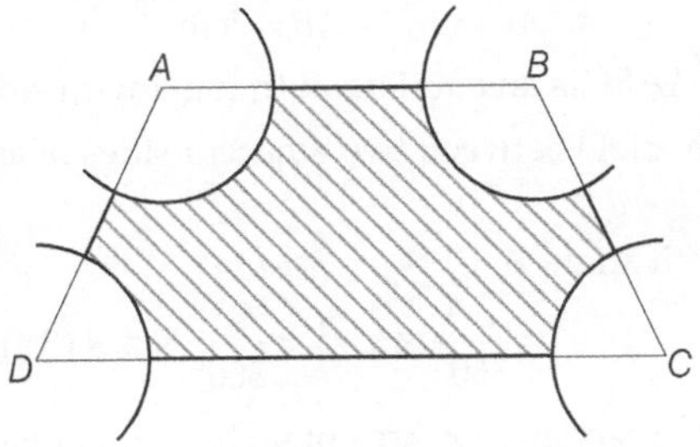

Ans. Given, $AB = 18$ cm, $DC = 32$ cm, height, $(h) = 14$ cm

and arc of radii = 7 cm

Since, $AB \parallel DC$

$\therefore$ $\angle A + \angle D = 180°$

and $\angle B + \angle C = 180°$

Note (*) *Topics related to these question have been removed from latest NCERT.*

$\therefore$ Area of sector with angle A and $D = \dfrac{\theta \times \pi r^2}{360°}$

$$= \frac{180°}{360°} \times \frac{22}{7} \times (7)^2$$

$$= 11 \times 7 = 77 \text{ cm}^2$$

Similarly, area of sector with angle B and $C = 77 \text{ cm}^2$

Now, Area of trapezium $= \dfrac{1}{2}(AB + DC) \times h$

$$= \frac{1}{2}(18 + 32) \times 14 = \frac{50}{2} \times 14 = 350 \text{ cm}^2$$

$\therefore$ Area of shaded region = Area of trapezium − (Area of sector points A and D + Area of sector points B and C)

$$= 350 - (77 + 77) = 196 \text{ cm}^2$$

Hence, the required area of shaded region is 196 cm^2.

*** Q.7** Three circles each of radius 3.5 cm are drawn in such a way that each of them touches the other two. Find the area enclosed between these circles.

Ans. Given that three circles are in such a way that each of them touches the other two.

Now, we join centre of all three circles to each other by a line segment. Since, radius of each circle is 3.5 cm.

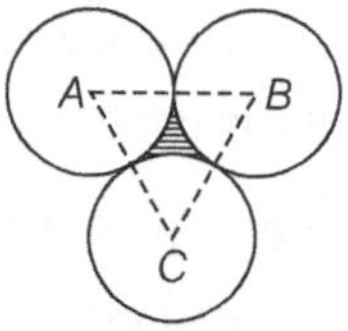

So; $AB = 2 \times \text{Radius of circle}$

$$= 2 \times 3.5 = 7 \text{ cm}$$

$\Rightarrow$ $AC = BC = AB = 7 \text{cm}$

which shows that, ΔABC is an equilateral triangle with side 7 cm.

We know that each angle between two adjacent sides of an equilateral triangle is 60°.

$\therefore$ Area of sector with angle A.

$$= \frac{\angle A}{360°} \times \pi r^2 = \frac{60°}{360°} \times \pi \times (3.5)^2 \qquad [\because \angle A = 60°]$$

So, total area of three sector = 3 × Area of sector with angle A.

$$= 3 \times \frac{60°}{360°} \times \pi \times (3.5)^2$$

$$= \frac{1}{2} \times \frac{22}{7} \times 3.5 \times 3.5$$

$$= 11 \times \frac{5}{10} \times \frac{35}{10} = \frac{11}{2} \times \frac{7}{2} = \frac{77}{4} = 19.25 \text{ cm}^2$$

Note (✱) *Topics related to these question have been removed from latest NCERT.*

and area of $\Delta ABC = \frac{\sqrt{3}}{4} \times (7)^2$ [$\because$ area of an equilateral triangle $= \frac{\sqrt{3}}{4}$ (side)^2]

$$= 49\frac{\sqrt{3}}{4} \text{ cm}^2$$

$\therefore$ Area of shaded region enclosed between these circles = Area of ΔABC − Total area of three sector

$$= 49\frac{\sqrt{3}}{4} - 19.25 = 12.25 \times \sqrt{3} - 19.25 = 21.2176 - 19.25 = 1.9676 \text{ cm}^2$$

Hence, the required area enclosed between these circles is 1.967 cm^2 (approx).

Q.8 Find the area of the sector of a circle of radius 5 cm, if the corresponding arc length is 3.5 cm.

Ans. Let the central angle of the sector be θ.

Given that, radius of the sector of a circle (r) = 5 cm

and arc length (l) = 3.5 cm

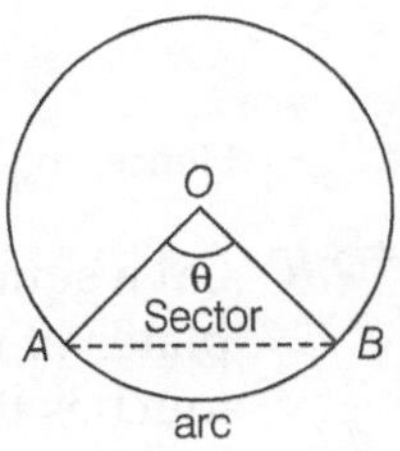

$\therefore$ Arc length $= \frac{\theta}{360^\circ} \times 2\pi r$

$$\Rightarrow \quad 3.5 = \frac{\theta}{360^\circ} \times 2 \times \frac{22}{7} \times 5$$

$$\Rightarrow \quad \theta = \frac{3.5 \times 360^\circ \times 7}{2 \times 22 \times 5} = \frac{35 \times 18^\circ \times 7}{10 \times 11} = \left(\frac{441}{11}\right)^\circ$$

Now, area of sector

$$= \frac{\pi r^2}{360^\circ} \times \theta = \frac{22}{7} \times \frac{(5)^2}{360^\circ} \times \left(\frac{441}{11}\right)^\circ = \frac{25 \times 7}{20} = \frac{175}{20} = 8.75 \text{ cm}^2$$

Hence, required area of the sector of a circle is 8.75 cm^2.

*** Q.9** Four circular cardboard pieces of radii 7 cm are placed on a paper in such a way that each piece touches other two pieces. Find the area of the portion enclosed between these pieces.

Ans. Given that, four circular cardboard pieces are placed on a paper in such a way that each piece touches other two pieces. Now, we join centre of all four circles to each other by a line segment. Since, radius of each circle is 7 cm.

So, $\quad AB = 2 \times \text{Radius of circle} = 2 \times 7 = 14$ cm

$\Rightarrow \quad AB = BC = CD = AD = 14$ cm

which shows that, quadrilateral $ABCD$ is a square with each of its side is 14 cm.

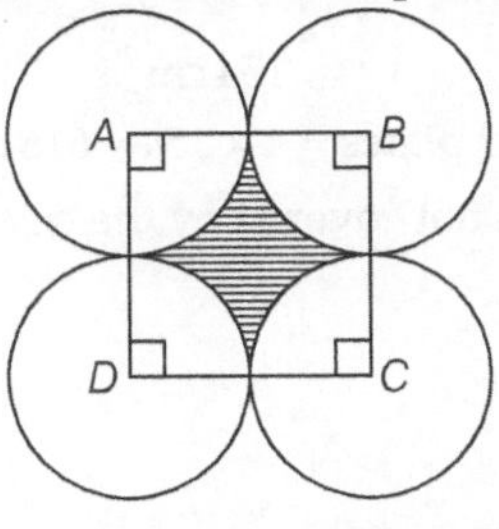

Note (*) *Topics related to these question have been removed from latest NCERT.*

We know that, each angle between two adjacent sides of a square is 90°.

$\therefore$ Area of sector with $\angle A$

$$= \frac{\angle A}{360°} \times \pi r^2 = \frac{90°}{360°} \times \pi \times (7)^2 \qquad [\because \angle A = 90°]$$

$$= \frac{1}{4} \times \frac{22}{7} \times 49 = \frac{154}{4} = \frac{77}{2}$$

$$= 38.5 \text{ cm}^2$$

$\therefore$ Area of all 4 sectors $= 4 \times$ Area of sector with $\angle A$

$$= 4 \times 38.5 = 154 \text{ cm}^2$$

and Area of square $ABCD =$ (side of square)^2

$$= (14)^2 = 196 \text{ cm}^2$$

So, area of shaded region enclosed between these pieces = Area of square $ABCD$ − Area of all 4 sector

$$= 196 - 154 = 42 \text{ cm}^2$$

Hence, required area of the portion enclosed between these pieces is 42 cm^2.

***Q.10** On a square cardboard sheet of area 784 cm^2, four congruent circular plates of maximum size are placed such that each circular plate touches the other two plates and each side of the square sheet is tangent to two circular plates. Find the area of the square sheet not covered by the circular plates.

Ans. $\because$ Area of square $= 784 \text{ cm}^2$

$\therefore$ $(\text{Side})^2 = (28)^2$

$\Rightarrow$ Side = 28 cm

Since, all four plates are congruent circular plates.

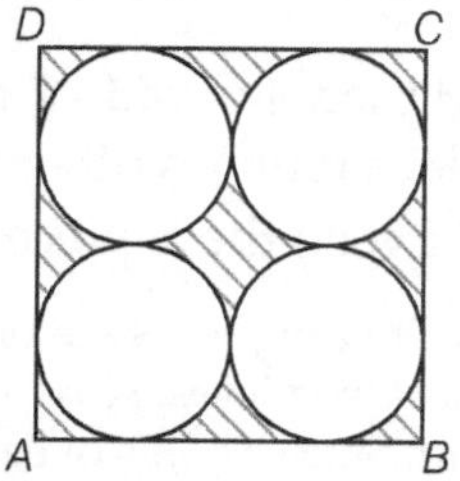

$\therefore$ Diameter of each circular plate = 14 cm

$\therefore$ Radius of each circular plate = 7 cm

Now, area of one circular plate $= \pi r^2 = \frac{22}{7}(7)^2$

$$= 154 \text{ cm}^2$$

$\therefore$ Area of four circular plates $= 4 \times 154 = 616 \text{ cm}^2$

$\therefore$ Area of the square sheet not covered by the circular plates $= 784 - 616 = 168 \text{ cm}^2$

Note (*) *Topics related to these question have been removed from latest NCERT.*

***Q.11** Floor of a room is of dimensions 5m × 4m and it is covered with circular tiles of diameters 50 cm each as shown in figure. Find area of floor that remains uncovered with tiles. (use $\pi = 3.14$)

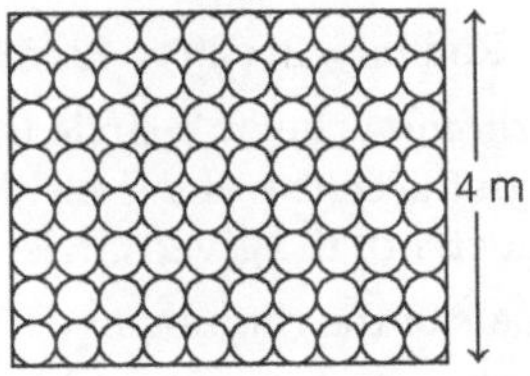

Ans. Given, floor of a room is covered with circular tiles.

Length of the floor of a room $(l) = 5$ m

and breadth of floor of a room $(b) = 4$ m

$\therefore$ Area of floor of a room $= l \times b$

$$= 5 \times 4 = 20 \text{ m}^2$$

Diameter of each circular tile = 50 cm

$\Rightarrow$ Radius of each circular tile $= \frac{50}{2} = 25$ cm [$\because$ diameter = 2 × radius]

$$= \frac{25}{100} \text{ m} = \frac{1}{4} \text{ m}$$

Now, area of a circular tile $= \pi$ (radius)^2

$$= 3.14 \times \left(\frac{1}{4}\right)^2 = \frac{3.14}{16} \text{ m}^2$$

$\therefore$ Area of 80 circular tiles $= 80 \times \frac{3.14}{16} = 5 \times 3.14 = 15.7 \text{ m}^2$

[$\because$ 80 congruent circular tiles covering the floor of a room]

So, area of floor that remains uncovered with tiles = Area of floor of a room – Area of 80 circular tiles

$$= 20 - 15.7 = 4.3 \text{ m}^2$$

Hence, the required area of floor that remains uncovered with tiles is 4.3 m^2.

***Q.12** All the vertices of a rhombus lie on a circle. Find the area of the rhombus, if area of the circle is 1256 cm^2. (use $\pi = 3.14$)

Ans. Let the radius of the circle be r.

Given that, area of the circle $= 1256 \text{ cm}^2$

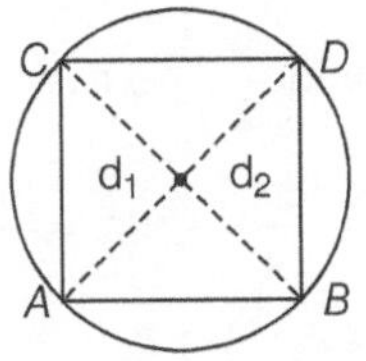

$\Rightarrow$ $\pi r^2 = 1256$

Note (*) *Topics related to these question have been removed from latest NCERT.*

$$\Rightarrow \quad r^2 = \frac{1256}{\pi} = \frac{1256}{3.14} = 400$$

$$\Rightarrow \quad r^2 = (20)^2$$

$$\Rightarrow \quad r = 20 \text{ cm}$$

$\therefore$So, the radius of circle is 20 cm.

$\Rightarrow$ Diameter of circle $= 2 \times \text{Radius} = 2 \times 20 = 40 \text{ cm}$

Since, all the vertices of a rhombus lie on a circle that means each diagonal of a rhombus must pass through the centre of a circle that is why both diagonals are equal and same as the diameter of the given circle.

Let d_1 and d_2 be the diagonals of the rhombus.

$\therefore \quad d_1 = d_2 = \text{Diameter of circle} = 40 \text{ cm}$

So, area of rhombus $= \frac{1}{2} \times d_1 \times d_2$

$$= \frac{1}{2} \times 40 \times 40 = 20 \times 40 = 800 \text{ cm}^2$$

Hence, the required area of rhombus is 800 cm^2.

***Q.13** An archery target has three regions formed by three concentric circles as shown in figure. If the diameters of the concentric circles are in the ratio 1 : 2 : 3, then find the ratio of the areas of three regions.

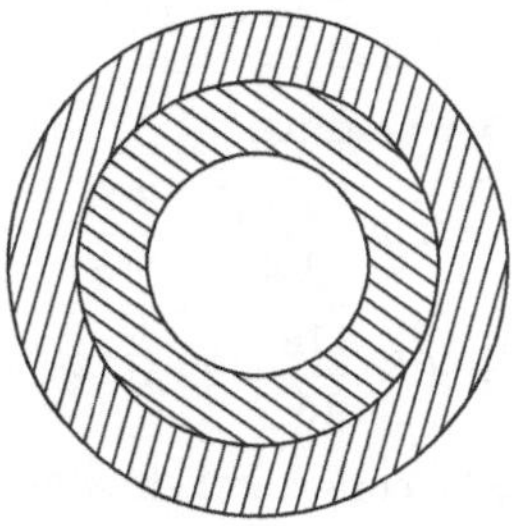

Ans. Let the diameters of concentric circles be k, $2k$ and $3k$.

$\therefore$Radius of concentric circles are $\frac{k}{2}$, k and $\frac{3k}{2}$.

$\therefore \quad$ Area of inner circle, $A_1 = \pi\left(\frac{k}{2}\right)^2 = \frac{k^2\pi}{4}$

$\therefore$ Area of middle region, $A_2 = \pi(k)^2 - \frac{k^2\pi}{4} = \frac{3k^2\pi}{4}$

[$\because$ area of ring $= \pi R^2 - \pi r^2$), where R is radius of outer ring and r is radius of inner ring]

and area of outer region, $A_3 = \pi\left(\frac{3k}{2}\right)^2 - \pi k^2$

$$= \frac{9\pi k^2}{4} - \pi k^2 = \frac{5\pi k^2}{4}$$

$\therefore \quad$ Required ratio $= A_1 : A_2 : A_3$

Note (*) *Topics related to these question have been removed from latest NCERT.*

Q.14 The length of the minute hand of a clock is 5 cm. Find the area swepts by the minute hand during the time period 6 : 05 am and 6 : 40 am.

Ans. We know that in 60 mins minute hand revolving = 360°

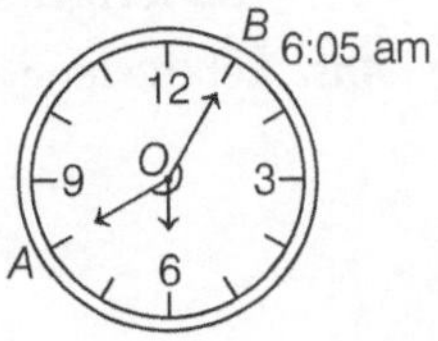

In 1 min, minute hand revolving $= \frac{360°}{60}$

$\therefore$ In (6:05 am to 6:40 am) = 35 minutes,

minute hand revolving $= \frac{360°}{60} \times 35 = 6° \times 35$

Given that, length of minute hand $(r) = 5\text{ cm}$.

$\therefore$ Area of sector $AOBA$ with angle $\angle O = \frac{\pi r^2}{360°} \times \angle O$

$$= \frac{22}{7} \times \frac{(5)^2}{360°} \times 6° \times 35$$

$$= \frac{22}{7} \times \frac{5 \times 5}{360°} \times 6° \times 35$$

$$= \frac{22 \times 5 \times 5 \times 5}{60°} = \frac{22 \times 5 \times 5}{12}$$

$$= \frac{11 \times 5 \times 5}{6} = \frac{275}{6} = 45\frac{5}{6}\text{ cm}^2$$

Hence, the required area swept by the minute hand is $45\frac{5}{6}\text{ cm}^2$.

Q.15 Area of a sector of central angle 200° of a circle is 770 cm^2. Find the length of the corresponding arc of this sector.

Ans. Let the radius of the sector $AOBA$ be r.

Given that, central angle of sector $AOBA = \theta = 200°$

and area of the sector $AOBA = 770\text{ cm}^2$

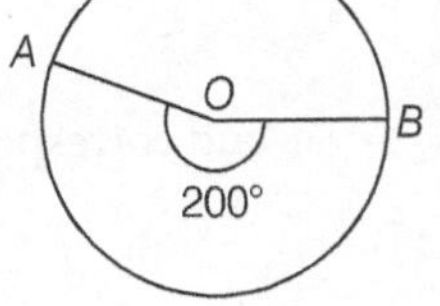

We know that area of the sector $= \frac{\pi r^2}{360°} \times \theta°$

$$\Rightarrow \quad 770 = \frac{\pi r^2}{360°} \times 200$$

$$\Rightarrow \quad \frac{77 \times 18}{\pi} = r^2$$

$$\Rightarrow \quad r^2 = \frac{77 \times 18}{22} \times 7 \Rightarrow r^2 = 9 \times 49$$

$$\Rightarrow \quad r = 3 \times 7$$

$$\therefore \quad r = 21\text{ cm}$$

So, radius of the sector $AOBA = 21\text{ cm}$.

Now, the length of the corresponding arc of this sector

$$= 2\pi r \times \frac{\theta}{360°} = 2 \times \frac{22}{7} \times 21 \times \frac{200°}{360°}$$

$$= \frac{2 \times 22 \times 5}{3} = \frac{220}{3} = 73\frac{1}{3}\text{ cm}$$

Hence, the required length of the corresponding arc is $73\frac{1}{3}$ cm.

Q.16 The central angles of two sectors of circles of radii 7 cm and 21 cm are respectively 120° and 40°. Find the areas of the two sectors as well as the lengths of the corresponding arcs. What do you observe?

Ans. Let the lengths of the corresponding arc be l_1 and l_2.

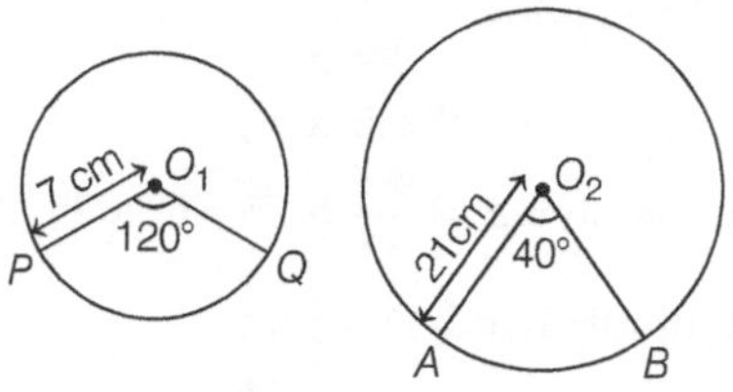

Given that, radius of sector $PO_1QP = 7$ cm

and radius of sector $AO_2BA = 21$ cm

Central angle of the sector $PO_1QP = 120°$

and central angle of the sector $AO_2BA = 40°$

$\therefore$ Area of the sector with central angle $\angle PO_1Q$

$$= \frac{\pi r^2}{360°} \times \theta = \frac{\pi (7)^2}{360°} \times 120°$$

$$= \frac{22}{7} \times \frac{7 \times 7}{360°} \times 120° = \frac{22 \times 7}{3} = \frac{154}{3} \text{cm}^2$$

and area of the sector with central angle $\angle AO_2B$

$$= \frac{\pi r^2}{360°} \times \theta = \frac{\pi (21)^2}{360°} \times 40° = \frac{22}{7} \times \frac{21 \times 21}{360°} \times 40°$$

$$= \frac{22 \times 3 \times 21}{9} = 22 \times 7 = 154 \text{ cm}^2$$

Now, corresponding arc length of the sector PO_1QP

$$= 2\pi r \times \frac{\theta}{360°} = 2 \times \frac{22}{7} \times 7 \times \frac{120°}{360°} = \frac{2 \times 22}{3} = \frac{44}{3} \text{ cm}$$

and corresponding arc length of the sector AO_2BA

$$= 2\pi r \times \frac{\theta}{360°} = \frac{2 \times 22}{7} \times 21 \times \frac{40°}{360°} = \frac{2 \times 22 \times 3}{9} = \frac{44}{3} \text{ cm}$$

Hence, we observe that arc lengths of two sectors of two different circles may be equal but their areas need not be equal.

***Q.17** Find the area of the shaded region given in figure.

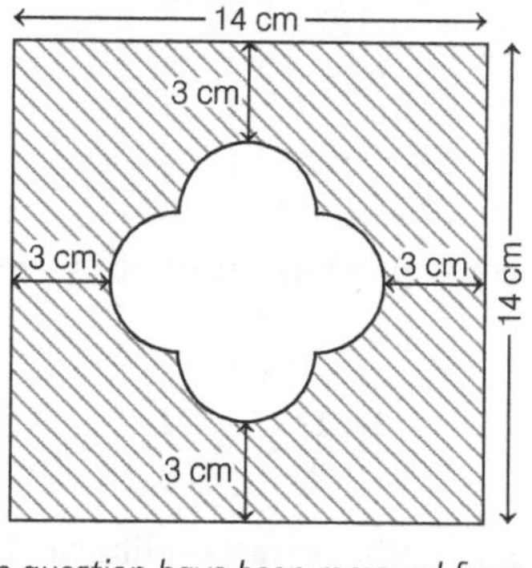

Note (*) *Topics related to these question have been removed from latest NCERT.*

Ans. Join *JK, KL, LM* and *MJ*.

Their are four equal semi-circles and *LMJK* formed a square.

$\therefore \quad FH = 14 - (3 + 3) = 8 \text{ cm}$

So, the side of inner square should be 4 cm and radius of semi-circles are 2 cm each.

$\therefore$ Area of square $JKLM = (4)^2 = 16 \text{ cm}^2$

Area of semi-circle $HJM = \frac{\pi r^2}{2} = \frac{\pi \times (2)^2}{2} = 2\pi \text{ cm}^2$

$\therefore$ Area of four semi-circle $= 4 \times 2\pi = 8\pi \text{ cm}^2$

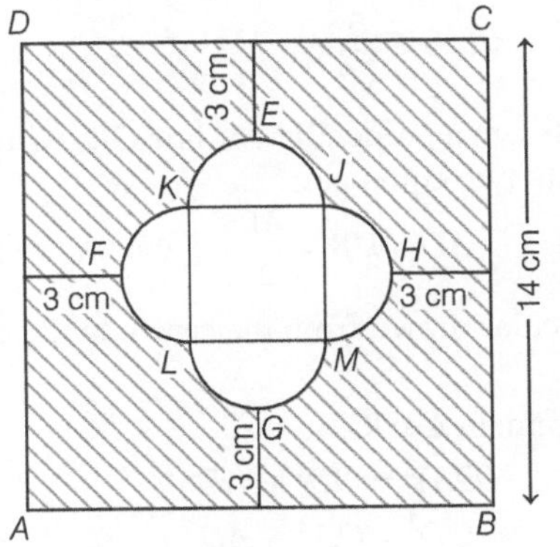

Now, area of square $ABCD = (14)^2 = 196 \text{ cm}^2$

$\therefore$ Area of shaded region = Area of square *ABCD*

– [Area of four semi-circle + Area of square *JKLM*]

$= 196 - [8\pi + 16] = 196 - 16 - 8\pi = (180 - 8p) \text{ cm}^2$

Hence, the required area of the shaded region is $(180 - 8\pi) \text{ cm}^2$.

***Q.18** Find the number of revolutions made by a circular wheel of area 1.54 m^2 in rolling a distance of 176 m.

Ans. Let the number of revolutions made by a circular wheel be n and the radius of circular wheel be r.

Given that, area of circular wheel = 1.54 m^2

$\Rightarrow \quad \pi r^2 = 1.54 \quad$ [$\because$ area of circular $= \pi r^2$]

$\Rightarrow \quad r^2 = \frac{1.54}{22} \times 7 \Rightarrow r^2 = 0.49 \therefore r = 0.7 \text{ m}$

So, the radius of the wheel is 0.7 m.

Distance travelled by a circlular wheel in one revolution = Circumference of circular wheel $= 2\pi r = 2 \times \frac{22}{7} \times 0.7 = \frac{22}{5} = 4.4 \text{ m}$ [$\because$ circumference of a circle $= 2\pi r$]

Since, distance travelled by a circular wheel = 176 m

$\therefore$ Number of revolutions $= \frac{\text{Total distance}}{\text{Distance in one revolution}} = \frac{176}{4.4} = 40$

Hence, the required number of revolutions made by a circular wheel is 40.

Note (*) *Topics related to these question have been removed from latest NCERT.*

Q.19 Find the difference of the areas of two segments of a circle formed by a chord of length 5 cm subtending an angle of 90° at the centre.

Ans. Let the radius of the circle be r.

$\therefore \quad OA = OB = r$ cm

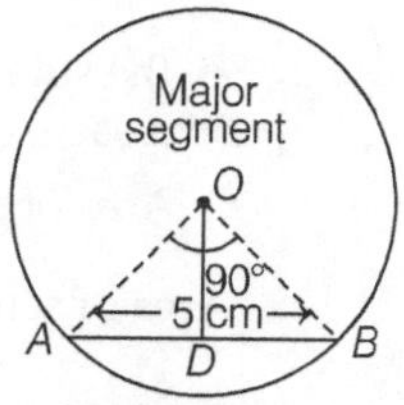

Given that, length of chord of a circle, $AB = 5$ cm

and central angle of the sector $AOBA$ $(\theta) = 90°$

Now, in ΔAOB $\quad (AB)^2 = (OA)^2 + (OB)^2$

[by Pythagoras theorem]

$$(5)^2 = r^2 + r^2 \Rightarrow 2r^2 = 25$$

$$\therefore \quad r = \frac{5}{\sqrt{2}} \text{ cm}$$

Now, in ΔAOB we drawn a perpendicular line OD, which meets at D on AB and divides chord AB into two equal parts.

So, $\quad AD = DB = \frac{AB}{2} = \frac{5}{2}$ cm

[since, the perpendicular drawn from the centre to the chord of a circle divides the chord into two equal parts]

By Pythagoras theorem, in ΔADO,

$$(OA)^2 = OD^2 + AD^2$$

$$\Rightarrow \quad OD^2 = OA^2 - AD^2$$

$$= \left(\frac{5}{\sqrt{2}}\right)^2 - \left(\frac{5}{2}\right)^2 = \frac{25}{2} - \frac{25}{4} = \frac{50-25}{4} = \frac{25}{4}$$

$$\Rightarrow \quad OD = \frac{5}{2} \text{cm}$$

$\therefore$ Area of an isosceles $\Delta AOB = \frac{1}{2} \times \text{Base} (= AB) \times \text{Height} (= OD)$

$$= \frac{1}{2} \times 5 \times \frac{5}{2} = \frac{25}{4} \text{ cm}^2$$

Now, area of sector $AOBA = \frac{\pi r^2}{360°} \times \theta = \frac{\pi \times \left(\frac{5}{\sqrt{2}}\right)^2}{360°} \times 90°$

$$= \frac{\pi \times 25}{2 \times 4} = \frac{25\pi}{8} \text{ cm}^2$$

$\therefore$ Area of minor segment = Area of sector $AOBA$ – Area of an isosceles ΔAOB

$$= \left(\frac{25\pi}{8} - \frac{25}{4}\right) \text{cm}^2 \quad \text{...(i)}$$

Now, area of the circle $= \pi r^2 = \pi \left(\frac{5}{\sqrt{2}}\right) = \frac{25\pi}{2}$ cm^2

$\therefore$ Area of major segment = Area of circle – Area of minor segment

$$= \frac{25\pi}{2} - \left(\frac{25\pi}{8} - \frac{25}{4}\right)$$

$$= \frac{25\pi}{8}(4-1) + \frac{25}{4} = \left(\frac{75\pi}{8} + \frac{25}{4}\right) \text{cm}^2 \quad \text{...(i)}$$

$\therefore$ Difference of the areas of two segments of a circle = | Area of major segment – Area of minor segment |

$$= \left|\left(\frac{75\pi}{8} + \frac{25}{4}\right) - \left(\frac{25\pi}{8} - \frac{25}{4}\right)\right|$$

$$= \left|\left(\frac{75\pi}{8} - \frac{25\pi}{8}\right) + \left(\frac{25}{4} + \frac{25}{4}\right)\right|$$

$$= \left|\frac{75\pi - 25\pi}{8} + \frac{50}{4}\right| = \left|\frac{50\pi}{8} + \frac{50}{4}\right|$$

$$= \left(\frac{25\pi}{4} + \frac{25}{2}\right)\text{cm}^2$$

Hence, the required difference of the areas of two segments is $\left(\frac{25\pi}{4} + \frac{25}{2}\right)\text{cm}^2$.

Q.20 Find the difference of the areas of a sector of angle 120° and its corresponding major sector of a circle of radius 21 cm.

Ans. Given that, radius of the circle $(r) = 21$ cm and central angle of the minor sector $AOBA$ $(\theta) = 120°$

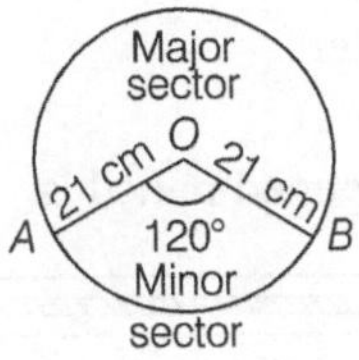

So, area of the circle $= \pi r^2 = \frac{22}{7} \times (21)^2 = \frac{22}{7} \times 21 \times 21$

$$= 22 \times 3 \times 21 = 1386\ \text{cm}^2$$

Now, area of the minor sector $AOBA$ with central angle 120°

$$= \frac{\pi r^2}{360°} \times \theta = \frac{22}{7} \times \frac{21 \times 21}{360°} \times 120°$$

$$= \frac{22 \times 3 \times 21}{3} = 22 \times 21 = 462\ \text{cm}^2$$

$\therefore$ Area of the major sector $ABOA$

= Area of the circle – Area of the minor sector $AOBA$

$= 1386 - 462 = 924\ \text{cm}^2$

$\therefore$ Difference of the areas of a minor sector $AOBA$ and its corresponding major sector $ABOA$

$= |$ Area of major sector $ABOA$ – Area of minor sector $AOBA |$

$= |924 - 462| = 462\ \text{cm}^2$

Hence, the required difference of two sectors is 462 cm^2.

Chapter 12

Surface Areas and Volumes

Multiple Choice Questions (MCQs)

Choose the correct answer from the given four options in the following questions:

Q.1 A cylindrical pencil sharpened at one edge is the combination of

(a) a cone and a cylinder
(b) frustum of a cone and a cylinder
(c) a hemisphere and a cylinder
(d) two cylinders

Ans. *(a)* Because the shape of sharpened pencil is

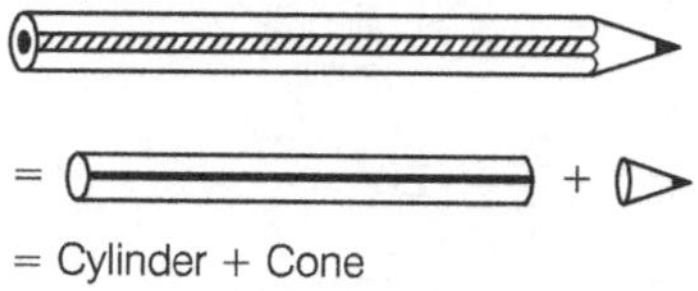

Q.2 A surahi is the combination of

(a) a sphere and a cylinder
(b) a hemisphere and a cylinder
(c) two hemispheres
(d) a cylinder and a cone

Ans. *(a)* Because the shape of surahi is

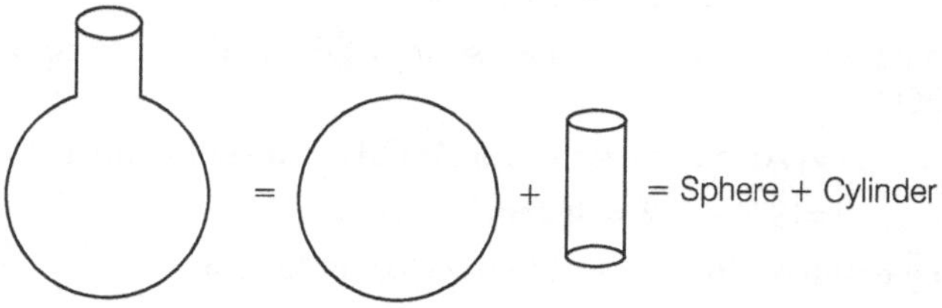

Q.3 A plumbline (sahul) is the combination of (see figure)

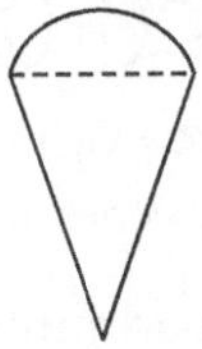

(a) a cone and a cylinder
(b) a hemisphere and a cone
(c) frustum of a cone and a cylinder
(d) sphere and cylinder

Ans. ***(b)***

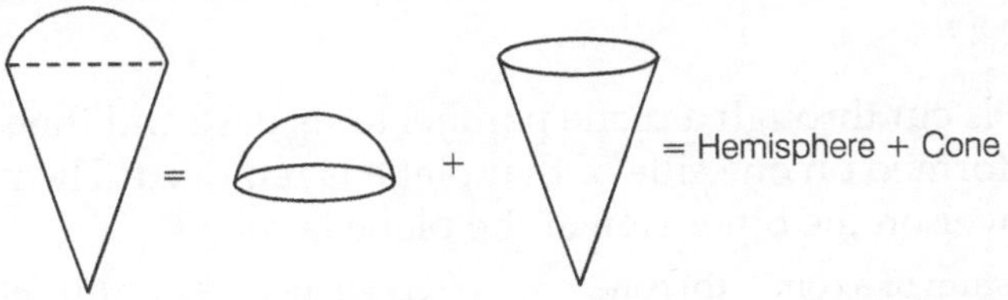

*** Q.4** The shape of a glass (tumbler) (see figure) is usually in the form of

(a) a cone
(b) frustum of a cone
(c) a cylinder
(d) a sphere

Ans. ***(b)*** We know that, the shape of frustum of a cone is

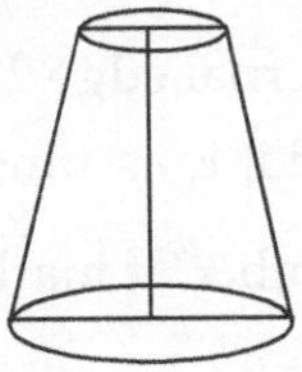

So, the given figure is usually in the form of frustum of a cone.

Q.5 The shape of a gilli, in the gilli-danda game (see figure) is a combination of

(a) two cylinders
(b) a cone and a cylinder
(c) two cones and a cylinder
(d) two cylinders and a cone

Note (*) *Topics related to these question have been removed from latest NCERT.*

Ans. *(c)*

= Cone + Cylinder + Cone

= Two cones and a cylinder

***Q.6** A shuttle cock used for playing badminton has the shape of the combination of

(a) a cylinder and a sphere (b) a cylinder and a hemisphere
(c) a sphere and a cone (d) frustum of a cone and a hemisphere

Ans. *(d)* Because the shape of the shuttle cock is equal to sum of frustum of a cone and hemisphere.

***Q.7** A cone is cut through a plane parallel to its base and then the cone that is formed on one side of that plane is removed. The new part that is left over on the other side of the plane is called

(a) a frustum of a cone (b) cone (c) cylinder (d) sphere

Ans. *(a)*

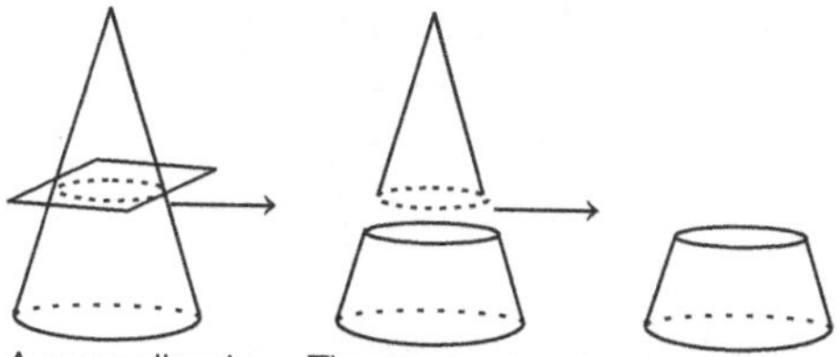

[when we remove the upper portion of the cone cut off by plane, we get frustum of a cone]

Q.8 If a hollow cube of internal edge 22 cm is filled with spherical marbles of diameter 0.5 cm and it is assumed that $\frac{1}{8}$ space of the cube remains unfilled. Then, the number of marbles that the cube can accomodate is

(a) 142296 (b) 142396 (c) 142496 (d) 142596

Thinking Process If we divide the total volume filled by marbles in a cube by volume of a marble, then we get the required number of marbles.

Ans. *(a)* Given, edge of the cube = 22 cm

$\therefore$ Volume of the cube $= (22)^3 = 10648 \text{ cm}^3$ [$\because$ volume of cube = (side)^3]

Also, given diameter of marble = 0.5 cm

$\therefore$ Radius of a marble, $r = \frac{0.5}{2} = 0.25$ cm [$\because$ diameter $= 2 \times$ radius]

Now, Volume of one marble $= \frac{4}{3}\pi r^3 = \frac{4}{3} \times \frac{22}{7} \times (0.25)^3$

[$\because$ volume of sphere $= \frac{4}{3} \times \pi \times (\text{radius})^3$]

Note (✱) *Topics related to these question have been removed from latest NCERT.*

$$= \frac{1.375}{21} \text{ cm}^3$$

$\Rightarrow$ Filled space of cube = Volume of the cube $- \frac{1}{8} \times$ Volume of cube

$$= 10648 - 10648 \times \frac{1}{8} = 10648\left(1 - \frac{1}{8}\right) = 10648 \times \frac{7}{8} = 9317 \text{ cm}^3$$

$\therefore$ Required number of marbles $= \dfrac{\text{Total space filled by marbles in a cube}}{\text{Volume of one marble}}$

$$= \frac{9317}{\frac{1.375}{21}} = 6776 \times 21 = 142296$$

Hence, the number of marbles that the cube can accomodate is 142296

Q.9 A metallic spherical shell of internal and external diameters 4 cm and 8 cm, respectively is melted and recast into the form a cone of base diameter 8 cm. The height of the cone is

(a) 12 cm (b) 14 cm

(c) 15 cm (d) 18 cm

Thinking Process When a solid shape is melted and recast into the form of other solid shape, then volume of both shapes are equal.

Ans. *(b)* Given, internal diameter of spherical shell = 4 cm

and external diameter of spherical shell = 8 cm

$\therefore$ Internal radius of spherical shell, $r_1 = \frac{4}{2}$ cm = 2 cm [$\because$ diameter = $2 \times$ radius]

and external radius of spherical shell, $r_2 = \frac{8}{2} = 4$ cm [$\because$ diameter = $2 \times$ radius]

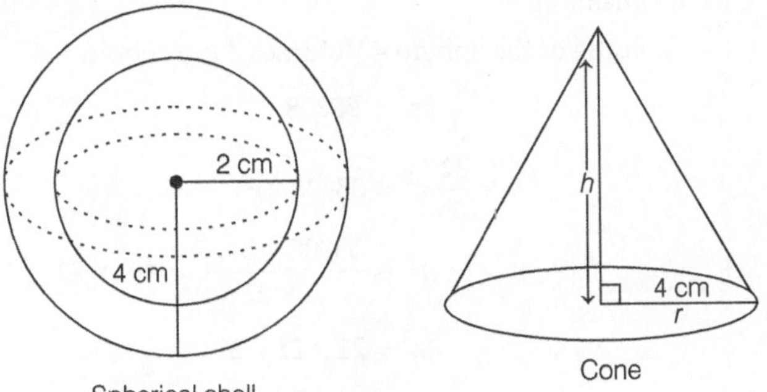

Spherical shell Cone

Now, volume of the spherical shell $= \frac{4}{3}\pi[r_2^3 - r_1^3]$

[$\because$ volume of the spherical shell $= \frac{4}{3}\pi$ {(external radius)^3 – (internal radius)^3}]

$$= \frac{4}{3}\pi(4^3 - 2^3) = \frac{4}{3}\pi(64 - 8)$$

$$= \frac{224}{3}\pi \text{ cm}^3$$

Let height of the cone = h cm

Diameter of the base of cone = 8 cm

$\therefore$ Radius of the base of cone $= \frac{8}{2} = 4$ cm [$\because$ diameter = $2 \times$ radius]

According to the question,

$$\text{Volume of cone} = \text{Volume of spherical shell}$$

$$\Rightarrow \quad \frac{1}{3}\pi(4)^2 h = \frac{224}{3}\pi$$

$$\Rightarrow \quad h = \frac{224}{16} = 14 \text{ cm}$$

[$\because$ volume of cone $= \frac{1}{3} \times \pi \times (\text{radius})^2 \times (\text{height})$]

Hence, the height of the cone is 14 cm.

Q.10 A solid piece of iron in the form of a cuboid of dimensions $49 \text{ cm} \times 33 \text{ cm} \times 24 \text{ cm}$, is moulded to form a solid sphere. Then, radius of the sphere is

(a) 21 cm (b) 23 cm

(c) 25 cm (d) 19 cm

Ans. *(a)* Given, dimensions of the cuboid = $49 \text{ cm} \times 33 \text{ cm} \times 24 \text{ cm}$

$\therefore$ Volume of the cuboid $= 49 \times 33 \times 24 = 38808 \text{ cm}^3$

[$\because$ volume of cuboid = length $\times$ breadth $\times$ height]

Let the radius of the sphere be r, then

Volume of the sphere $= \frac{4}{3}\pi r^3$ [$\because$ voulme of the sphere $= \frac{4}{3}\pi \times (\text{radius})^3$]

According to the question,

$$\text{Volume of the sphere} = \text{Volume of the cuboid}$$

$$\Rightarrow \quad \frac{4}{3}\pi r^3 = 38808$$

$$\Rightarrow \quad 4 \times \frac{22}{7} r^3 = 38808 \times 3$$

$$\Rightarrow \quad r^3 = \frac{38808 \times 3 \times 7}{4 \times 22} = 441 \times 21$$

$$\Rightarrow \quad r^3 = 21 \times 21 \times 21$$

$$\Rightarrow \quad r = 21 \text{ cm}$$

Hence, the radius of the sphere is 21 cm.

Q.11 A mason constructs a wall of dimensions $270 \text{ cm} \times 300 \text{ cm} \times 350 \text{ cm}$ with the bricks each of size $22.5 \text{ cm} \times 11.25 \text{ cm} \times 8.75 \text{ cm}$ and it is assumed that $\frac{1}{8}$ space is covered by the mortar. Then, the number of bricks used to construct the wall is

(a) 11100 (b) 11200

(c) 11000 (d) 11300

Ans. *(b)* Volume of the wall $= 270 \times 300 \times 350 = 28350000\ \text{cm}^3$

[$\because$ volume of cuboid=length $\times$ breadth $\times$ height]

Since, $\frac{1}{8}$ space of wall is covered by mortar.

So, remaining space of wall = Volume of wall – Volume of mortar

$$= 28350000 - 28350000 \times \frac{1}{8}$$

$$= 28350000 - 3543750$$

$$= 24806250\ \text{cm}^3$$

Now, volume of one brick $= (22.5 \times 11.25 \times 8.75)\ \text{cm}^3$

[$\because$ volume of cuboid=length $\times$ breadth $\times$ height]

$\therefore$ Required number of bricks $= \dfrac{24806250}{22.5 \times 11.25 \times 8.75} = 11200$

Hence, the number of bricks used to construct the wall is 11200.

Q.12 Twelve solid spheres of the same size are made by melting a solid metallic cylinder of base diameter 2 cm and height 16 cm. The diameter of each sphere is

(a) 4 cm (b) 3 cm

(c) 2 cm (d) 6 cm

Ans. *(c)* Given, diameter of the cylinder = 2 cm

$\therefore$ Radius = 1 cm and height of the cylinder = 16 cm [$\because$ diameter = 2 $\times$ radius]

$\therefore$ Volume of the cylinder $= \pi \times (1)^2 \times 16 = 16\pi\ \text{cm}^3$

[$\because$ volume of cylinder= $\pi \times (\text{radius})^2 \times$ height]

Now, let the radius of solid sphere $= r$ cm

Then, its volume $= \frac{4}{3}\pi r^3\ \text{cm}^3$ [$\because$ volume of sphere $= \frac{4}{3} \times \pi \times (\text{radius})^3$]

According to the question,

Volume of the twelve solid sphere = Volume of cylinder

$$\Rightarrow \quad 12 \times \frac{4}{3}\pi r^3 = 16\pi$$

$$\Rightarrow \quad r^3 = 1$$

$$\Rightarrow \quad r = 1\ \text{cm}$$

$\therefore$ Diameter of each sphere, $d = 2r = 2 \times 1 = 2$ cm

Hence, the required diameter of each sphere is 2 cm.

Mistake Alert! *Students may forget to find the diameter and assume that 1 cm will be the required answer.*

***Q.13** The radii of the top and bottom of a bucket of slant height 45 cm are 28 cm and 7 cm, respectively. The curved surface area of the bucket is

(a) 4950 cm^2 (b) 4951 cm^2

(c) 4952 cm^2 (d) 4953 cm^2

Note (*) *Topics related to these question have been removed from latest NCERT.*

Ans. *(a)* Given, the radius of the top of the bucket, $R = 28$ cm

and the radius of the bottom of the bucket, $r = 7$ cm

Slant height of the bucket, $l = 45$ cm

Since, bucket is in the form of frustum of a cone.

$\therefore$ Curved surface area of the bucket $= \pi\, l\,(R + r)$]

$= \pi \times 45\,(28 + 7)$

[$\because$ curved surface area of frustum of a cone $= \pi(R + r)l$]

$= \dfrac{22}{7} \times 45 \times 35 = 4950 \text{ cm}^2$

Q.14 A medicine-capsule is in the shape of a cylinder of diameter 0.5 cm with two hemispheres stuck to each of its ends. The length of entire capsule is 2 cm. The capacity of the capsule is

(a) 0.36 cm^3 (b) 0.35 cm^3

(c) 0.34 cm^3 (d) 0.33 cm^3

Ans. *(a)* Given, diameter of cylinder = Diameter of hemisphere = 0.5 cm

[since, both hemispheres are attach with cylinder]

$\therefore$ Radius of cylinder (r) = radius of hemisphere $(r) = \dfrac{0.5}{2} = 0.25$ cm

[$\because$ diameter $= 2 \times$ radius]

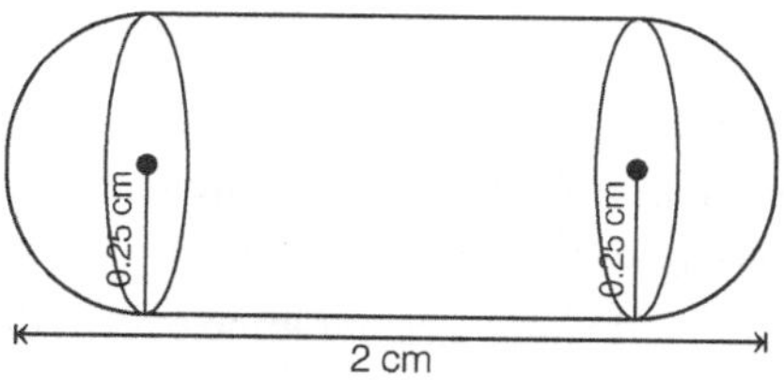

and total length of capsule = 2 cm

$\therefore$ Length of cylindrical part of capsule,

h = Length of capsule – Radius of both hemispheres

$= 2 - (0.25 + 0.25) = 1.5$ cm

Now, capacity of capsule = Volume of cylindrical part $+ 2 \times$ Volume of hemisphere

$= \pi r^2 h + 2 \times \dfrac{2}{3}\pi r^3$

[$\because$ volume of cylinder $= \pi \times (\text{radius})^2$

$\times$ height and volume of hemispere $= \dfrac{2}{3}\pi(\text{radius})^3$]

$= \dfrac{22}{7}\left[(0.25)^2 \times 1.5 + \dfrac{4}{3} \times (0.25)^3\right]$

$= \dfrac{22}{7}[0.09375 + 0.0208]$

$= \dfrac{22}{7} \times 0.11455 = 0.36 \text{ cm}^3$

Hence, the capacity of capsule is 0.36 cm^3.

Q.15 If two solid hemispheres of same base radius r are joined together along their bases, then curved surface area of this new solid is

(a) $4\pi r^2$ (b) $6\pi r^2$
(c) $3\pi r^2$ (d) $8\pi r^2$

Ans. *(a)* Because curved surface area of a hemisphere is $2\pi r^2$ and here, we join two solid hemispheres along their bases of radius r, from which we get a solid sphere.
Hence, the curved surface area of new solid $= 2\pi r^2 + 2\pi r^2 = 4\pi r^2$

Q.16 A right circular cylinder of radius r cm and height h cm (where, $h > 2r$) just encloses a sphere of diameter

(a) r cm (b) $2r$ cm (c) h cm (d) $2h$ cm

Ans. *(b)* Because the sphere encloses in the cylinder, therefore the diameter of sphere is equal to diameter of cylinder which is $2r$ cm.

Q.17 During conversion of a solid from one shape to another, the volume of the new shape will

(a) increase (b) decrease
(c) remain unaltered (d) be doubled

Ans. *(c)* During conversion of a solid from one shape to another, the volume of the new shape will remain unaltered.

***Q.18** The diameters of the two circular ends of the bucket are 44 cm and 24 cm. The height of the bucket is 35 cm. The capacity of the bucket is

(a) 32.7 litres (b) 33.7 litres (c) 34.7 litres (d) 31.7 litres

Ans. *(a)* Given, diameter of one end of the bucket,

$$2R = 44 \Rightarrow R = 22 \text{ cm} \qquad [\because \text{diameter} = 2 \times \text{radius}]$$

and diameter of the other end,

$$2r = 24 \Rightarrow r = 12 \text{ cm} \qquad [\because \text{diameter} = 2 \times \text{radius}]$$

Height of the bucket, $h = 35$ cm

Since, the shape of bucket is look like as frustum of a cone.

$\therefore$ Capacity of the bucket = Volume of the frustum of the cone

$$= \frac{1}{3}\pi h [R^2 + r^2 + Rr]$$

$$= \frac{1}{3} \times \pi \times 35 [(22)^2 + (12)^2 + 22 \times 12]$$

$$= \frac{35\pi}{3}[484 + 144 + 264] = \frac{35\pi \times 892}{3} = \frac{35 \times 22 \times 892}{3 \times 7}$$

$$= 32706.6 \text{ cm}^3 = 32.7 \text{ L} \qquad [\because 1000 \text{ cm}^3 = 1 \text{ L}]$$

Hence, the capacity of bucket is 32.7 L.

Mistake Alert! *Students may incorrectly apply the formula for volume of the frustum of the cone as* $\frac{1}{3}\pi h[R^2 + r^2 - Rr]$ *instead of* $\frac{1}{3}\pi h[R^2 + r^2 + Rr]$

Note (*) *Topics related to these question have been removed from latest NCERT.*

***Q.19** In a right circular cone, the cross-section made by a plane parallel to the base is a

(a) circle (b) frustum of a cone

(c) sphere (d) hemisphere

Ans. *(b)* We know that, if a cone is cut by a plane parallel to the base of the cone, then the portion between the plane and base is called the frustum of the cone.

Q.20 Volumes of two spheres are in the ratio 64 : 27. The ratio of their surface areas is

(a) 3 : 4 (b) 4 : 3

(c) 9 : 16 (d) 16 : 9

Ans. *(d)* Let the radii of the two spheres are r_1 and r_2, respectively.

$\therefore$ Volume of the sphere of radius, r_1 is $V_1 = \frac{4}{3}\pi r_1^3$ ...(i)

[$\because$ volume of sphere $= \frac{4}{3}\pi\,(\text{radius})^3$]

and volume of the sphere of radius, r_2 is $V_2 = \frac{4}{3}\pi\, r_2^3$ ...(ii)

Given, ratio of volumes $= V_1 : V_2 = 64 : 27 \Rightarrow \dfrac{\frac{4}{3}\pi r_1^3}{\frac{4}{3}\pi r_2^3} = \dfrac{64}{27}$ [using Eqs. (i) and (ii)]

$$\Rightarrow \quad \frac{r_1^3}{r_2^3} = \frac{64}{27} \Rightarrow \left(\frac{r_1}{r_2}\right)^3 = \left(\frac{4}{3}\right)^3 \Rightarrow \frac{r_1}{r_2} = \frac{4}{3} \quad \text{...(iii)}$$

Now, ratio of surface area $= \dfrac{4\pi r_1^2}{4\pi r_2^2}$ [$\because$ surface area of a sphere $= 4\pi\,(\text{radius})^2$]

$$= \frac{r_1^2}{r_2^2} = \left(\frac{r_1}{r_2}\right)^2 = \left(\frac{4}{3}\right)^2 \quad \text{[using Eq. (iii)]}$$

$= 16 : 9$

Hence, the required ratio of their surface area is 16 : 9.

Short Answer Questions with Reasoning

Write True or False and justify your answer in the following

Q.1 Two identical solid hemispheres of equal base radius r cm are stuck together along their bases. The total surface area of the combination is $6\pi r^2$.

Ans. *False*

Curved surface area of a hemisphere $= 2\pi r^2$

Here, two identical solid hemispheres of equal radius are stuck together. So, base of both hemispheres is common.

$\therefore$ Total surface area of the combination $= 2\pi r^2 + 2\pi r^2 = 4\pi r^2$

Note (✱) *Topics related to these questions have been removed from latest NCERT.*

Q.2 A solid cylinder of radius r and height h is placed over other cylinder of same height and radius. The total surface area of the shape, so formed is $4\pi rh + 4\pi r^2$.

Ans. *False*

Since, the total surface area of cylinder of radius, r and height, $h = 2\pi rh + 2\pi r^2$

height of the new cylinder $= 2h$ ($\because$ height and radius are same)

and radius of the new cylinder $= r$

$\therefore$ Total surface area of the new cylinder $= 2\pi r(2h) + 2\pi r^2 = 4\pi rh + 2\pi r^2$

Q.3 A solid cone of radius r and height h is placed over a solid cylinder having same base radius and height as that of a cone. The total surface area of the combined solid is $\pi r\left[\sqrt{r^2 + h^2} + 3r + 2h\right]$.

Ans. *False*

We know that, total surface area of a cone of radius, r and height, h = Curved surface Area + area of base $= \pi rl + \pi r^2$

where, $l = \sqrt{h^2 + r^2}$

and total surface area of a cylinder of base radius, r and height, h

= Curved surface area + Area of both base $= 2\pi rh + 2\pi r^2$

Here, when we placed a cone over a cylinder, then one base is common for both.

So, total surface area of the combined solid

$$= \pi rl + 2\pi rh + \pi r^2 = \pi r\,[l + 2h + r] = \pi r[\sqrt{r^2 + h^2} + 2h + r]$$

Q.4 A solid ball is exactly fitted inside the cubical box of side a. The volume of the ball is $\frac{4}{3}\pi a^3$.

Thinking process If a sphere is exactly or fitted inside a cube then the diameter of the sphere is equal to the side of the cube.

Ans. *False*

Because solid ball is exactly fitted inside the cubical box of side a. So, a is the diameter for the solid ball.

$\therefore$ Radius of the ball $= \frac{a}{2}$

So, volume of the ball $= \frac{4}{3}\pi\left(\frac{a}{2}\right)^3 = \frac{1}{6}\pi a^3$

***Q.5** The volume of the frustum of a cone is $\frac{1}{3}\pi h[r_1^2 + r_2^2 - r_1 r_2]$, where h is vertical height of the frustum and r_1, r_2 are the radii of the ends.

Ans. *False*

Since, the volume of the frustum of a cone is $\frac{1}{3}\pi\, h[r_1^2 + r_2^2 + r_1 r_2]$, where h is vertical height of the frustum and r_1, r_2 are the radii of the ends.

Note (*) *Topics related to these question have been removed from latest NCERT.*

Q.6 The capacity of a cylindrical vessel with a hemispherical portion raised upward at the bottom as shown in the figure is $\frac{\pi r^2}{3}[3h - 2r]$.

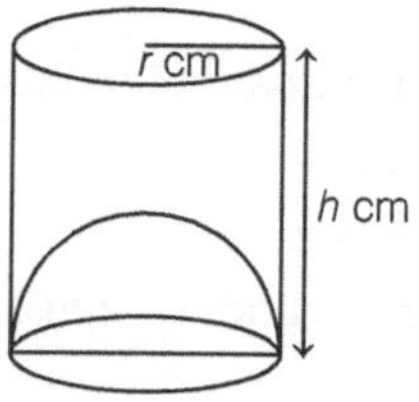

Ans. *True*

We know that, capacity of cylindrical vessel = $\pi r^2 h$

and capacity of hemisphere = $\frac{2}{3}\pi r^3$

From the figure, capacity of the cylindrical vessel = $\pi r^2 h - \frac{2}{3}\pi r^3 = \frac{1}{3}\pi r^2 (3h - 2r)$

***Q.7** The curved surface area of a frustum of a cone is $\pi l (r_1 + r_2)$, where $l = \sqrt{h^2 + (r_1 + r_2)^2}$, r_1 and r_2 are the radii of the two ends of the frustum and h is the vertical height.

Ans. *False*

We know that, if r_1 and r_2 are the radii of the two ends of the frustum and h is the vertical height, then curved surface area of a frustum is $\pi l(r_1 + r_2)$, where $l = \sqrt{h^2 + (r_1 - r_2)^2}$.

***Q.8** An open metallic bucket is in the shape of a frustum of a cone, mounted on a hollow cylindrical base made of the same metallic sheet. The surface area of the metallic sheet used is equal to curved surface area of frustum of a cone + area of circular base + curved surface area of cylinder.

Ans. *True*

Because the resulting figure is

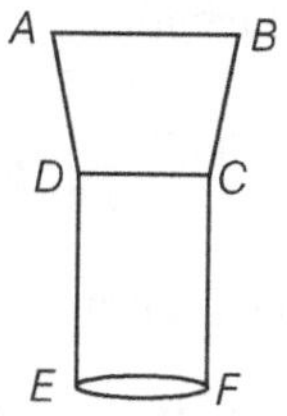

Here, *ABCD* is a frustum of a cone and *CDEF* is a hollow cylinder.

Note (*) *Topics related to these question have been removed from latest NCERT.*

Short Answer Questions

Q.1 Three metallic solid cubes whose edges are 3 cm, 4 cm and 5 cm are melted and formed into a single cube. Find the edge of the cube, so formed.

Ans. Given, edges of three solid cubes are 3 cm, 4 cm and 5 cm, respectively.

$\therefore$ Volume of first cube $= (3)^3 = 27 \text{ cm}^3$

Volume of second cube $= (4)^3 = 64 \text{ cm}^3$

and Volume of third cube $= (5)^3 = 125 \text{ cm}^3$

$\therefore$ Sum of volume of three cubes $= 27 + 64 + 125 = 216 \text{ cm}^3$

Let the edge of the resulting cube $= R$ cm

Then, volume of the resulting cube, $R^3 = 216 \Rightarrow R = 6$ cm

Q.2 How many shots each having diameter 3 cm can be made from a cuboidal lead solid of dimensions 9 cm × 11 cm × 12 cm?

Ans. Given, dimensions of cuboidal lead $= 9 \text{ cm} \times 11 \text{ cm} \times 12 \text{ cm}$

$\therefore$ Volume of cuboidal lead $= 9 \times 11 \times 12 = 1188 \text{ cm}^3$

and diameter of shot = 3 cm

$\therefore$ Radius of shot, $r = \frac{3}{2} = 1.5$ cm

Now, Volume of shot $= \frac{4}{3}\pi r^3$

$= \frac{4}{3} \times \frac{22}{7} \times (1.5)^3$

$= \frac{297}{21} \text{cm}^3$

$\therefore$ Required number of shots $= \dfrac{1188}{\frac{297}{21}} = 4 \times 21 = 84$

***Q.3** A bucket is in the form of a frustum of a cone and holds 28.490 litres of water. The radii of the top and bottom are 28 cm and 21 cm, respectively. Find the height of the bucket.

Ans. Given, volume of the frustum $= 28.490 \text{ L} = (28.490 \times 1000) \text{ cm}^3$ [$\because 1 \text{ L} = 1000 \text{ cm}^3$]

$= 28490 \text{ cm}^3$

and radius of the top $(r_1) = 28$ cm

radius of the bottom $(r_2) = 21$ cm

Let height of the bucket = h cm

Now, volume of the bucket $= \frac{1}{3}\pi h (r_1^2 + r_2^2 + r_1 r_2) = 28490$ [given]

$\Rightarrow \frac{1}{3} \times \frac{22}{7} \times h (28^2 + 21^2 + 28 \times 21) = 28490$

Note (*) *Topics related to these question have been removed from latest NCERT.*

$$\Rightarrow \quad h(784 + 441 + 588) = \frac{28490 \times 3 \times 7}{22}$$

$$\Rightarrow \quad 1813\,h = 1295 \times 21$$

$$\therefore \quad h = \frac{1295 \times 21}{1813} = \frac{27195}{1813} = 15 \text{ cm}$$

***Q.4** A cone of radius 8 cm and height 12 cm is divided into two parts by a plane through the mid-point of its axis parallel to its base. Find the ratio of the volumes of two parts.

Ans. Let *ORN* be the cone then, given radius of the base of the cone $r_1 = 8$ cm.

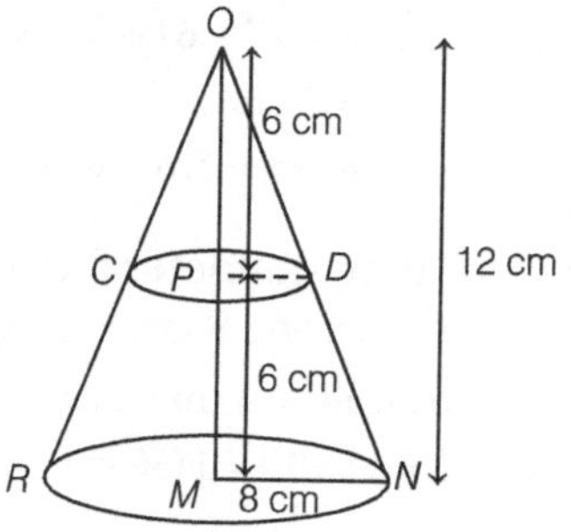

and height of the cone, (h) $OM = 12$ cm

Let P be the mid-point of OM, then

$$OP = PM = \frac{12}{2} = 6 \text{ cm}$$

Now, $\quad \Delta OPD \sim \Delta OMN$

$$\therefore \quad \frac{OP}{OM} = \frac{PD}{MN} \Rightarrow \frac{6}{12} = \frac{PD}{8}$$

$$\Rightarrow \quad \frac{1}{2} = \frac{PD}{8}$$

$$\Rightarrow \quad PD = 4 \text{ cm}$$

The plane along CD divides the cone into two parts, namely (i) a smaller cone of radius 4 cm and height 6cm and (ii) frustum of a cone for which

Radius of the top of the frustum, $r_1 = 4$ cm

Radius of the bottom, $r_2 = 8$ cm

and height of the frustum, $h = 6$ cm

$$\therefore \quad \text{Volume of smaller cone} = \left(\frac{1}{3}\pi \times 4 \times 4 \times 6\right) = 32\pi \text{ cm}^3$$

$$\text{and volume of the frustum of cone} = \frac{1}{3} \times \pi \times 6\,[(8)^2 + (4)^2 + 8 \times 4]$$

$$= 2\pi\,(64 + 16 + 32)$$

$$= 2\pi \times 112$$

$$= 224\,\pi \text{ cm}^3$$

$\therefore$ Required ratio = Volume of cone : Volume of frustum = $224\pi : 32\pi = 1:7$

Note (✱) *Topics related to these question have been removed from latest NCERT.*

Q.5 Two identical cubes each of volume 64 cm^3 are joined together end to end. What is the surface area of the resulting cuboid?

Ans. Let the length of a side of a cube = a cm

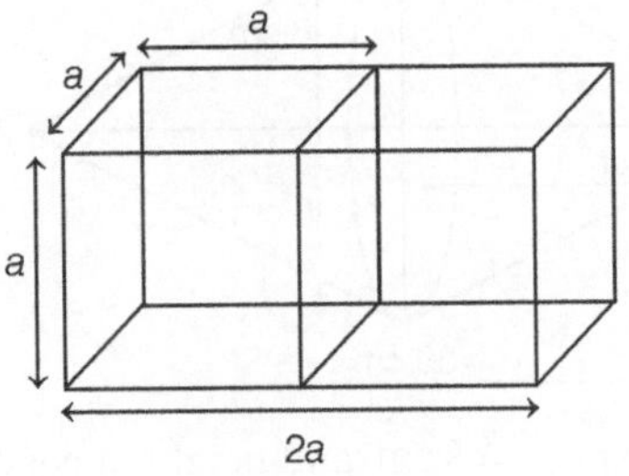

Given, volume of the cube, $a^3 = 64\ cm^3$

$\Rightarrow \quad a^3 = (4)^3$

$\Rightarrow \quad a = 4\ cm$

On joining two cubes, we get a cuboid whose length, $l = 2a$ cm, breadth, $b = a$ cm and height, $h = a$ cm

Now, surface area of the resulting cuboid = $2(lb + bh + hl)$

$$= 2(2a \cdot a + a \cdot a + a \cdot 2a)$$
$$= 2(2a^2 + a^2 + 2a^2) = 2(5a^2)$$
$$= 10a^2 = 10(4)^2 = 160\ cm^2$$

Mistake Alert! *Students mistakenly double all the dimensions of the cube to get the dimensions of new cuboid. However, only the length will be doubled, where as breadth and height will remain the same.*

Q.6 From a solid cube of side 7 cm, a conical cavity of height 7 cm and radius 3 cm is hollowed out. Find the volume of the remaining solid.

Ans. Given that, side of a solid cube $(a) = 7$ cm

Diameter $= 2 \times r = 2 \times 3 = 6$ cm

Height of conical cavity *i.e.*, cone, $h = 7$ cm

Radius of conical cavity *i.e.*, cone, $r = 3$ cm

$\therefore$ Volume of cube = $(\text{side})^3 = a^3 = (7)^3 = 343\ cm^3$

and volume of conical cavity *i.e.*, cone = $\frac{1}{3}\pi \times r^2 \times h$

$$= \frac{1}{3} \times \frac{22}{7} \times 3 \times 3 \times 7$$
$$= 66\ cm^3$$

$\therefore$ Volume of remaining solid = Volume of cube − Volume of conical cavity

$$= 343 - 66 = 277 cm^3$$

Hence, volume of remaining solid is 277 cm^3.

Q.7 Two cones with same base radius 8 cm and height 15 cm are joined together along their bases. Find the surface area of the shape, so formed.

Ans.

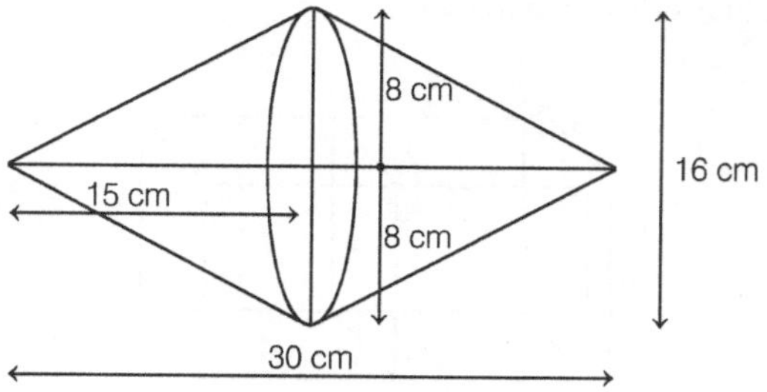

Given that, radius of cone, $r = 8\text{ cm}$ and height of cone, $h = 15$ cm

So, surface area of the shape so formed

$= \text{Curved area of first cone} + \text{Curved surface area of second cone}$

$= \pi rl + \pi rl$ [$\because$ both cones are identical]

$= 2 \times \pi rl = 2 \times \pi \times r \times \sqrt{r^2 + h^2}$ [$\because l = \sqrt{r^2 + h^2}$]

$= 2 \times \frac{22}{7} \times 8 \times \sqrt{(8)^2 + (15)^2}$

$= 2 \times \frac{22}{7} \times 8 \times \sqrt{64 + 225} = \frac{44}{7} \times 8 \times \sqrt{289}$

$= \frac{44}{7} \times 8 \times 17 = \frac{5984}{7} = 854.85\text{ cm}^2 = 855\text{ cm}^2$ (approx)

Hence, the surface area of shape so formed is 855 cm^2.

Mistake Alert! *Students may incorrectly assume the height as its slant height.*

Q.8 Two solid cones A and B are placed in a cylindrical tube as shown in the figure. The ratio of their capacities is 2 : 1. Find the heights and capacities of cones. Also, find the volume of the remaining portion of the cylinder.

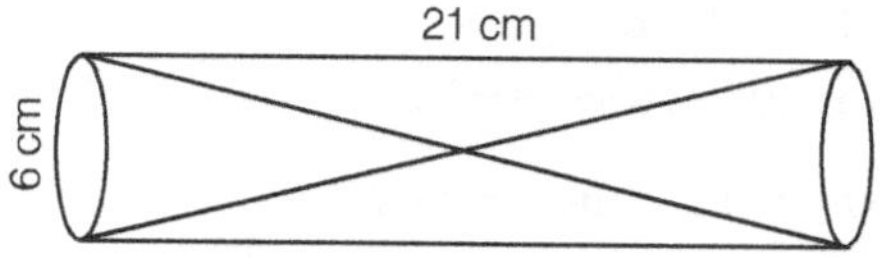

Ans. Let the volume of cone $A = 2V$

and volume of cone $B = V$ ($\because$ ratio of capacities is 2 : 1)

Also, let height of cone $A = h_1$ cm

and height of cone $B = (21 - h_1)$ cm

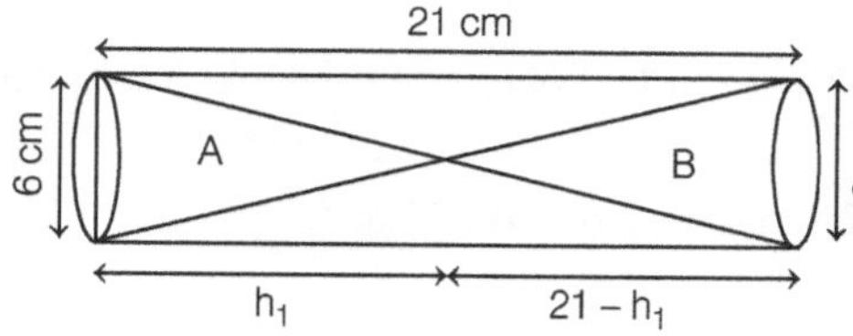

Given, diameter of the cone = 6 cm

$\therefore$ Radius of the cone $= \frac{6}{2} = 3$ cm

Now, volume of the cone $A = 2V = \frac{1}{3}\pi r^2 h = \frac{1}{3}\pi (3)^2 h_1$

$\Rightarrow$ $V = \frac{1}{6}\pi 9 h_1 = \frac{3}{2} h_1 \pi$ ...(i)

and volume of the cone $B = V = \frac{1}{3}\pi (3)^2 (21 - h_1) = 3\pi (21 - h_1)$ ...(ii)

From Eqs. (i) and (ii), we get

$$\frac{3}{2} h_1 \pi = 3\pi (21 - h_1)$$

$\Rightarrow$ $h_1 = 2(21 - h_1) = 42 - 2h_1$

$\Rightarrow$ $3h_1 = 42$

$\Rightarrow$ $h_1 = \frac{42}{3} = 14$ cm

$\therefore$ Height of cone $B = 21 - h_1 = 21 - 14 = 7$cm

Now, volume of the cone $A = \frac{1}{3} \times \frac{22}{7} \times 3^2 \times 14 = 3 \times 14 \times \frac{22}{7} = 132 \text{ cm}^3$

and volume of the cone $B = \frac{1}{3} \times \frac{22}{7} \times 9 \times 7 = 66 \text{ cm}^3$

Now, volume of the cylinder $= \pi r^2 h = \frac{22}{7} \times (3)^2 \times 21 = 594 \text{ cm}^3$

$\therefore$ Required volume of the remaining portion = Volume of the cylinder − (Volume of cone A + Volume of cone B)

$= 594 - (132 + 66) = 396 \text{ cm}^3$

Q.9 An ice-cream cone full of ice-cream having radius 5 cm and height 10 cm as shown in figure. Calculate the volume of ice-cream, provided that its $\frac{1}{6}$ part is left unfilled with ice-cream.

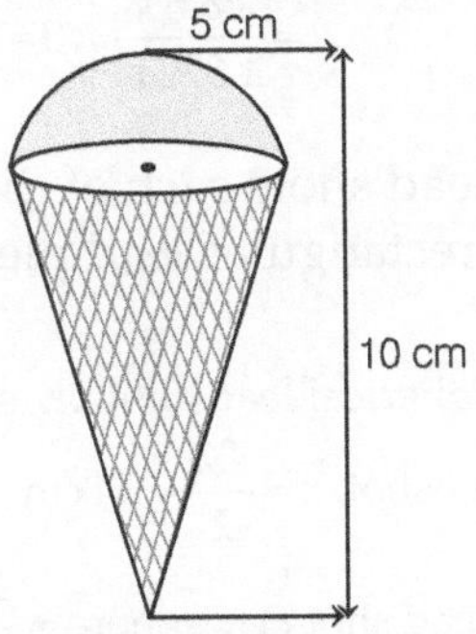

Ans. Given, ice-cream cone is the combination of a hemisphere and a cone.

Also, radius of hemisphere = 5 cm

$\therefore$ Volume of hemisphere $= \frac{2}{3}\pi r^3 = \frac{2}{3} \times \frac{22}{7} \times (5)^3 = \frac{5500}{21} = 261.90 \text{ cm}^3$

Now, radius of the cone = 5 cm

and height of the cone = 10 – 5 = 5 cm

∴ Volume of the cone $= \frac{1}{3}\pi r^2 h$

$$= \frac{1}{3} \times \frac{22}{7} \times (5)^2 \times 5 = \frac{2750}{21} = 130.95 \text{ cm}^3$$

Now, total volume of ice-cream cone = 261.90 + 130.95 = 392.85 cm^3

Since, $\frac{1}{6}$ part is left unfilled with ice-cream.

∴Required volume of ice-cream $= 392.85 - 392.85 \times \frac{1}{6} = 392.85 - 65.475$

$$= 327.4 \text{ cm}^3$$

Q.10 Marbles of diameter 1.4 cm are dropped into a cylindrical beaker of diameter 7 cm containing some water. Find the number of marbles that should be dropped into the beaker, so that the water level rises by 5.6 cm.

Ans. Given, diameter of a marble = 1.4 cm

∴ Radius of marble $= \frac{1.4}{2} = 0.7$ cm

So, volume of one marble $= \frac{4}{3}\pi (0.7)^3$

$$= \frac{4}{3}\pi \times 0.343 = \frac{1.372}{3}\pi \text{ cm}^3$$

Also, given diameter of beaker = 7 cm

∴ Radius of beaker $= \frac{7}{2} = 3.5$ cm

Height of water level raised = 5.6 cm

∴Volume of the raised water in beaker $= \pi (3.5)^2 \times 5.6 = 68.6\pi \text{ cm}^3$

Now, required number of marbles $= \frac{\text{Volume of the raised water in beaker}}{\text{Volume of one spherical marble}}$

$$= \frac{68.6\pi}{1.372\pi} \times 3 = 150$$

Q.11 How many spherical lead shots each of diameter 4.2 cm can be obtained from a solid rectangular lead piece with dimensions 66 cm, 42 cm and 21 cm?

Ans. Given that diameter of a spherical lead shot *i.e.*, sphere = 4.2 cm

∴ Radius of a spherical lead shot, $r = \frac{4.2}{2} = 2.1$ cm $\left[\because \text{radius} = \frac{1}{2}\text{diameter}\right]$

So, volume of a spherical lead shot *i.e.*, sphere $= \frac{4}{3}\pi r^3 = \frac{4}{3} \times \frac{22}{7} \times (2.1)^3$

$$= \frac{4}{3} \times \frac{22}{7} \times 2.1 \times 2.1 \times 2.1$$

$$= \frac{4 \times 22 \times 21 \times 21 \times 21}{3 \times 7 \times 1000}$$

Now, length of rectangular lead piece, $l = 66$ cm

Breadth of rectangular lead piece, $b = 42$ cm

Height of rectangular lead piece, $h = 21$ cm

$\therefore$ Volume of a solid rectangular lead piece *i.e.*, cuboid $= l \times b \times h = 66 \times 42 \times 21$

$$\text{Number of spherical lead shots} = \frac{\text{Volume of solid rectangular lead piece}}{\text{Volume of a spherical lead shot}}$$

$$\text{Number of spherical lead shots} = \frac{66 \times 42 \times 21}{4 \times 22 \times 21 \times 21 \times 21} \times 3 \times 7 \times 1000$$

$$= \frac{3 \times 22 \times 21 \times 2 \times 21 \times 21 \times 1000}{4 \times 22 \times 21 \times 21 \times 21}$$

$$= 3 \times 2 \times 250$$

$$= 6 \times 250 = 1500$$

Hence, the required number of spherical lead shots is 1500.

Q.12 How many spherical lead shots of diameter 4 cm can be made out of a solid cube of lead whose edge measures 44 cm.

Ans. Given that, diameter of a spherical lead shot = 4 cm

$\Rightarrow$ Radius of a spherical lead shot $(r) = \frac{4}{2}$

$\Rightarrow \quad r = 2$ cm $\quad$ [$\because$ diameter = 2 × radius]

So, volume of a spherical lead shot $= \frac{4}{3} \pi r^3$

$$= \frac{4}{3} \times \frac{22}{7} \times (2)^3 = \frac{4 \times 22 \times 8}{21} \text{ cm}^3$$

Now, since edge of a solid cube $(a) = 44$ cm

So, volume of a solid cube $= (a)^3 = (44)^3 = 44 \times 44 \times 44 \text{ cm}^3$

$$\text{Number of spherical lead shots} = \frac{44 \times 44 \times 44}{4 \times 22 \times 8} \times 21 = 11 \times 21 \times 11 = 121 \times 21 = 2541$$

Hence, the required number of spherical lead shots is 2541.

Q.13 A wall 24 m long, 0.4 m thick and 6 m high is constructed with the bricks each of dimensions 25 cm × 16 cm × 10 cm. If the mortar occupies $\frac{1}{10}$ th of the volume of the wall, then find the number of bricks used in constructing the wall.

Ans. Also, given that

Length of a wall $(l) = 24$ m,

Thickness of a wall $(b) = 0.4$ m,

Height of a wall $(h) = 6$ m

So, volume of a wall constructed with the bricks $= l \times b \times h$

$$= 24 \times 0.4 \times 6 = \frac{24 \times 4 \times 6}{10} \text{ m}^3$$

Now, $\frac{1}{10}$ th of volume of a wall $= \frac{1}{10} \times \frac{24 \times 4 \times 6}{10} = \frac{24 \times 4 \times 6}{100} \text{ m}^3$

and Length of a brick $(l_1) = 25 \text{ cm} = \frac{25}{100}$ m

Breadth of a brick $(b_1) = 16 \text{ cm} = \frac{16}{100}$ m

Height of a brick $(h_1) = 10 \text{ cm} = \frac{10}{100}$ m

So volume of a brick $= l_1 \times b_1 \times h_1 = \frac{25}{100} \times \frac{16}{100} \times \frac{10}{100} = \frac{25 \times 16}{10^5} \text{ m}^3$

Given that, a wall is constructed with the help of bricks and mortar.

$$\therefore \text{Number of bricks} = \frac{(\text{Volume of wall}) - \left(\frac{1}{10}\text{th of volume of wall}\right)}{\text{Volume of a brick}} \quad \text{...(i)}$$

$$\text{Number of bricks} = \frac{\left(\frac{24 \times 4 \times 6}{10} - \frac{24 \times 4 \times 6}{100}\right)}{\left(\frac{25 \times 16}{10^5}\right)} = \frac{24 \times 4 \times 6}{100} \times 9 \times \frac{10^5}{25 \times 16}$$

$$= \frac{24 \times 4 \times 6 \times 9 \times 1000}{25 \times 16} = 24 \times 6 \times 9 \times 10 = 12960$$

Hence, the required number of bricks used in constructing the wall is 12960.

Mistake Alert ! *Students may forget to convert cm into m.*

Q.14 Find the number of metallic circular disc with 1.5 cm base diameter and of height 0.2 cm to be melted to form a right circular cylinder of height 10 cm and diameter 4.5 cm.

Ans. Given, Base diameter of metallic circular disc = 1.5 cm

$\therefore$ Radius of metallic circular disc $= \frac{1.5}{2}$ cm [$\because$ diameter $= 2 \times$ radius]

and height of metallic circular disc = 0.2 cm

$$\therefore \quad \text{Volume of a circular disc} = \pi \times (\text{Radius})^2 \times \text{Height}$$

$$= \pi \times \left(\frac{1.5}{2}\right)^2 \times 0.2 = \frac{\pi}{4} \times 1.5 \times 1.5 \times 0.2$$

Now, height of a right circular cylinder $(h) = 10$ cm

and diameter of a right circular cylinder = 4.5 cm

$\Rightarrow$ Radius of a right circular cylinder $(r) = \frac{4.5}{2}$ cm

$$\therefore \text{Volume of right circular cylinder} = \pi r^2 h = \pi\left(\frac{4.5}{2}\right)^2 \times 10 = \frac{\pi}{4} \times 4.5 \times 4.5 \times 10$$

$$\therefore \text{Number of metallic circular disc} = \frac{\text{Volume of a right circular cylinder}}{\text{Volume of a metallic circular disc}}$$

$$= \frac{\frac{\pi}{4} \times 4.5 \times 4.5 \times 10}{\frac{\pi}{4} \times 1.5 \times 1.5 \times 0.2} = \frac{3 \times 3 \times 10}{0.2} = \frac{900}{2} = 450$$

Hence, the required number of metallic circular disc is 450.

Mistake Alert ! *Student may incorrectly assume circular disc as spherical in shape.*

Long Answer Questions

Q.1 A solid metallic hemisphere of radius 8 cm is melted and recasted into a right circular cone of base radius 6 cm. Determine the height of the cone.

- **Concept Insight** If a solid melted and recast into the form of other solid, then the volume of both solids are equal.

Ans. Let height of the cone be h.

Given, radius of the base of the cone = 6 cm

$\therefore$ Volume of circular cone $= \frac{1}{3}\pi r^2 h = \frac{1}{3}\pi(6)^2 h = \frac{36\pi h}{3} = 12\pi h \text{ cm}^3$

Also, given radius of the hemisphere = 8 cm

$\therefore$ Volume of the hemisphere $= \frac{2}{3}\pi r^3 = \frac{2}{3}\pi(8)^3 = \frac{512 \times 2\pi}{3} \text{ cm}^3$

According to the question,

Volume of the cone = Volume of the hemisphere

$$\Rightarrow \quad 12\pi h = \frac{512 \times 2\pi}{3}$$

$$\Rightarrow \quad h = \frac{512 \times 2\pi}{12 \times 3\pi}$$

$$\Rightarrow \quad h = \frac{256}{9} = 28.44 \text{ cm}$$

Q.2 A rectangular water tank of base 11 m × 6 m contains water upto a height of 5 m. If the water in the tank is transferred to a cylindrical tank of radius 3.5 m, find the height of the water level in the tank.

Ans. Given, dimensions of base of rectangular tank = 11 m × 6 m and height of water = 5 m

Volume of the water in rectangular tank $= 11 \times 6 \times 5 = 330 \text{ m}^3$

Also, given radius of the cylindrical tank = 3.5 m

Let height of water level in cylindrical tank be h.

Then, volume of the water in cylindrical tank $= \pi r^2 h = \pi (3.5)^2 \times h$

$$= \frac{22}{7} \times 3.5 \times 3.5 \times h$$

$$= 22 \times 0.5 \times 3.5 \times h = 38.5\, h \text{ m}^3$$

According to the question,

$330 = 38.5\, h$ [since, volume of water is same in both tanks]

$$\therefore \quad h = \frac{330}{38.5} = \frac{3300}{385}$$

$$\therefore \quad = 8.57 \text{ m or } 8.6 \text{ m}$$

Hence, the height of water level in cylindrical tank is 8.6 m.

Q.3 How many cubic centimetres of iron is required to construct an open box whose external dimensions are 36 cm, 25 cm and 16.5 cm provided the thickness of the iron is 1.5 cm. If one cubic cm of iron weights 7.5 g, find the weight of the box.

Ans. Let the length(l), breadth (b) and height (h) be the external dimension of an open box and thickness be x.

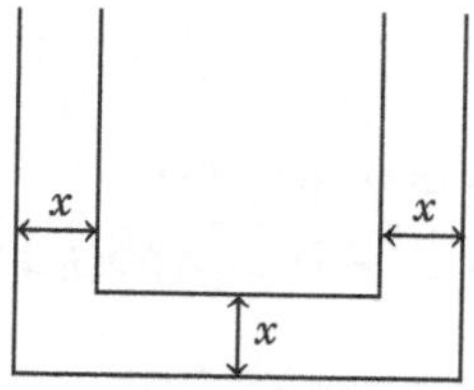

Given that,

external length of an open box $(l) = 36$ cm

external breadth of an open box $(b) = 25$ cm

and external height of an open box $(h) = 16.5$ cm

$\therefore$ External volume of an open box $= lbh$

$$= 36 \times 25 \times 16.5 = 14850 \text{ cm}^3$$

Since, the thickness of the iron $(x) = 1.5$ cm

So, internal length of an open box $(l_1) = l - 2x$

$$= 36 - (2 \times 1.5) = 36 - 3 = 33 \text{ cm}$$

Therefore, internal breadth of an open box $(b_2) = b - 2x$

$$= 25 - 2 \times 1.5 = 25 - 3 = 22 \text{ cm}$$

and internal height of an open box $(h_2) = (h - x)$

$$= 16.5 - 1.5 = 15 \text{ cm}$$

So, internal volume of an open box $= (l - 2x) \cdot (b - 2x) \cdot (h - x)$

$$= 33 \times 22 \times 15 = 10890 \text{ cm}^3$$

Therefore, required iron to construct an open box

= External volume of an open box – Internal volume of an open box

$= 14850 - 10890 = 3960 \text{ cm}^3$

Hence, required iron to construct an open box is 3960 cm^3.

Given that, 1 cm^3 of iron weights $= 7.5 \text{ g} = \frac{7.5}{1000} \text{ kg} = 0.0075 \text{ kg}$

$\therefore$ 3960 cm^3 of iron weights $= 3960 \times 0.0075 = 29.7$ kg

Q.4 The barrel of a fountain pen, cylindrical in shape, is 7 cm long and 5 mm in diameter. A full barrel of ink in the pin is used up on writing 3300 words on an average. How many words can be written in a bottle of ink containing one-fifth of a litre?

Ans. Given, length of the barrel of a fountain pen = 7 cm

and diameter $= 5 \text{ mm} = \frac{5}{10} \text{ cm} = \frac{1}{2}$ cm

$\therefore$ Radius of the barrel $= \dfrac{1}{2 \times 2} = 0.25\text{cm}$

Volume of the barrel $= \pi r^2 h$ [$\because$ Its shape is cylindrical]

$$= \frac{22}{7} \times (0.25)^2 \times 7 = 22 \times 0.0625 = 1.375\text{cm}^3$$

Also, given volume of ink in the bottle $= \dfrac{1}{5}$ of litre $= \dfrac{1}{5} \times 1000\text{ cm}^3 = 200\text{ cm}^3$

Now, 1.375 cm^3 ink is used for writing number of words = 3300

$\therefore 1\text{ cm}^3$ ink is used for writing number of words $= \dfrac{3300}{1.375}$

$\therefore 200\text{ cm}^3$ ink is used for writing number of words $= \dfrac{3300}{1.375} \times 200 = 480000$

Q.5 Water flows at the rate of 10 m/minute through a cylindrical pipe 5 mm in diameter. How long would it take to fill a conical vessel whose diameter at the base is 40 cm and depth 24 cm?

Ans. Given, speed of water flow = 10 m/min = 1000 cm/min

and diameter of the pipe = 5 mm $= \dfrac{5}{10}$ cm

$\therefore$ Radius of the pipe $(r) = \dfrac{5}{10 \times 2} = 0.25$ cm

$\therefore$ Area of the face of pipe $= \pi r^2 = \dfrac{22}{7} \times (0.25)^2 = 0.1964\text{ cm}^2$

Also, given diameter of the conical vessel = 40 cm

$\therefore$ Radius of the conical vessel $(R) = \dfrac{40}{2} = 20$ cm

and depth of the conical vessel $(H) = 24$ cm

$\therefore$ Volume of conical vessel $= \dfrac{1}{3}\pi R^2 H = \dfrac{1}{3} \times \dfrac{22}{7} \times (20)^2 \times 24$

$$= \frac{211200}{21} = 10057.14\text{ cm}^3$$

$\therefore$ Required time $= \dfrac{\text{Volume of the conical vessel}}{\text{Area of the face of pipe} \times \text{Speed of water}}$

$$= \frac{10057.14}{0.1964 \times 10 \times 100}$$

$$= 51.20\text{ min} = 51\text{ min}\left(\frac{20}{100} \times 60\right)\text{ s} = 51\text{ min } 12\text{ s}$$

Q.6 A heap of rice is in the form of a cone of diameter 9 m and height 3.5 m. Find the volume of the rice. How much canvas cloth is required to just cover heap?

Ans. Given, Height of a heap of rice *i.e.*, cone $(h) = 3.5$ m

and diameter of a heap of rice *i.e.*, cone = 9 m

Radius of a heap of rice *i.e.*, cone $(r) = \dfrac{9}{2}$ m

So, volume of rice $= \frac{1}{3}\pi \times r^2 h$

$$= \frac{1}{3} \times \frac{22}{7} \times \frac{9}{2} \times \frac{9}{2} \times 3.5 = \frac{6237}{84} = 74.25\,\text{m}^3$$

Now, canvas cloth required to just cover heap of rice

= Curved surface area of a heap of rice

$= \pi r l$

$$= \frac{22}{7} \times r \times \sqrt{r^2 + h^2} \quad [\because l = \sqrt{r^2 + h^2}]$$

$$= \frac{22}{7} \times \frac{9}{2} \times \sqrt{\left(\frac{9}{2}\right)^2 + (3.5)^2}$$

$$= \frac{11 \times 9}{7} \times \sqrt{\frac{81}{4} + 12.25} = \frac{99}{7} \times \sqrt{\frac{130}{4}} = \frac{99}{7} \times \sqrt{32.5}$$

$= 14.142 \times 5.7 = 80.61\,\text{m}^2$

Hence, 80.61 m^2 canvas cloth is required to just cover heap.

Q.7 A factory manufactures 120000 pencils daily. The pencils are cylindrical in shape each of length 25 cm and circumference of base as 1.5 cm. Determine the cost of colouring the curved surfaces of the pencils manufactured in one day at ₹ 0.05 per dm^2.

Ans. Given, Length of one pencil = 25 cm

and circumference of base = 1.5cm

$$\Rightarrow \quad r = \frac{1.5 \times 7}{22 \times 2} = 0.2386 \text{ cm} \quad [\because \text{Circumference of base} = 2\pi r]$$

Now, curved surface area of one pencil $= 2\pi rh$

$$= 2 \times \frac{22}{7} \times 0.2386 \times 25 = \frac{262.46}{7} = 37.49 \text{ cm}^2$$

$$= \frac{37.49}{100} \text{ dm}^2 \quad \left[\because 1 \text{ cm} = \frac{1}{10} \text{ dm}\right]$$

$= 0.375 \text{ dm}^2$

$\therefore$ Curved surface area of 120000 pencils $= 0.375 \times 120000 = 45000 \text{ dm}^2$

Now, cost of colouring 1 dm^2 curved surface of the pencils manufactured in one day

= ₹ 0.05

$\therefore$ Cost of colouring 45000 dm^2 curved surface $= 45000 \times 0.05 =$ ₹ 2250

Q.8 Water is flowing at the rate of 15 km/h through a pipe of diameter 14 cm into a cuboidal pond which is 50 m long and 44 m wide. In what time will the level of water in pond rise by 21 cm?

Thinking Process Speed of water flowing through the pipe will be taken as the length or height of the pipe.

Ans. Given, length of the pond $(l) = 50$ m and width of the pond $(b) = 44$ m

Depth required of water $(h) = 21 \text{ cm} = \frac{21}{100}$ m

$\therefore$ Volume of water in the pond $= \left(50 \times 44 \times \dfrac{21}{100}\right) = 462 \text{ m}^3$

($\because$ Volume of cuboid $= l \times b \times h$)

Also, given radius of the pipe $(R) = 7 \text{ cm} = \dfrac{7}{100}$ m

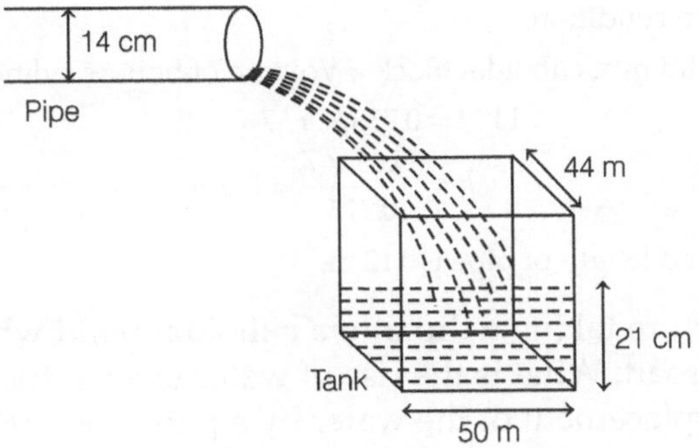

and speed of water flowing through the pipe $(H) = (15 \times 1000) = 15000$ m/h

Now, volume of water flow in 1 h $= \pi R^2 H$

$$= \left(\frac{22}{7} \times \frac{7}{100} \times \frac{7}{100} \times 15000\right)$$

$$= 231 \text{ m}^3$$

Since, 231 m^3 of water falls in the pond in 1 h.

So, 1 m^3 water falls in the pond in $\dfrac{1}{231}$ h.

Also, 462 m^3 of water falls in the pond in $\left(\dfrac{1}{231} \times 462\right)$ h $= 2$ h

Hence, the required time is 2 h.

Q.9 A solid iron cuboidal block of dimensions 4.4 m $\times$ 2.6 m $\times$ 1 m is recast into a hollow cylindrical pipe of internal radius 30 cm and thickness 5 cm. Find the length of the pipe.

Ans. Given, Length of cuboidal pipe $(l) = 4.4$ m

Breadth of cuboidal pipe $(b) = 2.6$ m and height of cuboidal pipe $(h) = 1$ m

So, volume of a solid iron cuboidal block $= l \times b \times h$

$$= 4.4 \times 2.6 \times 1 = 11.44 \text{ m}^3$$

Also, internal radius of hollow cylindrical pipe $(r_i) = 30 \text{ cm} = 0.3$ m

and thickness of hollow cylindrical pipe $= 5 \text{ cm} = 0.05$ m

So, external radius of hollow cylindrical pipe $(r_e) = r_i +$ Thickness

$$= 0.3 + 0.05 = 0.35 \text{ m}$$

$\therefore$ Volume of hollow cylindrical pipe = Volume of cylindrical pipe with external radius − Volume of cylindrical pipe with internal radius

$$= \pi r_e^2 h_1 - \pi r_i^2 h_1 = \pi (r_e^2 - r_i^2)\, h_1$$

$$= \frac{22}{7}[(0.35)^2 - (0.3)^2] \cdot h_1$$

$$= \frac{22}{7}[(0.35 + 0.3)(0.35 - 0.3)] \cdot h_1$$

$$= \frac{22}{7} \times 0.65 \times 0.05 \times h_1 = \frac{0.715}{7} \times h_1$$

where, h_1 be the length of the hollow cylindrical pipe.

Now, by given condition,

Volume of solid iron cuboidal block = Volume of hollow cylindrical pipe

$$\Rightarrow \quad 11.44 = 0.715 \times h / 7$$

$$\therefore \quad h = \frac{11.44 \times 7}{0.715} = 112 \text{ m}$$

Hence, required length of pipe is 112 m.

Q.10 **500 persons are taking a dip into a cuboidal pond which is 80 m long and 50 m broad. What is the rise of water level in the pond, if the average displacement of the water by a person is 0.04 m^3?**

Ans. Let the rise of water level in the pond be 'h' m, when 500 persons are taking a dip into a cuboidal pond.

Given that,

Length of the cuboidal pond = 80 m

Breadth of the cuboidal pond = 50 m

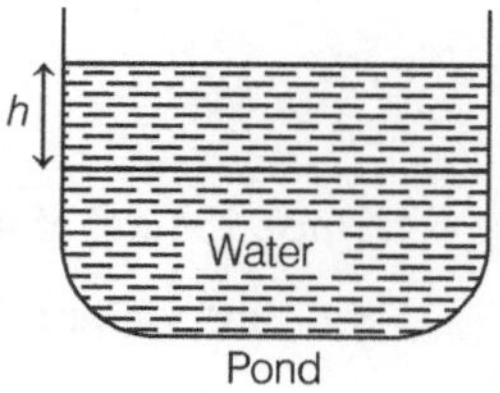

Now, volume for the rise of water level in the pond

$$= \text{Length} \times \text{Breadth} \times \text{Height}$$

$$= 80 \times 50 \times h = 4000\,h \text{ m}^3$$

and the average displacement of the water by a person $= 0.04 \text{ m}^3$

So, the average displacement of the water by 500 persons $= 500 \times 0.04 \text{ m}^3$

Now, by given condition,

Volume for the rise of water level in the pond = Average displacement of the water by 500 persons

$$\Rightarrow \quad 4000\,h = 500 \times 0.04$$

$$\therefore \quad h = \frac{500 \times 0.04}{4000} = \frac{20}{4000} = \frac{1}{200} \text{ m}$$

$$= 0.005 \text{ m}$$

$$= 0.005 \times 100 \text{ cm} = 0.5 \text{ cm}$$

Hence, the required rise of water level in the pond is 0.5 cm.

Q.11 **16 glass spheres each of radius 2 cm are packed into a cuboidal box of internal dimensions 16 cm × 8 cm × 8 cm and then the box is filled with water. Find the volume of water filled in the box.**

Ans. Given, dimensions of the cuboidal box = 16 cm × 8 cm × 8 cm

$\therefore$ Volume of the cuboidal (box) $= 16 \times 8 \times 8 = 1024 \text{ cm}^3$

Also, given radius of one glass sphere = 2 cm

$\therefore$ Volume of one glass sphere $= \frac{4}{3}\pi r^3 = \frac{4}{3} \times \frac{22}{7} \times (2)^3 = \frac{704}{21} = 33.523 \text{ cm}^3$

Now, volume of 16 glass spheres $= 16 \times 33.523 = 536.37 \text{ cm}^3$

$\therefore$ Required volume of water = Volume of cuboidal box – Volume of 16 glass spheres

$= 1024 - 536.37 = 487.63 \text{ cm}^3$

***Q.12** A milk container of height 16 cm is made of metal sheet in the form of a frustum of a cone with radii of its lower and upper ends as 8 cm and 20 cm, respectively. Find the cost of milk at the rate of ₹ 22 per litre which the container can hold.

Ans. Given that,height of milk container (h) = 16 cm,

Radius of lower end of milk container (r) = 8 cm

and radius of upper end of milk container (R) = 20 cm

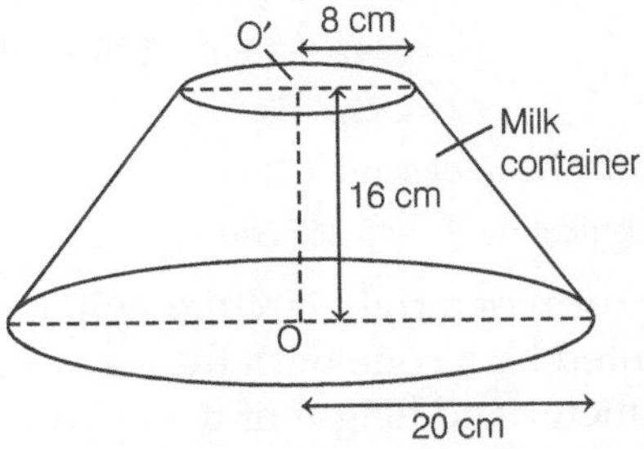

$\therefore$ Volume of the milk container made of metal sheet in the form of a frustum of a cone

$$= \frac{\pi h}{3}(R^2 + r^2 + Rr)$$

$$= \frac{22}{7} \times \frac{16}{3}[(20)^2 + (8)^2 + 20 \times 8]$$

$$= \frac{22 \times 16}{21}(400 + 64 + 160)$$

$$= \frac{22 \times 16 \times 624}{21} = \frac{219648}{21}$$

$= 10459.42 \text{ cm}^3 = 10.45942 \text{ L}$ $\quad [\because 1 \text{ L} = 1000 \text{ cm}^3]$

So, volume of the milk container is 10459.42 cm^3.

$\because$ Cost of 1 L milk = ₹ 22

$\therefore$ Cost of 10.45942 L milk = 22 × 10.45942 = ₹ 230.11

Hence, the required cost of milk is ₹ 230.11

Q.13 A cylindrical bucket of height 32 cm and base radius 18 cm is filled with sand. This bucket is emptied on the ground and a conical heap of sand is formed. If the height of the conical heap is 24 cm, find the radius and slant height of the heap.

Thinking Process Volume of the sand in the heap will be equal to volume of sand in conical heap.

Note (*) *Topics related to these question have been removed from latest NCERT.*

Ans. Given, radius of the base of the bucket = 18 cm

Height of the bucket = 32 cm

So, volume of the sand in cylindrical bucket $= \pi r^2 h = \pi (18)^2 \times 32 = 10368\pi$

Also, given height of the conical heap $(h) = 24$ cm

Let radius of heap be r cm.

Then, volume of the sand in the heap $= \frac{1}{3}\pi r^2 h = \frac{1}{3}\pi r^2 \times 24 = 8\pi r^2$

According to the question,

Volume of the sand in cylindrical bucket = Volume of the sand in conical heap

$$\Rightarrow \quad 10368\pi = 8\pi r^2$$

$$\Rightarrow \quad 10368 = 8 r^2 \Rightarrow r^2 = \frac{10368}{8} = 1296$$

$$\Rightarrow \quad r = 36 \text{ cm}$$

Again, let the slant height of the conical heap $= l$

Now, $\quad = (24)^2 + (36)^2 = 576 + 1296 = 1872$

$\therefore \quad l = 43.267$ cm

Hence, radius of conical heap of sand = 36 cm

and slant height of conical heap = 43.267 cm

Q.14 A rocket is in the form of a right circular cylinder closed at the lower end and surmounted by a cone with the same radius as that of the cylinder. The diameter and height of the cylinder are 6 cm and 12 cm, respectively. If the slant height of the conical portion is 5 cm, find the total surface area and volume of the rocket. (use $\pi = 3.14$)

Ans. Since, rocket is the combination of a right circular cylinder and a cone.

Given, diameter of the cylinder = 6 cm

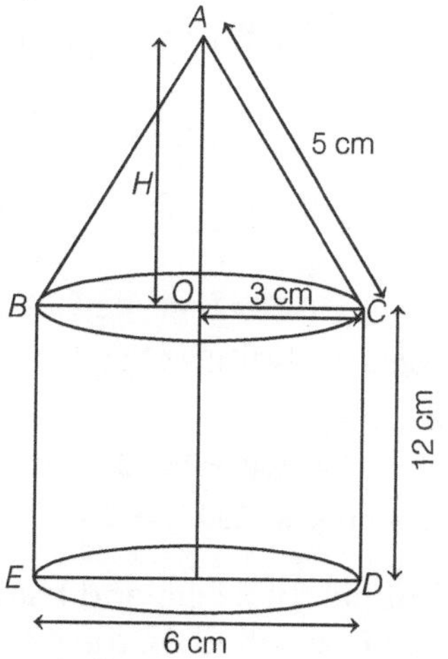

$\therefore$ Radius of the cylinder $= \frac{6}{2} = 3$ cm

and height of the cylinder = 12 cm

$\therefore$ Volume of the cylinder $= \pi r^2 h = 3.14 \times (3)^2 \times 12$

$= 339.12 \text{ cm}^3$

and curved surface area of cylinder $= 2\pi rh$

$$= 2 \times 3.14 \times 3 \times 12 = 226.08 \text{ cm}^2$$

Now, in right angled ΔAOC,

$$H = \sqrt{5^2 - 3^2} = \sqrt{25 - 9} = \sqrt{16} = 4 \text{ cm}$$

$\therefore$ Height of the cone, $H = 4$ cm

Radius of the cone, $R = 3$ cm

Now, volume of the cone $= \frac{1}{3}\pi R^2 H = \frac{1}{3} \times 3.14 \times (3)^2 \times 4 = \frac{113.04}{3} = 37.68 \text{ cm}^3$

and curved surface area of cone $= \pi rl = 3.14 \times 3 \times 5 = 47.1 \text{ cm}^2$

Area of base of cylinder $= \pi r^2 = 3.14 \times (3)^2 = 28.26 \text{ cm}^2$

Hence, total volume of the rocket

$$= 339.12 + 37.68 = 376.8 \text{ cm}^3$$

and total surface area of the rocket = CSA of cone + CSA of cylinder + Area of base of cylinder

$$= 47.1 + 226.08 + 28.26 = 301.44 \text{ cm}^2$$

Q.15 A building is in the form of a cylinder surmounted by a hemispherical vaulted dome and contains $41\frac{19}{21}$ m^3 of air. If the internal diameter of dome is equal to its total height above the floor, find the height of the building?

Ans. $\because$ Total height of the building = Internal diameter of the dome = $2r$m

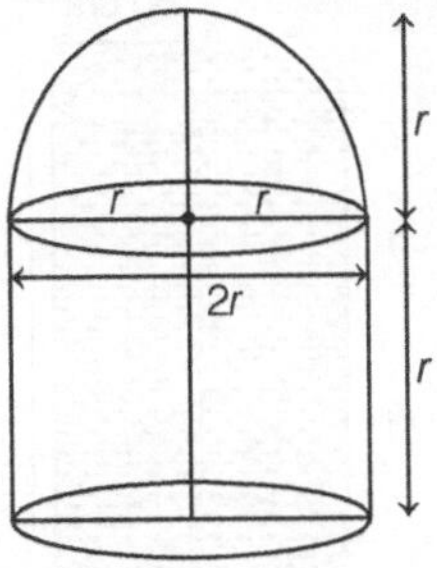

$\therefore$ Radius of building (or dome) $= \frac{2r}{2} = r$ m

Height of cylinder $= 2r - r = r$ m

$\therefore$ Volume of the cylinder $= \pi r^2 (r) = \pi r^3$ m^3 [$\because$ Volume of cylinder $= \pi r^2 h$]

and volume of hemispherical dome $= \frac{2}{3}\pi r^3$ m^3

$\therefore$ Total volume of the building

= Volume of the cylinder + Volume of hemispherical dome

$$= \left(\pi r^3 + \frac{2}{3}\pi r^3\right) \text{m}^3 = \frac{5}{3}\pi r^3 \text{ m}^3$$

According to the question,

Volume of the building = Volume of the air

$$\Rightarrow \quad \frac{5}{3}\pi r^3 = 41\frac{19}{21} \Rightarrow \frac{5}{3}\times\frac{22}{7}\times r^3 = \frac{880}{21}$$

$$\Rightarrow \quad r^3 = \frac{880\times 7\times 3}{21\times 22\times 5} = \frac{40\times 21}{21\times 5}$$

$$\Rightarrow \quad r^3 = 8 \Rightarrow r = 2$$

$\therefore$ Height of the building $= 2r = 2\times 2 = 4$ m

Q.16 A hemispherical bowl of internal radius 9 cm is full of liquid. The liquid is to be filled into cylindrical shaped bottles each of radius 1.5 cm and height 4 cm. How many bottles are needed to empty the bowl?

Ans. Given, radius of hemispherical bowl, $r = 9$ cm

and radius of cylindrical bottles, $R = 1.5$ cm and height, $h = 4$ cm

$\therefore$ Number of required cylindrical bottles $= \dfrac{\text{Volume of hemispherical bowl}}{\text{Volume of one cylindrical bottle}}$

$$= \frac{\frac{2}{3}\pi r^3}{\pi R^2 h} = \frac{\frac{2}{3}\times\pi\times 9\times 9\times 9}{\pi\times 1.5\times 1.5\times 4} = 54$$

Q.17 A solid right circular cone of height 120 cm and radius 60 cm is placed in a right circular cylinder full of water of height 180 cm such that it touches the bottom. Find the volume of water left in the cylinder, if the radius of the cylinder is equal to the radius to the cone.

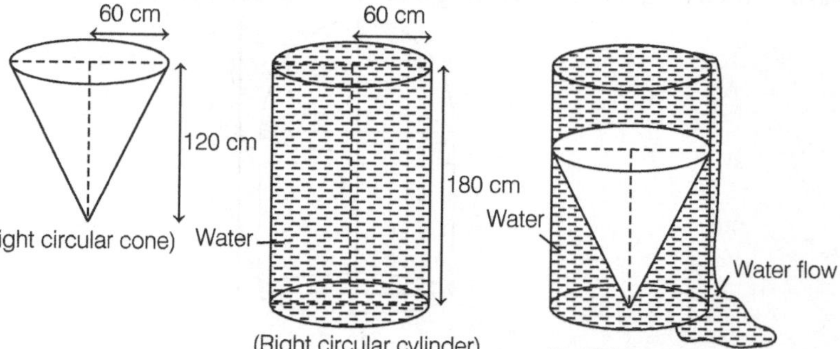

(Right circular cone) (Right circular cylinder) (Cylinder containing a cone)

Thinking Process

(i) Whenever we placed a solid right circular cone in a right circular cylinder with full of water, then volume of a solid right circular cone is equal to the volume of water falled from the cylinder.

(ii) Total volume of water in a cylinder is equal to the volume of the cylinder.

(iii) Volume of water left in the cylinder = Volume of the right circular cylinder − volume of a right circular cone.

Ans. Given, Height of a right circular cone $(h) = 120$ cm

Radius of a right circular cone $(r) = 60$ cm

$\therefore$ Volume of a right circular cone $= \dfrac{1}{3}\pi r^2 h$

$$= \frac{1}{3}\pi \times 60 \times 60 \times 120$$
$$= \pi \times 20 \times 60 \times 120$$
$$= 144000\pi \text{ cm}^3$$

$\therefore$ Volume of a right circular cone = Volume of water falled from the cylinder

$$= 144000\pi \text{ cm}^3$$

Given that, height of a right circular cylinder $(H) = 180$ cm

and radius of a right circular cylinder (r) = Radius of a right circular cone

$$= 60 \text{ cm}$$

$\therefore$ Volume of a right circular cylinder $= \pi r^2 H$

$$= \pi \times 60 \times 60 \times 180$$
$$= 648000\pi \text{ cm}^3$$

So, volume of a right circular cylinder = Total volume of water in a cylinder

$$= 648000\pi \text{ cm}^3$$

Now, Volume of water left in the cylinder

= Total volume of water in a cylinder − Volume of water falled from the cylinder when solid cone is placed in it

$$= 648000\pi - 144000\pi$$
$$= 504000\pi = 504000 \times \frac{22}{7}$$
$$= 1584000 \text{ cm}^3 = \frac{1584000}{(10)^6} \text{ m}^3 = 1.584 \text{ m}^3$$

Hence, the required volume of water left in the cylinder is 1.584 m^3.

Q.18 Water flows through a cylindrical pipe, whose inner radius is 1 cm, at the rate of 80 cm/sec in an empty cylindrical tank, the radius of whose base is 40 cm. What is the rise of water level in tank in half an hour?

Ans. Given, radius of tank, $r_1 = 40$ cm

Let height of water level in tank in half an hour $= h_1$

Also, given internal radius of cylindrical pipe, $r_2 = 1$ cm

and speed of water = 80 cm/sec *i.e.*, in 1 sec water flow = 80 cm

$\therefore$ In 30 min water flow $= 80 \times (60 \times 30) = 144000$ cm [$\because$ 1 min = 60 sec]

According to the question,

Volume of water in cylindrical tank = Volume of water flow from the circular pipe in half an hour

$$\Rightarrow \quad \pi r_1^2 h_1 = \pi r_2^2 h_2$$
$$\Rightarrow \quad 40 \times 40 \times h_1 = 1 \times 1 \times 144000$$
$$\therefore \quad h_1 = \frac{144000}{40 \times 40} = 90 \text{ cm}$$

Hence, the level of water in cylindrical tank rises 90 cm in half an hour.

Q.19 The rain water from a roof of dimensions 22 m × 20 m drains into a cylindrical vessel having diameter of base 2 m and height 3.5 m. If the rain water collected from the roof just fill the cylindrical vessel, then find the rainfall in cm.

Ans. Given, length of roof = 22 m and breadth of roof = 20 m

Let the rainfall be a cm.

$\therefore$ Volume of water on the roof $= 22 \times 20 \times \frac{a}{100}$

$$= \frac{22a}{5} \text{ m}^3 \qquad \left[\because 1 \text{ cm} = \frac{1}{100} \text{ m}\right]$$

Also, we have radius of base of the cylindrical vessel = 1 m

and height of the cylindrical vessel = 3.5 m

$\therefore$ Volume of water in the cylindrical vessel when it is just full

$$= \left(\frac{22}{7} \times 1 \times 1 \times \frac{7}{2}\right) = 11 \text{ m}^3$$

According to the question, volume of water on the roof = Volume of water in the vessel

$$\Rightarrow \qquad \frac{22a}{5} = 11$$

$$\therefore \qquad a = \frac{11 \times 5}{22} = 2.5 \quad [\because \text{volume of cylinder} = \pi \times (\text{radius})^2 \times \text{height}]$$

Hence, the rainfall is 2.5 cm.

Q.20 A pen stand made of wood is in the shape of a cuboid with four conical depressions and a cubical depression to hold the pens and pins, respectively. The dimensions of cubiod are 10 cm, 5 cm and 4 cm. The radius of each of the conical depressions is 0.5 cm and the depth is 2.1 cm. The edge of the cubical depression is 3 cm. Find the volume of the wood in the entire stand.

Ans. Given that, length of cuboid pen stand (l) = 10 cm

Breadth of cubiod pen stand (b) = 5 cm

and height of cuboid pen stand (h) = 4 cm

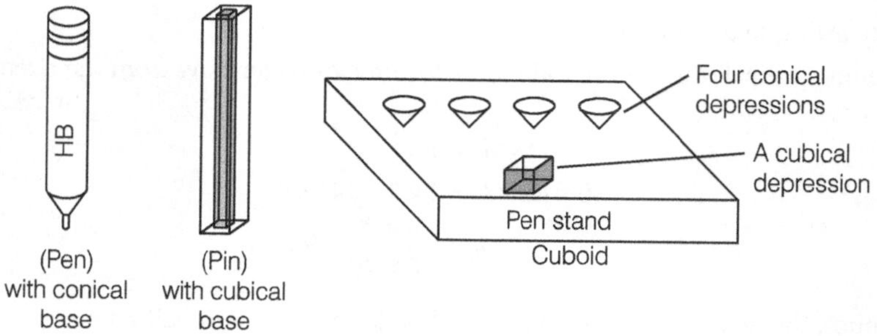

$\therefore$ Volume of cuboid pen stand $= l \times b \times h = 10 \times 5 \times 4 = 200\ \text{cm}^3$

Also, radius of conical depression $(r) = 0.5$ cm

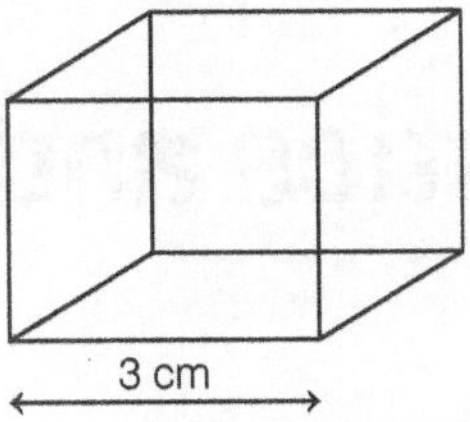

Cubical depression

and height (depth) of a conical depression $(h_1) = 2.1$ cm

$\therefore$ Volume of a conical depression $= \frac{1}{3}\pi r^2 h_1$

$$= \frac{1}{3} \times \frac{22}{7} \times 0.5 \times 0.5 \times 2.1$$

$$= \frac{22 \times 5 \times 5}{1000} = \frac{22}{40} = \frac{11}{20}\ \text{cm}^3$$

Also, given

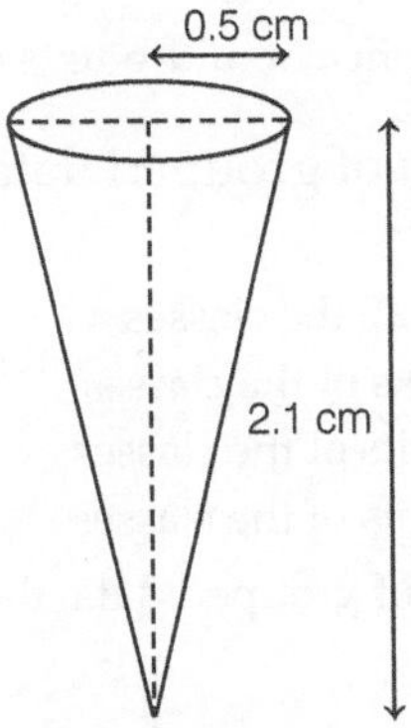

Conical depression

Edge of cubical depression $(a) = 3$ cm

$\therefore$ Volume of cubical depression $= (a)^3 = (3)^3 = 27\ \text{cm}^3$

So, volume of 4 conical depressions $= 4 \times$ Volume of a conical depression

$$= 4 \times \frac{11}{20} = \frac{11}{5}\ \text{cm}^3$$

Hence, the volume of wood in the entire pen stand

= Volume of cuboid pen stand – Volume of 4 conical depressions – volume of a cubical depressions

$$= 200 - \frac{11}{5} - 27 = 200 - \frac{146}{5}$$

$$= 200 - 29.2 = 170.8\ \text{cm}^3$$

So, the required volume of the wood in the entire stand is $170.8\ \text{cm}^3$.

Chapter

13

Statistics and Probability

Multiple Choice Questions (MCQS)

Choose the correct answer from the given four options in the following questions:

Q.1 In the formula $\bar{x} = a + \frac{\Sigma f_i d_i}{\Sigma f_i}$, for finding the mean of grouped data d_i's are deviation from a of

(a) lower limits of the classes
(b) upper limits of the classes
(c) mid-points of the classes
(d) frequencies of the class marks

Ans. *(c)* We know that, $d_i = x_i - a$

i.e., d_i's are the deviation from a of mid-points of the classes.

Q.2 While computing mean of grouped data, we assume that the frequencies are

(a) evenly distributed over all the classes
(b) centred at the class marks of the classes
(c) centred at the upper limits of the classes
(d) centred at the lower limits of the classes

Ans. *(b)* In computing the mean of grouped data, the frequencies are centred at the class marks of the classes.

Q.3 If x_i's are the mid-points of the class intervals of grouped data, f_i's are the corresponding frequencies and $\bar{x}$ is the mean, then $\Sigma(f_i x_i - \bar{x})$ is equal to

(a) 0 (b) –1 (c) 1 (d) 2

Ans. *(a)* $\because$ $\bar{x} = \frac{\Sigma f_i x_i}{n}$

$\therefore$ $\Sigma(f_i x_i - \bar{x}) = \Sigma f_i x_i - \Sigma\bar{x}$

$= n\bar{x} - n\bar{x}$ $[\because \Sigma\bar{x} = n\bar{x}]$

$= 0$

Q.4 In the formula $\bar{x} = a + h\left(\frac{\Sigma f_i u_i}{\Sigma f_i}\right)$, for finding the mean of grouped frequency distribution $u_i =$

(a) $\frac{x_i + a}{h}$ (b) $h(x_i - a)$ (c) $\frac{x_i - a}{h}$ (d) $\frac{a - x_i}{h}$

Ans. ***(c)*** Given, $\overline{x} = a + h\left(\dfrac{\Sigma f_i u_i}{\Sigma f_i}\right)$

Above formula is a step deviation formula.

$$\therefore \quad u_i = \frac{x_i - a}{h}$$

****Q.5*** The abscissa of the point of intersection of the less than type and of the more than type cumulative frequency curves of a grouped data gives its

(a) mean (b) median (c) mode (d) All of these

Ans. ***(b)*** Since, the intersection point of less than ogive and more than ogive gives the median on the abscissa.

Q.6 For the following distribution

Class	0 - 5	5 -10	10 -15	15 - 20	20 - 25
Frequency	10	15	12	20	9

the sum of lower limits of the median class and modal class is

(a) 15 (b) 25 (c) 30 (d) 35

Ans. ***(b)*** Here,

Class	Frequency	Cumulative frequency
0-5	10	10
5-10	15	25
10-15	12	37
15-20	20	57
20-25	9	66

Now, $\frac{N}{2} = \frac{66}{2} = 33$. The cumulative frequency just greater than 33 is 37, which lies in the interval 10-15. Therefore, lower limit of the median class is 10.

The highest frequency is 20, which lies in the interval 15-20. Therefore, lower limit of modal class is 15. Hence, required sum is 10 + 15 = 25.

Mistake Alert ! *Students may incorrectly select the modal class by selected the highest cumulative frequency instead of the highest frequency.*

Q.7 Consider the following frequency distribution

Class	0-5	6-11	12-17	18-23	24-29
Frequency	13	10	15	8	11

The upper limit of the median class is

(a) 17 (b) 17.5

(c) 18 (d) 18.5

Note (✱) *Topics related to these question have been removed from latest NCERT.*

Ans. *(b)* Given, classes are not continuous, so we make continuous by subtracting 0.5 from lower limit and adding 0.5 to upper limit of each class.

Class	Frequency	Cumulative frequency
–0.5-5.5	13	13
5.5-11.5	10	23
11.5-17.5	15	38
17.5-23.5	8	46
23.5-29.5	11	57

Here, $\frac{N}{2} = \frac{57}{2} = 28.5$. The cumulative frequency just greater than 28.5 is 38, which lies in the interval 11.5-17.5.

Hence, the upper limit is 17.5.

Q.8 For the following distribution

Marks	Number of students
Below 10	3
Below 20	12
Below 30	27
Below 40	57
Below 50	75
Below 60	80

the modal class is

(a) 10-20 (b) 20-30 (c) 30-40 (d) 50-60

Ans. *(c)*

Marks	Number of students	Cumulative frequency
Below 10	3 = 3	3
10-20	(12 – 3) = 9	12
20-30	(27 – 12) = 15	27
30-40	(57 – 27) = 30	57
40-50	(75 – 57) = 18	75
50-60	(80 – 75) = 5	80

Here, we see that the highest frequency is 30, which lies in the interval 30-40.

Hence, the modal class is 30-40.

Q.9 Consider the following data

Class	65-85	85-105	105-125	125-145	145-165	165-185	185-205
Frequency	4	5	13	20	14	7	4

The difference of the upper limit of the median class and the lower limit of the modal class is

(a) 0 (b) 19

(c) 20 (d) 38

Ans. *(c)*

Class	Frequency	Cumulative frequency
65-85	4	4
85-105	5	9
105-125	13	22
125-145	20	42
145-165	14	56
165-185	7	63
185-205	4	67

Here, $\frac{N}{2} = \frac{67}{2} = 33.5$. The cumulative frequency just greater than 33.5 is 42, which lies in the interval 125 -145.

Hence, upper limit of median class is 145.

Here, we see that the highest frequency is 20 which lies in 125-145. Hence, the lower limit of modal class is 125.

$\therefore$ Required difference = Upper limit of median class – Lower limit of modal class
= 145 – 125 = 20

Q.10 The time, in seconds taken by 150 atheletes to run a 110 m hurdle race are tabulated below

Class	13.8-14	14-14.2	14.2-14.4	14.4-14.6	14.6-14.8	14.8-15
Frequency	2	4	5	71	48	20

The number of atheletes who completed the race in less than 14.6 seconds is

(a) 11 (b) 71 (c) 82 (d) 130

Ans. *(c)* The number of atheletes who completed the race in less than 14.6 seconds
= 2 + 4 + 5 + 71 = 82

Q.11 Consider the following distribution

Marks obtained	Number of students
More than or equal to 0	63
More than or equal to 10	58
More than or equal to 20	55
More than or equal to 30	51
More than or equal to 40	48
More than or equal to 50	42

the frequency of the class 30-40 is

(a) 3 (b) 4
(c) 48 (d) 51

Ans. *(a)*

Marks obtained	Number of students
0-10	(63 – 58) = 5
10-20	(58 – 55) = 3
20-30	(55 – 51) = 4
30-40	(51 – 48) = 3
40-50	(48 – 42) = 6
50-60	42 = 42

Hence, frequency in the class interval 30-40 is 3.

Q.12 If an event cannot occur, then its probability is

(a) 1 (b) $\frac{3}{4}$ (c) $\frac{1}{2}$ (d) 0

Ans. *(d)* The event which cannot occur is said to be impossible event and probability of impossible event is zero.

Q.13 Which of the following cannot be the probability of an event?

(a) $\frac{1}{3}$ (b) 0.1 (c) 3% (d) $\frac{17}{16}$

Ans. *(d)* Since, probability of an event always lies between 0 and 1.

Q.14 An event is very unlikely to happen. Its probability is closest to

(a) 0.0001 (b) 0.001
(c) 0.01 (d) 0.1

Ans. *(a)* The probability of an event which is very unlikely to happen is closest to zero and from the given options 0.0001 is closest to zero.

Q.15 If the probability of an event is p, the probability of its complementary event will be

(a) $p-1$ (b) p (c) $1-p$ (d) $1-\frac{1}{p}$

Ans. *(c)* Since, probability of an event + probability of its complementary event = 1
So, probability of its complementary event = 1 – Probability of an event $= 1-p$

Q.16 The probability expressed as a percentage of a particular occurrence can never be

(a) less than 100 (b) less than 0
(c) greater than 1 (d) anything but a whole number

Ans. *(b)* We know that, the probability expressed as a percentage always lie between 0 and 100. So, it cannot be less than 0.

Q.17 If $P(A)$ denotes the probability of an event A, then

(a) $P(A) < 0$ (b) $P(A) > 1$ (c) $0 \le P(A) \le 1$ (d) $-1 \le P(A) \le 1$

Ans. *(c)* Since, probability of an event always lies between 0 and 1.

Q.18 A card is selected from a deck of 52 cards. The probability of its being a red face card is

(a) $\frac{3}{26}$ (b) $\frac{3}{13}$

(c) $\frac{2}{13}$ (d) $\frac{1}{2}$

Ans. *(a)* In a deck of 52 cards, there are 12 face cards *i.e.,* 6 red and 6 black cards.

So, probability of getting a red face card $= \frac{6}{52} = \frac{3}{26}$

Q.19 The probability that a non-leap year selected at random will contains 53 Sundays is

(a) $\frac{1}{7}$ (b) $\frac{2}{7}$ (c) $\frac{3}{7}$ (d) $\frac{5}{7}$

Ans. *(a)* A non-leap year has 365 days and therefore 52 weeks and 1 day. This 1 day may be Sunday or Monday or Tuesday or Wednesday or Thursday or Friday or Saturday. Thus, out of 7 possibilities, 1 favourable event is the event that the one day is Sunday.

$\therefore$ Probability of an event $= \frac{\text{Number of favourable}}{\text{Total number of outcomes}}$

$\therefore$ Required probability $= \frac{1}{7}$

Mistake Alert! *Students may get confused that the number of days in a non-leap year is 366 instead of 365.*

Q.20 When a die is thrown, the probability of getting an odd number less than 3 is

(a) $\frac{1}{6}$ (b) $\frac{1}{3}$ (c) $\frac{1}{2}$ (d) 0

Thinking process If a number is not divisible by 2, then the number is an odd number.

Ans. *(a)* When a die is thrown,then total number of outcomes = 6

Odd number less than 3 is 1 only.

$\therefore$ Number of possible outcomes = 1

$\therefore$ Required probability $= \frac{1}{6}$.

Q.21 A card is drawn from a deck of 52 cards. The event E is that card is not an ace of hearts. The number of outcomes favourable to E is

(a) 4 (b) 13 (c) 48 (d) 51

Ans. *(d)* In a deck of 52 cards, there are 13 cards of heart and 1 is ace of heart.
Hence, the number of outcomes favourable to $E = 52 - 1 = 51$

Q.22 The probability of getting a bad egg in a lot of 400 is 0.035. The number of bad eggs in the lot is

(a) 7 (b) 14 (c) 21 (d) 28

Ans. *(b)* Here, total number of eggs = 400

Probability of getting a bad egg = 0.035

$$\Rightarrow \quad \frac{\text{Number of bad eggs}}{\text{Total number of eggs}} = 0.035$$

$$\Rightarrow \quad \frac{\text{Number of bad eggs}}{400} = 0.035$$

$$\therefore \quad \text{Number of bad eggs} = 0.035 \times 400 = 14$$

Q.23 A girl calculates that the probability of her winning the first prize in a lottery is 0.08. If 6000 tickets are sold, how many tickets has she bought?

(a) 40 (b) 240 (c) 480 (d) 750

Ans. *(c)* Given, total number of sold tickets = 6000

Let she bought x tickets.

Then, probability of her winning the first prize $= \frac{x}{6000} = 0.08$ [given]

$$\Rightarrow \quad x = 0.08 \times 6000$$

$$\therefore \quad x = 480$$

Hence, she bought 480 tickets.

Q.24 One ticket is drawn at random from a bag containing tickets numbered 1 to 40. The probability that the selected ticket has a number which is a multiple of 5 is

(a) $\frac{1}{5}$ (b) $\frac{3}{5}$

(c) $\frac{4}{5}$ (d) $\frac{1}{3}$

Ans. *(a)* Total number of outcomes = 40

Multiples of 5 from 1 to 40 = 5, 10, 15, 20, 25, 30, 35, 40

∵ Total number of possible outcomes = 8

$$\therefore \quad \text{Required probability} = \frac{8}{40} = \frac{1}{5}$$

Q.25 Someone is asked to take a number from 1 to 100. The probability that it is a prime, is

(a) $\frac{1}{5}$ (b) $\frac{6}{25}$

(c) $\frac{1}{4}$ (d) $\frac{13}{50}$

Thinking process If a number is divisible by only 1 and the number itself, then the number is prime number.

Ans. *(c)* Total numbers of outcomes = 100

So, the prime numbers from 1 to 100 are 2, 3, 5, 7, 11, 13, 17, 19, 23, 29, 31, 37, 41, 43, 47, 53, 59, 61, 67, 71, 73, 79, 83, 89 and 97.

∵ Total number of possible outcomes = 25

$$\therefore \quad \text{Required probability} = \frac{25}{100} = \frac{1}{4}$$

Q.26 A school has five houses *A*, *B*, *C*, *D* and *E*. A class has 23 students, 4 from house *A*, 8 from house *B*, 5 from house *C*, 2 from house *D* and rest from house *E*. A single student is selected at random to be the class monitor. The probability that the selected student is not from *A*, *B* and *C* is

(a) $\frac{4}{23}$ (b) $\frac{6}{23}$ (c) $\frac{8}{23}$ (d) $\frac{17}{23}$

Ans. *(b)* Total number of students = 23

Number of students in house *A*, *B* and *C* = 4 + 8 + 5 = 17

∴ Remains students = 23 – 17 = 6

So, probability that the selected student is not from *A*, *B* and $C = \frac{6}{23}$

Short Answer Questions with Reasoning

Q.1 The median of an ungrouped data and the median calculated when the same data is grouped are always the same. Do you think that this is a correct statement? Give reason.

Ans. *Not always*, because for calculating median of a grouped data, the formula used is based on the assumption that the observations in the classes are uniformal distributed (or equally spaced).

Q.2 In calculating the mean of grouped data, grouped in classes of equal width, we may use the formula,

$$\bar{x} = a + \frac{\Sigma f_i d_i}{\Sigma f_i}$$

Where, *a* is the assumed mean, *a* must be one of the mid-points of the classes. Is the last statement correct? Justify your answer.

Ans. *No*, it is not necessary that assumed mean consider as the mid-point of the class interval. It is considered as any value which is easy to simplify it.

Q.3 Is it true to say that the mean, mode and median of grouped data will always be different? Justify your answer.

Ans. *No*, the value of these three measures can be same, it depends on the type of data.

Q.4 Will the median class and modal class of grouped data always be different? Justify your answer.

Ans. *Not always*, It depends on the given data.

Q.5 In a family having three children, there may be no girl, one girl, two girls or three girls. So, the probability of each is $\frac{1}{4}$. Is this correct? Justify your answer.

Ans. *No*, let *B* be boys and *G* be girls.

∴ Possible outcomes are

BBB, BGG, BBG, BGB, GBB,

GGG, GBG, GGB.

So, total number of outcomes = 8

Probability of no girl $= \frac{1}{8}$

Probability of 1 girl $= \frac{3}{8}$

Probability of 2 girls $= \frac{3}{8}$

Probability of 3 girls $= \frac{1}{8}$

So, probability of each is not $\frac{1}{4}$.

Q.6 A game consists of spinning an arrow which comes to rest pointing at one of the regions (1, 2 or 3) (see figure). Are the outcomes 1, 2 and 3 equally likely to occur? Give reasons.

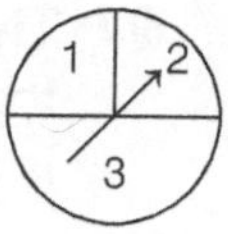

Ans. *No*, the outcomes are not equally likely to occur because 3 contains half part of the total region, so it is more likely than 1 and 2, since 1 and 2, each contains half part of the remaining part of the region.

Q.7 Apoorv throws two dice once and computes the product of the numbers appearing on the dice. Peehu throws one die and squares the number that appears on it. Who has the better chance of getting the number 36? Why?

Ans. Apoorv throws two dice once.

So, total number of outcomes = 36

Number of outcomes for getting product 36 $= 1(6 \times 6)$

∴ Probability of getting number 36 for Apoorv $= \frac{1}{36}$

Also, Peehu throws one die,

So, total number of outcomes = 6

Number of outcomes for getting square of a number is $36 = 1(6^2 = 36)$

∴ Probability of getting number 36 for Peehu $= \frac{1}{6} = \frac{6}{36}$

Hence, Peehu has better chance of getting the number 36.

Q.8 When we toss a coin, there are two possible outcomes-Head or Tail. Therefore, the probability of each outcome is $\frac{1}{2}$. Justify your answer.

Ans. *Yes*, probability of each outcome is $\frac{1}{2}$ because head and tail both are equally likely events.

Q.9 A student says that, if you throw a die, it will show up 1 or not 1. Therefore, the probability of getting 1 and the probability of not getting 1 each is equal to $\frac{1}{2}$. Is this correct? Give reasons.

Ans. No, this is not correct.

Suppose we throw a die, then total number of outcomes = 6

Possible outcomes = 1 or 2 or 3 or 4 or 5 or 6

$\therefore$ Probability of getting $1 = \frac{1}{6}$

Now, probability of not getting 1 = 1 − Probability of getting 1

$$= 1 - \frac{1}{6} = \frac{5}{6}$$

Q.10 I toss three coins together. The possible outcomes are no heads, 1 head, 2 heads and 3 heads. So, I say that probability of no heads is $\frac{1}{4}$. What is wrong with this conclusion?

Ans. I toss three coins together [given]

So, total number of outcomes $= 2^3 = 8$

and possible outcomes are $(HHH), (HTT), (THT), (TTH), (HHT), (THH), (HTH)$ and (TTT)

Now, probability of getting no head $= \frac{1}{8}$

Hence, the given conclusion is wrong because the probability of no head is $\frac{1}{8}$ not $\frac{1}{4}$.

Q.11 If you toss a coin 6 times and it comes down heads on each occasion. Can you say that the probability of getting a head is 1? Given reasons.

Ans. No, if let we toss a coin, then we get head or tail, both are equally likely events. So, probability of getting head or tail is $\frac{1}{2}$. If we toss a coin 6 times, then probability will be same in each case. So, the probability of getting a head is not 1.

Q.12 Sushma tosses a coin 3 times and gets tail each time. Do you think that the outcome of next toss will be a tail? Give reasons.

Ans. No, the outcome of next toss may or may not be tail, because on tossing a coin, we get head or tail so both are equally likely events.

Q.13 If I toss a coin 3 times and get head each time, should I expect a tail to have a higher chance in the 4th toss? Give reason in support of your answer.

Ans. No, let we toss a coin, then we get head or tail, both are equaly likely events. *i.e.*, probability of each event is $\frac{1}{2}$. So, no question of expecting a tail to have a higher chance in 4th toss.

Q.14 A bag contains slips numbered from 1 to 100. If Fatima chooses a slip at random from the bag, it will either be an odd number or an even number. Since, this situation has only two possible outcomes, so the probability of each is $\frac{1}{2}$. Justify.

Ans. Yes We know that, from 1 to 100, half numbers are even and half numbers are odd *i.e.*, 50 numbers (2, 4, 6, 8,...,96, 98, 100) are even and 50 numbers (1, 3, 5, 7,..., 97, 99) are odd. So, both events are equally likely.

So, probability of getting even number $= \frac{50}{100} = \frac{1}{2}$

and probability of getting odd number $= \frac{50}{100} = \frac{1}{2}$

Hence, the probability of each is $\frac{1}{2}$.

Short Answer Questions

Q.1 Find the mean of the distribution

Class	1-3	3-5	5-7	7-10
Frequency	9	22	27	17

- **Concept Insight** In this question we will use the formula $\bar{x} = \frac{\Sigma f_i x_i}{\Sigma f_i}$ to find the mean of the given distribution.

Ans. First find the class mark x_i, of each class and then proceed as follows.

Class	Class marks (x_i)	Frequency (f_i)	$f_i\, x_i$
1-3	2	9	18
3-5	4	22	88
5-7	6	27	162
7-10	8.5	17	144.5
		$\Sigma f_i = 75$	$\Sigma f_i x_i = 412.5$

Therefore, mean $(\bar{x}) = \frac{\Sigma f_i x_i}{\Sigma f_i} = \frac{412.5}{75} = 5.5$

Hence, mean of the given distribution is 5.5.

Q.2 Calculate the mean of the scores of 20 students in a mathematics test

Marks	10-20	20-30	30-40	40-50	50-60
Number of students	2	4	7	6	1

Ans. We first, find the class mark x_i of each class and then proceed as follows

Marks	Class marks (x_i)	Number of students (f_i)	$f_i\, x_i$
10-20	15	2	30
20-30	25	4	100
30-40	35	7	245
40-50	45	6	270
50-60	55	1	55
		$\Sigma f_i = 20$	$\Sigma f_i x_i = 700$

Therefore, $\text{mean}(\bar{x}) = \frac{\Sigma f_i x_i}{\Sigma f_i} = \frac{700}{20} = 35$

Hence, the mean of scores of 20 students in mathematics test is 35.

Mistake Alert! *Students calculating the class mark incorrectly using endpoints instead of the mid-point.*

Q.3 Calculate the mean of the following data

Class	4-7	8-11	12-15	16-19
Frequency	5	4	9	10

Ans. Since, given data is not continuous, so we subtract 0.5 from the lower limit and add 0.5 to the upper limit of each class.

Now, we first find the class mark x_i of each class and then proceed as follows.

Class	**Class marks (x_i)**	**Frequency (f_i)**	$f_i x_i$
3.5-7.5	5.5	5	27.5
7.5-11.5	9.5	4	38
11.5-15.5	13.5	9	121.5
15.5-19.5	17.5	10	175
		$\Sigma f_i = 28$	$\Sigma f_i x_i = 362$

Therefore, $\bar{x}\text{ (mean)} = \frac{\Sigma f_i x_i}{\Sigma f_i} = \frac{362}{28} = 12.93$

Hence, mean of the given data is 12.93.

Q.4 The following table gives the number of pages written by Sarika for completing her own book for 30 days.

Number of pages written per day	16-18	19-21	22-24	25-27	28-30
Number of days	1	3	4	9	13

Find the mean number of pages written per day.

Ans. Since, given data is not continuous, so we subtract 0.5 from the lower limit and add 0.5 to the upper limit of each class.

Class mark	**Mid-value (x_i)**	**Number of days (f_i)**	$f_i x_i$
15.5-18.5	17	1	17
18.5-21.5	20	3	60
21.5-24.5	23	4	92
24.5-27.5	26	9	234
27.5-30.5	29	13	377
Total		$\Sigma f_i = 30$	$\Sigma f_i x_i = 780$

$\therefore$ $\text{Mean}(\bar{x}) = \frac{\Sigma f_i x_i}{\Sigma f_i} = \frac{780}{30} = 26$

Hence, the mean number of pages written per day is 26.

Q.5 The daily income of a sample of 50 employees are tabulated as follows.

Income (in ₹)	1-200	201-400	401-600	601-800
Number of employees	14	15	14	7

Find the mean daily income of employees.

- **Concept Insight** In this question, we will use step deviation method to find the mean of the given distribution mean $(\overline{x}) = a + \frac{\Sigma f_i x_i}{\Sigma f_i} \times h$.

Ans. Since, given data is not continuous, so we subtract 0.5 from the lower limit and add 0.5 to in the upper limit of each class.

Now we first, find the class mark x_i of each class and then proceed as follows

Income (in ₹)	Class marks (x_i)	Number of employees (f_i)	$u_i = \frac{x_i - a}{h} = \frac{x_i - 300.5}{200}$	$f_i u_i$
0.5-200.5	100.5	14	−1	−14
200.5-400.5	$a = 300.5$	15	0	0
400.5-600.5	500.5	14	1	14
600.5-800.5	700.5	7	2	14
		$N = \Sigma f_i = 50$		$\Sigma f_i u_i = 14$

$\therefore$ Assumed mean, $a = 300.5$

Class width, $h = 200$

and total observations, $N = 50$

By step deviation method,

$$\text{Mean} = a + h \times \frac{1}{N} \times \sum_{i=1}^{5} f_i u_i = 300.5 + 200 \times \frac{1}{50} \times 14$$

$$= 300.5 + 56 = 356.5$$

Q.6 An aircraft has 120 passenger seats. The number of seats occupied during 100 flights is given in the following table.

Number of seats	100-104	104-108	108-112	112-116	116-120
Frequency	15	20	32	18	15

Determine the mean number of seats occupied over the flights.

Ans. We first, find the class mark x_i of each class and then proceed as follows.

Number of seats	Class marks (x_i)	Frequency (f_i)	Deviation $d_i = x_i - a$	$f_i d_i$
100-104	102	15	−8	−120
104-108	106	20	−4	−80
108-112	$a = 110$	32	0	0
112-116	114	18	4	72
116-120	118	15	8	120
		$N = \Sigma f_i = 100$		$\Sigma f_i d_i = -8$

$\therefore$ Assumed mean, $a = 110$,

Class width, $h = 4$

and total observation, $N = 100$

By assumed mean method,

$$\text{Mean}\,(\bar{x}) = a + \frac{\Sigma f_i d_i}{\Sigma f_i} = 110 + \left(\frac{-8}{100}\right) = 110 - 0.08 = 109.92$$

Alternate Method

We first, find the class mark (x_i) of each class and then proceed as follows.

Number of seats	Class marks (x_i)	Frequency (f_i)	$f_i x_i$
100-104	102	15	1530
104-108	106	20	2120
108-112	110	32	3520
112-116	114	18	2052
116-120	118	15	1770
		$\Sigma f_i = 100$	$\Sigma f_i x_i = 10992$

$$\therefore \text{Mean}\,(\bar{x}) = \frac{\Sigma f_i x_i}{\Sigma f_i} = \frac{10992}{100} = 109.92$$

Q. 7 The weights (in kg) of 50 wrestlers are recorded in the following table.

Weight (in kg)	100-110	110-120	120-130	130-140	140-150
Number of wrestlers	4	14	21	8	3

Find the mean weight of the wrestlers.

Ans. We first find the class mark x_i, of each class and then proceed as follows

Weight (in kg)	Number of wrestlers (f_i)	Class marks (x_i)	Deviations $d_i = x_i - a$	$f_i d_i$
100-110	4	105	–20	–80
110-120	14	115	–10	–140
120-130	21	$a = 125$	0	0
130-140	8	135	10	80
140-150	3	145	20	60
	$N = \Sigma f_i = 50$			$\Sigma f_i d_i = -80$

$\therefore$ Assumed mean $(a) = 125$,

Class width $(h) = 10$ and total observation $(N) = 50$

By assumed mean method,

$$\text{Mean}\,(\bar{x}) = a + \frac{\Sigma f_i d_i}{\Sigma f_i} = 125 + \frac{(-80)}{50} = 125 - 1.6 = 123.4 \text{ kg}$$

Alternate Method

We first, find the class mark (x_i) of each class and then proceed as follows.

Weight (in kg)	Class marks (x_i)	Number of wrestlers (f_i)	$f_i x_i$
100-110	105	4	420
110-120	115	14	1610
120-130	125	21	2625
130-140	135	8	1080
140-150	145	3	435
		$\Sigma f_i = 50$	$\Sigma f_i x_i = 6170$

$\therefore$ Mean $(\bar{x}) = \frac{\Sigma f_i x_i}{\Sigma f_i} = \frac{6170}{50} = 123.4$

So, the mean weight of the wrestlers is 123.4 kg

Q. 8 The mileage (km per litre) of 50 cars of the same model was tested by a manufacturer and details are tabulated as given below

Mileage (km/L)	10-12	12-14	14-16	16-18
Number of cars	7	12	18	13

Find the mean mileage.

The manufacturer claimed that the mileage of the model was 16 km/litre. Do you agree with this claim?

Ans.

Mileage (km/L)	**Class marks** (x_i)	**Number of cars** (f_i)	$f_i x_i$
10-12	11	7	77
12-14	13	12	156
14-16	15	18	270
16-18	17	13	221
Total		$\Sigma f_i = 50$	$\Sigma f_i x_i = 724$

Here, $\Sigma f_i = 50$

and $\Sigma f_i x_i = 724$

$\therefore$ $\text{Mean}(\bar{x}) = \frac{\Sigma f_i x_i}{\Sigma f_i} = \frac{724}{50} = 14.48$

Hence, mean mileage is 14.48 km/litre.

No, the manufacturer is claiming mileage 1.52 km/L more than average mileage.

Q.9 The following is the distribution of weights (in kg) of 40 persons.

Weight (in kg)	40-45	45-50	50-55	55-60	60-65	65-70	70-75	75-80
Number of persons	4	4	13	5	6	5	2	1

Construct a cumulative frequency distribution (of the less than type) table for the data above.

Ans. The cumulative distribution (less than type) table is shown below

Weight (in kg)	Cumulative frequency
Less than 45	4
Less than 50	$4 + 4 = 8$
Less than 55	$8 + 13 = 21$
Less than 60	$21 + 5 = 26$
Less than 65	$26 + 6 = 32$
Less than 70	$32 + 5 = 37$
Less than 75	$37 + 2 = 39$
Less than 80	$39 + 1 = 40$

Mistake Alert ! *Students may incorrectly calculate the 'less than' cumulative frequency from the end instead from the beginning.*

Q.10 The following table shows the cumulative frequency distribution of marks of 800 students in an examination.

Marks	Number of students
Below 10	10
Below 20	50
Below 30	130
Below 40	270
Below 50	440
Below 60	570
Below 70	670
Below 80	740
Below 90	780
Below 100	800

Construct a frequency distribution table for the data above.

Ans. Here, we observe that 10 students have scored marks below 10 *i.e.,* it lies between class interval 0-10. Similarly, 50 students have scored marks below 20. So, $50 - 10 = 40$ students lies in the interval 10 - 20 and so on.

The table of a frequency distribution for the given data is

Class interval	Number of students
0-10	10
10-20	50 – 10 = 40
20-30	130 – 50 = 80
30-40	270 – 130 = 140
40-50	440 – 270 = 170
50-60	570 – 440 = 130
60-70	670 – 570 = 100
70-80	740 – 670 = 70
80-90	780 – 740 = 40
90-100	800 – 780 = 20

Q.11 Form the frequency distribution table from the following data

Marks (Out of 90)	Number of candidates
More than or equal to 80	4
More than or equal to 70	6
More than or equal to 60	11
More than or equal to 50	17
More than or equal to 40	23
More than or equal to 30	27
More than or equal to 20	30
More than or equal to 10	32
More than or equal to 0	34

Ans. Here, we observe that, all 34 students have scored marks more than or equal to 0. Since, 32 students have scored marks more than or equal to 10. So, 34 – 32 = 2 students lies in the interval 0-10 and so on.

Now, we construct the frequency distribution table.

Class interval	Number of candidates
0-10	34 – 32 = 2
10-20	32 – 30 = 2
20-30	30 – 27 = 3
30-40	27 – 23 = 4
40-50	23 – 17 = 6
50-60	17 – 11 = 6
60-70	11 – 6 = 5
70-80	6 – 4 = 2
80-90	= 4

Q.12 Find the unknown entries a, b, c, d, e and f in the following distribution of heights of students in a class

Height (in cm)	**Frequency**	**Cumulative frequency**
150-155	12	a
155-160	b	25
160-165	10	c
165-170	d	43
170-175	e	48
175-180	2	f
Total	50	

Ans.

Height (in cm)	**Frequency**	**Cumulative frequency** (given)	**Cumulative frequency**
150-155	12	a	12
155-160	b	25	$12 + b$
160-165	10	c	$22 + b$
165-170	d	43	$22 + b + d$
170-175	e	48	$22 + b + d + e$
175-180	2	f	$24 + b + d + e$
Total	50		

On comparing last two tables, we get

$$a = 12$$

$\therefore$ $$12 + b = 25$$

$\Rightarrow$ $$b = 25 - 12 = 13$$

$$22 + b = c \Rightarrow c = 22 + 13 = 35$$

$$22 + b + d = 43$$

$\Rightarrow$ $$22 + 13 + d = 43$$

$\Rightarrow$ $$d = 43 - 35 = 8$$

and $$22 + b + d + e = 48$$

$\Rightarrow$ $$22 + 13 + 8 + e = 48$$

$\Rightarrow$ $$e = 48 - 43 = 5$$

and $$24 + b + d + e = f$$

$\Rightarrow$ $$24 + 13 + 8 + 5 = f$$

$\therefore$ $$f = 50$$

Q.13 The following are the ages of 300 patients getting medical treatment in a hospital on a particular day

Age (in years)	10-20	20-30	30-40	40-50	50-60	60-70
Number of patients	60	42	55	70	53	20

Form

(i) less than type cumulative frequency distribution.

(ii) More than type cumulative frequency distribution.

Ans. (i) We observe that the number of patients which take medical treatment in a hospital on a particular day with age less than 10 is 0. Similarly, less than 20 include the number of patients which take medical treatment from 0-10 as well as the number of patients which take medical treatment from 10-20.

So, the total number of patients with age less than 20 is $0 + 60 = 60$, we say that the cumulative frequency of the class 10-20 is 60. Similarly, for other class.

(ii) Also, we observe that all 300 patients which take medical treatment more than or equal to 10. Since, there are 60 patients which take medical treatment in the interval 10-20, this means that there are $300 - 60 = 240$ patients who take medical treatment more than or equal to 20. Continuing in the same manner.

(i) **Less than type**		(ii) **More than type**	
Age (in year)	**Number of students**	**Age** (in year)	**Number of students**
Less than 10	0	More than or equal to 10	300
Less than 20	60	More than or equal to 20	240
Less than 30	102	More than or equal to 30	198
Less than 40	157	More than or equal to 40	143
Less than 50	227	More than or equal to 50	73
Less than 60	280	More than or equal to 60	20
Less than 70	300		

Q.14 Given below is a cumulative frequency distribution showing the marks secured by 50 students of a class

Marks	Below 20	Below 40	Below 60	Below 80	Below 100
Number of students	17	22	29	37	50

Form the frequency distribution table for the data.

Ans. Here, we observe that, 17 students have scored marks below 20 *i.e.,* it lies between class interval 0-20 and 22 students have scored marks below 40, so $22 - 17 = 5$ students lies in the class interval 20-40 continuting in the same manner, we get the complete frequency distribution table for given data.

Marks	**Number of students**
0-20	17
20-40	$22 - 17 = 5$
40-60	$29 - 22 = 7$
60-80	$37 - 29 = 8$
80-100	$50 - 37 = 13$

Q.15 Weekly income of 600 families is tabulated below

Weekly income (in ₹)	Number of families
0-1000	250
1000-2000	190
2000-3000	100
3000-4000	40
4000-5000	15
5000-6000	5
Total	**600**

Compute the median income.

Ans. First we construct a cumulative frequency table.

Weekly income (in ₹)	Number of families (f_i)	Cumulative frequency (cf)
0-1000	250	250
1000-2000 = mid class	190 = f	250 + 190 = 440
2000-3000	100	440 + 100 = 540
3000-4000	40	540 + 40 = 580
4000-5000	15	580 + 15 = 595
5000-6000	5	595 + 5 = 600

It is given that, $n = 600$

$$\therefore \quad \frac{n}{2} = \frac{600}{2} = 300$$

Since, cumulative frequency 440 lies in the interval 1000 - 2000.

So, median class is 1000-2000.

Here, (lower limit of median class) $l = 1000$,

$f = 190$, $cf = 250$, (class width) $h = 1000$

and (total observation) $n = 600$

$$\therefore \quad \text{Median} = l + \frac{\left(\frac{n}{2} - cf\right)}{f} \times h$$

$$= 1000 + \frac{(300 - 250)}{190} \times 1000$$

$$= 1000 + \frac{50}{190} \times 1000$$

$$= 1000 + \frac{5000}{19}$$

$$= 1000 + 263.15 = 1263.15$$

Hence, the median income is ₹ 1263.15.

Q.16 The maximum bowling speeds, in km per hour, of 33 players at a cricket coaching centre are given as follows

Speed (in km/h)	85-100	100-115	115-130	130-145
Number of players	11	9	8	5

Calculate the median bowling speed.

Ans. First we construct the cumulative frequency table

Speed (in km/h)	**Number of players**	**Cumulative frequency**
85-100	11	11
100-115	9	11+ 9 = 20
115-130	8	20 + 8 = 28
130-145	5	28 + 5 = 33

It is given that, $n = 33$

$$\therefore \quad \frac{n}{2} = \frac{33}{2} = 16.5$$

So, the median class is 100-115.

where, lower limit $(l) = 100$,

frequency $(f) = 9$,

cumulative frequency $(cf) = 11$

and class width $(h) = 15$

$$\therefore \text{Median} = l + \frac{\left(\frac{n}{2} - cf\right)}{f} \times h = 100 + \frac{(16.5 - 11)}{9} \times 15$$

$$= 100 + \frac{5.5 \times 15}{9} = 100 + \frac{82.5}{9} = 100 + 9.17 = 109.17$$

Hence, the median bowling speed is 109.17 km/h.

Q.17 The monthly income of 100 families are given as below

Income (in ₹)	**Number of families**
0-5000	8
5000-10000	26
10000-15000	41
15000-20000	16
20000-25000	3
25000-30000	3
30000-35000	2
35000-40000	1

Calculate the modal income.

Ans. In a given data, the highest frequency is 41, which lies in the interval 10000-15000.

Here, $l = 10000$, $f_1 = 41$, $f_0 = 26$, $f_2 = 16$ and $h = 5000$

$$\therefore \quad \text{Mode} = l + \left(\frac{f_1 - f_0}{2f_1 - f_0 - f_2}\right) \times h$$

$$= 10000 + \left(\frac{41 - 26}{2 \times 41 - 26 - 16}\right) \times 5000$$

$$= 10000 + \left(\frac{15}{82 - 42}\right) \times 5000 = 10000 + \left(\frac{15}{40}\right) \times 5000$$

$$= 10000 + 15 \times 125 = 10000 + 1875 = 11875$$

Hence, the modal income is ₹ 11875.

Q.18 The weight of coffee in 70 packets are shown in the following table

Weight (in g)	**Number of packets**
200-201	12
201-202	26
202-203	20
203-204	9
204-205	2
205-206	1

Determine the model weight.

Ans. In the given data, the highest frequency is 26, which lies in the interval 201-202

Here, $l = 201,\ f_1 = 26,\ f_0 = 12,\ f_2 = 20$ and (class width) $h = 1$

$$\therefore \quad \text{Mode} = l + \left(\frac{f_1 - f_0}{2f_1 - f_0 - f_2}\right) \times h = 201 + \left(\frac{26 - 12}{2 \times 26 - 12 - 20}\right) \times 1$$

$$= 201 + \left(\frac{14}{52 - 32}\right) = 201 + \frac{14}{20} = 201 + 0.7 = 201.7$$

Hence, the modal weight is 201.7 g.

Q. 19 Two dice are thrown at the same time. Find the probability of getting

(i) same number on both dice.

(ii) different number on both dice.

Ans. Two dice are thrown at the same time. [given]

So, total number of possible outcomes = 36

(i) We have, same number on both dice.

So, possible outcomes are (1, 1), (2, 2), (3, 3), (4, 4), (5, 5) and (6, 6).

∴ Number of possible outcomes = 6

Now, Required probability $= \frac{6}{36} = \frac{1}{6}$

(ii) We have, different number on both dice.

So, number of possible outcomes

= 36 – Number of possible outcomes for getting same number on both dice

= 36 – 6 = 30

∴ Required probability $= \frac{30}{36} = \frac{5}{6}$

Q.20 Two dice are thrown simultaneously. What is the probability that the sum of the numbers appearing on the dice is

(i) 7? (ii) a prime number ? (iii) 1?

Ans. Two dice are thrown simultaneously. [given]

So, total number of outcomes = 36

(i) Sum of the numbers appearing on the dice is 7.

So, the possible outcomes are (1, 6), (2, 5), (3, 4), (4, 3), (5, 2) and (6, 1).

Number of possible outcomes = 6

$\therefore$ Required probability $= \frac{6}{36} = \frac{1}{6}$

(ii) Sum of the numbers appearing on the dice is a prime number *i.e.*, 2, 3, 5, 7 and 11.

So, the possible outcomes are (1, 1), (1, 2), (2, 1), (1, 4), (2, 3), (3, 2), (4,1), (1, 6), (2, 5), (3, 4), (4, 3), (5, 2), (6, 1), (5, 6) and (6, 5).

Number of possible outcomes = 15

$\therefore$ Required probability $= \frac{15}{36} = \frac{5}{12}$

(iii) Sum of the numbers appearing on the dice is 1.

It is not possible, so its probability is zero.

Q.21 Two dice are thrown together. Find the probability that the product of the numbers on the top of the dice is

(i) 6 (ii) 12 (iii) 7

Ans. Total number of outcomes = 36

(i) When product of the numbers on the top of the dice is 6.

So, the possible outcomes are (1, 6), (2, 3), (3, 2) and (6, 1).

Number of possible outcomes = 4

$\therefore$ Required probability $= \frac{4}{36} = \frac{1}{9}$

(ii) When product of the numbers on the top of the dice is 12.

So, the possible outcomes are (2, 6), (3, 4), (4, 3) and (6, 2).

Number of possible outcomes = 4

$\therefore$ Required probability $= \frac{4}{36} = \frac{1}{9}$

(iii) Product of the numbers on the top of the dice cannot be 7. So, its probability is zero.

Q.22 Two dice are thrown at the same time and the product of numbers appearing on them is noted. Find the probability that the product is less than 9.

Ans. Number of total outcomes = 36

When product of numbers appearing on them is less than 9, then possible outcomes are (1, 6), (1, 5) (1, 4), (1, 3), (1, 2), (1, 1), (2, 2), (2, 3), (2, 4), (3, 2), (4, 2), (4, 1), (3,1), (5, 1), (6, 1) and (2, 1).

Number of possible ways = 16

$\therefore$Required probability $= \frac{16}{36} = \frac{4}{9}$

Q.23 Two dice are numbered 1, 2, 3, 4, 5, 6 and 1, 1, 2, 2, 3, 3, respectively. They are thrown and the sum of the numbers on them is noted. Find the probability of getting each sum from 2 to 9, separately.

Ans. Number of total outcomes = $n(s) = 36$

(i) Let E_1 = Event of getting sum 2 = (1, 1), (1, 1) *i.e.*, 2 in number.

$$\therefore \quad P(E_1) = \frac{2}{36} = \frac{1}{18}$$

(ii) Let E_2 = Event of getting sum 3 = (1, 2), (1, 2), (2, 1), (2, 1) *i.e.*, 4 in number.

$$\therefore \quad P(E_2) = \frac{4}{36} = \frac{1}{9}$$

(iii) Let E_3 = Event of getting sum 4 = (2, 2), (2, 2), (3, 1), (3, 1), (1, 3), (1, 3) *i.e.*, 6 in number.

$$\therefore \quad P(E_3) = \frac{6}{36} = \frac{1}{6}$$

(iv) Let E_4 = Event of getting sum 5 = (2, 3), (2, 3), (4, 1), (4, 1), (3, 2), (3, 2) *i.e.*, 6 in number.

$$\therefore \quad P(E_4) = \frac{6}{36} = \frac{1}{6}$$

(v) Let E_5 = Event of getting sum 6 = (3, 3), (3, 3), (4, 2), (4, 2), (5, 1), (5, 1) *i.e.*, 6 in number.

$$\therefore \quad P(E_5) = \frac{6}{36} = \frac{1}{6}$$

(vi) Let E_6 = Event of getting sum 7 = (4, 3), (4, 3), (5, 2), (5, 2), (6, 1), (6, 1) *i.e.*, 6 in number.

$$\therefore \quad P(E_6) = \frac{6}{36} = \frac{1}{6}$$

(vii) Let E_7 = Event of getting sum 8 = (5, 3), (5, 3), (6, 2), (6, 2) *i.e.*, 4 in number.

$$\therefore \quad P(E_7) = \frac{4}{36} = \frac{1}{9}$$

(viii) Let E_8 = Event of getting sum 9 = (6, 3), (6, 3) *i.e.*, 2 in number.

$$\therefore \quad P(E_8) = \frac{2}{36} = \frac{1}{18}$$

Q.24 A coin is tossed two times. Find the probability of getting at most one head.

Ans. The possible outcomes, if a coin is tossed 2 times $(HH), (TT), (HT), (TH)$ *i.e.*, 4 in number

Let E = Event of getting at most one head

$$= (TT), (HT), (TH) \text{ i.e., 3 in number}$$

Hence, Required probability $= \frac{3}{4}$

Mistake Alert! *For 'at most one head' in one coin oin tossed twice, students might calculate the case of getting exactly one head.*

Q.25 A coin is tossed 3 times. List the possible outcomes. Find the probability of getting

(i) all heads (ii) at least 2 heads

Ans. The possible outcomes, if a coin is tossed 3 times are

$(HHH), (TTT), (HTT), (THT), (TTH), (THH), (HTH), (HHT)$ *i.e.*, 8 in number

(i) Let E_1 = Event of getting all heads = (HHH) *i.e.*, 1 in number.

$$\therefore \quad P(E_1) = \frac{1}{8}$$

(ii) Let E_2 = Event of getting at least 2 heads = $(HHT), (HTH), (THH), (HHH)$ *i.e.*, 4 in number

$$\therefore \quad P(E_2) = \frac{4}{8} = \frac{1}{2}$$

Q.26 Two dice are thrown at the same time. Determine the probability that the difference of the numbers on the two dice is 2.

Ans. The total number of outcomes $= 6 \times 6 = 36$

Let E = Event of getting the numbers whose difference is 2

$= (1, 3), (2, 4), (3, 5), (4, 6), (3, 1), (4, 2), (5, 3), (6, 4)$ *i.e.*, 8 in number

$$\therefore \quad P(E) = \frac{8}{36} = \frac{2}{9}$$

Q.27 A bag contains 10 red, 5 blue and 7 green balls. A ball is drawn at random. Find the probability of this ball being a

(i) red ball (ii) green ball (iii) not a blue ball

Ans. Total number of outcomes $= 10 + 5 + 7 = 22$

(i) Let E_1 = Event of getting a red ball

Number of favourable outcomes = 10

$$\therefore \quad \text{Required probability} = \frac{10}{22} = \frac{5}{11}$$

(ii) Let E_2 = Event of getting a green ball

Number of favourable outcomes = 7

$$\therefore \quad \text{Required probability} = \frac{7}{22}$$

(iii) Let E_3 = Event getting a red ball or a green ball *i.e.*, not a blue ball.

Number of favourable outcomes $= 10 + 7 = 17$

$$\therefore \quad \text{Required probability} = \frac{17}{22}$$

Q.28 The king, queen and jack of clubs are removed from a deck of 52 playing cards and then well shuffled. Now, one card is drawn at random from the remaining cards. Determine the probability that the card is

(i) a heart (ii) a king

Ans. If we remove one king, one queen and one jack of clubs from 52 cards, then the remaining cards left, $= 52-(1+1+1) = 49$

(i) Let E_1 = Event of getting a heart

Number of favourable outcomes = 13

$\therefore$ $$P(E_1) = \frac{13}{49}$$

(ii) Let E_2 = Event of getting a king

Number of favourable outcomes = 3 [since, out of 4 king, one club cards is already removed]

$\therefore$ $$P(E_2) = \frac{3}{49}$$

Q.29 Refer to Q.28. What is the probability that the card is

(i) a club (ii) 10 of hearts

Ans. (i) Let E_3 = Event of getting a club

Number of favourable outcomes = 13 – 3 = 10

$\therefore$ $$\text{Required probability} = \frac{10}{49}$$

(ii) Let E_4 = Event of getting '10' of hearts

Number of favourable outcomes = 1

[because in 52 playing cards only 13 are the heart cards and only one '10' in 13 heart cards]

$\therefore$ $$\text{Required probability} = \frac{1}{49}$$

Q.30 All the jacks, queens and kings are removed from a deck of 52 playing cards. The remaining cards are well shuffled and then one card is drawn at random. Giving ace a value 1 similar value for other cards, find the probability that the card has a value.

(i) 7

(ii) greater than 7

(iii) less than 7

Ans. In out of 52 playing cards, 4 jacks, 4 queens and 4 kings are removed, then the remaining cards are left $= 52 - 3 \times 4 = 40$.

(i) Let E_1 = Event of getting a card whose value is 7

= Card value 7 may be of a spade, a diamond, a club or a heart

$\therefore$ Number of favourable outcomes = 4

$\therefore$ $$P(E_1) = \frac{4}{40} = \frac{1}{10}$$

(ii) Let E_2 = Event of getting a card whose value is greater than 7

= Event of getting a card whose value is 8, 9 or 10

$\therefore$ Number of favourable outcomes $= 3 \times 4 = 12$

$\therefore$ $$P(E_2) = \frac{12}{40} = \frac{3}{10}$$

(iii) Let E_3 = Event of getting a card whose value is less than 7
= Event of getting a card whose value is 1, 2, 3, 4, 5 or 6

$\therefore$ Number of favourable outcomes $= 6 \times 4 = 24$

$\therefore$ $$P(E_3) = \frac{24}{40} = \frac{3}{5}$$

Q.31 An integer is chosen between 0 and 100. What is the probability that it is

(i) divisible by 7?

(ii) not divisible by 7?

Ans. The number of integers between 0 and 100 = 99

(i) Let E_1 = Event of choosing an integer which is divisible by 7
= Event of choosing an integer which is multiple of 7
= 7, 14, 21, 28, 35, 42, 49, 56, 63, 70, 77, 84, 91, 98 *i.e.*, 14 in number.

$\therefore$ $$P(E_1) = \frac{14}{99}$$

(ii) Let E_2 = Event of choosing an integer which is not divisible by 7

Number of favourable outcomes $= 99 - 14 = 85$

$\therefore$ $$P(E_2) = \frac{85}{99}$$

Q.32 Cards with numbers 2 to 101 are placed in a box. A card is selected at random. Find the probability that the card has

(i) an even number (ii) a square number

Ans. Total number of outcomes with numbers 2 to 101 = 100

(i) Let E_1 = Event of selecting a card which is an even number = 2, 4, 6,...100

[in an AP, $l = a + (n-1)d$, here $l = 100$, $a = 2$ and $d = 2 \Rightarrow 100 = 2 + (n-1)2$
$\Rightarrow (n-1) = 49 \Rightarrow n = 50$]

$\therefore$ Number of favouable outcomes = 50

$\therefore$ Required probability $= \frac{50}{100} = \frac{1}{2}$

(ii) Let E_2 = Event of selecting a card which is a square number
= 4, 9, 16, 25, 36, 49, 64, 81, 100
$= (2)^2, (3)^2, (4)^2, (5)^2, (6)^2, (7)^2, (8)^2, (9)^2, (10)^2$ *i.e.*, 9 in number

Hence, required probability $= \frac{9}{100}$

Mistake Alert! *Students may incorrectly take events as* $1^2, 2^2, 3^2, 4^2, 5^2, 6^2, 7^2, 8^2, 9^2, 10^2$ *instead of* $2^2, 3^2, 4^2, 5^2, 6^2, 7^2, 8^2, 9^2, 10^2$.

Q.33 A letter of English alphabets is chosen at random. Determine the probability that the letter is a consonant

Ans. We know that, in English alphabets, there are (5 vowels + 21 consonants) = 26 letters. So, total number of outcomes in English alphabets is 26.

Let E = Event of choosing an English alphabet, which is a consonant

= *b, c, d, f, g, h, j, k, l, m, n, p, q, r, s, t, v, w, x, y, z i.e., 21 in number.*

Hence, required probability $= \frac{21}{26}$

Q.34 There are 1000 sealed envelopes in a box, 10 of them contain a cash prize of ₹ 100 each, 100 of them contain a cash prize of ₹ 50 each and 200 of them contain a cash prize of ₹ 10 each and rest do not contain any cash prize. If they are well shuffled and an envelope is picked out, what is the probability that it contains no cash prize?

Ans. Total number of sealed envelopes in a box = 1000

Number of envelopes containing cash prize = 10 + 100 + 200 = 310

Number of envelopes containing no cash prize = 1000 − 310 = 690

$\therefore$ Required probability $= \frac{690}{1000} = \frac{69}{100} = 0.69$

Q.35 Box *A* contains 25 slips of which 19 are marked ₹ 1 and other are marked ₹ 5 each. Box *B* contains 50 slips of which 45 are marked ₹ 1 each and others are marked ₹ 13 each. Slips of both boxes are poured into a third box and reshuffled. A slip is drawn at random. What is the probability that it is marked other than ₹ 1?

Ans. Total number of slips in a box = 25 + 50 = 75

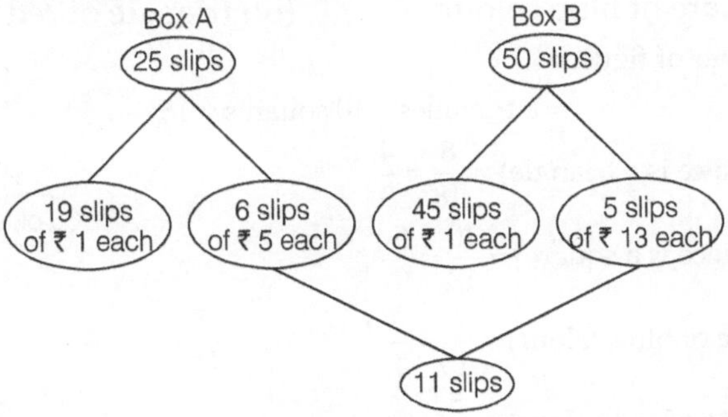

From the chart it is clear that, there are 11 slips which are marked other than ₹ 1.

$\therefore$ Required probability $= \frac{\text{Number of slips other than ₹ 1}}{\text{Total number of slips}} = \frac{11}{75}$

Q.36 A carton of 24 bulbs contain 6 defective bulbs. One bulb is drawn at random. What is the probability that the bulb is not defective? If the bulb selected is defective and it is not replaced and a second bulb is selected at random from the rest, what is the probability that the second bulb is defective?

Ans. $\because$ Total number of bulbs = 24

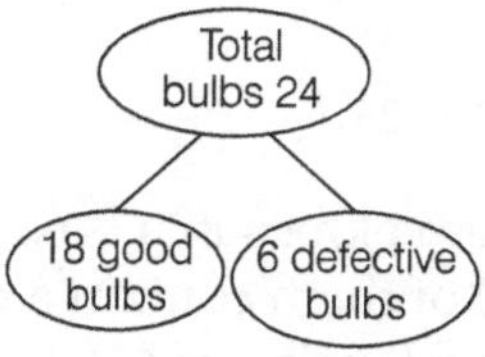

Let E_1 = Event of selecting not defective bulb = Event of selecting good bulbs *i.e.*, 18 in number

$$\therefore \quad P(E_1) = \frac{18}{24} = \frac{3}{4}$$

Suppose, the selected bulb is defective and not replaced, then total number of bulbs remains in a carton = 23.

In 23 bulbs, 18 are good bulbs and 5 are defective bulbs.

$\therefore$ P(selecting second defective bulb) $= \frac{5}{23}$

Q.37 A child's game has 8 triangles of which 3 are blue and rest are red, and 10 squares of which 6 are blue and rest are red. One piece is lost at random. Find the probability that it is a

(i) triangle (ii) square

(iii) square of blue colour (iv) triangle of red colour

Ans. Total number of figures

$$= 8 \text{ triangles} + 10 \text{ squares} = 18$$

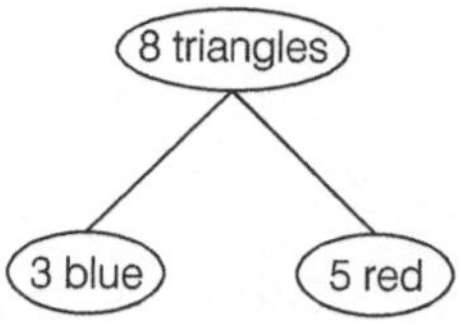

(i) P(lost piece is a triangle) $= \frac{8}{18} = \frac{4}{9}$

(ii) P(lost piece is a square) $= \frac{10}{18} = \frac{5}{9}$

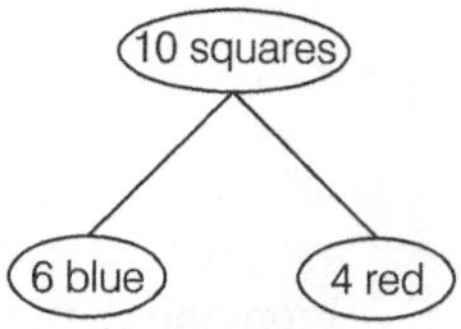

(iii) P(square of blue colour) $= \frac{6}{18} = \frac{1}{3}$

(iv) P(triangle of red colour) $= \frac{5}{18}$

Q.38 In a game, the entry fee is of ₹ 5. The game consists of a tossing a coin 3 times. If one or two heads show, Sweta gets her entry fee back. If she throws 3 heads, she receives double the entry fees. Otherwise she will lose. For tossing a coin three times, find the probability that she

(i) loses the entry fee. (ii) gets double entry fee.

(iii) just gets her entry fee.

Ans. Total possible outcomes of tossing a coin 3 times are

$(HHH), (TTT), (HTT), (THT), (TTH), (THH), (HTH), (HHT)$ *i.e.*, 8 in number.

(i) Let E_1 = Event that Sweta loses the entry fee

= She tosses tail on three times

$= (TTT)$

$$P(E_1) = \frac{1}{8}$$

(ii) Let E_2 = Event that Sweta gets double entry fee

= She tosses heads on three times = (HHH) *i.e.*, 1 in number.

$$\therefore \quad P(E_2) = \frac{1}{8}$$

(iii) Let E_3 = Event that Sweta gets her entry fee back

= Sweta gets heads one or two times

$= (HTT), (THT), (TTH), (HHT), (HTH), (THH)$ i.e., 6 in number.

$$\therefore \quad P(E_3) = \frac{6}{8} = \frac{3}{4}$$

Q.39 A die has its six faces marked 0, 1, 1, 1, 6, 6. Two such dice are thrown together and the total score is recorded.

(i) How many different scores are possible?

(ii) What is the probability of getting a total of 7?

Ans. Given, a die has its six faces marked 0, 1, 1, 1, 6, 6.

$\therefore$ Total number of outcomes $= 6^2 = 36$

(i) The different score which are possible are 6 scores *i.e.*, 0,1,2,6,7 and12.

(ii) Let E = Event of getting a sum 7

$= (1,6),(1,6),(1,6),(1,6),(1,6),(1,6),(6,1),(6,1),(6,1),(6,1),(6,1),(6,1)$

i.e., 12 in number.

$$\therefore \quad P(E) = \frac{12}{36} = \frac{1}{3}$$

Q.40 A lot consists of 48 mobile phones of which 42 are good, 3 have only minor defects and 3 have major defects. Varnika will buy a phone, if it is good but the trader will only buy a mobile, if it has no major defect. One phone is selected at random from the lot. What is the probability that it is

(i) acceptable to Varnika?

(ii) acceptable to the trader?

Ans. Given, total number of mobile phones = 42 + 3 + 3 = 48

(i) Let = Event that Varnika will buy a mobile phone

= Varnika buys only, if it is good mobile

Number of favourable outcomes = 42

$$\therefore P(E_1) = \frac{42}{48} = \frac{7}{8}$$

(ii) Let E_2 = Event that trader will buy only when it has no major defects

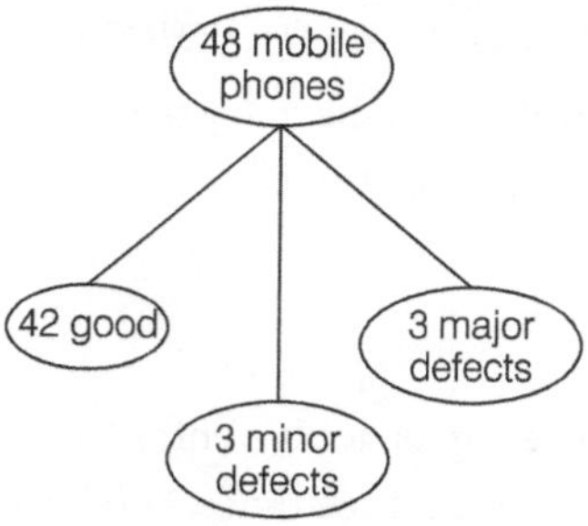

Number of favourable outcomes = 42 + 3 = 45

$$\therefore \quad P(E_2) = \frac{45}{48} = \frac{15}{16}$$

Q.41 A bag contains 24 balls of which x are red, $2x$ are white and $3x$ are blue. A ball is selected at random. What is the probability that it is

(i) not red? (ii) white?

Ans. Given that, total number of balls in a bag = 24

Number of red balls in a bag = x

Number of white balls in a bag = $2x$

and number of blue balls in a bag = $3x$

By condition, $x + 2x + 3x = 24 \Rightarrow 6x = 24$

$\therefore \quad x = 4$

$\therefore$ Number of red balls = x = 4

Number of white balls = $2x = 2 \times 4 = 8$

and number of blue balls = $3x = 3 \times 4 = 12$

So, total number of outcomes = 24.

(i) Let E_1 = Event of selecting a ball which is not red *i.e.*, can be white or blue.

= Number of white balls + Number of blue balls

$\Rightarrow \quad = 8 + 12 = 20$

$\therefore$ Required probability $= \frac{20}{24} = \frac{5}{6}$

(ii) Let E_2 = Event of selecting a ball which is white

$\therefore$ Number of white balls = 8

So, required probability $= \frac{8}{24} = \frac{1}{3}$

Q.42 At a fete, cards bearing numbers 1 to 1000, one number on one card, are put in a box. Each player selects one card at random and that card is not replaced. If the selected card has a perfect square greater than 500, the player wins a prize. What is the probability that

(i) the first player wins a prize?

(ii) the second player wins a prize, if the first has won?

Ans. Total number of outcomes = 1000

If the selected card has a perfect square greater than 500, then player wins a prize.

(i) Let E_1 = Event first player wins a prize = Player select a card which is a perfect square greater than 500

$= 529, 576, 625, 676, 729, 784, 841, 900, 961$

$= (23)^2, (24)^2, (25)^2, (26)^2, (27)^2, (28)^2, (29)^2, (30)^2, (31)^2$ *i.e.*, 9 in number.

So, Required probability $= \frac{9}{1000} = 0.009$

(ii) First, has won *i.e.*, one card is already selected, greater than 500, has a perfect square. Since, repeatition is not allowed. So, one card is removed out of 1000 cards. So, number of remaining cards is 999.

$\therefore$ Total number of remaining outcomes = 999

Let E_2 = Event the second player wins a prize, if the first has won.

= Remaining cards has a perfect square greater than 500 are 8.

Number of favourable outcomes = 9 – 1 = 8

So, required probability $= \frac{8}{999}$

Long Answer Questions

Q.1 Find the mean marks of students for the following distribution

Marks	Number of students	Marks	Number of students
0 and above	80	60 and above	28
10 and above	77	70 and above	16
20 and above	72	80 and above	10
30 and above	65	90 and above	8
40 and above	55	100 and above	0
50 and above	43		

Ans.

Marks	Class marks (x_i)	f_i	$f_i\ x_i$
0-10	5	3	15
10-20	15	5	75
20-30	25	7	175
30-40	35	10	350
40-50	45	12	540
50-60	55	15	825
60-70	65	12	780
70-80	75	6	450
80-90	85	2	170
90-100	95	8	760
100-110	105	0	0
			$\Sigma f_i x_i = 4140$

$\therefore$ Mean $= \frac{\Sigma f_i x_i}{\Sigma f_i} = \frac{4140}{80} = 51.75$

Q.2 Determine the mean of the following distributio

Marks	Number of students
Below 10	5
Below 20	9
Below 30	17
Below 40	29
Below 50	45
Below 60	60
Below 70	70
Below 80	78
Below 90	83
Below 100	85

Ans. Here, we observe that, 5 students have scored marks below 10 *i.e.*, it lies between class interval 0-10 and 9 students have scored marks below 20.

So, $(9-5)=4$ students lies in the class interval 10 - 20. Continuing in the same manner, we get the complete frequency distribution table for given data.

Marks	Number of students (f_i)	Class marks (x_i)	$u_i=\frac{x_i-a}{h}=\frac{x_i-45}{h}$	f_iu_i
0-10	5	5	-4	-20
10-20	$9-5=4$	15	-3	-12
20-30	$17-9=8$	25	-2	-16
30-40	$29-17=12$	35	-1	-12
40-50	$45-29=16$	$a=45$	0	0
50-60	$60-45=15$	55	1	15
60-70	$70-60=10$	65	2	20
70-80	$78-70=8$	75	3	24
80-90	$83-78=5$	85	4	20
90-100	$85-83=2$	95	5	10
	$N=\Sigma f_i=85$			$\Sigma f_iu_i=29$

Here, (assumed mean) $a=45$

and (class width) $h=10$

By step deviation method,

$$\text{Mean}\ (\overline{x})=a+\frac{\Sigma f_i u_i}{\Sigma f_i}\times h=45+\frac{29}{85}\times 10=45+\frac{58}{17}=45+3.41=48.41$$

Q.3 Find the mean age of 100 residents of a town from the following data

Age equal and above (in years)	0	10	20	30	40	50	60	70
Number of persons	100	90	75	50	25	15	5	0

Ans. Here, we observe that, all 100 residents of a town have age equal and above 0. Since, 90 residents of a town have age equal and above 10.

So, 100 – 90 = 10 residents lies in the interval 0-10 and so on. Continue in this manner, we get frequency of all class intervals. Now, we construct the frequency distribution table.

Class interval	Number of persons (f_i)	Class marks (x_i)	$u_i = \frac{x_i - a}{h}$	$f_i u_i$
0-10	100 – 90 = 10	5	– 3	– 30
10-20	90 – 75 = 15	15	– 2	– 30
20-30	75 – 50 = 25	25	– 1	– 25
30-40	50 – 25 = 25	35 = a	0	0
40-50	25 – 15 = 10	45	1	10
50-60	15 – 5 = 10	55	2	20
60-70	5 – 0 = 5	65	3	15
	$N = \Sigma f_i = 100$			$\Sigma f_i u_i = -40$

Here, (assumed mean) $a = 35$

and (class width) $h = 10$

By step deviation method,

$$\text{Mean}(\bar{x}) = a + \frac{\Sigma f_i u_i}{\Sigma f_i} \times h$$

$$= 35 + \frac{(-40)}{100} \times 10 = 35 - 4 = 31$$

Hence, the required mean age is 31 years.

Q.4 The weights of tea in 70 packets are shown in the following table

Weight (in gram)	Number of packets
200-201	13
201-202	27
202-203.0	18
203-204	10
204-205	1
205-206	1

Find the mean weight of packets.

Ans. First, we find the class marks of the given data as follows.

Weight (in gram)	Number of Packets (f_i)	Class marks (x_i)	Deviation ($d_i = x_i - a$)	$f_i d_i$
200-201	13	200.5	– 3	– 39
201-202	27	201.5	– 2	– 54
202-203	18	202.5	– 1	– 18
203-204	10	a = 203.5	0	0
204-205	1	204.5	1	1
205-206	1	205.5	2	2
	$N = \Sigma f_i = 70$			$\Sigma f_i d_i = -108$

Here, (assume mean) $a = 203.5$
and (class width) $h = 1$
By assumed mean method,

$$\text{Mean}(\bar{x}) = a + \frac{\Sigma f_i d_i}{\Sigma f_i}$$
$$= 203.5 - \frac{108}{70}$$
$$= 203.5 - 1.54 = 201.96$$

Hence, the required mean weight is 201.96 g.

*** Q.5** Refer to the table below Draw the less than type ogive for this data and use it to find the median weight.

Weight (in g)	**Number of packets**
200-201	13
201-202	27
202-203	18
203-204	10
204-205	1
205-206	1

Ans. We observe that, the number of packets less than 200 is 0. Similarly, less than 201 include the number of packets from 0-200 as well as the number of packets from 200-201.

So, the total number of packets less than 201 is 0 + 13 = 13. We say that, the cumulative frequency of the class 200-201 is 13. Similarly, for other class.

Less than type	
Weight (in g)	**Number of packets**
Less than 200	0
Less than 201	0 + 13 = 13
Less than 202	27 + 13 = 40
Less than 203	18 + 40 = 58
Less than 204	10 + 58 = 68
Less than 205	1 + 68 = 69
Less than 206	1 + 69 = 70

To draw the less than type ogive, we plot the points (200, 0), (201, 13), (202, 40) (203, 58), (204, 68), (205, 69) and (206, 70) on the paper and join by free hand.

$\because$ Total number of packets $(n) = 70$

Note (*) *Topics related to these question have been removed from latest NCERT.*

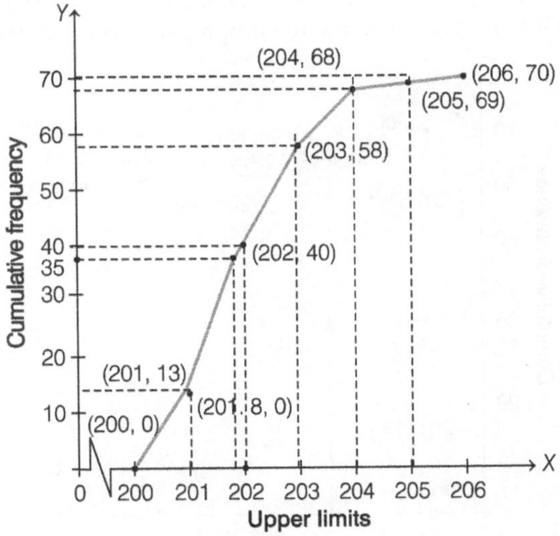

Now, $\frac{N}{2} = 35$

Firstly, we plot a point (0, 35) on Y-axis and draw a line $y = 35$ parallel to X-axis. The line cuts less than ogive curve at a point. We draw a line on that point which is perpendicular to X-axis. The foot of the line perpendicular to X-axis is the required median.

∴ Median weight = 201.8 g

***Q.6** Refer to Q.2 above. Draw the less than type and more than type ogives for the data and use them to find the meadian weight.

Ans. For less than type table we follow the Q.2.

Here, we observe that, the weight of all 70 packets is more than or equal to 200. Since, 13 packets lie in the interval 200-201. So, the weight of 70 – 13 = 57 packets is more than or equal to 201. Continuing in this manner we will get remaining more than or equal to 202, 203, 204, 205 and 206.

(i) **Less than type**		(ii) **More than type**	
Weight (in g)	**Number of packets**	**Number of packets**	**Number of students**
Less than 200	0	More than or equal to 200	70
Less than 201	13	More than or equal to 201	70 – 13 = 57
Less than 202	40	More than or equal to 202	57 – 27 = 30
Less than 203	58	More than or equal to 203	30 – 18 = 12
Less than 204	68	More than or equal to 204	12 – 10 = 2
Less than 205	69	More than or equal to 205	2 – 1 = 1
Less than 206	70	More than or equal to 206	1 – 1 = 0

To draw the less than type ogive, we plot the points (200, 0), (201, 13), (202, 40), (203, 58), (204, 68), (205, 69), (206, 70) on the paper and join them by free hand.

Note (✱) *Topics related to these question have been removed from latest NCERT.*

To draw the more than type ogive plot the points (200, 70), (201, 57), (202, 30), (203, 12), (204, 2), (205, 1), (206, 0) on the the graph paper and join them by free hand.

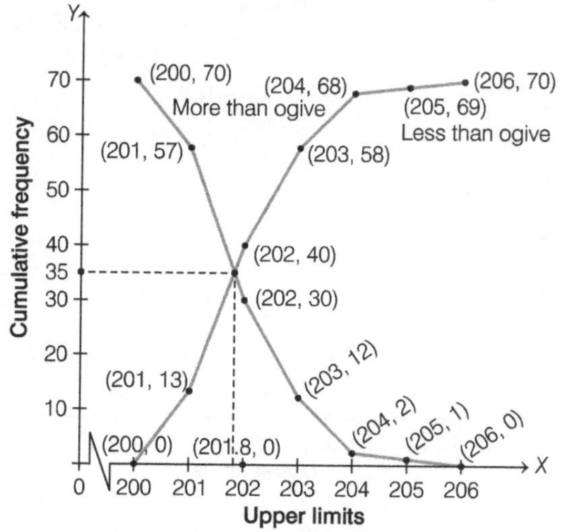

Hence, required median weight = Intersection point of X-axis = 201.8 g.

Q.7 The table below shows the salaries of 280 persons.

Salary (in ₹ thousand)	**Number of persons**
5-10	49
10-15	133
15-20	63
20-25	15
25-30	6
30-35	7
35-40	4
40-45	2
45-50	1

Calculate the median and mode of the data.

Ans. First, we construct a cumulative frequency table

Salary (in ₹ thousand)	**Number of persons** (f_i)	**Cumulative frequency** (cf)
5-10	$49 = f_0$	$49 = cf$
10-15	$f_1 = 133 = f$	133 + 49 = 182
15-20	$63 = f_2$	182 + 63 = 245
20-25	15	245 + 15 = 260
25-30	6	260 + 6 = 266
30-35	7	266 + 7 = 273
35-40	4	273 + 4 = 277
40-45	2	277 + 2 = 279
45-50	1	279 + 1 = 280
	$N = 280$	

Note (✱) *Topics related to these question have been removed from latest NCERT.*

$$\therefore \quad \frac{N}{2} = \frac{280}{2} = 140$$

(i) Here, median class is 10-15, because 140 lies in it.

Lower limit (l) = 10, Frequency (f) = 133,

Cumulative frequency (cf) = 49 and class width (h) = 5

$$\therefore \quad \text{Median} = l + \frac{\left(\frac{N}{2} - cf\right)}{f} \times h$$

$$= 10 + \frac{(140 - 49)}{133} \times 5 \quad = 10 + \frac{91 \times 5}{133}$$

$$= 10 + \frac{455}{133} = 10 + 3.421$$

$$= ₹\ 13.421 \text{ (in thousand)}$$

$$= 13.421 \times 1000$$

$$= ₹\ 13421$$

(ii) Here, the highest frequency is 133, which lies in the interval 10-15, called modal class.

Lower limit (l) = 10, class width (h) = 5, $f_1 = 133$, $f_0 = 49$, and $f_2 = 63$.

$$\therefore \text{Mode} = l + \left(\frac{f_1 - f_0}{2f_1 - f_0 - f_2}\right) \times h = 10 + \left\{\frac{133 - 49}{2 \times 133 - 49 - 63}\right\} \times 5$$

$$= 10 + \frac{84 \times 5}{266 - 112} = 10 + \frac{84 \times 5}{154} = 10 + 2.727$$

$$= ₹\ 12.727 \text{ (in thousand)}$$

$$= 12.727 \times 1000 = ₹\ 12727$$

Hence, the median and modal salary are ₹ 13421 and ₹ 12727, respectively.

Q.8 The mean of the following frequency distribution is 50 but the frequencies f_1 and f_2 in classes 20-40 and 60-80, respectively are not known. Find these frequencies, if the sum of all the frequencies is 120.

Class	0-20	20-40	40-60	60-80	80-100
Frequency	17	f_1	32	f_2	19

Ans. First we calculate the class mark of given data

Class	Frequency (f_i)	Class marks (x_i)	$u_i = \frac{x_i - a}{h}$	$f_i u_i$
0-20	17	10	− 2	− 34
20-40	f_1	30	− 1	$-f_1$
40-60	32	$a = 50$	0	0
60-80	f_2	70	1	f_2
80-100	19	90	2	38
	$\Sigma f_i = 68 + f_1 + f_2$			$\Sigma f_i u_i = 4 + f_2 - f_1$

Given that, sum of all frequencies = 120

$$\Rightarrow \quad \Sigma f_i = 68 + f_1 + f_2 = 120$$

$$\Rightarrow \quad f_1 + f_2 = 52 \quad \text{...(i)}$$

Here, (assumed mean) $a = 50$

and (class width) $h = 20$

By step deviation method,

$$\text{Mean} = a + \frac{\Sigma f_i u_i}{\Sigma f_i} \times h$$

$$\Rightarrow \quad 50 = 50 + \frac{(4 + f_2 - f_1)}{120} \times 20$$

$$\Rightarrow \quad 4 + f_2 - f_1 = 0 \Rightarrow -f_2 + f_1 = 4 \quad \text{...(ii)}$$

On adding Eqs. (i) and (ii), we get

$$2f_1 = 56 \Rightarrow f_1 = 28$$

Put the value of f_1 in Eq. (i), we get

$$f_2 = 52 - 28 \Rightarrow f_2 = 24$$

Hence, $f_1 = 28$ and $f_2 = 24$.

Q.9 The median of the following data is 50. Find the values of p and q, if the sum of all the frequencies is 90.

Marks	Frequency
20-30	p
30-40	15
40-50	25
50-60	20
60-70	q
70-80	8
80-90	10

Ans.

Marks	Frequency	Cumulative frequency
20-30	p	p
30-40	15	$15 + p$
40-50	25	$40 + p = cf$
50-60	$20 = f$	$60 + p$
60-70	q	$60 + p + q$
70-80	8	$68 + p + q$
80-90	10	$78 + p + q$

Given, $N = 90$

$$\therefore \quad \frac{N}{2} = \frac{90}{2} = 45$$

Lower limit, $l = 50$, $f = 20$, $cf = 40 + p$, $h = 10$

$\therefore$ $$\text{Median} = l + \frac{\left(\frac{N}{2} - cf\right)}{f} \times h$$

$\Rightarrow$ $$50 = 50 + \frac{(45 - 40 - p)}{20} \times 10 \Rightarrow 0 = \frac{5 - p}{2}$$

$\therefore$ $$p = 5$$

Also, $78 + p + q = 90$ [given]

$\Rightarrow$ $78 + 5 + q = 90 \Rightarrow q = 90 - 83$

$\therefore$ $q = 7$

***Q.10** The distribution of heights (in cm) of 96 children is given below

Height (in cm)	**Number of children**
124-128	5
128-132	8
132-136	17
136-140	24
140-144	16
144-148	12
148-152	6
152-156	4
156-160	3
160-164	1

Draw a less than type cumulative frequency curve for this data and use it to compute median height of the children.

Ans.

Height (in cm)	**Number of children**
Less than 124	0
Less than 128	5
Less than 132	13
Less than 136	30
Less than 140	54
Less than 144	70
Less than 148	82
Less than 152	88
Less than 156	92
Less than 160	95
Less than 164	96

To draw the less than type ogive, we plot the points (124, 0), (128, 5), (132, 13), (136, 30), (140, 54), (144, 70), (148, 82), (152, 88), (156, 92), (160, 95), (164, 96) and join all these point by free hand.

Note (*) *Topics related to these question have been removed from latest NCERT.*

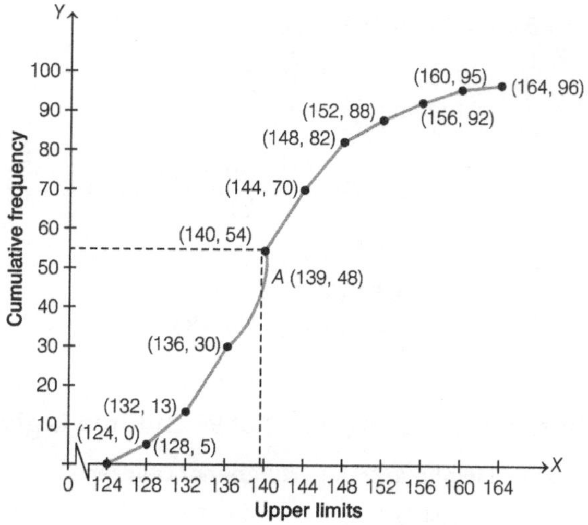

Here, $$\frac{N}{2} = \frac{96}{2} = 48$$

We take, $y = 48$ in y-coordinate and draw a line parallel to X-axis, meets the curve at A and draw a perpendicular line from point A to the X-axis and this line meets the X-axis at the point which is the median *i.e.*, median = 139.

Q.11 Size of agricultural holdings in a survey of 200 families is given in the following table:

Size of agricultural holdings (in hec)	**Number of families**
0-5	10
5-10	15
10-15	30
15-20	80
20-25	40
25-30	20
30-35	5

Compute median and mode size of the holdings.

Ans.

Size of agricultural holdings (in hec)	**Number of families** (f_i)	**Cumulative frequency**
0-5	10	10
5-10	15	25
10-15	30	55
15-20	80	135
20-25	40	175
25-30	20	195
30-35	5	200

(i) Here, $N = 200$

Now, $\frac{N}{2} = \frac{200}{2} = 100$, which lies in the interval 15-20.

Lower limit, $l = 15$, $h = 5$, $f = 80$ and $cf = 55$

$$\therefore \quad \text{Median} = l + \left(\frac{\frac{N}{2} - cf}{f}\right) \times h = 15 + \left(\frac{100 - 55}{80}\right) \times 5$$

$$= 15 + \left(\frac{45}{16}\right) = 15 + 2.81 = 17.81 \text{ hec}$$

(ii) In a given table 80 is the highest frequency.

So, the modal class is 15-20.

Here, $l = 15$, $f_1 = 80$, $f_0 = 30$, $f_2 = 40$ and $h = 5$

$$\therefore \quad \text{Mode} = l + \left(\frac{f_1 - f_0}{2f_1 - f_0 - f_2}\right) \times h$$

$$= 15 + \left(\frac{80 - 30}{2 \times 80 - 30 - 40}\right) \times 5$$

$$= 15 + \left(\frac{50}{160 - 70}\right) \times 5$$

$$= 15 + \left(\frac{50}{90}\right) \times 5 = 15 + \frac{25}{9}$$

$$= 15 + 2.77 = 17.77 \text{ hec}$$

***Q.12** The annual rainful record of a city for 66 days is given in the following table.

Rainfall (in cm)	0-10	10-20	20-30	30-40	40-50	50-60
Number of days	22	10	8	15	5	6

Calculate the median rainfall using ogives (of more than type and of less than type).

Ans. We observe that, the annual rainfall record of a city less than 0 is 0. Similarly, less than 10 include the annual rainfall record of a city from 0 as well as the annual rainfall record of a city from 0-10.

So, the total annual rainfall record of a city for less than 10 cm is $0 + 22 = 22$ days. Continuing in this manner, we will get remaining less than 20, 30, 40, 50, and 60.

Also, we observe that annual rainfall record of a city for 66 days is more than or equal to 0 cm. Since, 22 days lies in the interval 0-10. So, annual rainfall record for $66 - 22 = 44$ days is more than or equal to 10 cm. Continuing in this manner we will get remaining more than or equal to 20, 30, 40, 50 and 60.

Note (✱) *Topics related to these question have been removed from latest NCERT.*

Now, we construct a table for less than and more than type.

(i) **Less than type**		(ii) **More than type**	
Rainfall (in cm)	**Number of days**	**Rainfall** (in cm)	**Number of days**
Less than 0	0	More than or equal to 0	66
Less than 10	0 + 22 = 22	More than or equal to 10	66 – 22 = 44
Less than 20	22 + 10 = 32	More than or equal to 20	44 – 10 = 34
Less than 30	32 + 8 = 40	More than or equal to 30	34 – 8 = 26
Less than 40	40 + 15 = 55	More than or equal to 40	26 – 15 = 11
Less than 50	55 + 5 = 60	More than or equal to 50	11 – 5 = 6
Less than 60	60 + 6 = 66	More than or equal to 60	6 – 6 = 0

To draw less than type ogive we plot the points (0, 0), (10, 22), (20, 32), (30, 40), (40, 55), (50, 60), (60, 66) on the paper and join them by free hand.

To draw the more than type ogive we plot the points (0, 66), (10, 44), (20, 34), (30, 26), (40, 11), (50, 6) and (60, 0) on the graph paper and join them by free hand.

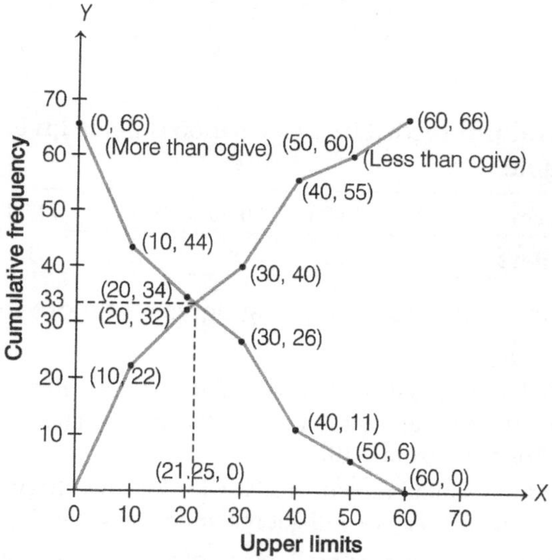

∵ Total number of days $(n) = 66$

Now, $\frac{n}{2} = 33$

Firstly, we plot a line parallel to X-axis at intersection point of both ogives, which further intersect at (0, 33) on Y-axis. Now, we draw a line perpendicular to X-axis at intersection point of both ogives, which further intersect at (21.25, 0) on X-axis. Which is the required median using ogives.

Hence, median rainfall = 21.25 cm.

***Q.13** The following is the frequency distribution of duration for 100 calls made on a mobile phone.

Duration (in seconds)	**Number of calls**
95-125	14
125-155	22
155-185	28
185-215	21
215-245	15

Calculate the average duration (in sec) of a call and also find the median from a cumulative frequency curve.

Ans. First, we calculate class marks as follows

Duration (in sec)	**Number of calls** (f_i)	**Class marks** (x_i)	$u_i = \frac{x_i - a}{h}$	$f_i u_i$
95-125	14	110	– 2	– 28
125-155	22	140	– 1	– 22
155-185	28	$a = 170$	0	0
185-215	21	200	1	21
215-245	15	230	2	30
	$\Sigma f_i = 100$			$\Sigma f_i u_i = 1$

Here, (assumed mean) $a = 170$,

and (class width) $h = 30$

By step deviation method,

$$\text{Average } (\bar{x}) = a + \frac{\Sigma f_i u_i}{\Sigma f_i} \times h$$

$$= 170 + \frac{1}{100} \times 30$$

$$= 170 + 0.3$$

$$= 170.3$$

Hence, average duration is 170.3 seconds.

For calculating median from a cumulative frequency curve

We prepare less than type or more than type ogive.

We observe that, number of calls in less than 95 secs is 0. Similarly, in less than 125 secs include the number of calls in less than 95 secs as well as the number of calls from 95-125.secs. So, the total number of calls less than 125 secs is 0 + 14 = 14. Continuing in this manner, we will get remaining in less than 155, 185, 215 and 245 secs.

Note (✱) *Topics related to these question have been removed from latest NCERT.*

Now, we construct a table for less than ogive (cumulative frequency curve).

Less than type	
Duration (in s)	**Number of calls**
Less than 95	0
Less than 125	0 + 14 = 14
Less than 155	14 + 22 = 36
Less than 185	36 + 28 = 64
Less than 215	64 + 21 = 85
Less than 245	85 + 15 = 100

To draw less than type ogive we plot them the points (95, 0), (125, 14) (155, 36), (185, 64), (215, 85), (245, 100) on the paper and join them by free hand.

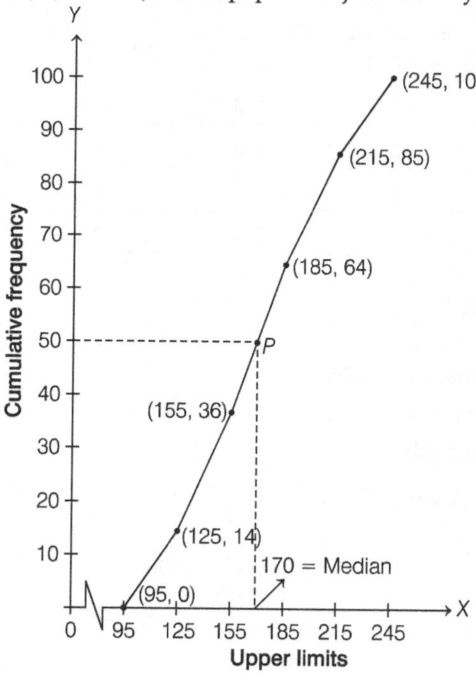

∵ Total number of calls (n) = 100

∴ $$\frac{n}{2} = \frac{100}{2} = 50.$$

Now, point 50 taking on Y-axis draw a line parallel to X-*axis* meet at a point P and draw a perpendicular line from P to the X-*axis*, the intersection point of X-*axis* is the median.

Hence, required median is 170 .

***Q.14** 50 students enter for a school javelin throw competition. The distance (in metres) thrown are recorded below

Distance (in m)	0-20	20-40	40-60	60-80	80-100
Number of students	6	11	17	12	4

(i) Construct a cumulative frequency table.
(ii) Draw a cumulative frequency curve (less than type) and calculate the median distance drawn by using this curve.
(iii) Calculate the median distance by using the formula for median.
(iv) Are the median distance calculated in (ii) and (iii) same?

Ans. (i)

Distance (in m)	**Number of students** (f_i)	**Cumulative frequency** (cf)
0-20	6	6
20-40	11	17
40-60	17	34
60-80	12	46
80-100	4	50

(ii)

Distance (in m)	**Cumulative frequency**
Less than 0	0
Less than 20	6
Less than 40	17
Less than 60	34
Less than 80	46
Less than 100	50

To draw less than type ogive, we plot the points (0, 0), (20, 6), (40, 17), (60, 34), (80, 46), (100, 50), join all these points by free hand.

Now, $\frac{N}{2} = \frac{50}{2} = 25$

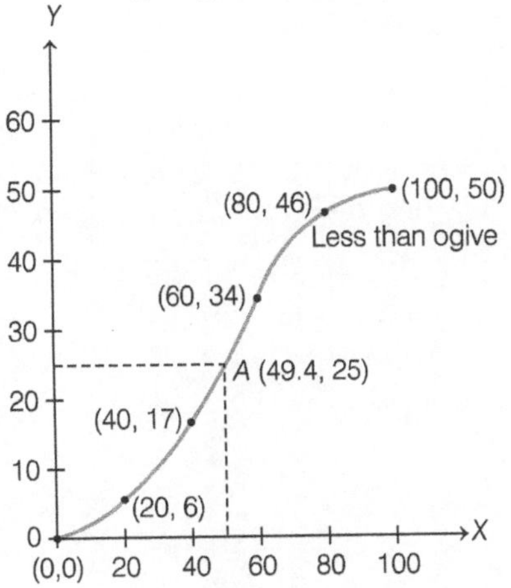

Note (*) *Topics related to these question have been removed from latest NCERT.*

Taking $Y = 25$ on Y-axis and draw a line parallel to X-*axis*, which meets the curve at point A. From point A, we draw a line perpendicular to X-*axis*, where this meets that point is the required median *i.e.*, 49.4.

(iii) Now, $$\frac{N}{2} = \frac{50}{2} = 25$$

which lies is the interval 40-60.

$\therefore$ $$l = 40,\ h = 20,\ cf = 17 \text{ and } f = 17$$

$\therefore$ $$\text{Median} = l + \left(\frac{\frac{N}{2} - cf}{f}\right) \times h$$

$$= 40 + \frac{(25 - 17)}{17} \times 20$$

$$= 40 + \frac{8 \times 20}{17}$$

$$= 40 + 9.41$$

$$= 49.41$$

(iv) *Yes*, median distance calculated by parts (ii) and (iii) are same.